POETRY
for Students

Advisors

Jayne M. Burton is a teacher of secondary English and an adjunct professor for Northwest Vista College in San Antonio, TX.

Klaudia Janek is the school librarian at the International Academy in Bloomfield Hills, Michigan. She holds an MLIS degree from Wayne State University, a teaching degree from Rio Salado College, and a bachelor of arts degree in international relations from Saint Joseph's College. She is the IB Extended Essay Coordinator and NCA AdvancEd co-chair at her school. She is an IB workshop leader for International Baccalaureate North America, leading teacher training for IB school librarians and extended essay coordinators. She has been happy to serve the Michigan Association for Media in Education as a board member and past president at the regional level, advocating for libraries in Michigan schools.

Greg Bartley is an English teacher in Virginia. He holds an M.A.Ed. in English Education from Wake Forest University and a B.S. in Integrated Language Arts Education from Miami University.

Sarah Clancy teaches IB English at the International Academy in Bloomfield Hills, Michigan. She is a member of the National Council of Teachers of English and Michigan Speech Coaches, Inc. Sarah earned her undergraduate degree from Kalamazoo College and her Master's of Education from Florida Southern College. She coaches the high-ranking forensics team and is the staff adviser of the school newspaper, *Overachiever*.

Karen Dobson is a teen/adult librarian at Plymouth District Library in Plymouth, Michigan. She holds a Bachelor of Science degree from Oakland University and an MLIS from Wayne State University and has served on many committees through the Michigan Library Association.

Tom Shilts is the youth librarian at the Okemos branch of Capital Area District Library in Okemos, Michigan. He holds an MSLS degree from Clarion University of Pennsylvania and an MA in U.S. History from the University of North Dakota.

POETRY
for Students

**Presenting Analysis, Context, and Criticism
on Commonly Studied Poetry**

VOLUME 55

Kristin B. Mallegg, Project Editor

Foreword by David J. Kelly

GALE
CENGAGE Learning·

Farmington Hills, Mich • San Francisco • New York • Waterville, Maine
Meriden, Conn • Mason, Ohio • Chicago

Poetry for Students, Volume 55

Project Editor: Kristin B. Mallegg

Rights Acquisition and Management:
Ashley Maynard, Carissa Poweleit

Composition: Evi Abou-El-Seoud

Manufacturing: Rita Wimberley

Imaging: John Watkins

© 2017 Gale, Cengage Learning

ALL RIGHTS RESERVED. No part of this work covered by the copyright herein may be reproduced, transmitted, stored, or used in any form or by any means graphic, electronic, or mechanical, including but not limited to photocopying, recording, scanning, digitizing, taping, Web distribution, information networks, or information storage and retrieval systems, except as permitted under Section 107 or 108 of the 1976 United States Copyright Act, without the prior written permission of the publisher.

Since this page cannot legibly accommodate all copyright notices, the acknowledgments constitute an extension of the copyright notice.

For product information and technology assistance, contact us at
Gale Customer Support, 1-800-877-4253.
For permission to use material from this text or product,
submit all requests online at **www.cengage.com/permissions.**
Further permissions questions can be emailed to
permissionrequest@cengage.com

While every effort has been made to ensure the reliability of the information presented in this publication, Gale, a part of Cengage Learning, does not guarantee the accuracy of the data contained herein. Gale accepts no payment for listing; and inclusion in the publication of any organization, agency, institution, publication, service, or individual does not imply endorsement of the editors or publisher. Errors brought to the attention of the publisher and verified to the satisfaction of the publisher will be corrected in future editions.

Gale
27500 Drake Rd.
Farmington Hills, MI, 48331-3535

ISBN-13: 978-1-4103-2847-2
ISSN 1094-7019

This title is also available as an e-book.
ISBN-13: 978-1-4103-2852-6
Contact your Gale, a part of Cengage Learning sales representative for ordering information.

Printed in Mexico
1 2 3 4 5 6 7 21 20 19 18 17

Table of Contents

Just a Few Lines on a Page

I have often thought that poets have the easiest job in the world. A poem, after all, is just a few lines on a page, usually not even extending margin to margin—how long would that take to write, about five minutes? Maybe ten at the most, if you wanted it to rhyme or have a repeating meter. Why, I could start in the morning and produce a book of poetry by dinnertime. But we all know that it isn't that easy. Anyone can come up with enough words, but the poet's job is about writing the *right* ones. The right words will change lives, making people see the world somewhat differently than they saw it just a few minutes earlier. The right words can make a reader who relies on the dictionary for meanings take a greater responsibility for his or her own personal understanding. A poem that is put on the page correctly can bear any amount of analysis, probing, defining, explaining, and interrogating, and something about it will still feel new the next time you read it.

It would be fine with me if I could talk about poetry without using the word "magical," because that word is overused these days to imply "a really good time," often with a certain sweetness about it, and a lot of poetry is neither of these. But if you stop and think about magic—whether it brings to mind sorcery, witchcraft, or bunnies pulled from top hats—it always seems to involve stretching reality to produce a result greater than the sum of its parts and pulling unexpected results out of thin air. This book provides ample cases where a few simple words conjure up whole worlds. We do not actually travel to different times and different cultures, but the poems get into our minds, they find what little we know about the places they are talking about, and then they make that little bit blossom into a bouquet of someone else's life. Poets make us think we are following simple, specific events, but then they leave ideas in our heads that cannot be found on the printed page. Abracadabra.

Sometimes when you finish a poem it doesn't feel as if it has left any supernatural effect on you, like it did not have any more to say beyond the actual words that it used. This happens to everybody, but most often to inexperienced readers: regardless of what is often said about young people's infinite capacity to be amazed, you have to understand what usually does happen, and what could have happened instead, if you are going to be moved by what someone has accomplished. In those cases in which you finish a poem with a "So what?" attitude, the information provided in *Poetry for Students* comes in handy. Readers can feel assured that the poems included here actually are potent magic, not just because a few (or a hundred or ten thousand) professors of literature say they are: they're significant because they can withstand close inspection and still amaze the very same people who have just finished taking them apart and seeing how they work. Turn them inside out, and they will still be able to come alive, again and again. *Poetry for*

Students gives readers of any age good practice in feeling the ways poems relate to both the reality of the time and place the poet lived in and the reality of our emotions. Practice is just another word for being a student. The information given here helps you understand the way to read poetry; what to look for, what to expect.

With all of this in mind, I really don't think I would actually like to have a poet's job at all. There are too many skills involved, including precision, honesty, taste, courage, linguistics, passion, compassion, and the ability to keep all sorts of people entertained at once. And that is just what they do with one hand, while the other hand pulls some sort of trick that most of us will never fully understand. I can't even pack all that I need for a weekend into one suitcase, so what would be my chances of stuffing so much life into a few lines? With all that *Poetry for Students* tells us about each poem, I am impressed that any poet can finish three or four poems a year. Read the inside stories of these poems, and you won't be able to approach any poem in the same way you did before.

David J. Kelly
College of Lake County

Introduction

Purpose of the Book

The purpose of *Poetry for Students* (*PfS*) is to provide readers with a guide to understanding, enjoying, and studying poems by giving them easy access to information about the work. Part of Gale's "For Students" Literature line, *PfS* is specifically designed to meet the curricular needs of high school and undergraduate college students and their teachers, as well as the interests of general readers and researchers considering specific poems. While each volume contains entries on "classic" poems frequently studied in classrooms, there are also entries containing hard-to-find information on contemporary poems, including works by multicultural, international, and women poets.

The information covered in each entry includes an introduction to the poem and the poem's author; the actual poem text (if possible); a poem summary, to help readers unravel and understand the meaning of the poem; analysis of important themes in the poem; and an explanation of important literary techniques and movements as they are demonstrated in the poem.

In addition to this material, which helps the readers analyze the poem itself, students are also provided with important information on the literary and historical background informing each work. This includes a historical context essay, a box comparing the time or place the poem was written to modern Western culture, a critical overview essay, and excerpts from critical essays on the poem. A unique feature of *PfS* is a specially commissioned critical essay on each poem, targeted toward the student reader.

To further help today's student in studying and enjoying each poem, information on audio recordings and other media adaptations is provided (if available), as well as reading suggestions for works of fiction and nonfiction on similar themes and topics. Classroom aids include ideas for research papers and lists of critical and reference sources that provide additional material on the poem.

Selection Criteria

The titles for each volume of *PfS* are selected by surveying numerous sources on notable literary works and analyzing course curricula for various schools, school districts, and states. Some of the sources surveyed include: high school and undergraduate literature anthologies and textbooks; lists of award-winners, and recommended titles, including the Young Adult Library Services Association (YALSA) list of best books for young adults.

Input solicited from our expert advisory board—consisting of educators and librarians—guides us to maintain a mix of "classic" and contemporary literary works, a mix of challenging and engaging works (including genre titles that are commonly studied) appropriate for different age levels, and a mix of international, multicultural and women authors. These advisors also consult on each volume's entry list, advising on which titles are most studied, most appropriate, and meet the broadest interests across secondary (grades 7–12) curricula and undergraduate literature studies.

How Each Entry Is Organized

Each entry, or chapter, in *PfS* focuses on one poem. Each entry heading lists the full name of the poem, the author's name, and the date of the poem's publication. The following elements are contained in each entry:

Introduction: a brief overview of the poem which provides information about its first appearance, its literary standing, any controversies surrounding the work, and major conflicts or themes within the work.

Author Biography: this section includes basic facts about the poet's life, and focuses on events and times in the author's life that inspired the poem in question.

Poem Text: when permission has been granted, the poem is reprinted, allowing for quick reference when reading the explication of the following section.

Poem Summary: a description of the major events in the poem. Summaries are broken down with subheads that indicate the lines being discussed.

Themes: a thorough overview of how the major topics, themes, and issues are addressed within the poem. Each theme discussed appears in a separate subhead.

Style: this section addresses important style elements of the poem, such as form, meter, and rhyme scheme; important literary devices used, such as imagery, foreshadowing, and symbolism; and, if applicable, genres to which the work might have belonged, such as Gothicism or Romanticism. Literary terms are explained within the entry, but can also be found in the Glossary.

Historical Context: this section outlines the social, political, and cultural climate in which the author lived and the poem was created. This section may include descriptions of related historical events, pertinent aspects of daily life in the culture, and the artistic and literary sensibilities of the time in which the work was written. If the poem is

a historical work, information regarding the time in which the poem is set is also included. Each section is broken down with helpful subheads.

Critical Overview: this section provides background on the critical reputation of the poem, including bannings or any other public controversies surrounding the work. For older works, this section includes a history of how the poem was first received and how perceptions of it may have changed over the years; for more recent poems, direct quotes from early reviews may also be included.

Criticism: an essay commissioned by *PfS* which specifically deals with the poem and is written specifically for the student audience, as well as excerpts from previously published criticism on the work (if available).

Sources: an alphabetical list of critical material quoted in the entry, with full bibliographical information.

Further Reading: an alphabetical list of other critical sources which may prove useful for the student. Includes full bibliographical information and a brief annotation.

Suggested Search Terms: a list of search terms and phrases to jumpstart students' further information seeking. Terms include not just titles and author names but also terms and topics related to the historical and literary context of the works.

In addition, each entry contains the following highlighted sections, set apart from the main text as sidebars:

Media Adaptations: if available, a list of audio recordings as well as any film or television adaptations of the poem, including source information.

Topics for Further Study: a list of potential study questions or research topics dealing with the poem. This section includes questions related to other disciplines the student may be studying, such as American history, world history, science, math, government, business, geography, economics, psychology, etc.

Compare & Contrast: an "at-a-glance" comparison of the cultural and historical differences between the author's time and culture and late twentieth century or early twenty-first century Western culture. This box includes pertinent parallels between the major scientific, political, and cultural movements of the time or place the poem was written, the time or place the poem was set (if a historical work), and modern Western culture. Works written after 1990 may not have this box.

What Do I Read Next?: a list of works that might give a reader points of entry into a classic work (e.g., YA or multicultural titles) and/ or complement the featured poem or serve as a contrast to it. This includes works by the same author and others, works from various genres, YA works, and works from various cultures and eras.

Other Features

PfS includes "Just a Few Lines on a Page," a foreword by David J. Kelly, an adjunct professor of English, College of Lake County, Illinois. This essay provides a straightforward, unpretentious explanation of why poetry should be marveled at and how *PfS* can help teachers show students how to enrich their own reading experiences.

A Cumulative Author/Title Index lists the authors and titles covered in each volume of the *PfS* series.

A Cumulative Nationality/Ethnicity Index breaks down the authors and titles covered in each volume of the *PfS* series by nationality and ethnicity.

A Subject/Theme Index, specific to each volume, provides easy reference for users who may be studying a particular subject or theme rather than a single work. Significant subjects from events to broad themes are included.

A Cumulative Index of First Lines (beginning in Vol. 10) provides easy reference for users who may be familiar with the first line of a poem but may not remember the actual title.

A Cumulative Index of Last Lines (beginning in Vol. 10) provides easy reference for users who may be familiar with the last line of a poem but may not remember the actual title.

Each entry may include illustrations, including photo of the author and other graphics related to the poem.

Citing Poetry for Students

When writing papers, students who quote directly from any volume of *PfS* may use the

following general forms. These examples are based on MLA style; teachers may request that students adhere to a different style, so the following examples may be adapted as needed.

When citing text from *PfS* that is not attributed to a particular author (i.e., the Themes, Style, Historical Context sections, etc.), the following format should be used in the bibliography section:

"Grace." *Poetry for Students*. Ed. Sara Constantakis. Vol. 44. Detroit: Gale, Cengage Learning, 2013. 66–86. Print.

When quoting the specially commissioned essay from *PfS* (usually the first piece under the "Criticism" subhead), the following format should be used:

Andersen, Susan. Critical Essay on "Grace." *Poetry for Students*. Ed. Sara Constantakis. Vol. 44. Detroit: Gale, Cengage Learning, 2013. 77–80. Print.

When quoting a journal or newspaper essay that is reprinted in a volume of *PfS*, the following form may be used:

Molesworth, Charles. "Proving Irony by Compassion: The Poetry of Robert Pinsky." *Hollins Critic* 21.5 (1984): 1–18. Rpt. in *Poetry for Students*. Ed. Sara Constantakis. Vol. 44. Detroit: Gale, Cengage Learning, 2013. 189–92. Print.

When quoting material reprinted from a book that appears in a volume of *PfS*, the following form may be used:

Flora, Joseph M. "W. E. Henley, Poet." *William Ernest Henley*. New York: Twayne, 1970. 119–41. Rpt. in *Poetry for Students*. Ed. Sara Constantakis. Vol. 43. Detroit: Gale, 213. 150–52. Print.

We Welcome Your Suggestions

The editorial staff of *Poetry for Students* welcomes your comments and ideas. Readers who wish to suggest poems to appear in future volumes, or who have other suggestions, are cordially invited to contact the editor. You may contact the editor via E-mail at: **ForStudentsEditors@cengage.com**. Or write to the editor at:

Editor, *Poetry for Students*
Gale
27500 Drake Road
Farmington Hills, MI 48331-3535

Literary Chronology

1809: Edgar Allan Poe is born on January 19 in Boston, Massachusetts.

1825: Frances Ellen Watkins Harper is born on September 24 in Baltimore, Maryland.

1840: Thomas Hardy is born on June 2 in Upper Bockhampton, Dorset, England.

1849: Edgar Allan Poe dies of unknown causes on October 7 in Baltimore, Maryland.

1864: Frances Harper's "Bury Me in a Free Land" is published in *Liberator*.

1875: Edgar Allan Poe's "Alone" is published in *Scribner's Monthly*.

1879: Sarojini Naidu is born on February 13 in Hyderabad, India.

1881: Juan Ramón Jiménez is born on December 27 in Moguer, Spain.

1893: Dororthy Parker is born on August 22 in Long Branch, New Jersey.

1900: Yvor Winters is born on October 17 in Chicago, Illinois.

1901: Sterling Brown is born on May 1 in Washington, DC.

1911: Frances Harper dies of natural causes on February 22 in Philadelphia, Pennsylvania.

1912: Sarojini Naidu's "In the Bazaars of Hyderabad" is published in *The Bird of Time: Songs of Life, Death & The Spring*.

1914: Thomas Hardy's "The Wall" is published in *Satires of Circumstance*.

1917: Juan Ramón Jiménez's "I Am Not I" is published in *Eternidades*.

1926: Dororthy Parker's "Love Song" is published in *Enough Rope*.

1928: Thomas Hardy dies of cardiac syncope on January 11 in Dorchester, England.

1934: Saadi Youssef is born in Abulkhasib, Iraq.

1934: Nellie Wong is born on September 12 in Oakland, California.

1934: Amiri Baraka is born on October 7 in Newark, New Jersey.

1936: Sterling Brown's "Southern Cop" is published in *Partisan Review*.

1947: Rae Armantrout is born on April 13 in Vallejo, California.

1947: Yusef Komunyakaa is born on April 29 in Bogalusa, Louisiana.

1949: Sarojini Naidu dies of a heart attack on March 2 in Lucknow, India.

1951: Garrett Hongo is born on May 30 in Volcano, Hawaii.

1955: Yvor Winters's "At the San Francisco Airport" is published in *Hudson Review*.

1955: Carol Ann Duffy is born on December 23 in Glasgow, Scotland.

1956: Juan Ramón Jiménez is awarded the Nobel Prize in Literature..

ca. 1957: Diane Burns is born in Lawrence, Kansas.

1958: Juan Ramón Jiménez dies of cancer on May 29 in San Juan, Puerto Rico.

1967: Dorothy Parker dies of a heart attack on June 7 in New York, New York.

1968: Yvor Winters dies of throat cancer on January 25 in Palo Alto, California.

1969: Amiri Baraka's "Incident" is published in *Black Magic*.

1981: Nellie Wong's "When I was Growing Up" is published in *This Bridge Called My Back*.

1982: Garrett Hongo's "Yellow Light" is published in *Yellow Light*.

1983: Diane Burns's "Sure You Can Ask Me a Personal Question" is published in *Songs from this Earth on Turtle's Back: Contemporary American Indian Poetry*.

1989: Sterling Brown dies of leukemia on January 13 in Takoma Park, Maryland.

1992: Yusef Komunyakaa's "Blackberries" is published in *Magic City*.

1993: Carol Ann Duffy's "Valentine" is published in *Mean Time*.

1994: Yusef Komunyakaa is awarded the Pulitzer Prize for Poetry for *Neon Vernacular*.

1998: Saadi Youssef's "The Fence" is published in *Agni*.

2006: Diane Burns dies of kidney and liver failure on December 22 in New York, New York.

2009: Rae Armantrout's "Unbidden" is published in *Versed*.

2010: Rae Armantrout is awarded the Pulitzer Prize for Poetry for *Versed*.

2014: Amiri Baraka dies of complications following surgery on January 9 in Newark, New Jersey.

Acknowledgements

The editors wish to thank the copyright holders of the excerpted criticism included in this volume and the permissions managers of many book and magazine publishing companies for assisting us in securing reproduction rights. We are also grateful to the staffs of the Detroit Public Library, the Library of Congress, the University of Detroit Mercy Library, Wayne State University Purdy/Kresge Library Complex, and the University of Michigan Libraries for making their resources available to us. Following is a list of the copyright holders who have granted us permission to reproduce material in this volume of *PFS*. Every effort has been made to trace copyright, but if omissions have been made, please let us know.

COPYRIGHTED EXCERPTS IN PFS, VOLUME 55, WERE REPRODUCED FROM THE FOLLOWING PERIODICALS:

African American Review, Vol. 30, No. 2, Summer 1996, p. 302. © 1996 Maryemma Graham, Gina Rossetti. —*AGNI*, Vol. 56, 2002. © 2002 Reprint with permission from Saadi Youssef. —*American Visions*, Vol. 14, No. 5, October 1999. © 1999 American Visions. —*Booklist*, Vol. 93, No. 12, February 15, 1997. © 1977 American Library Association - ALA. —*Bulletin of Hispanic Studies*, Vol. 80, No. 4, September 2003. © 2003 Liverpool University Press. —*Common-Place*, Vol. 15, No. 4, Summer 2015. © 2015 American Antiquarian Society. —*Globe & Mail*, December 6, 2003. © 2003 Dennis Lee. —*G-Spot*, August 6, 2002. ©

2002 Nellie Wong. —*Iris*, Vol. 47, FallWinter 2003. © 2003 Jolie Sheffer. —*Library Journal*, Vol. 137, No. 8, November 1, 2012. © 2012 Library Journals LLC. —*London Evening Standard*, September 22, 2011. © 2011 Solo Syndication. —*Progressive*, Vol. 67, No. 3, March 2003. © 2003 The Progressive. —*Publishers Weekly*, Vol. 244, No. 2, January 13, 1997. © 1997 PWXYZ, LLC. —*Publishers Weekly*, Vol. 249, No. 47, November 25, 2002. © 2002 PWXYZ, LLC. — *Socialist Worker*. © The Socialist Worker (socialistworker.co.uk). —*Telegraph*, February 14, 2010. © 2010 Daily Telegraph. —*Villager*, Vol. 76, No. 38, February 1420, 2007. © 2007 The Villager / Diane Burns. —*World Literature Today*, Vol. 74, No. 4, Fall 2000. © 2000 World Literature Today. —*World Literature Today*, Vol. 75, SummerAutumn 2001. © 2001 World Literature Today.

COPYRIGHTED EXCERPTS IN PFS, VOLUME 55, WERE REPRODUCED FROM THE FOLLOWING BOOKS:

Armantrout, Rae. From *Versed*. © Wesleyan University Press. — Bolden, Tony. From *Afro-Blue: Improvisations in African American Poetry and Culture*. © 2009 University of Illinois Press. — Brito, Manuel. From *A Suite of Poetic Voices: Interviews with Contemporary American Poets*. © 1992 Rae Armantrout. — Brown, Sterling A. *The Collected Poems of Sterling A. Brown - Southern Cop*. © Northwestern University Press. — Buranelli, Vincent. From *Edgar Allan*

Poe. © 1997 The Gale Group. — Clements, Patricia. From *The Poetry of Thomas Hardy*. © 1980 Patricia Clements. — Davis, Dick. From *Wisdom and Wilderness: The Achievement of Yvor Winters*. © 1983 Ohio University Press/Swallow Press/University of Georgia Press. — Hardy, Thomas. From *Thomas Hardy: The Complete Poems*. 2011 Courtesy of Palgrave Macmillan. — Harper, Frances Ellen Watkins. From *A Brighter Coming Day*. Courtesy of Feminist Press at CUNY. — Hongo, Garrett Kaoru. From *Yellow Light*. © Wesleyan University Press. — JimÕnez, Juan Ramœn. © Representante de los Herederos de Juan Ramœn JimÕnez. — Kinney, Arthur F. From *Dorothy Parker, Revised*, © 1998 The Gale Group. — Komunyakaa, Yusef. From *Pleasure Dome: New and Collected Poems*. © 2001 Wesleyan University Press. — Maio, Samuel. From *Creating Another Self: Voice in Modern American Personal Poetry*. © 1995 Wesleyan University Press, Truman State University Press. — Miller, Nina.

From *Making Love Modern: The Intimate Public Worlds of New York's Literary Women*. © 1998 Northwestern University Press. — Naidu, Sarojini. From *The Bird of Time: Songs of Life, Death & the Spring*. Courtesy of William Heinemann. — Pettit, Rhonda S. From *A Gendered Collision: Sentimentalism and Modernism in Dorothy Parker's Poetry and Fiction*. © 2000 Associated University Press. — Poe, Edgar Allan. From *Poetry and Tales*. 1984 Courtesy of Library of America. — Roberts, Katrina. From *Because You Asked: A Book of Answers on the Art & Craft of the Writing Life*. © 2015 Lost Horse Press. — Salas, Angela M. From *Flashback through the Heart: The Poetry of Yusef Komunyakaa*. © 2004 Associated University Press. — Smethurst, James E. From *Race and the Modern Artist*. © 2003 Oxford University Press. — Symons, Arthur. From *The Flute and the Drum: Studies in Sarojini Naidu's Poetry and Politics*. Courtesy of William Heinemann.

Contributors

Bryan Aubrey: Aubrey holds a PhD in English. Entry on "At the San Francisco Airport." Original essay on "At the San Francisco Airport."

Rita M. Brown: Brown is an English professor. Entries on "Alone" and "When I Was Growing Up." Original essays on "Alone" and "When I Was Growing Up."

Klay Dyer: Dyer is a freelance writer specializing in topics relating to literature, popular culture, and the relationship between creativity and technology. Entry on "Valentine." Original essay on "Valentine."

Kristen Sarlin Greenberg: Greenberg is a freelance writer and editor with a background in literature and philosophy. Entry on "Yellow Light." Original essay on "Yellow Light."

Amy L. Miller: Miller is a graduate of the University of Cincinnati. Entries on "Blackberries," "The Fence," and "Incident." Original essays on "Blackberries," "The Fence," and "Incident."

Michael J. O'Neal: O'Neal holds a PhD in English. Entry on "The Walk." Original essay on "The Walk."

Jeffrey Eugene Palmer: Palmer is a scholar, freelance writer, and teacher of high school English. Entries on "Bury Me in a Free Land" and "Unbidden." Original essays on "Bury Me in a Free Land" and "Unbidden."

April Paris: Paris is a freelance writer with a degree in classical literature and a background in academic writing. Entries on "Southern Cop" and "Sure You Can Ask Me a Personal Question." Original essays on "Southern Cop" and "Sure You Can Ask Me a Personal Question."

Bradley A. Skeen: Skeen is a classicist. Entries on "I Am Not I," "In the Bazaars of Hyderabad," and "Love Song." Original essays on "I Am Not I," "In the Bazaars of Hyderabad," and "Love Song."

Alone

EDGAR ALLAN POE
1829

Edgar Allan Poe is perhaps the most famous of all American poets, the best known in popular culture, though admittedly through only a handful of poems. Peter Ackroyd, at the beginning of his biography *Poe: A Life Cut Short*, sums up the received image of Poe as a man and as a writer: "Edgar Allan Poe has become the image of the *poète maudit*, the blasted soul, the wanderer. His fate was heavy, his life all but insupportable." Poe, deeply immersed in the romantic movement, wrote "Alone" in 1829 when he was nineteen years old in the autograph book of a friend of his, and it was not discovered and published until a generation after his death, in 1875. The poem is a careful channeling of adolescent anxiety and rage into a declaration of romantic principles, championing nature over the human world. It can be found in any complete collection of Poe's verse.

AUTHOR BIOGRAPHY

Poe was born on January 19, 1809, in Boston. His parents, David and Elizabeth, were actors in a traveling troupe. Within two years, Poe's father would abandon the family, and his mother would die of consumption (tuberculosis). Poe and his older brother, William Henry, were taken in as orphans by a slave dealer in Richmond, Virginia, John Allan (hence Poe's

Edgar Allan Poe *(©Everett Historical / Shutterstock.com)*

illegitimate children better than he did Poe, who had been raised by his wife, and the two became permanently estranged.

While he was at West Point, Poe took up a subscription from his fellow students to pay for the publication of a second volume of poetry, a procedure unusual only in its supporters (and which might be compared to modern crowdfunding), which this time received some critical notice. Poe left West Point, which entailed arranging for his own court-martial for desertion, and determined to make his living as writer, an unheard-of project at the time. Poe began to publish more poetry and some prose in newspapers as well as the new weekly and monthly magazines. He came to the attention of the wealthy patron John Kennedy, and through him got a job as assistant editor at the *Southern Literary Messenger*. Over the next few years, Poe moved from magazine to magazine and attempted to start his own. He finally bought the *Broadway Journal*, but it collapsed from previous debt. Poe's business moves were certainly partly motivated by ambition, but they were also conditioned by his alcoholism, with employers making it clear to him on more than one occasion that he had to leave or be fired. Poe quickly adapted to the new short-story genre, tailored to magazine publication, and invented the detective story (the Mystery Writers of America's annual award is called the Edgar in his honor) and contributed to the formation of the science-fiction genre. In 1845 he published "The Raven," which became an immediate national sensation, though, with copyright laws in their infancy and generally unenforced, he profited only the nine dollars he was paid for the initial publication.

In 1835, Poe married his cousin Virginia, who was thirteen years old at the time (a less startling age then than now). She died of consumption in 1842. The deaths of his mother, stepmother, and wife are often thought to be linked to the main theme of Poe's "The Raven," "Ulalume" (1847), and "Annabel Lee" (1849), which all concern mourning for a dead wife or lover.

The circumstances of Poe's death are highly mysterious. He was found lying in the street in Baltimore on October 3, 1849, and taken to a hospital, where he remained delirious until he died on October 7. It was suggested at the time that Poe died from a drinking binge or possibly from the use of laudanum (an oral form of morphine), which he began taking because he was

middle name), but they were not legally adopted. Poe received an excellent secondary education, particularly at schools in England, where the family stayed while Poe was sixteen and seventeen years old. Allan, who had a private fortune equivalent to at least several tens of millions of dollars in modern money, balked at paying tuition at the University of Virginia for Poe, citing Poe's gambling and drinking as an excuse. Thus, Poe was to attend only one semester of college.

Left without resources, Poe joined the army, where he served for two years. Poe was posted to Boston and there published *Tamerlane and Other Poems* in 1827. This was a self-publication for which Poe paid the costs, but that was not unusual at the time (and might be compared today to publishing an e-book rather than a modern vanity-press book). By November 1829, Poe's regiment was moved to South Carolina, and he stopped in Baltimore to visit relatives of his mother in the city. This must be the time when Poe wrote "Alone" in the autograph book of Lucy Holmes. John Allan's wife died in 1830, and this effected a sentimental reconciliation between him and Poe, during which time Allan bought Poe an appointment to West Point. Poe soon went out of his way to provoke Allan, claiming that Allan supported his several depressed over the death of his wife. A rather fantastic literature has grown up suggesting that he died of poisoning, rabies, or some other unlikely cause. Rufus Griswold, a rival editor, wrote an obituary and later a biography of Poe, portraying him as a depraved drug addict; it was filled with exaggerations and fabrications, many of which nevertheless became common currency in popular beliefs about Poe.

Poe's fame as a writer only increased after his death, especially with "The Raven," the short story "The Gold Bug," and other works set as standard school texts. In 1875, the magazine writer Eugene L. Didier discovered and published the manuscript of "Alone."

POEM TEXT

```
From childhood's hour I have not been
As others were—I have not seen
As others saw—I could not bring
My passions from a common spring—
From the same source I have not taken        5
My sorrow—I could not awaken
My heart to joy at the same tone—
And all I lov'd—I lov'd alone—
Then—in my childhood—in the dawn
Of a most stormy life—was drawn             10
From ev'ry depth of good and ill
The mystery which binds me still—
From the torrent, or the fountain—
From the red cliff of the mountain—
From the sun that 'round me roll'd          15
In its autumn tint of gold—
From the lightning in the sky
As it pass'd me flying by—
From the thunder, and the storm—
And the cloud that took the form            20
(When the rest of Heaven was blue)
Of a demon in my view—
```

POEM SUMMARY

The text used for this summary is from *Poetry and Tales*, edited by Patrick F. Quinn, Library of America, 1984, p. 60. A version of the poem can be found on the following web page: http://www.eapoe.org/works/poems/alonea.htm.

The main idea of the poem is the speaker's isolation from his fellow human beings in connection with his unique and rare inner nature. The speaker of the poem (who must essentially be regarded as a fictional character, no matter

how closely he aligns with Poe himself as the author) states that he has known he is different from other people from the time of his childhood. In a series of grammatically complete sentences, which Poe nevertheless punctuates with dashes to simulate the urgency of impassioned speech, the speaker gives the particular details in which this difference consists. He says that he does not see in the same way as other people. *Seeing*, here, is probably in the first instance a metaphorical reference to the difference in worldview or disposition between the speaker and others. Given the morbid and fantastic descriptive passages in Poe's later poetry and fiction, however, it can be taken in a literal sense also. The speaker is aware that the things that make him happy or sad are different from the things that make those around him happy or sad. He attempts to think like others, but it is impossible. Above all, he loves things that are different from what the world loves.

Beginning in line 9 the speaker again identifies his childhood, the start of a tempestuous life, as the time when he became different. His life has been lived under the impression of a mysterious force that seems to proceed from nature and from the entire world: everything that is either good or bad. The reader may suppose that this phrase is used to indicate the distinction that the speaker would call good what the world calls bad and vice versa. The poet then lists a series of natural phenomena from which the mystery came to him: from raging rivers and whirlpools and the sources of rivers, from the red cliffs and mountains of the American West (which Poe had never visited), from the sun and gold color it imparts to leaves in the fall, as well as from lightning and storms. This does not quite complete the list, but some observations about these items are in order.

For the most part, these are things that generally impart fear and which people avoid, yet they are the very things that have hold of the speaker. Rapids on a river are considered dangerous. The great American desert, as the West was then called, was, in the 1820s, considered uninhabitable and the abode of savage Indians. While lightning storms are dangerous, the sun seems out of place on the list. That is explained by different cultural attitudes between Poe's time and today. Traditionally, sunburn was abhorred by Western elites because it marked workers who spent all their time at labor in the fields. The Greek poet Homer, for example, describes beautiful women as white-armed and silver-footed because women in elite households spent all of their time indoors weaving and were thus shielded from the sun. This changed late in the nineteenth century when railroads made it possible for members of the elite class in England or the American Northeast to vacation during the middle of winter in southern France or Florida, where they would spend time lying in the sun at the beach. Thus, having a moderate sunburn, rechristened by the less pejorative term *suntan*, became a marker of elite status. In Poe's time, the rays of the sun were considered destructive rather than health promoting. This list also has a metaphysical significance. It should be pointed out that Poe is scarcely alone in finding storms, whirlpools, and the destructive power of nature an inspiring spectacle. The idea is characteristic of romantic era literature. The preference for the inhuman, destructive part of nature supports the poem's mood of alienation.

However, in another connection, the disturbed waters, the mountains, the sun, and the storms refer to the traditional elements of Greek cosmology—water, earth, fire, and air—and hence constitute a complete description of the natural world. This leads to the last of the natural phenomena that inspire mystery in the poem's speaker: a cloud in the shape of a demon, significantly of such a shape that only the speaker can recognize what it is. Although this is sometimes read with reference to the fallen spirits of Christian and Semitic tradition, the preceding list of the four elements, as well as the generally Greek metaphysics that informs Poe's poetry, dictate that this entity be understood in a Greek sense. For the Greeks, an entity called a *daimon* (conventionally transliterated as "daemon" or "demon") existed as an intermediary between gods and human beings. They were often associated with natural phenomena like weather. They were neither good nor evil but could certainly work against human interests if it suited them. Since the Renaissance, such beings have played a large part in English literature, represented by the character of Ariel in Shakespeare's *The Tempest* or the spirits that Manfred encounters inhabiting the wild mountains he crosses in George Gordon, Lord Byron's play *Manfred* (an important source for "Alone"). Demons were thought by Greek philosophers to have bodies composed of a fifth element, called the quintessence by Aristotle and more generally *aether*, so this entity completes the list of the Greek elements. Demons in this sense

are also responsible for poetic inspiration, so in the final lines of the poem the speaker is perhaps appealing to a demon as the personification of the inspiration he receives from wild nature.

THEMES

Alienation

The main theme of "Alone" is the speaker's alienation from human society. Instead of communing with his fellow men, he ends up bound to nature by a mystery that sets him apart and which other people are not able to comprehend. Therefore, they do not understand how he thinks and feels any more than he understands how they think and feel. Yet he recognizes from lifelong experience that he and they—he and the world—are different. The poet finds himself drawn to what is destructive, though inspiring, in nature: tempests and thunderbolts, the very things that others fear (and, to reduce them to the mundane way of thinking the poet shuns, the very things that people take out insurance against). The urge to flee ordinary human existence for destructive nature, for death, in other words, would become a main theme in Poe's work as a whole. Bettina L. Knapp, in her *Edgar Allan Poe*, observes that Poe is obsessed by

> a deeply felt need for psychological death, for an eclipse of the ego and a schizophrenic disintegration of consciousness. Step by step Poe takes the reader from the realm of the living into a spectral world of shadows, from the existential sphere to that of the subliminal universe whose primal waters dissolve and absolve.

It is not hard to see this literary theme played out in Poe's life—in his alcoholism and his tendency to go on a drunken binge at the very moment he needed to work to achieve success. At the same time, it is rarely possible to know enough about a writer to fully understand his character and how it is both expressed and concealed in his work.

Confession

Among Poe's marginalia (brief pieces written as filler for magazines or newspapers), he penned a note that may throw some light on "Alone." He begins the half-page-long essay by asserting that "if any ambitious man have a fancy to revolutionize, at one effort, the universal world of human thought, human opinion, and human sentiment," he may easily do so. Poe

TOPICS FOR FURTHER STUDY

- Poe was a great favorite of the Argentinian author Jorge Luis Borges and a major influence on his work. Select one of his poems—the majority can be found in both the original Spanish and English translation in *Selected Poems* (2000), edited by Alexander Coleman—and write an essay comparing it to Poe's "Alone."

- Augustine, the fifth-century bishop of Hippo in North Africa, wrote in his *Confessions*: "People are moved to wonder by mountain peaks, by vast waves of the sea, by broad waterfalls on rivers, by the all-embracing extent of the ocean, by the revolutions of the stars. But in themselves they are uninterested" (10.8.15). A thousand years later, Petrarch (*Epistolae familiares* 4.1) cited this passage as antithetical to the medieval mind (from his viewpoint the modern mind), which he insisted was unable to find beauty in the natural world. Find and further study these passages and write an essay relating them to Poe's "Alone."

- The main theme of "Alone" is the poet's alienation, and it is undeniable that this is in some measure an adolescent feeling on the part of the nineteen-year-old Poe. Using an Internet search term like "teen angst" or "teen alienation," one can find an enormous amount of relevant poetry posted on blogs (and even more so in electronic publishing formats, which you could look at if you have access). The genre is so ubiquitous that many of the top hits are satires of it. Present your class with a prospectus of the kind of poetry you find, always bearing in mind similarities to and differences from "Alone."

- Poe's essay "The Philosophy of Composition" purports to give instruction on how to write a best-selling poem, though it is often taken as satire. In any case, he gives general instructions and then deals with the particular case of his own poem "The Raven." Write an essay analyzing "Alone" from the viewpoint of the procedure outlined in Poe's essay.

- Many anthologies for young adults feature poetry about nature, such as *Poems about the Natural World* (2014), edited by Evan T. Voboril, or Jane Yolen's *A Mirror to Nature: Poems about Reflection* (2009). Write a paper comparing the views of nature in a sampling of these poems with that expressed by Poe in "Alone."

tells him how: "All that he has to do is to write and publish a very little book. Its title should be simple—a few plain words—'My Heart Laid Bare.' But—this little book must be *true to its title*." Yet Poe is confident that this will never happen: "No man dare write it. No man ever will dare write it. No man *could* write it, even if he dared. The paper would shrivel and blaze at every touch of the fiery pen." Poe means that the difference between a man's interior self and the self he presents to the world is an unbridgeable gulf. The attempt would set the paper ablaze because it would bring the combustible material world into contact with the pure fire of the spirit.

This impossible distance between the true self and the self that one presents to the world would also become a major theme of Poe's work and one in deep discussion with the philosophy of his day. Jeffrey Steele, in *The Representation of the Self in the American Renaissance*, reflects on the deep division between Poe's view and that of the philosopher Ralph Waldo Emerson, who saw the visible individual as a faithful reflection of his interior. Poe, Steele says, instead views "the self as an opaque mask that reflects social demands and refracts unconscious impulses. Personality is not effaced [in his writing]; rather, the human face is imagined as a disguise."

The image of the fountain, rather than peaceful, is foreboding (©Phase4Studios / Shutterstock.com)

Herman Melville seems to agree with Poe, when he says in *Moby Dick*:

> All visible objects...are but as pasteboard masks. But in each event—in the living act, the undoubted deed—there, some unknown but still reasoning thing puts forth the mouldings of its features from behind the unreasoning mask. If man will strike, strike through the mask! How can the prisoner reach outside except by thrusting through the wall?

Here the mask is the world, concealing its true nature in the form of God, and tearing it away would be an act as destructive of the world as setting the burning pen to paper. "Alone" is an attempt by the poet to tear through the mask, to show the smoldering divinity within himself. Perhaps one reason Poe never published the poem is that as a more mature poet he realized he had not succeeded in setting the paper on fire because, as he says, it is not humanly possible to do so.

STYLE

Juvenilia

The term *juvenilia* usually refers to childhood writings by an author who achieved fame in later life. Naturally, such writing tends to survive only in manuscript form, since it was never intended for publication. A great mass of such writing does survive, for example, from the Brontë sisters, and its study forms almost a separate specialty. In contrast, while it is known that John Keats prepared a complete translation of Virgil's *Aeneid* during the summer break from school when he was fourteen years old, no trace of it survives. "Alone," a poem written when Poe was nineteen years old in a friend's autograph book, would certainly qualify as juvenilia for Poe, except for the extraordinary fact that already at nineteen he was a published poet.

"Alone" is juvenile in another sense, however, and that is in its adolescent sensibility. However much Poe exceeds his peers in the sophistication of the form of expression, the poem develops the typically adolescent sentiment that other people just do not realize how special the author is. If only they could see his real self, then they would understand. Poe, however, did turn out to have something special to show the world. Yet there remains something of the adolescent in Poe's sense of alienation. Lewis Leary, writing in the *Southern Literary Journal* for 1972, saw avatars of Poe in the "hippie" students walking around American college campuses of that era, in the student who

> communicates only with those who share his vision of a world unlike the world he has inherited. To those separated from him by gaps of age or understanding, he is likely to be disrespectful, sometimes viciously condescending.

Lewis sees "Alone" as an anthem of youthful alienation.

Taking a different tack in perhaps the most famous critical judgment of Poe, T. S. Eliot, in the *Hudson Review*, finds Poe's appeal to the adolescent in the reader:

> I believe the view of Poe taken by the ordinary cultivated English or American reader is something like this: Poe is the author of a few, a very few short poems which enchanted him for a time when he was a boy, and which do somehow stick in the memory. I do not think that he re-reads these poems...; his enjoyment of them is rather the memory of an enjoyment which he may for a moment recapture. They

seem to him to belong to a particular period when his interest in poetry had just awakened. Certain images, and still more certain rhythms, abide with him.

Eliot admits that this is not the most useful way to read Poe and that Poe is understood very differently by French critics, but it remains a reading pertinent to "Alone."

Poetics

Poe is famous as a poetic stylist and for his control of the formal qualities of poetry, such as meter and diction, entirely subordinated to the sound of poetry. It is for this reason that Poe is often hated by modern critics. The realization of modern poetry was that ideas, not sounds, make poetry, so the modern ear is unnerved by the careful attention Poe pays to sound. The prominent Poe scholar Daniel Hoffman at first dismissed Poe for this reason, considering him a hack who threw meaning away in favor of sound, distorting language for the sake of meter and rhyme. His opinion changed when he realized that Poe was also using language in ways that assisted ideas (for example, the repetitive ballad form of "Ulalume" that provides the context of the ballad tradition for the poem), but he still insisted that in order to appreciate Poe the reader has to work through Poe's linguistic mastery, which he considered a hindrance in and of itself. In the nineteenth century, however, the sound of poetry was as important as its meaning, in part because poetry was still typically read aloud, and Poe is perfectly clear that metrical showpieces like "Ulalume" and "The Bells" were intended for recitation.

Poe's prosody in "Alone" may not rise to the levels of those masterworks, but it is very sophisticated metrically for a poem of its era and still more for a poem written by a nineteen-year-old. Thomas Ollive Mabbott, in his edition of Poe's works, judges regarding "Alone" that "the metrical structure of the verses, with the many runlines, is one of Poe's earliest bold experiments and a most successful one." The poem is written in eleven rhyming couplets. Each line is a tetrameter, with four poetic feet. The first six couplets are ordinary iambic lines (generally unstressed followed by stressed syllables), but then the meter reverses itself and becomes trochaic (stressed followed by unstressed). The last four couplets are catalectic, that is, they end with a so-called limping foot, which has only the initial stressed syllable with no following unstressed

syllable. This means that the poem in the middle switches from the most conventional cadence of English poetry to a headlong rush—but a rush to nowhere, since there is no metrical or thematic resolution to the poem, which simply stops short, shocking the reader into thinking it might otherwise have moved on to matters that cannot be spoken about or which simply cannot be conveyed in language.

HISTORICAL CONTEXT

Magazines and Autographs

Poe is often mentioned as the first American writer who attempted to support himself entirely through the commercial proceeds of writing, rather than from the gifts of a wealthy patron. This was possible for the first time in history because advances in printing technology coincided with the rise of an educated middle class, fostering the invention of the modern magazine. The vast explosion of magazine publishing in the early nineteenth century led to a proportionate increase in paying work in both nonfiction and fiction, allowing writers like Mary Shelley and Nikolai Gogol to earn a living from their short stories. Poe attempted to follow in their footsteps, though with limited success. Kurt Vonnegut observed that, in the mid-twentieth century, he himself was in the last generation of magazine writers, as television eclipsed magazine publishing. Now, of course, magazines are almost completely dead because of the Internet, where there is a far greater amount of writing but very little of it paid.

Poe did not attempt to publish "Alone," but the circumstances of its publication were nevertheless shaped by the history of the century of magazines. The manuscript was discovered by a hack writer (a term of the era for a freelancer) named Eugene L. Didier, who in the 1870s was trying to make a living in magazine publication and had written a series of inconsequential articles on Poe. After some negotiation, he sold the manuscript to *Scribner's Magazine* for one hundred dollars (probably about equal to several months of his usual income). I. B. Cauthen, in his article in *Studies in Bibliography*, describes the surprisingly detailed documentation about the poem that survives in the correspondence of the *Scribner's* editor who negotiated with Didier and used his range of contacts in the publishing

The speaker feels a mysterious dread that is drawn from far and wide, from the mountains and the sky
(©Martin M303 | Shutterstock.com)

world to test the validity of the writer's claims. Didier, however, proved still more adept at exploiting the new periodical economy, and after selling the piece to *Scribner's*, sold it a second time to the *Sunday News*, a Baltimore newspaper, which actually published a transcription of the poem (rather than an engraving of the manuscript photograph) the day before the September 1875 issue of *Scribner's* went on sale.

"Alone" was written in the autograph book of Lucy Holmes, a middle-class woman of Poe's acquaintance in the 1820s and 1830s. If the term *autograph book* has meaning today, it is as a small book in which a fan would collect the autographs of celebrities, approaching them, if they are actors, from the crowd at a Hollywood premier or reception, or, if they are athletes, at a sports game or convention or in a similar venue. But in nineteenth-century America, an autograph book would be kept by someone for their friends to write meaningful comments in, perhaps interspersed with the owner's comments. It is not unusual, therefore, that Poe would have written a poem in such a book. Indeed, the book contained more than seventy other

poems, including one by Poe's older brother, William, that Poe had copied onto the page facing "Alone." The book was also filled with Holmes's own comments, other notes from her acquaintances, and hand-drawn copies of their visiting cards. This kind of autograph book has a close analog today in the Facebook page.

CRITICAL OVERVIEW

The most substantive study of Poe's "Alone" is I. B. Cauthen's article in *Studies in Bibliography*. Cauthen found the original manuscript (which is still in private hands) and established beyond doubt the authenticity of the poem. This was necessary because the original publisher of the poem, Eugene L. Didier, had altered the manuscript, writing his title for the work, "Alone," and a date probably derived from the Holmes family tradition for the writing of the poem, March 17, 1829. Cauthen established that this date is obviously wrong, since Poe was with his military unit in Boston at that time; however, a

COMPARE
&
CONTRAST

- **1820s:** Friends often exchange personal communications in a more lasting form than written correspondence, such as in a remembrance book or autograph book.

  Today: This kind of slightly more formal personal exchange of communication between friends often takes place on an Internet platform like Facebook, with people leaving public messages on each other's pages.

- **1820s:** The prairies in the middle of North America and the more arid regions in the Southwest (then in Mexico) are called the great American desert and are considered uninhabitable, and the Native Americans living there are characterized as bloodthirsty savages.

  Today: Despite the ecological disaster caused by poor farming practices in prairie regions in the Depression era (the dust bowl), the upper Midwest and West are productive and populous parts of the United States.

- **1820s:** The discoloration of the skin by exposure to intense sunlight is called *sunburning* and is avoided by elites as a marker of working-class status.

  Today: Since sunbathing in tropical climates in the middle of winter was first made possible for the middle and upper classes, originally by rail transport in the nineteenth century and now by air, the new term *suntanning* is used to indicate the display of disposable income that having a suntan in winter entails.

---

somewhat later date in 1829, when he is known to have visited Baltimore, is likely. Cauthen also describes the manuscript and summarizes a good deal of its history as well as the correspondence between editors at *Scribner's*, Didier, and various experts about the poem at the time of its publication. Cauthen also suggested the poem's inspiration in Lord Byron's *Manfred*. The publication was described as a facsimile, but while photography was involved in the process, the poem was ultimately printed from a hand-engraved plate, and its correspondence to the original is only approximate. Cauthen confirmed that the handwriting in the manuscript poem was Poe's, as was that of the poem of Poe's brother, to which was added a note that Poe copied it into the book. By the time Cauthen saw the manuscript in the 1950s, Didier's title and date, originally penciled in, had been erased, but traces of them were still visible on the page.

Perhaps because Poe never published the poem, or because it can be dismissed as derivative, or for whatever reason, "Alone" is not nearly as extensively studied as the several other well-known Poe poems, although it certainly approaches them in popularity and presence in the classroom. "Alone" is not mentioned, for example, in any of the essays in *The Cambridge Companion to Edgar Allan Poe*. Floyd Stovall, in his 1969 volume *Edgar Poe the Poet*, comments on the few manuscript poems of Poe's that survive:

> Little need be said about the half dozen early poems that Poe never collected.... The first three were written in albums, and it is quite possible that Poe did not keep a copy of any of them. Even if he did he would probably not have thought them good enough to be published in editions issued subsequent to their composition.

Stovall concedes that "'Alone' is perhaps the best of the three, but it is undistinguished even among the early poems in either meaning or form." However, Daniel Hoffman, in his important (if curiously titled) critical study *Poe Poe Poe Poe Poe Poe Poe*, has a different, if still difficult, relationship with "Alone." He was originally repulsed by what he considered the preciousness of the poem's nineteenth-century poetics but eventually came to the opinion that "the Poem is nearly a success." He holds that its tone echoes that of Thomas Hood or Tom Moore, poets of that era whom Hoffman (and many other critics) consider second rate, but in the last six lines it moves in the direction of William Blake—of genius, in other words. Hoffman is willing to make great allowances for the poem, as it is a youthful work in which Poe is still learning how to write poetry. Hoffman recognizes the poem's overwhelming theme of alienation: the poet is "not alienated by the neglect of a materialist Bourgeois society—that is the case of course, though here he doesn't complain of it—but alienated because of the fated specialness of his own nature." Poe, Hoffman thinks,

> is a marked man, one of the Chosen. Chosen to enjoy what others cannot even sense, chosen to suffer what others know not, to love whom he loves in an isolation as complete as that in which he feels suffering and joy.

CRITICISM

Rita M. Brown

Brown is an English professor. In the following essay, she situates Poe's "Alone" within the context of romanticism.

The romantic movement, in philosophy as well as literature and the arts, began in Germany and England in the late eighteenth century and ended, at least in its first phase in the 1820s or early 1830s, with the deaths of major figures such as Johann Wolfgang von Goethe, George Gordon, Lord Byron, and John Keats. The influence of German and British romanticism created new movements during the next generation, especially in France and the United States. In America, the romantic movement is part of the American Renaissance, in which philosophers like Henry David Thoreau and Ralph Waldo Emerson were prominent, as well as littérateurs like Herman Melville, Nathaniel Hawthorne, and Poe. Of these, Poe was certainly the premiere poet, and poetry may be regarded as the most prestigious literary expression of romanticism. Poe's "Alone" can be fully understood only within the context of romanticism.

As a philosophy, romanticism, like Marxism, embraced Georg Wilhelm Friedrich Hegel's dialectical analysis of history. Hegel established a historical typology based on the salvation

THE POET'S ALIENATION IS ALIENATION

FROM MODERNITY."

history outlined in the New Testament. The fall from the Garden of Eden contains within it the seeds of its own opposite, namely salvation, and the two will come together to produce the final state of a redeemed world. Hegel saw this progression as akin to a dialectical syllogism in which a major thesis can be combined with a minor thesis to produce a new, previously unknown synthesis, which will be true if the two premises are true. Marx provides an example of concrete historical analysis using this dialectical scheme. For instance, he held that the major medieval thesis of feudalism gave rise to a new merchant class that acted as a minor thesis, and the interaction between the feudal and merchant classes gave rise to the synthesis of bourgeois capitalism. Marx used dialectical analysis to project the process into the future, where bourgeois society, which has given rise to the industrial working class, will be overturned in the new and final synthesis of communism.

The romantic analysis of history is the same in its methods but reaches a very different conclusion. For the romantics, the Enlightenment was a turning point in history, in which analysis became the primary mode of human thought. Someone in the Middle Ages, to the contrary, was to the romantics naïve or innocent. Such people might have believed in Christianity without any conscious thought or analysis because they did not give any thought to finding another way to believe. The Enlightenment began to ask questions. Does the received account of Christian history agree with the historical account that can be rationally constructed by investigation of the evidence? Do the fundamental doctrines of Christianity agree with philosophical and scientific investigation? A person who asks these questions might remain a Christian, but his relationship with Christianity will be fundamentally changed. The same kind of distancing through systematic investigation can apply to any area of life, including class, government, or social relations generally. In concert with the rise

WHAT DO I READ NEXT?

- Sarah Crossan's *The Weight of Water* (2012) is a young-adult novel about a girl's family's move from Poland to England and the theme of alienation. Although the text constitutes a novel, it is written in verse.

- David Perkins's *English Romantic Writers*, 2nd ed. (1995), is a standard anthology and textbook of Keats, Byron, and other English romantics meant to introduce students to the writers of this school and provide an introduction to the movement that Poe's work grows out of.

- The main theme of the work of the Japanese novelist Haruki Murakami, such as in his 2014 novel *Colorless Tsukuru Tazaki and His Years of Pilgrimage*, is alienation from the modern world. He views modernity as a system built on greed and social control, which can be combated only through constructing a separate, self-determined identity apart from one's socially imposed role.

- Bertell Ollman's *Alienation: Marx's Conception of Man in Capitalist Society* (1971) is a standard textbook on Marxism (since one of Ollman's aims is to demystify Marx's elaborate technical language) and focuses on the problems of the modern human being's alienation in an industrial society, the great area of overlap between Marxism and romanticism.

- Another great American romanticist was Nathaniel Hawthorne, whose works have been collected into two volumes in the Library of America series: *Tales and Sketches* (1982) and *Collected Novels* (1983).

- David Luke's translations in the Johann Wolfgang von Goethe collection *Selected Poetry* (2005) present an overview of Goethe's romantic ideology as expressed in his poetry.

- *The Letters of Edgar Allan Poe* (1966), edited by John Ward Ostram, collects Poe's correspondence, giving insight into his personal, artistic, and professional life.

of analytic thought, industrialization was so radically changing society that it would be literally impossible to maintain received traditions and received social structures. If the life of a peasant is tied to the land, to the calendar of his parish church, to the churchyard where his ancestors are buried, to the motions of the sun throughout the day and the changing seasons, what meaning will his life have when he moves a hundred miles away to work tending machines on the night shift in a factory in Birmingham? The very circumstances of his life demand that tradition give way to something new.

The romantics viewed history as a dialectic with the major thesis being the primitive or naïve unreflective mental state, characterized as antiquity or tradition, and the modern critical, self-reflective mental state being the minor thesis. It was realized that the two were irreconcilable, but both seemed to have virtues. The naïve world was genuine and authentic (if fixed and immobile), while the modern world was critically engaged and produced an ever-growing body of knowledge. While the leaders of the Enlightenment in the generation previous to the romantics had been aware of the same dichotomy, their solution had been simply to throw tradition out as a hindrance. The romantics were, as they said, sentimentally attached to the simple and direct world of tradition. Therefore, they thought that it would be possible to achieve a synthesis between tradition and modernity, and that synthesis would be romanticism. The project could never be realized. William Wordsworth might speak from time to time as if he were simultaneously experiencing a reflective and unreflective perception in some sort of ecstatic state, but he would soon lose sight of it in a bout of depression. John Keats's "Ode to a Nightingale" describes a state where the poet ascends to a paradise where the synthesis is taking place, but he is not permitted to see it and is eventually cast back down in the dark world of modernity.

No romantic poem presents the whole dialectical scheme in a single image or narrative. One consequence of existing in modernity is that the whole can be glimpsed only in fragments, and a given romantic poem will show only a single aspect or view of the romantic totality. Seen in this light, Poe's "Alone" is a romantic fragment poem. Poe describes the integration of the traditional world, where everything is bound together into a single whole. The

Though for everyone around him the sky is blue, the speaker sees a frightening devil in the clouds
(©Pictureguy / Shutterstock.com)

lightning and the sunlight are part of the poet, and the poet is part of the lightning and the sunlight. This is something that the poet remembers from his infancy, in other words, from the traditional stage of development of human thought. The speaker of the poem, as a romantic, is different from other people, the modern people around him, because he is still bound to the natural world, not separated from it as they are. The poet's alienation is alienation from modernity. He feels out of place in the modern world, because the modern world is cut off from the natural unity of which he is part. The unspoken corollary is that modern people are just as out of place, because they are alienated from nature. The mystery in the poem is precisely the romantic reconciliation of tradition and modernity, the new thing that would make the world make sense again but which he cannot understand or, in any case, cannot reveal (since a mystery is not to be spoken).

Much of Poe's formal expression borrows ideas and forms from the ancient philosophy of Neoplatonism. The Enlightenment historian Edward Gibbon had ridiculed Neoplatonism because it accepted the existence of magic and the supernatural. The romantics embraced it for that very reason. The idea of the individual's participating in a cosmic whole, where he becomes part of the same organism as the storm and the mountain and all are alive together, is a basic principle of Neoplatonism. The organization of the world into four elements, an essential framework for the structure of "Alone," while it is more generally Greek, certainly came to Poe from Plato and his followers. Poe's use of the idea of the demon betrays its Neoplatonic origin. This Greek idea was particularized in Neoplatonism as a figure intermediary between the human and the divine worlds, and it is in this capacity that the demon appears in "Alone." It is a figure beckoning the poet to become one with nature.

Poe's "Alone" is deeply indebted to English romanticism in another way too. The poem is closely based on a scene in Byron's verse play *Manfred* (act 2, scene 2). In the play, the hero Manfred is wandering through the wild mountains and encounters a demonic figure identified as a witch who demands that he give an account of himself. Poe's use of this source was first noticed by I. B. Cauthen in his article on "Alone" in *Studies in Bibliography*. One can hardly read "Alone" and *Manfred* together without thinking of Eliot's famous maxim (from *The Sacred Wood*): "Immature poets imitate; mature poets steal." While Poe was certainly an immature poet at the time, there is an undeniable act of theft in the poem (perhaps one reason he never published it). One is just as strongly reminded, however, of Eliot's less well-known continuation of the line of thought: "Bad poets deface what they take, and good poets make it into something better, or at least something different." In the opening section of "Alone" Poe echoes Byron quite closely.

Poe changes a great deal also. Byron's misanthropy, expressed in his hatred of his own humanity and being brought back down to the human level just as he thought he was escaping upwards, is removed, and the passage is changed from an arrogant boast to a wail of sorrow and perplexity. Poe echoes also *Manfred*'s praise of the wilderness, but in Byron, the wild world is principally a place of escape from other human beings. It is wild and untamed, but especially it is unpeopled. In Poe, the wilderness is transformed into the living organism of a natural world of which the poet is a part.

Another mystery contained in "Alone," then, is the poet's link to the romantics of the past and their human achievements. The poet remains alone because he does not want to see that it is to the human world that he is necessarily connected. Crowded among men, he remains alone in his alienation from the natural world to which he seeks a connection that no human being can achieve. If he had truly achieved the romantic synthesis, he would be alienated neither from man nor from nature, neither from tradition nor from modernity.

Source: Rita M. Brown, Critical Essay on "Alone," in *Poetry for Students*, Gale, Cengage Learning, 2017.

Vincent Buranelli

In the following excerpt, Buranelli analyzes Poe's theories about poetry and its meaning.

. . . The writer of so much *ad hoc* copy aimed at meeting deadlines could not avoid self-contradiction, much less the apparent inconsistencies that spring from the uses of language, especially from forgetfulness about how one has defined

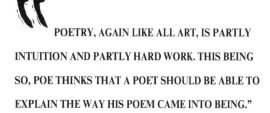

POETRY, AGAIN LIKE ALL ART, IS PARTLY INTUITION AND PARTLY HARD WORK. THIS BEING SO, POE THINKS THAT A POET SHOULD BE ABLE TO EXPLAIN THE WAY HIS POEM CAME INTO BEING."

words in the past. That is one caveat. A second touches the question of intellectual development, and this is an acute problem in a discussion of Poe's poetry, because the longest career he enjoyed during his comparatively brief life was that of a poet. The youthful author of "Tamerlane" is not identical with the mature author of "Ulalume," nor can their attitudes toward poetry as an art be meshed without friction.

Still, there are constants throughout, and by identifying and interpreting these we may arrive at a systematic statement that Poe himself possibly would not have rejected, and that, should he have done so, might fairly be argued as something forced upon him by his own principles.

In his famous "Letter to B——," written as early as 1831, Poe offers a few hints about the attributes by which poetry may be recognized:

> A poem, in my opinion, is opposed to a work of science by having, for its *immediate* object, pleasure, not truth; to romance, by having for its object an *indefinite* instead of a *definite* pleasure, being a poem only so far as this object is attained: romance presenting perceptible images with definite, poetry with indefinite sensations, to which end music is an *essential*, since the comprehension of sweet sound is our most indefinite conception. Music, when combined with a pleasurable idea, is poetry; music without the idea is simply music; the idea without the music is prose from its very definitiveness.

When Poe wrote this passage he was a young romantic poet, strongly influenced by Bryon, Moore and Shelley in his practice, just as strongly influenced by Schlegel, Shelley and Coleridge in his theory. The passage starts him to theorizing about poetry, and is fundamental enough in his continuing thought to be used as a point of reference for what he says later on. It deserves, therefore, to be examined clause by clause.

The distinction between poetry and science ties in directly with his broad philosophy of aesthetics. Less than anywhere else in creative literature will he allow the "heresy of *The Didactic*" to contaminate poetry. The poem must neither teach nor preach, truth and goodness being pertinent only if they arise indirectly from the text. The poet must be a committed true believer in art for art's sake.

What is the object of poetry? The "Letter to B——" says that pleasure is the immediate object. "The Poetic Principle" says that beauty is the "province of the poem," and defines poetry as "*The Rhythmical Creation of Beauty*." The same work adds that "through the poem" the reader experiences a kind of divine joy. The obvious inconsistencies of these *dicta* have caused Poe to be severely criticized for a confused thinker.

But the inconsistencies are not so radical as they seem, for they come out of different contexts. If the effect on the reader is under discussion, then it is correct to say that pleasure is the object. Since this pleasure is caused by beauty, it is correct to say that beauty is the object. Since the poem is a construct in verse, it may properly be defined as the rhythmical creation of beauty. Since the elements out of which the poet makes his construct are not themselves created by him, the idea of creation has to be modified, therefore, by the thought that what the poet manufactures is the poem, and that what the poem does is to suggest an already existent beauty. The poem thus becomes a pipeline connecting the reader with the beautiful, and the beautiful is arrived at through, rather than in, the poem.

Poe follows the Platonic tradition. He agrees with Plato that there is a higher world of perfect Ideas, of which the world in which we live is but a copy. Things suggest Ideas; and beautiful things suggest the Idea of beauty. Between things and Ideas exists the world of art, the world that would not exist but for the work of the poet, the musician, the painter. The function of the poet, then, is to put words together in such a way as to give his reader a glimpse of Platonic beauty, and thereby to rouse in him the pleasure and the elevation of the soul that come from contact with the beautiful.

Poe holds that the poet differs from the prose writer because he employs means that suggest indefinite, rather than definite, ideas and emotions. Both literary artists want to produce a desired effect. The story writer—whether his purpose is to amuse, to frighten, or to cause any other reaction—can pursue his aim with the

unencumbered directness of Poe writing "The Cask of Amontillado." He can do this because he is working on manageable human reactions like humor and fear. He is in pursuit of a definite, unequivocal, emotional reaction; and he has a clear view of both his objective and the best way to reach it.

The poet, on the contrary, is trying to reveal an eternal beauty that he himself has never seen except in intermittent and oblique flashes. He cannot achieve his purpose except by capturing, as far as the resources of language permit, those intangible feelings that defy direct description. He must try to arouse the sense of beauty by indirection, by being suggestive and symbolical, by choosing his words so that their associations and sounds may carry overtones beyond their dictionary meanings.

This is one of Poe's essential ideas, and one of his most influential, for it hints at the later development of poetry into symbolism and impressionism. Especially in France, with Baudelaire and Mallarmé and Valéry, poetry entered into the domain of psychology that Poe had identified. All of these poets subordinated the direct statement in favor of a suggestiveness that ranged beyond the limits of direct speech. The handling of words became more subtle and refined as the search went on for new ways to perpetuate new experiences. Form began to dominate content as never before in the history of poetry.

The theory is obviously not as all-embracing as Poe thought. It fits his own best poetry well enough, and the poetry of those inspired by him; but it does not cover the greatest poets of world literature. There is much more than Poe's concept of poetry in Homer, Dante, Shakespeare, and Goethe, all of whom are capable of doing what Poe says is impossible: expressing emotions like terror through genuine poetry. *King Lear*, to cite a clear case, bursts the bounds of poetry set by Poe. One of the most proper criticisms of Poe is that he is too addicted to identifying his personal art with universal art.

Indefiniteness implies music. This is another basic proposition of Poe's artistic creed, for he believes that music is the most indefinite of the arts, and therefore that poetry can catch some of this quality by being infused with music. He makes this point in "The Poetic Principle."

It is in Music, perhaps, that the soul most nearly attains the great end for which, when inspired by the Poetic Sentiment, it struggles—the creation of supernal Beauty. It *may* be, indeed, that here this sublime end is, now and then, attained *in fact*. We are often made to feel, with a shivering delight, that from an earthly harp are stricken notes which *cannot* have been unfamiliar to the angels. And thus there can be little doubt that in the union of Poetry with Music in its popular sense, we shall find the widest field for the Poetic development.

Poe puts the stages of poetry in the same ratio with music. Just as music finds its lowest level with program music (naturalistic music attempting to imitate the sounds of the world around us) and ascends by degrees to the highest level where it enters an artistic universe of pure form—just so does poetry rise from the definite imagery of the open eye to the indefinite impressions filtered "through the veil of the soul." Appropriately, several composers have been inspired by Poe to set his verses to music, and Ravel and Debussy have testified to his influence on their composition. "Edgar Allan Poe," wrote Debussy, "had the most original imagination in the world; he struck an entirely new note. I shall have to find its equivalent in music."

Poetry differs from music by using ideas, and from prose by using music. Poe, naturally, does not mean that poetry presents clear ideas to be judged as true or false. He means that, for all his talk about indefiniteness and the flight of the imagination, poetry is knowledge. It is an insight into something objective—the eternal beauty that the poet wants to unveil as far as he can by means of his poetry. In Poe's review of Joseph Rodman Drake, he defines the love of poetry as "the sentiment of Intellectual Happiness here, and the Hope of a higher Intellectual Happiness hereafter." Poetry is one result of "the unconquerable desire—*to know*." From this thought sprang a more intellectualistic handling of poetry than romanticism had ever produced. The seeds of Neo-Realism are here.

Poe denies passion to the poet for the same reason that he denies it to any artist. *As a man*, of course, the poet must be passionate; he must perceive the existence of a Platonic world of ideal beauty; and he must feel ecstatic during his moments of enlightenment by it. *As an artist*, he must sit down to his work in the mood of a cool-headed craftsman able to think about the end he has in view and about the means that will take him most expeditiously to it. There is no contradiction in calling passion the enemy of poetry: It is the enemy of all art, once the artist has begun to put his vision into expressive form.

Poetry, again like all art, is partly intuition and partly hard work. This being so, Poe thinks that a poet should be able to explain the way his poem came into being. "The Philosphy of Composition" claims to do precisely that with "The Raven": Poe will take us into his workshop and show us how this one of his productions was conceived and executed. Whether or not Poe's memory was accurate, whether or not "The Raven" actually came into existence by the process he describes, "The Philosophy of Composition" reveals the way in which he considered a poem ought to be written.

He begins by mounting one of his hobby horses—that of length. Just as he stands for brevity in prose, for the magazine story, he stands for brevity in poetry, for the poem that can be read in a single sitting. He calls the long poem a contradiction in terms since its object, the elevation of the soul, cannot be sustained for any degree of time. As might be expected, he argues also that unity fails. The epics of Homer and Milton he categorizes as successions of short poems divided by spaces that are prose but presented in poetic form.

His criterion is confused because he does not keep separate the poem as an objective thing and the psychological reaction of the reader. A long poem might be a true poem throughout, and the reader's interest might still flag through sheer weariness. Poe does not consider this possibility, or the possibility of a special aesthetic pleasure in coming back to a long poem over several sessions. As for unity, the *Iliad* has an architectonic unity with an aesthetic value of its own.

Poe says he began "The Raven" by deciding that he wanted about a hundred lines and that he ended with a hundred and eight. His objective is to elevate the souls of his readers by suggesting to them intimations of the perfect beauty that lies beyond this world. He here adds that the tone of the highest beauty in poetry is sadness and that melancholy, therefore, is "the most legitimate of all the poetical tones."

This is another point of confusion. There would be no need to cavil at his principle that, since poetry reveals eternal joys that are now beyond us, there lies deep within it, therefore, the cause of sorrow. It has always been one of the fundamental aesthetic ideas that great art is closely connected with the tragic sense of life—Virgil's *lachrimae rerum,* "the tears of things." But this feeling is too profound a commentary on man's fate to be identified with melancholy in Poe's sense. It is only on a more superficial level that his theory can be sustained.

Poe's notion of the function of melancholy in poetry leads him to ask himself what is the most melancholy of subjects. "Death—was the obvious reply." He next asks when death is most poetical. "When it most closely allies itself to *Beauty*: The death, then, of a beautiful woman is, unquestionably, the most poetical topic in the world—and equally is it beyond doubt that the lips best suited for such a topic are those of a beareaved lover."

This argument is so faulty that one may well feel that he ought to guard himself against the possibility that "The Philosophy of Composition" is another of Poe's hoaxes. To reduce the notion of beauty to that of feminine beauty is almost bathetic; and it is obvious that the death of a *good* woman (Desdemona's tragedy) is at least as moving as the death of a *beautiful* woman. This brand of aesthetics has validity only for Poe and for those who think as he does.

He echoes in his theory the practice of his poems and stories. He has in mind his young, beautiful, doomed women like Annabel Lee, Eleanora and Madeline Usher. His remarks about the death of a beautiful woman must be seen against his related principle that the loftiest beauty always has something strange about it. The beauty he experiences certainly is infused with a strong dose of the strange, and he handles it with such consummate art that he would have been in an invulnerable position if he had restricted his theory to cover his own poetry and nothing more.

"The Philosophy of Composition" purports to show how Poe took the above ideas, added to them those he entertained about versification, and wrote "The Raven." That there are defects in his analysis has been shown. Again, he perhaps does himself an injustice in expounding so mechanical a process. He never touches intuition—imaginative insight—even though elsewhere he explicitly declares this to be a necessary part of poetry. The work is useful, however, for understanding Poe, once the exaggerations have been discarded and the confusions exposed; for, wherever his inspiration came from in the first place, it seems indubitable that as a craftsman he did work in some such fashion as that outlined in "The Philosophy of Composition."

The main lines of its theory of poetry can be checked against "The Poetic Principle" and against his reviews. The treatment of versification appears in lengthy exposition in "The Rationale of Verse." It is a pity that he wasted so much time on this essay, which, although it says much that is sound about poetizing, proves that he had no conception of the difference between English verse (based on accent) and Greek and Latin verse (based on syllabic length). Fortunately his ear for the sounds of his own language was better than his "Rationale of Verse."

Poe wrote in "Marginalia" that genius is much more abundant than we think. He means that poetic inspiration is more widespread than the industry to exploit it; he means that potential poets are too lazy to make use of their gifts. He himself was not one of them. "The Philosophy of Composition" would be enough to tell us that if the rest of his works had vanished....

Source: Vincent Buranelli, "Lyric Strains," in *Edgar Allan Poe*, Twayne Publishers, 1977, pp. 89–95.

SOURCES

Ackroyd, Peter, *Poe: A Life Cut Short*, Chatto & Windus, 2008, pp. 7–8.

Augustine, *Confessions*, translated by Henry Chadwick, Oxford University Press, 1992, p. 187.

Bandy, W. T., "Poe's *Alone*: The First Printing," in *Papers of the Bibliographical Society of America*, Vol. 70, January 1, 1976, pp. 405–406.

Byron, George Gordon, *Manfred: A Dramatic Poem*, John Murray, 1817, pp. 33–34.

Cauthen, I. B., "Poe's *Alone*: Its Background, Source, and Manuscript," in *Studies in Bibliography*, Vol. 3, 1950/1951, pp. 284–91.

Eliot, T. S., "From Poe to Valéry," in *Hudson Review*, Vol. 2, No. 3, Fall 1949, pp. 327–42.

———, *The Sacred Wood: Essays on Poetry and Criticism*, Alfred A. Knopf, 1921, p. 114.

Hoffman, Daniel, *Poe Poe Poe Poe Poe Poe Poe*, Louisiana State University Press, 1998, pp. 31–33.

Knapp, Bettina L., *Edgar Allan Poe*, Frederick Ungar, 1984, pp. 114–17.

Leary, Lewis, "Edgar Allan Poe: The Adolescent as Confidence Man," in *Southern Literary Journal*, Vol. 4, No. 2, Spring 1972, pp. 3–21.

Mabbott, Thomas Ollive, ed., Notes to *Collected Works of Edgar Allan Poe*, Vol. 1, *Poems*, Belknap Press of Harvard University Press, 1969, p. 145.

Melville, Herman, *Moby Dick; or, The Whale*, Harper Brothers, 1851, Vol. 1, p. 181.

Poe, Edgar Allan, "Alone," in *Poetry and Tales*, edited by Patrick F. Quinn, Library of America, 1984, p. 60.

———, "Marginalia," in *The Works of the Late Edgar Allan Poe*, Vol. 3, *The Literati*, Redfield, 1857, p. 508.

Steele, Jeffrey, *The Representation of the Self in the American Renaissance*, University of North Carolina Press, 1987, p. 2.

Stovall, Floyd, *Edgar Poe the Poet: Essays New and Old on the Man and His Work*, University Press of Virginia, 1969, p. 209.

twentieth century, such as the Russian Revolution and the rise of the Nazi Party in Germany, can in part be traced back to romanticism (which is not to say that either was a legitimate expression of romanticism).

Hayes, Kevin J., ed., *The Cambridge Companion to Edgar Allan Poe*, Cambridge University Press, 2002.
    This is a collection of introductory essays to Poe's life and writings.

Melville, Herman, *Timoleon, Etc.*, Caxton Press, 1891.
    Although it was compiled only at the end of his life, this little-known poetry collection—available at the University of Nebraska–Lincoln's DigitalCommons—is a prime part of the poetic legacy of the third great American romantic besides Poe and Hawthorne. The poems clearly show the influence of Poe on Melville's ear, highlighting the very aspect of Poe's poetry most thoroughly rejected by modernity.

FURTHER READING

Bartlett, Irving H., *The American Mind in the Mid-Nineteenth Century*, 2nd ed., H. Davidson, 1982.
    Bartlett provides the standard account of American intellectual history in the period in which Poe emerged.

Berman, Marshall, *All That Is Solid Melts into Air: The Experience of Modernity*, Simon & Schuster, 1982.
    This well-respected political-science-oriented meditation on the intellectual revolutions of the nineteenth century shows how romanticism helped to create not the hoped-for romantic synthesis, but a more acute form of modernity, to the degree that many social disasters of the

SUGGESTED SEARCH TERMS

Edgar Allan Poe

"Alone" AND Poe

American Renaissance

alienation AND poetry

Neoplatonism

four elements

romanticism

nature AND poetry

Byron AND Manfred

At the San Francisco Airport

YVOR WINTERS

1955

"At the San Francisco Airport" is a poem by American mid-twentieth-century poet Yvor Winters. It was first published in the *Hudson Review* in the spring of 1955 and was reprinted in Winters's *Collected Poems* (1960) and *The Selected Poems of Yvor Winters* (1999). The poem is written in traditional rhyme and meter, which Winters adopted in his later poetry, and is one of several poems he wrote about his family. The poem describes the poet's feelings as he takes his daughter to the San Francisco Airport for a trip that she is to make without him. She is focusing on the journey while he reflects stoically on the fact that she will soon be gone, taking whatever journey in life awaits her, and he will be left behind.

AUTHOR BIOGRAPHY

Poet and literary critic Arthur Yvor Winters was born on October 17, 1900, in Chicago. His father, Harry Lewis Winters, was a trader on the Chicago Stock Exchange. His mother was Faith Evangeline Ahenfeldt Winters. Winters grew up in Chicago and was educated at Evanston and Nicholas Senn high schools. He then attended the University of Chicago from 1917 to 1918, where he was a member of the Poetry Club and continued the habit of writing poems, which he had begun in high school. In the winter of

Winters dedicated the poem to his daughter, which shows the difficulty he had in saying goodbye
(©Serhii Moiseiev / Shutterstock.com)

1918–1919 he suffered from tuberculosis and was sent to California and then to New Mexico for treatment. He recuperated over the next five years, during which his first book of poetry, *The Immobile Wind* (1921), and *The Magpie's Shadow* (1922) were published. Winters taught in high school in New Mexico for two years beginning in 1923 and then resumed his education, attending the University of Colorado at Boulder and graduating with a BA and MA in romance languages. He taught as an instructor in French and Spanish at the University of Idaho, Moscow, from 1925 to 1927. In June 1926, he married the poet and novelist Janet Lewis. They had first met in Santa Fe, New Mexico, where Lewis, who also had contracted tuberculosis, had gone to improve her health.

The couple moved to California in 1927, where Winters enrolled in a PhD program at Stanford University, also working as an instructor in the English department. He published four volumes of poetry over the next seven years: *The Bare Hills* (1927), *The Proof* (1930), *The Journey and Other Poems* (1931), and *Before Disaster*

(1934). He also cofounded the literary journal *Gyroscope* in 1929. After completing his PhD in 1934, Winters continued to teach in the English department. He ran poetry workshops, and among his students were the poets J. V. Cunningham, Robert Pinsky, and Thom Gunn. His students acknowledged him as an outstanding teacher, and he became a full professor in 1949.

Beginning in the late 1930s, Winters also distinguished himself as a critic, publishing *Primitivism and Decadence: A Study of American Experimental Poetry* (1937), *Maule's Curse: Seven Studies in the History of American Obscurantism* (1938), and *The Anatomy of Nonsense* (1943). He was actually more admired for his criticism than for his poetry, although he continued to publish the latter, including *Poems* (1940) and *The Giant Weapon* (1943). His *Collected Poems* was published in 1952 and revised in 1960, for which he was awarded the 1961 Bollingen Prize for Poetry. *Collected Poems* contained "At the San Francisco Airport," which was first published in the *Hudson Review* in the spring of 1955.

Winters retired from teaching in 1966. His volume *The Early Poems of Yvor Winters, 1920–1928*, was published in that year also. His final book, a work of literary criticism, was *Forms of Discovery* (1967). Winters died of throat cancer on January 25, 1968, in Palo Alto, California. He was survived by his wife, his daughter (born in 1931) and son (born in 1938).

POEM SUMMARY

The text used for this summary is from *The Selected Poems of Yvor Winters*, Swallow Press, p. 107. A version of the poem can be found on the following web pages: http://www.poetry foundation.org/poems-and-poets/poems/detail/ 47785, http://www.poemhunter.com/poem/at-the-san-francisco-airport/, and http://www.ohios wallow.com/extras/0804010129_excerpt.pdf.

The poem is in five stanzas of five lines each. In the first stanza, the poet and his daughter arrive at the San Francisco Airport terminal. In the first three lines, the poet comments on the glare of the artificial light and how easy it is to see everything. All the metal surfaces gleam. There is, however, something false about this light, because it is unlike natural light. (The reader may assume that the poet is accompanied by his daughter, because the poem is dedicated to her, with a date, 1954, after it, which suggests that the poet was drawing on an actual incident in his life. The poet's daughter would have been about twenty-three years of age in 1954.) Lines 4 and 5 mention all the airplanes that are waiting outside, in the darkness that contrasts with the light in the terminal.

In stanza 2, the poet mentions that his daughter is with him. He thinks of her as small and delicate and imagines that she is occupied in thinking about things that he cannot fully remember, although he offers no explanation of what those might be. She is focused on the journey she is about to undertake. The final line offers an observation about the situation he is in; as his daughter goes off on some new adventure, he feels he is now part of her past, and there seems to be a finality about it in his mind. He and his daughter have reached a turning point in their relationship.

Having established in stanza 2 that father and daughter are about to be separated, in stanza 3 the poet looks at the situation from a different point of view, laying out some of the things that he and his daughter share and which join them together. It is as if they are both driven on, in a certain state of anxiety, to do whatever it is they have to do in life. They both have the same determination and enthusiasm; they acquire whatever skills they need, and they face up to things even when it is not easy, because they know that doing so is better than shirking tasks that are absolutely necessary.

In stanza 4 the poet concentrates on what is going on in his own mind. It seems from the first two lines that for a moment he is lost in confusion or despair or some other negative emotion. But then, at the end of line 2 and in line 3, clarity is restored. He has the simple realization that whatever is going to happen will happen, no matter what he thinks or feels about it. The second part of line 3 along with lines 4 and 5 seem to expand on this point, looking further ahead at what might be lost in this endless progression of life's experiences. Eventually, all is lost, because death will bring an end to the intellect—the means by which he knows what he knows—and everything else about him.

The last stanza repeats the beginning of the first stanza, with its reference to the terminal, but in this stanza the emphasis is not on the airport terminal but on the fact that the moment marks a termination of one stage in the relationship between father and daughter. The daughter must take the way that is marked out for her— she can do nothing else—and he must remain behind, contemplating the event. He has a good, clear, intellectual grasp of what is going on as he stands in the glare of the terminal lights, but it is a sober, difficult, lonely moment for him nonetheless. There is a sense that although he stands in the light at this moment, the light of his intellect is all that stands between him and a darkness all around.

THEMES

Father-Child Relationships
Central to the poem is the poet's relationship with his daughter; this is what stimulates his thoughts about how life is moving on and changing. It seems likely that the daughter is a young adult, because it appears that she is making the airplane trip by herself. She is not presented in any detail, however, and is seen entirely through

TOPICS FOR FURTHER STUDY

- Write a poem in traditional rhyme and meter (not necessarily iambic tetrameter) from the point of view of a young woman who is saying goodbye to her father in a context that resembles in some way the situation in "At the San Francisco Airport." In other words, examine a similar situation but from the daughter's perspective, rather than that of the father. What thoughts and feelings does she have at this important moment in their lives?

- Write a free-verse lyric poem in the first person ("I") that describes and explores a particular emotion or feeling prompted by something else—a memory, an experience or observation in nature, or anything else that inspires you. Then try to write the poem in formal verse, with regular meter and rhyme. Give a class presentation in which you read both poems and discuss the relative merits of free verse and formal verse. Which is the better of your two poems? Which was harder to write and why? Which poem is the better one when read aloud?

- Select another poem by Winters and write a brief essay in which you compare and contrast it with "At the San Francisco Airport." One suggestion for comparison is "Much in Little," a poem about nature that can be found at the Poetry Foundation website, at http://www.poetryfoundation.org/poems-and-poets/poems/detail/47783.

- Consult *Roots & Flowers: Poets and Poems on Family* (2001), an anthology of poems edited by Liz Rosenberg that is aimed at young-adult readers. Forty poets are represented, and in addition to their poems they each make a statement about how their families have affected their poetry. Take one or two poems that you like and read them aloud to your class, explaining why you selected them. Also write a statement, like those in the book, about how your family has influenced your own writing. Upload the statement to your blog and invite others to comment on it.

---

the eyes of the father, who describes what he thinks must be going on in her mind. It is clear that he feels protective toward her, because he refers to her as "small," and he is aware of what he sees as her vulnerability. He also believes, as stanza 3 makes clear, that he and his daughter share some of the same personality traits, such as determination and the desire for knowledge, and a vision of what they need to do in life as well as a certain edgy sensibility (conveyed in line 2) that seems to drive them on. These shared qualities, at least in the opinion of the father, bind them together and create a feeling in him that they are, in a way, like one person. After all, she likely inherited these qualities from her father.

Given the closeness to her that he feels and that he is attached to his protective role as father, it is hard for him to let his daughter go; doing so

likely represents the end of an era for him in his personal life. The feelings he has no doubt resemble those of many parents when they send their children off to college; they must acknowledge that their son or daughter is no longer a child and must begin to make his or her way in the world. The days of living closely together as a family unit have gone and will probably never return. It is not surprising, then, that the father's thoughts have something of a melancholy hue. He knows his daughter is intent on doing whatever new task awaits her, and it seems he feels that he is no longer important for her, as the last line of stanza 2 suggests. He is being left behind, or so he feels, and is part of what the young woman has grown out of. (It should be noted again that the poem consists entirely of the father's own thoughts about the subject; it is

Night is falling, and the planes outside are in the dark, though inside the lights are bright

(©Sergey Peterman / Shutterstock.com)

The latter part of the poem might be thought to convey the idea that for all that a person knows, there is so much more that he or she does not know, and even what is known will one day no longer be obtainable. A little island of light burns brightly in the conscious mind, and the poet uses it to understand his life rationally, as best he can, using his intellect and whatever other tools he can muster. But surrounding this light of understanding is a great darkness, as if the island is threatened with being overwhelmed by waters that will obliterate it. For the moment the poet is fully awake and alert to life, as he stands in the garish light of the airport terminal, holding darkness at bay (stanza 5, line 5), but perhaps the last line of the first stanza, about the airplanes being "already" in the darkness, has now acquired a more ominous meaning, for darkness will come to all at some point.

not a dialogue between them, so it is possible that the father is mistaken about how his daughter feels.) The challenge for the father, after he watches his daughter go through the departure gate, is going to be how to construct a meaningful life for himself now that the close day-to-day relationship he had with his daughter is over.

Change

The imminent parting of father and daughter at the airport represents a concrete, observable change in the lives of both, and the poet uses this as a jumping-off point for more abstract considerations of change in a larger context. Everything is transient; nothing lasts forever, including memory, for there are already things the poet has half-forgotten (stanza 2). An unknown destiny awaits all. At the present moment, though, he is in full possession of his intellectual faculties, and it seems that this is what he prides himself on, because they function as the tools with which he can understand at least a small part of his world. There is a sense, nevertheless, that human knowledge is always limited because the container of that knowledge, the individual intellect, is vulnerable. It is subject to the same inexorable change that is—just to give one instance—taking the father's daughter off on a new phase of her life.

STYLE

Meter

The meter is iambic tetrameter, meaning that there are four iambic feet in each line. Iambic meter is the most common meter in English poetry. Each iambic foot consists of an unstressed syllable followed by a stressed syllable.

Caesura

A caesura is a pause in the middle of a line, indicated by some mark of punctuation, such as a comma, colon, or period. In this poem, there are quite a lot of caesuras. The colon in the first line of the first stanza is one example. The periods in lines 2 and 3 in stanza 4 are also caesuras. (This is the only stanza that contains more than one sentence.) Each stanza has at least one caesura, most commonly a comma. Employing a caesura helps to vary the rhythm of a poem and avoid monotony, especially in a poem such as this, where the meter is very regular.

Rhyme

The rhyme scheme is the same in all five stanzas. The last syllable of line 1 rhymes with lines 3 and 5, and lines 2 and 4 rhyme. The pattern can thus be described as *ababa*. Most of the rhymes (all of them in stanzas 1, 2, and 5) occur with monosyllabic words.

COMPARE & CONTRAST

- **1950s:** While Winters near the end of his poetic career writes in traditional rhyme and meter, Allen Ginsberg, one year after the publication of "At the San Francisco Airport," publishes "Howl" (1956), a long, ambitious Whitmanesque free-verse poem that announces his arrival as a formidable force on the American literary scene. Ginsberg is one of the Beat poets, who provide fresh energy to American poetry in the 1950s.

  Today: Free verse is the dominant poetic form in American poetry, but owing to the movement known as New Formalism, which flourished mostly in the 1980s and 1990s, more poetry is published today in traditional rhyme and meter than was the case in the 1960s and 1970s. For example, West Chester University in Pennsylvania holds a large annual poetry conference with several hundred participants that focuses on New Formalism. Some New Formalist poets who led the movement in the late twentieth century are still publishing. These poets include Dana Gioia, who publishes *Pity the Beautiful* in 2012 and *99 Poems: New and Selected* in 2016. Another contemporary New Formalist poet is A. E. Stallings, who publishes *Olives* in 2012.

- **1950s:** In addition to the emergence of the Beat poets, a relatively young poet, Elizabeth Bishop, publishes her second collection of poems, *Poems: North & South—A Cold Spring* in 1955, for which she receives the Pulitzer Prize. A well-established poet, Marianne Moore, publishes *Like a Bulwark* in 1956. Several of Winters's students also begin to publish around this time. Edgar Bowers publishes *The Form of Loss* (1956); Thom Gunn publishes *Fighting Terms* in 1954 and *The Sense of Movement* in 1957; Donald Hall, who spent a year in the early 1950s as a Creative Writing Fellow at Stanford, studying under Winters, publishes *Fantasy Poets Number Four* in 1952 and *Exiles and Marriages* in 1955.

  Today: Leading American poets in this decade, as measured by the winners of the Pulitzer Prize for Poetry, include Peter Balakian, who wins the 2016 prize for his *Ozone Journal*, his seventh poetry collection. Earlier volumes of his verse include *Ziggurat* (2010). Other Pulitzer Prize winners in the 2010s include Rae Armantrout, Kay Ryan, Tracy K. Smith, Sharon Olds, Vijay Seshadri, and Gregory Pardlo.

- **1950s:** A new terminal is completed at San Francisco International Airport in 1954. A three-day celebration marks the event and includes an exhibition of forty-three aircraft on the airfield. In that year, two million passengers pass through the airport.

  Today: San Francisco International Airport is the second-busiest airport in California, after Los Angeles International Airport. It is the seventh-largest airport by number of passengers in the United States, with nearly forty-five million passengers in 2013. A remodeled Terminal 2 opens in 2011. It includes a collection of fine art and a museum gallery. In 2012 a quiet space for yoga practitioners is created in Terminal 2.

HISTORICAL CONTEXT

American Poetry in the 1950s

During the 1950s Winters did not write many poems, but he continued to publish literary criticism, such as *The Function of Criticism* in 1957. Winters was one of a number of poets of the time who were also well known as critics and university teachers of literature. These included R. P. Blackmur, who taught at Princeton University from the 1940s to the 1960s; John Crowe Ransom, who taught at Kenyon College in the

The airport setting is cold and artificial (©Perfect Gui | Shutterstock.com)

1950s; and Theodore Roethke, who taught for fifteen years at the University of Washington in Seattle. Other poet-critics of the period included Allen Tate, with whom Winters frequently corresponded, and Robert Penn Warren. Many of these outstanding teachers had students who went on to distinguish themselves as poets. In this decade it became more common for poets to gain employment at universities as teachers of literature and creative writing. This meant that they became part of the academic establishment rather than having to make a living at some other occupation. In contrast, for example, William Carlos Williams and Wallace Stevens, two of the most prominent American poets of a generation earlier than Winter, who were still publishing in the 1950s, were a doctor and an insurance executive, respectively.

The work of Williams and Stevens, as well as the later work of modernist poets such as Ezra Pound, Robert Frost, and Marianne Moore, made up a large part of the American poetry landscape in the 1950s. One of the most popular of verse forms was the lyric poem, a brief meditation on an object or a scene in nature or on

some incident encountered by the poet, presented in a way that explained and clarified the poet's feelings. Like "At the San Francisco Airport," these poems were often written in formal, rhymed verse, although free verse was also becoming more popular.

In addition to the established poets, newer poetic voices were emerging among a generation of poets born between about 1900 and 1920. These included Richard Wilbur, who published *Things of This World*, which won the Pulitzer Prize for Poetry and the National Book Award in 1957. Other poets of this younger generation included Elizabeth Bishop, John Berryman, Randall Jarrell, Karl Shapiro, and Robert Lowell. These mainstream poets did not form any new poetic movement, even though the heyday of modernism was well in the past. However, during the 1950s and into the 1960s new perspectives emerged in the form of the Beat poets, who included Allen Ginsberg and Gary Snyder. The publication of Ginsberg's visionary *Howl and Other Poems* in 1956 was a landmark in the history of post–World War II American poetry. Interestingly, Ginsberg started his poetic career writing traditional rhyming quatrains before unleashing the long, unrhymed lines of the free-verse "Howl." This was the exact opposite of Winters's poetic journey, which started with free verse and ended in formal verse. (Winters abandoned writing free verse in the late 1920s.)

Also influential were the Black Mountain poets, named as such because Charles Olson, the founder of this school, taught at Black Mountain College in North Carolina. Olson's influential manifesto *Projective Verse* was published in 1950. Robert Creeley and Denise Levertov were two prominent poets associated with this movement. In addition, Lowell's *Life Studies* (1959) is considered a seminal work of the confessional poetry movement that gathered strength in the 1960s. Confessional poets revealed in their verse the most painful aspects of their personal lives, including traumatic events such as divorce and mental illness.

CRITICAL OVERVIEW

Winters's poetry has been respected by other poets and critics without ever gaining widespread popularity. After the publication of Winters's *Collected Poems* in 1952, literary critic David Daiches hailed it as "the equal of anything in the United States since Emily Dickinson" (as quoted by Elizabeth Isaacs in *An Introduction to the Poetry of Yvor Winters*), which is high praise indeed. Daiches opined that the poems "work by limitation ... precise, restricted, remarkable technical accomplishment and control." However, Jan Schreiber noted in *Contemporary Poetry Review* in 2004 that after Winters's death, it did not take long for interest in his poetry to dip, and *Poetry*, a well-known anthology compiled by R. S. Gwynn in 1998, included poetry of a number of Winters's former students but omitted Winters. Yet Schreiber notes that some of Winters's poems, including "At the San Francisco Airport," "still reward the thoughtful reader and should be preserved."

Over the years, several literary critics have commented favorably on the poem. Helen Pinkerton Trimpi, in her introduction to *The Selected Poems of Yvor Winters*, calls it "the exemplar of Winters's high art." Elizabeth Isaacs, in *An Introduction to the Poetry of Yvor Winters*, notes that "At the San Francisco Airport" is one of a number of poems Winters wrote

in which the subjects of the poems are members of his own family. These poems "testify to the seriousness with which he took his family relationships and the depth of his affection. In these poems there is no modern mawkishness, no Freudian frustration; simply honest dedication."

Dick Davis, in *Wisdom and Wilderness: The Achievement of Yvor Winters*, selected the poem as an example of the "tact and tenderness" apparent in Winters's poems about his own family, poems that are notable for "their poignant sense of the uniqueness and fragility of individual lives." Davis finds the "understated stoicism of the end ... very moving" and also comments on the final image of the poem, which

> is not only a fine evocation of the father left alone, momentarily fixed in private thought, withdrawn from the airport's public glare, but it suggests too that light of the intellect which had become Winters's chief concern, the intellect which sees and understands but knows that it is cut off from the life it loves and watches.

Terry Comito, *In Defense of Winters: The Poetry and Prose of Yvor Winters*, offers the view that "At the San Francisco Airport" is a representative poem of the last years of Winters's career, in which he "is forced ... to acknowledge that all his certainties are inscribed in an unknowable darkness." The image in the poem of the "hard limited glare" is the "characteristic image for the straitened place we are able to make for ourselves ... a wakefulness that seems to him merely to make more intense the night all around it." Comito comments further,

> This solitary brightness is ... the clarity of an intensely felt absence: the absence, precisely, of what the poet has brought into being (his daughter, his self) and now finds from moment to moment slipping away from him.

CRITICISM

Bryan Aubrey

Aubrey holds a PhD in English. In the following essay, he discusses the theme of stoicism in "At the San Francisco Airport."

In 2003, Dana Gioia, David Mason, and Meg Schoerke compiled and edited for McGraw-Hill *Twentieth-Century American Poetry*, a massive, nearly twelve-hundred-page anthology, with critical commentary, which presented the whole range of American poetry across the twentieth

WHAT DO I READ NEXT?

- "A Prayer for My Son" is one of the poems, like "At the San Francisco Airport," that Winters wrote about his own family. The poem is a tender one, appealing for divine protection for his young son, who will eventually have to make his own way in a difficult world. The poem can be found in *The Collected Poems of Yvor Winters* (1978), with an introduction by Donald Davie.

- "The Marriage" is another touching poem by Winters about family, this time about the relationship between husband and wife that celebrates how well they loved each other. The poet also is aware that one day death will bring an end to it all, but he issues instructions that their ashes be gathered in one urn, because they were one spirit. "The Marriage" can be found in *The Collected Poems of Yvor Winters* (1978), with an introduction by Donald Davie.

- "Promises" is a poem by African American poet Rita Dove. It is written from the point of view of a woman named Beulah, who tells of the advice given to her by her father at her wedding ceremony. However, unlike the apparent close relationship between father and daughter in "At the San Francisco Airport," Beulah does not have warm feelings for her father, regarding his words as insincere. The poem appears in a collection of poems that tell the story of Beulah and her husband, who are based on Dove's grandparents. *Thomas and Beulah* (1986) won the Pulitzer Prize for Poetry in 1987.

- *Essential Love: Poems about Mothers and Fathers, Daughters and Sons* (2000), edited by Ginny Lowe Connors, is a collection of about 150 poems by American poets on the theme of parent-child relationships. Poets featured include Donald Hall, Robert Hass, Maxine Kumin, Galway Kinnell, and Sharon Olds.

- In "At the San Francisco Airport," the father is about to go through a significant transition in his life, now that his daughter is grown and ready to pursue her own goals. He may have to make some changes in his life and his attitude in order to come to terms with this new reality. In her best-selling book *Passages: Predictable Crises of Adult Life* (1976, reprinted in 2006), Gail Sheehy explores the various crises that are likely to arise in adult life as people move through their twenties, thirties, forties, and fifties and explains how to cope with such challenges.

- "A Prayer for My Daughter," is a poem by Irish poet W. B. Yeats about his infant daughter. He prays for her as she sleeps in her cradle, wishing her, as all fathers do, a future happiness. The poem, which can be found in Yeats's *Selected Poems* (1995) in the Everyman's Library Pocket Poets series, can be compared to Winters's "A Poem for My Son," although it is very different in form and Yeats was not a poet that Winters counted as an influence on his own work.

- *Poetry for Young People* (2013), by well-known American poet Maya Angelou, consists of twenty-five poems, with an introduction and annotations by Edwin Graves Wilson and illustrations by Jerome Lagarrigue.

century. The anthology did not include a single poem by Yvor Winters, although it alluded several times to Winters's work as a critic. None of Winters's poems appear in another major anthology, the eighth edition of *The Norton Anthology of*

American Literature (2012) either, squeezed out by bigger names of the period, such as Robert Frost, Wallace Stevens, William Carlos Williams, Ezra Pound, and some of the poets from a younger generation such as Elizabeth Bishop, Randall

> PERHAPS THE POET CONSIDERED IT A MORAL SITUATION BECAUSE THE FATHER IS DUTY-BOUND NOT TO OPPOSE THE DEPARTURE OF HIS DAUGHTER, EVEN THOUGH SEEING HER GO LEAVES HIM WITH THOUGHTS THAT MIGHT BE DESCRIBED AS MELANCHOLY OR AT LEAST SOBER."

Jarrell, and Richard Wilbur, among others. However, another large anthology, the *Oxford Book of American Poetry*, edited by David Lehman and published in 2006, does feature four poems by Winters, including "At the San Francisco Airport." One might conclude from this that Winters's place as a poet is by no means secure in the collective cultural memory, and undergraduates may not encounter his work very often, although it cannot be said that he is an entirely forgotten poetic voice.

Admirers of "At the San Francisco Airport" will hope that Winters's name as a poet will live on for some time yet. This would be in addition to the place he holds as one of the leading literary critics of his day, who helped to shape the literary canon as it is known today. Interestingly, one of the admirers of the poem was no less than the poet himself, who commented on it in a letter dated April 21, 1958, to his friend fellow literary critic Allen Tate. Winters remarks that he had sent the poem in typescript to Tate, and Tate had not liked it; then he notes that Frederick Morgan, editorial director of the *Hudson Review*, said it was the best poem the journal had published. Winters then offers his own view that the poem is one of the fifteen or eighteen best poems he wrote. He also analyzes it, and because poets do not usually offer detailed analyses of their own poems and Winters was himself a prominent critic, his comments are worth exploring.

Winters writes that stanzas 2 and 3 of the poem are "almost wholly in abstract language; they are a close and quick analysis of a certain moral situation, roughly similar to what one might expect to find in Wyatt or Jonson." He is referring to sixteenth-century English poet

Thomas Wyatt (1503–1542) and Ben Jonson (1572–1637), a later English poet and dramatist, both of whom were known for their lyric poetry and were greatly admired by Winters. "The closely ordered rational structure of the whole poem may resemble Jonson," Winters added, revealing the high place he accorded the rational element in poetry, in contrast to the romantic emphasis on emotion. Winters describes the remaining three stanzas as "largely a matter of physical detail (although the fourth stanza is partly abstract). The sensory imagery, however, is . . . not Renaissance imagery."

The "moral situation" the poet refers to here is the imminent parting of father and daughter, who are close but must be separated because life is moving on and the former relationship of father and child cannot be maintained. Perhaps the poet considered it a moral situation because the father is duty-bound not to oppose the departure of his daughter, even though seeing her go leaves him with thoughts that might be described as melancholy or at least sober. He knows how much they have in common as individuals and has a feeling of being left behind as his daughter's new independence manifests in the trip she is about to take on her own. Perhaps this is a moment that all parents (and sons and daughters) know in some form or another at some point in their lives, which gives the poem a certain universal quality. The individual aspect of such a situation is how different people might respond to it. What is noticeable about "At the San Francisco Airport" is the self-control exerted by the father. He does not give direct expression to his emotions; he seems to hold them in, even as he is acutely aware of them. (In Winters's poetry, the undisciplined expression of emotion was something he was at pains to avoid.) It seems also that this is a private moment for the father, not something he is going to share with his daughter (notwithstanding the fact that the poem is addressed to her). Indeed, there is no dialogue in the poem; the situation is seen entirely from the point of view of the father, who is determined to remain stoic in the face of this personal loss, because he knows it is inevitable and part of their respective destinies.

In her book *An Introduction to the Poetry of Yvor Winters*, Elizabeth Isaacs has taken up the theme of stoicism in Winters's poetry, writing that the "development of stoic strength" stands

The airport's artificial light makes everything seem unnatural to the speaker (©Wayne0216 / Shutterstock.com)

out as one of six major themes in his poetry, becoming prominent in the later poems. She notes, for example, that in two poems addressed to Herman Melville, including "A Portrait of Melville in My Library," "he seeks for his own restless spirit the quiet contemplation that he imagined the older poet had finally achieved." This is not dissimilar to the way in which the father in the poem reflects on his situation; emotion is present, no doubt, but it is held in check, filtered through a rational consciousness that philosophically accepts the way things must be and finds some solace in that. This appears to have been Winters's ideal, both in poetry and in life. He was distrustful of emotions and the role they played in life, preferring reason.

In "Notes on Contemporary Criticism," one of his essays that later appeared in *Uncollected Essays and Reviews* (1976), as quoted by Dick Davis in *Wisdom and Wilderness: The Achievement of Yvor Winters*, he discussed reason and emotion in the context of Roman Catholic

ethics, to which he adhered. In terms of good and evil, he ascribed evil to the emotions and good to "the power of rational selection in action." To attain such a thing, a person must eliminate emotion to the extent that that was possible, he wrote. It was not possible to eliminate emotion entirely, but it should be reduced "to a minimum." The end result would be "a controlled and harmonious life," as the ancient Greek Stoic philosophers had argued. Commenting on this, Davis calls it a Socratic notion that what stops a man from choosing the good and instead choosing evil "is emotion, which blurs his perception and persuades him that a lesser good (for example, the satisfaction of his own desire) is greater than an in fact greater good (for example, honesty)."

By the same token, calm submission to whatever fate and destiny may decree would be considered a greater good than indulging in a particular emotion that might lead to an impulsive and therefore inadvisable action—in terms of the poem, trying to stop the daughter from striking out on her own, making her feel guilty about doing so, or any one of a variety of other reactions that might stem from an emotional reaction to the situation.

Another reason that Winters admired and cultivated stoicism was that, in his view, as explained by Terry Comito in *In Defense of Winters: The Poetry and Prose of Yvor Winters*, "what we know is grounded, as the very condition of its possibility, in what we do not and cannot know." In other words, although a person may gain clarity about a particular situation (as the father does in "At the San Francisco Airport") it is knowledge of a limited kind, because so many other vital and ultimate matters of life and death must remain unknown and unobtainable.

It is this wisdom, such as it is, that Winters wished to pass on through his work. As Donald Davie, a fellow poet who knew Winters, wrote in an introduction to the 1978 edition of Winters's *Collected Poems*—alluding first to Winters's status as a well-known literary critic—"Winters's poems were not written for class-room use or . . . as models or *exempla* or illustrations of 'how to write,' but as considered statements of how to *live*, or of how the business of living had been experienced by one thoughtful and feelingful man." "At the San Francisco Airport" might be considered an example of exactly that.

Source: Bryan Aubrey, Critical Essay on "At the San Francisco Airport," in *Poetry for Students*, Gale, Cengage Learning, 2017.

Dick Davis

In the following excerpt, Davis explores Winters's depiction of nature in his later works.

The poems of my second suggested group clearly indicate this ambiguity in Winters's response to the external and natural world. These poems are mostly concerned with the past, and their tone is more or less constantly nostalgic. They are either concerned with the poet's own biography, or with episodes from California history. As Winters had spent part of his early childhood in California, the two subjects were probably associated for him. In these poems the natural world is less a threat than a symbol of lost beatitude, often indistinguishable from the traditional romantic beatitude of childhood. The implication of a lost Eden is reinforced in certain of the poems on

BY THIS INTRODUCTION OF THE PAST WINTERS PREPARES US FOR THE APPEARANCE OF HIS FATHER IN THE POEM, AND HE PREPARES US TOO FOR THE TONE OF QUIET RESPECT WITH WHICH HE TREATS HIS FATHER'S VALUES AND LIFE."

California history by the descriptions of a fall—the sudden and violent transformation of California during the latter half of the nineteenth century. Of the autobiographical poems in *The Journey* the most important are "On a View of Pasadena from the Hills," "The Marriage," and the title poem, in which, however, the relation of the mind to external reality is more that of questing exploration than nostalgic revery. Of the autobiographical poems from the later volumes, which share the sense of nature as a benign presence, the most important seem to me to be "On Re-reading a Passage from John Muir" and "A Summer Commentary."

If we except the satire "The Critiad," which Winters did not reprint after its appearance in *The Journey*, "On a View of Pasadena from the Hills" is his longest and most ambitious poem in heroic couplets. In it he combined both personal and more public topographical history to make a poem that is a homage simultaneously to a particular landscape and its way of life, and to his own father. It is surely psychologically significant that the most substantial poem he retained from *The Journey* (1931, the year of his father's death; the volume is dedicated partly to his memory)—the volume in which his commitment to tradition becomes explicit and complete—should be in honor of his father.

The poem opens with a narrator watching, from a height, the gradual illumination of the valley below him as dawn approaches. His situation reminds us of that of the child at the opening of "The Slow Pacific Swell," who similarly watches the sea "from a hill / At thirty miles or more." In both cases there is a sense of the observer being at once above what he sees (literally and also in the hierarchical sense that he is a consciousness above the existence he perceives), but also excluded from any intimacy of knowledge. The first stanza describes the coming of dawn, and suggests in certain of its details the postsymbolist method, to use Winters's terminology as defined by Howard Kaye. The details have their own fidelity to sensory experience but simultaneously indicate Winters's deeper concerns... where the darkness is given the unmistakable connotation of the undefined in general. In a similar way the approach of dawn indicates the intellect's gradual comprehension of its subject—experience, or the world—and the moment chosen (the moment when darkness gives way to light) is like the shore of "The Slow Pacific Swell," the peculiar province of the poet.

The imagery of the first stanza is significant. The approach of dawn suggests images of flow and change ("the darkness spills / Down the remoter gulleys"), and these images suggest and are associated with images of growth, the growth of the young gardens illuminated by the dawn. But contrasted with these images of flow and natural growth are images of definition; there is the "frame" in the above quotation, and the "concrete walls" of the stanza's closing couplet...

This juxtaposition ("seeping," "bastions") is an encapsulation of one of Winters's chief preoccupations: the mind's attempts to define what is elusive, to be hypersensitively aware of flux, and at the same time to insist on the definitions and categories by which we necessarily live. It is the concern that underlies the title of his first book, *The Immobile Wind*, and which Thom Gunn summarized in his poem "To Yvor Winters, 1955," to "keep both Rule and Energy in view."

The second stanza contrasts the ordered gardens of the poem's opening with a memory of an older and more haphazard rural existence—an existence which even in its heyday seemed removed from reality...

The dust that muffled leaves and roads was a literal sign of this landscape's isolation from more urgent concerns, a sign of its Eden-like status. And the sense of observing a dreamworld is increased by our knowledge that the picture evoked belongs to an irrecoverable past...

The expostulation "Peace to all such" is a sign of how Winters has come to terms with reality in these poems. The attitude evinced is not of a mind's hypnotized absorption in the minutiae of sensory experience (as in the earliest poems), nor of that hysterical horror of the undefined which we notice in many of the poems of *The Proof*. Rather we see that sense of propriety, of the mind's tact before experience and the world, which I have suggested is a persistent aim in Winters's later poetry. In saying "Peace to all such" the poet bids farewell to his own childhood's pastoral idyll (and its attendant pantheist musings), and to a traditional world now lost—a world he can respect and not hector. By this introduction of the past Winters prepares us for the appearance of his father in the poem, and he prepares us too for the tone of quiet respect with which he treats his father's values and life. What we witness is the poet's acknowledgment of the public and real world of humanity beyond himself. In the earlier, virtually solipsistic poems this world hardly exists—when other characters appeared they seemed mere paradigms for the poet's own emotions, or reminders of his mortality. But in this calm evocation of a vanished life, and in the poet's grave and tender reverence towards it and its representative (his father), we have the best evidence that Winters had been able to break out of the obsessive inwardness of his twenties into a more humane and civilized consciousness of the world beyond the poet, and the poet's role vis-à-vis that world.

The next two stanzas again contrast past and present. The past is evoked in images of a dusty, dreamlike landscape...

The "powdered ash, the sift of age" in its dry crumbling is an image of the landscape's distance from present life, and this is confirmed by the ghostly unreality of the "soft explosion" as the friable, dead plants disintegrate. The present hillsides now visible to the poet are evoked in opposing images of damp and vivid growth, and the stanza ends with a fish pond, the schematic opposite of the past's "burning ashes."

So far in the poem we have had a description of dawn illuminating the gardens of the hills flanking the valley, and this present scene of ordered vigorous growth has been contrasted with memories of a more haphazard pastoral landscape, which, whatever its attractions, is associated with a dreamlike sense of death and disintegration. The last stanza of the poem continues the description of the scene now present to the poet's eyes—"the city, on the tremendous valley floor"—but before this stanza there interposes a passage about the poet's father. Up to this point the poem has contrasted past and present, but now we understand that the garden just described is that of the poet's father. That is, the past's representative is associated with, and is indeed responsible for, the present growth described in the poem. In the poem's weaving together of past and present we are shown that it is the past, or at least one aspect of it, that sustains the present. The past is presented as beguiling, then dreamlike and deathly, then as a sustaining force that informs and orders the present.

The poem ends with a description of the city, which is just emerging from night. It has passed from haphazard pastoral, to a garden, to the wholly man-made, each stage recognizably more ordered than the last. But this does not imply the poet's commitment to this subjugation of the natural world. The dead pastoral of the "powdered ash" and the more vivid order of his father's garden seem, each in their own way, to command more of his allegiance. The poem's close is reminiscent of the end of "The Invaders," another poem concerned with man's mastery of nature, in which Winters appeared as simultaneously fascinated and appalled by man's power. The final lines, in their suggestion of hubris and arrogance, and with their echo of the imagery at the end of "The Slow Pacific Swell," read as an admonishing reminder of the limits of man's capacities to transform the natural world . . .

Source: Dick Davis, "The Later Poetry: Nature as a Benign Presence," in *Wisdom and Wilderness: The Achievement of Yvor Winters*, University of Georgia Press, 1983, pp. 102–105.

SOURCES

"Airport Traffic Report," Port Authority of NY and NJ website, April 2014, p. 36, http://www.panynj.gov/air ports/pdf-traffic/ATR2013.pdf (accessed May 17, 2016).

Barth, R. L., ed., *The Selected Letters of Yvor Winters*, Swallow Press, 2000, p. 372.

Breslin, James E. B., "Poetry: 1945 to the Present," in *Columbia Literary History of the United States*, edited by Emory Elliott, Martha Banta, Terence Martin, et al., Columbia University Press, 1988, pp. 1079–1100.

"A Brief Guide to New Formalism," Poets.org, February 21, 2014, https://www.poets.org/poetsorg/text/brief-guide-new-formalism (accessed May 14, 2016).

Comito, Terry, *In Defense of Winters: The Poetry and Prose of Yvor Winters*, University of Wisconsin Press, 1986, p. 192.

Davie, Donald, "The Poetry of Yvor Winters," in *The Collected Poems of Yvor Winters*, Swallow Press, 1978, p. 3.

Davis, Dick, *Wisdom and Wilderness: The Achievement of Yvor Winters*, University of Georgia Press, 1983, pp. 67, 144–47.

"History of SFO," SFO, http://www.flysfo.com/about-sfo/history-sfo (accessed May 16, 2016).

Isaacs, Elizabeth, *An Introduction to the Poetry of Yvor Winters*, Swallow Press, 1981, pp. 66, 73, 80, 86.

Schreiber, Jan, "The Absolutist: The Poetry and Criticism of Yvor Winters," in *Contemporary Poetry Review*, 2004, http://www.cprw.com/Schreiber/win ters.htm (accessed May 17, 2016).

Trimpi, Helen Pinkerton, Introduction to *The Selected Poems of Yvor Winters*, edited by R. L. Barth, Swallow Press, 1999.

Winters, Yvor, "At the San Francisco Airport," in *The Selected Poems of Yvor Winters*, edited by R. L. Barth, Swallow Press, 1999, p. 107.

FURTHER READING

Gunn, Thom, Introduction to *Yvor Winters: Selected Poems*, Library of America, 2003.

   Thom Gunn is a British poet who was once a student of Winters, and this introduction serves as a concise introduction to Winters's poetry.

Parkinson, Thomas, *Hart Crane and Yvor Winters: Their Literary Correspondence*, University of California Press, 1982.

   Parkinson reproduces forty-four letters written by the American modernist poet Hart Crane to Winters between 1926 and 1930, two years before Crane died. Winters's side of the correspondence has not survived, however, and it is left to Parkinson to fill in the gaps, speculating, with the help of Winters's wife, Janet Lewis, and the critic Allen Tate, on what Winters may have written to his fellow poet.

Powell, Grosvenor, *Language as Being in the Poetry of Yvor Winters*, Louisiana State University Press, 1980.

   This analysis of Winters's poetry, which includes how it changed and developed over the years, includes generous selections from Winters's work, and some poems are quoted in full.

Winters, Yvor, *In Defense of Reason*, Swallow Press, 1987.

   First published in 1947, this book contains most of Winters's major critical works. It consists of studies of experimental poetry and poetic structure, nineteenth-century poets and novelists, and modernist poets of the twentieth century.

SUGGESTED SEARCH TERMS

Yvor Winters

"At the San Francisco Airport" AND Winters

iambic foot

tetrameter

formal verse

New Formalism

lyric poem

American poetry 1950s

Blackberries

YUSEF KOMUNYAKAA
1992

Pulitzer Prize–winning poet Yusef Komunyakaa's "Blackberries," published in his 1992 collection *Magic City*, tells the story of a young blackberry picker brought to transcendent bliss by the dewy beauty of the early morning fields and the miracle of plump blackberries falling into his cupped hands. His pleasure is quickly replaced by pain, however, when—standing on the side of the road, selling his harvest with berry-stained hands—he is mocked by two children his own age, who sit in cool, clean comfort in the back of a luxurious, air-conditioned car. Komunyakaa, widely celebrated for his ear for language, captures both the wild union of boy and blackberry and the sudden, spiraling shame he feels when he sees himself through the eyes of his wealthy peers.

AUTHOR BIOGRAPHY

The oldest of five children, Komunyakaa was born on April 29, 1947, in Bogalusa, Louisiana, as James Willie Brown Jr. Originally named after his father, Komunyakaa later changed his name to honor his grandfather, who arrived in America as a stowaway on a ship from the West Indies. Komunyakaa grew up in the oppressive heat and racial segregation of the South, surrounded by storytelling and jazz traditions. Because African Americans were barred from

Yusef Komunyakaa *(©James Keyser | | Time Life Pictures | Getty Images)*

entering the local public library, Komunyakaa relied on a small church's library for reading material as a child, where he discovered James Baldwin and the Harlem Renaissance. His mother encouraged his education, buying him a set of encyclopedias. He graduated from high school in 1965, then served in the United States Army in 1969 as a correspondent and managing editor of the military paper *Southern Cross* during the Vietnam War. He earned a Bronze Star for his work and returned home in 1970.

Komunyakaa earned his bachelor's degree in English and sociology from the University of Colorado Springs in 1975, before publishing his first poetry collection in 1977, titled *Dedications & Other Darkhorses*. He went on to publish a second collection, *Lost in the Bonewheel Factory*, in 1979. He earned his master's degree in creative writing from the University of Colorado Springs and his master of fine arts degree from the University of California, Irvine, in 1980, before returning in 1981 to Louisiana, where he taught at the University of New Orleans. There he met his wife of ten years, the Australian novelist Mandy Sayer.

His breakthrough collection, *Copacetic*, debuted in 1984. Inspired by his childhood in the Deep South during the birth of the civil rights movement, the collection earned Komunyakaa a reputation as a jazz poet of immeasurable skill. Many collections followed, including *I Apologize*

for the Eyes in My Head (1986) and *Dien Cai Dau* (1988), a collection of poems focused on his experiences in Vietnam that remains one of the most important and influential examples of Vietnam War poetry. "Blackberries" was first published in *Magic City* in 1992, a collection that draws on Komunyakaa's childhood for inspiration.

Neon Vernacular: New and Selected Poems, published in 1993, earned Komunyakaa the 1994 Pulitzer Prize for Poetry, the William Faulkner Prize, and the Kingsley Tufts Award. In 1999, he was elected chancellor of the Academy of American Poets. Following his divorce from Sayer in 1995, Komunyakaa's relationship with the poet Reetika Vazirani ended in tragedy in 2003 when she took her own life along with the life of their two-year-old son.

Following the publication of *Pleasure Dome* in 2001, Komunyakaa published *Taboo: The Wishbone Trilogy, Part 1* in 2006, *Warhorses* in 2008, *The Chameleon Couch* in 2011, and *The Emperor of Water Clocks* in 2015. He received the 2011 Wallace Stevens Award, the Ruth Lily Poetry Prize, the Levinson Prize, the Shelley Memorial Award, the Hanes Poetry Prize, and the Thomas King Forçade Award, as well as fellowships from the Louisiana Arts Council, the National Endowment for the Arts, and the Fine Arts Work Center. He has taught at Indiana University, Washington University in St. Louis, Princeton University, and New York University. He lives in New York City.

POEM TEXT

They left my hands like a printer's
Or thief's before a police blotter
& pulled me into early morning's
Terrestrial sweetness, so thick
The damp ground was consecrated   5
Where they fell among a garland of thorns.

Although I could smell old lime-covered
History, at ten I'd still hold out my hands
& berries fell into them. Eating from one
& filling a half gallon with the other,   10
I ate the mythology & dreamt
Of pies & cobbler, almost

Needful as forgiveness. My bird dog Spot
Eyed blue jays & thrashers. The mud frogs
In rich blackness, hid from daylight.   15
An hour later, beside City Limits Road
I balanced a gleaming can in each hand,
Limboed between worlds, repeating *one dollar.*

The big blue car made me sweat.
Wintertime crawled out of the windows.   20
When I leaned closer I saw the boy
& girl my age, in the wide back seat
Smirking, & it was then I remembered my
      fingers
Burning with thorns among berries too ripe to
      touch.

POEM SUMMARY

The text used for this summary is from *Pleasure Dome: New and Collected Poems*, Wesleyan University Press, 2001, pp. 280–81. A version of the poem can be found on the following web page: https://www.ibiblio.org/ipa/poems/komunyakaa/blackberries.php.

"Blackberries" begins with a description of the appearance of the speaker's hands after a morning picking blackberries. His fingers are stained dark as if he worked at a printer's shop or as if he were a thief who had been caught and fingerprinted by the police. Early in the morning the ground is still damp with dew. The plump blackberries fall to the ground, blessing the earth with their sweetness where they land among the thorns.

The speaker can smell the recent layer of lime, spread by the farmer as fertilizer for the field. Because he is an impulsive ten-year-old, he indulges himself by eating blackberries as they fall into his hands. He eats from one hand as he fills up his half gallon pail with the other. He eats the mythology of blackberries, dreaming of future pies and cobblers.

As he picks blackberries, his bird dog, Spot, watches blue jays and thrashers with interest. Below, frogs hide from the sun in the cool black mud. After an hour of picking, the speaker stands on the side of City Limits Road, selling cans of blackberries for one dollar. He shouts it at passing cars holding a shining can in each hand, feet balanced in limbo between worlds.

A big blue car pulls up. The speaker sweats, though the air-conditioning rolls out of the open window like winter. When the speaker leans closer to the car, he sees a boy and girl his age smirking at him smugly from the ample backseat. Suddenly the speaker remembers how the thorns bit his fingers as he tried to reach for berries too ripe to be picked.

THEMES

Inequality

When the speaker is confronted by two wealthy ten-year-olds who look down on him from the comfortable backseat of a big, air-conditioned car, he begins to doubt his own self-worth. Class separates the three children, and though the boy has had a wonderful morning picking blackberries, he feels ashamed of himself and his poverty at the sight of the boy and girl. The memory of scratching his hands on thorns in an attempt to reach overripe berries overwhelms him. These berries are too good for him, too well protected by thorns and out of his reach. This is symbolic of the wealth of the children, which is certainly out of reach of a young boy selling cans of blackberries by the side of the road for one dollar.

The poem would be lopsided with the sheer inequality between the classes were it not for the boy's genuine spiritual connection to the act of blackberry picking. He feels a joy so distracting that he neither notices how hot, dirty, and scratched he is by thorns nor does he particularly care how he looks until he is confronted by his smug peers. The spirituality of the land provides him with an understanding of the inequality he feels through the out-of-reach blackberries. The boy will recover from the shame he feels by the side of the road, but he may think of those smirking faces next time before he reaches deep into the brambles for the overripe berries surrounded by thorns. The children's smirks are the first appearance of cruelty in the poem—after all, whoever is driving the car has stopped to make a purchase, supporting his cause. The children's cruelty is followed rapidly by the memory of the bite of the thorns, but until they sneered at him, the pain of blackberry picking had not mattered to the boy in his spiritual pleasure. The poem illustrates how such inequality breeds cruelty in the wealthy and low self-esteem in the poor. The boy has put in a hard day's work and enjoyed himself in the process. He has nothing to feel ashamed of, yet he is made to feel bad simply because he was not born rich like the children in the backseat, who have not felt the heat of the day on their skin.

Nature

Through his joyful celebration of the act of picking blackberries, the boy worships the natural world around him, of which he himself is a part. The first three stanzas are filled with images of

TOPICS FOR FURTHER STUDY

- Read Christopher Paul Curtis's young-adult novel *The Watsons Go to Birmingham— 1963* (2000). What do the speaker of "Blackberries" and Kenny Watson have in common? What sets them apart? How are segregation, race relations, and class difference depicted in each of the works? Organize your answers into an essay.

- What type of jazz music do you think matches the style and sound of "Blackberries?" Using the YouTube website, listen to the work of different jazz musicians in search of a song that you think fits the poem well. Once you have found an artist and song that you believe fits, make an audio recording of yourself reading the poem with the song playing in the background. Some artists to try in your search include Thelonious Monk, Charlie Parker, John Coltrane, Ernie K-Doe, Billie Holiday, Kermit Ruffins, Art Tatum, Dizzy Gillespie, Duke Ellington, and Louis Armstrong. Some jazz genres to try include bebop, swing, experimental, free, Dixieland, and blues. Along with your recording, write a paragraph-long explanation of why you chose the artist, song, and style.

- Create a blog devoted to a different poem from *Magic City*. Write five to seven posts about the poem, one of which should list and explain the poem's theme, one the speaker, one the style in which the poem is written, and the remaining posts on topics of your choosing. Include relevant photos to make your blog posts visually compelling and cite any sources that you use. When you are finished making your posts, visit three classmates' blogs and leave a thoughtful comment on a post you found interesting. Be sure to respond to any comments you receive. Free blogspace is available at blogger.com.

- What is the significance of Komunyakaa's choice of blackberries as opposed to another type of fruit? How would the meaning of the work change if he were picking apples, for example? Write an essay in which you answer these questions and explicate the blackberry image as it relates to the poem's themes, language, and meaning.

- Write a poem about an experience from your childhood in which you use at least one simile and one metaphor. The poem may be any style or length, as long as the required elements of figurative language are present.

nature: berries, thorns, morning dew, lime, birds, a dog, frogs, mud, and sunshine. The only danger present in the scene is that of the thorns. The poem is idyllic and pastoral in its presentation of a peaceful morning spent berry picking. Surrounded by nature, the boy feels an ecstatic freedom—a sense of belonging to something greater than the mundane world. Komunyakaa achieves this effect through the use of metaphors that compare the blackberries to religion: they bless the ground they fall on, and their taste contains an entire mythology. In a world of already pleasant, enjoyable nature, the blackberries are the most decadent offering imaginable to

the boy. They fall into his hands as if they have been waiting impatiently for him to come. He belongs in this natural world and not in the society he must enter to sell the berries. When he does emerge from the field to sell the berries, he keeps one foot in the beauty of nature, straddling his world and that of society in limbo—a place between worlds, neither wholly one or the other. It is here that, much as in the story of Adam and Eve, he suddenly realizes how he is dirty and scratched from his hours in the field, his fingers stained dark from juices. He feels shame for the first time in the poem and relates it to the unreachable overripe berries that

The fruit represents limitless possibility as the boy dreams of treats *(©Robert Lucian Crusitu / Shutterstock.com)*

tempted him deeper into the thorns. In acknowledgment of his poverty, the natural imagery of the poem is no longer suggestive of beauty and peace but of exclusion and pain. The boy's perception of himself creates the reality around him: seeing blackberries when he is happy and thorns when he is sad. The natural landscape is the center around which the boy's life revolves and through which he understands the more complex outside world.

Wealth

Wealth takes two forms in the text of "Blackberries": monetary wealth in the form of the big blue car and natural wealth in the form of blackberries. Each of these images is presented in decadent detail. Komunyakaa lingers over the car's icy air-conditioning and the wide and comfortable backseat. Likewise, the abundance of blackberries allows the boy to eat his fill while simultaneously filling up a half gallon pail with the fruit. There are berries to spare, and the boy revels in nature's bounty. The versions of wealth

cross, however, when the boy emerges from the field to sell cans of blackberries for one dollar on the side of the road. When the large car pulls up, the boy feels uncomfortable—sweating in response to the cool air that pours out of the windows. In the presence of such coldness, he feels the heat that did not bother him as he worked in his field. When he sees the children smirking at him from the backseat, he feels inferior. Suddenly the memories of nature that had his mood soaring provide no relief from the shame he feels toward his poverty. Just as the car's air-conditioning makes him sweat, the sight of wealthy children and their smugness makes him feel his poverty acutely. Yet there is a third kind of wealth in the poem that challenges the perception that the monetary wealth of the two children is somehow superior to the natural wealth of the blackberries. Spiritual wealth is on the side of nature, living among the berries and thorns. Even the speaker's shame is expressed through the natural and spiritual lens of blackberry picking—with the children's affluence represented by overripe berries too well protected by thorns to reach. Their wealth is simply not available to him.

STYLE

Juxtaposition

Juxtaposition in a poem occurs when two images are presented side by side in order to emphasize the similarities or differences between them. In "Blackberries," the young speaker is juxtaposed with two children his age in the backseat of the air-conditioned car. Their smug attitude toward him deflates the joy he felt while he was alone in the field. The juxtaposition of the three children illustrates the harsh reality that exists for the speaker outside the blackberry field, because the boy's poverty is striking only when he is compared with the wealthy children. Before they appear, he is contented and carefree. Through the juxtaposition of rich and poor children, the reader sees the speaker for the first time from the eyes of a judgmental society, as does the speaker himself. This leads him to feel a sense of shame that was not present amid the joy he felt prior to their arrival.

Metaphor

Metaphor is a type of figurative language in which two unrelated things are directly compared, so that the primary item is described as a second item in order to accentuate its important traits. In "Blackberries" Komunyakaa uses several metaphors; for example, he describes the car's air-conditioning as wintertime, an important distinction from his summertime pleasure in picking blackberries. The blackberries themselves are described as a mythology as well as consecrating the ground among the thorns, an indirect reference to Jesus's crucifixion. Through these religious metaphors, the blackberries take on a sacred context, belonging to a secret and mystical plane of existence. The boy worships the blackberries as a devotee; the solitude and peace of the field form his church and blackberry-picking day his holy day. Through his veneration of the berries the boy worships nature; when he sells them on the road, he has a foot in each world—one in the church of nature and one in the secular society in which blackberries are merely a commodity and the boy is misunderstood, judged by his appearance rather than the content of his soul.

Simile

A simile is a type of figurative language in which two unlike things are compared using "like" or "as." The poem begins with two similes as the speaker first compares his berry-stained hands to the hands of a printer and then to a thief who has been caught and fingerprinted by the police. In each of these similes, the blackberry juice is like dark ink, but the implications behind the comparisons are drastically different. A printer is master of a trade in which stained hands are all part of a day's work. A thief gets his fingers stained with ink only if he is caught. His ink stains are thus a symbol of his guilt. The boy plays both of these roles as he picks blackberries: eating blackberries with one hand (thief) as he collects blackberries in a pail with his other hand (worker). Both of these occupations are sneered at by the upper-class children, who see the boy's stained hands simply as a sign of poverty.

HISTORICAL CONTEXT

Segregation

Komunyakaa came of age in the racially segregated Deep South, before the birth of the civil rights movement in the 1950s. Jim Crow laws were established following the Civil War in order to prevent newly freed African Americans from attaining status, wealth, power, or even a standard of living equal to whites, and they remained in effect from approximately 1874 to 1965. The laws called for separate schools, churches, and public facilities such as restrooms and water fountains. Additionally, African Americans were made to sit in a separate section of restaurants (if they were served at all) and at the back of the public buses. Komunyakaa was not allowed to enter the public library in his hometown of Bogalusa, Louisiana, as African Americans could neither check out books nor sit inside to read.

Nominally, these laws created a separate but equal environment in which blacks and whites would exist without interacting. In truth, the public facilities for African Americans were always more poorly maintained than their white counterparts, African American schools were given no funding by their local and state governments, and African Americans who broke the Jim Crow laws were punished with more severity than whites. The Supreme Court upheld

COMPARE & CONTRAST

- **1992:** Though great steps have been made toward equality between races, thanks in large part to the civil rights movement that saw the end of segregation, no African American has yet held the highest position in the country—that of the president of the United States.

  Today: Barack Obama, forty-fourth president of the United States, is sworn into office in January 20, 2009, serving two terms as the first African American president of the United States.

- **1992:** Between 1992 and 1994, the state of Louisiana's average poverty rate is a staggering 25.5 percent, making it the most impoverished state in the nation.

  Today: At 19.8 percent, five percentage points higher than the national average,

Louisiana ranks as the third most impoverished state in the United States. Approximately one of five adults and one of four school-age children live below the poverty line.

- **1992:** Jazz is a popular but widely diverse genre of music, with everything from straight-ahead jazz to jazz fusion played throughout the United States and internationally. Jazz remains an important part of Louisiana culture, celebrated annually at the New Orleans Jazz and Heritage Festival.

  Today: Following the devastating effects of Hurricane Katrina in 2005, New Orleans has experienced a rebirth of its musical traditions. The New Orleans Jazz and Heritage Festival is set to celebrate its fifty-year anniversary in 2020.

---

the constitutionality of separate but equal laws in *Plessy v. Ferguson* (1896), a decision based on the widespread belief in the United States at the time that blacks were genetically inferior to whites. Segregation was a fact of life in the United States for decades, until the civil rights movement was formed following the end of World War II. Implied by the inspiration of *Magic City*—Komunyakaa's childhood in segregated Louisiana—but not directly stated in "Blackberries" is the race of the three children. A poor African American boy selling blackberries by the side of the road in the Deep South being looked on with contempt by affluent white children would be a normal scene in a time when racism was the unshakable law of the land.

Jazz Poetry

Jazz poetry, which incorporates the sounds of jazz music into poetic verse, emerged as a genre in the 1920s. Harlem Renaissance poet Langston Hughes is widely acknowledged as the father of the genre, and his first collection, *The Weary Blues* (1926), is considered the first collection of

jazz poetry. Jazz poetry, beloved by the Harlem Renaissance, became a popular style in several later poetry movements, including the poetry of the Beats, the Black Arts movement, and slam poetry. Taking as its inspiration the music of jazz legends such as Charlie Parker, John Coltrane, Jelly Roll Morton, Miles Davis, Dizzy Gillespie, Billie Holiday, Louis Armstrong, and Bessie Smith, as well as the work of local and up-and-coming jazz musicians, jazz poetry attempts to recreate in language the musicality and laissez-faire attitude of jazz. Langston Hughes characterized jazz as a limitless ocean, capable of taking in all forms of expression in his speech "Jazz as Communication," at the 1956 Newport Jazz Festival: "Jazz is a great big sea.... Throw it all in the sea, and the sea'll keep on rolling along toward the shore and crashing and booming back into itself again."

Komunyakaa, growing up near the jazz-rich city of New Orleans and heavily influenced by Louisiana's celebrated musical culture, incorporates jazz poetry into many of his collections, the

---

The blackberry bushes give the boy an overwhelming harvest—enough to eat and gather—and still some fall to the ground *(©Serguei Levykin / Shutterstock.com)*

first of which was *Copacetic* in 1984. Tomeiko Ashford writes in her biography of the poet for the Internet Poetry Archive:

> Komunyakaa uses his childhood experiences to inform many of his works: . . . the musical environment afforded by the close proximity of the jazz and blues center of New Orleans provide[s] fundamental themes for several of his volumes.

Other notable jazz poets include Mina Loy, James Baldwin, Ishmael Reed, Amiri Baraka, Sonia Sanchez, Jack Kerouac, Marilyn Hacker, and many more.

CRITICAL OVERVIEW

Komunyakaa is among the most well respected and decorated contemporary American poets. Winner of the 1994 Pulitzer Prize for Poetry, the Kingsley Tufts Award, the William Faulkner Prize, the Hanes Poetry Prize, the Morton Dauwen Zabel Award, the Levinson Prize, the Thomas King Forçade Award, the Shelley Memorial Award, and the Ruth Lily Poetry Prize, he has been favorably compared by critics to such legendary poets as Gwendolyn Brooks, Langston Hughes, Ezra Pound, William Carlos Williams, and Amiri Baraka, among others. He was named chancellor of the American Academy of Arts and Letters in 1999. Ashford describes his uniquely optimistic poetic vision of the world:

> Komunyakaa maintains that the whole of humanity is a conglomeration of differing—but not necessarily warring—parts. By juxtaposing his varied experiences, he attempts to form meaning and to lend insight where others find only chaos.

Like many critics and scholars, Philip Metres is especially impressed by the wide scope of Komunyakaa's poetic subjects. He writes in the *Plain Dealer*:

> He's written poems for Michael Jackson and Mahmoud Darwish. . . . What connects the work is Komunyakaa's search to find or create new structures of freedom—in music, in literature, in relationships and in the sensual world.

In "Songs of Rage and Tenderness: The Poetry of Yusef Komunyakaa," Elizabeth Hoover admires the many settings Komunyakaa conjures effortlessly from his own experiences and rich imagination: "With remarkable concision, he summons entire landscapes for readers to explore: Landscapes of the rural South, the jungles of Vietnam, and even ancient Persia."

The diversity of language in Komunyakaa's poems is another fascinating aspect of his talent. Eric Miles Williamson writes in his review of Komunyakaa's collection *The Chameleon Couch*:

> Few living poets, or poets from any other epoch...have the range of ear we find in Komunyakaa: he hears the cadences of the slave, of the aesthete, of the child, the matron, and the master.

Bruce Weber summarizes Komunyakaa's singular commitment to poetry in "A Poet's Values: It's the Words over the Man" for the *New York Times*: "He acknowledges poetry to be the most inaccessible of literary forms....But he himself is committed to the relentless plumbing of ideas and the language needed to express them." It is this tireless dedication to his craft that makes Komunyakaa a respected master of poetry.

CRITICISM

Amy L. Miller

Miller is a graduate of the University of Cincinnati. In the following essay, she discusses Komunyakaa's use of complex imagery to mimic the thick brambles in "Blackberries" and traces this imagery through the appearance of the big blue car that brings winter to the speaker's perfect summer day.

In Komunyakaa's "Blackberries," the natural world is a sacred playground for the young speaker. Early in the morning, between the rows of brambles, the speaker finds heaven on earth in blackberries so plump and plentiful that they fall like raindrops into his cupped hands. To the speaker, the blackberries are priceless treasures: they represent wealth, nature, contentment, and freedom. Through metaphor, they are connected to the sacred blood of Jesus in the Christian tradition as well as to a secret mythology of their own. The taste, touch, smell, and sight of blackberries overwhelms each of the four stanzas, but the first half of the poem is especially abundant with fruit. As the speaker travels

> TO THE SPEAKER, THE BLACKBERRIES ARE PRICELESS TREASURES: THEY REPRESENT WEALTH, NATURE, CONTENTMENT, AND FREEDOM. THROUGH METAPHOR, THEY ARE CONNECTED TO THE SACRED BLOOD OF JESUS IN THE CHRISTIAN TRADITION AS WELL AS TO A SECRET MYTHOLOGY OF THEIR OWN."

further from the brambles, the blackberry imagery all but disappears, until the smirking children bring the speaker's reality crashing to the front of his mind. His fingers begin to sting from the memory of reaching out for blackberries that cannot be picked as the truth of his poverty steals away the innocent fun of his day. Komunyakaa's use of ampersands, figurative language, juxtaposition, and enjambment together with religious imagery adds layers of meaning onto a seemingly simple poem.

The poem's imagery can be divided into what is familiar and what is alien to the speaker. He can navigate the blackberry brambles, name the animals that live there by their breed, and recognize the scent of lime fertilizer. He knows Christian symbolism, the hazards in the lives of printers and thieves, and the taste of blackberry cobbler. He knows how to get to City Limits Road and how much to sell his blackberries for when he gets there. For a ten-year-old boy he is a remarkably self-sufficient entrepreneur. Komunyakaa emphasizes the ease with which he exists together with nature through long, lavish descriptions of the world the boy inhabits inside his mind and within the brambles. The frogs hide from sunlight in the shadows of rich, black mud, much as the boy hides from the truth of his poverty in the richness of the blackberries. Natural wealth extends not only to the frogs and boy but also to his bird dog, Spot, who watches two types of birds with interest from the speaker's side. Everything is plentiful in the poem's ecosystem.

Hoover writes of Komunyakaa: "He grew up surrounded by the rich musical and storytelling tradition of the Deep South." In the tradition of great storytellers, Komunyakaa sets the scene early for the hero's tragic fall. The first two lines

WHAT
DO I READ
NEXT?

- *Poetry for Young People: Langston Hughes* (2012), edited by David Roessel and Arnold Rampersand, combines twenty-six poems from the ingenious Harlem Renaissance author and father of jazz poetry with illustrations by Benny Andrews, background information, definitions of vocabulary and terms, and notes from Hughes himself.

- In Komunyakaa's *Neon Vernacular* (1993) the Vietnam War haunts the poet's memory, driving him to create a new poetic language in which to express both the horrors and the kindness he has witnessed in the thick jungles and wide rice fields. The collection earned Komunyakaa the 1994 Pulitzer Prize for Poetry as well as the prestigious Kingsley Tufts Award.

- Palestinian poet Mahmoud Darwish's collection *If I Were Another* (2009) shares, with stunning lyrical beauty, the personal grief of exile and war. Considered one of the greatest Arab poets, Darwish gives voice to the voiceless Palestinian people through the heartache found in his work: a poetic manifestation of the physical and spiritual longing he felt as an exile for his lost home.

- An early but significant influence on Komunyakaa's life and writing was James Baldwin, whose collection of nonfiction essays *Nobody Knows My Name* (1961) covers a variety of topics—writing, reading, segregation, the Harlem Renaissance, and American identity.

- Winner of the 2007 Pulitzer Prize for Poetry, Natasha Trethewey, in her collection *Native Guard: Poems* (2006), tells two tales of the Deep South based on her childhood in Mississippi: that of the all-black Civil War regiment the Mississippi Native Guards and that of her mother's illegal marriage to a white man. With a keen eye for the overlooked and all but forgotten, Trethewey sheds light on the past as she looks to her own future following her mother's death.

- Gwendolyn Brooks's *Selected Poems* (2006) collects the work this Pulitzer Prize–winning poet known for her dedication to the subjects of the civil rights movement, race relations, poverty, and the position of black women in American society. Her compassion, optimism, and enormous talent are evident in this collection.

- In *This Is My Century: New and Collected Poems* (1989), Margaret Walker's devotion to folklore and oral traditions are on display as she paints a vibrant portrait of the culture of the South and African American history. The first African American to win a national award for literary writing, Walker is a groundbreaking and monumental figure in the American literary canon.

- *The Collected Poems of Sterling A. Brown* (1980) gathers the work of a poet responsible for bringing African American oral traditions into the literary limelight. Full of soulful intelligence, sharp insight, and rich imagery, Brown's poetry cleared the path for countless African American poets to follow.

- Countee Cullen's *My Soul's High Song* (1990) is the work of a Harlem Renaissance master who infuses his poems with questions of personal identity, whether racial, spiritual, national, or political. This volume includes notes, essays, speeches, and an interview of the poet conducted by James Baldwin.

- Amiri Baraka's *SOS: Poems 1961–2013* (2016) collects the work of the controversial firebrand poet and leader of the Black Arts movement of the 1960s, from his days as a Beat poet through his radicalization following the assassination of Malcolm X to become a fierce defender of civil rights.

reveal in a series of two similes that, in the process of his morning blackberry picking, the speaker's hands are dyed with the dark juices. Though he knows this, and shares this information with the reader first before ever describing the bramble, he soon forgets his own appearance entirely in his religious devotion to picking berries. Komunyakaa underscores the importance of this detail with a pair of similes: the ink-stained hands of printers and thieves. A printer specializes in knowledge and a thief in deception, and both are marked as a result of their occupation. The combination of knowledge and deception subtly suggests the story of Adam and Eve who, eating from the Tree of Knowledge and deceiving God, were cast from the Garden of Eden. The speaker's stained hands represent his guilt—not of being bad, but of being poor. The children interpret his stained hands as a symbol not of knowledge or deception but of poverty, and they smirk at him as if they know something that he does not. Indeed, until that unpleasant moment leaning in to the car, he had forgotten his berry-stained hands. When he does remember, it is not just that they are stained with juice but that they are also slashed with thorns. The children catch him literally red-handed and judge him guilty of poverty, worthy of their contempt as his punishment. His straddling of the two worlds (familiar and alien) with a can of blackberries in each hand looks to the children less like a prophet bringing the word of God to his people and more like a juggler trying to make them laugh.

Thus, from the first lines, the hammer is poised to fall on the speaker, yet Komunyakaa—even while setting the boy up for heartbreak—revels along with him in the morning's natural beauty. Ampersands curl like brambles through the long poetic clauses, adding themselves to the pleasing visual effect of the nearly uniform line lengths, neat as a farmer's rows. Additionally, blackberry brambles may come in neat rows but within those rows the vines twist and meander. The poem does the same: the lines at once heavy with ripe images, spiked with ampersands, and wandering with free associations. When the big blue car arrives, these rolling sentences come to an abrupt halt. The enjambment of lines that has kept the reader's eye moving down the page stops for two curt sentences, one line each, in which the speaker's discomfort is clear. Bruce Weber writes of Komunyakaa's style: "In the language of his poems . . . is a sense of struggling to embrace complexity, images layered on images to create depth rather than simple revelation." In the brambles, the imagery is dense enough to be ambiguous: blackberries, mythologies, dreams, frogs, and dew mix together unpredictably but with a dark and decadent beauty. As the speaker moves away from the brambles, however, the imagery begins to untangle. The road, unlike the farm, has a name, and the blackberries have a price. The fever dream of the field has broken to reveal the method behind the earlier madness: a can of blackberries for one dollar, sold by a ten-year-old boy standing alone on the side of the road. The speaker, his mood still elevated from the morning's work, feels he is the lone occupant of a limbo between the natural world and society. He is, in fact, standing at the outermost edge of what he knows and what remains a mystery to him.

The freewheeling imagery left over from the poetic heights of the brambles drains away as the big blue car approaches. The car upsets the speaker immediately. The poem comes to a halt as the window rolls open and wintertime rolls out, freezing the scene in place. Wintertime means the death of the blackberries, the death of the boy's escapism in the brambles, and the death of his blissful mornings alone. It suggests birds migrating north, frogs disappearing under the mud, and no hot sun to hide from in the relief of the dark shade. While the poem's other metaphors compare nature to religion, this metaphor for air-conditioning compares technology to nature. The car and its air-conditioning represent the alien—something the bright, curious boy has little knowledge of and no opportunity to research further. When he tries to see more, leaning in toward the cold air, he sees the children smirking back at him from a comfortable seat. The cold air makes his skin sweat, and the sight of other children fills him with shame. He is operating far outside his comfort zone, having stepped over the threshold from nature to limbo to the outside world. Now he is bombarded with unfamiliar sensations: artificial cold; strange, smirking children; and shame. In a boy proven to be especially emotionally responsive to his environment, this sensory overload catapults him backward in memory to the brambles. In his earlier joy, he forgot to feel the sting of the thorns as sharply as he does now, hours later. He worships nature as it is while others worship technology designed to replace it with whatever season they want to feel at the moment. What's worse, these children look down on him as a poor country boy with stained fingers, unaware of his emotional, intellectual, and—above all—spiritual depths. But it is they who sit on an ample throne and the boy who stands outside the car, gawking. He remembers then the berries that cannot be picked and the reason he hides from the world in the solitude of the brambles.

Weber writes that Komunyakaa is

pleased by ambiguity, complexity, resonance without clarity. His poems, many of which are built on fiercely autobiographical details... deal with the stains that experience leaves on a life, and they are often achingly suggestive without resolution.

It is the stains of experience that give the speaker his roughshod appearance, making the children laugh. Stained by poverty and the labor of his day, he stands outside the car in a cold sweat, burning with the memory of thorns lashing at his fingers. Komunyakaa has taken him from the center of his spiritual being on a journey to the superficial edge of his existence: from nature's bounty of blackberries falling on him like rain to children laughing at him for his poverty. The poem ends with a return to the bramble patch, but this time the circumstances are not nearly as sweet. The final metaphor of the poem, which compares the children's wealth to the berries that elude the speaker's determined fingers, suggests a surrender to his position in the world as a poor boy on the roadside. Having faced his judgment and felt ashamed, he has left the garden unwillingly to join the harsh world outside.

Source: Amy L. Miller, Critical Essay on "Blackberries," in *Poetry for Students*, Gale, Cengage Learning, 2017.

Angela M. Salas

In the following excerpt, Salas stresses Komunyakaa's empathetic outlook, which is reflected in his poems.

... Yusef Komunyakaa's literary career reveals a specific aesthetic attempt to achieve an unmediated connection with his readers: a connection informed, but not determined, by his life and experiences as an African American man. These attempts are in some way akin to those of James Baldwin. As a teenager, Komunyakaa read Baldwin's *Nobody Knows My Name* (from which the first epigraph was taken) in the segregated public library of his home town of Bogalusa, Louisiana; he has cited Baldwin's work as instrumental in the formation of his

> KOMUNYAKAA WRITES AS A JEREMIAH RATHER THAN A JOURNALIST, REMINDING READERS OF THE HUMAN COST OF THE VIETNAM WAR, A COST INSCRIBED ON VIETNAMESE BODIES AS WELL AS ON AMERICAN ONES."

consciousness. Komunyakaa has traveled widely, to such places as Mexico, Vietnam, Japan, and Australia; it is notable, however, that he has not needed to become an expatriate, as did Baldwin, to become a successful writer. Perhaps Baldwin's account of his own dilemmas gave Komunyakaa the mental space to map out his human journey; more likely, the phenomenal, if uncompleted, changes in the social and racial status quo in the United States have given the younger writer an emotional and psychological liberation Baldwin lacked.

While drawing strength from the particularity of his experience as an African American and a Southerner, and as a veteran of the American war in Vietnam, Komunyakaa nonetheless insists that he can function imaginatively from many different positions, not all of which derive from autobiography. In his career, Komunyakaa has taken on the personae of many people, including a female Vietnamese rape victim, tricksters, a white member of a lynch mob, combat veterans, and his remembered childhood self, a feat he accomplishes in *Magic City* (1992). Indeed, Komunyakaa maintains that a poet must have a capacity for human empathy, saying that "the world is so large, and we are so small. How dare an artist *not* imagine the world from the perspective of someone other than himself? It's all part of the ongoing dialogue we must have between ourselves and the world." Race, gender, age, experience, and upbringing inform our perceptions of the world, but they needn't contain our imaginations and sympathies. Thus, while sternly rendering racial intimidation in the Jim Crow South in "History Lessons," from *Magic City*, Komunyakaa also imagines the dreams of Vietnamese refugees, in *Dien Cai Dau*'s "Boat People" (1988). Komunyakaa enlarges *our* imaginations to encompass both a

The smug faces of the boy and girl in the car take away the speaker's joy (©sergeisimonov | Shutterstock.com)

frightened grandmother . . . to the youth who faces down a bullying white deliveryman, and the Vietnamese refugees who . . .

While Komunyakaa's attempts to imagine the world from other perspectives have sometimes been audacious, as in the poems "You and I Are Disappearing" and "Re-creating the Scene." in *Dien Cai Dau*, they have also evolved over the course of his career. Since the publication of *I Apologize for the Eyes in My Head* (1986), Komunyakaa has moved from singular racial and gender identities, to still more imaginative "hyphenated" positions rooted in his own

experiences, to a projected identity that seeks to erase the specificity of the narrator and, as importantly, the reader. The first lines of the first poem in *I Apologize* are a rebuke . . ; The enumeration of the things the speaker is and *is* and is *not* gestures to his identity, beyond the confines of his race. . .

In short, the speaker's life and his actions have moved him outside the trivial sorts of labeling devices with which people limit themselves, or are limited by others. You cannot call me "X" the speaker asserts, because that name does not take into account the things I have done and experienced—things that are beyond the rigid signifiers you might wish to apply to me. Importantly, the narrator's humanity is tied to his *masculinity*, evidenced by his demand to be introduced as a *man*; he will allow neither his masculinity nor his humanity to be called into question. This suggests that at the time Komunyakaa wrote this piece, which opens his first widely reviewed volume of poetry, he was still learning to render experience beyond the signifiers of gender, despite being quite clear-eyed about the problems presented by racial signifiers. His narrator seeks to transcend race, yet frames his disclaimer in terms of masculine prowess, ... In this poem, Komunyakaa invokes a long-standing tradition in African American literary and civic life by framing his antiracist critique with the assertion "I am a man." Clearly, Komunyakaa is not seeking to deny or diminish the fact of his dark skin and all that such skin means in the United States; he is, rather, asserting himself beyond the generic signifiers of "person" or "human being," signifiers which, as Susan Gubar suggests, actually imply *whiteness* as the universal human condition.

The poems ends ... suggesting an attempt on the poet's part to claim his body and everything that comes with it as his own—to wrest his black, male body away from the gaze of a world preoccupied with the bodies of black men, whether as aesthetic and sexual objects or as the objects of fear and mistrust. Being a *man* and possessing a male body are not necessarily the same thing; thus, Komunyakaa's narrator claims himself as a space his "body believes in." In short, his boundaries, and the boundaries of the love of which he speaks in the final lines of the poem, are not fixed by corporeal barriers. The poet is more than the experiences of which he writes, although it is these experiences ... that contribute to his status as *a man*. It may be that Komunyakaa himself needed to celebrate his masculinity and assert the privileges that come with it before he could undertake the task of rendering the subjectivities of others; each volume since *I Apologize for the Eyes in My Head* has evidenced increasingly bold attempts to encompass the world in all its complexity. Indeed, while Komunyakaa's narrators are never "raceless" and never fall into the "default position" of implied whiteness, their observations are not bounded by their race. They are, rather, enriched by it.

When Komunyakaa published *Dien Cai Dau*, a volume addressing the experiences and observations of an African American serviceman during the Vietnam War, he was beginning to immerse himself in the experiences of people whose lives were different from his own. "Re-creating the Scene" is one example of a poem in which Komunyakaa began a strikingly active imaginative engagement with the perspectives of other people. In "Re-creating the Scene," discussed more fully in chapter 3, Komunyakaa imagines the scene of a Vietnamese woman's rape and subsequent murder by American soldiers. The juxtaposition of a protective mother as a frail "torn water flower" and her rapists as "gods" inside their tank ... (defiling both her body and her family name) is startling and apt. While these U.S. soldiers may be the victims of a racist and classist nation, they do untold, irreparable damage to those who are smaller and weaker than they are; they shore up their own wounded self-regard through sexual assault. Komunyakaa suggests to readers that these soldiers may be sinned against, may be small and vulnerable as combatants in a frightening foreign land, but that they also sin—and terribly.

Throughout "Re-creating the Scene," Komunyakaa simultaneously attempts to render the experience of a person not often seen in American literature, while suggesting the ultimate impossibility of truly "knowing" this experience. The poem rejects any impulse to tidy, or to corral its meanings for readers; thus, it is an unsettling poem, and one that manifests Komunyakaa's decision to transcend the particularity of the experience he offered in "Unnatural State of the Unicorn." "Recreating the Scene" is not a mea culpa, as the narrator has had nothing to do with this crime, and it is not an apologia for the soldiers (on the order of "pity these poor young men, made into brutes and rapists by the horrors of the war in Vietnam"). Rather, the poem is an arresting look at the sordidness of the rape ... and how useless the rules against war crimes are to a female civilian. It is a basic human right that one not be raped, and a basic legal right to seek redress should this right be transgressed; however, should the woman attempt to claim her rights, she is likely to be killed, or to endanger the rest of her family. The rules do not matter, and the laws do not protect her.

It is notable that Komunyakaa's narrator, a military journalist, remains outside of these events, never claiming to understand anything, from the motivations of the soldiers to the ultimate fate of their victim. The details he lays, one by one, are all conjecture, as the poem's title makes clear. Still, it is a powerful, wrenching poem, and the fact that the narrator *must* recreate the scene in the victim's absence adds to, rather than detracts from, its power. One wonders about this woman, and about her child, who "grabs the air, / searching for a breast" and one gets no answer, except for a certain, sinking feeling that both are the long dead victims of what we in the United States still attempt to see as a noble cause undertaken by fine young men and a highly principled Unites States government.

Another stunning poem from *Dien Cai Dau* is "You and I Are Disappearing," which was subsequently included in Elliot Goldenthal's *Fire, Paper, Water: A Vietnam Oratorio* (1996). The poem describes the death of a Vietnamese woman by napalm, and in it Komunyakaa's narrator is like a piece of film, marked forever by what it has captured and been captured by. "You and I Are Disappearing" is an account of an experience that the narrator must remember again and again, despite the anguish such remembering causes him... Komunyakaa piles simile upon simile to describe the woman's death; such a device places the reader apart from, yet witness to, the woman's horrifying death. In Komunyakaa's narrative, she burns...

It is as though mere words, words absent of symbol and simile, will never be enough to truly show the violent catastrophe of death by napalm. The propulsive layering of similes upon each other suggests, indeed creates, a certain narrative frenzy. If the victim is rendered not-human, it is because of the napalm, not because Komunyakaa lacks the imagination to do her justice. Indeed, Komunyakaa elevates the ever-dying woman to biblical status when he finally describes her as burning...; These lines remind us of God made manifest in the burning bush of the book of Exodus, but they also empty that allusion of its hopeful promise of liberation. Moses received instruction and guidance from the burning bush; the horror of this woman's death simply replays itself, ad infinitum, in the appalled narrator's mind.

"You and I Are Disappearing" is a haunting poem, turned into a frightening lament by Elliot Goldenthal's score for *Fire, Water, Paper*. The narrator attests to having been a witness to this

death...and he attempts to find the words to match this horrible spectacle. The choices Komunyakaa makes, and the similes he uses, speak to the trauma that the sight has inflicted upon the speaker; however, this narrator does not make himself the central character in the poem. This is not a poem about how terrible it was for the narrator to witness a civilian's horrible death. What matters in the poem is the dying "girl," the fact that she is Vietnamese, and that she is immolated by a chemical manufactured to permit Americans to kill from a safe distance. It is the woman's suffering, not the narrator's, which Komunyakaa reanimates for readers. In "You and I Are Disappearing" Komunyakaa writes as a Jeremiah rather than a journalist, reminding readers of the human cost of the Vietnam War, a cost inscribed on Vietnamese bodies as well as on American ones....

Source: Angela M. Salas, "Human Empathy and Negative Capability: Yusef Komunyakaa's Poetry," in *Flashback through the Heart: The Poetry of Yusef Komunyakaa*, Susquehanna University Press, 2004, pp. 48–54.

Andrea Shaw

In the following review, Shaw highlights Komunyakaa's use of religious imagery and themes in one of his collections.

Talking Dirty to the Gods is poet Yusef Komunyakaa's twelfth book, and it follows an illustrious sequence of publications that include his Pulitzer Prize-winning collection *Neon Vernacular*. Born in Bogalusa, Louisiana in 1947, Komunyakaa writes verse which pulsates with the rich folklore and mystery that attended his childhood in the South, and the collection is suffused in ancient mythology, especially incorporating gods from the Greek pantheon. *Talking Dirty to the Gods* consists of 132 four-quatrain poems that destabilize traditional Western notions regarding the nature of the divine. Through retelling myths and recontextualizing various aspects of human existence, Komunyakaa situates God in the mundane interstices of our life while concomitantly defiling sacrosanct imaginings of the divine.

"Ode to the Maggot" suggests that this creature's subsistence on decaying matter metaphorically functions as an equalizing agent, exacting upon human beings the same lack of regard for social stature that God is assumed to perpetuate. Both "beggars and kings" are subjected to the same deterioration process, and this egalitarian posture is a prerequisite for human spiritual evolution: "No decree or creed can outlaw you / As you take every living thing apart. Little / Master of earth, no one gets to heaven / Without going through you first." Several other pieces challenge our appropriation of life forms and objects as not inconsequential to the universe, and "The God of Broken Things" infers the vitality of society's rejects, situating elements of the divine among the discards in a junk shop.

Talking Dirty to the Gods locates gratifying the flesh as a path to experiencing God, and in several pieces religious and sexual passion are conflated, desecrating—by traditional Western standards—the chastity of the religious arena. In "Shiva" the deity's spiritual magnetism is combined with his sexual prowess, and "spell-bound women" are drawn to him, "This beggar with the erect penis." The poem "Sex Toys" implicitly links sex and religion, connoting that sexual and religious stimulation emerge from the same locale: "these instruments / Raise temples beneath reason & skin."

Komunyakaa's collection also challenges the sanctity of society's modern gods such as time and physical beauty. In "Vainglory" the goal of cosmetic perfection is likened to the hollow desire for a "perpetual orgasm," and "Venus of Willendorf" resists Western esthetic standards by referencing a fat female body, associating that body with fertility, and imbuing it with spiritual allure. In "The Devil's Ball" the idea of time's being equivalent to money is revisited; however, it is not saving time that is rendered as valuable, but savoring it, specifically through the act of artistic production.

Talking Dirty to the Gods insists upon a reconceptualization of the divine and those icons that are associated with religiosity. By rendering gods that are not dichotomized into simplistic good and evil strata, Komunyakaa uses his collection to present an astounding contemplation of the fluid boundaries in which our godlike figures reside.

Source: Andrea Shaw, Review of *Talking Dirty to the Gods*, in *World Literature Today*, Vol. 75, Summer–Autumn 2001, p. 153.

SOURCES

"A Brief Guide to Jazz Poetry," Poets.org, https://www.poets.org/poetsorg/text/brief-guide-jazz-poetry (accessed April 28, 2016).

Ashford, Tomeiko, "Biography: Yusef Komunyakaa," Internet Poetry Archive, http://www.ibiblio.org/ipa/poems/komunyakaa/biography.php (accessed April 28, 2016).

Hansen, J. E., "Jim Crow Laws and Racial Segregation," Social Welfare History website, 2011, http://www.socialwelfarehistory.com/eras/civil-war-reconstruction/jim-crow-laws-andracial-segregation/ (accessed April 29, 2016).

Hoover, Elizabeth, "Songs of Rage and Tenderness: The Poetry of Yusef Komunyakaa," August 31, 2010, http://www.sampsoniaway.org/literary-voices/2010/08/31/songs-of-rage-and-tenderness-the-poetry-of-yusef-komunyakaa/ (accessed April 28, 2016).

Hughes, Langston, "Jazz as Communication (1956)," Poetry Foundation, October 13, 2009, http://www.poetryfoundation.org/resources/learning/essays/detail/69394 (accessed April 28, 2016).

"Income, Poverty, and Valuation of Noncash Benefits," U.S. Department of Commerce, 1993, p. xviii.

Komunyakaa, Yusef, "Blackberries," in *Pleasure Dome: New and Collected Poems*, Wesleyan University Press, 2001, pp. 280–81.

Lawson, Steven F., "Segregation," National Humanities Center website, May 2010, http://nationalhumanitiescenter.org/tserve/freedom/1865-1917/essays/segregation.htm (accessed April 29, 2016).

Metres, Philip, "Poet Yusef Komunyakaa Brings His Keen Eye and Sense of Craft to a Reading Tuesday at John Carroll," in *Plain Dealer*, October 20, 2014, http://www.cleveland.com/books/index.ssf/2014/10/poet_yusef_komunyakaa_brings_h.html (accessed April 28, 2016).

"1 in 5 Louisianans Lived in Poverty Last Year: Census Data," NOLA website, September 15, 2015, http://www.nola.com/politics/index.ssf/2015/09/louisiana_poverty_rate.html (accessed April 28, 2016).

Pruyn, Cassie, "Poetry Profile: Yusef Komunyakaa, 2016 Festival Poetry Judge," Tennessee Williams Festival website, November 10, 2013, http://www.tennesseewilliams.net/poetry-profile-yusef-komunyakaa-2016-festival-poetry-judge (accessed April 28, 2016).

Span, Paula, "The Failing Light: Why Did a Rising Young Poet Plunge into Despair, Taking Her Own Life and the Life of Her 2-year-old Son?," in *Washington Post*, February 15, 2004, https://www.washingtonpost.com/lifestyle/magazine/the-failing-light-why-did-a-rising-young-poet-plunge-into-despair-taking-her-own-life-and-the-life-of-her-2-year-old-son/2015/01/15/2575a388-9d1f-11e4-96cc-e858eba91ced_story.html (accessed April 28, 2016).

Weber, Bruce, "A Poet's Values: It's the Words over the Man," in *New York Times*, May 2, 1994, http://www.nytimes.com/1994/05/02/books/a-poet-s-values-it-s-the-words-over-the-man.html?pagewanted = all (accessed April 28, 2016).

Williamson, Eric Miles, "Eric Miles Williamson on Yusef Komunyakaa's *The Chameleon Couch*," in *Critical Mass*, March 6, 2012, http://bookcritics.org/blog/

archive/ eric-miles-williamson-on-yusef-komunyakaas-the-chameleon-couch1 (accessed April 28, 2016).

"Yusef Komunyakaa," Poetry Foundation, http://www.poetryfoundation.org/bio/yusef-komunyakaa (accessed April 28, 2016).

FURTHER READING

Feinstein, Sascha, and Yusef Komunyakaa, *The Jazz Poetry Anthology*, Indiana University Press, 1991.
This anthology of 132 poets covers a range of jazz styles, including free jazz, blues, experimental, Dixieland, and beyond. Poets collected include James Baldwin, Mina Loy, Langston Hughes, Sonia Sanchez, and Ishmael Reed.

Hale, Grace Elizabeth, *Making Whiteness: The Culture of Segregation in the South, 1890–1940*, Vintage, 1999.
Hale examines the ways in which white Americans, faced with the citizenship of freed slaves following the Civil War, created a new system of disenfranchisement and inequality in order to preserve their own economic and social status within society through preventing African Americans a chance at true equality.

Komunyakaa, Yusef, *Blue Notes: Essays, Interviews, and Commentaries*, University of Michigan Press, 2000.
Blue Notes provides background context and personal notes for many of Komunyakaa's poems written by the poet himself, as well as a collection of essays from artists who have influenced Komunyakaa's development, including Thelonious Monk, Langston Hughes, and Ma Rainey.

Komunyakaa, Yusef, *Dien Cai Dau*, Wesleyan, 1988.
Komunyakaa's 1988 collection confronts his time in Vietnam and is considered one the best literary works ever written on the subject. *Dien Cai Dau* means "crazy" in Vietnamese, a phrase the locals called the American soldiers often. After years of avoiding the topic, Komunyakaa found that once he started writing poetry about the Vietnam War, he could not stop.

Myers, Walter Dean, *Jazz*, Holiday House, 2008.
This picture book of jazz poetry combines the bright illustrations of Christopher Myers with surprising typography and an accompanying CD of music and narration. A glossary and time line of important moments in jazz history are included.

SUGGESTED SEARCH TERMS

Yusef Komunyakaa

Komunyakaa AND "Blackberries"

Komunyakaa AND Magic City AND Pleasure Dome

nature poetry

jazz poetry

jazz music

segregation AND civil rights movement

Louisiana AND poverty

Bury Me in a Free Land

FRANCES ELLEN WATKINS HARPER

1864

"Bury Me in a Free Land" is the best-known poem of influential writer and abolitionist Frances Ellen Watkins Harper. An enduring rallying cry for racial equality during the period of Reconstruction after the Civil War and through the civil rights movement of the following century, the poem was first published in 1864 to small readership in the Boston-based antislavery newspaper the *Liberator*. Two years later, in 1866, fellow abolitionist and women's rights activist Lydia Maria Francis Child included the poem in her recently revived *The Freedmen's Book*.

In keeping with the larger body of Harper's contributions to both poetry and literature, "Bury Me in a Free Land" is largely concerned with propagating a political viewpoint and encouraging humanitarian ends. Her verse is highly lyrical, written in the first person and containing elements of musicality, and heavily indebted to the ancient tradition of dramatic poetry. The oral quality of the poem helps to at once express the personal convictions of the narrator and universalize the message for an implied audience that spans the breadth of an entire nation. The accessible language of "Bury Me in a Free Land," coupled with its predictable and hypnotic rhyming couplets, grounds the composition in the language of the everyday American.

Harper famously gifted a copy of the poem, a stirring testament to the freedom of the human spirit that transcends even death, to a condemned

Frances Ellen Watkins Harper (©*Library of Congress /*
Getty Images)

abolitionist who had participated in John Brown's armed insurrection against the South. The composition became a mainstay of Harper's extensive lecture circuit and gained considerable popularity during her decades as a public activist. In the troubled era of American Reconstruction following the Civil War, a time marred by widespread disenfranchisement, mourning, and renewed racial animosities, Harper's public recitations sought to soothe and to heal a devastated national psyche. In this spirit of hope and of healing, "Bury Me in a Free Land" combines uncompromising humanistic sentiments with a nonjudgmental delivery inviting the participation of all Americans regardless of political faction or race. The poem remains a sentimental favorite to the present day and is still recited in memory of a great woman and her everlasting commitment to freedom.

AUTHOR BIOGRAPHY

Revered as a poetess, lecturer, and lifelong advocate of human rights, Harper was born to free African American parents in Baltimore,

Maryland, on September 24, 1825. At the tender age of four, Harper suffered the loss of her mother and was entrusted to the care of her uncle, a well-known abolitionist of the day. Harper grew to adulthood steeped in her uncle's views and soon came to share his commitment to the ideals of freedom and equality. As a young teenager, the budding activist pledged her domestic service to a family of local Quakers who allowed her free rein of the household library and encouraged her inborn gift for the arts of writing and rhetoric. It was during these years that Harper first began to publish her compositions in local magazines and newspapers. Her first collection of poetry, *Forest Leaves*, was released in 1845 and was soon lost to history until the early 2000s.

In 1850, with the passing of the Fugitive Slave Act, which legalized the reenslavement of freed and escaped African Americans in southern states, Harper left Maryland with her family, moving initially to Ohio and later to Pennsylvania. She continued to write during this time and earned her keep as a teacher at various schools and as a well-respected lecturer on civil rights issues. It was in Philadelphia that the young woman became directly engaged with the abolitionist movement and assisted many prominent activists in allowing African Americans to escape bondage through the Underground Railroad. In the years following the outbreak of the Civil War, Harper traveled, lectured extensively, and gained critical acclaim and monetary success as a writer of both prose and poetry. Her 1854 *Poems on Miscellaneous Subjects* became an instant classic and commercial success, whereas her 1859 "The Two Offers" made history as the first short story published by an African American woman.

In 1860, Harper met the man who was to be her husband, a widower with three children, and moved with her new family to settle in Ohio during the years of the Civil War. She gave birth to her only daughter, Mary, in 1862 but lost her husband two years later, in 1864. That same year, she published her most celebrated individual poem, "Bury Me in a Free Land" in the abolitionist newspaper the *Liberator*.

After the victory of the Union over the Confederacy, Harper toured the devastated American South with her family and sought to assist in the slow, painful process of Reconstruction. With the decisive victory of the Union over the

Confederacy and the tenuous reforging of a unified America, Harper recognized the enormity of the struggle still confronting the nation. Her work from this period onward reflected her desire not only to ease the ongoing trials and tribulations of the long-suffering African American community but also to help heal the American sense of common identity and bring solace to a bloodied and impoverished South. In particular, Harper's 1872 collection of verse, *Sketches of Southern Life*, sought to universalize the diminished way of life afflicting millions in the years following America's most bloody and divisive war.

As both an African American and a woman, Harper was remarkable in an age of deep inequality and prejudice for reaching so broad an audience and for attaining a high degree of monetary self-sufficiency and success through her work. In 1859, Harper published what is widely acknowledged to be the first short story by an African American woman to appear in a magazine, "The Two Offers," and expanded and serialized the landmark work into a complete novel two decades later. Harper's 1892 success, *Iola Leroy; or, Shadows Uplifted*, marked the apex of her literary success and brought together the many strands of activism championed by Harper in over half a century of humanitarian involvement.

Harper continued to give voice to the oppressed through writing and lectures until the end of her life and was instrumental in advancing causes of both national and local import. She eventually settled in Philadelphia, the city most closely associated with her memory, and became heavily involved in organizations promoting racial equality and desegregation, temperance, and political involvement for women. Harper died on February 22, 1911, one of the most prominent voices in the history of American civil liberties. She was laid to rest in Philadelphia's Eden Cemetery, next to her daughter who had died some years earlier, in a simple grave consistent with the sentiments expressed by "Bury Me in a Free Land."

POEM TEXT

Make me a grave where'er you will,
In a lowly plain or a lofty hill,
Make it among earth's humblest graves,
But not in a land where men are slaves.

I could not rest, if around my grave   5
I heard the steps of a trembling slave;
His shadow above my silent tomb
Would make it a place of fearful gloom.

I could not sleep, if I heard the tread
Of a coffle-gang to the shambles led,   10
And the mother's shriek of wild despair
Rise, like a curse, on the trembling air.

I could not rest, if I saw the lash
Drinking her blood at each fearful gash;
And I saw her babes torn from her breast,   15
Like trembling doves from their parent nest.

I'd shudder and start, if I heard the bay
Of a bloodhound seizing his human prey,
And I heard the captive plead in vain,
As they bound, afresh, his galling chain.   20

If I saw young girls from their mother's arms
Bartered and sold for their youthful charms,
My eye would flash with a mournful flame,
My death-paled cheek grow red with shame.

I would sleep, dear friends, where bloated Might 25
Can rob no man of his dearest right;

POEM SUMMARY

The text used for this summary is from *A Brighter Coming Day*, Feminist Press, 1993, p. 177. Versions of the poem can be found at the following web pages: http://www.poemhunter.com/poem/bury-me-in-a-free-land/ and https://www.poets.org/poetsorg/poem/bury-me-free-land.

Lines 1–4

The poet instructs the audience to make her grave in a location according to their own preference. She expresses her equal willingness to be interred on a depressed plane or on an elevated hill overlooking the countryside. The poet then makes it clear that she seeks a humble grave as much as a grandiose one but will not tolerate being laid to rest in a land where human enslavement still endures.

Lines 5–8

The poet claims that her final rest would be disturbed by the feet of terrified slaves treading the earth above her body, their fleeing shadows casting a pall of gloom over an already unquiet grave.

Lines 9–12

The sound of clinking chains binding enslaved workers would disturb the rest of the deceased poet. This sound is interrupted by the wail of a bereaved mother, her cry a lingering curse on the air.

Lines 13–16

The poet evokes the sense of sight in the fourth stanza and bears witness to the horrific whipping of the aforementioned slave mother, the rawhide drawing vivid blood upon each impact. The speaker of the verse watches as the woman's children are torn from her breast. She likens their shaking bodies to those of doves fallen from a familiar nest.

Lines 17–20

The speaker shudders in her grave at the triumphant barking of dogs fallen on their human quarry. She hears the futile pleading of the escaped slave as he is once again committed to chains by his unnamed masters.

Lines 21–24

In this next stanza, the poet envisions young girls separated from the loving embrace of their mothers to be bartered like goods and sold to lustful and cruel masters. This shameful spectacle is enough to bring a flush of indignation to a cheek made colorless by death.

Lines 25–28

The speaker of the poem directly addresses her friends to express the possibility of her undisturbed rest under specific circumstances. Only in a land freed from slavery and ruled by moral conviction rather than strength, the poet asserts, can she go to her grave in peace.

Lines 29–32

In the poem's final stanza, the poet comes full circle to once again outline the specifications for her grave. She rejects the prospect of its being marked by an impressive monument and seems equally uninterested in the recognition of either casual passersby or posterity. Cut loose from mortal concerns of vanity, her spirit seeks only to be tied to a plot of earth free from the taint of slavery.

THEMES

Enslavement

"Bury Me in a Free Land" is first and foremost a poem about the horrors of human enslavement. By calling upon all the senses to bear witness to the trauma of slavery, Harper immerses her readers in the full injustice and cruelty human beings so wantonly inflict upon their fellows. The poet relates various scenarios of suffering and demonstrates the impact of enslavement on individuals, families, and society itself. To this end, Harper makes no specific reference to the racial differences between the oppressors and the oppressed in her poem and refuses to cast blame. She establishes slavery as an evil in its own right and thereby brings a degree of universality to its continuing implications for the dignity of the human race.

Harper's depiction of slavery is rooted in both its graphic physicality and its emotional trauma. Vivid and disturbing imagery of violence combines in the poet's verse with the clink of chains, the baying of hounds, and the cries of the bereaved to instill terror and disgust in its audience. In the inescapability of the poem's assault upon the senses and the conscience, "Bury Me in a Free Land" simulates the hopeless confinement of the slave within the experience of the reader.

Death

The poem's fixation with death and an unquiet grave extends slavery's implications beyond life itself and into the hereafter. The poem opens and closes as a last testament of sorts, providing instructions for the ideal burial of the narrator. The simplicity of the central desire expressed by this testament, namely to be buried in earth free from the taint of slavery, contrasts with the grandiose ideal of a grand funeral and imposing marble monument. The spirit of the narrator is divorced from personal concerns of mortality and seeks only to better the existence of still-living, still-suffering slaves.

At the same time, the poem deals so heavily in the imagery of the grave that it elevates the importance of life over death and trivializes the desire for enduring fame. The drab, static imagery of mortality utilized by Harper serves as a contrast to the vitality and horror of the experience of slavery still endured above ground.

TOPICS FOR FURTHER STUDY

- "Bury Me in a Free Land" is a poem powerfully rooted in the senses, immersing readers in the sights, sounds, and sensations of the horrific institution of slavery. After deliberation with a partner, agree on a pressing injustice confronting the world today that you both would like to see resolved. Make use of an online template to compose a "sense poem" on a large sheet of paper concerning your chosen issue, using simple but visceral language in the style of Harper. When you are finished, take turns reading your compositions aloud to your classmates and respond to any questions.

- Using a suggested medium of clay, construct what you believe to be a fitting monument to one of your personal heroes. Make your creation as ornate or as simple as you desire, but strive to make sense of your choice within the context of your hero's life choices and beliefs. Explain your reasoning on an index card to be attached to your creation. Finally, arrange your monuments and written explanations around the room in the manner of an art gallery and circulate to participate in a class-wide viewing.

- Reflect on a plot of earth—whether in your backyard, a public park, or a distant vacation spot—that holds deep personal significance for you. In a brief but visually dense journal entry, describe this locale and give voice to either its positive or negative connotations in terms of your experience. With a partner, rehearse reading your entry aloud in an attempt to imbue your description with the appropriate emotion and effective narrative flow. Reflect on some of the similar choices Harper might have made in reading her poetry aloud and inspiring audiences and how these techniques contribute to the art of rhetoric.

- "Bury Me in a Free Land" was seldom read by Harper in isolation but rather as part of a larger demonstration or human rights rally. In this spirit, design a performative reading of the poem intended to achieve maximum effect and capture the excitement and gravity of the event. In groups of two or three, implement your unique vision using whatever effects, props, or costumes you deem appropriate. Have one member of your group record the production using a cell phone, iPad, or other recording device. As a class, create a YouTube channel devoted to your efforts and post each of your group videos. After watching all the performances in turn, devote discussion time to discussing what worked and what did not in terms of engaging the audience.

- "Bury Me in a Free Land" deals both with mortality and immortality, evoking unquiet graves, marble monuments, and the long-denied sleep of a tortured spirit. Read Natalie Babbitt's 1975 classic of young-adult literature, *Tuck Everlasting*, for comparison to Harper's poem, and take note of their individual views on life and death, brevity, and longevity. Construct a Venn diagram outlining these differences and similarities to share with your classmates in a group discussion.

- Harper's composition derives strength from its imagery of containment and claustrophobia. It is a poem narrated from the dark embrace of the grave and recounting the horrors of inescapable human bondage. Cut a piece of construction paper into ribbons of equal size and divide them up among classmates. Each student will then select an especially striking scene from the poem to draw on their slip of paper. When finished with their individual drawings, the class will create a paper chain—representing a manacle—from their various artistic renderings to serve as reminder of the legacy of slavery in America.

The poem includes many images of slavery *(©Bakhur Nick / Shutterstock.com)*

This reversal suggests that life, and not its end, is the true source of both suffering and salvation.

Peace

Despite its horrific subject matter, "Bury Me in a Free Land" is not without a note of optimism and the possibility of redemption. The restlessness that saturates the earlier portions of the poem is a result of the injustices still carried out above the narrator's unquiet grave. Initially, death is cast not in the light of a peaceful sleep but a vivid nightmare, with the deceased unable either to wake up and act or achieve the comfort of full oblivion. As a result, the poem's speaker becomes a tortured and helpless participant in a cycle of almost unimaginable cruelty. Much to the relief of the reader, the same measure of peace denied by the first stanzas of "Bury Me in a Free Land" is restored in the poem's closing lines. With the hope of right triumphing over might and the passing of the institution of slavery from the earth, Harper conjures up a world where peace is at last attainable.

STYLE

Imagery

Harper's use of imagery, striking visual representations rendered through words, is intentionally brutal and relentless. The helplessness and terror inherent to the life of a slave is simulated through a barrage of upsetting images of laborers straining under the weight of chains, families being torn apart, and whips and the fangs of bloodhounds tearing into human flesh. So, too, the grandiose image of the tomb represented by a marble monument serves to offset the narrator's true desire for a peaceful, unmarked grave in a land free from the evils of slavery.

Motif

The poem's central motif, the characterizing theme or style of its writing, is that of the grave. By casting her verse within the context of a final will and testament, Harper makes her easy sleep conditional on the healing of the land's injustices. The impotence and confinement inherent to the grave serve also to

COMPARE
&
CONTRAST

- **1860s:** The notion of a self-sufficient African American woman in the 1860s is almost unprecedented. Not only is Harper able to support her family after the death of her husband, but she even gains a degree of renown and financial prosperity from her tireless writing and lecturing efforts.

  Today: Talk show host and media icon Oprah Winfrey holds the distinction of being one of the wealthiest and most influential African Americans in the country, dedicating her impressive speaking career and countless millions to further philanthropic causes of all stripes.

- **1860s:** The Fugitive Slave Act of the previous decade is still in effect and results in the forceful return to bondage of countless escaped slaves along the border states.

  Today: An estimated 5 to 10 percent of American farm workers are still subject to some form of forced labor and undocumented human rights abuses.

- **1860s:** Along with championing issues of racial equality in the years following the American Civil War, Harper turns her efforts towards promoting political participation for women.

  Today: Members of all races and genders granted the right to vote, and African American president Barack Obama takes office for two terms starting in 2009; female candidate Hillary Clinton makes a bid to be the next in line for the presidency.

emphasize the similar condition of bondage, a sort of living death for millions of enslaved African Americans. Harper suggests through her motif of the grave that the soul is immortal and yearns to remedy injustice both in this world and in the next.

Polemic

"Bury Me in a Free Land" is a polemic of sorts, an uncompromising examination of the issue of slavery, which threatened to divide the nation in the years leading up to the American Civil War. The poem's fearless treatment of this controversial theme and unyielding moral pronouncements on right and wrong mark it as a declaration of war against an unjust institution. At the same time that she condemns the evils of slavery, however, Harper's polemic refuses to directly assign blame or single out guilty parties for punishment.

Rhyme

Harper's poem is composed of stanzas containing two sets of couplets each, an unassuming but powerful rhyme scheme that complements the gravity of its subject matter. This lends a direct, almost childlike air of simplicity to the verse that obscures none of the poet's moral assertions and makes the message clear to all. Because Harper was fond of presenting this particular composition at her various lectures, the rhyme scheme enhances the pleasant musicality of "Bury Me in a Free Land" when recited aloud.

HISTORICAL CONTEXT

Although the Underground Railroad was instituted as early as the 1780s as a network to help slaves escape to free northern states, the efforts of the organization intensified greatly in the years leading up to the American Civil War. With considerable support from the Quaker community and well-known abolitionists from all races and creeds, the network was instrumental in freeing thousands of enslaved African Americans in the space of only a few decades. With the institution of the 1850 Fugitive Slave

The image of doves—symbols of peace—taken from their nest is a metaphor for children taken from their enslaved parents (©*Bob Denelzen* | *Shutterstock.com*)

Act, support for the Underground Railroad increased dramatically to combat the active recapture of slaves seeking sanctuary in border regions. When President Abraham Lincoln was elected in 1860 and the southern states seceded, which soon after culminated in the American Civil War, the Underground Railroad was forced into temporary inactivity because of the outbreak of open hostilities.

By 1864 and the publication of "Bury Me in a Free Land," the Emancipation Proclamation officially freeing American slaves was already in effect, but the outcome of the war was still uncertain. In the difficult years to follow, Harper renewed her abolitionist efforts to help heal the South during Reconstruction and bring a degree of racial understanding to a resentful and decimated population. She devoted her considerable skills of oratory and empathy to combating widespread lynching and the passing of restrictive racial laws aimed at barring African Americans from equality and upward mobility. "Bury Me in a Free Land" became a well-loved fixture of many of Harper's lectures during this period.

The Reconstruction Act, a piece of landmark legislation passed in 1867, allowed African American men full voting rights and participation in government as a movement towards universal male suffrage. Southern states were required to comply with the terms of this new act to be admitted back into the Union and receive federal aid and funding for continued reconstruction. In response to these conditions imposed upon the South, homegrown organizations like the infamous Ku Klux Klan emerged to inflict violence on the agents of this change and preserve the antebellum way of life. Outspoken activists like Harper were instrumental during this period in helping to curb the renewed outbreaks of violence and protect newly emancipated African Americans from murder at the hands of their own communities.

The women's suffrage movement in the United States, though it predated the Civil War by as much as three decades, became subsumed in the abolitionist cause and the reconstruction of national identity in the years following the outbreak of open conflict between the Union and the Confederacy. Only during the 1890s did the advocates of universal suffrage, Harper a prominent voice among them, regroup and renew pushing their agenda in earnest. By the time of Harper's death in 1911, only a handful of states had extended women the right to vote, and it was not until 1920 that the Nineteenth Amendment was ratified, granting all American women full political representation.

CRITICAL OVERVIEW

Because of the comparatively obscure publication of "Bury Me in a Free Land" in 1864 and its subsequent popularity at abolitionist meetings and lectures, Harper's poem is better known to later scholars than to contemporary reviewers. In a retrospective review published only a few years after Harper's death, Benjamin Brawley outlines what he sees as the defining characteristics of Harper's poetry and her contribution to the growing body of African American literature. According to Brawley's "Three Negro Poets: Horton, Mrs. Harper, and Whitman," the immense popularity of the poet is diminished by a certain simplicity of style and an inability to reach true technical mastery. In this way, the critic compares Harper to other poets of the era and finds her lacking. Brawley writes of Harper,

> Her verse was very popular, not less than ten thousand copies of her booklets being sold. It was decidedly lacking in technique, however.... Mrs. Harper was best when most simple.

In her "Black Woman Poets from Wheatley to Walker," scholar Gloria T. Hull takes a more generous and dynamic view of Harper's poetry within the context of the day. In addition to lauding Harper for the precision and pointed accessibility of her verse, Hull explains the importance of the iconic poet in bringing her message to the people, evoking the abolitionist spirit of the times, and creating poetry well adapted to public reading. Hull writes,

> Essentially this poetry is message verse, dependent on an oratorical and histrionic platform delivery for its effect. Harper leans heavily on the poetic and emotional appeal of sensory imagery, as can be seen in ... "Bury Me in a Free Land."

While acknowledging the points of the aforementioned critics—Harper's reliance on public delivery over technical superiority in her verse—scholar Patricia Liggins Hill seeks to establish the lineage of the poet's work as well as its influence upon later African American poets. In her article "'Let Me Make the Songs for the People': A Study of Frances Watkins Harper's Poetry," Hill explains,

> Just as these latter-day poets base their oral protest poetry primarily on direct imagery, simple diction, and the rhythmic language of the street to reach the masses of black people, Harper relies on vivid, striking imagery, simplistic language, and the musical quality and form of the ballad.

In a similar vein of enduring national resonance, Donald Yacavone of the Massachusetts Historical Society stresses the inherent strength and defiance of Harper's work, in particular "Bury Me in a Free Land," and its implications for the future of a nation reforged. In his essay "Sacred Land Regained: Frances Ellen Watkins Harper and 'The Massachusetts Fifty-fourth,' a Lost Poem," Yacavone acknowledges the role of the poem in consecrating land once infected by the evils of slavery.

Despite the poem's enormous role in promoting national healing, advancing human rights, and inspiring hope in America during Reconstruction, contemporary reception of Harper's body of work and its subsequent interpretation by a more modern age are colored by the same racial and gender-based insecurities Harper worked so tirelessly to combat. Attempting to make their own mark on the growing canon of American literature and measure up to the perceived greatness of the famously florid literary giants of white society, a new generation of African American poets dominating the early twentieth century actively shunned Harper's work for its simplicity of style and emphasis on gender and race equality.

Fellow activist, writer, and cofounder of the enormously influential National Association for the Advancement of Colored People (NAACP), W. E. B. Du Bois eulogized Harper and gave voice to the grudging respect shared by many of his contemporaries for their literary predecessor. Forced to acknowledge the undeniable conviction and dedication expressed by Harper through her life and work, Du Bois nevertheless expresses hesitancy to laud what he views as crude craftsmanship in her poems. In a 1911 edition of the NAACP publication *Crisis*, he writes, "She was not a great singer, but she had some sense of song; she was not a great writer, but she wrote much worth reading. She was, above all, sincere."

Likewise, Harper's tendency to depict protagonists of mixed race and soften the otherwise sharp divide between victim and victimizer proved unpopular among later African American poets and critics, and much of her work faded gradually into obscurity. Fueled in large part by the publication of *Iola Leroy* in mass-market paperback, a collection of articles discussing the legacy of Harper's work in the late 1980s, along with the painstaking recovery of Harper's first collection of poetry, *Autumn Leaves*, the reputation of the poet has achieved a newfound popularity among casual readers and scholars alike.

CRITICISM

Jeffrey Eugene Palmer

Palmer is a scholar, freelance writer, and teacher of high school English. In the following essay, he examines themes of undead longing in Toni Morrison's Beloved *and "Bury Me in a Free Land."*

Although the unnamed narrator of Harper's "Bury Me in a Free land" physically occupies a plot of earth, her essence cannot be contained by the grave while injustice persists in her native land. Her spirit seems at once nowhere and everywhere in the vivid imagery and sensory output of the poem, resonant in the cry of a bereaved mother, trembling in the limbs of a terrified child, and tasting the brine of sweat and jewels of blood on a slave's flayed back. The visceral and universal nature of Harper's verse, its horrific inescapability, are key components to its tremendously popular reception by contemporary audiences of a large and diverse makeup.

Amplifying its horrors, even the solace of oblivion is denied the suffering slaves of the poem. The earth itself is poisoned by injustice, by the proverbial blood of Cain calling out from the ground, and will abide no peaceful interment. The unquiet grave of Harper's composition evokes another, more contemporary representation of the theme of the tortured undead in African American literature. In Toni Morrison's celebrated 1987 novel *Beloved*, the victim of an infanticide returns as a dazzling

> WHEREAS MORRISON'S NOVEL CENTERS ON A HAUNTING, WILLINGLY PERPETUATED BY ILL WILL AND AN INSATIABLE HUNGER FOR VENGEANCE, HARPER'S POEM PREACHES THE NEED FOR PURIFICATION AND THE RENUNCIATION OF A CYCLE OF CRUELTY AND UNSPEAKABLE INJUSTICE."

but deadly abomination to plague her mother and steal back a life denied. Herself a victim of cruel enslavement, the girl's mother, Sethe, attempts to atone for the sin she committed out of desperation and love by submitting willingly, even readily, to this vampiric reversal of circumstance. The physical site of this bygone tragedy, a house shunned by neighbors and designated by the number 124, is haunted by the memory of a time without reason or hope, a time when mothers murdered their children rather than submit them to slavery.

Harper's more contemporary portrayal of the restless dead differs from Morrison's tale of undying animosity in several crucial respects. Foremost among them are their disparate portrayals of blame and culpability, retribution and redemption. Whereas *Beloved* vilifies both Sethe and her abusive master, known only as "Schoolteacher," Harper's "Bury Me in a Free Land" makes no explicit distinction between victim and victimizer. Tellingly, any mention of race is entirely absent from the poem, and the burden of blame and culpability falls upon all men, regardless of the color of their skin.

Morrison twists the hopeful theme of racial indifference in Harper's poem by transforming it into a horrifyingly literal representation of featureless corpses and men flayed of all skin. Unlike the narrator of "Bury Me in a Free Land," whose spirit dwells above the earth to share in the suffering of the living, *Beloved's* shade is preoccupied primarily with her deceased neighbors. Through a horrifying stream of consciousness, the murdered girl describes every detail of those who dwell in the dirt, their moldering jewelry, tapered, shining teeth, and general absence of skin or distinguishing features.

WHAT DO I READ NEXT?

- Renowned historian Howard Zinn's *A People's History of the United States* was first published in 1980 but remains a definitive, best-selling masterwork of American history from the perspective of the poor, the disenfranchised, and the enslaved.

- The haunting 1853 memoir of freeman-turned-slave Solomon Northup, *Twelve Years a Slave*, recounts the unique horror of the Fugitive Slave Act and its implications for a divided country on the brink of civil war.

- Harper Lee's enduring 1960 classic *To Kill a Mockingbird* is a story of racial prejudice, injustice, and redemption in the troubled southern hamlet of Maycomb, Alabama.

- *The Confessions of Nat Turner* is a 1967 novel by southern author William Styron that attempts to tell the story of the most infamous slave uprising in the history of the United States from the perspective of its charismatic, controversial leader.

- Toni Morrison's 1987 *Beloved* is a moving story of family, community, and an unspeakable act of love committed by a former slave for her children.

- Famed Harlem Renaissance poet Jean Toomer published his novelistic masterpiece *Cane* in 1923, a decade after Harper's death. It remains a compelling, complex portrait of African American life in a new century fueled by hope but overshadowed by the memory of a painful past.

- Phillis Wheatley's *Complete Writings* was edited by Vincent Carretta and published in 2001 as a definitive anthology of the work of America's first, and perhaps most influential, African American poetess.

- A renowned novelist, poet, and speaker, Alice Walker is the literary and ideological heir to earlier figures like Wheatley and Harper. Walker's collection *Her Blue Body Everything We Know: Earthling Poems* was published in 2004 and melds historical currents of African American sentiment with the triumphs and tribulations of a more modern age.

- A young-adult classic, Ann Rinaldi's 2007 *The Ever-After Bird* is the tale of one girl's painful, poignant initiation into the truths of slavery and her growing involvement in the abolitionist movement.

- *The Wars of Reconstruction: The Brief, Violent History of America's Most Progressive Era* was authored by Douglas R. Egerton and published in 2015. The work provides a comprehensive, compelling picture of a nation recovering from the institution of slavery and a devastating civil war.

Tellingly, the ghost in *Beloved* comes to fixate on the corpse of one woman whose face she envies, attempting to enter the cold body and animate it with the warmth of the living. For the purpose of Morrison's novel, then, bodilessness and the erosion of personal identity is a state to be dreaded and avoided at any cost. The elimination of self for *Beloved*'s ghost is also the elimination of her all-consuming need for personal vengeance, a drive that, by contrast, is discouraged in every line of Harper's "Bury Me in a Free Land."

The selfishness inherent to the tragic and terrifying figure of *Beloved* is in no way echoed by Harper's poem. Rather than filling a single body and reveling in the joys denied her in life, the narrator of the poem infuses her essence with that of many individuals to share in their almost unbearable suffering. The visceral empathy and selflessness of this act divorces the poem's shade from personal concerns of comfort and universalizes the plight of an enslaved people. Unlike the spirit in *Beloved*, who wears a face of great

The speaker does not want a grand memorial on her grave, only the knowledge that all people are free in her country (©Stuart Monk / Shutterstock.com)

beauty and revels in her body, the sleepless spirit of "Bury Me in a Free Land" is faceless, bodiless, and a willing participant in the pain of all of humanity.

Whereas Morrison's novel centers on a haunting, willingly perpetuated by ill will and an insatiable hunger for vengeance, Harper's poem preaches the need for purification and the renunciation of a cycle of cruelty and unspeakable injustice. Although the reality that blood calls out for blood is reflected equally in both works, the similarity ends there. House 124 is an evil place, tainted by the memory of murder, enslavement, and human greed. Although suffering greatly from the abuses of the malevolent spirit within the walls of 124, Sethe and her living daughter, Dallas, cling to the grim comfort of the familiar and express little desire to escape. The land described by Harper, although it is no less evil, is a place resonant with the possibility of redemption and hope for a brighter

future. The poem actively seeks a peace long denied and refuses to settle for the familiarity of a corrupted and age-old system of injustice. Through her verse, Harper seeks to consecrate the land and exorcise the spirits of a traumatic, turbulent past. In his historical analysis of the poem "Sacred Land Regained: Frances Ellen Watkins Harper and 'The Massachusetts Fifty-Fourth,' A Lost Poem," Donald Yacavone echoes this understanding:

> "Bury Me in a Free Land" reflected the remorse and sadness that blacks felt, but also expressed their defiant stand not to accept slavery and racism as fixed features of American life. "Bury Me in a Free Land" was not a poem of hopelessness and despair, but of tragedy and resistance. This nation, the very ground itself was poisoned by the institution of slavery and blacks would have none of it.

In this same vein, whereas Morrison's ghost in *Beloved* is obsessed with looking back, with reliving and perpetuating the trauma of a recently concluded age, "Bury Me in a Free Land" dwells exclusively in the present and stretches towards a brighter future. The horrible injustices of the moment are decried and proclaimed unacceptable, the poem, and by extension the nation itself, contained in a stasis until justice and healing are realized. In this way, Harper's narrator-shade expresses both optimism and unyielding conviction, refusing to relive the past, determined to right the present, and tirelessly appealing to a tomorrow defined by peace and equality for all.

This essential difference between two works composed more than a century apart is explainable, in large part, by the contemporary realities of their authors. While Morrison's work is retrospective, recalling the era of Reconstruction in which the institution of slavery had ceased to exist but widespread injustice persisted, Harper's is contemporary with that era and actively engaged with burning issues of the day. The need for healing and forgiveness in the rebuilding of a devastated nation figures largely in "Bury Me in a Free Land" and explains its emphasis on the future rather than the past, the softening of blame, and the universalization of issues affecting all Americans, regardless of the color of their skin, in the difficult years to come.

Significantly, and despite their glaring differences in the portrayal of the restless dead and traumatic memory, both *Beloved* and "Bury Me in a Free Land" pose nearly identical solutions to the issue of societal persecution and injustice. Although she is a woman of color living among a largely African American community, Sethe is cruelly shunned by her neighbors for her act of murder fueled by desperation and love. The apathy and often blatant contempt the community demonstrates towards the tortured mother of four is inextricably intertwined with the germinating seed of evil contained in the breast of her daughter's ghost and the enduring shadow over 124. The return of Paul D, a girlhood friend of Sethe's, is enough to keep the evil at bay for a time, but this relationship is soon discouraged by the community, and the affliction of 124 resumes with a vengeance.

Only by coming together in common cause to redeem Sethe and exorcise the foul spirit plaguing her home is a degree of peace and closure achieved at the end of the novel. In much the same way, "Bury Me in a Free

> *FOREST LEAVES* IS ILLUSTRATIVE OF THE SUCCESS OF THE ANTEBELLUM BLACK FIGHT FOR LITERACY AND EDUCATION, WHILE ADDING TO THE FIELD OF EARLY AFRICAN AMERICAN LITERATURE."

Land" preaches that a nation divided by old prejudices and even the foulest of bygone injustices can never endure to see a brighter tomorrow. As the specters of the past are conjured by a collective will, so too, in compassion and unanimity, must they be laid to rest.

Source: Jeffrey Eugene Palmer, Critical Essay on "Bury Me in a Free Land," in *Poetry for Students*, Gale, Cengage Learning, 2017.

Johanna Ortner

In the following essay, Ortner describes the recovery of a collection of Harper's poetry.

In her poem titled "Yearnings for Home," Frances Ellen Watkins Harper describes how she longs to be back home in her mother's cot in order to pass away peacefully in the familiar surroundings of home. Harper beautifully depicts the rural landscape that surrounds her mother's little house as a heavenly, blissful place. Those who know Frances Harper and her literary works might feel taken aback by the above-mentioned poem, because it was not printed in any of her known literary publications before or after the Civil War. Indeed, "Yearnings for Home" is only included in Harper's first pamphlet, titled *Forest Leaves*, which was deemed lost to history for more than 150 years. This article introduces that long-lost publication to readers, scholars, and archivists.

A LOST TEXT FOUND

As I began to research my dissertation, "'Whatever concerns them, as a race, concerns me:' The Life and Activism of Frances Ellen Watkins Harper," which chronicles Harper as a seminal figure in black women's protest tradition and aims to highlight her political activism, I started in Maryland, the state of her birth. To be honest, I had no clear concept of how to go about conducting archival research on a figure like Harper, who did not leave behind, as far as we know, any personal papers, other than letters and speeches, some of which were published in newspapers, such as *The Christian Recorder* and *The National Anti-Slavery Standard*.

I decided to begin with the Maryland Historical Society, which is located in Harper's hometown of Baltimore. Having done my secondary source reading on her, I knew that *Forest Leaves* was deemed lost. Call it my naiveté as a young graduate student, but I figured I might as well type in the title in the society's catalogue. *Voilà*, it came up, together with a collection number. Even as I stared at the number on my screen, I thought that it could not be the "real deal," but instead was maybe a copy of the cover, or a newspaper clipping discussing the pamphlet (my naiveté knew no bounds). Fast forward to when the MDHS special collections archivist placed an envelope with the call number in front of me. I opened it up, peeked inside and wanted to let out a high-pitched squeal that I had enough sense to repress at the last second. The pamphlet slid right out of the envelope into my hands and there it was, staring me in the face. The term surreal is appropriate for how I felt when I first perused the pages of *Forest Leaves*. As I am writing this essay, I still catch myself looking at my copy, double-checking the cover of the pamphlet, making sure that I am not imagining the title. I have to reassure myself that I am not hallucinating: finally, scholars and students will be able to read Harper's first published work and include it in their teachings and studies alike.

A KEY TO HARPER'S EARLY LIFE

The retrieval of *Forest Leaves* not only gives us an earlier starting point for Harper's writings, but it is also the only primary source we have from her young life in Baltimore, before she joined the abolition movement in 1854 and began her decades-long career as a committed writer and activist for major social reform movements during the nineteenth century. Harper was raised by her uncle William Watkins, who took her in after she became an orphan at the age of three in 1828. Watkins was a renowned minister, educator, and avid abolitionist in Baltimore. He taught in his own school, the Watkins Academy for Negro Youth, which, according to Frances Smith Foster "was well known for its emphasis upon biblical studies, the classics, and elocution." Harper was one of his students until she was about thirteen years old and began to work

as a domestic servant for a couple who owned a bookstore in the city.

Very little is known about Harper's childhood and young adulthood in antebellum Baltimore, where she lived with her uncle William Watkins' family in the city's eleventh ward. Being born in a city with the largest free black population in the nation in the decades leading up to the Civil War, Harper grew up in an environment that displayed an intimate geographic proximity to slavery, since Maryland was a slave state. While we do not have autobiographic sources by Harper describing the first—roughly—twenty-five years of her life in Maryland, it is safe to state that her uncle had a great influence in shaping the young Harper's mind and writing development. Due to Watkins' position as the founder of his own academy, Harper had the advantage of receiving a formal education at a time when access to schools was either greatly restricted or impossible to obtain for African American children. Leroy Graham lists the subjects taught at Watkins' academy as "History, Geography, Mathematics, English, Natural Philosophy, Greek, Latin, Music, and Rhetoric" and describes Watkins as "a grammarian of such precision in the way of etymology, syntax, prosody, and so on, that one of his former pupils wrote humorously of the old leather strap Watkins used to correct grammar misuses." This account of the teacher's strict expectations allows us to safely assume that Harper not only learned basic literacy in her uncle's school, but was also taught the composition and style that is needed to write well-developed poems. The rediscovered pamphlet testifies to Harper's access to a strong formal education, which made her stand out from the majority of the nation's black population, who were denied such access. She was not the first one in her family to use the medium of print in order to have her voice heard. Her uncle William Watkins had his letters published in newspapers like *Freedom's Journal* and *The Liberator*, discussing the need for abolition and expressing his strong dislike for colonization—the plan to repatriate all free black people to Africa. One could argue that Harper must have been familiar with Watkins' activism and publications and perhaps this was the inspiration for her to seek to have her own work read outside of her family's household. While the pamphlet was written by Harper herself, one has to acknowledge how her familial surroundings helped her develop and nurture her growing desire to write for public consumption.

Forest Leaves gives us insight into Harper's desire to publish her works for a public readership while she was still living in Baltimore and had not, as yet, joined the abolition movement.

INSIGHTS INTO NINETEENTH-CENTURY BLACK PRINT CULTURE AND HARPER'S BODY OF WORK

The pamphlet functions as our "new" starting point for Harper's introduction into African American literary history and allows us the opportunity to discuss how she was able to distribute her first poems within the nation's burgeoning print culture. *Forest Leaves* was published by printer James Young, who founded and lead [sic] temperance organizations in Baltimore. As Patricia Dockman Anderson has shown, Young owned a printing business, but was also a leader in the Maryland temperance movement, helping to found Maryland's branch of the Sons of Temperance organization in Harper's hometown. According to the title page of *Forest Leaves*, Young's printing business was at the corner of Baltimore and Holliday streets. An advertisement in the *Baltimore Wholesale Business Directory* for 1845 lists Young's printing press at No. 3 South Gay Street and states that he would "execute every description of printing as cheap and well as any other establishment in the city." It's likely that the prospect of an affordable print run influenced Harper's choice of Young's business for her first collection of poems. Having books and pamphlet printed was not a low-cost venture for writers during that time, and Harper certainly could not have paid high prices on her domestic servant's salary.

Forest Leaves does not include a publication year, but the found copy of the pamphlet is likely not from the year 1845, which initially was proposed as the publishing date by other scholars, since James Young's shop was located on Gay Street during that year, and not at Baltimore and Holliday as stated in the pamphlet. This could either mean that *Forest Leaves* was not originally published in 1845, or that a different printer printed it that year and no record survived. In the following year, 1846, Young printed an almanac, published by J. Moore, still citing his Gay Street address. In 1853, he printed a lecture by Harry Young on the rise in crime, and the printing location is the same as in *Forest Leaves*. This indicates that James Young moved his

business from No. 3 Gay Street to the corner of Baltimore and Holliday Streets sometime between 1846 and 1853, and that he printed this copy of *Forest Leaves* during that time period. Keeping in mind that Harper moved to Ohio to teach at Union Seminary in 1851, it is safe to state that her first pamphlet was published sometime in the latter half of the 1840s, when she was in her early twenties. The publication of *Forest Leaves* provides a prehistory for the other literary works Harper wrote when she became one of the most well-known black women activists of the nineteenth century. After Harper left Baltimore to eventually work as a traveling lecturer for the Maine Anti-Slavery Society and later the Pennsylvania Anti-Slavery Society during the mid to late 1850s, she published her second pamphlet, titled *Poems on Miscellaneous Subjects*, in 1854. After the Civil War ended and slavery was officially abolished, Harper became active in the women's rights and temperance movements and continued to publish (serialized) novels, such as *Minnie's Sacrifice*, *Sowing and Reaping*, *Trial and Triumph*, and *Iola Leroy*, as well as collections of poems. Harper died in Philadelphia in 1911. Frances Smith Foster points out that "Harper's literary aesthetics were formed during the first half of the nineteenth century, and her commitment to a literature of purpose and of wide appeal remained constant." This constancy is evidenced by a writing style, which, we can now see, did not change much after her first pamphlet. However, while her later publications, including her novels, were certainly more political and focused on black life, her first pamphlet centers heavily on Christianity. Importantly, *Forest Leaves* marked the first stepping-stone of a literary career that would earn her a spot as one of the most influential and celebrated African American women writers.

A CASE STUDY IN THE POLITICS OF AUTHENTICATION

Forest Leaves provides a new site to discuss the practice of authenticating black writers' literary productions during the antebellum period. Black writers like Phillis Wheatley, Ann Plato, and Harriet Jacobs, who published their works during the 1770s, the 1840s, and the 1860s respectively, relied on well-respected community leaders/activists to write prefaces that would vouch for their intellectual writing capabilities. Harper's own 1854 pamphlet *Poems on*

Miscellaneous Subjects includes such a preface by none other than abolitionist William Lloyd Garrison, most likely because of her emerging public persona as an abolitionist lecturer and the use of the pamphlet as a piece of literature that spoke out against the enslavement of millions of African Americans in the South. Yet *Forest Leaves* has no such authenticating material. Does the lack of a preface in *Forest Leaves* suggest that Harper did not mean for it to be published for public consumption? Or, we might ask, did she actively opt *not* to have an authority like her well-known uncle vouch for her authenticity as an author?

In *The Underground Railroad*, William Still wrote that "the ability [Harper] exhibited in some of her productions was so remarkable that some doubted and others denied their originality." With this in mind, Harper's omission of a preface for *Forest Leaves* can be read as a conscious effort to distance herself, as a young black woman in her early twenties, from white America's desire and need to have (predominately) white men function as creditors for black intellectual publications. She could very well have viewed her pamphlet as her first foray into the literary world and was content with publishing her creative expression without someone else's written stamp of approval.

NEW POEMS, AND NEW ORIGINS FOR KNOWN WORK

The content of *Forest Leaves* itself provides a rich new site of study for scholars of African American literature and history, and for researchers of book history and print culture. To begin with, we now have earlier versions of poems scholars are familiar with through her already known literary productions. *Forest Leaves'* poem "The Soul" was republished in the *Christian Recorder* in 1853, according to Foster's citation of Daniel Payne in *A Brighter Coming Day*. "Bible Defence of Slavery," "Ethiopia," "That Blessed Hope," and "The Dying Christian" were republished in Harper's 1854 pamphlet, *Poems on Miscellaneous Subjects*. Two poems from *Forest Leaves*, namely "He Knoweth Not That The Dead Are There" and "For She Said If I May But Touch Of His Clothes I Shall Be Whole," were also included in her second pamphlet, but with different titles, "The Revel" and "Saved By Faith," respectively.

According to an advertisement in the newspaper the *National Anti-Slavery Standard* from

June 6, 1857, *Poems on Miscellaneous Subjects* was for sale at the Philadelphia Anti-Slavery Office for 37 cents and could "be had at short notice and at the current price, by applying at this office." Her poem "Ruth and Naomi" was included in the pamphlet's 1857 edition. Also, "I Thirst" resurfaces, with minimal corrections from the original version in *Forest Leaves*, in the *National Anti-Slavery Standard* on October 9, 1858, and is reprinted in Harper's 1873 edition of her publication *Sketches of Southern Life*. The poem "A Dialogue" was republished in the *Christian Recorder* on July 3, 1873, as stated in *A Brighter Coming Day*. While Harper republished "I Thirst" in an anti-slavery newspaper a few years after the publication of *Forest Leaves*, it is interesting to note that she held on to "A Dialogue" for more than twenty years before republishing it again in a newspaper. Further, the content of "A Dialogue" shares clear commonalities with her short story "Shalmanezer, Prince of Cosman," which, according to Melba Boyd, "is concerned with the pitfalls of man's materialism," and is published in the 1887 edition of *Sketches of Southern Life*. Thus, one can see how her earliest work continued to influence and inspire her later literary productions. Because of the pamphlet's discovery, we know now that none of these already known poems were reproduced in their original form, but were revised in various ways for the 1854 publication. Further, most of these poems were at least one verse longer in *Forest Leaves*, and Harper altered punctuations as well as various words in her revisions. This discovery alters our understanding of these previously studied poems, as they now must be understood as revisions of earlier works. Harper's choice to reprint these early works allows for the conclusion that she was, despite some alterations, satisfied with her literary productions before she formally joined the abolition movement and became one of the most well-known nineteenth-century black women writers. The fact that "Bible Defence of Slavery" was originally written for *Forest Leaves* testifies to the young writer's growing activist mindset, exemplifying her critique of slavery while she was still living in Baltimore. Further, it shows her uncle's influence on Harper's evolving thoughts on slavery, as Watkins himself published various letters in *Frederick Douglass' Paper* in which he voiced his contempt for Christians and ministers who used the Bible to justify the enslavement of millions of African Americans.

The ten new poems are, of course, exciting additions to Harper's body of work. Half of the newly recovered poems in *Forest Leaves* focus on religion and Christianity, which function as dominant themes throughout her career as a writer. Harper's focus on Christianity as a central topic in her first pamphlet emphasizes the fact that religion played—as it still does to this day—a key component in the lives of African Americans. According to Frances Smith Foster, biblical studies were part of the Watkins Academy's school curriculum. William Watkins was also a minister at Baltimore's Sharp Street Methodist Episcopal Church and thus religion was probably a central part of his family's life, which is reflected in the Christian themes of most of the poems in *Forest Leaves*. Further, Harper stays within the limits of female respectability by writing about religion, which is not surprising for a young, free black woman who was consciously defying societal norms by publishing her literary works for a potentially broad audience. This fact is further underlined by her use of romanticism and sentimentalism in the poems "Let Me Love Thee" and "Farewell, My Heart Is Beating." These works could be expressions of a young Harper's awakening sense of love and romance, something she did not address again in her subsequent poems; by exploring these topics in her writing, she again remains within the boundaries of proper femininity, while expressing herself through the public medium of print culture.

In sum, *Forest Leaves* represents a new vista for scholarship on Frances Ellen Watkins Harper by not only expanding the cannon of her literary work, but by also adding to a broader genealogy of antebellum black women's literature. Writing in the decades leading up to the Civil War, African American men and women affirmed and fought for their right to be seen as full citizens in a country that continuously portrayed them as inferior and lacking in intellectual capabilities. Education became one of the crucial pillars of the black freedom struggle. Due to people like Harper's Uncle Watkins, the succeeding generation of black activists, which included Harper, were able to put their demands, thoughts, and ideas into writing, defying stereotypes. *Forest Leaves* is illustrative of the success of the antebellum black fight for literacy and education, while adding to the field of early African American literature.

Source: Johanna Ortner, "Lost No More: Recovering Frances Ellen Watkins Harper's *Forest Leaves*," in *Common-Place*, Vol. 15, No. 4, Summer 2015.

Denolyn Carroll

In the following review, Carroll asserts that Harper's poetry is still relevant today.

This reissue of Frances Harper's 1895 book presents 42 verses and an in-depth biographical introduction by columnist and author Emma Wisdom. Referred to as "the most popular African-American writer of the 19th century, but also one of the most important women in United States history," Harper—lecturer and orator, activist, abolitionist, novelist, essayist and poet—devoted her life to anti-slavery and abolitionist causes, freedmen's and freedwomen's rights and Christian temperance. Her poems highlight her firm belief in God—the Savior, the Redeemer—and have the formal, structured verses, rhyme schemes and cadences typical of her time. Yet, from "A Double Standard" (where she speaks of gender inequality and sexual morality) to "The Martyr of Alabama" (about blacks being murdered for sport) to "The Burdens of All" (where she calls for racial unity), Harper's work is still relevant-almost two centuries later.

Source: Denolyn Carroll, Review of *Poems*, in *American Visions*, Vol. 14, No. 5, October 1999, p. 35.

Maryemma Graham and Gina M. Rossetti

In the following essay, Graham and Rossetti describe the discovery in the 1990s of three previously unknown novels by Harper.

As an act of literary archaeology, Frances Smith Foster has brought forth three previously unaccounted for novels by Frances E. W. Harper. Foster's text *Minnie's Sacrifice, Sowing and Reaping, Trial and Triumph: Three Rediscovered Novels by Frances E. W. Harper* is instrumental to the study of African American literature not only because it expands the canon of its most popular nineteenth-century writer, but also because it focuses attention on what many have considered the least successful aspect of her work, fiction writing. Between 1854 and 1901, Harper wrote continuously while she was in the forefront of radical Black and women's movements as a lecturer and public spokesperson. The resulting eleven books of poetry and prose serve as a testament to this remarkable woman. While Harper was regarded by her

> IN ADDITION TO THE OTHER CHALLENGES WHICH FOSTER'S TEXT PRESENTS, IT PROBLEMATIZES THE NOTION THAT HARPER'S NOVEL PROJECT CAME AT THE END OF HER CAREER. A QUESTION WORTH RAISING IS, OF WHAT IMPORTANCE IS THE FACT THAT HARPER WROTE NOVELS ALTERNATELY WITH POETRY?"

peers as a supremely oral poet and known for her professional activism in the cause of human rights for Black people, women, and the poor, criticism of *Iola Leroy, Or Shadows Uplifted*, the one novel previously attributed to Harper, has been either biographical or in reaction to her use of sentimental literary conventions. Harper employs what appear to be rudimentary literary devices through which she examines the two issues in her fiction: racial uplift and Christian temperance. However, as Melba Joyce Boyd, Hazel Carby, and others have suggested, Harper was as much a "race woman" as she was the prototypical feminist.

All three of the rediscovered stories recall the themes common in the early African American novel: revision of biblical tales and the role of the talented tenth. *Minnie's Sacrifice*, published in 1869, is a revision of the Moses story, a device and theme Harper used later, as her 1869 poem "Moses: A Story of the Nile" indicates. Although Harper continues with the biblical motif in *Sowing and Reaping* (1876–1877), she is more outspoken about the problem she sees as a second slavery: alcoholism. In *Trial and Triumph* (1888–1889). Harper explores the damaging effects of both racism and sexism. It is important to note that these three novels were originally published in the *Christian Recorder*, the journal of the African Methodist Episcopal Church. Clearly written for a Black audience, Harper's texts uncover more evidence that there was a literate, educated Black reading audience during the nineteenth century; and as a result African American writers were not necessarily writing for an exclusively white audience. Furthermore, these three novels allow one

to re-examine the reason that Harper's 1892 text *Iola Leroy* is the only novel to have originally survived. We might consider several possibilities for this. First, the newly discovered novels may have been "lost" due to the fact that they were published in a Black religious journal. As such, these novels can be easily "written off" and/or forgotten as being too ecclesiastical or too sentimental (especially when one considers that the novels are serialized fiction). Second, *Iola Leroy* has survived because its surface tale of family reunions satisfies the literary tastes of her time. In other words, *Iola Leroy* can be read as a "safe" novel, whereas the other three speak more boldly about racial discrimination and temperance. In them, Harper uses fewer devices to conceal/mask her arguments.

Minnie' Sacrifice and *Sowing and Reaping* not only revise biblical tales, but they also serve as "lesson-teaching" stories for the treatment and behavior of African Americans during Reconstruction. At the beginning of *Minnie's Sacrifice*, Camilla, the slave owner's daughter, "rescues" Louis, a mulatto boy, from slavery. Harper uses the story of the enslaved Jews and the emergence of their future deliverer to criticize the current condition/treatment of African Americans. As a result, Harper establishes the two mulatto characters, Louis and Minnie, as individuals who choose not to "pass" and are instead committed to helping the African American community. Minnie and Louis predate Iola and Dr. Latimer, who also establish a school for African Americans. In *Sowing and Reaping*, Harper turns to issues of public morality, most notably Christian temperance. Harper's characters, who are drawn in racially ambiguous terms, must contend with the notion that "one reaps what one sows." The characters who do not succumb to alcohol, either by consumption or profit, are rewarded. Despite his financial difficulties, Paul Clifford refuses to enter into the saloon business because he places his beliefs in Christian temperance over greed. Likewise, Belle Gordon refuses a marriage proposal from the eligible and wealthy Charles Romaine because she objects to his frequent drinking.

In *Trial and Triumph*, Harper changes her formula as she considers the implications of being both an African American and a woman. The main character, Annette, faces both racism and sexism: As a mulatto, her association with the African American community makes it difficult for her to receive and/or keep a teaching position; as a woman, her desire for an education and a career is constantly questioned because she is not content to live within the gender limits that are assigned to her. Annette's remedy is a re-affirmation of genuine Christianity. This solution is female-gendered. In male narratives, such as those of Frederick Douglass, the male figure overcomes his obstacles and acquires person-hood by first achieving/asserting manhood; in other words, the African American male in such texts subverts the servile stereotype by physically attacking and/or breaking free from those who promote such myths, as Douglass defends himself against Mr. Covey. For Annette/Harper, the solution is different. The woman acquires personhood as she remains true to Christian values. It is through her right-eous behavior that she subverts racist acts done in the name of Christianity. She, as a result, not only pinpoints the hypocrisy of racist-oriented "Christianity," but she also serves as an educator to her community by teaching moral beliefs and racial pride.

In addition to the other challenges which Foster's text presents, it problematizes the notion that Harper's novel project came at the end of her career. A question worth raising is, Of what importance is the fact that Harper wrote novels alternately with poetry? In an earlier crit-ical text on Harper, Foster has argued that in Harper's poetry from 1853 to 1864 one sees an "emphasis upon acts of ordinary individuals whose integrity and conviction give them strength and courage they need to perform heroically in the face of evil." It is our assertion that Harper's poetry occasions and foregrounds her fiction. Harper's two 1869 works "Moses: A Story of the Nile" and *Minnie's Sacrifice* are more than just revisions of the Moses tale. They are also vehicles through which Harper "rends the veil" that not only separates African Americans from the white majority, but also African Americans from each other. Harper's use of the analogy between the Jewish and Afri-can diasporas is a mask that conceals her larger purpose: a political commentary on the state of race relations. She brings her original African American audience back to the mountaintop to make a covenant with God: "And we all, with unveiled face, beholding the glory of the Lord, are being changed into His likeness from one degree of glory to another; for this comes from the Lord who is the Spirit" (2 Corinthians 3:18). This reveals several possibilities: First, Harper creates African Americans as the "chosen"

people; second, she thwarts white racism and casts away the veil that yields African Ameri-cans, as Du Bois puts the matter, "no true self-consciousness, but only lets [them] see [themselves] through the revelation of the other world . . . a world that looks on in amused con-tempt and pity." One must also consider the relationship between Harper's 1859 short story "The Two Offers" and her newly discovered novels. In "The Two Offers," Harper argues for the independent Black woman, who does not feel obligated to achieve comfort through marriage. In fact, she sees marriage for a woman is a source of dependence. This appeal for independent African American women also manifests itself in such later women characters as Belle Gordon and Iola Leroy. This is important to note for two reasons: First, this ideology is coextensive with Harper's lecturing activities; second, it compli-cates what would later be known as the "New Negro Movement." The second point is partic-ularly salient because the theories espoused by Alain Locke and James Weldon Johnson focused only on the plight of the African Amer-ican male, who then served as the universal—i.e., everyman—for all African Americans. Thus, Locke, Johnson, and other male leaders did not attend to gender issues; in fact, their theories obscured the work of Amy Jacques Garvey, whose manifesto for the "New Negro Woman" is actually a later articulation of precepts that were originally put forth by Harper. In other words, Harper's novels prefigure these later arguments, and this calls into question the com-monly held belief that Harper never wrote polit-ical fiction; it also documents the fact that Harper actively considers the racial and gender implications of racial equality.

Minnie's Sacrifice, Sowing and Reaping, Trial and Triumph: Three Rediscovered Novels by Frances E. W. Harper causes one to re-assess nineteenth-century African American women's writing. Moreover, Harper boldly weaves the political debates of her time into the central fabric of her fiction. This suggests that Harper was conscious of and catered to a predominantly Black audience at the same time that she was intensely involved in the writing of poetry and, second, that she was actively engaged in fiction writing throughout her professional career and not simply at the end; it also raises questions about the reasons that Harper's work did not originally survive. Thus, Foster's text allows one to consider Harper not only as a writer of "protest" poetry, but also as an author of "political" fiction.

Source: Maryemma Graham and Gina M. Rossetti, Review of *Minnie's Sacrifice; Sowing and Reaping; Trial and Triumph: Three Undiscovered Novels by Frances E.W. Harper*, in *African American Review*, Vol. 30, No. 2, Summer 1996, p. 302.

SOURCES

Brawley, Benjamin, "Three Negro Poets: Horton, Mrs. Harper, and Whitman," in *Journal of Negro History*, Vol. 2, No. 4, 1917, pp. 384–92.

Du Bois, W. E. B, "Editorials: Writers," in *Crisis*, Vol. 1, No. 6, 1911, p. 20, http://library.brown.edu/pdfs/1274706888875000.pdf (accessed August 18, 2016).

"Forced Labour in the United States Agricultural Industry," in *Anti-Slavery.org*, http://www.antislavery.org/english/campaigns/take_action/background_forced_and_exploitative_labour_in_us_agriculture.aspx (accessed May 15, 2016).

"Frances Ellen Watkins Harper," Maryland Women's Hall of Fame Website, http://msa.maryland.gov/msa/educ/exhibits/womenshall/html/harper.html (accessed May 15, 2016).

"Frances E. W. Harper," in *Bio.com*, http://www.biography.com/people/frances-ew-harper-40710 (accessed May 15, 2016).

"Fugitive Slave Acts," in *History.com*, http://www.history.com/topics/black-history/fugitive-slave-acts (accessed May 15, 2016).

Groschmeyer, Janeen, "Frances Harper," in *Dictionary of Unitarian and Universalist Biography*, http://uudb.org/articles/francesharper.html (accessed May 15, 2016).

Harper, Frances Ellen Watkins, "Bury Me in a Free Land," in *A Brighter Coming Day*, Feminist Press, 1993, p. 177.

Hill, Patricia Liggins, "'Let Me Make the Songs for the People': A Study of Frances Watkins Harper's Poetry," in *Black American Literature Forum*, Vol. 15, No. 2, 1981, pp. 60–65.

Hull, Gloria T., "Black Women Poets from Wheatley to Walker," in *Negro American Literature Forum*, Vol. 9, No. 3, 1975, pp. 91–96.

Mitchel, John, "Underground Railroad," in *HistoryNet*, http://www.historynet.com/underground-railroad (accessed May 15, 2016).

"Reconstruction," in *History.com*, http://www.history.com/topics/american-civil-war/reconstruction (accessed May 15, 2016).

Yacavone, Donald, "Sacred Land Regained: Frances Ellen Watkins Harper and 'The Massachusetts Fifty-fourth,' a Lost Poem," in *Pennsylvania History*, Vol. 62, No. 1, Winter 1995, p. 103, https://journals.psu.edu/phj/article/download/25194/24963 (accessed August 19, 2016).

FURTHER READING

Child, Lydia Maria, *The Freedmen's Book*, Arno Press, 1968.

> Originally compiled by abolitionist Lydia Maria Francis Child in 1866, *The Freedmen's Book* was intended to inspire newly liberated African Americans. It contains "Bury Me in a Free Land" and many other enduring classics of the anti-slavery movement.

Garrison, William Lloyd, *William Lloyd Garrison and the Fight against Slavery: Selections from "The Liberator"*, Bedford Books of St. Martin's Press, 1994.

> *William Lloyd Garrison and the Fight against Slavery: Selections from "The Liberator"* was released in 1994 and edited by William E. Cain. It contains many of the most influential articles of *The Liberator*, the antislavery newspaper that first published Harper's poem, as edited by her fellow abolitionist William Lloyd Garrison.

Harper, Frances Ellen Watkins, *Iola Leroy; or, Shadows Uplifted*, Tredition, 2011.

> Known by the alternate titles *Iola Leroy* and *Shadows Uplifted* and detailing the journey of self-discovery of a heroine of mixed race, Harper's novel was published in 1892 to considerable acclaim and no small degree of monetary success.

Yellin, Jean Fagan, and John C. Van Horne, *The Abolitionist Sisterhood: Women's Political Culture in Antebellum America*, Cornell University Press, 1994.

> Edited by scholars Jean Fagan Yellin and John C. Van Horne and published in 1994, *The Abolitionist Sisterhood: Women's Political Culture in Antebellum America* provides a comprehensive overview of the same circles of reform frequented by Harper.

SUGGESTED SEARCH TERMS

Frances Ellen Watkins Harper

"Bury Me in a Free Land" AND Frances Harper

Frances Harper AND abolition

Frances Harper AND women's rights

American Civil War AND slavery

American Reconstruction

Fugitive Slave Act

Underground Railroad

The Fence

SAADI YOUSSEF

1998

In Iraqi poet Saadi Youssef's "The Fence," first published in *Agni* (1998), a man's house and prized garden of red carnations are exposed to the invasive elements of the street: cats, dogs, insects, and dust. Considered one of the greatest living Arabic poets, Youssef has lived in exile from his homeland of Iraq since 1979, following Saddam Hussein's rise to power. A voice of lyrical tenderness and quiet power, Youssef, in his long partnership with translator Khaled Mattawa, has created mesmerizing translations from the original Arabic verse to the English language. The invasion of the man's home and garden in "The Fence" subtly references the political upheaval and chaos in Iraq in the country's tumultuous history of war and uprisings.

AUTHOR BIOGRAPHY

Youssef was born in Abulkhasib, a village near the city of Basra, Iraq, in 1934. Positioned near the border of Iran, the area is well known for its ancient canals and natural beauty. Youssef's family grew dates, wheat, and grapes, and he traveled by bus to Basra for school. He began to write poetry as a teenager, just when classic Arabic poetry began to give way to modern verse in the 1950s. However, his first collection, *Al-Qursan* (*Pirate*), was written in the strictly structured classical style and published in 1952. He

Saadi Yousef (©*JONAS EKSTROMER* | *AP Images*)

earned a degree in Arabic from the teachers college at Baghdad University in 1954, before publishing his second collection, *Ughniyat Laysat lil-Akharin* (*Songs Not for Others*) in 1955. *Songs Not for Others* was written in the new, modern style of Arabic poetry: *taf'ila*, or free verse. Without set limits on rhyme, meter, or structure, Youssef found he enjoyed experimenting with repetition, style, and image association.

In 1957, Youssef took an unauthorized trip to Moscow for a youth conference but was not allowed to enter Iraq upon his return. He spent a year in Kuwait until the 1958 revolution in Iraq allowed him to reenter the country safely. He was imprisoned for his Marxist political views, after which he moved to Algeria, where he found work as a journalist and high school teacher. In 1971, he returned once again to Iraq to work in the Ministry of Culture. When Saddam Hussein rose to power in the late 1970s, Youssef began to receive visitors at work, pressuring him to join

Saddam's Ba'ath Party. When he refused, he was first demoted from a ministry director to an assistant manager in a government library. When he refused again, he was told he had ten days to join before the Ba'ath security forces came for him. In response, he fled the country permanently in 1979, after taking one last walk through his home village of Abulkhasib.

Since 1979, Youssef has lived as an exile, traveling widely. He lived in Yemen, where he felt particularly at home before the country erupted into civil war, as well as in France, where he was forced to leave after a club of Iraqi expatriates he had started drew the attention of the French Interior Ministry. He lived in Syria, Lebanon, Tunisia, Cyprus, Jordan, and Yugoslavia, before settling down in England. Throughout his travels, he continued to write and publish poetry, earning a reputation as one of the greatest living poets writing in Arabic. He has published over thirty collections of poetry and prose, including

The Memoirs of the Castle's Prisoner (2000), *The Fifth Step* (2003), *My Choices* (2007), *The Poems of the Public Park* (2009), and *In the Wilderness Where the Thunder Is* (2010). "The Fence" was published in 1998 in *Agni*. In addition to his renown as a poet, he has become known as a translator of English literature into Arabic, including the work of Walt Whitman, George Orwell, and Federico García Lorca.

POEM TEXT

His house was exposed to dust from the street.
His garden, blooming with red carnations,
was open to dogs
and strange insects,
open to cat claws.   5
The red carnations, when they bloomed for
   two days,
were a feast to the dogs
and strange insects,
a feast to cats and their claws.
Dust from the street invading the tender petals.   10
Salt on the flowers,
salt on hair,
salt on a moon turning in its clothes.

One day he remembered
how his grandfather built the family house.   15

POEM SUMMARY

The text used for this summary, translated by Khaled Mattawa, is from *Agni*, Vol. 48, 1998. A version of the poem can be found on the following web page: http://www.bu.edu/agni/poetry/print/2002/56-youssef.html.

"The Fence" begins with the speaker describing a man's house, which sits exposed to the dust of the street. His garden, full of blooming, red carnations, is unprotected from stray dogs, strange insects, and cats with their sharp claws. When the red carnations bloom for a couple of days, the dogs, insects, and cats feast upon them, leaving nothing worthy of admiration behind. The dust from the road blows onto the carnations' new petals. There is salt everywhere: on the flowers, in hair, and in the moon as it turns in its clothes. The moon turning in its clothes is a metaphor for the changing phases of the moon, underscoring how the salt never ceases to blow. One day the man remembers how his grandfather had built this house for his family. The fence of the title would

solve the man's problems—protecting his home and fragile garden from wild animals as well as dust and salt—but it is not mentioned in the text of the poem itself.

THEMES

Destruction

In "The Fence," the destruction of the garden serves as an allegory of the destruction and never-ending strife in the Middle East. The beautiful garden of red carnations, the house, and the man himself are exposed to erosive dust and salt, which blows in from the street. The dust settles in the crevices of the house and between the petals of the flowers. The salt clings to everything: the carnations, the man's hair, and even the nighttime air beneath the changing moon. That the salt clings to the moon itself as it cycles through its phases indicates that—unlike the carnations that bloom for only two days—the salt creeps in constantly, a relentless force of destruction eating away at the house, as well as the suffering man.

In addition to the salt and dust, there are unfamiliar insects, dogs, and cats with sharp claws that wander into the garden from the street. As soon as the red carnations bloom, they are consumed by the animals, which feast on the flowers as if they were raw meat, a delicacy they find especially delicious. Between the dust, salt, and rampaging animals, the house is never left at peace, always agitated by some outside force. The destruction threatens the man's ancestral home, and thus the actions of the invaders are acts of desecration against a site of spiritual significance for him.

In an allegorical sense, the acts of destruction are against the land itself (the garden), its people (the man), and its institutions (the house). In short, everything that makes up the country is under attack, from domestic forces (cats and dogs), foreign interests (strange insects), and the air itself (bombs dropped from above and the pervasive paranoia of wartime). The man must watch helplessly as his beautiful flowers are destroyed, but he can potentially save his garden by remembering his grandfather's pride in building the house and taking defensive action.

TOPICS FOR FURTHER STUDY

- Read D. J. Murphy's young-adult novel *A Thousand Veils* (2008). How is exile portrayed in the novel? How does the author illustrate the danger of living under Saddam Hussein's regime in Iraq? What comparisons can you draw between the novel and "The Fence"? Can you find similar imagery, themes, or language? Organize your thoughts into an essay.

- Create a time line of the Iraq War, beginning with the invasion on March 20, 2003, and ending with the withdrawal of the final American troops in December 18, 2011. Choose ten important events from the war to place on your time line along with a description of the event and its significance. Be sure to cite any sources you use. Free infographics are available at easl.ly.

- Create a blog focused on a major city in Iraq. Create a minimum of seven blog posts about its climate, history, government, significant monuments and architecture, religious sites, and economy and how they affected by the Iraq War, along with a post on a topic of your own choosing. Include photos and links to relevant sources of additional information. After you have made your post, go to three of your classmates'

blogs and leave a thoughtful comment on the posts you found most interesting. Be sure to respond to any comments you receive. Major Iraqi cities to consider for your blog include Baghdad, Basra, Mosul, Arbil, Kirkuk, Sulaymaniya, Hilla, Karbala, Najaf, or Al Nasiriya. Free blogspace is available at blogger.com.

- In small groups, explore the image of salt in the poem. What effect does salt have on flowers, hair, and the moon? Where does the salt come from? Can you think of any cultural, historical, or religious implications of salt that might shed light on the image? Brainstorm as many relevant meanings, connections, and theories on the image as you can in the time you are given. Take notes in preparation for a group discussion.

- What is your interpretation of the poem's final stanza? What do you think happens next? Write a sequel to "The Fence" in poem form in which you pick up the narrative of the man and his house where it leaves off and explain what happens after the man remembers his grandfather. Make an effort to match Youssef's language and style in your poem.

Invasion

The invading forces of "The Fence" ransack the garden and insinuate themselves into the house. They destroy all that they touch, taking what they like for themselves without regard for the man's right to a peaceful home. They do not speak the same language or share the same beliefs. (For example, the man does not wish to eat the carnations; rather he grows them for the pleasure of their beauty.) They are enemies engaged in a hostile takeover, their attention fixed on their goal. A cat, for example, can make a pleasant companion, but not when its claws are out. Likewise, salt is a

necessary part of anyone's life, but too much of it will rub skin raw and sting the eyes. The combined force of the invaders overwhelms the man, until he remembers that his grandfather built the house and in his family's honor he must defend it.

The invasion is cyclical, based on the life cycle of the carnations, as well as the phases of the moon, but these cycles move too quickly to provide the man with relief. There is always an enemy at this doorstep, fully engaged in a plot to take over his land. Without relief in sight, the man grows more frustrated. In a poem of only fifteen lines, the animals and the dust attack

The garden is open to neighborhood pets (©*Boris-B* / *Shutterstock.com*)

twice, and the salt insinuates itself into every-thing. To fight off one enemy would be to let another sneak past, and so the man does nothing but look on bitterly as what is rightfully his is taken away by invaders too numerous to effectively repel.

Vulnerability

The house is vulnerable on all sides. Nothing prevents dust from the street from blowing onto the property. Nothing stands in the way of the insects, cats, and dogs that roam freely into the garden to eat the carnations. The mandibles of insects, jaws of dogs, claws of cats, and the fine grain of dust consume the house's unguarded treasure trove of carnations as soon as they bloom. The house and the man who owns it are battered by the salty wind. The first stanza of the poem is crowded with the house, garden, flowers, man, cats, dogs, insects, dust, and sand. These elements overlap each other and interact with each other, all piled together in the space of thir-teen lines. Nothing separates the man, his house, and his garden from outside forces, and nothing

defends against the constant invasion. The solu-tion is hinted at in the poem's second stanza: two peaceful lines free of attacking forces, in which the man remembers his grandfather's legacy. Thus, structurally, the poem introduces its first and only line of defense against the animals and corrosive elements. The space between the first and second stanza separates the chaos of life with-out a fence and the potential calm of a life lived within a fence's protection.

STYLE

Allegory

An allegory is a work of literature in which the characters, setting, and other elements serve as a set of symbols that can be interpreted to reveal a hidden meaning, often with moral implications. "The Fence" is an allegory in which the house represents Iraq, a familial home built by a grand-father (a founder or leader) and passed down through the family (the civilians) through generations. This house, however, has no fence (strong, defensive force) to protect its precious red carnations (natural resources). As a result, the cat, dog, and insect pests (invaders—both domestic and foreign) come to feast on the red carnations, destroying the garden (the natural landscape) in the process. Because it is unprotected, the house and its occupant are battered by outside elements while pests destroy their natural resources. The fence is the solution—a strong defensive force—but the poem ends before it is built, an accurate reflection of the state of Iraq not only in 1998 but even today.

Free Verse

Free verse refers to poetry without rhyme or meter (the pattern of stressed and unstressed syllables in poetry) that has varying line lengths and structure. In Arabic poetry, free verse is known as *taf'ila*, which emerged as a style in the mid-twentieth century in opposition to the strict structure of classical Arabic poetry. Youssef is a master of free-verse poetry in Arabic, of which "The Fence" is a prime example. The lines are unrhymed, the two stanzas are mismatched in size, and the line length is unpredictable. Free verse allows the poet to make his own choices, a freedom that Youssef uses to his advantage to alternate long lines describing the house and its blooming flowers with short lines describing the pests—insects, cats, dogs, dust, and salt. This helps convey the mood of frustration through the clipped repeated interruptions of the garden invaders.

Mood

Mood in a poem is the emotional atmosphere created within the work through its syntax, imagery, themes, speaker, and other poetic elements. The mood of "The Fence" is frustration and anger as the garden with its tender blooms is savaged by wild animals and by dust blown in from the street. By including the detail that the flowers bloom for only two days, Youssef emphasizes the bitterness of the man, who, rather than enjoy the blooming flowers, must bear witness to their destruction. The softness of the flower imagery contrasted with the harsh descriptions of the outside elements and invading animals creates the mood of frustration, which finds reprieve in the poem's final lines as the man remembers his ancestral pride in the home and—it is implied—makes plans to end the cycle of destruction and frustration by constructing a fence.

HISTORICAL CONTEXT

Iraq History

The history of Iraq stretches back to the dawn of human civilization in Mesopotamia over five thousand years ago. The site of advanced ancient civilizations, including the Sumerian, Assyrian, and Babylonian Empires, Iraq contains artifacts from 4000 BCE to this day. The Babylonian Empire fell in 539 BCE to Cyrus the Great, followed by Alexander the Great in 333 BCE. The land was annexed to the Persian Empire, of which it was a part until it was conquered by Muslims in 651 CE. The city of Baghdad, the capital of Iraq, was founded in 762 and became one of the largest cities in the world, with an advanced aquifer system that allowed for massive agricultural production. A cultural and intellectual hub, Baghdad attracted philosophers, artists, mathematicians, and scientists to its prestigious schools and libraries. The city boasted a population of over one million.

In 1258, invading Mongols led by Genghis Khan sacked Baghdad, leaving the city and its population in absolute ruin. Neglected under Mongol rule and unable to farm because of the destruction of the irrigation system, Iraq reverted to a tribal society. Between 1509 and 1638, the Safavid Empire and Ottoman Empire traded control of Iraq in a protracted series of invasions. Eventually, the Ottoman Empire routed the Safavids and ruled Iraq until the end of World War I. An ally of Germany, the Ottoman Empire found itself on the losing side of the war. The defeated empire was handed to the British to be partitioned and ruled. Ignoring the sentiment of nationalists who hoped to create their own state in Iraq, Britain set up the new Iraqi government and defined its borders without intimate knowledge of the terrain.

When British administration ended in 1932, Iraq became a kingdom under the rule of the elected king, Faisal ibn Hussein. In 1936, during the reign of Ghazi I, Saudi Arabia and Iraq signed a treaty of nonaggression and brotherhood, promoting Pan-Arabism and Arab federation. Amid the debate between taking the British or German side at the start of World War II, the royalty of Iraq was overthrown by the military on April 1, 1941, but—though the royals did not return—newly elected Prime Minister Rashid Ali al-Gaylani soon took back control. Following his regime's collapse, the British intervened militarily and reestablished a pro-British government in

COMPARE
&
CONTRAST

- **1998:** Suspicious of Iraq's potential for harboring biological weapons and hoping to increase domestic support for a war in Iraq, Madeleine AlBright, William Cohen, and Samuel Berger, three high-ranking members of President Bill Clinton's cabinet, discuss their options in a town meeting at Ohio State University. An enraged crowd protests their plan, making it clear that the public will not support a war in Iraq.

  Today: Though Bill Clinton warned against a preemptive strike against Iraq, President George W. Bush and a US-led coalition of allies invade the country, beginning the Iraq War (2003–2011). Public support of the war drops steadily with each passing year, as the situation overseas proves interminable and unstable. Following the withdrawal of American troops, the country returns to violent infighting between major political factions, though the American-backed Iraqi government remains in power.

- **1998:** After Saddam Hussein refuses to cooperate with UN weapons inspectors, military targets within Iraq are bombed for four days by the United States and Britain in Operation Desert Fox.

Today: Following an inconclusive Iraqi general election, the United Nations joins the United States and other interested nations in urging the creation of a new Iraqi government under Haider al-Abadi. Al-Abadi becomes prime minister in September of 2014 in a peaceful transition of power from Prime Minister Nouri al-Maliki.

- **1998:** Saddam Hussein, hated virulently by the Western world, rules Iraq with an iron fist, committing regular acts of violence and brutality against his own people and those of other nations.

  Today: Hussein is tried and executed by hanging in December 2006. In place of his rule, elections are held in 2005 for the first prime minister under the new federal parliamentary government. However, the Islamic terrorist organization known as ISIS (or ISIL) gains control of much of the al-Hawija district, committing atrocities against the Iraqi people, including public executions, beheadings, and the 2016 capture of over three thousand people attempting to flee ISIS territory.

1952. However, the new government was unstable, leading to decades of civil unrest and a series of both violent and nonviolent coups between rival political parties.

Saddam Hussein

Born April 28, 1937, in a village near Tikrit, Saddam Hussein would become the fifth president of the Republic of Iraq and an infamously brutal dictator. He joined the Socialist Ba'ath Party at the age of twenty and was sentenced to six months in prison for the murder of his brother-in-law at the age of twenty-one. After fleeing Iraq following his involvement in an unsuccessful assassination attempt on an Iraqi

general in 1959, Hussein returned four years later but was captured and imprisoned from 1964 until his escape in 1967. On July 17, 1968, the Ba'ath Party successfully overthrew Abdul Rahman Arif's regime, and Ahmed Hassan al-Bakr, Hussein's cousin, was named president. Under al-Bakr's regime, Hussein took over internal security and gradually became more powerful, aiding the aging al-Bakr in performing the duties of the president. Saddam became president of Iraq on July 16, 1979, and set about purging hundreds of members of his own party in mass executions. Youssef fled Iraq that year after the Ba'ath Party threatened his life.

The blooming carnations are lovely, but they are "invaded" by the street dust and animals
(©Aleksei Verhovski | Shutterstock.com)

Hussein's dictatorship was marked by war and genocide, the gruesome details of which are still being uncovered. In 1980, he invaded Iran, setting off the Iran-Iraq War (1980–1988), in which he committed a number of atrocities, including the use of child soldiers on the front lines and chemical weapons against civilians in the village of Halabja, killing approximately five thousand people and injuring ten thousand more. Following the end of the war, which resulted in a stalemate, Hussein invaded Kuwait in 1990, sparking the Gulf War. The United States and its allies under George H. W. Bush came to Kuwait's aid in 1991, driving Iraqi forces back into the country and invading Iraq in the hope of ousting Hussein, but the attempt was unsuccessful. As a result of the loss, Hussein was forced to comply with United Nations Resolution 687, which required him to provide information on his weapons of mass destruction.

Insulted by accusations of noncompliance from the United Nations Special Commission charged with assessing Hussein's weapons program, Hussein accused the weapons inspectors sent by the United Nations of spying. In the meantime, the Iraqi people were bombarded with propaganda and punished severely if caught speaking out against the president. Gerald Butt, in his article "Saddam Hussein—His Rise to Power" for the BBC, characterized Hussein in 1998 as the "world's best known and most hated Arab leader. And in a region where despotic rule is the norm, he is more feared by his own people than any other head of state."

In December 1998, after negotiations failed once again, President Bill Clinton ordered a four-day air strike against Iraqi military targets. By 2002, Hussein remained obstinate in his refusal to cooperate. A dummy election held that year in which Hussein received 100 percent of the vote ensured he stayed in power. Tensions reached their peak on March 17, 2003, when President George W. Bush gave Hussein twenty-four hours to step down. When Hussein refused, the United States invaded on March 20, 2003. Hussein went into hiding but was captured on December 13, 2003, near Tikrit. He was tried and executed by hanging on December 30, 2006. His legacy of war devastated the country, crippling Iraq economically and, as Sinan Antoon and Peter Money write in their introduction to *Nostalgia, My Enemy*, "[The Iraq War] and the compounded effects of dictatorship and genocidal sanctions (1991–2003) have scarred Iraqi collective memory. This tragic history has challenged Iraqi writers... who try to grapple with its enormity."

CRITICAL OVERVIEW

With a celebrated career that began with publication of his first collection in 1952 and continues to the present day, Youssef is a beloved and prominent figure in the world of Arabic poetry. Antoon and Money write, "He has become one of the greatest living poets writing in Arabic. His prolific output... has influenced generations of Arab poets and shaped the trajectory of modern Arabic poetry." In praise of the immense body of work Youssef has produced over six decades, Khaled Mattawa writes in his introduction to *Without an Alphabet, Without a Face*:

> Comprising about forty volumes of poetry, numerous works of translation, memoir, criticism, and fiction, Saadi's output is an impressive component of modern Arabic literature. His high status is... in contrast to the subtlety of his works.

A poet tied inexorably to Iraq, Youssef's opinion is regularly sought following outbreaks of political turmoil, violence, and war in his country, as Charis Bredin notes in her review of *Nostalgia, My Enemy* in *Banipal*: "In exile in London, Youssef's response to the atrocities suffered by his country has ranged from angry political invectives in essay form to tender poems, recuperating his fractured memories of Iraq." "The Fence" is of the latter category, casting the country's history of unrest as the annoyance of common garden pests destroying a man's garden.

In "A Poet of Light, Earth and Sea" for *Banipal*, Stephen Watts writes in admiration of Youssef's unbreakable artistic spirit, despite the trials he has faced: "Youssef is a poet of subtle, daily, lyric-rich freedoms in the face of intense unfreedom.... His poetry matters to us greatly."

In "Tonight We Rest Here—An Interview with Poet Saadi Youssef," Joy E. Stocke summarizes the remarkable contrast between the poet's towering reputation and calm, humble demeanor: "Considered by many to be the greatest living

THE IMAGERY IN 'THE FENCE' SERVES DOUBLE-DUTY BOTH AS ILLUSTRATIVE OF THE TALE OF A MAN'S PERSONAL STRUGGLE TO CONTROL A DIFFICULT DOMESTIC SITUATION AND AS SYMBOLS IN AN ALLEGORY FOR THE NEVER-ENDING UNREST IN IRAQ."

Arabic poet, Youssef speaks quietly and deliberately, as if each word holds the weight of his lifetime."

CRITICISM

Amy L. Miller

Miller is a graduate of the University of Cincinnati. In the following essay, she examines the simultaneously personal and political implications of the invasion of the garden by wild animals in Youssef's "The Fence."

Known for the surprising subtlety of his poetry, given his status as an exile from one of the most embattled countries in the world, Youssef puts his calm but mighty verbal power on display in "The Fence," a short allegorical poem overflowing with imagery and symbolism. The speaker describes a man and his property under constant attack. Though the invaders are not particularly exceptional enemies—cats, dogs, strange insects, dust from the road—they are numerous and relentless enough to keep the man in a constant state of frustrated anger as they eat the flowers in his garden. By the end of the crowded first stanza, the man is cursing the air itself, until he remembers that the property was passed down to him from his grandfather. Whatever the frustrations, he must defend his family's home.

The imagery in "The Fence" serves double-duty both as illustrative of the tale of a man's personal struggle to control a difficult domestic situation and as symbols in an allegory for the never-ending unrest in Iraq. Because the poem is as difficult to solve as the situation it describes, its abstract imagery is better understood using the heart rather than straining the mind over why, for example, dogs and cats would want to

WHAT DO I READ NEXT?

- In Mary Sullivan's young-adult novel *Dear Blue Sky* (2013), an American girl named Cassie watches her family's gradual collapse following her brother's deployment to Iraq. She begins an unexpected online friendship with an Iraqi girl called Blue Sky whose determination to survive amidst the chaos of war inspires Cassie to see her life through a new perspective, which she uses to enact positive change in her world.

- In Youssef's *Nostalgia, My Enemy* (2012), translated by Sinan Antoon and Peter Money, the poet addresses the invasion of Iraq by the United States, as he witnesses the Iraq War from his exile in London. Torn between gladness at the end of Saddam Hussein's regime and horror at the atrocities committed at Abu Ghraib, Youssef attempts to locate the beautiful, beloved homeland of his memories through the smoke and dust of war.

- Famed Spanish poet Federico García Lorca's *Selected Verse* (2004) provides readers with the wide scope of the poet's skill, as he transitions effortlessly between subjects and styles, genres, and themes. His modernist poetry, noted for its linguistic gymnastics, captivates the ear and eye as well as the heart, as he lives, loves, and mourns without holding anything back.

- *Imagining Iraq: Literature in English and the Iraq Invasion*, by Suman Gupta (2011), examines the literature published in English (in the United States and Britain) during the heated debate leading up to the invasion of the country by US-led forces in 2003. Poetry, drama, fiction, and film are discussed in this wide-ranging study of literature on the brink of war.

- Mahmoud Darwish's *Almond Blossoms and Beyond* (2009) collects the later work of one of the greatest Arabic poets in history as well as the voice of displaced Palestinians across the globe. Known for his passionate verses in which he proudly proclaims his own identity despite the odds set against him, Darwish teaches the world the meaning of resilience while reassuring his own people that they, too, could stand up and be heard.

- In *And the Mountains Echoed*, by Khaled Hosseini (2014), Afghan families separated by poverty, war, and greed must reinvent themselves or perish in the shifting sands of political chaos and the turmoil of war. Set in Afghanistan, France, Greece, and the United States over the course of decades, the characters' reunions never go as planned and yet yield fantastical results all the same.

- *The World's Embrace: Selected Poems*, by Abdellatif Laabi (2003), collects the work of the leader of the North African avant-garde movement, a poet who was imprisoned and tortured for seven years by the Moroccan government. His poetry reflects these pains as well as his hope to one day see a world rid of such injustice.

- In *Here, Bullet* (2005), Iraqi War veteran Brian Turner's poetry on his experiences in the United States Army's infantry touches on issues of shared humanity, invasion, violence, and death in unflinchingly realistic terms. An important voice in Iraq War poetry, Turner's raw style yields moments of surprisingly delicate beauty as he reports on the horrors of war.

- In Ghassan Kanafani's *Men in the Sun and Other Palestinian Stories* (1999), the inhumanity faced by refugees from Palestine is rendered in heartbreaking detail as those who sacrificed their homes and lives in order to survive the unthinkable horrors of war find themselves drifting in an often hostile world blind to their suffering.

eat flowers. Youssef's skill as an artist lies in his ability to fuse personal and political crises into works of soft-spoken universality.

The poem's two stanzas stand in direct opposition. The first stanza, at thirteen lines, packs its imagery in tightly: the man, house, garden, flowers, cats, dogs, insects, dust, salt, street, moon, and hair are the main subjects. The man spends the stanza under attack. In the poem's first line, the dust blows in off the street, and dust—the reader soon learns—is the least of the man's concerns. However, by the end of the stanza, the man has grown so frustrated with the destruction of his carnations by the wild animals that it is not the dust, but the salt in the dust that finally breaks him. He rails against the salt, the least avoidable of all his problems, in an emotional breakdown. Written with Youssef's subtle touch, this is a man of the desert complaining about sand. As Khaled Mattawa writes in his introduction to Youssef's *Without an Alphabet, Without a Face*, "Open-ended and inconclusive as his poems may seem, they nonetheless leave us with an echoing impression of familiarity with their subject matter."

The man's breakdown separates the poem's initial conflict from the suggestion of a solution. From an allegorical standpoint, the emotional outburst represents the thinnest barrier between the poem's symbolic and literal meanings: sometimes a person simply has had enough—of war, of salt, of the coarse things in life that sting the eyes. To complain not about the dust but the smaller particles within the dust is an example of knowing the situation too well for one's own good, to have suffered too much for too long. Youssef's salt represents the petty but personal annoyances of war, not the large-scale destruction or catastrophic loss of life but the gradual erosion of the mind, spirit, and body, until a person either explodes with impotent rage like the man in "The Fence" or lies down in surrender and dies.

In their introduction to *Nostalgia, My Enemy: Poems by Saadi Youssef*, Sinan Antoon and Peter Money write: "While not a nationalist in any traditional sense, many of Youssef's late poems are variations on a central question: What has become of Iraq and how can one confront its reality?" In "The Fence," following the speaker's outburst, the second stanza offers him a solution. Two lines long, at first seemingly disconnected from the poem entirely, the stanza is in fact everything the man wants: his house and himself, alone. Without the other images crowding,

attacking, feasting, the only images left are the man and his home, undisturbed. The stanza seems disconnected because it is designed purposefully by Youssef to achieve this effect. The solution is not escape but defense—to dig in deeper and remember why he fights: to defend his grandfather's house, passed down to him. Allegorically, this is a call for Iraqi pride, to remember their heritage and hold fast, though the battle may be exhaustive and without end. The fence mentioned in the poem's title is not physically present in the poem's text, though the demarcation between the first and second stanzas forms a symbolic fence that emphasizes the effectiveness of the man's memory of his grandfather's pride in the home he built. This fence keeps the invaders, as well as the man's frustration, on one side of the poem, while on the other side is simplicity and peace.

The invaders are, with the exception of the strange insects, familiar sights. Feral cats and dogs run wild in the city, while all roads collect dust that is disturbed by those who use them. These invaders are the wildness that lives untamed in urban areas, easily kept out by a fence, potentially dangerous to life and property without one. The feral animals, together with the road dust, attack the man's prized carnations. The flowers, in Youssef's gentle, abstract rendering, represent natural beauty as well as sought-after natural resources that would draw invaders both domestic and foreign to a place (for example, oil). Significantly, carnations are poisonous to cats and dogs if ingested in large quantities, meaning the animals' feast may be their last. In their greed for the consumption of natural resources, they did not recognize how they poisoned themselves.

In a review of *Nostalgia, My Enemy*, Charis Bredin writes: "[Youssef's] poetry is inseparable from Iraq's recent turbulent history but it also captures the eternal and ephemeral moments of existence." The image of a frenzied, bacchanalian feast carried out on a bed of bright red flowers by a strange alliance of invaders is particularly prophetic of the 2003 Iraq invasion by the United States and its allies, but Iraq—centrally located in the Middle East, home of the ancient civilization of Mesopotamia, and sitting atop the second-largest reserves of oil in the world—has had a long and violent history of rebellion, uprisings, and war. The image is as personal as it is political: the flowers represent something wonderful and deeply cherished that is not simply taken away but indeed destroyed before the owner's eyes. This could be a loved one killed, a village bombed, a government toppled, or simply a flower shredded by the claws of a hungry alley cat. Though it is never stated outright, the flowers may be grown as a source of income to the man, thus making their destruction a symbol of financial devastation as well. Perhaps the lack of a fence is due to a lack of funds, and the man is caught in a perpetual cycle in which he needs the money from the flowers to build a fence, yet cannot grow flowers to sell without a fence to protect them.

As Mattawa explains, "Not aiming to write ideas, rather to suggest them, Youssef provides the reader with meditations constructed through musical and imagistic associations." The poem exists on two planes at once: that of the personal and that of the political. Also, it allows for multiple interpretations of its many images. The last line of the first stanza—describing the salt on the moon as it turns in its clothes—is a particularly abstract image, best understood as salt lingering in the air through all of the moon's phases. As the moon turns, showing more or less of its naked form throughout the month, the salt remains, an example of how the man gets no relief from his struggles. In addition, the presence of the moon suggests that the man struggles against his situation at night in addition to his daytime strife (indicated by the open petals of the carnations). However, the exact meaning, whether literal or symbolic, behind any one image is less important than the emotional thrust of the poem. To have a personal vulnerability taken advantage of by one's enemies is a universal fear, and one way to conquer it is through overcoming that vulnerability through self-confidence. The man in "The Fence" finds his confidence in the memory of his grandfather, a man who acted rather than standing idly by. The man's decision to reclaim his grandfather's legacy is sure to end well, as the poem's title points towards a solution to the problem.

Whether describing a domestic problem between an exasperated man and some tenacious garden pests or an international crisis between nations, the poem's subtle language hides volumes of meaning. The optimism of the final stanza, following on the heels of such unending strife, reflects Youssef's incredible ability to find the goodness in humanity, the resilience of those who have known great loss, and the strength found through self-reliance. Mattawa summarizes Youssef's impact: "Writing in a country ... torn between

powerful and power-hungry ideological currents, Youssef's reclamation of lived experience and defense of individual integrity make him one of the most important Arab poets today."

Source: Amy L. Miller, Critical Essay on "The Fence," in *Poetry for Students*, Gale, Cengage Learning, 2017.

Jonathan Maunder and Saadi Youssef

In the following interview, Youssef talks about culture and censorship in Iraq.

Saadi Youssef is one of Iraq's most well known poets and his work is renowned throughout the Middle East and beyond. He has translated numerous writers into Arabic including George Orwell, Federico Garcia Lorca and Walt Whitman. He fled Iraq in 1979 after Saddam Hussein tightened his hold on power, and lived subsequently in numerous countries. He now lives just outside London.

With current events in Lebanon in mind, when we met I began by asking Saadi about his time in Beirut during the first Israeli invasion in 1982. "I was there for three months of the siege. In that situation you can't be safe for a moment, there is constant fear. One time I was walking on the street and a mortar bomb landed fifty yards from me. The writers and poets at the time played a very important role. There were many journals, which would publish work by the poets in Beirut; these would be sent out to those on the front line resisting Israel. They were very influential in this sense. The Lebanese Communist Party printed a daily newspaper, and during the siege many poets played a crucial role in maintaining it, as many of the journalists were out fighting. Writing poetry was a way of maintaining hope at a time of great horror." How does he view the current Israeli offensive? "I think that what is going on at the moment is similar to what happened in 1918 after WW1 and the collapse of the Ottoman Empire. Then the whole region was redrawn and colonized by the west. Today I think we are seeing something similar, an attempt to re-colonies [sic] the region. It's not only the US but the Europeans too. The French could be going back into Lebanon just as they did in 1918!"

Saadi started writing poetry in his late teens. I ask what caused him to start writing. "People, especially poor people in Iraq, appreciate poetry. It started for me as a political expression but after a while poetry reaches a kind of independence of artistic form. You can't sacrifice art to politics." The natural environment of southern

Unusual insects infest the garden (©Shutterschock / Shutterstock.com)

Iraq—its date palms, birds, marshes—is a major influence on Saadi's poetry, but he finds it hard to separate it from political realities, "I can be observing a tree, and watch how it is blown by the wind, and how it looks, but then I can hear the sound of war planes overhead. I believe nature repairs what war does to you. So it is hard to separate out my poetry and politics. On a surface level they are separate. But I think in a deeper sense they are very interwoven. Personal experience is the normal way of beginning any work of art."

"When I write poetry sometimes it can mean meditating on an idea for a few days and then writing, or it can be writing first and then developing it. People need poetry; it helps people who maybe cannot get to a theatre or cinema to get in touch with an artistic form. Poetry is accessible." Why does he think poetry is so central to Middle Eastern culture? "The oral tradition is very important. Partly this stems from censorship. With poetry, you can smuggle it across borders. The first thing to be searched for at Arab airports is not drugs or guns, but books! Novels can be censored easily, but poetry stays in the head.

People respect poets more than politicians, who are usually corrupt."

We talk about his life in Iraq. "When I was in secondary school in Basra in the 1940s around a third of the students in my class were Jewish. Later, when Israel was created in 1948, the Israeli's did a deal with the Iraqi government to transfer the Iraqi Jews to Israel. Half a million were transferred. The Iraqi government got a £5 commission for every ticket they sold to an Iraqi Jew to go to Israel. Today the young generation in Israel aren't taught about their roots in the Arab world, even though their grandparents may have come from there."

"I went to study at the University of Baghdad in the mid 1950s. Cultural life in Iraq was rich then. I and many other students were also very active in political life. There were many strikes at that time which we helped to lead. I was a member of the Iraqi Communist Party, as many of the youth were. It was a major political party at that time. Communist party members led all the Trade Unions and peasant organizations. There were a number of famous clerics who were also in the party. In the late 1960s the US assisted the Baathists in destroying the party."

Where does he see Iraq going under the occupation? "Under the Ottoman empire Iraq was divided into three separate regions. The current talk of sectarian division is to prepare the ground once again for the division of Iraq. In terms of access to oil, a federal structure is easier to manipulate than a central government, but Iraq has no history of sectarian division."

"In Iraq at the moment there is 'bullet censorship.' Two women Iraqi writers who I know and respect have recently fled. One is a novelist, the other a journalist. There is a reign of terror going on. The occupation is turning a blind eye to it. As in the old days the fight for political and artistic freedom is the same."

Alongside military and economic colonization there is cultural colonization. Saadi says, "There was recently a gathering of important Iraqi cultural figures in Jordan who have links to the occupation. There was top security and a very small audience. I think the majority of Iraqi poets are against the occupation but there is no real organization between them. There is a need for a central, organized opposition to the occupation."

He says of America, "There is much I love about America, like the Jazz culture for example, I have great respect for the American people; I just oppose the American war machine." This is reflected in his poem 'America, America' where he condemns the first Gulf War but also writes about the feelings of a US soldier disillusioned with the fighting. I finish by asking him about the future of poetry in the Middle East. "There are a lot of younger poets today who send me their work. They are from North Africa as well as the Middle East. For the last twenty years this poetry has had a gloomy atmosphere, expressing feelings of dislocation and frustration. But when politics gets hotter, the poets will come out of their cocoons."

Source: Jonathan Maunder and Saadi Youssef, "Saadi Youssef's Interview in the *Socialist Worker*," Saadi Youssef website, 2016.

Sadiq Alkorigi

In the following review, Alkorigi describes Youssef's work as that of a "transformative voice in poetry.

Leading Arabic poet Youssef (*Without an Alphabet, Without a Face*) uses the physical aspects of the everyday to evoke a flowing narrative of a lost home. His native Iraq is a recurring theme—"On this Sunday, wet like a shepherd's dog/I miss my country." Youssef reveals bruised feelings about a homeland that he was forced to leave decades ago for his political views and that he now sees as wounded by invasion. (Currently, he lives in London.) Youssef's language recalls that of William Carlos Williams in its clarity, precision, and unwavering attention to the small things: "on my house door/the spider weaves/his naked clothes/for the air to pass through." Youssef repeatedly hints and reveals, suggests and declares, sometimes blurring the line between ideological statements and poetry. Ultimately, however, Youssef's work is innovative and immediate, distilling bright details drawn from memory into poems pulsing with life. VERDICT This beautifully translated work serves as an excellent introduction to a transformative voice in poetry. Highly recommended, especially for readers interested in Middle Eastern literature.

Source: Sadiq Alkorigi, Review of *Nostalgia, My Enemy*, in *Library Journal*, Vol. 137, No. 8, November 1, 2012, p. 72.

Amanda Laughtland

In the following review, Laughtland points out that Youssef's poetry reminds us to heed the viewpoint of individuals.

Born near Basra, Iraq, in 1934, Saadi Youssef has published nearly forty books, but for most American readers, *Without an Alphabet, Without a Face* will likely serve as an introduction to the work of this skilled poet. Youssef writes lyric poems in which personal and sociopolitical life collide. The relatively large size of this collection works to Youssef's benefit as it allows the details to accrue and the different poems to function together as a diverse whole.

Though Youssef currently lives in London, his work continues to reveal a knowing perspective on life in Iraq. In a poem from 1995 called "America, America," he writes: "Of the surface of the earth, generals know only two dimensions: / whatever rises is a fort, / whatever spreads is a battlefield."

Translated by Khaled Mattawa, who also provides a fourteen-page introduction that balances critical assessment with biographical detail, the poems of Youssef remind us of the importance of listening to the thoughts of one individual, a rare opportunity in a time when dissenting voices are often drowned out in the clamor of news bites.

Source: Amanda Laughtland, Review of *Without an Alphabet, Without a Face: Selected Poems*, in *Progressive*, Vol. 67, No. 3, March 2003, p. 44.

Publishers Weekly

In the following review, the anonymous author praises the translation of this collection, which captures of complex layers of meaning in Youssef's work.

Born in 1934 in Basra, Iraq, Youssef has recently settled in London after a peripatetic adult existence. These poems drawn from his 30 books are organized by date and place of composition: Baghdad (1972–1979), Algeria (1980), Yemen (1981–1982), Beirut (1979–1982), with later stops in Paris, Amman, Damascus, Berlin, Belgrade and Cairo. The poems work brilliantly through their differing times and places, pushing unflinching description through a steady determination to foment a more just world: "This watered wine/awaits its moment,/maybe in the lines of a song/or in a narrow bed." Often, Youssef will address anonymous figures he comes across, creating a sense of fellowship and shared longings from the slightest of materials: "Think about it:/Can we talk in a restaurant/ or find a river to dip our hands in?/ Or should we be content with breathing,/or let ourselves be snuffed out with a question?" The Libyan-born Mattawa (Ismailia Eclipse) emigrated to the U.S. in 1979, and does an excellent job rendering the layered complexity of the poems. Mattawa's translations of Youssef's declarative iterations— "The room shivers/from distant explosions./The curtains shiver./ Then the heart shivers./Why are you in the midst of all this shivering?"—create a center around which these poems move.

Forecast: Visa issues may prevent Youssef from touring in support of this book, but Mattawa, who has been published these translations in literary journals and who is based at the University of Texas at Austin, is available; look for strong support from campus reading series and post-colonial literature courses.

Source: Review of *Without an Alphabet, Without a Face: Selected Poems*, in *Publishers Weekly*, Vol. 249, No. 47, November 25, 2002, p. 59.

Marilyn Booth

In the following review, Booth asserts that Youssef does not receive the recognition he deserves.

In a 1973 poem translated from the Arabic in this collection, the Iraqi poet Sa'di Yusuf (b. 1934) offers an autobiographical reflection: "Dans les visages que je redoute / mon pays que je redoute / j'ai vule vieux train qui quitte Bagdad et m'amene / parfois a l'eau et parfois aux tribunaux / passer la vie en exil est un metier" ("La distance"). The four translators describe *Loin du premier ciel* as a retracing of the poet's "itinerary," of a long journey both literary and literal.

This is a voice that has been greatly influential to younger poets throughout the Arabic-speaking world. Yusuf's earliest poetry collection dates to 1952, as free verse was becoming the Mecca of avant-garde Arab poets; in his prolific career since then, he has consistently drawn upon the material imagery of rural southern Iraq and the colors of everyday existence as he has continued to experiment with new forms, yoking free verse and prose poetry in his memoiristic poetic journey. Incarcerated in Iraq, forced to work in his schoolteacher metier elsewhere, and after returning to Iraq exiled for the last time in 1979, Yusuf joined the Palestinian resistance and shared the forced wanderings of the fida'iyyin. His poems invoke not only Basra but the capitals of Arab exile: Beirut, Algiers, Aden. The new collection includes some short, imagistic poems that capture moments of reflection, lament, and memory, but puts more focus on the longer poetic reflections that trace journeys across space and time. The translators draw from seventeen collections (Yusuf has published at least twenty-five); their choices span, in chronological order, the years 1953–93, giving most space to the 1970s and 1980s.

Scholars of modern Arabic poetry recognize Sa'di Yusuf as having introduced a lower, more individual register into the poetry of resistance in Arabic, while they lament that he has not generally received the credit which is his due in the modern pantheon. Yusuf has been fearless in privileging the language and the cultural forms of everyday life, as well as mundane images, in complexly structured polyphonic poems. He anchors his poetic journey in geographies of exile, memory, and history; equally, for Yusuf, human sojourns are rooted in the processes and images of nature. In a poem interrogating the celebrated pre-Islamic poet, fighter, wanderer, and victim of assassination Imru'l-Qays, the poet assesses the "gallery of mirrors" that his existence has become, typically through nature images that not only cluster around but also give life to the architecture and the tastes of human sociability: "Des nuages fixes comme des montagnes de craie / l'hirondelle s'elance / atteint le clocher de l'eglise au bout du quartier / puis trois petits cedres /—je les dessinerai un jour—/ Mon cendrier est rempli d'escargots / la matinee est blanche / la plante verte tremble."

I would have liked to see more of Yusuf's most compressed poems here; yet any set of choices would have to omit some wonderful texts, and *Loin de premier ciel* seems a fair sampling. Perhaps some translations do not fully convey the street-life brusqueness and beauty of Yusuf's poetic voice; the sonority and the interruptions and the collision of forms and voices in, for example, "La maison de mon oncle" are muted. But this is a hard task, and the translators are to be thanked for making available in a European language a poetic voice whose tones ought to be heard more loudly everywhere.

Source: Marilyn Booth, Review of *Loin de premier ciel*, in *World Literature Today*, Vol. 74, No. 4, Fall 2000, p. 904.

SOURCES

Al-Muttalibi, Khaloud, "Saadi Yousef," in *The Contemporary Iraqi Poetry Movement: The Future of the Past*, Hurst and Hawk Publishing, 2012, p. 27.

Antoon, Sinan, and Peter Money, Introduction to *Nostalgia, My Enemy: Poems by Saadi Youssef*, Graywolf Press, 2012, pp. vii–xii.

Bredin, Charis, Review of *Nostalgia, My Enemy*, in *Banipal*, Vol. 43, 2012, http://www.banipal.co.uk/book_reviews/102/nostalgia-my-enemy/ (accessed April 11, 2016).

Butt, Gerald, "Saddam Hussein—His Rise to Power," BBC, November 17, 1998, http://news.bbc.co.uk/2/hi/events/crisis_in_the_gulf/decision_makers_and_diplomacy/216328.stm (accessed April 11, 2016).

Dearden, Lizzie, "ISIS 'Captures 3,000 Civilians' Trying to Escape Its Territory in Iraq," in *Independent*, August 5, 2016, http://www.independent.co.uk/news/world/middle-east/isis-captures-3000-civilians-trying-to-escape-its-territory-in-iraq-hawija-kirkuk-peshmerga-war-a7173321.html (accessed August 5, 2016)

"Iraq History," Arabic Media website, http://arabic-media.com/iraq_history.htm (accessed April 11, 2016).

"Key Events in the Life of Saddam Hussein," in *Guardian*, December 14, 2003, http://www.theguardian.com/world/2003/dec/14/iraq.iraq3 (accessed April 11, 2016).

Mattawa, Khaled, Introduction to *Without an Alphabet, Without a Face: Selected Poems of Saadi Youssef*, Graywolf Press, 2002, pp. xi–xxiv.

———, "Meet the Poet-Stranger: Three Stories and Their Aftermath," in *Kenyon Review*, Fall 2014, http://www.kenyonreview.org/kr-online-issue/2014-fall/selections/khaled-mattawa-essay-2-656342/ (accessed April 11, 2016).

Review of *Without an Alphabet, Without a Face: Selected Poems of Saadi Youssef*, in *Publishers Weekly*, http://www.publishersweekly.com/978-1-55597-371-1 (accessed April 11, 2016).

"Saadi Youssef," Poetry Foundation website, http://www.poetryfoundation.org/bio/saadi-youssef (accessed April 11, 2016).

"Saadi Youssef," Words without Borders website, http://www.wordswithoutborders.org/contributor/saadi-youssef (accessed April 11, 2016).

"Saddam Hussein Executed in Iraq," BBC website, December 30, 2006, http://news.bbc.co.uk/2/hi/middle_east/6218485.stm (accessed April 11, 2016).

Salama, Vivian, and Sameer N. Yacoub, "Tensions High in Iraq as Support for New PM Grows," in *Stars and Stripes*, August 13, 2014, https://web.archive.org/web/20140813212654/http://www.stripes.com/tensions-high-in-iraq-as-support-for-new-pm-grows-1.297997 (accessed April 11, 2016).

Stocke, Joy E., "Tonight We Rest Here—An Interview with Poet Saadi Youssef," in *Wild River Review*, August 1, 2007, http://www.wildriverreview.com/4/worldvoices-saadiyoussef.php (accessed April 11, 2016).

Watts, Stephen, "A Poet of Light, Earth and Sea," in *Banipal*, Vol. 17, Summer 2003, http://www.banipal.co.uk/book_reviews/23/a-poet-of-light-earth-and-sea/ (accessed April 11, 2016).

Youssef, Saadi, "The Fence," translated by Khaled Mattawa, in *Agni*, Vol. 48, 1998, http://www.bu.edu/agni/poetry/print/2002/56-youssef.html (accessed April 11, 2016).

FURTHER READING

Adonis, *Adonis: Selected Poems*, translated by Khaled Mattawa, Yale University Press, 2002.

> An exiled Syrian poet living in Paris, Adonis is a titan of Arabic literature, a respected contemporary of Youssef, and a leader of the modernist movement in Arabic poetry. This anthology includes poems from throughout his long and influential career.

Mattawa, Khaled, *Ismailia Eclipse: Poems*, Sheep Meadow, 1995.

> Mattawa's beautiful, haunting poetry written in English expresses both the longing of an exile for home as well as the eagerness of immigrants to become one with their new country. Arriving in the United States from Libya at the age of fifteen, Mattawa has used his knowledge of Arabic and English to become one of the

foremost translators of Arabic poetry as well as a respected author of Arab American poetry in his own right.

Mikhail, Dunya, *Fifteen Iraqi Poets*, New Directions, 2013.
Collecting fifteen poems from fifteen contemporary Iraqi poets, Mikhail's *Fifteen Iraqi Poets* provides an excellent introduction to the modern poetry of Iraq, complete with contextual and biographical introductions to each work.

Polk, William R., *Understanding Iraq: The Whole Sweep of Iraqi History, from Genghis Khan's Mongols to the Ottoman Turks to the British Mandate to the American Occupation*, Harper Perennial, 2006.
Written by a former adviser of John F. Kennedy and passionate student of Middle Eastern culture and history, *Understanding Iraq* is a comprehensive guide to the embattled country's long history of instability, insurgency, and war. With a particular focus on Iraqi culture, dialects, and traditions, Polk brings to light a people overshadowed by the political chaos of their homeland.

Youssef, Saadi, *Without an Alphabet, Without a Face: Selected Poems of Saadi Youssef*, translated by Khaled Mattawa, Graywolf Press, 2002.
Poems from throughout Youssef's career are collected in *Without an Alphabet, Without a Face* and organized by the place in which they were written during the poet's extended travels following his exile from Iraq. Sections include Yemen, Beirut, Paris, Berlin, Cairo, Algeria, and, of course, Baghdad, among many more.

SUGGESTED SEARCH TERMS

Saadi Youssef

Saadi Youssef AND poetry

Saadi Youssef AND Iraq

Saadi Youssef AND "The Fence"

Saadi Youssef AND Khaled Mattawa

Iraq AND Arabic poetry

Iraq AND Saddam Hussein

war AND poetry

I Am Not I

JUAN RAMÓN JIMÉNEZ
1918

Juan Ramón Jiménez's "I Am Not I" (1918) is the masterpiece of a Nobel Prize–winning poet. It is also the centerpiece marking the author's place in the history of Spanish poetry. Part of the Generation of '98, Jiménez moves with his *Eternidades* ("Eternities") volume (in which "I Am Not I" was published) from *modernismo*, the reception of French symbolist poetry, to *ultraismo*, the Spanish conversation with the European avant-garde. The work builds on the typical Neoplatonic metaphysics of the symbolists to create a paradox (evident in the title) that presages surrealism. The poem itself concerns the separation (which is also a unity) between the poet himself and his poetry. Jiménez explores the possibilities of other selves to be found in his own soul and in his love affair with the female embodiment of poetry. Indeed, in the case of Jiménez, this metaphysical concept was entangled with the person of his wife; as he confessed in his speech sent to the Nobel Prize award ceremony two days after her devastating death, he could not distinguish his wife, Zenobia, from his own work. At the same time, "I am Not I" is a specimen of pure poetry, a work stripped of everything except the evocative power of art. The poem appears in *Lorca and Jiménez: Selected Poems* (Beacon, 1973).

Juan Ramón Jiménez *(©Everett Collection Historical | Alamy Stock Photo)*

AUTHOR BIOGRAPHY

Juan Ramón Jiménez Mantecón was born on December 23, 1881, in Moguer, a village near Huelva, Spain, a seaside resort town in Andalusia. In 1900, Jiménez left his studies at the University of Seville without taking a degree; published his first book of poetry, *Almas de violeta* ("Souls of Violet") with the help of Nicaraguan poet Rubén Darío; and suffered the death of his father. He entered a clinical depression and was hospitalized for a time in France, then at a convent hospital in Spain. His poems of this period dwell on his affairs, whether real or imagined, with the nurses and even the nuns that attended him. He soon returned to the serious

composition of poetry, writing in the French symbolist style adopted by the prevailing movement in Spain of *modernismo*. In 1916, he began writing in his new style, expressing his own concept of *poesía desnuda* ("unveiled poetry"), based on the French concept of pure poetry. *Desnuda* carries with it in Spanish the connotation of the mystic stripping away the unnecessary parts of life to prepare to ascend to God. Jiménez soon came to be regarded as the most important poet in Spain. In particular, Jiménez would, in his turn, act as the patron of Federico García Lorca.

In 1917, Jiménez married Zenobia Camprubí. She was an important writer herself and translated the Bengali poetry of the Nobel laureate Ribindranath Tagore into Spanish.

Jiménez had an unusually close relationship with his wife, and she embodied for him the whole art of poetry in human, feminine form. "Yo no soy yo" ("I am Not I") was originally published in Jiménez's *Eternidades* ("Eternities," 1918). Jiménez was offered the post of ambassador to the United States by the Republican government, but he had to flee Spain at the outbreak of the civil war before anything could come of that. When they left, Jiménez and his wife took a dozen orphans with them, having to hurriedly adopt them to speed up the necessary paperwork, and they later established a foundation to care for them. They lived in Cuba until 1939 and then moved to the United States, where Zenobia became a professor of Spanish at the University of Maryland and Jiménez held various academic positions. In 1961, the couple moved to Puerto Rico, where Jiménez accepted a position as a literature professor at the University of Puerto Rico, through which he shaped a generation of Puerto Rican writers, including Manuel Ramos Otero and Giannina Braschi.

In 1956, Jiménez received the Nobel Prize in Literature, but he was not able to attend the award ceremony in Stockholm because Zenobia died of ovarian cancer just two days after the announcement of the award was made. Jaime Benitez, rector of the University of Puerto Rico, attended in his place and read a statement on his behalf, including this appreciation of his lifelong companion, "My wife Zenobia is the true winner of this Prize. Her companionship, her help, her inspiration made, for forty years, my work possible. Today, without her, I am desolate and helpless." Aristotle says in *Nicomachean Ethics* that a friend is another self; in Jiménez's case, his other self was undoubtedly Zenobia. Jiménez died on May 29, 1958, also of cancer and in the same Puerto Rican hospital where Zenobia had preceded him. Both are buried in Moguer.

POEM SUMMARY

The text used for this summary is from *Lorca and Jiménez: Selected Poems*, translated by Robert Bly, Beacon, 1973, pp. 76–77. A version of the poem can be found on the following website: http://www.poetryfoundation.org/poems-and-poets/poems/detail/51759.

Jiménez's poem "I Am Not I" is a short lyric poem that does not use the conventions of traditional poetry, like meter or rhyme, but is written in the modern manner, using other considerations of language, meaning, and form to define its poetic character. Its highly evocative text is filled with paradox and relies on figurative language, striking words and phrases that misdirect and redirect the reader's understanding, to create its poetic effect.

The first line of "I Am Not I" is also used as the title. The line presents a paradox because, by the law of identity, I must be I. However, the poet offers a different meaning for *I*. *I* is not the poet himself—or not only the poet himself—but is or is also another entity that accompanies the self. The text of the poem proceeds to contrast the actions of the two selves. In fact, this contrast is built into the very structure of the poem. The typesetting of its first two lines is odd compared with the following lines. Both are only half as long as the rest. Moreover, the second line is offset so that it begins in the position its first letter would have occupied if it had been printed in line with the first line of text. Thus, the first two lines are really one line of poetry split in two. The first identifies the *I who is not I*, while the second line identifies *this I*, which may be termed the *I who is I*. The very printing of the poem is meant to show how the self can simultaneously be a single and a double entity. The poet refers to both entities by the pronoun *I* even within the same sentence, where they govern different, particularly opposite, verbs. He goes further than this in lines 2 and 3 and makes *I* both the subject and object of the same verb. The *I* who is not *I* walks beside me (presumably meaning the *I* that is *I*), but the *I* who is *I* does not see the *I* who is not *I*. It is not possible to build a clear distinction between this *I* and that *I*, however, which is as Jiménez intends. This entity must be simultaneously collapsed into one and doubled into two.

The subject of the clauses in lines 4 and 5 seems to be the *I* who is *I*, that is, the more normal self-perception of consciousness that most readers would simply identify as *I*. This *I* sometimes manages to visit the other *I*. This is probably meant to express that there are moments of communion or unity between them. At other times, *I* forgets the other *I*, that is, the simple *I* acts or thinks with reference only to itself and not its unseen companion or counterpart. The two act and think, or can act and think, in opposite ways. While the *I* that is *I* talks, the other *I* remains undisturbed and quiet. Quiet and talking are natural opposites, but in this construction (line 6), calmness also has to be taken as the opposite of talking. This suggests that talking might be seen as a response to a disturbance of interior or emotional calmness. A difference between the two *I*'s is that the other *I* is superior to the normal sense of self because it remains calm while the other is moved to speak. This is made clearer in line 7, in that the *I* who is not *I* forgives when the *I* who is *I* hates. The forgiveness is given gently, which ties back in with the calmness of the silence in the preceding line. In the Spanish text, in fact, the two lines are precisely parallel in construction, and the terms literally meaning "serenely" and "sweetly" link to each other more naturally than the terms used by Bly in the translation.

The final two lines of the poem view the relationship of this *I* with that *I* in an even broader context. One *I* walks where the other *I* does not, which most obviously means that one *I* exists where the other *I* does not. It is hard to read this line except in a metaphorical sense, derived from the Hebrew Bible, in which *walking* means "behaving." That reading reinforces the difference in attitude between the two selves highlighted in the earlier lines: one is virtuous. whereas the other is a sinner. This kind of religious reading seems confirmed by the last line, which says that the *I that is not I* will continue to exist (using the biblical metaphor of standing for existing) when the *I that is I* has died.

THEMES

Neoplatonism

Jiménez's "I Am Not I" is paradoxical and obscure and one of its intended effects is to baffle the reader. Still, some sense can be made out of the poem within the framework of the ancient Greek philosophy of Neoplatonism. If this at first seems to the reader like replacing one unknown for another, it is at least certain that Jiménez intended the poem to be read that way, because he said of himself (in a letter quoted in Howard T. Young's *The Line in the Margin*), "Soy, fui, y seré Platónico" ("I am, have been, and will be a Platonist"). The double self in Jiménez's poem grows out of the Platonic conception of the human being, specifically the

relation between a person's body and those parts of a person that are not the body.

Plato taught that a person has three parts: a body (*soma*), a soul (*psyche*), and an intellect (*nous*). The soul is what a modern person would call the mind, a person's consciousness of himself and his place in the world as well as his discursive reasoning, his power to think and talk. (What we would call the unconscious mind with its drives and instincts, Plato located in the body.) For Plato, the soul was originally in heaven with the gods, was seduced into falling into a body, and will eventually be freed from the body (perhaps after a series of reincarnations) to be restored to its place in heaven. The intellect, however, is something else again. While the soul is in a body, it has no consciousness of its own intellect (except in the case of the philosopher who is able to glimpse it through mystical contemplation). The intellect is pure spirit and cannot be touched by matter; thus it always remains in heaven, and the higher part of the soul (the part that will eventually be returned) is attached to it. The intellect is the true human being in the same way that the heavenly world is the true world, of which the physical world perceived by the senses is only a fallen copy. The only way that the discursive reasoning of the soul is able to understand the chaotic physical world is through the order in the world of forms (archetypes of physical existence) that it can dimly remember from the time before it was in a body.

The two *I*'s in "I am Not I" are the soul and intellect. They are both parts of a single self but are nevertheless discrete entities. All of these ideas are present in the works of Plato, often as speculation, but the Neoplatonists, especially Plotinus (who lived in the third century, about seven hundred years after Plato) developed them into a formal system. The *I* in Jiménez's poem who cannot see, who has to commune with the other self, who forgets, who talks, who hates (i.e., feels passions), and who will die is the soul, but the *I* who walks (exists) alongside the other, who remains silent, who forgives, and who will remain after the other dies is the intellect. Death in this case means not ceasing to exist but instead the soul's liberation from the body as from a prison, at which time it will return to the other *I*. The intellect, in contrast, remains in its own state of being, since it was never in the body.

TOPICS FOR FURTHER STUDY

- The Argentinian writer Jorge Luis Borges's prose poem "Borges and I" (available in his *Selected Poems*, edited by Alexander Coleman, 2000) is very similar to Jiménez's "I Am Not I" and was likely partially inspired by it. Write a paper comparing the two works.

- The Nobel Prize Committee maintains a website with extensive information about all Nobel laureates in literature. (This link is to the site index: http://www.nobelprize .org/nobel_prizes/literature/laureates/index .html.) Using this site as a source, make a presentation to your class about the Nobel laureates who wrote in Spanish, including Jiménez. Pay special attention to how they are connected both by personal links and within the framework of the history of modern Spanish literature.

- The Cuban poet José Martí stood on the opposite side from the generation of '98. While the Spanish poets were energized by shame over the loss of the colonial empire in the Spanish-American War, Martí died as a guerrilla fighting in Cuba for freedom from Spain. He also produced a politically engaged poetry opposite in many respects to the character of pure poetry. He wrote a cycle of poems specifically for young adults that has been translated by Manuel A.

- Tellechea as *Versos Sencillos: Simple Verses* (1997). Make a presentation to your class contrasting the political and purely aesthetic poetry of Martí and Jiménez.

- Rewrite "I Am Not I" as a sonnet with regular scansion and rhyme scheme. Append a commentary to your poem discussing how the use of traditional forms clashes with the ideals of pure poetry embodied in the original.

- Jiménez considered himself a Neoplatonist and "I am Not I" is deeply involved with Neoplatonic philosophy. There are many online resources on Neoplatonism, including the collection of links to Neoplatonic texts maintained by the International Society for Neoplatonic Studies (http://www. isns.us/texts.htm) and the relevant entries in the *Stanford Encyclopedia of Philosophy* on Neoplatonism and various Neoplatonic thinkers, including Numenius, Plotinus, Porphyry, Iamblichus, Pseudo-Dionysius the Areopagite, Proclus, and Ammonius Saccas. Familiarize yourself with the basic ideas of Neoplatonism from these or similar resources found by searching on the Internet. (Searches for strings like "Neoplatonism self" will return results directly applicable to Jiménez.) Present your findings in a PowerPoint presentation to your class.

Silence

The poem's denigration of human speech in preference for silence seems an odd idea for a poet, whose business is language, to hold. But the Neoplatonic background of "I Am Not I" helps to explain it. Speech is something that arises in the soul because it is ignorant and confused. In Plato's famous parable of the cave in *The Republic*, he describes the soul, while it is trapped in a body, as being like a man who can see only the shadows of reality and has to try, without much success, to figure out what they are. Once the soul is set free by the death of the

body and returns to the heavenly world of forms, it will see everything clearly in the bright light and understand, like the man who having seen only shadows will do once he finally sees the people, animals, and objects that made the shadows. The *I who is I*, the Platonic soul, has to use speech and reason in its attempt to understand what it cannot fully perceive in life. Talking comes about as a way of explaining things to one's self and to others, things that are not immediately understood. If they were understood, there would be no need for discourse about them. No form of speech or discursive reasoning

The speaker seems to be alone, but he imagines another beside him (©Eugene Sergeev / Shutterstock.com)

is necessary, however, for the intellect in its celestial home; there the intellect directly apprehends everything. Plotinus explains this directly in his philosophical essays (called the *Enneads*):

> Very surely the deliberation of doubt and difficulty which they practice here [on earth] must be unknown to them There [in heaven].... They will know, each, what is to be communicated from another by present consciousness. Even in our own case here, eyes often know what is not spoken; and There the whole body (the heaven) is pure, and every being is, as it were, an eye, nothing is concealed or sophisticated, there is no need of speech, everything is seen or known.

Thus the lack of speech, and in its place clear understanding, is the ideal, superior even to the language of poetry.

STYLE

Profundity

One of the goals of Jiménez's *poesía desnuda* (unveiled poetry) is to use poetry to produce a powerful emotional effect apart from any discursive meaning of the poem. A technique of

doing this is to use simple language that makes a bold declarative statement but also with elements of paradox in order to create an impression of profundity, an effect that seems simultaneously mysterious and meaningful. There are many examples of this in literature. When Moses asks God to tell him his name, he responds, "I am that I am" (Exodus 3:14 KJV) While this works as a pun on the actual divine name Yahweh in Hebrew, the simple statement, which is both easy and impossible to understand, immediately produces a more profound effect than any actual name could. A similar effect was used more prosaically in the comic strip *Popeye*, whose main character had the slogan "I am what I am," which made him seem both wise and humble. Poetic examples include Shakespeare's "To be or not to be" (from *Hamlet*); this could hardly be a more simple statement, the repetition of the infinitive *to be* with one instance negated, but at the same time it is a consideration of the most profound choice of life and death. It is no accident that this is the most famous line of poetry in the world. Similar is the opening of Catullus's poem 85, "Odi et amo" ("I hate her and I love her"). This is even simpler with the

COMPARE
&
CONTRAST

- **1910s:** Spain is a constitutional monarchy with one of the most ineffectual and reactionary governments in Europe.

  Today: Spain is a constitutional monarchy, with the king largely reduced to a head of state position with little executive power and with a political spectrum in the European mainstream.

- **1910s:** After the aesthetic reforms of the Generation of '98, Spanish letters are moving toward the forefront of the European cultural scene.

  Today: While Spain has its share of distinguished poets, it is not in the middle of an artistic ferment similar to what it experienced a century ago.

- **1910s:** Jiménez develops his theory of *poesía desnuda*, of which "I Am Not I" is an expression, in part from resonances with the physical rhythmic motions of ship and train travel during his honeymoon in the United States.

  Today: The kind of worldwide travel that Jiménez undertook on his honeymoon would more likely be done in airplanes.

---

two short verbs that contain their contradiction in themselves and, of course, deal with the two most intense human emotions. With the first line of Jiménez's poem, which also serves as the title, "I Am Not I" ("Yo soy no yo"), he aims at the same kind of profound effect as these other passages. He combines a simple grammatical structure with a paradoxical meaning and immediately sets readers the task of trying to understand what cannot be understood, fully engaging their faculties as they try to come to grips with the text.

Language

Whether or not human thought and the human imagination is in any sense limited, their expression to other human beings is decidedly limited by the structure of language. The problem is most obvious in the case of religious mysticism, where the mystic complains that mental experience cannot be communicated in words or even transcends articulate thoughts. The experience of the intense feelings of love is similarly often said to be beyond words. In "I Am Not I," Jiménez pushes at the same boundary between thought and expression. In the first line, he breaks the law of identity, one of the fundamental bases of logic, by creating two specimens of *I* that are not identical. To describe the situation,

one would have to use a plural of *I*, which in the sense required does not exist in either Spanish or English. The reader might object that *we* is the plural of *I*, but *we* is always equivalent to *you and I together*, not *an I and another I*. There is no word for two *I's*. The concept is grammatically impossible, because the same entity would have to become simultaneously the subject and object of the same sentence, as Jiménez demonstrates when he talks about *I walking beside me* and *I not seeing me*.

HISTORICAL CONTEXT

The history of modern Spanish poetry is dominated by three schools that are called generations: the Generation of 1898, the Generation of 1927, and the Generation of 1950. The dates refer not to poets born at that time but to those who then reached artistic maturity. These were all calls for the reform of Spanish poetry in response to political and cultural events of the period in question. The Generation of '98 had to deal with the loss of the Spanish colonial empire and what they perceived as Spain's national humiliation in the Spanish-American War. The Generation of '27 tried to come to terms with the

---

The speaker imagines another presence listening when he talks, though it is unclear whether this presence is God, an alternate self, a soul, or some kind of ghost (©Jaroslav Franicsko / Shutterstock.com)

European, particularly the French, avant-garde. The Generation of '50 saw their calling as chronicling the injustice of the Franco dictatorship and had to write in a highly allusive and allegorical style to outwit government censorship. Jiménez, born in 1881 and publishing "I Am Not I" in 1918, falls between the first two periods. Antonio Machado was a leading figure of the Generation of '98. His work begins in the symbolist school, comparable to the work of an English writer like Oscar Wilde, and by the time of the civil war in 1936 had moved in the direction of cataloguing Spanish peasant life in an almost anthropological fashion. Symbolism, the French school that created a new and rich aesthetic vocabulary for the expression of emotion, found its equivalent in Spanish *modernismo*, which dominated the early Generation of '98 period.

A leader of *modernismo* was the Nicaraguan Rubén Darío, who acted as Jiménez's patron, assisting him with the publication of his first volume of poetry, *Almas de violeta* (1900). However, a movement known as *ultraismo* eventually opposed *modernismo* and called

for following the French avant-garde. Led by the Argentinian writer Jorge Luis Borges, *ultraismo* by 1917 had become the primary artistic movement in Spain. Jiménez's "I Am Not I" clearly and avowedly belongs to *ultraismo*. Before the Generation of '27, Spain was forced to react to artistic movements in France and elsewhere. But Federico García Lorca, undoubtedly the leading poet of that era and a follower of Jiménez, did not have to take second place to any other poet in the world in the 1930s. Jiménez's later award of the Nobel Prize shows how quickly Spanish letters were able to catch up with the rest of the world before all progress was halted by the fascist dictatorship. The Generation of '27 built on the base of *ultraismo* and pure poetry to move in the direction of the French and Italian avant-garde and eventually became itself a formative force on surrealism through the work of the painter Salvador Dali and the filmmaker Luis Buñuel. One can see the outlines of surrealism already in Jiménez's use of paradox in "I Am Not I" and his fascination with the obscure and abandoned ancient philosophy of Neoplatonism.

CRITICAL OVERVIEW

Jiménez, as a Nobel Prize winner, has been extensively studied by critics, especially in Spanish-language publications (and note that many studies written in English will quote only the original Spanish text of his poems). Catherine Jaffe, in her study in *Hispania* (1990), argues that Jiménez

> frequently identified woman, "la mujer", with his work, "la Obra". As object of erotic or spiritual desire, image of beauty, symbol of love, and form of the Ideal, "la mujer" is as central to his poetic discourse as "la Obra", his life as poetry, and "la muerte" his preoccupation with death.

Further, "'La poesía desnuda' [unveiled poetry] first practiced in *Diario de un poeta recién casado* (1916) and *Eternidades* (1917) [source of 'I Am Not I'], is grounded metaphorically in the nude female figure." Howard T. Young, in one of the most frequently cited studies of Jiménez in English, *The Line in the Margin* (1980), takes "I Am Not I" as an important or at least emblematic work by the poet, saying, "As every devotee of Juan Ramón's poetry knows, there is a second *yo* [*I*] in his work. On occasion, this *desdoblamiento* [doubling] is of a Platonic goodness," also emphasizing the poem's background in Platonic metaphysics. Citing "I Am Not I" as an example, he points to division between the self and an ideal self as a main theme of Jiménez's work: "Much of Juan Ramón's poetry discusses how to reconcile, protect, and cultivate that *yo eterno* [eternal *I*] . . ., that inner paradigm against which all others must be matched."

Jaffe follows Young's analysis that Jiménez tends to divide, or rather duplicate, his poetic persona into a self (more or less corresponding to the poet) and an ideal self, with the *Other* ideal self standing for the poetic text. Jaffe's main argument is that this turns Jiménez's poetry into a love affair between a male poet and a female poem, citing "I Am Not I" as her example, creating special difficulties for women reading Jiménez:

> For a female reader experiencing the doubling process when the represented object is a woman, the female Other is more (un)comfortably familiar than a male Other. Only by rejecting her own feminine identity can she feel the same strange pull of wondering and erotic desire that for the poet is the mystical reality of the attraction. Or she must substitute as male any female Other in order to not end up contemplating self as object of desire.

"JIMÉNEZ FOLLOWS NOT THEORY, BUT NATURE."

Of course, queer readings of poetry were not yet mainstream in the early 1990s, although Jiménez suggested in his own writings that, in his terms, a female poet would be a lesbian. Mervyn Coke-Enguidanos, in his *Word and Work in the Poetry of Juan Ramon Jimenez* (1982), views the two *I*'s in "I Am Not I" as "the self of world-experience and the projected literary self." He sees a parallel between Jiménez's poem and Jorge Luis Borges's prose poem "Borges y yo" ("Borges and I"), in which the author is divided into his authentic self and the public persona forced upon him by his celebrity. Leo R. Cole, in *The Religious Instinct in the Poetry of Juan Ramón Jiménez*, suggests that the clear distinction of the *I* that will die and the *I* that will remain in "I Am Not I" is in distinction to other poems of Jiménez that blur distinctions between the self and another. He also refers the metaphysics of the poem to the influence of the New Age figures George Gurdjieff and P. D. Ouspensky.

CRITICISM

Bradley A. Skeen

Skeen is a classicist. In the following essay, he places Jiménez's poem "I Am Not I" in the context of the pure poetry movement.

Jiménez's "I Am Not I" is generally classed under the category of pure poetry. The manifesto of this movement is the essay "Pure Poetry," by Frenchman Paul Valéry, in which he summarizes or gives definitive form to a movement he had perceived developing among European poets for some time. Because the term *pure poetry* itself is, not accidentally, so simple, the phrase is often used in other senses, so Valéry is quick to define what he means by it: "I use the word *pure* in the sense in which the physicist speaks of pure water." He is clear it has nothing to do with moral purity.

WHAT DO I READ NEXT?

- The Nicaraguan ultraist poet Rubén Darío acted as Jiménez's literary patron. His own poetry, comparable to the work of the English decadent and symbolist Oscar Wilde, has been neglected by translators, but there have been two partial translations, both confusingly published with the title *Selected Poems of Rubén Darío*. One was published by Lysander Kemp in 1965 and the other by Alberto Acereda and Will Derusha in 2001; the latter is a bilingual edition of the selected texts.

- Giannina Braschi was one of Jiménez student's at the University of Puerto Rico. Her *Yo-Yo Boing!* (1998) is a postmodern novel. It takes the form of a series of dialogues without setting or character discussing various topics of postmodern interest, including feminism, racism, and colonialism. It also occasionally gives critical overviews of various figures in the history of Spanish literature, including Jiménez. It is best known as the most important literary work written in Spanglish, a style in which bilingual speakers code-switch, alternating between English and Spanish, even in the same sentence. The book was entirely translated into English in 2011 by Tess O'Dwyer.

- Federico García Lorca was the most important of Jiménez's disciples and one of the leading poets of the twentieth century. He developed his own avant-garde style of poetry, studiously avoiding the surrealism developed by his friends Salvador Dali and Luis Buñuel. He was murdered by fascists at the beginning of the Spanish Civil War. A substantial collection of his poetry is published, together with English translations by Christopher Mauer, in *The Collected Poems, A Bilingual Edition* (2002).

- Juan Felipe Herrera, former poet laureate of the United States, wrote *Laughing Out Loud, I Fly* (1998), a collection of poems for young adults concerning the maintenance of a Spanish identity in American culture.

- The Chilean poet Pablo Neruda (himself a Nobel laureate in 1971) never studied with Jiménez, but he could not, like all Spanish poets of his generation, escape the influence of *poesía desnuda*—though he was forced to abandon its principles in the political climate created by the Spanish Civil War and the later fascist coup in his own country. This is the subject of his essay "Toward an Impure Poetry," translated by Ben Belitt in *Pablo Neruda: Five Decades, a Selection (Poems: 1925–1970)*, published in 1974.

- Antonio Machado was among the most prominent poets of the initial *modernismo* phase of the Generation of '98. A corpus of his work is available in English, translated by Willis Barnstone in *Border of a Dream: Selected Poems of Antonio Machado* (Spanish and English edition) published in 2003.

Valéry says that when one calls a landscape or an old ruin or anything else *poetic*, one means it elicits an internal emotional state of excitement or enchantment. He calls poetry the use of language for "artificially producing this kind of emotion." Poetic language is able to do this because it creates an illusion of the world, "a *world* in which events, images, beings, and things, although resembling those which people the ordinary world, are in an inexplicable but intimate relationship with the whole of our sensibility." Pure poetry, then, is language that takes as its goal the artificial creation of such emotions and nothing else, poetry that does not use language in any discursive way to analyze, consider, or describe, or anything else that the mass of people ordinarily do with language. Pure poetry is language stripped of anything that is not poetic, including narrative, discourse, or argument, which are attributes of prose but which would exclude epics like the poems of Homer or *Beowulf* or drama. One of the sources of pure poetry was the work of Edgar Allan Poe, a figure regarded much more seriously in France than in the United States. A poem like Poe's "The Bells" achieves one effect that pure purity aimed at. It has no discursive content at all, and it would therefore be impossible to summarize. (One could say it describes the sensation of hearing bells, but that would only be misleading.) Instead, it uses language to evoke feeling and mood in the reader or, better, the hearer to the exclusion of any other purpose.

In practice, the language of works that are intended to be pure poetry is extremely spare and stripped down, removing even what one may think as defining characteristics of older poetry like meter and rhyme, sacrificing everything for emotional or aesthetic effect. Pure poetry must strive to do with language what the musician does with music. Valéry says,

> *if a pure sound*, that is, a relatively exceptional sound, *is heard, a particular atmosphere is immediately created, a particular state of expectation is produced in our senses, and this expectation tends*, in some way, *to provoke sensations of the same order, and of the same purity as the first. If a pure sound is heard in a hall, everything in us is changed.*

If in the middle of the performance one hears a noise that is not music, for example, a musician knocking over a chair, the entire effect is destroyed: "*a universe is shattered*, a spell is abolished." One can see, or rather hear, precisely what Valéry means by listening to the prelude to Richard Wagner's *Das Rheingold* or the first movement of Wolfgang Amadeus Mozart's *Requiem*. Pure poetry then, is the same as music without noise. The poet must write poetry being careful not to knock over any chairs. Valéry insists that a poem entirely pure of nonpoetic language is impossible to achieve and is a goal that the poet can never reach but only aim for. One can certainly make out that Jiménez aimed for pure purity in "I Am Not I." The language of the poem is purely evocative and not at all discursive, to the degree that it actively resists mere comprehension. It is based on paradoxes, a suitable nondiscursive element because pure prose would demand such seeming contradictions be

unraveled while pure poetry flourishes by leaving them unresolved.

Jiménez thought deeply about the nature of pure poetry and produced his own theoretical works on the subject. W. Douglas Barnette, in *A Study of the Works of Manuel Mantero*, a work that deals in part with Jiménez's influence on Mantero, traces it back to the influence of the nineteenth-century poet Gustavo Adolfo Bécquer on Jiménez. In particular, he quotes Bécquer's wish to aim at a poetry "desnuda de aritficio" ("stripped of artifice"). This Spanish context provides the launching point for Jiménez's own poetic trajectory. Howard T. Young, in his study of Jiménez poetry, *The Line in the Margin*, points out that Jiménez paid lip service to the current term *pure poetry* but created his own aesthetic he more precisely described with his own term *poesía desnudo* ("unveiled poetry"). Young provides an important insight into Jiménez's theory of poetry, based on his writings in Spanish that have not yet been translated. Jiménez, in Young's words, offered that

> his writing took place in response to the movement of the waves during his ocean voyage.... He speaks of the rhythmic monotony of the train rattling onward, and proclaims also another source: the naked female form and the rhythm of its movement.

Jiménez follows not theory, but nature. On precisely this point, Young identifies a vital difference between Jiménez and Valéry: "In casting about for a name for a poetry divested of anecdote, elevated in tone, select in diction, and restricted in theme, Juan Ramón hesitated to import the phrase *poésie pure*." Jiménez modified Valéry's concept with Bécquer's langue to produce his own description of his poetry, *poesía desnuda*, or unveiled poetry. Young continues,

> Nothing, however, could be more indicative of a basic underlying difference than the chemical connotation of the term "pure" as described in French poetics and the sensual source of *desnudo*. Both notions posit a privation and an uncovering, but only one holds forth the paradigm of the naked human form divine.

Jiménez believed that the sexual act could lead to something greater and found confirmation of this idea in the Neoplatonic aesthetics of poets such as Percy Bysshe Shelley and William Butler Yeats, for whom it led to the contemplation of an abstract, ideal, timeless beauty. As a Platonist, Jiménez agrees with Plato's teaching in *The Symposium* that the desire to experience

When the speaker is angry or hateful, he imagines the shadow figure as forgiving (©Jaroslav Franicsko / Shutterstock.com)

beauty in other human beings leads upward to the desire to experience beauty itself.

In his intellectual autobiography, *Time & Space*, Jiménez emphasizes what may be called the erotic nature of poetry. He approaches poetry as he would a woman he is in love with:

> A "manly" poetry, delicate, exquisitely natural, spontaneously perfect; what is usually called feminine poetry, namely, manly poetry. I take poetry (life, death, beauty) as being a woman, I cannot see it otherwise, because I am a man. We must not forget that "poetry" is feminine.

He means that in Spanish (as in Latin and its ultimate source, Greek), the word *poesía* has a feminine grammatical gender. In writing poetry, he both exploits and transcends the two human genders in a way that has tended to baffle modern feminist critics. Conversely, Jiménez imagines that the female poet must take the opposite stance: "A woman, on the other hand, must see poetry, illusion, in the shape of a man, and the poetry called 'masculine' must be written by a woman." Above all, he concludes, "Poetry is

love. I am in love with her and I must, therefore, see her as feminine." Jiménez returns again to the Platonic theme of philosophy, or for Jiménez poetry, as a flight through the universe from a physical lover to the love of the beautiful or of God, which for Plato was the same thing:

> When we kiss our own woman on the lips we kiss the lips of god, the whole visible and invisible universe; and love is the only way to eternity and as a matter of fact I do not believe there is any other eternity but love, and if we feel death as a defect it is because we are left without the action of love, because our lips are no longer able to be in voluntary and dynamic contact with the lips of the world.

If this discussion seems digressive, it leads back finally to "I Am Not I." In that poem, the other *I*, the unseen self, which is wiser and more spiritual than Jiménez and which is immortal and divine, is his own intellect—which takes the form of his poetry, his feminine other half linking him to the divine world. The other *I* is the poem itself, which has the quality of being even more present to the reader than the *I* that is the poet.

The idea of silence in "I Am Not I" might at first seem of secondary importance, but it relates to the overall meaning of the poem; silence has a meaning in Platonic philosophy too, as a description of the contemplation by the intellect of the beautiful, which does not need the noise of language, although in the shadow world of matter it can be communicated, imperfectly, only through language. If poetry were truly unveiled, truly pure, it would be just that vision of beauty, with no need of veiled or impure language at all. This is a theme of considerable importance to Jiménez, and he discusses it at length in his collection of anecdotes and aphorisms, *The Complete Perfectionist*. One way to think of the silence he means is as the union between poet and beauty, which needs no talk, similar to the quiet sought by the Christian mystic in union with God. He establishes a hierarchy for speaking, dreaming, or thinking and reading:

> Better to be quiet than to speak; to dream than to be quiet; to read than to dream or think. When we read, silence itself grows quiet, and we can think or dream in company.

The three items are ranked in terms of the silence they permit or indeed require. As a poet, Jiménez naturally uses reading as a metaphor for contemplation. He says that "unity is the noble daughter of silence; dispersion, the mad stepchild of noise," because his goal is union with the beautiful, which is destroyed by the fragmentation of the sensory world. He emphasizes this when he again says, "Noise shatters my day and brain into a thousand irreparable little pieces." But silence allows the one who enjoys it to rise above the time and space of the material world to the contemplation of the eternal:

> Silence does not waste time, it fills it. Yes. And the only thing that fills time is silence. So that time shared with noise is time lost. But silence conquers time, puts it back together, and makes it whole.

Jiménez returns finally to Valéry's metaphor of music's emotional elicitation for the effect of pure poetry, in a final paradox: "True music is the music of silence, the silent but well-heard music of thought in the head, passion in the body, reverie in the soul."

Source: Bradley A. Skeen, Critical Essay on "I Am Not I," in *Poetry for Students*, Gale, Cengage Learning, 2017.

John C. Wilcox

In the following review, Wilcox discusses the different effects of two varying translations of Jiménez's work.

In 1923, with the publication in Madrid of *Poesia and Belleza (En verso) 1917–1923*, Juan Ramon Jimenez effectively placed a seal on the mid-period of his poetic evolution. An introductory note listed fifteen unpublished volumes of verse from which *Poesia and Belleza* had been selected. *La realidad invisible*, the first of the fifteen, was finally published 25 years after the poet's death, in 1983, owing to the tenacity of Antonio Sanchez Romeralo, the distinguished editor of Jimenez's "recreated" *Obra* (called *Metamorfosis*), who in 1976 submitted his critical edition of the text to Tamesis. The latter contained 144 poems, half of which had not previously been published; it also provided a photocopy of the manuscript for every text, and a meditated "lectura interpretativa" on each poem edited. Imprenta Aguirre, which in 1936 had printed Jimenez's *Cancion*, the last volume of poetry he was destined to publish in his own country, printed the book and set the poems in the same Elzevirian type Jimenez made popular in Spain. In short, Sanchez Romeralo's was an edition for scholars and bibliophiles.

Martinez Torron's has the advantage of being a Catedra paperback. It contains all the poems included by Sanchez Romeralo, plus thirteen additional ones, most of which have not previously been published. He claims that his edition differs from Sanchez Romeralo's in that he is following the poet's final corrections and, moreover, that he abides by the textual criteria authorized by Jimenez's heirs. My assessment is that Sanchez Romeralo was guided by his own refined sensibility to produce a text that is consonant with a 1920s' aesthetic. Martinez Torren [sic] includes extra syntagmas—Jimenez's afterthoughts— which break the delicate tone and allusive appeal of such "pure" or "naked" poetry. So, students should compare both versions.

Sanchez Romeralo's introduction to *La realidad invisible* was clear and straightforward: it provided historical background to the volume, situated the poetry within Jimenez's poetic trajectory and briefly categorized its major themes and preoccupations. Martinez Torren's [sic] introduction meanders and is tendentious. He believes that Juan Ramon is a lay mystic, a late San Juan; accordingly, his discussions emphasize the "invisible" or celestial aspect of these poems but are scant on their "realidad," or terrestrial component. Hence, he avoids confronting numerous metaphors in the volume inspired by coitus. Also, his commentary is weakened by too frequent self-reference. However, there are useful sections in which he limits himself to reviewing previous interpretations of the concept "invisible reality" and to tracing its evolution in Jimenez's extensive prose writings. Also, I welcome, for its accessibility, the inclusion in the appendix of the poem "Nada"—"A veces, un gusto amargo, un olor malo"—a fragment of which introduces Carmen Laforet's *Nada* (1945).

La realidad invisible consists of three sections in which Jimenez struggled to fuse the "real" (life, love, house, relationships, grief and joy) with the "invisible" (dream, beauty, poetry, the other, the infinite, dying). It deserves a separate study, and it is to be hoped that Martinez Torren's edition with Catedra might inspire one.

Source: John C. Wilcox, Review of *La realidad invisible*, in *Bulletin of Hispanic Studies*, Vol. 80, No. 4, September 2003, p. 595.

Publishers Weekly

In the following review, the anonymous author explains that Jiménez believed that striving toward perfection helps one do one's absolute best.

Fastidious, prolific, hypochondriacal Andalusian poet Jimenez (1881–1958), who won a Nobel Prize in 1956, was an obsessive perfectionist, a mentor to Federico Garcia Lorca and Jorge Guillen, translator of Blake and Tagore, a self-exiled enemy of fascism who spent his last two decades in New York, Havana, Florida and Puerto Rico, indifferent to worldly success. This elegantly translated selection of his aphorisms, vignettes, prayers and poems, organized around such themes as self, nature, writing and memory, is a profound meditation on the quest for perfection in art, work and daily life. An idealist who believed that one person's striving for absolute perfection can lead to profound social change, Jimenez saw work as an essential means of self-definition and social renewal—a process that involves the harnessing of dream, instinct and reverie to practical intelligence. Maurer (*The Art of Worldly Wisdom*), a Vanderbilt University professor of Spanish, has fashioned a gem of a book, a fertile source of insights for perfection-seekers in many fields.

Source: Review of *The Complete Perfectionist: A Poetics of Work*, in *Publishers Weekly*, Vol. 244, No. 2, January 13, 1997, p. 62.

Patricia Monaghan

In the following review, Monaghan praises the collection The Complete Perfectionist *as embodying a "natural type of perfection."*

The Nobel Prize–winning Spanish poet Juan Ramon Jimenez sought perfection in his work. His was no stale and static perfection however, but an organic one that permitted deviations from regularity, and the pursuit of it was an ever-changing quest for the right action at the right time. For much of his life, Jimenez recorded his thoughts about this quest in aphorisms that redoubtable translator Maurer (his version of the seventeenth-century Jesuit Baltasar Gracian's *Art of Worldly Wisdom* [1992] was something of a bestseller) here gathers and categorizes. Maurer also provides ample context for Jimenez's maxims, so that we begin to know Jimenez as a person and a poet as well as a philosopher. The aphorisms are marvelous nuggets of wisdom—"Treat the least significant things you do as though they were permanent and they will endure," for example, and "When a noise breaks into your silence, make it immediately a natural part of your silence." Jimenez redefines perfectionism by embracing a marvelously natural type of perfection.

Source: Patricia Monaghan, Review of *The Complete Perfectionist: A Poetic of Work*, in *Booklist*, Vol. 93, No. 12, February 15, 1997, p. 994.

SOURCES

Barnette, W. Douglas, *A Study of the Works of Manuel Mantero: A Member of the Spanish Generation of 1950*, Edwin Mellen, 1995, p. 18.

Coke-Enguidanos, Mervyn, *Word and Work in the Poetry of Juan Ramon Jimenez*, Tamesis, 1982, pp. 97–99.

Cole, Leo R., *The Religious Instinct in the Poetry of Juan Ramón Jiménez*, Dolphin, 1967, p. 66.

Jaffe, Catherine, "Lyric Reading: Woman and Juan Ramón Jiménez," in *Hispania*, Vol. 74, No. 3, September 1990, pp. 593–604.

Jiménez, Juan Ramón, *The Complete Perfectionist: A Poetics of Work*, edited and translated by Christopher Mauer, Doubleday, 1990, pp. 51–60.

————, "I Am Not I," in *Lorca and Jiménez: Selected Poems*, translated by Robert Bly, Beacon, 1973, pp. 76–77.

————, Nobel Prize Banquet Speech, http://www.nobel prize.org/nobel_prizes/literature/laureates/1956/jimenez-speech.html (accessed June 10, 2016).

————, *Time & Space: A Poetic Autobiography*, edited and translated by Antonio T. de Nicolás, Paragon House, 1988.

Plotinus, *The Enneads*, translated by Stephen MacKenna, Penguin, 1991, p. 271.

Valéry, Paul, "Pure Poetry," in *The Art of Poetry*, translated by Denise Folliot, Bollingen Series XLV, Pantheon, 1948, Vol. 7, pp. 184–92.

Wallis, R. T., *Neoplatonism*, 2nd edition, Gerald Duckworth, 1995, pp. 52–53.

Young, Howard T., *The Line in the Margin: Juan Ramón Jiménez and His Readings in Blake, Shelley, and Yeats*, University of Wisconsin Press, 1980, pp. 77–78, 218, 247, 268.

FURTHER READING

Florit, Eugenion, *Introduction to Spanish Poetry: A Dual-Language Book*, Dover, 1991.
> This helpful introduction gives sample poems from the leading Spanish poets from the Middle Ages to the late twentieth century, introduced by short biographies of the authors.

Fogelquist, Donald F., *Juan Ramón Jiménez*, Twayne, 1976.
> This survey of Jiménez, intended primarily for students, is organized around the poet's biography, dealing with individual works where they fit in that chronology.

O'Meara, Dominic J., *Plotinus: An Introduction to the Enneads*, Clarendon, 1995.
> O'Meara is one of the most distinguished contemporary scholars of Neoplatonism. This volume serves as an introduction to the Neopaltonic metaphysics embraced by Jiménez.

Wilcox, John C., *Self and Image in Juan Ramón Jiménez: Modern and Post Modernist Readings*, University of Illinois Press, 1987.
> Wilcox's postmodernist reading of Jiménez divides his work into two periods, an earlier one dominated by a positive solar aestheticism and a later one dominated by a negative lunar aestheticism. He classes "I Am Not I" in the later period.

SUGGESTED SEARCH TERMS

Juan Ramón Jiménez

"I Am Not I" AND Jiménez

pure poetry

ultraist

symbolist

Generation of '98

Generation of '27

Neoplatonism

Incident

AMIRI BARAKA

1969

In Amiri Baraka's "Incident," first published in his 1969 collection *Black Magic*, a community left rattled by a man's murder helplessly repeat the details of what they know to be true—the killer, the gun, the victim falling to the ground, bleeding—without understanding the reason behind the death. The community's confusion in "Incident" reflects the distress of a nation caught in a series of assassinations, riots, and cultural uprisings in the 1960s. Especially significant for Baraka's development as a member of the Black Arts movement were the 1965 assassination of Malcolm X and the 1967 Newark riot. "Incident" encapsulates the violence of the time in which it was written yet remains undeniably relevant to American society today.

AUTHOR BIOGRAPHY

Baraka was born in Newark, New Jersey, on October 7, 1934, as Everett LeRoi Jones. After graduating from high school, he earned his bachelor's degree in English from Howard University in 1954. That year he joined the US Air Force, serving three years before he was dishonorably discharged after Communist literature was found in his possession. Baraka moved to Greenwich Village, where he became fast friends with Allen Ginsberg, joining the bohemian Beat movement. Along with his wife, Hettie Cohen,

Amiri Baraka (© *Richard Levine / Alamy Stock Photo*)

Baraka founded a literary magazine, *Yugen*, and he published his first volume of poetry, *Preface to a Twenty Volume Suicide Note*, in 1961 under the name LeRoi Jones, as which he was yet known.

In 1963 he published *Blues People: Negro Music in White America*, a highly regarded guide to blues and jazz history and culture in the United States. As the civil rights movement gained power, Baraka's work became more focused on race relations and often took on confrontational tones. In 1964 he received widespread recognition for his play *Dutchman*, in which a white woman baits a middle-class black man into an outburst of rage before murdering him on a subway car. The play won a *Village Voice* Obie Award for best off-Broadway play and was later adapted into a film.

Baraka became a devoted member of the Black Power movement following the assassination of Malcolm X in 1965. He divorced his wife, leaving her with their two children, and left the Greenwich Village bohemia in favor of Harlem.

To mark his departure from Beat poetry, he published two works of fiction: *The System of Dante's Hell* (1965) and *Tales* (1967). In Harlem, he founded the Black Arts movement, the creative arm of the Black Power movement, and opened the Black Arts Repertory Theatre/School in 1967. A haven for artistic expression, the theater featured open-air poetry readings, plays, concerts, and community classes in art, literature, music, history, and martial arts. Though it was short-lived, the theater inspired similar organizations to open throughout the country and had a considerable impact on diversifying American literature and art. Baraka's 1969 collection *Black Magic*, in which "Incident" first appeared, addressed his transformation from Beat poet to black nationalist with politically driven poems.

Baraka converted to Islam in the late 1960s, changing his name from LeRoi Jones to Ameer Barakat, later changed to Amiri Baraka. He married the poet Sylvia Robinson—later Amina Baraka—and began to get involved in politics. He worked on the campaign to elect the first African American mayor of Newark in 1970, and in 1972 he helped to organize the National Black Political Convention in Gary, Indiana. In 1980 he abandoned black nationalism in favor of Communism.

Beginning in 1985, Baraka taught at the State University of New York at Stony Brook for twenty years. He was named poet laureate of New Jersey in 2002. However, after a poem he had written in response to the September 11 terrorist attacks titled "Somebody Blew Up America" drew heated controversy, his position was abolished in 2003. Baraka died at the age of seventy-nine on January 9, 2014, in Newark, New Jersey.

POEM SUMMARY

The text used for this summary is from *Black Magic*, Bobbs-Merrill, 1969, p. 118. A version of the poem can be found on the following web page: http://www.poetryfoundation.org/poems-and-poets/poems/detail/42558.

"Incident" begins with the speaker saying that an unnamed man came back and shot another man. The man fell. He stumbled past a dark wood (or past dark wood) and fell to the ground, dying. Then he was dead, completely. He came to a full stop.

He died, bleeding, after being shot and falling to the ground. He died after falling, after being shot in the face by a bullet. When he was shot in the face, the bullet tearing his skin, blood sprayed onto the shooter in the gray light.

There are pictures of the dead man everywhere—presumably in the media, perhaps elsewhere as well. His restless spirit absorbs the light. However, he died in the dark, in a darkness more dark than his soul. When he died, everything was plunged with him blindly into darkness, falling down the dark stairs.

The people have no news of the man's killer, except that he returned from somewhere to kill the man. He shot only one time, into the victim's eyes, and left him to bleed until his blood ran out, departing quickly after.

Additionally, the people know the killer knew what he was doing. He was fast, silent, and skilled with a gun. They assume the victim knew his murderer. Apart from these scant facts, the haunting vision of the victim's sour expression caked in blood, and the surprise indicated by the position of his hands and fingers, the people know nothing.

THEMES

Death

Death courses through "Incident" in the narrator/community's repetitive listing of the details of the murder. As they work through what they know again and again, the man dies over and over, resurrected in their collective memory just to be shot again. The death of a man is upsetting by itself, but his violent death at the hands of another person whose motives remain unclear makes the death exceptional. In fact, this man's death is so exceptional as to be beyond normal comprehension. The speaker, a member of *we*—the community affected by the murder—claims to know nothing even after listing the many gruesome and terrifying details of the crime. Surely knowing these details counts as knowing something, but the word *nothing* itself in this context also suggests the nothingness of death: the unknowable. Nothingness is exactly what the community has witnessed—a man passing from existence into death, into nothing, his face frozen

in its last expression. Death is further emphasized by the alliteration of the letter *d* throughout the poem, especially in words related to death and darkness. The finality of the hard *d* sound only adds to the definitive theme of death, an inescapable and certain end, which the man faced in a mysterious if ultimately public way. Although they know exactly what happened in the physical act of the murder, the community does not know why the man died, why it had to be so, their confusion echoing the questions of a child first learning about death and struck by the injustice of it. Yet death cannot be stopped, and the poem's victim—whether he knew why he was targeted by his murderer or not—cannot answer the bewildered questions of the community. They are left to watch him die again and again in their mind's eye without ever knowing why.

Helplessness

In the act in question, the murderer proves skilled, so much so that the victim has no time to defend himself or flee. He is helpless to prevent his death, once the man comes back determined to kill him. The victim's hands are set in a position of surprise, while his expression is sour, as if he is at once shocked by and resigned to his fate. Either way, no one can save him. He is dead from the poem's first stanza onward.

The community, too, is helpless. They can neither erase from their memory what they know of the murder nor find closure through knowledge of the murderer's identity or his motive for the crime. Significantly, not only the murderer but also his victim goes unnamed in the poem, as if his name were stripped away by the violence of his death. This anonymity further emphasizes how little is known about the dead man. Although the community knows many details of the murder, some mundane but mostly horrific, they do not know the details that could help bring the murderer to justice, and they also do not know anything that could explain why the man was killed. They are helpless in the sense that they are not helpful. They have no critical information aside from the facts they repeat, mantra-like, in their shock.

Every character in the poem, from shooter to victim to the community, is helplessly caught in a culture of violence, as repetitive as the poem and just as focused on death, in which one man, dissatisfied with an argument, can simply return with a gun and open fire. The poem's repetitive

TOPICS FOR FURTHER STUDY

- Read Jerry Spinelli's young-adult novel *Maniac Magee* (1990). How are racial tensions and violence presented in the novel? What forms of prejudice or discrimination does Magee encounter in his search for a home? What thematic similarities can you find between the novel and "Incident"? Organize your thoughts into an essay.

- Can you find five recent stories in the news that parallel the events of "Incident"? Do online research to find local and national articles with similar details. Create a blog in which each of your posts is devoted to one of the articles you have found and a discussion of the details the story shares with Baraka's poem. Be sure to make a minimum of five posts and include links to the articles you have found. Free blog space is available at Blogger.

- Visit Poetry Slam Inc online to learn more about performance poetry. Compose a free-verse poem in which you use repetition and alliteration to describe an event you have witnessed and then film yourself performing your poem in the style of a slam poet. Upload the video to YouTube in preparation for presenting it to your class.

- Choose a different poem in *Black Magic* to read and explicate. Write an essay in which you summarize the poem; discuss the major themes, style, and historical context; and draw comparisons with "Incident." Do the poem you chose and "Incident" share language, images, subject matter, thematic elements, and other facets? Conclude your essay with a brief discussion of which poem you prefer and why.

- In small groups, choose one of the three-line stanzas in "Incident" to examine more closely. What information is given in the stanza that does not appear elsewhere in the work? What examples of repetition or alliteration can you find? Which of the poem's characters (killer, victim, community) are included in the stanza and what are their roles in the action? Make a list of your discoveries in preparation for a class discussion on the poem's structure.

---

convulsions, as if the text itself is in its death throes, reflect in one incident the problems of a violent society as a whole.

Violence

The violence of the victim's death is described in vivid detail. The action verbs—*shot, dying, bleeding, tumbled, sprayed, stumbling*—indicate the excessive force of the shooter and the reeling confusion of the victim as both play their role in the murder. The shooter, the speaker says, is practiced in violence and an efficient, effective killer. However, no matter how quickly or skillfully the deed is done, he still leaves the scene covered in his victim's blood. The blood runs throughout the poem, which is otherwise deeply shaded in black, white, and gray. The shocks of color imitate the shock of violence. The fact that the shooter stays to watch his victim bleed to death indicates his comfort level with this kind of violence, the kind that leaves the community reeling. The victim is shot in the face, the shooter aiming into his glare. This is an unfair fight, in which one man is armed with a glare and the other a gun. The damage the bullet causes is described in minute detail. After he has died, the man wears a sour expression, with his hands raised in surprise or perhaps in surrender to the imminent violence. The murderer escapes, while the victim is left on the ground to bleed, the community to repeat the details of the violence as if to coat themselves in it and be camouflaged for when death, like the shooter, comes back.

The style of the poem reflects how shaken people are after witnessing the incident (©ja-images / Shutterstock.com)

STYLE

Repetition

The most immediately evident stylistic feature of "Incident" is the poem's reliance on repetition, which begins in the very first line. The fact that the killer shot the victim is repeated four times in the first stanza. The fact that the victim dies and thus is dead is repeated three times in the third line alone. The facts of the incident are repeated as if being passed back and forth between witnesses, all verifying the story with the others while trying to process what they have learned of the murder. The repeated information is clung to because of how little else is known. Without names, motives, or a suspect, the only facts that remain are those that are the most concrete and observable: a man shot another man, who fell down dead. The rest is a mystery.

Alliteration

Alliteration is a poetic device in which a sound or letter is repeated. In "Incident," the repeating *d* sound is an example of alliteration. The effect of

alliteration in "Incident" is to emphasize the death of the shooting victim through words like *dying, dead, died, darker, darkness,* and *down.* These words, like the hard *d* sound itself, suggest an inescapable finality, a change of state from life to death, from light to dark, from up to down. This is the transformation the man experiences as he, dying, falls down in the dark. The alliterative effect gives the poem an incantatory rhythm, further heightened by the many repeated images, so that it resembles a spell or song.

Enjambment

Enjambment occurs in a poem when a sentence or phrase is interrupted by a line break and continued in the next line. Enjambment causes the reader's eye to move more quickly down the page in search of the end of the interrupted thought. In addition, it causes a jolting, disjointed sensation, as sentences do not pause or end where expected. "Incident" features enjambment throughout the text, adding a further layer of disorientation to the repeating images. The choppy effect of the

COMPARE
&
CONTRAST

- **1969:** Baraka's Black Arts Repertory Theatre/School, established in 1965 as the center around which the Black Arts movement would revolve, has failed owing to issues of funding and internal disagreement. However, the idea of a creative outpost for the voices of authors, playwrights, and poets disenfranchised by the dominant culture spreads widely. Similar enclaves of African American artists and writers form throughout the country, harnessing their combined power to stage readings, plays, and concerts, as well as to teach community classes in the creative arts. Though the Black Arts Repertory Theatre/School is no more, the Black Arts movement remains strong, effecting change on the local and national levels.

  Today: The Black Arts movement and the Black Arts Repertory Theatre/School have inspired other minority groups to use their blueprint in order to establish cultural and artistic presences. LGBTQ artists, Latinos and Latin Americans, Asians and Asian Americans, and Native Americans, among others, have become more visible in a literary landscape once dominated almost exclusively by white males. In addition to adding their voices to the cultural conversation, these literary and artistic groups perform community outreach to help others express themselves creatively, using the same methodologies as the Black Arts movement.

- **1969:** Baraka works tirelessly on the mayoral campaign of Kenneth A. Gibson, who becomes, in 1970, the first African American mayor of Newark, New Jersey. The poverty-stricken city continues to suffer from high tension between citizens and the police force in the wake of the riots of 1967, which left twenty-six people dead and over one thousand injured and caused ten million dollars in property damage.

  Today: Baraka's son, Ras Baraka, is elected mayor of Newark on May 13, 2013. He is sworn into office on July 1, 2014, for a four-year term. Newark remains a city deeply troubled by poverty.

- **1969:** Following the assassination of Malcolm X in 1965, the widespread race riots of the 1960s, and the assassination of Martin Luther King Jr. in 1968, the civil rights movement and Black Power movement continue to fight for the end of discrimination against African Americans and the acknowledgment of their equal rights as citizens of the United States.

  Today: In the summer of 2014, the shooting of Michael Brown by Officer Darren Wilson sparks days of both violent and nonviolent protest in Ferguson, Missouri, as well as across the country. Michael Brown's death, on the heels of the controversial 2012 death of Trayvon Martin, an unarmed high-school student shot dead by George Zimmerman, a member of a neighborhood watch who was acquitted of the murder, gives rise to the Black Lives Matter campaign, a national effort to raise awareness of police brutality against African Americans.

enjambment mimics the movement of the victim as he stumbles after being shot before falling to the ground. In addition, the enjambment emphasizes the community's shock and confusion by making the poem purposefully more confusing to the reader, so that the reader, like the speaker, is left searching for meaning.

HISTORICAL CONTEXT

Black Arts Movement

The Black Arts movement was the artistic wing of the Black Power movement, founded by Baraka in the 1960s. In response to the proliferation of art, literature, and visual iconography based

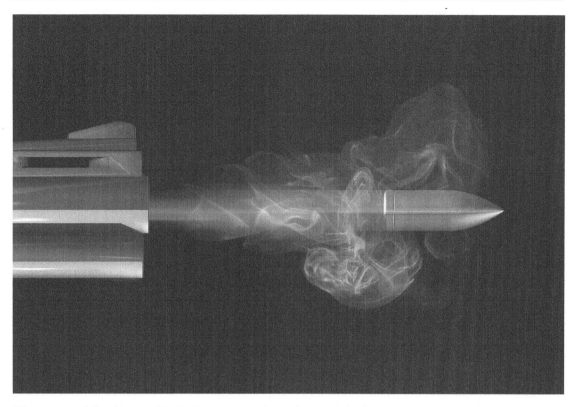

The image of the unstoppable bullet captures the violence of the scene (©*Phil McDonald | Shutterstock.com*)

on and made by the dominant white culture, the Black Arts movement tasked itself with creating an entirely new aesthetic to reflect African American experience. Larry Neal, one of the movement's most integral members, summarized its mission in the *Drama Review* in 1968 in "The Black Arts Movement":

> It envisions an art that speaks directly to the needs and aspirations of Black America. In order to perform this task, the Black Arts Movement proposes a radical reordering of the western cultural aesthetic. It proposes a separate symbolism, mythology, critique, and iconology.

On April 30, 1965, Baraka opened the Black Arts Repertory Theatre/School in Harlem, with the financial backing of friends as well as a government grant through the Harlem Youth organization HARYOU-ACT. The theater provided community outreach as well as classes in history, poetry, painting, martial arts, and music. Members staged poetry readings, dances, concerts, and plays written and performed by African Americans for African American audiences. Although the theater closed within the

year due to a combination of funding issues and disagreements between the members, Baraka opened Spirit House in Newark to continue the theater's mission. Additionally, similar organizations were opened around the country in order to further the cause of Black Arts visibility and independence. Members of the Black Arts movement include Maya Angelou, Gwendolyn Brooks, Nikki Giovanni, Marvin X, Calvin Hicks, Rita Dove, Lorenzo Thomas, Tom Dent, Ron Karenga, Mari Evans, Sonia Sanchez, and many more.

The Assassination of Malcolm X

Malcolm X was one of the most influential African American leaders in the history of the United States. After his father was murdered and his mother was committed to a mental hospital, Malcolm X entered the foster-care system. A deeply troubled youth, he was arrested at the age of twenty for larceny and sentenced to prison. While imprisoned he joined the Nation of Islam, a controversial Muslim black supremacy group, in which, upon his release, Malcolm X became a prominent leader. Rejecting the message of peace, nonviolence, and integration put forth by Martin Luther King Jr., the most prominent leader of the civil rights movement, Malcolm X believed that blacks should attempt not to appeal to white sensibilities, but rather to embrace their own identity and live separately. His fame grew immeasurably, until he was a professional speaker and household name, overshadowing more senior members of the Nation of Islam. He grew disillusioned with the Nation after learning that its leader, Elijah Muhammad, was disobeying his own religious teachings. Malcolm X officially left the Nation of Islam on March 8, 1964. Soon after, he began receiving threats to his safety. His home was firebombed on February 14, 1965. Then, on February 21, at a regular speaking engagement for his Organization of Afro-American Unity at the Audubon Ballroom in Manhattan, three members of the Nation of Islam charged the stage and shot Malcolm X to death.

Scott Sherman, in "A Turbulent Life: On Amiri Baraka" for *Dissent* magazine, writes: "The murder of Malcolm X in 1965 radicalized Jones. He jettisoned his Beat identity, left Greenwich Village for Harlem, and eventually changed his name to Amiri Baraka. . . . Black liberation was his new fixation." Malcolm X's assassination was followed by a series of riots as racial tensions escalated in major cities throughout the 1960s. Baraka himself was badly beaten in the 1967 Newark riots, in which twenty-six people were killed, sparked by a possible incident of police brutality against an African American cab driver. Amid the chaos of the riots, the Black Power movement emerged, with Malcolm X as the inspiration. The Black Arts movement was heavily influenced by Malcolm X's energetic oratory style, and tapes of his speeches were played regularly at the Black Arts Repertory Theatre/School.

CRITICAL OVERVIEW

Baraka was awarded the Langston Hughes Award, the Rockefeller Foundation Award for Drama, the PEN/Faulkner Award, and the Before Columbus Lifetime Achievement Award. He served as the poet laureate of New Jersey from 2002 to 2003, was a member of the American Academy of Arts and Letters, and received fellowships from the Guggenheim Foundation and the National Endowment for the Arts.

He left behind a body of work that spans decades, genres, movements, and styles. With his habit of total creative reinvention combined with a history of controversy that often eclipses his literary work, no two critics agree on the subject of Baraka's poetry, as Margalit Fox remarks in her obituary of him for the *New York Times*: "Among reviewers, there was no firm consensus on Mr. Baraka's literary merit, and the mercurial nature of his work seems to guarantee that there can never be." In *All Things Considered* on NPR, Neda Ulaby discussed the effect of the poet's ever-shifting identity and the seemingly paradoxical confidence with which he changed his mind: "Over his life, Amiri Baraka would express an extremely broad range of beliefs— some offensive, some achingly beautiful."

No matter his controversial image, Baraka's commitment to and success in changing the literary and social landscape for African American artists cannot be denied. In his obituary for Baraka in the *Washington Post*, Matt Schudel writes: "As much as anyone, Mr. Baraka helped define a modern, militant sense of self-identity and empowerment among African Americans seeking to break free of white cultural and social norms."

In an interview with Amy Goodman and Juan González on *Democracy Now!* following Baraka's death, the poet Sonia Sanchez mourned the passing of her friend and colleague in the Black Arts movement: "His words carried the spirit of creation. You know, he sewed himselves into the sleeves of history and change." William J. Harris summarizes the change that Sanchez speaks of in his introduction to *The LeRoi Jones/Amiri Baraka Reader*: "Acting as an energetic artist-critic-spokesman, Baraka almost single-handedly changed both the nature and the form of post–World War II Afro-American literature."

Harris goes on to say, on the subject of his poetry: "Baraka has also created an original body of work that belongs in the forefront of innovative avant-garde writing, regardless of ethnic background." In his preface to the Baraka collection *SOS: Poems 1961–2013*, Paul Vangelisti succinctly summarizes the legacy of a man at once suspected and respected by the literary establishment. He writes that Baraka is simply "one of the most important and least understood American poets of the past century."

CRITICISM

Amy L. Miller

Miller is a graduate of the University of Cincinnati. In the following essay, she discusses how Baraka renders the effects of gun violence in a community through broken verse in his poem "Incident."

In "Incident," Baraka uses repetition, alliteration, and enjambment to unsettle the reader's easy progress through the poem in an imitation of the dying man's last moments. Rather than allow the reader to scan through the poem at an even pace, Baraka uses unpredictable syntax to slow down the reader's eye and enjambment to speed up the eye. This causes an uneven, jolting rhythm that brings to mind the victim's stumbling. In addition, the excessive repetition of information and alliteration of words related to dying and darkness make the poem's grim subject matter inescapable. There is subtlety in the poem, but not in the case of its major themes. Instead, Baraka forces the reader to confront the death of the victim alongside the community. The reader joins the collective *we*, after hearing the details of the murder, because the reader now knows all that can be known. *We* may be close enough to know the victim's last expression, but *we* can get no closer, separated from the action by the nature of the collective consciousness of the poem. While the victim and the murderer are distinct individuals with private, unknowable information about the crime, *we* know only what can be observed on a superficial level, and those observations—unlike the knowledge of the victim and murderer—are picked over in the poem as if to uncover something new. "Incident" defines violence as the loss of knowledge. As the murderer stands over his victim to watch his blood run out, he is simultaneously watching the man's ability to identify him, to explain what happened, and to speak the truth drain away.

As a member of the Black Arts movement, Baraka aimed in his poetry to express the experiences of African Americans frequently ignored or misunderstood by the mainstream media of the 1960s. "Incident" accomplishes this goal in portraying an act of gun violence through the eyes of the community affected by the crime rather than through the language of an objective journalist listing the details. While an article in a newspaper might summarize the events of

> WHILE THE VICTIM AND THE MURDERER ARE DISTINCT INDIVIDUALS WITH PRIVATE, UNKNOWABLE INFORMATION ABOUT THE CRIME, *WE* KNOW ONLY WHAT CAN BE OBSERVED ON A SUPERFICIAL LEVEL, AND THOSE OBSERVATIONS—UNLIKE THE KNOWLEDGE OF THE VICTIM AND MURDERER—ARE PICKED OVER IN THE POEM AS IF TO UNCOVER SOMETHING NEW."

"Incident" in a headline as "Man shot and killed, police search for killer," the community's retelling is fearful, confused, and fraught with pain. The palpably frantic testimony of the speaker resembles an interview with a shocked witness. In fact, "Incident" is a crime report written entirely from the witnesses' or survivors' side, with the reporter's objectivity excised. The dominant voice in the poem is the community's voice. What *we* have seen is all that can be known. In this way, the poem indirectly challenges the idea of objectivity itself: when every party involved in a murder (victim, murderer, reacting community) has a subjective experience, why would a community outsider report on the event in static terms? This subtle rejection of mainstream white society's approach to reporting crime in an African American community illustrates why the collection in which Baraka published "Incident" is so highly regarded, as Vangelisti writes: "*Black Magic* [is] the quintessential volume of his Nationalist period and one of the most influential publications of the Black Arts movement." Baraka achieves a black aesthetic in "Incident" in focusing on the internal struggle of the community exclusively.

The poem's narrative collapses on itself already in the first stanza, overcome by the crime. The word *shot* appears four times in the stanza's three sentences. Although the victim was shot only once by the murderer, the poem shoots him again and again. The man dies in every stanza through the power of the community's obsessive retelling. This obsession, illustrated not only by the constant repetition of

WHAT DO I READ NEXT?

- Belinda Rochelle's young-adult poetry anthology *Words with Wings: A Treasury of African-American Poetry and Art* (2001) pairs twenty poems with twenty works of art by notable African American poets and artists from the nineteenth century to the present day. Poets featured include Rita Dove, Paul Lawrence Dunbar, Countee Cullen, Jacob Lawrence, and many others.

- *The Autobiography of Malcolm X* (1987), as told to Alex Haley, tells the surprising true tale of Malcolm Little, a thief and misguided youth who, after serving time in prison, emerged into the world as Malcolm X, a luminary of the Nation of Islam preaching self-reliance to African Americans and growing to become famous as well as infamous for his fiery rhetoric.

- Baraka's *Dutchman & The Slave: Two Plays* (1964) combines two of his early plays on the subject of race. Winner of the Obie Award for best off-Broadway play the year of its debut in 1964, *Dutchman* tells the story of a white woman and black man driving each other to acts of rage and violence on the subway. In *The Slave*, first performed the same year, a black revolutionary leader breaks into the house of his white ex-wife and her new husband.

- Originally published in 1984, Sonia Sanchez's *Homegirls & Handgrenades* was awarded an American Book Award. A member of the Black Arts movement, Sanchez writes with charismatic power about the lives of impoverished African American women who retain a sense of dignity, community, and optimism against the stresses of a society that often seems blind to their existence.

- *The August Sleepwalker* (1990), by China's most influential voice of government protest, Bei Dao, collects the early work of the now exiled poet, who is considered partly responsible for inciting the student protests in Tiananmen Square in 1989 that led to an infamous massacre when soldiers opened fire on the gathering. Bei Dao's surrealist, individualistic poetry flies in the face of a government based on collectivist obedience.

- In *The Collected Poems of Langston Hughes* (1994), over eight hundred of Hughes's poems, some never before published, are collected and annotated by Arnold Rampersad and David E. Roessel. A star of the Harlem Renaissance, Hughes is a master of language and style, whether his subject is tragic or comic, familiar or profound. His unique voice has earned him an incontestable seat among the best American poets of all time.

- *The Collected Poetry of Nikki Giovanni, 1968–1998* (2003) combines five of her previously published collections into one extensive volume. Her revolutionary work as a member of the Black Arts movement and outspoken hero of the underrepresented and underappreciated has made her into a champion of the common people, a poet-heroine who can find the extraordinary in the most ordinary of lives. A predecessor of the slam poets of today, she is particularly well known for her exuberant poetry readings.

- Maya Angelou's *The Complete Poetry* (2015) collects the work of an inspirational icon of black women's independence and power. Her poetry fans the fires of passion just as often as it soothes old wounds, and through it all Angelou's unforgettably original voice sings a song of freedom.

- *Transfigurations: Collected Poems* (2000), by Jay Wright, weaves African American past and present together along with Mexican, European, African, and Native American influence in search of a shared human spirituality. A former jazz musician and member of the Black Arts movement, Wright has an unparalleled ear for rhythm and language.

information but also by the poem's alliteration, is a coping mechanism against the victim's horrific death. By controlling the narrative, the community feels control over an incident that was truly out of their control. By knowing the facts of the death, the community can pretend to have some control over their lives—lives in which a murder so gruesome could occur, and the killer walk away—when the facts of the matter point toward the opposite. The person with the most control over the situation is the murderer, yet even he is subject to the chaos he has created when the victim's blood stains his clothes.

The alliterative effect of words related to death and darkness drive the poem's stumbling rhythm, the repetitions hypnotic but not calming. The poem becomes a morbid incantation, appropriate for a collection titled *Black Magic*, as Harris writes: "[The] blackening and politicalization of Baraka's art is formal as well as thematic. The poetic line becomes longer as the verse imitates the chant." Spoken by the community, the chant bears witness to the death of a man who was at once a member of their collective group and an individual. He, like them, does not have a name. However, unlike the *we*, he acts alone. He is described as the owner of a dark soul, but not a soul darker than death. The murderer's soul, however, may indeed be darker. He is imagined watching the death of his enemy passionlessly, in no hurry to flee the scene of his crime.

Vangelisti writes: "Masterful turn after masterful turn, Baraka drives the stakes higher, pushing one to feel the sounds of an increasingly discomforting, ridiculous, and monstrous world." The murderer steals away in the night with the knowledge the community desires, having stolen it from the victim at the cost of his life. With the victim's voice silenced, the story will remain incomplete forever. The killer, if caught, would tell his side. The community could recite what they know. But the victim's knowledge is lost to the world through the violence of his death. Pictures of the dead man are circulated as if he were a missing person who could be returned by a watchful neighbor, but these pictures only suck up the light, reminding the community of their own helplessness. They are forced to admit, by the poem's end, despite the impressive amount of information gleaned from the scene of the crime, that they in fact know

nothing. They are the community, not the participants, and anything less than the real reasons behind the conflict, the felt emotions of killer and victim, is nothing more than what a newsman from outside the community might rattle off, standing in front of the police tape and flashing lights at the scene of the crime.

The poem is written in shades of black: light absorbed by the victim's spirit, gray light, shadows, and darkness are the colors used to paint the portrait of this murder, with the exception of the victim's red blood—the ultimate symbol of violence. The scene is lit dimly, owing not only to the nature of the darkness in which it takes place but also to the absence of knowledge illuminating the actions of the two men. Both murderer and victim take light away: the murderer through his flight from the scene along with any explanation for what happened and the victim through his spirit's thirsty drinking of light from those who would search for answers. As a result, the community is left in the dark. The poem mimics this in remaining frustratingly elusive despite being written in accessible language. The words themselves are simple, but their organization is purposefully disjointed. Nearly every line of the poem ends in enjambment, disorienting the reader so as to further the sense of distress caused by the poem's thematic and stylistic elements. Vangelisti writes: "Baraka's lyrical gift remained always *of* and *for* the world, and the people's music that daily inspired it." This is in part the dark music of fear and death, an unknowable world, and a mysterious end. The poem is, for all its darkness, nevertheless an accurate depiction of a world in which gun violence is a reality, in which the pettiest of arguments can be settled instantaneously and permanently, depicted in the poem by the murderer's action of coming back. The murderer left the scene to get his gun before the action of the poem begins, and then, as the poem begins, he comes back to shoot the man.

Baraka illustrates the way in which violence in a community robs it of knowledge and replaces that knowledge with fear. Left to repeat the details of the crime to each other, the speaker, part of a *we*, admits to knowing nothing, surrendering to the chaos of the world in which they live. A reflection of society in the turbulent 1960s, "Incident" remains relevant to society today, as the United States continues to struggle

The victim falling down the stairs makes the death seem that much more tragic *(©Roman Tsubin / Shutterstock.com)*

with gun violence in both major cities and small communities across the country. Everyone loses in "Incident": the victim dies wearing a bitter expression, the murderer must flee or risk capture, and the community struggles to process the crime. Baraka ensures, through his ingenious mimicking of the victim's final moments in the poem's repetitive yet unpredictable style, that the reader shares the community's anxiety and distress following the unexplained murder of a man so close to home.

Source: Amy L. Miller, Critical Essay on "Incident," in *Poetry for Students*, Gale, Cengage Learning, 2017.

SOURCES

"About the Black Lives Matter Network," Black Lives Matter website, http://blacklivesmatter.com/about/ (accessed April 26, 2016).

Ali, Zaheer, "What Really Happened to Malcolm X?," CNN website, February 17, 2015, http://www.cnn.com/2015/02/17/opinion/ali-malcolm-x-assassination-anniversary/ (accessed April 26, 2016).

Als, Hilton, "Amiri Baraka's First Family," in *New Yorker*, January 11, 2014, http://www.newyorker.com/books/page-turner/amiri-barakas-first-family (accessed April 26, 2016).

"Amiri Baraka," Poetry Foundation website, http://www.poetryfoundation.org/bio/amiri-baraka (accessed April 26, 2016).

"Biography: An Abridged Biography of Malcolm X," Malcolm X website, http://malcolmx.com/biography/ (accessed April 27, 2016).

Fox, Margalit, "Amiri Baraka, Polarizing Poet and Playwright, Dies at 79," in *New York Times*, January 9, 2014, http://www.nytimes.com/2014/01/10/arts/amiri-baraka-polarizing-poet-and-playwright-dies-at-79.html?_r=0 (accessed April 26, 2016).

Goodman, Amy, Juan González, Larry Hamm, Felipe Luciano, Sonia Sanchez, and Komozi Woodard, "Amiri Baraka (1934–2014): Poet-Playwright-Activist Who Shaped Revolutionary Politics, Black Culture," *Democracy Now!* website, January 10, 2014, http://www.democracynow.org/2014/1/10/amiri_baraka_1934_2014_poet_playwright (accessed April 26, 2016).

Harris, William J., ed., Introduction to *The LeRoi Jones/Amiri Baraka Reader*, Basic Books, 2009, pp. xvii–xxx.

Hartman, David, and Barry Lewis, "A Walk through Newark," Thirteen website, http://www.thirteen.org/newark/history3.html (accessed April 26, 2016).

Jones, LeRoi, "Incident," in *Black Magic*, Bobbs-Merrill, 1969, p. 118.

Mack, Dwayne, "Baraka, Amiri (1934–2014)," BlackPast.org, http://www.blackpast.org/aah/baraka-amiri-1934 (accessed April 26, 2016).

Neal, Larry, "The Black Arts Movement," Part 1, in *Drama Review*, Summer 1968, http://nationalhumanities center.org/pds/maai3/community/text8/blackartsmovement.pdf (accessed April 26, 2016).

Salaam, Kalamu ya, "Historical Background of the Black Arts Movement (BAM)—Part II," in *Black Collegian*, https://web.archive.org/web/20000420003430/http://www.black-collegian.com/african/bam2_200.shtml (accessed April 26, 2016).

Schudel, Matt, "Amiri Baraka, Poet and Firebrand, Dies at 79," in *Washington Post*, January 9, 2014, https://www.washingtonpost.com/entertainment/books/amiri-baraka-poet-and-firebrand-dies-at-79/2014/01/09/930897d2-796e-11e3-af7f-13bf0e9965f6_story.html (accessed April 26, 2016).

Sherman, Scott, "A Turbulent Life: On Amiri Baraka," in *Dissent*, Spring 2002, https://www.dissentmagazine.org/article/a-turbulent-life (accessed April 26, 2016).

Ulaby, Neda, "Amiri Baraka's Legacy Both Controversial and Achingly Beautiful," NPR website, January 9, 2014, http://www.npr.org/2014/01/09/261101520/amiri-baraka-poet-and-co-founder-of-black-arts-movement-dies-at-79 (accessed April 26, 2016).

Vangelisti, Paul, Preface to *SOS: Poems 1961–2013*, by Amiri Baraka, Grove Press, 2014, pp. xiii–xix.

Williamson, Marcus, "Amiri Baraka: Writer," in *Independent* (London, England), January 10, 2014, http://www.independent.co.uk/news/obituaries/amiri-baraka-writer-9052670.html (accessed April 26, 2016).

Wulfhorst, Ellen, "Mayor Faces Complexities of Poverty, Crime in Reviving N.J.'s Largest City," Reuters website, June 25, 2015, http://www.reuters.com/article/us-usa-newark-baraka-idUSKBN0P51AL20150625 (accessed April 26, 2016).

FURTHER READING

Baraka, Amiri, *The Autobiography of LeRoi Jones*, Lawrence Hill Books, 1997.

When it was first published in 1984, Baraka's autobiography suffered from cuts made to the text by the publisher. The 1997 edition recovers what was initially left out and includes a new introduction by the author. Baraka tells the story of his childhood in Newark, his struggle with both university and military institutions, his rise to prominence among the Beats through his friendship with Allen Ginsberg, his reinvention as a founder of the Black Arts movement following the assassination of Malcolm X, and his further evolution into an advocate of Communism, as well as the details of his marriages and family life.

Jones, LeRoi, *Blues People: Negro Music in White America*, Harper Perennial, 1999.

Originally published in 1963, Baraka's celebrated guide to blues in America traces the genre from the arrival of African slaves on American shores to the civil rights movement of the 1960s, weaving the history of African Americans' fight for civil rights into the development of blues, jazz, and rock 'n' roll. Baraka explains how, along with the white American population's embrace of black music, African American values and culture passed into the mainstream.

Mumford, Kevin, *Newark: A History of Race, Rights, and Riots in America*, New York University Press, 2008.

This study of Newark from its founding in 1666 to the present day explores the roles of the civil rights and Black Power movements in the shaping of the city's proud culture, as well as the violence and endemic poverty that have plagued its streets. Mumford draws on public and private documents, letters, flyers, campaign posters, photographs, and newspapers in his survey of Newark's history.

Ongiri, Amy Abugo, *Spectacular Blackness: The Cultural Politics of the Black Power Movement and the Search for a Black Aesthetic*, University of Virginia Press, 2010.

Ongiri uncovers the history of the Black Power movement's creation of a visible black aesthetic presence in the arts through the development of visual icons, film, music, art, prose, and poetry dedicated to reflecting the African American experience.

Smethurst, James, *The Black Arts Movement: Literary Nationalism in the 1960s and 1970s*, University of North Carolina Press, 2005.

Smethurst recounts the formation, rise, and impact of the Black Arts movement, with a particular focus on regional manifestations of this powerful force of change. Putting the movement in the context of the political and social atmosphere of the United States following World War II, as well as its place within the civil rights and Black Power movements, *The Black Arts Movement* is a thorough study of how the dedicated artists of the movement made a place for themselves within the literary landscape of their country.

SUGGESTED SEARCH TERMS

Amiri Baraka

LeRoi Jones

LeRoi Jones AND Black Magic

LeRoi Jones AND "Incident"

Black Arts movement AND Amiri Baraka

Beat poetry

Black Power AND Black Arts

Newark AND poverty AND riots

Malcolm X and black liberation

In the Bazaars of Hyderabad

SAROJINI NAIDU

1912

Sarojini Naidu's "In the Bazaars of Hyderabad" (1912) can be approached on many levels. It is most often appreciated for its glittering and sensuous descriptions of the products of Indian craftspeople, but a deeper reading reveals its political and even philosophical significance in the movement for Indian independence. Naidu purposely wrote the work to appeal to the English taste for orientalism and exoticism and to offer an ideal vision of a free India. This kind of skillful balancing of opposites made Naidu the most popular as well as the most important Indian poet of her generation to write in English. Dissatisfied with mere literary achievement, however, Naidu abandoned poetry in 1917 and became one of the leading followers of Mahatma Gandhi in his struggle for Indian Home Rule and an important politician in her own right. The poem is an important example of Indian English literature, which refers to works written by Indians in English as opposed to the work of English writers about India, such as E. M. Forester's *A Passage to India*. The poem is available in Naidu's *The Bird of Time: Songs of Life, Death & the Spring*, republished in 2015 by Andesite Press.

AUTHOR BIOGRAPHY

Naidu (née Chattopadhyay) was born on February 13, 1879, in Hyderabad, India. Her father, Aghore Nath Chattopadhyay, was born into a

Sarojini Naidu and Mahatma Gandhi *(©Imagno / Getty Images)*

poor family but went through the Indian educational system on scholarship and completed a PhD in chemistry at the University of Edinburgh in 1877. He immediately set to work founding and serving as the first head of Hyderabad College (renamed Nizam College), the equivalent of a college at Oxford or Cambridge University. Naidu's mother, Barada Sundari Devi, was a poet who wrote in Bengali and was an early advocate of Indian independence. Although both of Naidu's parents came from poor backgrounds, they were of the Brahman caste, the highest rank in the social-religious system that stratified traditional Indian society. Naidu's father had a definite career path in mind for his daughter, to become a mathematician or a physical scientist like him. Naidu's interest in literature made this impossible. Moreover, her father sent her to study in Madras to separate her from a suitor, Govindarajulu Naidu, who, though he was a medical doctor, was of a lower caste. Naidu nevertheless married him in 1898.

There were at least two periods when Naidu missed several years of education because of illness, and she never took a degree. In 1895, Naidu, like her father, went to Britain to study and attended King's College, London. There she met the poet and critic Edmund Gosse, who became her patron and her connection to the literary and artistic world of London. Following Gosse's advice to become what England expected of what he called an Indian poetess, Naidu wrote three books of verse that became best sellers in England as well as in India. The first of these was *The Golden Threshold* (1905). The second, *The Bird of Time: Songs of Life, Death & the Spring* (1912) contained "In the Bazaars of Hyderabad." The third was *The Broken Wing: Songs of Love, Death & Destiny* (1917).

Like many Indians, Naidu was shocked by the partition of the state of Bengal in 1905. The partition was an open attempt by the British to create separate and hostile Muslim and Hindu communities in India to make British rule easier by playing the two factions against each other. Naidu spent increasing amounts of time touring and lecturing on independence but also on social welfare and the rights of women. She became a member of the Congress Party and as a nationally famous figure was welcomed into the inner circle around its leaders Gandhi, Muhammad Ali Jinnah, and Jawaharlal Nehru. Gandhi famously called her the nightingale of India. After 1917, Naidu announced that she no longer had time for poetry and devoted herself entirely to her political work. She was awarded the Hind Kesari medal in 1928.

After independence was achieved in 1947, Naidu became the governor of the United Provinces of Agra and Oudh (later called Uttar Pradesh), the most populous state in India. She died of a heart attack working at her desk in the capital in Lucknow on March 2, 1949. In 1961 Naidu's daughter Padmaja (who also became a provincial governor in India) published a posthumous volume of her mother's poetry, *The Feather of the Dawn*. Many hospitals and university schools in India are named after Naidu, and her works are central to the Indian education system.

POEM TEXT

What do you sell, O ye merchants?
Richly your wares are displayed.
Turbans of crimson and silver,
Tunics of purple brocade,
Mirrors with panels of amber,   5
Daggers with handles of jade.

What do you weigh, O ye vendors?
Saffron and lentil and rice.
What do you grind, O ye maidens?
Sandalwood, henna, and spice.   10
What do you call, O ye pedlars?
Chessmen and ivory dice.

What do you make, O ye goldsmiths?
Wristlet and anklet and ring,
Bells for the feet of blue pigeons,   15
Frail as a dragon-fly's wing,
Girdles of gold for the dancers,
Scabbards of gold for the king.

What do you cry, O ye fruitmen?
Citron, pomegranate, and plum.   20
What do you play, O musicians?
Cithár, sarangi, and drum.
What do you chant, O magicians?
Spells for the æons to come.

What do you weave, O ye flower-girls   25
With tassels of azure and red?
Crowns for the brow of a bridegroom,
Chaplets to garland his bed,
Sheets of white blossoms new-gathered
To perfume the sleep of the dead.   30

POEM SUMMARY

The text used for this summary is from *The Bird of Time: Songs of Life, Death & the Spring*, William Heinemann, 1912, pp. 62–63. A version of the poem can be found on the following web page: https://archive.org/stream/birdoftime00-naid#page/62/mode/2up.

Naidu's "In the Bazaars of Hyderabad" is a lyric poem divided into five unnumbered stanzas of six lines each. It is a conversation between customers in the bazaars, who ask the merchants what they have for sale, and the merchants, who respond with lists of wares. A bazaar is a traditional open-air market where merchants set up displays to sell their goods. Hyderabad, like any large city, had several bazaars, typically one large one in a central location but also smaller ones in individual neighborhoods. The bazaar is based on an economic model whereby local craftspeople sell their products directly to the public. (It may be that the seller works only part-time and sells part-time or that a spouse or other family member sells the goods.) Some goods, especially in the main bazaar, may be brought from elsewhere by professional merchants who buy and resell them; these would be in the minority.

Stanza 1

Stanza 1 begins with the most general question the shoppers ask: What is being sold? Even here the questioner comments on the visually appealing displays that the merchants have laid out. The merchants' answers begin to develop a highly visual emphasis on beauty. They are selling, not coincidentally, typically Indian as opposed to English-style garments, and these are made of fabrics dyed with bright colors like red and purple. The shininess of the goods is also emphasized, because some of the cloth is also silver, and the other wares—a mirror and a dagger—incorporate gemstones in their construction. This list of wares has a problem that hovers over the poem and is never really addressed by the poet or by later critics. The items for sale are all costly goods that could be purchased only by members of an elite class, whether Indian or British. Like anyone else, Naidu had human failings and was repeatedly criticized throughout her career for her ostentatious dress and display of jewelry as inconsistent with Congress Party positions on social justice.

Stanza 2

Stanza 2 consists of three questions and three answers divided into individual couplets. The first question, about what they are weighing out, is addressed most generally to the vendors,

which could mean anyone selling anything in the bazaar. The answer is the most traded of all goods, staple foods. In this case, that means beans and rice together with spices. Saffron may seem like an exotic spice to Western readers, but it is a common item in Hyderabad. The food is marked by its simplicity. The diet is vegetarian not so much because of Hindu dietary restrictions (Hindus can certainly eat mutton and other meats, just not beef) but mainly because of the poverty of most of the shoppers. This is in contrast to the costly items mentioned in stanza 1 and serves as a reminder that just as no religious difference is apparent to an observer at the bazaars, all classes live more or less together and shop in the same bazaar.

The next couplet is addressed to young girls who, before marriage, might work at simple jobs such as the incessant manual grinding necessary for all sorts of production. The items that they grind are incense, dyes used in cosmetics and cloth manufacture, and generic spice, meaning pepper and similar items. This couplet illustrates the problem with the economic model celebrated in the poem: people who are employed all day long grinding solid materials into powder by hand are never going to be able to rise out of poverty.

In the last couplet, the peddlers (the alternative spelling "pedlars" is used in the poem) are asked what they are selling. This hawking of wares, or calling out what is for sale, is the everyday practice that the theme of the poem is built on. These vendors are selling hand-carved ivory chess sets and dice, that is, more items for the luxury trade.

Stanza 3

Stanza 3, line 1 asks the goldsmiths about their wares. Lines 2–6 are devoted to the answer. These wares are highly varied. Traditionally, what little wealth a poor Indian family might possess would be stored in the form of gold jewelry worn by its female members; these are the first class of items mentioned. The next item seems to be an impossibly ostentatious display of vast wealth: golden bells worn by pet pigeons. The last two are directed toward temple dancers and the monarchy (religion and government), showing the integration of all society within the bazaar.

Stanza 4

Stanza 4 is also divided into three question-and-answer couplets. The first addresses fruit sellers, who mention fruits that may seem exotic in the West but are grown locally in Hyderabad. The second couplet asks musicians what they play, and they answer with the names of typically Indian musical instruments. For Naidu, the life of the bazaar is not merely commercial but is a microcosm of the life of India, so it must contain all of the arts. The third couplet addresses Indian holy men, who commonly beg in bazaars in recompense for the spiritual gifts they bestow on their community. To characterize them as magicians and their prayers as spells as Naidu does is a highly orientalizing motif that would seem to the Western reader to discredit them, though that is probably not Naidu's ultimate intention. On the other hand, the use of the Western term does not require Naidu to differentiate between Hindu yogis and Islamic fakirs.

Stanza 5

In stanza 5, girls weaving wreaths of flowers are questioned about their merchandise. They reply that they are making garlands for bridegrooms and wedding beds but also flowers for funerals. This stanza conveys the larger meaning of the poem and of the bazaar as a symbol that stands for the whole cycle of life and death.

THEMES

Orientalism

In his book *Orientalism* (1979) and in other works, Edward Said was the first leading critic to recognize the importance and character of orientalism. Orientalism is a concept that Western writers developed to define non-Western cultures as an other, something that is alien and that has the quality of being primitive—perhaps in some degree in a positive sense as being original and authentic but above all in the sense of being undeveloped and inferior to the West. Orientalism is a colonialist discourse, one that is used to justify Western conquest and exploitation with the same logic by which parents must care for their helpless children. Non-Western peoples are denied any agency, any possibility of effectively governing themselves. They become what Rudyard Kipling called in an 1899 poem the white man's burden, making Europeans responsible for educating the primitive people of the world, to protect them from their own inferiority by conquering and ruling them.

In the nineteenth century, writers from the elite classes in India, for the most part educated in English schools and universities, perhaps surprisingly adopted this orientalist attitude about their own country. This was the background of Naidu's own education. The daughter of the director of a school in the princely state of Hyderabad, Naidu told the story that as a little girl she refused to learn English, but when she was eight years old, her father sent her to her room as a punishment, and she soon emerged speaking English fluently. Thereafter, she spoke to her parents only in English, though they responded to her in Hindustani, the national language of the administration imposed on India by the British, although the ancestral language that all three spoke was Bengali. The story is no doubt apocryphal, with a political rather than a literal historical meaning.

While she was at university in England, Naidu blossomed as a poet and was referred for tutelage to Edmund Gosse, who was an important poet and far more important critic and who sat at the center of the English literary and artistic worlds. Gosse dismissed the works she showed him as too imitative of contemporary English poets. Instead, he advised her, as he recalls in the introduction of her anthology *The Bird of Time* (1912), to write what the English expected of an Indian poetess:

> some revelation of the heart of India, some sincere penetrating analysis of native passion, of the principles of antique religion and of such mysterious intimations as stirred the soul of the East long before the West had begun to dream that it had a soul.

He also advised her to address her spirit, "to the exposition of emotions which are tropical and primitive." In short, Gosse advised her to offer a safe, controllable, orientalist vision of India, and, as far as Gosse was concerned, that is the kind of poetry Naidu began to write. "In the Bazaars of Hyderabad" has the orientalist feature of presenting India in the guise of an ideal past, supposedly representing a simpler, idyllic time. The text describes the wares on sale at the market in Hyderabad, and they are typically exotic pieces of local color, such as hand-worked gold anklets and ivory chess sets. So the poem is entirely successful on the level that Gosse thought proper for Naidu's efforts, although that is not necessarily the totality of the poem's meaning.

TOPICS FOR FURTHER STUDY

- Many students in India have made and posted videos to YouTube and other video-hosting sights in which they read the text of "In the Bazaars of Hyderabad" over a montage of images depicting the bazaar merchandise mentioned in the poem. Others have used the poem to construct a miniature diorama of a bazaar (*The Hindu*, February 2, 2002, http://www.thehindu.com/thehindu/lf/2002/02/23/stories/2002022300100200.htm). Carry out a similar project (which may work best as a group assignment) and share it with your class.

- Despite its title, *The Puffin Book of Poetry for Children: 101 Poems* (2005), with poems by writers such as T. S. Eliot, Rupert Brooke, and W. H. Auden, is intended for young adults. It was edited by Eunice de Souza, a prominent Indian poet, and about a third of the poems (including de Souza's "From Pahari Parrots" and "Peacock," by Harindranath Chattopadhyay, Naidu's youngest brother) are by contemporary Indian poets. If all of Naidu's poems were ultimately subordinated to the cause of Indian independence, these poems have a very different tone and theme. Report to your class on a survey of the Indian poems in this collection, perhaps one or a few of them that you found interesting or important.

- Prepare a report for your class on Naidu's brother, Virendranath Chattopadhyaya. Unlike Naidu and her Congress Party allies, her brother sought to expel the British by violent revolution and spent most of his life abroad trying to enlist the aid of Britain's enemies to support an armed rebellion in India. During World War I, he was well received in Germany, though that country was never in a position to intervene in India. Thereafter, Chattopadhyaya pinned his hopes on Russia and an Indian Communist revolution, but he was executed in 1937 during the dictator Joseph Stalin's purge of the Communist Party.

- Ananda Coomaraswamy, besides being an Indian nationalist and art historian, was also a founder of the traditionalist school of philosophy. Traditionalists consider that modernity has been a disaster and are waiting for the moment when the past can be used as the model to create a new and better future. The overlap between traditionalism and Naidu's poetry is extensive. For instance, traditionalism holds that all religious traditions are equally valid expressions of a single original or authentic revelation. This would make it possible to reconcile Islam and Hinduism into a homogeneous whole, as Naidu evidently tends to do. Write a paper exploring affinities between traditionalist ideas and "In the Bazaars of Hyderabad" (and possibly other poems). Mark Sedgewick's *Against the Modern World* (2009) is the standard academic treatment of traditionalism, and many of Coomaraswamy's books are available on the Internet.

Decadence

Although Naidu began to write poetry that fit the orientalist mode Gosse recommended, she did not abandon her association with contemporary English poetry and the poets to whom Gosse introduced her. Critics often mention the influence on Naidu of decadent writers like Oscar Wilde, and this influence can easily be seen in this poem. The poem is essentially an evocative description of oriental luxury goods, emphasizing their exotic, sensual attractiveness, meant to evoke an ideal past and an idealized India, an India that consists only of pleasures and beauties. Wilde included many such passages in his work. For example, in the novel *The Picture of Dorian Gray* (1890), Wilde lists

The poem's title sets the scene in Hyderabad, India (©Waj | Shutterstock.com)

in detail the various classes of art treasure Gray owns, including

> dainty Delhi muslins, finely wrought with gold-thread palmates, and stitched over with irides-cent beetles' wings; the Dacca gauzes, that from their transparency are known in the East as "woven air," and "running water," and "evening dew"; strange figured cloths from Java; elaborate Chinese hangings.

These wares are exactly comparable to the wares in the Hyderabad bazaar, particularly in the fanciful description of their construction. The cloth that improbably incorporates beetle wings especially compares with Naidu's gold jewelry wrought as fine as dragonfly wings.

STYLE

Poetics

"In the Bazaars of Hyderabad," notwithstanding Naidu's inscription that it could be sung to a piece of traditional Indian music, is entirely English in its poetic features. It satisfies Gosse's advice to Naidu to become what the English

audience expects of an Indian poetess. The basic line of the poem is iambic trimeter, or the repetition of three iambs (an unstressed followed by a stressed syllable, the basic units of English meter) in each line. Each stanza consists of six lines. The poem consists of alternating questions and answers about the products sold by each class of vendor in the bazaar. The answer presented, sometimes in a block, sometimes interspersed in single lines, consists of three to five lines of each stanza. In each stanza, either the answering three lines rhyme, or the answers are arranged in *abab* rhyming couplets.

Street Cries

The framework of this poem is that vendors hawk their wares by calling out lines of poetry describing them. This structure can be understood within an English context. Naidu refers to the practice directly when the bazaar merchants are asked what they call, that is, what they call out to attract customers. Another poem of Naidu's on the same subject is "Street Cries." This was probably an actual practice in London markets, since repetitive traditional speech often takes the form of

COMPARE
&
CONTRAST

- **1910s:** India is British crown colony.

  Today: India has gained its independence and fragmented along communal religious lines established by the British into the nations of India, Pakistan, and Bangladesh (corresponding to the British-era province of East Bengal).

- **1910s:** Voting rights under colonial rule in India are more theoretical than practical; suffrage is limited to a small group of men.

- **Today:** The Indian constitution adopted in1950 guarantees full voting rights to women.

- **1910s:** Hyderabad is the capital of a theoretically, but not practically independent princely state ruled by the Nazim.

  Today: Having been forcibly incorporated into India in 1948, Hyderabad is the capital of an Indian province.

poetry. Indian folk traditions are less likely to take on the formal characteristics of poetry, such as meter, but it is more to the point that English literary and musical tradition imposed this form of speech on poor people working as merchants in the city streets. This is most famously evidenced in the 1880s English music hall song known as "Molly Malone" (after its main character), "In Dublin's Fair City" (after its first line), or "Cockles and Mussels" (after its refrain). The song is distinctly English, though it is set in Ireland, another colonized, exoticized nation. An American example is the hawking songs sung by the street vendor Peter in Ira and George Gershwin's opera *Porgy and Bess* (1935), in which the practice helps to characterize the poor black community as an other.

For this poem, Naidu worked in the English tradition. She headed the poem with an inscription linking the text to the traditional music of the bazaars, to which it could not have any very close relation (Indian songs are not written in iambic trimeter), representing what can best be seen as the representation of English working class tradition in foreign disguise. The transference of a rejected part of Western culture (in this case because it is not elite) onto a foreign other is a typical feature of orientalism. But the question-and-answer structure of the poem also works toward the same goal. It is easiest to imagine the questioner as an aristocratic English woman shopping for luxury goods in the bazaars. This

is suggested by the gold jewelry and household objects made of precious materials. A dagger with a jade handle, for example, could hardly be anything except a costly souvenir.

HISTORICAL CONTEXT

The Indian Independence Movement

In the seventeenth century, a joint stock company called the East India Company was created in Britain for the purpose of economically exploiting India. Originally, it established factories in the country to manufacture cloth, which was then traded farther east for spices that could be profitably sold in Britain. The company bought rights from the local governments to establish bases and factories in Indian port cities. By the middle of the eighteenth century, the company had a private army (which more or less fought alongside British government forces, for example, against Napoleon in Egypt). It also began to intervene in the politics of the numerous small local governments in India. It established nominees in some states and annexed others outright (so that this private corporation effectively had dictatorial control over a nation's population). The company came to terms with still other states, whose rulers offered submission to the company in exchange for not being attacked. These were the so-called princely states. They had a degree of autonomy in local affairs, but a company official was present

The bazaars of Hyderabad have been fixtures of the city for hundreds of years (©steve estvanik / Shutterstock.com)

at court to make sure they did nothing outside their borders against company interests.

Hyderabad in southern India was the largest princely state. Within a century, company rule of India was so oppressive that it sparked the India Mutiny (1857–1858), which was suppressed at the cost of hundreds of thousands of Indian lives. After the mutiny, the British government directly took over India and made it a crown colony. The mercantile policies of Britain ended any serious industrial development in the colony, which was henceforth treated as a market for British manufactures. The British did, however, begin giving the children of Indian elites a British education so that they could assist the British in the administration of the country. Within a generation, this educated class increasingly began to call for independence from Britain and gained steadily increasing popular support, especially as British efforts to suppress dissent became more and more violent and manipulative.

One strategy the British government used was to turn Muslim and Hindu Indians into blocks defined by religious identity so that their efforts could be directed at fighting each other rather than the British. This resulted in the separation of India and Pakistan and entailed a terrible humanitarian crisis, a series of wars after independence, and an ongoing nuclear standoff. This policy of divide and rule manifested itself in the breakup of the province of Bengal into Muslim and Hindu sections in 1905, an event that radicalized many Indians, including Naidu. Already a world famous poet, Naidu joined the Congress Party, the center of Gandhi's resistance to colonial rule. She was soon welcomed into the party's inner circle and became a close companion of Gandhi's, devoting herself to public speaking on behalf of independence and to the equality of women. In 1925, she served as president of the Congress Party.

Naidu supported Gandhi's policy of nonviolence (*satyagraha*, which means showing the truth, that is, the truth that oppressive rule is based on violence) and the boycott of British manufactured goods (*swadeshi*, or self-sufficiency). In 1930, Gandhi organized a march through India to the sea to make salt, an illegal act because the crown administration held a monopoly on salt. Naidu accompanied Gandhi and can be seen in the same frame of most of the famous photographs taken of him at the time. Because this action did not provoke the British authorities to violence, Gandhi determined to use nonviolence to shut down a government salt factory in Gujarat. The British tried to preempt the effort by arresting Gandhi in the middle of the night before the march, but the march went on under Naidu's leadership. (Gandhi chose her to promote the political equality of women.) A police line (composed of Indian soldiers in imperial service) in the marchers' path made it clear that the British would not permit the protest. Naidu (quoted in Peter Ackerman and Jack DuVall's *A Force More Powerful*) addresses the marchers: "You must not use any violence under any circumstances. You will be beaten but you must not resist: you must not even raise a hand to ward off blows." When they approached, the police attacked, beating the protesters with clubs in full view of Western and Indian reporters and newsreel film crews. Dozens of people were killed and hundreds injured. This event is seen as the turning point in world opinion against British rule in India.

Throughout the 1930s, the British began to prepare for independence, allowing an Indian self-government, which in practice had little power but which at least established regular popular elections that included women and Dalits (the lowest traditional caste in India, which faced and in the twenty-first century continues to face a large measure of discrimination in Indian society). During World War II, Gandhi announced that the independence movement would not compromise the British during their crisis (realizing that the fascist government of Japan that would likely take over India if the British faltered would hardly be an improvement), but he and Congress Party leaders, including Naidu, were nevertheless put under arrest for the duration of the war (with typical humor, when Naidu was released, she asked to stay in prison a bit longer so she could see the flowers she had planted blossom). India finally gained independence in 1947, and Naidu served as governor of the United Provinces (renamed Uttar Pradesh in 1950). The British gave the choice to the rulers of the princely states to join either Pakistan or India or to become independent countries. The Nizam of Hyderabad (Naidu's home region) was the only Indian ruler to choose the third option, resulting in the territory's military conquest by India in 1948.

CRITICAL OVERVIEW

Helen Eullis, in a 1913 *New York Times* review of *The Bird of Time*, noted Gosse's advice to Naidu (repeated in the introduction to the collection) to write in an orientalist manner acceptable to the English public. She remarks on how successfully Naidu seems to have followed the advice:

> To us of a colder, soberer clime the very name of this singer of "the oldest land" brings a suggestion of color and perfume, of strange twilights, of all the mystery and magic and swift bestowals of life and death that we traditionally associate with India.

She adds that "In the Bazaars of Hyderabad" "shines like an Oriental gem." Eullis's review demonstrates the orientalist character, that is, the lack of authenticity that the Western reading public demanded of Indian authors. Western readers wanted nothing authentic but only the oriental mirage: "Our own English poets have taught us . . . what Oriental poetry should be like. If it turns out not to be like that, why, then, so

much the worse for Oriental poetry." Eullis also recognized the decadent affinities in Naidu's work when she compared her to Algernon Swinburne.

There has been no shortage of scholarship on Naidu, as one of the leading literary and political figures of her generation in India, but it has avoided "In the Bazaars of Hyderabad," no doubt because it seems so successful as an orientalist work. The main theme of essays about Naidu's poetry has been her rejection of orientalism. Recent readings of Naidu's verse do see her work as a foundation for an independent, unified India (which was not to be). Ellen Brinks, in the 2013 monograph, *Anglophone Indian Women Writers, 1870–1920*, pointed out that the earlier generation of Indian writers, such as Cornelia Sorabji, characterized their acceptance of British imperialism and of ideological orientalism through the use of a family metaphor in which Queen Victoria was accepted as the mother of an India in need of maternal care. But,

> in the writings of Sarojini Naidu . . . kinship tropes also assume centrality. Naidu's family unit however is radically different than the one envisioned by Sorabji. The imperial parent figure is gone; in its place is an Indian mother.

Although Brinks cannot find a particular traditional song to which "In the Bazaars of Hyderabad" could become lyrics, she believes that Naidu is here, as in many other poems, invoking the oral culture of the common people of India.

Because of Naidu's importance as an Indian English poet and her importance as a Congress politician, "In The Bazaars of Hyderabad" is often used in Indian school curriculums and civil service examinations. A considerable body of literature from India-based publishers is available both on paper and at websites to assist students in the study of the poem, but the works generally do not attempt a thorough analysis. A typical example of this literature is Vishwanthe S. Naravane's *Sarojini Naidu* (1980), which does little more than summarize the poem and emphasize the sensual nature of its descriptions, a suggestion that could easily be developed into a brief essay on an examination paper.

CRITICISM

Bradley A. Skeen

Skeen is a classicist. In the following essay, he shows how Naidu's "In the Bazaars of Hyderabad"

WHAT DO I READ NEXT?

- In 1966, Padmini Sathianadhan Sengupta published *Sarojini Naidu: A Biography*, which is one of the basic sources of information about Naidu's life but does not provide much historical analysis or aesthetic criticism.

- *The Golden Threshold* (1905) is Naidu's first collection of poetry.

- The most important pieces of Naidu's correspondence have been published in *Selected Letters: 1890s to 1940s* (1996), edited by Makarand Paranjape, but the volume is not widely available outside of India.

- Toru Dutt's *Ancient Ballads and Legends of Hindustan* (1882) is a collection from ancient Sanskrit texts translated into English verse. This volume, like Naidu's *The Bird of Time*, had a laudatory introduction by Edmund Gosse and formed the model of what an Indian poetess ought to be for the English audience that Gosse later fostered onto Naidu.

- Nirode K. Barooah's *Chatto: The Life and Times of an Indian Anti-Imperialist in Europe* (2004) is a biographical study of Virendranath Chattopadhyaya, Naidu's brother, who parted political ways with his sister in seeking a violent overthrow of British rule in India.

- Rudyard Kipling's *The Jungle Book* (1894), usually reprinted with *The Second Jungle Book* (1895) under the title *The Jungle Books*, is a collection of short stories for young adults in the form of animal fables. It represents the epitome of the British orientalist conception of India.

---

promotes the idea of swadeshi *(self-sufficiency)* in the particular form advocated by the art historian Ananda Coomaraswamy.

"In the Bazaars of Hyderabad" is a particularly difficult poem because it seems to perfectly embody the orientalism recommended to Naidu by her mentor Edmund Gosse—who

called on Naidu to become the kind of Indian poetess the English reading public expected—and to mark the poetry of the prior generation in the work of poets like Toru Dutt. Although Gosse and many English readers were able to read Naidu's work without recognizing this truth, the main thrust of her poetical work, as well as her later political career, was to oppose orientalism and the colonial purpose it served in keeping India subdued as a British colony. Because of this inherent difficulty, the poem has been either ignored outright or accepted as an orientalist trifle and celebrated for its sensuous descriptions. Even Brinks, in *Anglophone Indian Women Writers, 1870–1920,* did not analyze it beyond noticing its valorization of the working class. So it is a worthwhile question to ask whether the poem is a piece of lazy orientalism or has a more serious political purpose.

One way to begin is to look a little more carefully at the use of orientalist ideology in the British administration of India, which is the background for understanding all of Naidu's work.

A central feature of orientalism was to define India with reference to the country's most ancient literature, the Vedas and a few other works, all more than fifteen hundred years old, so the true India could be safely pushed back into a remote past. Brahman pundits, part of the native elite class in India, were happy to go along with the characterization because their caste could be the most easily associated with this ancient, almost mythical India. In contrast to this ancient ideal, modern India was seen to be ripe for dependency because it had supposedly declined culturally, intellectually, spiritually, and in every other way. Administrators in the East India Company had had to learn Indian languages and so were the first to discover that Indian and European languages were closely related, descended from a language (now reconstructed by a comparative model) called Proto-Indo-European that existed thousands of years ago. In the atmosphere of the nineteenth century, this idea took on a racial component that could be used to make several spurious arguments that were taken seriously until well into the twentieth century.

One of the spurious arguments was that India was a land without a history and that its racial development had stopped at a level similar, perhaps, to Homeric Greece and needed the

GIVEN THE ORIENTALIST IDEOLOGY
AND ITS PRACTICAL EFFECT IN THE SUBJUGATION
OF INDIA, HOW WAS NAIDU TO FIGHT AGAINST IT
WITH MERE POETRY?"

help of Europeans to catch up. A particularly unfortunate version of this idea was that the cultural arrest was caused by the mixing of the pure Aryan racial stock of the invaders who had conquered northern India around 1000 BCE and produced Sanskrit literature and the dark-skinned inferior peoples they conquered. This would suggest that the English, who according to this idea had not compromised their pure Aryan identity, had a natural right to rule India. *Aryan* is a linguistic rather than a racial term and refers to the stage of language between Proto-Indo-European and Avestan and San-skrit. No people either speaking an Aryan lan-guage or calling themselves Aryan ever existed in Europe except in the confused imaginations of racist ideologues in the nineteenth and twentieth centuries. It is possible to draw a contrary con-clusion from the relation between languages that because Indians were the equals of Europeans in speaking Indo-European languages, they ought to be treated as equals. Some politicians and bureaucrats did propose this, but because it would count as an argument against the colonial exploitation of India, it did not receive much serious attention. The generally accepted think-ing on the racial status of India was expressed by Herbert Risley, a high-ranking civil servant (director of ethnography) in the imperial admin-istration in India, in the monograph *The People of India* (1915):

> As each wave of conquerors, Greek, Scy-thian, Arab, Moghal, that entered the coun-try by land became more or less absorbed in the indigenous population, their physique degenerated, their individuality vanished, their energy was sapped, and dominion passed from their hands into those of more vigorous successors. *Ex Occidente Imperium*; the genius of Empire in India has come to her from the West; and can be maintained only by constant infusions of fresh blood from the same source.

Thus the justification for British rule in India rested on a false, even nonsensical, reading of history (Risley devoted much space to debat-ing the relative shapes of the heads of primitive tribesmen, half of whom existed only in his imag-ination and the rest of whom had certainly never had their craniums measured) that is an expres-sion of orientalist ideology.

Islam was another element of Indian culture subject to orientalist analysis in a crown colony that included the modern states of Pakistan and Bangladesh. The orientalist reading of Islam was two-sided. On the one hand, Islam was denounced as despotic, fanatical, and warlike. On the other hand, the relatively enlightened Mughal period of Indian history, when much of the subcontinent was unified under Islamic rule, was presented as a model for British rule, and the particular qual-ities attributed to Muslims could be turned around to view their religion as pure and unspoiled and their warlike actions as bravery.

Communalism was the idea operative in the British administration that Muslims and Hindus belonged to their own communal groups and could not form a common political or social body. This view was used to attack the independ-ence movement on the ground that it was impos-sible for anybody to speak for a unified India. It also led to political actions, such as the partition of Bengal, that were seen as aimed at making the job of British rule more difficult in India by creating rival hostile factions that could be pitted against each other.

Given the orientalist ideology and its prac-tical effect in the subjugation of India, how was Naidu to fight against it with mere poetry? Unsurprisingly, Gosse advised Naidu to attempt nothing of the kind and avoid a political or revolutionary aesthetic. As early as 1905, how-ever, Naidu responded to him in a letter that "all talents and enthusiasms should concentrate themselves on some practical end for the imme-diate and obvious good of the nation" (quoted in Brinks's *Anglophone Indian Women Writers, 1870–1920*), *the good of the nation* being a euphe-mism for self-rule and independence. Naidu was adamant that Indians could not afford to be distracted by any lesser cause: not by religious particularism or even by religious unity, except to the degree that served the cause of independ-ence, and not even by feminism or economic justice. So what does "In the Bazaars of Hyder-abad" look like from this perspective?

The most notable feature of Naidu's poem is that it does not mention the supposedly irreconcilable communes of Hinduism and Islam. For Naidu, these differences of religion and differences of race were trivial compared with the shared Indianness of the two groups. Brinks mentions that

> in speaking as and for India, Naidu's speakers [in her poems] are particularly invested in constituting an India where religious factionalism between Hindus and Muslims, seen as one of the prime obstacles to national unity, is either non-existent or overcome.

Although Brinks did not specify "In the Bazaars of Hyderabad" as the subject of her comment, she certainly identified a key element of the poem.

In her Hindu family, Naidu grew up embedded in the cultural matrix of Hyderabad, which under the patronage of the Nazim was the leading center for Islamic culture in India. Unity between members of the two religions seemed natural and inevitable to her, except for British interference. Following the fashions of the city, her Hindu family was indistinguishable in dress and appearance from Muslims, and the first poets she read were Sufi mystics. Naidu's poetry transcends orientalism by presenting Hyderabad as an apex of higher social and moral development in an enriching cultural unity instead of the cultural division that the British wanted to drag India down to. Among the few poems in which Naidu does mention Islam and Hinduism are "The Call to Evening Prayer," which refers to an Islamic practice and begins with the muezzin's call but goes on to include prayers of Hinduism, Christianity, Zoroastrianism, and every religion in India, all mixed together in a single song. Similarly, "Love Song" is the story of a marriage between a mixed Hindu and Muslim couple.

Another idea expressed in "In the Bazaars of Hyderabad" is *swadeshi*. The word means self-sufficiency, and its political meaning was the belief that Indians should buy products made in India rather than those imported from Britain. This began in the late nineteenth century and became a widespread practice after 1905 in protest of the split of Bengal. It was finally taken up by Gandhi as the basis for a boycott of all British goods as an economic tool to be used against the colonial government. Gandhi summarized the idea in a single simple action that the masses could immediately understand. He did

not say, but rather showed, that Indians should wear clothes made of homespun cloth rather than clothes manufactured in the British Midlands. He showed it by his own constant work at a spinning wheel, which is still the most famous image of Gandhi. Spinning was traditionally women's work, so Gandhi's spinning sent a feminist message in concert, not in conflict, with the message of independence. In Naidu's poems, all of the goods being sold in the bazaars are Indian national products, not imports.

The wares offered in "In the Bazaars of Hyderabad," however, are made not of simple homespun cloth but are the most extravagant luxury goods. Although not with direct reference to this poem, Naidu (quoted by Vishwanthe S. Naravane in *Sarojini Naidu*) explains in a speech given many years later:

> For me Swadeshi begins with Mahatma Gandhi's *charkha* [spinning wheel] but does not end there.... It means reviving every art and craft of the land. It means giving a livelihood to every craftsman—the dyer, the embroiderer, the goldsmith, the man who makes tassels for your weddings.... For me it means the renaissance of our literature, the revival of our music, a new vision of architecture that is in keeping with our modern ideas of life.

This elaboration of *swadeshi* goes a long way toward explaining Naidu's poem. She emphasized the beauty and excellence of each item produced for sale in the bazaar because it is Indian and not British. It does not have to refer to an idealized past but to a future to hope for and a present to strive for.

The ideas that Naidu expresses in poetic form stem from the work of the art historian and cofounder of the traditionalist school of philosophy, Ananda Coomaraswamy. Naidu knew Coomaraswamy personally, though not well, but any educated Indian of that time would have been familiar with his works, which revolutionized the perception of Indian art in the West. In 1912, Coomaraswamy published the monograph *Art and Swadeshi*, which developed his views on the subject. He began by describing *swadeshi* as it was actually practiced, usually meaning buying inferior copies of British products that had been manufactured in India. But the same shabbiness infected Indian craft work:

> If you go into one of those shops frequented by tourists in Indian towns, you will find ... flimsy wood carving and shallow brass work, the cheap

The poems lists the staggering variety of goods available (©Jaroslaw Grudzinski | Shutterstock.com)

enamels and the overloaded embroideries which are outward manifestations of the degradation of Indian craftsmanship.

This is precisely the opposite of the wares offered in Naidu's poetic Hyderabad, which seems to be an idealized perfection compared with this degraded reality. For Coomaraswamy, the practice of *swadeshi* revealed how British rule destroyed Indian art: "Modern India, Anglicised India, has produced no beauty and romance, but has gone far to destroy the beauty and romance which are our heritage from the past." Coomaraswamy's description of the nearly lost tradition of Indian craftsmanship seems to be a direct inspiration for Naidu's poem when he mourns:

> the wealth and beauty which the Indian craftsman used to lavish on the simplest articles of daily use, the filmy muslins or the flowerwoven silks with which we used to worship the beauty of Indian women, the brazen vessels from which we ate and drank, the carpets on which we trod with bare feet or the pictures that revealed to us the love of Radha, or the soul of the eternal snows.

Because the Indians must cooperate with the British, even in the act of *swadeshi* as Indians are reduced to imitating British manufactures, commerce must destroy art. In Coomaraswamy's view, "it is the outward sign of the merely material ideal of prosperity which is too exclusively striven for by our economists and politicians." Coomaraswamy observes that "India, politically and economically free, but subdued by Europe in her inmost soul is scarcely an ideal to be dreamt of, or to live, or die for," so *swadeshi* must move beyond the merely economic sphere. He asks his readers,

> Has it never occurred to you that it is as much your duty to make your lives and your environment beautiful as to make them moral, in fact that without beauty there can be no true morality, without morality no true beauty?

Naidu gives her answer in "In the Bazaars of Hyderabad."

Source: Bradley A. Skeen, Critical Essay on "In the Bazaars of Hyderabad," in *Poetry for Students*, Gale, Cengage Learning, 2017.

Arthur Symons
In the following essay, which originally appeared as the introduction to Naidu's collection The

HER BODY WAS NEVER WITHOUT SUFFERING,

OR HER HEART WITHOUT CONFLICT; BUT NEITHER

THE BODY'S WEAKNESS NOR THE HEART'S VIOLENCE

COULD DISTURB THAT FIXED CONTEMPLATION, AS

OF BUDDHA ON HIS LOTUS-THRONE."

Golden Threshold, *Symons describes the poet's unique spirit.*

It is at my persuasion that these poems are now published. The earliest of them were read to me in London in 1896, when the writer was seventeen; the later ones were sent to me from India in 1904, when she was twenty-five; and they belong, I think, almost wholly to those two periods. As they seemed to me to have an individual beauty of their own, I thought they ought to be published. The writer hesitated. "Your letter made me very proud and very sad," she wrote. "Is it possible that I have written verses that are 'filled with beauty,' and is it possible that you really think them worthy of being given to the world? You know how high my ideal of Art is; and to me my poor casual little poems seem to be less than beautiful—I mean with that final enduring beauty that I desire." And in another letter, she writes: "I am not a poet really. I have the vision and the desire, but not the voice. If I could write just one poem full of beauty and the spirit of greatness, I should be exultantly silent for ever; but I sing just as the birds do, and my songs are as ephemeral." It is for this bird-like quality of songs, it seems to me, that they are to be valued. They hint, in a sort of delicately evasive way, at a rare temperament, the department of a woman of the East, finding expression through a Western language and under partly Western influences. They do not express the whole of that temperament; but they express, I think, its essence; and there is an Eastern magic in them.

Sarojini Chattopadhyay was born at Hyderabad on February 13, 1879. Her father, Dr. Aghorenath Chattopadhyay, is descended from the ancient family of Chattorajes of Bhramangram, who were noted throughout Eastern Bengal as patrons of Sanskrit learning, and for their practice of Yoga. He took his degree of Doctor of Science at the University of Edinburgh in 1877, and afterwards studied brilliantly at Bonn. On his return to India he founded the Nizam College at Hyderabad, and has since laboured incessantly, and at great personal sacrifice, in the cause of education.

Sarojini was the eldest of a large family, all of whom were taught English at an early age. "I," she writes, "was stubborn and refused to speak it. So one day when I was nine years old my father punished me—the only time I was ever punished—by shutting me in a room alone for a whole day. I came out of it a full-blown linguist. I have never spoken any other language to him, or to my mother, who always speaks to me in Hindustani. I don't think I had any special hankering to write poetry as a little child, though I was of a very fanciful and dreamy nature. My training under my father's eye was of a sternly scientific character. He was determined that I should be a great mathematician or a scientist, but the poetic instinct, which I inherited from him and also from my mother (who wrote some lovely Bengali lyrics in her youth) proved stronger. One day, when I was eleven, I was sighing over a sum in algebra; it *wouldn't* come right; but instead a whole poem came to me suddenly. I wrote it down.

"From that day my 'poetic career' began. At thirteen I wrote a long poem *a la* 'Lady of the Lake'—1300 lines in six days. At thirteen I wrote a drama of 2000 lines, a full-fledged passionate thing that I began on the spur of the moment without forethought, just to spite my doctor who said I was very ill and must not touch a book. My health broke down permanently about this time, and my regular studies being stopped I read voraciously. I suppose the greater part of my reading was done between fourteen and sixteen. I wrote a novel, I wrote fat volumes of journals. I took myself very seriously in those days."

Before she was fifteen the great struggle of her life began. Dr. Govindarajulu Naidu, now her husband, is, though of an old and honourable family, not a Brahmin. The difference of caste roused an equal opposition, not only on the side of her family, but of his; and in 1895 she was sent to England, against her will, with a special scholarship from the Nizam. She remained in England, with an interval of travel in Italy, till 1898, studying first at King's College, London, then, till her health again broke down, at Girton. She returned to Hyderabad in September 1898, and in the December of that year, to the scandal of all India, broke through the bonds of caste, and married Dr. Naidu. "Do you know I have some very beautiful poems floating in the air," she wrote to me in 1904; "and if the gods are kind I shall cast my soul like a net and capture them, this year. If the gods are kind—and grant me a little measure of health. It is all I need to make my life perfect, for the very 'Spirit of Delight' that Shelley wrote of dwells in my little home; it is full of the music of birds in the garden and children in the long arched verandah." There are songs about the children in this book; they are called the Lord of Battles, the sun of Victory, the Lotus-born, and the Jewel of Delight.

"My ancestors for thousands of years," I find written in one of her letters, "have been lovers of the forest and mountain caves, great dreamers, great scholars, great ascetics. My father is a dreamer himself, a great dreamer, a great man whose life has been a magnificent failure. I suppose in the whole of India there are few men whose learning is greater than his, and I don't think there are many more beloved. He has a great white beard and the profile of Homer, and a laugh that brings the roof down. He has wasted all his money on two great objects; to help others, and on alchemy. He holds huge courts every day in his garden of all the learned men of all religions—Rajahs and beggars and saints and downright villains all delightfully mixed up, and all treated as one. And then his alchemy! Oh dear, night and day the experiments are going on, and every man who brings a new prescription is welcome as a brother. But this alchemy is, you know, only the material counterpart of a poet's craving for Beauty, the eternal Beauty. 'The makers of gold and the makers of verse,' they are the twin creators that sway the world's secret desire for mystery; and what in my father is the genius of curiosity—the very essence of scientific genius—in me is the desire for beauty. Do you remember Pater's phrase about Leonardo da Vinci, 'curiosity and the desire of beauty'?"

It was the desire of beauty that made her a poet; her "nerves of delight" were always quivering at the contact of beauty. To those who knew her in England, all the life of the tiny figure seemed to concentrate itself in the eyes; they turned towards beauty as the sun-flower turns towards the sun, opening wider and wider untill

one saw nothing but the eyes. She was dressed always in clinging dress of Eastern silk, and as she was so small, and her long black hair hung straight down her back; you might have taken her for a child. She spoke little, and in a low voice, like gentle music; and she seemed, wherever she was, to be alone.

Through that soul I seemed to touch and take hold upon the East. And first there was the wisdom of the East. I have never known any one who seemed to exist on such "large draughts of intellectual day" as this child of seventeen, to whom one could tell all one's personal troubles and agitations, as to a wise old woman. In the East, maturity comes early; and this child had already lived through all a woman's life. But there was something else, something hardly personal, something which belonged to a consciousness older than the Christian, which I realised, wondered at, and admired, in her passionate tranquillity of mind, before which everything mean and trivial and temporary caught fire and burnt away in smoke. Her body was never without suffering, or her heart without conflict; but neither the body's weakness nor the heart's violence could disturb that fixed contemplation, as of Buddha on his lotus-throne.

And along with this wisdom, as of age or of the age of a race, there was what I can hardly call less than an agony of sensation. Pain or pleasure transported her, and the whole of pain or pleasure might be held in a flower's cup or the imagined frown of a friend. It was never found in those things which to others seemed things of importance. At the age of twelve she passed the Matriculation of the Madras University, and awoke to find herself famous throughout India. "Honestly," she said to me, "I was not pleased; such things did not appeal to me." But here, in a letter from Hyderabad, bidding one "share a March morning" with her, there is, at the mere contact of the sun, this outburst; "Come and share my exquisite March morning with me; this sumptuous blaze of gold and sapphire sky; these scarlet lilies that adorn the sunshine; the voluptuous scents of neem and champak and serisha that beat upon the languid air with their implacable sweetness; the thousand little gold and blue and silver breasted birds bursting with the shrill ecstasy of life in nesting time. All is hot and fierce and passionate, ardent and unashamed in its exulting and importunate desire for life and love. And, do you know that the scarlet lilies are woven petal by petal from my heart's blood, these little quivering birds are my soul made incarnate music, these heavy perfumes are my emotions dissolved into aerial essence, this flaming blue and gold sky is the 'very me,' that part of me that incessantly and insolently, yes, and a little deliberately, triumphs over that other part—a thing of nerves and tissues that suffers and cries out, and that must die to-morrow perhaps, or twenty years hence."

Then there was her humour, which was part of her strange wisdom, and was always awake and on the watch. In all her letters, written in exquisite English prose, but with an ardent imagery and a vehement sincerity of emotion which make them, like the poems, indeed almost more directly, un-English, Oriental, there was always this intellectual, critical sense of humour, which could laugh at one's own enthusiasm as frankly as that enthusiasm had been set down. And partly the humour, like the delicate reserve of her manner, was a mask or a shelter. "I have taught myself," she writes to me from India, "to be common place and like everybody else superficially. Every one thinks I am so nice and cheerful, so 'brave,' all the banal things that are so comfortable to be. My mother knows me only as 'such a tranquil child, but so strong-willed.' A tranquil child!" And she writes again, with deeper significance: "I too have learnt the subtle philosophy of living from moment to moment. Yes, it is a subtle philosophy, though it appears merely an epicurean doctrine: 'Eat, drink, and be merry, for to-morrow we die.' I have gone through so many yesterdays when I strove with Death that I have realised to its full the wisdom of that sentence; and it is to me not merely a figure of speech, but a literal fact. Any tomorrow I might die. It is scarcely two months since I came back from the grave: is it worth while to be anything but radiantly glad? Of all things that life or perhaps my temperament has given me I prize the gift of laughter as beyond price."

Her desire, always, was to be "a wild free thing of the air like the birds, with a song in my heart." A spirit of too much fire in too frail a body, it was rarely that her desire was fully granted. But in Italy she found what she could not find in England, and from Italy her letters are radiant. "This Italy is made of gold," she writes from Florence, "the gold of dawn and daylight, the gold of the stars, and now dancing in weird enchanting rhythms through this magic month of May, the gold of fireflies in the perfumed darkness—'aerial gold.' I long to catch the subtle music of their fairy dances and make a poem with a rhythm like the quick irregular wild flash of their sudden movements. Would it not be wonderful? One black night I stood in a garden with fireflies in my hair like darting restless stars caught in a mesh of darkness. It gave me a strange sensation, as if I were not human at all, but an elfin spirit. I wonder why these little things move me so deeply? It is because I have a most 'unbalanced intellect,' I suppose." Then, looking out on Florence, she cries, "God! how beautiful it is, and how glad I am that I am alive to-day!" And she tells me that she is drinking in the beauty like wine, "wine, golden and scented, and shining, fit for the gods; and the gods have drunk it, the dead gods of Etruria, two thousand years ago. Did I say dead? No, for the gods are immortal, and one might still find them loitering in some solitary dell on the grey hillsides of Fiesole. Have I seen them? Yes, looking with dreaming eyes, I have found them sitting under the olives, in their grave, strong, antique beauty—Etruscan gods!"

In Italy she watches the faces of the monks, and at one moment longs to attain to their peace by renunciation, longs for Nirvana; "then, when one comes out again into the hot sunshine that warms one's blood, and sees the eager hurrying faces of men and women in the street, dramatic faces over which the disturbing experiences of life have passed and left their symbols, one's heart thrills up into throat. No, no, no, a thousand times no! how can one deliberately renounce this coloured, unquiet, fiery human life of the earth?" And, all the time, her subtle criticism is alert, and this woman of the East marvels at the woman of the West, the beautiful wordly women of the West" whom she sees walking in the Cascine, "taking the air so consciously attractive in their brilliant toilettes, in the brilliant coquetry of their manner!" She finds them "a little incomprehensible," "profound artists in all the subtle intricacies of fascination," and asks if these "incalculable frivolities and vanities and coquetries and caprices" are, to us, an essential part of their charm? And she watches them with amusement as they flutter about her, petting her as if she were a nice child, a child or a toy, not dreaming that she is saying to herself sorrowfully: "How utterly empty their lives must be of all spiritual beauty *if* they are nothing more than they appear to be."

She sat in our midst, and judged us, and few knew what was passing behind that face "like an awakening soul," to use one of her own epithets. Her eyes were like deep pools, and you seemed to fall through them into depths below depths.

Source: Arthur Symons, "Sarojini Naidu's Poetry," in *The Flute and the Drum: Studies in Sarojini Naidu's Poetry and Politics*, edited by V. A. Shahane and M. N. Sarma, Avon Printing Works, 1980, pp. 81–88.

SOURCES

Ackerman, Peter, and Jack DuVall, *A Force More Powerful: A Century of Nonviolent Conflict*, Palgrave Macmillan, 2000, p. 90.

Brinks, Ellen, *Anglophone Indian Women Writers, 1870–1920*, Ashgate, 2013, pp. 36–41, 171–207.

Coomaraswamy, Ananda, *Art and Swadeshi*, Ganesh, 1912, pp. 1–9.

Eullis, Helen, "Poet of India," in *New York Times*, April 27, 1917, http://query.nytimes.com/mem/archive-free/pdf?res=9E04EEDA173FE633A25754C2A9629C946296D6CF (accessed May 5, 2016).

Gosse, Edmund, Introduction to *The Bird of Time: Songs of Life, Death & the Spring*, by Sarojini Naidu, William Heinemann, 1912, pp. 1–8.

Naidu, Sarojini, "In the Bazaars of Hyderabad," in *The Bird of Time: Songs of Life, Death & the Spring*, William Heinemann, 1912, pp. 62–63.

Naravane, Vishwanthe S., *Sarojini Naidu*, Orient Blackswan, 1980, pp. 85, 145.

Risley, Herbert, *The People of India*, 2nd ed., edited by W. Crooke, W. Thacker, 1915, p. 53.

Roy, Parama, *Indian Traffic: Identities in Question in Colonial and Postcolonial India*, University of California Press, 1889, pp. 130–51.

Said, Edward, *Orientalism*, Vintage, 1979, pp. 1–112.

Wilde, Oscar, *The Picture of Dorian Gray*, Ward Lock, 1891, pp. 201–208.

FURTHER READING

Coomaraswamy, Rama P., ed., *The Essential Ananda K. Coomaraswamy*, World Wisdom, 2004.
    In this volume, Ananda's son Rama collects examples of his father's art historical and philosophical writings.

Gandhi, Mohandas K., *The Story of My Experiments with Truth*, Public Affairs Press, 1948.
    In this autobiographical work, Gandhi covers his life from 1921 and states the philosophical and political principles that he applied in his struggles for Indian rights in South Africa. It was originally published in Gandhi's journal *Young India* (a name chosen to contest the orientalist conception of India as an ancient country) from 1925 to 1929. His assassination prevented Gandhi from chronicling his part in the struggle for Indian independence and his association with Naidu.

Grover, Verinder, and Ranjana Arora, eds., *Sarojini Naidu: Great Woman of Modern India*, Deep and Deep, 1993.
    The first half of this volume, published in India, collects selected political speeches by Naidu. The second half comprises a series of articles focused on political analysis of Naidu's life and career.

Naidu, Sarojini, *The Broken Wing: Songs of Love, Death & Destiny, 1915–1916*, William Heinemann, 1917.
    This is the third and final collection of poetry Naidu published during her lifetime.

SUGGESTED SEARCH TERMS

Sarojini Naidu

Naidu AND "In the Bazaars of Hyderabad"

English Indian literature

orientalism

Hyderabad

Indian independence

swadeshi

Edmund Gosse

Ananda Coomaraswamy

Gandhi

Love Song

DOROTHY PARKER

1926

Dorothy Parker is a legendary figure from the Jazz Age: a member of the famous literary circle of the Algonquin Round Table, a best-selling poet, and then a screenwriter, whose career was finally extinguished by the McCarthy-era blacklist, one of the most shameful episodes in American history. One of the first people whom radio and periodical syndication made famous for being famous, Parker's name is recognized by many (in the 1990s her life was the subject of two motion pictures), but her work is less well known. A poem such as her "Love Song" can seem today like a mere trifle, as it seemed to many reviewers when it was published. Nonetheless, it carries a serious message of embryonic feminism and creates a modern form of the ancient poetic epigram in an authentic, conversational language. Originally published in her volume *Enough Rope* (1926), the poem can also be found in her *Collected Poems: Not So Deep as a Well* (1936).

AUTHOR BIOGRAPHY

The parents of Dorothy Rothschild, as she was first named, Jacob and Eliza Rothschild, lived in Manhattan, but their daughter was born at their summer cottage in Long Branch, New Jersey, on August 22, 1893. Jacob was a successful garment manufacturer and a doctor of Talmudic law.

Dorothy Parker (©Hansel Mieth / Getty Images)

Eliza, a Protestant, died when Dorothy was five, and the girl soon acquired a stepmother, Eleanor. The adult Dorothy would leave no doubt that she loathed her father and stepmother as well as her half siblings. She felt that her father was a bully and her stepmother spent too much effort trying to convert her to fundamentalist Christianity. She also blamed her father for the discrimination she experienced as a Jew. Dorothy nevertheless received a first-class education, at private Catholic schools, but after she graduated from high school, she struck out on her own.

She began her working life as a pianist at a dancing school. She sold her first poem to *Vanity Fair* in 1914 and quickly became hired as an editorial assistant at *Vogue* and as a staff writer and theater critic at *Vanity Fair* in 1916. In 1917, she married Edwin Parker but separated from him when he went overseas to serve in World War I just a few months later. (They divorced in 1928.) Through the 1920s, Dorothy Parker became nationally known as a critic, poet,

short-story writer, and member of the literary circle called the Algonquin Round Table. In 1926, she published her first poetry collection, *Enough Rope*, which became a national best seller (to the tune of forty-seven thousand copies that year, a very large print run at the time). *Enough Rope* contains "Love Song." Her short story "Big Blonde" won the O. Henry Award in 1929.

Throughout this period, despite what can only be described as phenomenal professional success, Parker suffered from depression, resulting in serious bouts of alcoholism and several suicide attempts. Parker frequently underwent psychotherapy, including Freudian psychoanalysis. By the early 1930s, Parker was also a regular guest making the rounds of radio shows. Sondra Melzer, in *The Rhetoric of Rage*, describes Parker's life in this period:

> Dazzling, flippant, reckless, and rebellious on the outside, inside, her life was marked by abject sadness, incurable pessimism, failed relationships with men, mordant moodiness, self-doubt, and self-punishment. As her life fed her fiction, her fiction elucidated elements of life.

In 1934, Parker married Alan Campbell, and the two moved to Hollywood and worked as a screenwriting team, making up to five thousand dollars per week in the depths of the Great Depression. They were nominated, along with cowriter Robert Carson, for an Academy Award for the script of *A Star Is Born* (1937). Although there were some periods of estrangement, Parker would remain linked with Campbell until his suicide in 1963.

Always sensitive to anti-Semitism, Parker helped to found the Hollywood Anti-Nazi League in 1936 and traveled to Spain, reporting from the antifascist side in the Spanish Civil War. She also worked for charities that resettled Spanish war orphans and Loyalist soldiers after the fascists' victory in Spain. For these reasons, she was seriously investigated as a Communist agent in 1940 by J. Edgar Hoover's FBI. In 1950, Parker's Hollywood career, and to a large degree her career as a writer, came to a halt because she was blacklisted. The blacklist was promulgated by the House Un-American Activities Committee (HUAC). This was an official organ of the government that without trial or investigation decided that certain Americans were Communists (which was never a crime) and therefore their very existence was contrary to American values. The committee produced the blacklist, and the Hollywood studios voluntarily enforced it, firing or never hiring anyone whose name appeared on it, in unofficial exchange for not being formally investigated by HUAC. None of the people on the list were Communist spies or regarded themselves as enemies of the United States, but the reactionary, authoritarian members of the committee recognized that their subjects' liberal impulses made them different, an alien *other*, and so smeared them with the convenient label *Communist*.

The nature and extent of the authoritarian hysteria of the period can be seen in the writings of critic and cultural historian Edmund Wilson. Politically far to the left, Wilson had written a sympathetic history of Communism and was himself highly suspected, and from 1955 to 1965 he would go on a tax strike to protest the erosion of civil liberties in the United States represented by the blacklist and similar Cold War measures. Nevertheless, in 1950, in his *Classics and Commercials: A Literary Chronicle of the Forties*, Wilson was able to write of Parker:

> She succumbed to the expiatory mania that has become epidemic with film-writers and was presently making earnest appeals on behalf of those organizations which talked about being "progressive" and succeeded in convincing their followers that they were working for the social revolution, though they had really no other purpose than to promote the foreign policy of the Soviet Union.

Even Wilson could not see at that time the difference between wanting to reform society to promote equality between the sexes and races, the only political radicalism Parker ever engaged in, and being an agent of a hostile ideological power. Parker still wrote sporadically for magazines such as *Esquire*, but her literary output suffered from her increasing alcoholism as much as her status as a political pariah. Parker died of a heart attack in New York City on June 7, 1967. She left her estate to the civil rights activist Martin Luther King Jr., and it was eventually passed on to the National Association for the Advancement of Colored People.

POEM SUMMARY

The text used for this summary is from *Collected Poems: Not So Deep as a Well*, Viking, 1936, p. 63. A version of the poem can be found on the following web page: http://www.poetry foundation.org/poems-and-poets/poems/detail/44831.

MEDIA ADAPTATIONS

- There is a recording of "Love Song" being read aloud by an unidentified actress on its page on the Poetry Foundation website (http://www.poetryfoundation.org/poems-and-poets/poems/detail/44831.). The reading is one minute and eighteen seconds long.

"Love Song" is divided into three stanzas, each of four couplets, or eight lines. The poem is in the voice of a woman, describing her lover or husband. (The speaker's gender is never identified in the poem, but in a work from the 1920s that she is female can be taken for granted.) In each stanza, she begins with outlandish praise of the man but by the end expresses increasing distaste for him, before renewing the praise in the next stanza.

Lines 1–8

In the first stanza, the speaker begins to describe the man she is in love with. She relates his character to a particular stereotype, the decisive man of action who boldly acts as soon as he has made up his mind, without wasting much time on deliberation or forethought. While this trait is often singled out as attractive to women and as something possessed by men who are natural leaders—the kind of thing that defines a "real man"—in society decisiveness must be tempered with caution. Perhaps Parker singles out this decisiveness because in isolation it can be reckless or hasty, and she is building up to the rejection of the man described. (This kind of personality is certainly, though not exclusively, the ideal of fascist masculinity, though Parker was naturally not as concerned with fascism in 1926 as she would later be.)

The speaker next praises what can be described as the man's rhetorical effectiveness: his speech is persuasive, and his demeanor is attractive. The likening of the man's mood to a flag flowing in the breeze is a conventional appeal to patriotism. Altogether, it is hard not to believe that Parker is purposefully describing the authoritarian personality type, which indeed is commonly presented as an ideal in society but one that does not hold up on closer examination. Parker is relying on her audience's first casual reading of the text to suggest that all of these traits might be positive, only to force the reader to reconsider after the punch line at the end of the stanza. The speaker finishes this stanza's praise by noting that the man would make an immediate and lasting impression on any woman and stating that her life completely revolves around his—which, though flattering to the man, is not the kind of relationship liable to result in much happiness for the speaker. She concludes by saying she wishes she had never met the man.

Lines 9–16

In the first line of the second stanza, Parker's meaning becomes a bit difficult to unravel, since so many things are going on at once. She returns to praising the man, but now she says that he is "mad." In this case, it is easier to understand the secondary, negative reading that Parker wants to promote, namely, that he is either enraged or insane, and harder to read the word positively. She may be trying to invoke the kind of meaning found in the idiom *he's mad for her*, meaning madly in love with her, or she may simply be tempering her praise with straight talk about his character. *Fleet* at the end of the line must mean "athletic," which is an obvious point of masculine praise, but in particular it suggests that he is *fleet of foot*, or liable to take off and at a decent clip, which rings more like a criticism. The word *fleet* may also have been chosen for its rhyme. In a sense this would count as satire, if Parker is making the poem hypercorrect in its poetic character to accentuate the humor.

In the next few lines, Parker heightens the satirical effect, bursting into an imitation of classical pastoral, as if the man were a mythological hero born to a wood nymph. The unspoken corollary is that someone reared outside of human society would be uncouth and boorish, like Paris, the prince of Troy and suitor of Helen, who was left exposed at birth and reared by a she-bear. The elevated imitation of classical language continues with the man's feet being given the epithet *roaming*, which is easily read as indicating that he betrays his lover through adultery. The speaker says that the world is beautiful and

sunny for the man, leaving the implication that it is not that way for her. Finally, the man is compared to the sweet smell of acacia, which has been used since antiquity in manufacturing perfume and incense. This fits in well with the bucolic turn of this stanza, but it is also possible that Parker is giving a second meaning here as well, since acacia leaves contain cyanide and will kill any livestock that are allowed to feed on them. In the stanza's final couplet, the speaker reveals that she is so obsessed with the man that she dreams of him, but really would prefer that he be separated from her by being on the other side of the world.

Lines 17–24

At the beginning of the third stanza, the speaker describes her lover as being like the passing of a beautiful June day. This perhaps conditions her earlier description of him as "fleet" by suggesting that her love for him (or vice versa) is, or ought to be, fleeting. Similarly, the man is unacquainted with unhappiness, which has the secondary implication that he ignores the unhappiness of those around him, specifying the results of the rashness praised in the first stanza. The next four lines function mainly as a satire of elevated poetic language, but they reinforce the ideas of inflexibility and pigheadedness that go along with making quick decisions. In the final couplet, the speaker restates her obsessive love for the man but wishes that someone would release her from it by shooting him.

THEMES

Feminism

Women have, since the beginning of human culture, been legally and socially disadvantaged compared with men, but the arc of history has generally bent towards establishing equality between the sexes. The nineteenth century saw the beginning of a positive feminist movement in which women campaigned for an equal social position. Today, these movements are generally known as first-wave feminism. In this period, women were concerned with gaining legal equality, and this came in the United States in the form of women's property rights (under English and earlier American law, married women's property and wages technically belonged to their husbands) and the right to vote in elections

TOPICS FOR FURTHER STUDY

- In 1992, a new book of Greek epigrams, believed to be mostly by the Hellenistic epigrammatist Posidippus of Pella, was acquired by the University of Milan. It was preserved because the book had been torn up and used as mummy wrappings (cartonage) in ancient Egypt. It contains 112 poems and is the largest discovery of ancient Greek poems since the town dump of the Egyptian city of Oxyrhynchus was excavated over a century ago. Although the text received a formal initial publication in 2001, the Center for Hellenic Studies at Harvard has carried out an experiment in online publication with the text, publishing a constantly updated edition together with a series of web pages containing a vast amount of research on and resources for studying the document (http://www.chs.harvard.edu/CHS/article/display/1347; a search there for Posidippus will return additional results), including English translations (http://www.chs.harvard.edu/CHS/article/display/1723). Make a presentation to your class describing Posidippus's work and its epigrammatic character as well as giving an overview of the resources available on the Center for Hellenic Studies website.

- The Japanese haiku, a staple of contemporary literature instruction in the United States, is, in Japanese literature, linked with epigrammatic subject matter. The third line reveals a new meaning for the first two. Write and share with your class a haiku (which can be simply thought of in English as a poem with three lines consisting of five, seven, and five syllables, though in Japanese those numbers quantify the number of characters and their calligraphic execution is an integral part of the composition)

that is epigrammatic in character. William Ninnis Porter's *A Year of Japanese Epigrams* (1911) provides sample haikus and a discussion of the haiku form in relation to the Western epigram.

- The Dorothy Parker Society (http://dorothyparker.com/) maintains an unusual website devoted to Parker's life in New York. The site hosts biographical and other material about Parker, including sound recordings of Parker reading more than thirty of her poems, but is more generally devoted to New York as Parker experienced it, with pages on various apartments she lived in as well as bars and cafés she frequented. There are regular updates on events at the Algonquin Hotel. The society hosts parties and other events (chronicled in a monthly newsletter) meant to emulate Parker's Jazz Age lifestyle. Use the resources at the site to make a presentation introducing your class to Parker's New York.

- "Phrases and Philosophies for the Use of the Young" is a short collection of epigrams by Oscar Wilde, which was published in 1907, together with prose epigrams drawn from Wilde's other writings, in the first edition of his collected works (*The Writings of Oscar Wilde*, https://archive.org/details/epigramsphrasesp00wild). Because the work was intended for a young-adult audience, Wilde was closely questioned about it at his trial for homosexuality as the prosecutor attempted to prove that Wilde was morally corrupt. Using Wilde's and Parker's epigrams as models, write several epigrams that expose some overlooked but essential truths in your own life experience.

---

equally with men. This was granted in 1920 through the Nineteenth Amendment to the Constitution. Women still faced inequality in

unofficial matters, however. For instance, very few women were able to pursue professional careers—as doctors, lawyers, or engineers, for example—because it was expected that they would sooner or later leave work to become mothers and housewives.

Writing and the entertainment industry had always been an exception, and Parker exploited that exception to pursue her own highly successful career. Even so, it remained true that even a woman like Parker was still widely viewed as subordinate to or dependent on men, and Parker unquestionably felt that way herself, having internalized the mores of her generation. Until the awakening of a greater consciousness through the second-wave feminism of the 1950s and 1960s, calls for women's freedom and equality in the social, rather than merely legal, sphere were often dismissed as radical.

Nevertheless, in "Love Song" Parker expresses feminist social concerns. In her poetry as well as in her short stories, Parker was able to indirectly express women's dissatisfaction with their social limitations. Sondra Melzer, in *The Rhetoric of Rage*, points out that Parker's work can provide insight into the internalized or repressed stage of feminism between the first and second wave: "Dorothy Parker's stories seen from the perspective of modern feminist theory, shed new light on the way in which a woman's image, status, social roles, sexual behavior and relationships are to be read in literature." The speaker of "Love Song" is a woman who is trapped in a relationship with an emotionally abusive and authoritarian partner, which she cannot easily leave either because of legal obstacles (divorce being rare, especially outside the upper classes) or social pressures. She can express her desire to leave him, however strongly felt, only ironically, as a fantastic wish.

Emotions

In Parker's "Love Song," it is clear that the speaker of the poem despises the man she is describing. She seems to have been seduced into loving him at one time, but she wishes now that he were dead or at least far away from her. Whatever the nature of their relationship, however, she cannot bring this separation about. Therefore, she must dissemble her former feeling of affection to the man and to the world, while carefully hiding her true feelings; they slip out only in the joke-like punch lines at the end of each stanza. In short, the speaker has to use humor to veil the hostility that she feels but

The speaker implies that the sun shines just for her lover (©Elenamiv / Shutterstock.com)

cannot express because of her second-class feminine status within the relationship. Melzer observes that this use of humor is common throughout Parker's work: "While drawing playful attention to the stereotypical behavior of women, Parker's ironic humor disguised implicit criticism and outrage toward a repressive and patriarchal society."

STYLE

Poetics

Parker's "Love Song" takes a highly conventional approach to meter. The poem is arranged in three stanzas, each of four couplets, or eight lines. The rhyme scheme is *abab*, meaning that the first line rhymes with the third, the second with the fourth, and so on. One can find descriptions of the poem (especially online) that state that it is in common measure (a line of iambic quadrameter followed by a line of iambic trimeter), but all of the lines are quadrameters. This means that each line consists of four feet, iambs in particular. The iamb, an unstressed syllable followed by a stressed syllable, is the basic unit of English meter. Within any iambic verse, some substitution of other poetic feet is allowed.

Parker follows traditional poetic form with great meticulousness—indeed, too strictly, which produces a sort of singsong quality of exaggerated meter meant to be satirical compared with the lines of a poet like William Shakespeare or John Keats. Similarly, Parker uses unexpected and unlikely rhymes that seem forced and nearly impossible, as if she were desperately searching for a rhyme rather than for meaning. By the 1920s, leading poets in English like T. S. Eliot and Ezra Pound either abandoned or greatly modified traditional poetic conventions such as meter and rhyme because they came to seem artificial and a hindrance to the true purpose of poetry, conveying meaning through figurative language. Parker's poem is purposely quaint in comparison, as if it were still possible to seriously write an old-fashioned popular poem like Ernest Thayer's "Casey at the Bat." On the other hand, "Love Song" is also satirical of the nature of poetry as figurative language. In the second stanza, she satirizes the elevated poetic language of ancient pastoral, putting high-sounding phrase to ridiculous use. Her model for this is inevitably the Roman poet Virgil in his *Eclogues* and *Georgics*, collections that Parker, like most of her middle-class audience in the 1920s, would have read in Latin in school. In the last stanza of "Love Song," Parker uses combinations of obscure words and convoluted phrasings that may, to a casual reader, at first pass as serious poetic language but which collapse under their own weight into satire as one tries to untangle them. The last line of each stanza, the punch line, is rendered in everyday highly colloquial speech specifically to bring the reader back from the poetic realm to the real world, as the speaker expresses her wishes that she had never met her lover, that he would go away, that someone would kill him.

Irony

Irony is the technique of presenting a text (in the broadest sense, including any form of communication) that seems to have one very definite surface meaning but which actually means exactly the opposite. The discerning reader is meant to experience humor, astonishment, or some other emotion as he figures out for himself the relation between truth and the appearance of truth in the ironic statement. Parker's "Love Story" is ironic on every level. It seems to be a woman praising the virtues of a man she loves, but in fact she is describing how insufferable she finds the man and how she longs to be rid of him, to the point of wishing someone would murder him. The title "Love Story" suggests a story in which two

people fall in love, but instead the poem shows what must be taken as the death of the woman's love for her partner. The individual tropes of praise are just as ironic. The man makes an overwhelming impression that would persuade any woman to love him, but the same words more carefully considered mean that he is thoughtless, manipulative, and demanding. The man is fleet of foot, but this makes him faster to run to other women and betray his lover.

HISTORICAL CONTEXT

The Algonquin Round Table

At the height of her popularity in the 1930s, Parker had greater fame as a celebrity—someone whose fame depends more on being written about frequently in newspapers and magazines and mentioned on the radio than on any actual achievements—than reputation as a poet. This celebrity can hardly be disentangled from her membership in the Algonquin Round Table. This unofficial body consisted of a number of professional writers who met for regular luncheons in the Oak Room (later the Rose Room) at the Algonquin Hotel in New York throughout the 1920s and early 1930s. Several of the members, besides Parker, had regular newspaper columns or regularly wrote nationally syndicated articles, such as Franklin Pierce Adams and Alexander Woollcott, while member Harold Ross was the founder and editor of the *New Yorker*, so the various jokes and witticisms told by the Round Table members became known across the country. Much of their humor was quite cutting and tended towards practical jokes, so the members informally called each other the "vicious circle," but the term Algonquin Round Table comes from press reporting about them.

Besides Ross and Parker, the Pulitzer Prize– and Tony Award–winning playwright and director George S. Kaufman is probably the member of the Round Table best known today. Kaufman wrote and directed the stage versions of the Marx Brothers' Broadway shows *The Cocoanuts* and *Animal Crackers* and hence was a friend of Harpo Marx, whom he introduced to the group, though his attendance was sporadic. Many of the members, like Parker, left for a career in Hollywood. Contemporary critics of the Round Table, such as writer James Thurber,

The speaker compares her love to a flying flag *(©L F File | Shutterstock.com)*

critiqued the group as more or less a publicity stunt so that members could promote each other's celebrity, the original case of becoming famous for being famous.

In an Associated Press interview towards the end of her life, Parker undercut the reputation of the Round Table group, saying:

> People romanticize it. It was no Mermaid Tavern, I promise you, these were no giants. Think of who was writing in those days—Lardner, Fitzgerald, Faulkner, and Hemingway. Those were the real giants. The Round Table was just a lot of people telling jokes and telling each other how good they were. Just a bunch of loudmouths showing off, saving their gags for days, waiting for a chance to spring them. It was not legendary. I don't mean that—but it wasn't all that good. There was no truth in anything they said. It was the terrible day of the wisecrack, so there didn't have to be any truth, you know. There's nothing memorable about them.

The Mermaid Tavern was the home of a Jacobean literary group that included John Donne and Ben Jonson. (Shakespeare's membership is probably apocryphal.) Aviva Slesin's 1987

film *The Ten-Year Lunch* is a documentary about the Algonquin Round Table that won the Academy Award for Best Documentary. Alan Rudolph's film *Mrs. Parker and the Vicious Circle* (1994) tells a fictional version of the story of the Round Table from Parker's perspective.

CRITICAL OVERVIEW

Sondra Melzer, author of *The Rhetoric of Rage*, one of the few scholarly monographs on Parker, indeed points out that "there is a notable absence of substantive scholarship on Parker in American literary criticism." In addition, she finds,

> It is astonishing that Dorothy Parker's universe remains essentially unexplored as serious literature about women. . . . Virtually no critics have sought to furnish serious consideration of the view of women in the works of Dorothy Parker or to explore her treatment of women from a feminist perspective.

Melzer's work is addressed to correcting these omissions and provides a feminist analysis of several of Parker's short stories, all of which

COMPARE & CONTRAST

- **1920s:** First-wave feminism accomplishes its goal of obtaining women's suffrage with the passage of the Nineteenth Amendment in 1920.

  Today: Third-wave feminism aims to bring about complete equality between men and women now that many legal and social barriers have been removed by earlier feminist efforts.

- **1920s:** Sigmund Freud's technique of psychoanalysis is a popular fad in American intellectual circles.

Today: In America, psychoanalysis still has a dedicated following, and many of its ideas seem permanently fixed in popular consciousness, but Freudian psychoanalysis has generally fallen out of favor.

- **1920s:** Thanks to radio and the proliferation of national magazines, the first celebrities emerge who are, so to speak, famous for being famous.

  Today: Among millennials, social media have created a culture in which Facebook *likes* and YouTube *views* have become a way to measure social status or fame.

---

deal with the same theme as "Love Song," namely, a woman trapped in a dependent and ultimately destructive relationship that she cannot escape and against which society permits her to defend herself with nothing more than ironic humor. About Parker's best-selling poetry anthology *Enough Rope* (which contains "Love Song"), Melzer observes:

> People bought it because the author was a media celebrity, and they seemed to appreciate it more for the voguish humor, rather than for the subtle details of the subtext, which touched upon the little, painful, and poignant struggles of women's life.

Arthur F. Kinney, in his study *Dorothy Parker, Revised* (alongside Kinney's earlier *Dorothy Parker*, the only other monograph devoted entirely to her work), deals more extensively with the collection *Enough Rope* as a whole. Kinney gives a good survey of contemporary reviews of *Enough Rope*, which are not easily accessible today since they were published in popular periodicals (often defunct) and are not on the Internet or in any but the largest research libraries. Kinney observes that reviewers often deemed the book trivial but entertaining and did not consider themes like suicide or the oppression of women to reflect Parker's lived experience. A few reviews do catch Parker's darker undertones. Kinney's

own discussion of the collection points towards the influence of the Latin epigrammatic tradition on it. He concludes that "Roman poetry lies just behind the epigrammatic poems of Dorothy Parker."

Nina Miller, in her essay "Making Love Modern: Dorothy Parker and Her Public," again focuses on common themes that permeate Parker's voluminous work without narrowing in on "Love Song," which nevertheless also expresses them. Miller begins by reminding the reader that Parker's very first sale of a poem was a satire of love poetry called "War Song," which was so popular it led *Vanity Fair* to commission a whole series of *war songs* from her, beginning Parker's publishing career. Miller's thesis is that the women's magazine culture of the early twentieth century was striving to form a concept she calls Modern Love, which was meant to make readers feel superior to old Victorian stereotypes about romance in received culture. She says, "Foundational to the ideology of Modern Love was the assumption that gender relations were permanently and intrinsically flawed." Women were meant to feel the superior, if put-upon, party over thoughtless, infantilized men. "As a popular discourse," Miller says, "Modern Love rendered a vision of heterosexuality toward which one could only assume a stance of cynical detachment; in a word, Modern Love flatteringly inscribed its readers as sophisticates."

The *character* of Dorothy Parker, which Miller locates not only as the speaker of Parker's poems but as a persona she created in her journalistic writing and radio appearances, one which was far from representing her true identity, perfectly embodied Modern Love through her cynicism and ironic distance from feeling. In particular, "she successfully projected beauty and style, a near-total preoccupation with love and men, and a ladylike suppression of hostility (expressed only in 'confidence' to her audience)"—a statement that applies as much to "Love Song" as to any of Parker's other works.

CRITICISM

Bradley A. Skeen

Skeen is a classicist. In the following essay, he places Parker's "Love Song" in its context as an epigrammatic poem and analyzes its wit based on Freud's theory of humor.

To the casual modern reader, Parker's "Love Song" may not look as if it has much to do with ancient poetry. It has none of the archaic language that the popular audience might associate with translations of Greek and Latin works. But "Love Song," as well as Parker's poetic work as a whole, is deeply indebted to Latin satirists like Martial and Horace, poets whose work is not widely read today but whose language is just as modern, just as chatty and informal, as Parker's. Arthur F. Kinney, in his *Dorothy Parker, Revised*, argues that

> two classical traditions merged during the period that Parker advanced from her light verse to her mature and substantial poetry; although no one has yet paid sufficient attention, these two strains caused a remarkable revival in interest in Roman poetry in the earlier part of the twentieth century. One tradition, the more learned and serious, stemming from Catullus, arose with [E. A.] Housman and reached Parker largely through the work of [Edna St. Vincent] Millay and Elinor Wylie. The other, beginning with Eugene Field's imitations of Horace, reached Parker through later imitations by F.P.A. [Franklin P. Adams, a member of the Algonquin Round Table and dedicatee of *Not So Deep as a Well*.] Her best poems marry both traditions, display both voicings.

THE JOCULAR LANGUAGE OF 'LOVE SONG'

INVITES THE READER TO UNDERSTAND

THE EPIGRAM AS A JOKE."

Kinney judges that Parker possessed "the precision and distillation characteristic of Martial at *his* succinct best."

Parker's "Love Song" is an epigram. This is an ancient genre of poetry that was first developed in classical Greece. It attempts to put in more formal terms the wit of everyday speech and in its first stage was used in public inscriptions. One of the first and most famous epigrams was written by Simonides to serve as an inscription on the tomb for the Spartan soldiers who died at the battle Thermopylae, and is preserved in the text of the historian Herodotus (VII.228). It takes the form of two lines of verse and is written as if it were spoken by the dead Spartan warriors to anyone visiting the grave site. It instructs the reader to go to Sparta and tell the assembly there, who had ordered the soldiers to defend the mountain pass at Thermopylae without retreating, that they are still in place obeying the orders they were given. (Each soldier was buried at the place his body was found about a year later, after the Greeks had resecured the area, presumably the same place he had died.) Despite its serious theme, it has a punch line. The reader must make the mental leap to understand that the Spartan soldiers are not still at their posts but rather died at their posts and so will be there forever. This turning of the tables on the reader, to make him finally reinterpret the setup in a different way than he might have, is the essence of the epigram, as well as of the joke.

The form was very popular and was often written in graffiti (a combination of a popular joke with the more formal origins of the epigram in inscriptions). A particular graffito was written several times on the graffiti-covered walls of the Roman city of Pompeii in the years before it was buried in the ash of a volcanic eruption. The poet asks the wall how it is able to stand up under the weight of so much poetry written on it. Martial's late-first-century literary epigrams are more developed but still take the form of a joke. To cite a brief example, one poem (II.43) is

WHAT DO I READ NEXT?

- Like all biographical studies of Parker yet written, John Keats's *You Might as Well Live: The Life and Times of Dorothy Parker* (1970), though based on research, is popular rather than scholarly. Writing shortly after Parker's death, Keats had the advantage of being able to interview some of Parker's contemporaries.

- The epigrams of the Roman poet Martial give insight into Parker's poetic models and represent the highest achievement of Latin satire to which Parker aspired. An excellent modern translation is D. R. Shackleton Bailey's three-volume set *Epigrams* (1993), in the Loeb Classical Library, which prints the original Latin and the translation on facing pages.

- *The Coast of Illyria*, written with Ross Evans, is Parker's only Broadway play. (It was never performed in her lifetime but is occasionally staged today.) It tells the story of the tragic lives of Mary and Charles Lamb, who in 1807 wrote *Tales from Shakespeare*, the still-popular introduction for children. The play's themes of depression

and alcoholism also reflect Parker's own life. An edition of the play was published in 1990.

- The Japanese haiku is a form of poetry that parallels the Western epigram. Harry Behn's translation of a collection of haiku for young adults, *Cricket Songs: Japanese Haiku* (1964), was an influential book in infusing the haiku form into American schools.

- Randall Calhoun's *Dorothy Parker: A Bio-bibliography* (1993) is a fundamental resource for future critical work on Parker.

- *The Collected Dorothy Parker*, published most recently in a 2001 edition, is the most comprehensive modern text of Parker's work. Based on *The Portable Dorothy Parker* (1944), it includes some later short stories and articles as a sample of her criticism. An edition of Parker's complete works, which would include hundreds of pages of literary and theater reviews as well as several volumes' worth of screenplays, has not been attempted.

---

addressed to a politician who dyes his gray hair to look younger (still a topical issue today), but, Martial tells him, he is not going to fool the underworld goddess Proserpina, who will soon receive him when he dies of old age even with his fake black hair. In the same way, "Love Song" turns the tables on the reader in the last line of each stanza. The speaker of the poem makes the reader realize that all the praise of her partner was ironic when in the last line she wishes he would disappear or die.

The jocular language of "Love Song" invites the reader to understand the epigram as a joke. A joke is by no means a simple or innocent literary form, as Sigmund Freud, himself a sort of celebrity in 1920s America, explained. Freud is the father of modern psychology, and

his ideas were especially fashionable in the United States in the 1920s; Parker, like many people of her class and background, underwent his analytic treatment as much because of its novelty and faddism as because they were in need of psychological help. While the effectiveness of analytical therapy is debatable, and many of Freud's ideas would have to be drastically revised if modern analysts did the work of reconciling their practice with contemporary discoveries about neurophysiology, Freud brought directly to public attention a basic fact that had long been known to creative artists (as Freud himself well understood): that the human mind has an unconscious component of which people are generally unaware, but which is vital in maintaining their identity as

Her love makes his way through life as if performing a lively dance *(©300dpi | Shutterstock.com)*

individuals as well as social animals. Unconscious mechanisms prevent the consciousness from being overwhelmed by an impossibly wide range of detailed tasks and at the same time locate meaning in the outside world in a system of symbolic connections that are ultimately based on the brain's organization of memory. The work of the unconscious in supporting consciousness can be seen in the simple act of looking at another person's face and, without having to think about it, recognizing the meaning of a smile.

One of Freud's most popular books among the lay audience was *Wit and Its Relation to the Unconscious* (also translated as *Jokes and Their Relation to the Unconscious*), which explains the psychological function of humor. For Freud, the essence of wit is the turning of the tables seen in the epigram form. To a degree, an epigram could be called simply a formalized joke. Freud is naturally interested in the psychological mechanisms and structures that lie behind humor. Freud characterizes humor as typically aggressive. Jokes very often are at someone's expense and consist of attacking that person in a way

that, if it were in any normal form of discourse, would create an unpleasant scene filled with social tension. To the contrary, a joke discharges that tension. Humor is a safety valve that allows the expression of aggression that could not otherwise be put into words and more fundamentally takes the place of, and therefore prevents, actual violence. In the context of modern civilization, Freud says:

> Society, as the third and dispassionate party in the combat to whose interest it is to safeguard personal safety, prevents us from expressing our hostile feelings in action; and hence . . . there has developed a new technique of invectives, the aim of which is to enlist this third person against our enemy. By belittling and humbling our enemy, by scorning and ridiculing him, we indirectly obtain the pleasure of his defeat by the laughter of the third person, the inactive spectator.

Freud sees humor as a social-psychological mechanism as much to preserve mental health in the face of adversity as to preserve the cohesion of the community.

As Freud indicates in the quoted passage, a joke depends on three persons or groups: the joke teller, the victim or butt of the joke, and the audience to which the joke is addressed. Humor takes a truth that has been repressed, that is consciously ignored by the joke teller as well as his audience, and suddenly and unexpectedly brings it out into the open. The speaker is able to overcome the forces that hold the truth in a state of repression because of the reward of pleasure received by telling the truth. A similar wave of pleasure experienced by the audience gets the audience on the speaker's side, at least momentarily. The pleasure derived from the joke is not simple, however. The original act of repression creates anxiety, the psychological unease at having to pretend that something which is true is not true. Telling the joke, momentarily admitting the truth, discharges the anxiety and brings about a feeling of euphoric relief.

The original repression inhibited the statement of fact that the joke makes because the revelation of the truth would be damaging, either directly to the butt of the joke, or more generally to the speaker, because the joke involves a break from social conventions or mores that may reflect badly on the speaker's role in society. Obtaining the approval of the audience, however brief or limited, for breaking taboos instead of upholding them is part of the motive for humor. Moreover, the person who makes the joke can dismiss one's own aggression by saying *it was just a joke* and thereby allowing the previous repression to reassert itself.

Parker's "Love Song" corresponds quite closely to the description of humor given by Freud. The speaker of the poem, the joke teller, is trapped in a romantic relationship. She cannot simply leave it because of the social stigma attached to divorce in the 1920s, because her peers expect her to stay in the relationship, because she is financially dependent on her partner, or for whatever reasons. Yet she desperately wants out because, while she may have once been happy with her partner, a time recalled by the surface content of her apparent praise of him, she now loathes him. This is the secret, the repressed aggression that she shares with her audience in the turning of the tables in the last line of each stanza. By stating this truth, she feels relief and makes the audience feel relief on her behalf and sympathize with her, though it is not a truth she could tell directly, outside of a

> THEIR FORM, IMAGERY, AND SUBJECT
> MATTER ARE WELL WITHIN THE SENTIMENTAL
> TRADITION, YET IN EACH POEM PARKER EXPLORES
> A NEW WAY TO PRESENT A FAMILIAR STORY—USING
> A MARGINAL VOICE, A PROPHETIC MARY, AND A
> DEROMANTICIZED SETTING."

humorous context, either to her audience or especially to her partner.

Source: Bradley A. Skeen, Critical Essay on "Love Song," in *Poetry for Students*, Gale, Cengage Learning, 2017.

Rhonda S. Pettit

In the following excerpt, Pettit explains that though Parker's poetry was often humorous and sometimes shocking, she worked within certain restrictions of gentility.

... The Boundary of Gentility examines the region of permissible topics for women poets of the nineteenth century, the ways in which these poets try to extend this boundary, and the extent to which this sense of propriety continues into the twentieth century. This category includes a discussion of themes noted by Emily Stipes Watts, Cheryl Walker, and Sandra Gilbert and Susan Gubar: religion, domestic issues, forbidden love, and the tension between sexual reticence and sexual exuberance. Alicia Ostriker provides the title for this category when she notes, in *Stealing the Language*, that the sexual theme is one of the primary "strains" exercised by women poets against the "boundaries of gentility." The ways in which Parker's poetry makes similar moves is discussed in this section.

We are so accustomed to thinking of Parker as a wisecracking, at times shocking wit that the concept of gentility seems inappropriate in a discussion of her poetry. However, Parker worked within a range of acceptable methods and topics having parallels to the kinds of restrictions imposed on nineteenth-century women poets. The type and diction of Parker's poems suggests the extent to which she was aware of or guided by such restrictions. A number of her poems are songs—"A Very Short

Song," "Somebody's Song," "Spring Song," "Love Song," "Song of One of the Girls," and "Song in a Minor Key" are six examples from *Enough Rope* alone. *Not Much Fun* contains eighteen songs. The song poem has a rich and complicated role in the lyric tradition. The Elizabethan songs of Wyatt, Shakespeare, and Jonson, among others, expressed simple emotion in a direct and musical manner, thus offering an acceptable model for women poets to use. Blake's *Songs of Innocence and of Experience* lent a dark underside to the form, while Whitman's song poems added a mystical dimension. The free verse and irony in Eliot's "The Love Song of J. Alfred Prufrock" stripped the song of its simplicity and recurring musical pattern. Parker's songs retain the accessibility or familiarity of formal verse patterns, but often contain a dark undercurrent that negates the simple romance of Elizabethan songs, or the transcendent powers of nature described in many nineteenth-century poems. Thus, her use of "song" in the titles of her poems is as ironic as Eliot's, yet the poems' form and complaint echoes that of nineteenth-century women poets in Cheryl Walker's nightingale tradition.

In terms of diction, one of the notable characteristics of Parker's poetry is the frequency with which she uses the word "Lady." The term is not used merely to assign gender; in Parker's poems "Lady" connotes a different set of assumptions than that found in, for example, her use of "girl." In *Enough Rope*, her first collection of poetry, Parker includes fifteen poems that either have "Lady" in the title, or address or refer to a "Lady" in the poem. Five poems are titled with, or address or describe a "girl." Parker's ladies tend to be proper, delicate, passive victims of love; her girls are more inclined toward modern moral looseness, as seen previously in "The Dark Girl's Rhyme" and "Prologue to a Saga." At times the speaker in Parker's Lady poems may console or offer advice to the suffering lady, as in "To a Much Too Unfortunate Lady," thus bestowing a Victorian sense of fragility and sympathy to the figure. At other times, Parker seems to be satirizing this delicacy, as in "Epitaph for a Darling Lady." Her satires are suggestive of the eighteenth-century tradition of satirizing "ladies" seen in the poetry of Alexander Pope, John Gay, and Edward Young, among others. In Parker's Lady and Girl poems we find two conflicting notions of feminine behavior, one suggesting the propriety of a nineteenth-century drawing room, the other suggesting the fast life in a speakeasy.

Some of Parker's poems deal with themes a nineteenth-century audience would find wholly acceptable. Other poems deal with male/female relationships outside of marriage, and while these seem far from genteel, their reticent approach to sexuality and admissions of promiscuity suggest that Parker was conscious of a code of behavior or expectation, no doubt enforced, as in the nineteenth century, by magazine editors. Like some of her nineteenth-century predecessors, Parker at times pushed against the boundary of gentility without breaking through it.

One of the very acceptable topics for women poets of the nineteenth century was religion, a topic not normally considered one of Parker's concerns. One religious motif seen in sentimental women writers is anxiety about reunion or reconciliation in the afterlife. Parker touches on this theme in "Garden-Spot," a poem originally published in *Death and Taxes.* . . .

"Garden-Spot" is markedly different in tone from the smarty-pants poetry for which Parker is famous. The poem's opening image—"God's acre"—may have been borrowed from Henry Wadsworth Longfellow's poem with that title, linking Parker's poem to a male sentimentalist. No satiric or ironic phrases or final couplet undercut the sentiment of spiritual isolation. The "Garden-Spot" variety of spiritual isolation differs from that associated with modernist texts. The denial of burial in "consecrated ground" suggests the subject is being isolated by the rules of religious convention, in this case, the rules regarding burial after a suicide. In the texts of Eliot, Joyce, and Pound, isolation occurs when an individual finds the conventions no longer useful and chooses to reject them. Parker's poem is thus more closely tied to the sentimental tradition, but it presents an opportunity to examine how the sentimental and the modern intersect. If "Garden-Spot" had been one of her earlier poems, published, for example, in *Vanity Fair*, one could argue that its sentimental aspects were older influences yet to be discarded, that she had yet to "kill" her literary predecessor, as Harold Bloom argues in *The Anxiety of Influence*. But "Garden-Spot" came late, appearing in Parker's last individual poetry book among other poems that both continue and reject the sentimental tradition. A Bloomian analysis of Parker might thus conclude that she was a weak writer, grounds for dismissing her from the canon of "great works." A more accurate interpretation is that poems like "Garden-Spot" suggest ways in which twentieth-century literature incorporates aspects of the sentimental tradition. Its presence in the work of a writer also known for modernist sensibilities and modernist form in fiction suggests that the theme of spiritual isolation is not purely a modernist characteristic, nor a radical break from the past, but rather a different manifestation of a nineteenth-century concern.

Parker also maintains this consistency of tone, and comes closest to extolling the domestic and Christian virtues associated with nineteenth-century sentimentalism, in three of her Christmas poems: "The Maid-Servant at the Inn," "The Gentlest Lady," and "Prayer for a New Mother." "The Maid-Servant at the Inn" differs from the other two poems in that it gives voice to a marginal figure, a female we might compare with one of William Wordsworth's "common" people. The poem presents a conventional retelling of the birth of Jesus from the point of view of the maid-servant who, according to one traditional version of the events leading up to the Nativity, worked at the inn that denied lodging to Mary and Joseph. There is nothing surprising, however, in the maid's sentiments. Mary is described as "such a gentle thing,"...

The image of a mother and child, associated with "tears," can be found in numerous poems and stories by nineteenth-century women. Parker maintains this emotional force through the end of the poem, where it becomes clear that the maid is recalling the birth at the approximate time of Christ's crucifixion. Thus, two holidays, Christmas and Easter, merge into one without a humorous punch line to counter the poem's serious intentions. Though it is steeped in sentimental language and imagery, this poem is part of a tradition of Christmas poetry, as outlined by Robert Pinsky, that "expresses the idea of despair underlying religious celebration." The "dark beauty of Christmas," the ambivalence associated with sources of transformation, conflicts with and complicates the feel-good impulse of the season and of many seasonal poems. Parker's Christmas poem, read within the tradition Pinsky defines, takes on a more complicated matrix.

On the one hand, the image of death is certainly associated with the sentimental tradition. On the other hand, the presence of death in Parker's poem—part of its sentimental language—undercuts to some degree the coziness of the poem's Christmas sentiment. In light of this reading, defining the sentimental in a pejorative sense becomes more of a challenge.

As the titles indicate, both "The Gentlest Lady" and "Prayer for a New Mother" also focus on the mother figure. Again, Parker presents the expected virtues of Mary as mother in terminology readers of nineteenth-century sentimental poetry would recognize in "The Gentlest Lady":...

Parker uses the conventional, sentimental imagery of a mother and child, a sheltering breast, and a breaking heart, but she also invests Mary with knowledge of the future.

"Prayer for a New Mother" asks that Mary be allowed to boast and plan like any mother, and to forget what she knows of the past. Again we have sentimental language revising what is typically a sentimentally rendered scene. The sense of wonder, the pastoral shepherds, and the noble wise men are replaced with more negative images: "The voices in the sky, the fear, the cold, / The gaping shepherds, and the queer old men / Piling their clumsy gifts of foreign gold." This revision strategy can be usefully compared with that of T. S. Eliot in "The Journey of the Magi," where the hardships of the journey to the Nativity and its aftermath are emphasized. In contrast to "The Gentlest Lady," "Prayer for a New Mother" offers a prayer that Mary will have no vision of the troubled future her son faces:...

Within the realm of what is considered serious poetry, these poems could be dismissed as seasonal lyrics, occasional verse, or magazine verse. But if we set aside classification by poetic types for a moment, the critical biases against them become less important to our reading of the poems. Our attention can then focus on other characteristics the poems possess. Their form, imagery, and subject matter are well within the sentimental tradition, yet in each poem Parker explores a new way to present a familiar story—using a marginal voice, a prophetic Mary, and a deromanticized setting. These aren't the poems that come to mind if we think of Parker as primarily a sophisticated wit, or as a hard-living, precariously loving, magazine personality. As part of her poetic oeuvre, however, they forge significant links to an American woman's tradition even as they strain against some of its conventions. Some of Parker's love poetry also makes a connection to this tradition, but in a slightly different manner . . . .

Source: Rhonda S. Pettit, "The Sentimental Connection I: Dorothy Parker's Poetry and the Sentimental Tradition," in *A Gendered Collision: Sentimentalism and Modernism in Dorothy Parker's Poetry and Fiction*, Fairleigh Dickinson University Press, 2000, pp. 96–101.

Nina Miller

In the following excerpt, Miller compares Parker's relationship with the public to romantic love.

. . . Parker was a great admirer of Edna Millay (newly famous at the start of Parker's career), of whom she once remarked, "Millay did a great deal of harm with her double-burning candles" (a reference to "First Fig"), making "poetry seem so easy that we could all do it but, of course, we couldn't." We might as well take this as a judgment on the larger project of public New Womanhood, for Parker was, indeed, to become a poet of equal stature, with equal cultural responsibility for the serious business of feminine transgression and heterosexual reconciliation—though in a sardonic mode which turned Millay's lyricism on its ear. Parker herself put it more humbly: "I was following in the exquisite footsteps of Miss Edna St. Vincent Millay, unhappily in my own horrible sneakers." Embedded within Round Table discourse, such an identification might also have resonated with the midtown mockery of Village idealism, suggesting the possibility of a more pointed edge to Parker's emulation. But however variegated this identification, Parker's choice of a professional path occurred with full benefit of Millay's warning about public life, that "a person who publishes a book willfully appears before the populace with his pants down [*sic*]"; she had, moreover, the lesson of Millay's literary imitativeness to signal the degree of determining force exerted by the poetic tradition. For Parker, a woman writer attempting to project and sustain a highly public and appropriately sophisticated identity, lyric love poetry—and, more generally, the traditional literary role of woman lover—had its own inherent problems, founded as it was on feminine self-effacement. While Millay drew her New Womanly strategies out of the

> WITH LOVE ESTABLISHED AS MORE OR LESS A DEAD END, PARKER'S POEMS CHANNEL THEIR ENERGY TOWARD THE MORE INTERESTING TASK OF ELABORATING A LIFE IN PUBLIC."

literary tradition, Parker mined the possibilities of her public context. Through figurations and rhetorical modes that incorporated the public into her poetics, Parker provided her speakers the possibility of self-definition outside the heterosexual dyad. As we shall see, to the extent that this was a deliberate gesture toward public identity and speech, it was an identity defined not as sexual, but civic.

Within the legacy of romanticism, love has conventionally been premised on the uniqueness of the lover for the Other, and the context for mutual recognition of this uniqueness has been the dyadic intersubjective relationship. Roland Barthes's *A Lover's Discourse* captures the critical interdependence of love and individual identity for the amorous modern subject, expressed here in the text's characteristically cumulative, collage style.

> "Ah, whatever I know, anyone may know—[but] I alone have my *heart*."
>
> I divine that the true site of originality and strength is neither the other nor myself, but our relation itself.
>
> Once, speaking to me of ourselves, the other said: "a relation of quality"; this phrase was repugnant to me: it came suddenly from outside, flattening the specialty of the rapport by a conformist formula.
>
> The other whom I love and who fascinates me is *atopos*. I cannot classify the other, for the other is, precisely, Unique, the singular Image which has miraculously come to correspond to the specialty of my desire. The other is the figure of my truth and cannot be imprisoned in any stereotype (which is the truth of others).

Within the ideology Barthes describes, lovers are not answerable to common moral or aesthetic standards—"the world and I are not interested in the same thing"—but perceive themselves as inhabiting an intersubjective space with its own private ethos. The romantic relationship, then, is seen as irreducible to objective cultural criteria of worth and compatibility. Most important, it is inaccessible to outsiders.

But within such a hermetic universe, differential positions become crucially important. Critic Jan Montefiore has called the traditional literary expression of heterosexual romance the "I-Thou dyad." Focusing on the love sonnet in particular, Montefiore argues for the historically entrenched and psychoanalytically overdetermined nature of the gender polarity these poems employ.

> The love poem as it appears in the Western tradition of poetry represented by Petrarch and Sidney is characteristically spoken by a male poet celebrating the beauty and virtue of an unattainable woman who is at once the object of his desire, the cause of his poetry and the mirror which defines his identity....Problems arise [for the woman poet] from the complex processes of self-definition at work in the classic love poems. In the great tradition of Petrarch and Shakespeare, the lover-poet is principally concerned with defining his own self through his desire either for the image of his beloved or for his own image mediated through her response to him.

The male speaker, then, is the subjective "I" to the female addressee's objectified "Thou," a dyad in which the woman is reduced to a function of her lover's narcissism. John Brenkman identifies this one-sided dynamic as a form of "cultural domination," an aesthetic of love that "refus[es] the play of the desire of the other in all its negativity and conflict"—refuses, that is, the productive exchange that occurs when both lovers are accorded full status as subjects. Montefiore notes, moreover, "the obvious difficulty of speaking in a form which defines one as muse, not maker."

Feminist criticism has identified a wealth of women's strategic responses to the gendered character of the traditional canon, from literary cross-dressing to subversion of the genres themselves. At the broadest level, Parker undercut her own ascension to muse or loved object through her irony, a stance built into her subcultural imperative to perform as a humorist. More important, in sacrificing the sober intensity of romantic love to humor, she broke up the loving dyad with the implied intervention of her audience, for whom the jokes were staged. Thus

triangulated, the lovers lose the psychodynamic logic supporting their lopsided interrelation. Humor about love—not the dramatic irony attending the spectacle of bunglers but the acerbic wit of a sophisticated lover-narrator—has the power to rupture the charmed circle of intersubjectivity by constructing its audience as a complicitous third party to the ridicule of one lover (the man) by the other (the woman).

Parker also refused the passivity and objectification that the love tradition would assign her at the thematic level of her work, where her historical-discursive manipulations were most evident and particularized. Her explicit response to the romantic love tradition often went beyond protest of her designated position as female within the dyad to rejection of the very form of hermetic intersubjectivity itself. The profoundly jaundiced notion of love structuring Modern Love discourse gave Parker license to displace the heterosexual relationship as the necessary center of her poems and, instead, make the poems' public the site of her primary psychological investment.

Parker's self-declared lesser-little-sister relation to Millay translated quite directly into a poetry of the antilyric, which evoked key lyric conventions only to invert them. Intended for public consumption, lyric poetry nevertheless issues from an intensely private voice traditionally understood as "not heard but overheard." Parker's most significant manipulation of the lyric was to foreground the listening audience that was usually suppressed. Her very fame carried with it the spectral presence of the public which constituted her as a "personality," while her writing actively transformed the solitary musings of a speaker addressing only herself or the figure of her lover into essentially public space and speech.

In "Plea," humor constitutes the female speaker's first level of resistance to her lover's attempt to impose upon her a tyranny of privacy....

In this first stanza, the speaker mockingly renders her lover's self-indulgence in the terms of his own self-justification, terms the contemporaneous audience must recognize as a species of "enlightened" Free Love: the couple are to have no "secrets" to keep them "apart," anything that would sustain their separateness being self-evidently a bad thing. But as the poem so clearly demonstrates, this relation is not one of equality, and modern mutual honesty appears to be neither actively mutual nor, strictly speaking, honest. Rather, we see the male lover, under the guise of Free Love intimacy, attempt to reduce the woman to a function of his own psychic economy, an ego ideal to whom he can confess himself a sexual adventurer and thus emerge "luxuriously clean of heart."

Parker's speaker is conscious of her lover's instrumental use of her but goes beyond a mocking tone and the joke she has with her audience at his expense....

The Round Table ethos mitigated against anything so humorless as direct protest of gender oppression, but note how this requisite aloofness dovetails with Parker's own desideratum for the love relationship. Underlying the ironic depiction of gross inequality in "Plea" is an almost palpable disgust with the sort of relationship this modern love affair implies, even in its ideal (that is, genuinely mutual) form. It is not merely the self-serving use to which it is put in this instance but the very idea of "the intimate places of [the lover's] heart" that is held at a critical distance; the speaker's distaste is clearly and extensively drawn around the idea of intimacy as such.

Read in terms of the relationship's gender inequality, the speaker's relative passivity may be seen as a function of her femininity and the exclusion of her own "contribution" as anything more than confessor. But her silence may also be deliberate reticence: beyond her marginalization within the relationship as defined and controlled by her lover, the language of the poem suggests that, in fact, she imposes her own alternative framework on their interactions. Stanza one is devoted exclusively to the male lover's construction of love. The first word. *Secrets*, deliberately set off by a comma, signals the lover's self-infatuated exhibition to come. Lines like "Kneeling, you bared to me, as in confession," and "Luxuriously clean of heart once more" join images of sensuality and religious asceticism in a way that renders both faintly obscene. Ironically, this sense carries over to the programmatically unashamed Free Love paganism underwriting the lover's revelations of "clinging arms" and "kisses gladly given." The speaker's repugnance is thus plainly evident from the poem's beginning; when in stanza two she goes on to speak from within her own, more dignified

model of love, it stands as a reproof to the version that preceded it.

Leaving the lover to stand "before [her], shriven," she establishes a loving arena according to her own terms before making the request with which the poem culminates. In defiance of her lover's attempts to contain her within his narcissism, the female speaker chooses to view their relationship in the discreet and lyrical terms of flower imagery ("love, that bloomed so fair"), oppositional in its invocation of emphatically traditional rather than modern love paradigms. Here it becomes apparent that the struggle to set the terms of love in this poem goes beyond the opposition of romantic intersubjectivity and its absence in Modern Love. The model the speaker offers combines the cool cynicism of Modern Love with the traditional lyricism of love poetry. The essence of this hybrid mode is *decorum*, continuous with the drawing room dimension of Round Table identity. As we have seen, a mannered and proprietary aesthetic functioned for the group as a whole to establish their modernist "aristocratic" detachment. But for Parker in particular, decorum provided the foundation for an intrinsically social alternative to private love.

Stanza two of "Plea" highlights the stark difference of the speaker's assumptions about the status of this affair in her life. The lover uses the ostensible telos of unbounded and unending mutuality to justify his lurid self-revelations, a pretext mocked by the very nature of the confessions themselves. The female speaker, by contrast, augments the dignified distance she puts between herself and him by assuming, with lyrical calm, the unlamented finitude of their affair. She makes no pretense of being absorbed with him in particular but explicitly derives her pleasure from the experience of love itself. Their affair at its height is *her* "day of happiness," and the love that blooms, then wilts, as the metaphor suggests, has its own objective existence and its own immanent course to run independently of either of them. The assertion that she has "given so much, and asked so little" apparently expresses (ironic) feminine self-effacement but more pointedly functions to emphasize—even to flaunt—her restraint and self-sufficiency. Her protest to him to, "For Heaven's sake," keep their affair secret from his next lover, is ostensibly a plea for her own future privacy, but the force behind the expletive, the force that has been building steadily throughout the previous stanzas, derives from her disgust with the absence of privacy in their present interactions. One hears in this woman's voice the distinctly preromantic echo of Congreve's Millamant, who demanded of her husband-to-be that they "be very strange [reserved] and well bred: let us be as strange as if we had been married a great while," she says, "and as well bred as if we were not married at all."

Intersubjective love, what one Parker poem refers to as the "mist of a mutual dream," places its practitioners in an unbounded relation to each other while sequestering them away from the emotional reach of the ordinary world. But Parker's writing works actively toward a more viable sexual-literary praxis through her characteristic bitterness and the theme of an endless series of doomed relationships. Thus surrounded by the apparatus of love and men, the Parker persona remains legitimately within the sphere of "women's concerns," and she addresses her audience unquestionably as a woman. But by virtue of her amorous "failures," she is free from the all-consuming rapture that would bar her access to the world (though granting her the "success" of submersion in a single adored man.) With love established as more or less a dead end, Parker's poems channel their energy toward the more interesting task of elaborating a life in public . . . .

Source: Nina Miller, "'Oh, Do Sit Down, I've Got So Much to Tell You!': Dorothy Parker and Her Intimate Public," in *Making Love Modern: The Intimate Public Worlds of New York's Literary Women*, Oxford University Press, 1998, pp. 122–27.

Arthur F. Kinney
In the following excerpt, Kinney points out the discipline of Parker's language.

"To look upon life with the eye of understanding is to see men the prey to passions and delusions,—the very comment on which can be nothing else but satire." This remark in a popular 1922 book on Horace, one of Dorothy Parker's favorite poets, summarizes the perspective common to all of her writing: essays, verse, drama, fiction, criticism. The premise, a loose summing of Horace's first satire, recalled for her those classical roots she had learned at Miss Dana's, roots that she could translate into the demands of those popular, sophisticated magazines where most of her early work appeared. But, as she knew, this form of

> HER ACHIEVEMENT IS NOT CONSISTENT. BUT AT HER BEST—IN THE ART OF THE EPIGRAM OR THE BRIEF WORD PORTRAIT—SHE IS WITHOUT PEER IN HER TIME."

humor had its own demarcations. Aldous Huxley, among others, made this clear in an essay she also knew: "[S]atire, the comedy of manners, and wit are not creative, like pure comedy. Satire and the comedy of manners depend on the actual life they portray and mock at, with greater or less ferocity; while wit is an affair of verbal ingenuity." Parker's contribution to the humor of her period was a combination of classical practices with her own very personal tone, often using her own experience to expose the personal and public failings of her subjects. Frequently but not always this results in the persona of the self-declared (or self-implied) victim, for Parker a common profile and a recognizable hallmark that especially pleased her early readers and thus can, at times, become mannered. But embedded in her works are also the implied reasons for such conditions of life and spirit and even, at a deeper and still more subtle level, the mistaken emotions or judgments that make her characters, like Mimi and Steve in "The Lovely Leave," self-victims. It is this continual mingling of effect and cause, public and private, that raise in her work questions of consequence and responsibility and so give to it a toughness and intricacy both enduring and unmatched by most of her contemporaries, including the other members of the Algonquin Round Table.

Parker's work is also grounded in a world of taste and manners—in a world where values, integrity, and discipline are not only admirable but necessary. This perspective may stem directly from her life at Miss Dana's where classes discussing the promises of socialism and the shortcomings of capitalism, the need for ethics and the irrelevance of institutionalized religion to the sufferings and weaknesses of mankind were held in a highly disciplined class day set amidst the Oriental rugs and glass chandeliers of the well-to-do. As if her writing arose from such discussions, her work observes social facts and customs, sees them representatively rather than in particularities, and then invites the knowingly sympathetic or scornful laughter of criticism. She invites people (as a generality or type) to change, just as she urges the imperatives of change in social and political life. Amusement comes from performances and conditions. Her satire preserves through exposure and revelation. Her friend Gilbert Seldes wrote in 1924 that "[s]atire is like parody in admitting the integrity of the subject; it is a pruning knife for the good of the tree." That idea, too, is classical in origin.

Parker's writing, therefore, sanctions and insists on interrogation through compassion and proper behavior—"proper" meaning both "functional" and "refined." Usually her works insinuate her criticism, providing their own sense of decorum, while she herself practices a restraint, balance, and attempted urbanity that lends her work an air of control even in the use of conversational diction. What she strives for is a telling casualness. The discrepancy between the seriousness of her aim and the playful tone of her presentation provides not only a kind of cool satire but a forceful, because constricted, irony. Indeed, her work is so cool in its fundamental bitterness that she has from the first appealed to a very wide audience—both those wishing simple amusement and those who recognize her sardonic wit.

To locate Parker's unique flavor, it is simplest to keep in mind her short poems where, despite the compactness of the form, all her attitudes and techniques are in play. Here as elsewhere she concentrates on a specific situation or moment, the foreground sharply focused in time and space. Her images and her diction (formal or informal) are synecdochical: she has a fine gift for appropriate selectivity of detail. Often, but not always, she extends her canvas by burlesque, pun, or paradox; often too the wit is reflexive, and irony becomes irony of the self (and even of the poem, of poetry). By restricting her scope, her concentration on the paraphernalia of life never clutters her line as it never clutters her point of view. An underlying and contrasting voice is introduced dialogically through the incongruity of situation and observation, action and thought, or parenthesis—a

technique she learned from the popular nineteenth-century poet Thomas Hood—or what seems a surprise twist or sardonic remark. But the "surprise ending" in Parker is never a surprise entirely, for it grows out of the dialogism on which a poem or story has rested since it was first conceived.

What *is* complicated, then, are the levels on which even her simplest poems and stories function. At first reading, they are commentaries about what is open to ridicule, about the ridiculous. They expose correctable human failings; her chief means are repetition ("I Live on Your Visits"), dullness (*Close Harmony*), and hyperbole ("One Perfect Rose"). By such means we not only see but see through the pretense or shallowness she describes in her stories and dramatizes in poems and plays. Pushed harder, her works discuss failings not only of a poem's persona or a story's protagonist but equally of us, of her readers. When we are amused by her work (and only amused) we are trapped, because we are never meant to agree with her characters. Sympathy, for her, does not mean consent. Our involvement, potentially if not actually, is what supplies irony to her work, gives it the double edge, the sardonic twist. Pushed hardest, the third level at which her works operate reveals her as author and her insistent desire to expose, which, because it becomes universal, reveals the mordant quality of her own mind. Here the tone is neither angry nor despairing; there is, rather, a rueful acceptance, an edged stoicism. It is this quality that has led some critics to find a certain "smartness" or "urbanity" in her work. Such descriptions may be accurate as far as they go, but the hardness they are describing is not so much an easy formula for writing as it is a consequence of her polyphonic perspective. All of these characteristics are relatively available to the careful reader of "Neither Bloody nor Bowed."...

It is easy, in reading such a poem, to suppose we are to agree with the attitude of sophisticated flippancy. A quick reading, for enjoyment, will be content with this. But it is not the poem. Friends who "accumulate dividends" are business people who quantify things—not only wrong in Parker's lexicon but presumably also in our own. So the source of wisdom in the poem is tainted. There are other clues: we could hardly admire someone whose reputation depends on "parlor games," but to align this with science and art suggests the shallowness—not the wise flippancy—of the persona. The word *nice* is so limp, moreover, that the poem itself is not, finally, fully accomplished. Such are the clues we must look for in a corpus as carefully crafted as Parker's. As for the last two lines, they are a cheap theatrics, a gesture meant to secure the superficiality of the earlier lines through its irrelevant comment at the close; their colloquialism, moreover, not only extends the possible subjects of the poem but attracts the hasty reader to acknowledge the conditions for satire through the discrepant dialogic tones.

When Parker wishes, her language has a kind of classical purity and vigor, a fine power of expression stemming from simplicity, lucidity, and economy; for her, disciplined language is also a matter of taste. Like Horace, she writes satires that are seen as a form opposed not to tragedy (that would be comedy) but to epic. She deals with the commonplace, the everyday, even the trivial if it reveals something useful. In "For a Sad Lady" no word is out of tune, everything is carefully placed. . . .

Here the risk is not to be taken too lightly but to be considered too sentimental. Yet look carefully. The commonplace language of the first two lines melds into—but is not discrepant from—the biblical diction of the last two lines. The irony is clear if we see the conflicting uses of "her" in lines 1 and 4; even the internal rhyme of "loves" and "above" (lines 1, 2) suggest how the obvious ignores the meaningful. Because the poem's chief irony is that the woman could give things no one wished, she is a "lady"—it gives new significance to a clichéd word of the 1920s. Her willingness to be ignored, Parker is saying, suggests the depth of her love—always ready to nourish as bread does—even as it points to the shallowness of "love" by the "loves." Their shallowness is caught in the act of providing a grave marker that misunderstands and so, not properly honoring the lady, gravely critiques those providing the memorial, as well as the takers in life who are easily reconciled to their donors.

Like Horace, Parker weighs every word; she employs both its conventional context and the context in which she places it; she notes the attitude of the persona, the reader, and the poet. Hers is an art that *unwinds* or *progressively reveals* it meanings through concealed or exposed multiple perspectives. Like Horace, her work only appears extemporaneous; it is really skillfully *fashioned*. And like Horace, who wanted to become Rome's leading satirist by applying his personal stamp, she finds her own tone, reveals her own sensibility. Repeatedly her attitude is that of a woman who is lazy or carefree but is nevertheless put upon, exploited, unfortunate in life and love. When Parker is careless, her work goes flat, words function unequally, and her attitude can collapse into sentimentality. The poems, plays, and stories become thin or, worse, maudlin and bathetic. Her achievement is not consistent. But at her best—in the art of the epigram or the brief word portrait—she is without peer in her time . . . .

Source: Arthur F. Kinney, "Her Apprenticeship: Essays, Light Verse, Drama," in *Dorothy Parker, Revised*, Twayne Publishers, 1998, pp. 54–58.

SOURCES

Allen, Kelcey, "Algonquin Round Table," in *Broadway: Its History, People, and Places; An Encyclopedia*, 2nd ed., edited by Ken Bloom, Routledge, 2004, pp. 10–11.

Freud, Sigmund, *Wit and Its Relation to the Unconscious*, translated by A. A. Brill, Moffat, Yard, 1916, pp. 151, 204–206, 230–32.

Frewin, Leslie, *The Late Mrs. Dorothy Parker*, Macmillan, 1986, pp. 3–9, 143, 166–69.

Kinney, Arthur F., *Dorothy Parker, Revised*, Twayne Publishers, 1998, pp. 23, 86–102.

Martial, *Epigrams*, edited and translated by D. R. Shackleton Bailey, Loeb Classical Library, Harvard University Press, 1999, Vol. 1, p. 231.

Melzer, Sondra, *The Rhetoric of Rage: Women in Dorothy Parker*, Peter Lang, 1997, pp. 1–9.

Miller, Nina, "Making Love Modern: Dorothy Parker and Her Public," in *American Literature*, Vol. 64, No. 4, December 1992, pp. 763–84.

Parker, Dorothy, "Love Song," in *Not So Deep as a Well*, Viking Press, 1936, p. 63.

Weaver, Angela, "'Such a Congenial Little Circle': Dorothy Parker and the Early-Twentieth-Century Magazine Market," in *Women's Studies Quarterly*, Vol. 38, Nos. 3–4, Fall/Winter 2010, pp. 25–41.

Wilson, Edmund, *Classics and Commercials: A Literary Chronicle of the Forties*, Farrar, Straus, 1950, p. 170.

FURTHER READING

Fitzpatrick, Kevin C., *A Journey into Dorothy Parker's New York*, 2nd ed., Roaring Forties Press, 2013.

    Fitzpatrick gives a social history of New York's intelligentsia in the 1920s and early 1930s, surveying the still-intact buildings they frequented and reprinting rarely read newspapers and magazine stories together with little-known photographs of the era, using Parker and the Algonquin Round Table as her focus.

Meade, Marion, *Dorothy Parker: What Fresh Hell Is This?*, Villard Books, 1988.

    Meade's popular biography of Parker concentrates on the private life of her subject and, to the degree that she does deal with Parker's career, focuses her effort through the lens of the Algonquin Round Table.

Nixon, Paul, *A Roman Wit: Epigrams of Martial Rendered into English*, Houghton Mifflin, 1911.

    This volume would have been a standard text on Martial in Parker's day. Arthur Kinney, in his *Dorothy Parker, Revised*, uses Nixon's volume to gauge the likely reception of the Roman satirist by Parker and her audience.

Pettit, Rhonda S., *A Gendered Collision: Sentimentalism and Modernism in Dorothy Parker's Poetry and Fiction*, Fairleigh Dickinson University Press, 2000.

    Pettit furthers the work of redefining Parker as a feminist and a modernist. In particular, she sees Parker's poetry as a sort of combination of two nineteenth-century poetic values: sentimentalism and decadence.

SUGGESTED SEARCH TERMS

Dorothy Parker

"Love Song" AND Parker

Algonquin Round Table

Jazz Age

Jazz Age AND feminism

epigram AND satire

Freudian psychoanalysis

McCarthyism AND black list

haiku AND epigram

Southern Cop

STERLING BROWN

1936

"Southern Cop" is a free-verse poem by Sterling Brown, the scholar and poet who helped draw attention to the importance of African American works in the literary landscape. The poem first appeared during the Great Depression and examined the racially motivated violence of the time. Brown uses irony as he narrates the events surrounding the shooting of an innocent African American man by a police officer. He successfully exposes the ugliness and hypocrisy of racism while also expressing his personal feelings of anger at injustice. First published in 1936 in *Partisan Review*, the poem "Southern Cop" is now available in *The Collected Poems of Sterling Brown*, published by TriQuarterly Books in 2000.

AUTHOR BIOGRAPHY

Brown was born on May 1, 1901, in Washington, DC. Although he lived during the era of segregation, his family was considered middle class, according to John Edgar Tidwell, writing in "Sterling A. Brown's Life and Career." His father was the Reverend Sterling Nelson Brown, who served at Howard University as a professor of religion and was a minister at Lincoln Temple Congregational Church. Brown excelled at academics as a child and attended Dunbar High School. In 1922, he graduated from Williams

Sterling Brown (front row, left) *(©Everett Collection Historical | Alamy Stock Photo)*

College as a Phi Beta Kappa. Brown went on to earn a master's degree from Harvard in 1923.

After Harvard, Brown traveled south, where he taught at Virginia Theological Seminary and College. Leela Kapai, in "Sterling A. Brown (1901–1989)," writes that it was "at Virginia Seminary that he met his wife, Daisy Turnbull, who was his companion and his inspiration for over fifty years." Kapai also notes that the African Americans of the South inspired his work. Brown also taught at Lincoln University and Fisk University before settling in 1929 at Howard University, where he would work until his retirement.

Brown began writing for *Opportunity* and other journals in the 1920s. His first collection of poetry, *Southern Road*, was published in 1932. He continued sending poems to journals during this time. "Southern Cop" appeared in *Partisan Review* in 1936. Brown also worked as one of the editors of Negro affairs for the Federal Writers'

Project from 1936 to 1939. In 1937, he earned a Guggenheim Fellowship and wrote *The Negro in American Fiction* and *Negro Poetry and Drama*. According to Robert Stepto in *American National Biography Online*, "From the 1940s into the 1960s Brown was no longer an active poet, in part because his second book, 'No Hidin' Place,' was rejected by his publisher." During this time, he focused his work on creating essays and teaching his students. His most famous essay was "The New Negro in Literature (1925–1955)." According to Stepto, "In this essay he argued that the Harlem Renaissance was in fact a New Negro Renaissance, not a Harlem Renaissance, because few of the significant participants, including himself, lived in Harlem or wrote about it."

Brown retired in 1969, but a renewed interest in his work during the 1970s brought him back in 1974, which is the same year *Southern Road* was reprinted. *The Last Ride of Wild Bill* and *Eleven Narrative Poems* made their debut the following year, and *Collected Poems* was published in 1980. After a battle with leukemia, Brown died in Takoma Park, Maryland, on January 13, 1989.

POEM TEXT

Let us forgive Ty Kendricks.
The place was Darktown. He was young.
His nerves were jittery. The day was hot.
The Negro ran out of the alley.
And so he shot.   5

Let us understand Ty Kendricks.
The Negro must have been dangerous.
Because he ran;
And here was a rookie with a chance
To prove himself a man.   10

Let us condone Ty Kendricks
If we cannot decorate.
When he found what the Negro was running for,
It was too late;
And all we can say for the Negro is   15
It was unfortunate.

Let us pity Ty Kendricks.
He has been through enough,
Standing there, his big gun smoking,
Rabbit-scared, alone,   20
Having to hear the wenches wail
And the dying Negro moan.

POEM SUMMARY

The text used for this summary is from *The Collected Poems of Sterling A. Brown*, Northwest University Press, 2000, pp. 185–86. A version of this poem can be found on the following web page: http://www.usprisonculture.com/blog/2013/08/21/poem-of-the-day-southern-cop-by-sterling-brown/.

"Southern Cop" is a narrative free-verse poem divided into four separate stanzas as it tells the story of a police officer's killing of an unarmed man. Although it does not follow a traditional metrical and rhyme scheme, certain patterns are apparent. Stanza 1 has five lines. Line 1 names the police officer who shot a man and ironically asks that readers absolve the officer. The irony is evident, because the call for forgiveness is insincere. A period, acting as an end stop, completes the line. The first

sentence in line 2 establishes the setting. The location is an African American neighborhood. The break between the first and second sentence is a caesura and pauses for emphasis. The second sentence describes the officer's youth and inexperience. The two-sentence line with caesura is repeated in line 3. The first sentence describes the officer's mindset at the time of the shooting. He is nervous and jumpy because he is afraid of the neighborhood. The second sentence indicates that the high temperature influenced the following events. Additionally, the final word of line 3 rhymes with the final word of line 5. In line 4, an African American man dashed past the officer, which is why the officer shoots in line 5. Both line 4 and line 5 end with an end stop.

Stanza 2 is also made up of five lines, but here the speaker explains the officer's motivations for shooting an unarmed man. Line 6 repeats line 1 except for a change in the third word. More than imparting forgiveness, the poet asks the reader to comprehend this policeman. Again the speaker is ironic in his statement. In line 7 and line 8, the racist mindset of the officer is revealed. The African American man is automatically considered threatening in line 7, and a comma at the end of the line creates a brief pause before introducing the reason behind the officer's assumption. The man is considered a threat simply because of the speed of his pace and not because of any violent behavior. A semicolon ends line 8, which has only three words and a great deal of blank space. Line 8 rhymes with line 10. Line 9 and line 10 are linked without any punctuation, following a thought through to completion, which is an example of enjambment. The idea carries over from one line to the next. In line 9, the officer is described as young and new to his job, but he sees an opportunity. In line 10, the opportunity that the officer discovers is the chance to demonstrate his manhood by killing someone.

Six lines make up stanza 3. Line 11 repeats line 1 except for the third word. This time the reader is asked to support the officer's action. Again, the speaker uses irony to communicate the opposite of his words. Line 12 rhymes with line 14, and line 16 is an example of eye rhyme: the final word ends with the same letters as the other two lines but does not have the same sound. Brown ironically encourages pardoning the officer, and enjambment between line 11 and line 12 links the lines. In line 12, the speaker mentions that it is not possible for the officer to receive an award for his decision to shoot an unarmed man, which is why he must be excused for his behavior. Here, the irony of the poem continues. A period acts as an end stop and completes the line before introducing the events that took place after the shooting.

Line 13 is a dependent clause that communicates that the officer eventually did discover why the man was moving so quickly when he passed through the street. The comma at the end of the line creates a very short pause before introducing the independent clause of line 14. Once the officer discovers the truth, the man has already been killed despite his being innocent. Like line 8, line 14 ends with a semicolon and has visual blank space before introducing the dead man.

Enjambment connects line 15 and 16. Here, the speaker shifts from describing the police officer to speaking about the dead man. In line 15, the speaker introduces the African American that the officer shot and what can be communicated about his death. In line 16, the only response that the speaker has is to call it unlucky. Understating the impact of the dead man's suffering and its effect on the people in his life reflects common sayings used when people have been shot by the police.

Stanza 4 also has six lines; just like the preceding stanzas, it repeats line 1 while changing only the third word in line 17. The reader is encouraged to feel sorry for the officer. Again, the speaker is using irony when he calls upon his readers to have sympathy for the police officer who shot an innocent man. This thought continues through line 18, where the speaker says that there is no reason to punish the officer for his actions any further because he has been punished sufficiently. The comma at the end of line 18 introduces the officer's experiences after firing.

In line 19, the officer remains in the place of the shooting. A comma creates a pause before introducing the fact that the weapon he recently fired still has smoke coming out of it. The comma at the end of the line creates a pause while continuing to characterize the officer's suffering. Line 20 and line 22 rhyme. The first word

of line 20 is hyperbole, comparing the shooter to a frightened rabbit. The comma in the line creates a pause before introducing that the officer was by himself at the scene of the shooting. A comma ends the line and introduces line 21. Here, the officer is forced to listen to women cry. The final two words of the line begin with the letter *w* and provide an example of alliteration. Enjambment connects line 21 with line 22. As the man hears the women weep, he also has to listen to the sounds the man he shot is making while he dies.

THEMES

Anger

Anger at injustice is a clear theme throughout Brown's poem. The speaker's ire comes through in the ironic tone that he uses to narrate the events of an innocent man's death. For example, in line 21 and line 22, the speaker's irony mocks how the officer suffered when listening to the shooting victim groan while he died and how he had to hear the women crying over the violent act.

The speaker's description of the scene indicates that it is not an isolated incident. The title of the poem gives the impression that the officer named in this poem is like many others in the South during this time. The fatal shootings by law enforcement officials of African American men who posed no threat appears to have been a common occurrence. Published in 1936, "Southern Cop" was a reflection of the public perception during a time when segregation was legal and racially motivated violence common. As Allan Burns says in *Thematic Guide to American Poetry*, "The poem addresses the black community, telling them how they should respond to this tragic and, as it becomes clear, racist incident."

The officer is obviously guilty of murder or, at the very least, manslaughter, and the speaker's irony serves to highlight this guilt in the minds of his readers and remind them of their personal losses. As Burns explains, "The narrator makes us participate all the more acutely in the great ineffable pang of loss." As the poet reveals his personal anger at this all too common racially motivated incident, he encourages his readers to examine their own. Addressing the hypocrisy of

TOPICS FOR FURTHER STUDY

- Read *Monster* (1999), by Walter Dean Myers. This young-adult novel tells the story of Steve Harmon, a teenager who is on trial for murder. Working with a partner, write a blog for Brown and one for Steve. Consider what each one would post on his blog and what they would say to each other.

- Brown is associated with the Harlem Renaissance despite his never having lived in Harlem. Research the poets of the movement and their impact on American culture and society. Pay attention to prevalent themes and differences in style. Create a web page that provides an overview of influential authors and their works. Be sure to include a link for Brown.

- Read the young-adult novel *The Absolutely True Diary of a Part-Time Indian* (2007), by Sherman Alexie. The main character, Junior, experiences racism and isolation in his community but expresses his feelings in writing and drawing. Create your own comic that includes Junior and someone from "Southern Cop." The images may be hand-drawn, or you can use a computer program.

- Read *Poetry Speaks Who I Am: Poems of Discovery, Inspiration, Independence, and Everything Else* (2010). This young-adult volume is edited by Elise Paschen and Dominique Raccah. Choose a poem to compare and contrast with "Southern Cop." Write an essay that examines the differences and similarities between the poems. Pay attention to the themes and style of each poem and present your essay to the class.

- Research the history of the United States in the 1930s. Take note of demographic, economic, and civil rights movements in society. How do they relate to one another, and how are they reflected in "Southern Cop"? Use the tools at the easlly website to create graphics that organize your information and present your findings to the class.

the event shines a light on the events motivated by Jim Crow laws as well as the emotions that they inspire.

Racism

One of the main themes of "Southern Cop" is racism. The police officer who is named in the first line of the poem is white, and the man he shoots is African American. The officer's actions are evidently racially motivated, because he makes assumptions about the unnamed man he killed that prompted him to fire his weapon. Starting in line 2, the officer is clearly uncomfortable about being in a predominately African American neighborhood. The setting alone is enough for the officer to feel uncomfortable and fear for his safety, even though there is no direct threat to his life—which the poet makes clear in line 3 when he describes how nervous the police officer is and why. It is this feeling of unease around African Americans that causes the police officer to kill an unarmed man for no reason other than seeing him sprint. An innate but unfounded fear results in the death of an innocent man.

Many of the speaker's ironic statements reflect the racially charged comments used when innocent African American men are shot by the police. For example, line 15 and line 16 only call the death of an innocent man at the hands of a police officer regrettable. This emotionless disregard for a dead man stands in stark contrast to the calls for mercy for the officer who took the shot without any provocation. For example, in line 2 and line 3, the officer's youth and nervous state are held up as excuses for his actions. In this way, the poet's ironic statements serve to showcase how many Americans care more about the welfare of the man who has pulled the trigger than they do about the man who has died.

The racist ideas that motivate the officer are repeated in the poem. For example, stanza 2 explains his mindset. In line 7 and line 8, the belief is that any African American man is a risk, and running is a sign of guilt. Additionally, shooting a man is seen as the way to prove his manhood. The idea that the man may be innocent never enters the officer's mind because of the racism entrenched in society and in his mind.

The poem at first seems to forgive the officer's actions, in part because of his youth (© LifetimeStock / Shutterstock.com)

STYLE

Irony

According to William Harmon's *A Handbook to Literature*, irony is "a figure of speech in which the actual intent is expressed in words that carry the opposite meaning. . . . Characteristically, it speaks words of praise to imply blame and words of blame to imply praise." The first line of each stanza is clearly said ironically. The speaker asks that his readers give the police officer the benefit of the doubt and show tolerance. In reality, however, the poem goes on to remind readers of the police officer's guilt, encouraging them to identify the racist motivations behind the officer's actions.

Enjambment

Brown uses enjambment between lines 9 and 10 as well as between line 11 and line 12. It also appears between line 15 and line 16 and between line 21 and line 22. "Enjambment occurs in run-on lines and offers contrast to end-stopped

lines," according to Harmon. Brown blends the ideas between two lines to link them and create the proper emphasis.

Hyperbole

Harmon defines hyperbole as "exaggeration," explaining that "the figure may be used to heighten effect." The hyperbole in "Southern Cop" appears in line 20, when the police officer is described as a frightened animal. The expression comparing the officer to a timid animal stands in contrast to his true position as a hunter, as described in line 19.

HISTORICAL CONTEXT

1930s Segregation

Segregation and Jim Crow laws date back to the nineteenth century. Many southern states created laws racially segregating African Americans and other minorities. The Supreme Court case *Plessy v. Ferguson* in 1896 provided federal protection for segregation, favoring "separate but equal" communities. According to "Jim Crow Laws" at the *American Experience* PBS website, "Public facilities for blacks were almost always inferior to public facilities for whites, when they existed at all." Segregation affected every area of life, including education, shops, transportation, public facilities, and access to work.

The Great Depression had particularly devastating effects on African Americans in the 1930s. Franklin Roosevelt's New Deal programs were created to bolster the economy, but segregation still negatively affected African Americans. As Walter A. Jackson explains in *Gunnar Myrdal and America's Conscience*, "Blacks often faced segregation and discrimination in New Deal programs. Local relief administrators in the South made it more difficult for blacks to receive assistance and offered blacks smaller benefits than whites." Many people migrated to the North because of Jim Crow laws. In fact, *The Oxford Encyclopedia of American Social History* notes that "from 1915 to 1945, 1.75 million African Americans moved from the rural South." Even beyond the South, segregation still affected people. One work relief program was the Civilian Conservation Corps, employing young men in jobs related to the development of natural resources

COMPARE
&
CONTRAST

- **1930s:** Segregation and Jim Crow laws lead to migrations of African Americans from southern states. Many people still face discrimination and segregation in states without Jim Crow laws.

  Today: With the Civil Rights Act of 1964, racial segregation and discrimination are no longer legally protected. Sadly, there is still racial prejudice and inequality, and Americans still fight for social justice and equality.

- **1930s:** The Great Depression is particularly devastating for African Americans. There is a higher rate of unemployment, and African Americans face discrimination from relief administrators.

Today: In the wake of the 2008 economic downturn, or Great Recession, many Americans have lost their jobs and homes. According to the *New York Times*, the recession has been worse for African Americans.

- **1930s:** Legally protected segregation and prejudice lead to racially motivated violence. Race riots occur, and antilynching laws are fought in Congress, leaving African Americans unprotected from mob violence.

  Today: Racial tension still exists and is a political talking point. Organizations protest police violence and other inequalities that minority citizens face in the United States.

---

on rural government-owned land. Jackson explains that Civilian Conservation Corps camps remained segregated in some areas, and, in the North, Federal Housing Administration projects were racially segregated. The difficulties associated with legally protected segregation could easily turn to violence.

1930s Racial Violence

The migration of African Americans often led to racial conflict. In 1936, when Brown's poem was first published, racial violence was relatively common. Race riots, violent discrimination, and lynching were all potential threats that African Americans faced. One example of racial violence occurred in Harlem in 1935. According to the "Harlem Race Riot of 1935," the incident took place when a boy was accused of stealing a penknife, but the store owner and police let him leave. Rumors spread that the police killed him, and protests began. "When it ended, 125 people had been arrested, more than 100 people had been injured, and 3 individuals were dead— all of them black."

In the South, violence against African Americans was often legally protected,

particularly in cases of lynching. Over the years, antilynching laws were proposed at the federal level, but they never passed. As reported by the Virginia Center for Digital History, in 1933 the civil rights advocate Walter White, executive secretary for the NAACP, "determined to channel the NAACP's piecemeal efforts into a concerted federal lobbying campaign" when "lynching once more soared to a record high after dipping to a low of 10 the year before." He gained enough support to bring a bill forward, but it faced harsh resistance. The legislation "proposed federal trials for mob members where local authorities refused to act, fines or jail terms for officers who failed to discharge their duties, and damage claims against counties where lynchings occurred." The president, however, had a rocky relationship with civil rights advocates. Roosevelt was often hesitant to support civil rights issues, such as antilynching laws, because he feared losing support for his New Deal legislation. In the end, the legislation failed to pass, and lynchings continued for the next three decades before ceasing in the 1960s.

The cop's prejudice makes him assume that a running African American man must be a threat
(©mimagephotography | Shutterstock.com)

CRITICAL OVERVIEW

Brown was both an academic and an artist. His work, both poetic and critical, had a profound impact on the landscape of American literature. Brown's first volume of poetry, *Southern Road*, was not without its controversies when it was published in 1932. As Henry Louis Gates Jr. says in "Songs of a Racial Self," "'Dialect,' the unique form of English that Afro-Americans spoke, was thought by whites to reinforce assumptions about the Negro's mental inferiority. Middle-class blacks considered dialect an embarrassment." Still, Brown chose to include dialect in his poetry, and he persuaded critics such as Alain Locke of dialect's literary significance. In *The Collected Poems of Sterling A. Brown*, Michael S. Harper quotes Locke: "Here for the first time is that much-desired and long-awaited acme attained or brought within actual reach."

Despite the critical acclaim of his first collection of poetry, the second volume, *No Hiding Place*, was rejected for publication in 1937. He published other poems in journals, such as "Southern Cop" in the *Partisan Review* in 1936, but he soon began focusing on academic writings. Brown's other books should not be overlooked, because they helped cultivate a respect for African American literature. For example, B. A. Botkin's review (as quoted in Jerrold Hirsch's *Portrait of America*) of *The Negro in American Fiction* and *Negro Poetry and Drama* (both published in 1937) for *Opportunity* claims that Brown "inaugurated a new era in Negro literary criticism."

In her entry for *African American Authors, 1745–1945*, Leela Kapai notes that Brown "did not get the acclaim he richly deserved until the late 1960s, when the political activists of the black power movement and the aestheticians of the black arts movement brought his works to public attention." In 1975, he began publishing poetry again, and *The Collected Poems of Sterling A. Brown* appeared in 1980 to great acclaim. As Gates points out, "This impressive collection at last makes it possible to review the whole of Sterling Brown's work, after years when his books remained out-of-print or difficult to get."

CRITICISM

April Paris

Paris is a freelance writer with a degree in classical literature and a background in academic writing. In the following essay, she examines how the use of irony allows Brown to expose racism in "Southern Cop."

In the poem "Southern Cop," Brown takes a realistic look at what life was like for African Americans in the Jim Crow South as well as the racist assumptions that helped shape this unjust society. Although the poem presents a bleak and honest account of a man's death, the speaker does not directly attack the racially charged violence it describes. Rather, the poet chooses to employ irony in an attempt to develop a clear disdain for the man guilty of murder and the system that not only created him but also forgives and condones such thoughtless and unjust behavior.

Brown is a poet known for his use of realism. As Phillip M. Richards notes in "Sterling Brown, Past and Present," Brown believed that realism "provided a significant style of cultural self-description: a humane aesthetic interpretation of social disorganization and dislocation...to embody cultural crisis." In this narrative poem, he tells the story of an officer shooting an unarmed African American man for one simple reason: the man was running. The scene in the poem is not an isolated incident; neither is it a surprising one, for that matter. Racial inequality in the South was prevalent after Reconstruction, but the economic depression of the 1930s made life even harder for African Americans, particularly in the Jim Crow South. The weak economy, blended with unjust laws, prompted a migration of African Americans out of the rural South, according to *The Oxford Encyclopedia of American Social History*.

Leela Kapai points out in "Sterling A. Brown (1901–1989)" that "a common thread that runs through many of the poems is a desire to escape from the surrounding bleak conditions." In "Southern Cop," however, the dead man was never able to escape from the cruelty of the Jim Crow South, as did those who migrated from the area. As Mark Sanders explains in *Afro-Modernists Aesthetics and the Poetry of Sterling Brown*, "The urban South creates its own system of confinement where...the location determines a poignantly delimited fate."

IN THE POEM 'SOUTHERN COP,' BROWN TAKES A REALISTIC LOOK AT WHAT LIFE WAS LIKE FOR AFRICAN AMERICANS IN THE JIM CROW SOUTH AS WELL AS THE RACIST ASSUMPTIONS THAT HELPED SHAPE THIS UNJUST SOCIETY."

The very act of running is enough to cost the man his life. This tragedy is far too real and far too familiar given the setting of the poem, and Brown's poem uses irony to reveal the actual burden that African Americans in the South are forced to bear.

The speaker in "Southern Cop" addresses his audience directly in the narrative poem. Line 1 repeats at the beginning of every stanza with only a minor change. This repeated line is a call to action from the readers. The use of repetition recalls the style of African American sermons, which have often been imitated by poets throughout the years. The speaker in this poem, however, is not sincere in his call to action. The request to absolve the police officer of his crime in the first line is said ironically. In this way, the poet uses the Christian command to forgive as a vehicle to express his anger and expose the injustice of societally sanctioned beliefs and actions that cause the deaths of innocent people.

The events of the death are outlined in the remaining lines of the first stanza. An inexperienced white police officer is alone in a predominately African American area. He is nervous, and the heat is damaging his view of the world. When an African American man suddenly runs out of an alleyway, the officer shoots him without a thought. In the second stanza, the speaker calls for understanding from his readers as he reveals the police officer's mindset both before and during the shooting. "The poem's embittered speaker notes that the boy must have been dangerous because he ran, a deadpan way of identifying and implicitly denouncing the twisted, racist logic" of the police officer, according to Allan Burns, writing in *Thematic Guide to American Poetry*. In addition to the idea that moving fast is proof of guilt, the officer also considers one more angle. He views firing his

WHAT DO I READ NEXT?

- *Before We Were Free*, by Julia Alvarez, is the story of Anita de la Torre, a young girl living under the authoritarian dictatorship in the Dominican Republic. Published in 2002, the young-adult novel explores the idea of suppression and freedom.

- *After Winter: The Art and Life of Sterling A. Brown*, edited by John Edgar Tidwell and Steven C. Tracy, examines the life and work of Brown. Published in 2009, the text includes a collection of essays about Brown and his work.

- Republished in 1974, *Southern Road* is Brown's first collection of poetry. The collection showcases the early poetry of the author that gained acclaim from contemporaries.

- Published in 1971, *Harlem Renaissance*, by Nathan Irvin Huggins, examines the literature, music, and history of the Harlem Renaissance. The nonfiction text provides insight into Brown's contemporaries.

- *Select Poems*, a collection by the Harlem Renaissance poet Claude McKay, was published in 1999. McKay was a peer of Brown's and wrote about similar subjects and themes.

- *Harlem Renaissance: Four Novels of the 1930s* is a collection of writings by Harlem Renaissance authors edited by Rafia Zafar. The volume was published in 2011 and includes the work of Langston Hughes, Arna Bontemps, Rudolph Fisher, and George S. Schuyler.

pistol and killing someone as a way to prove his manhood and shift his status from that of an inexperienced officer to that of a seasoned law-enforcement professional. With the young man's guilt existing as a foregone conclusion in the officer's mind, shooting him is an opportunity that presents itself without any risk. He knows that the society in which he lives will not see him as a criminal. He is acting in self-defense because the man he killed was African American.

The police officer's racial and social status provides him with an assumed innocence. This fact is apparent in the first two lines of stanza 3. Here, the speaker admonishes his audience to accept the officer's action because he cannot be decorated for killing an unarmed young man who was African American. Additionally, the speaker points out that the officer had no way of knowing that he was firing at an innocent man until after the shooting. Mark Sanders argues that the words of the speaker are "feigning empathy and justice while perpetuating the very racism that conditioned Ty Kendricks for murder." The irony of the speaker's words, however, do more than "feign empathy"; they show the hypocrisy of a mindset that can so easily justify the death of an innocent young man and ignore the impact that it has on his family and community.

As Burns contends, the speaker in "Southern Cop" demonstrates how "society, for reasons having to do with race and official sanctions of power, stands helpless before an individual." The police officer is the only person named in the poem. In this way, he is the only character with status and authority. The officer is only one person, but he terrorizes an entire area because of his race and his position as a law-enforcement officer. Remember that the incident does not take place near his home. The officer is walking in a community that he is not any part of when he chooses to fire at a young man who poses no threat. This jumpy officer's act of murder is inexcusable, but the community has no power to stop him or others like him in the context of the racist society that created him. The young police officer is free to kill without any repercussions. Again, this "trigger-happy white police officer," as Burns calls him, represents a significant problem that Jim Crow laws helped create and then to sustain.

Sanders notes that in "Southern Cop" the speaker presents the point of view of the white citizen of the South, albeit while using an ironic tone to show how unjust the accepted discriminatory behavior is. By imitating the word and ideas of white southerners, the speaker "displays their blindness and resulting inability to appreciate the humanity of African Americans." As already noted, the officer who fired his weapon is the only person named in the poem. The young man who died is simply referred to by two words

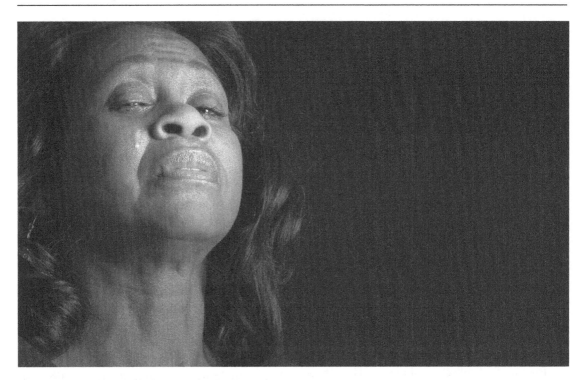

By the final stanza, with the women of the community mourning the victim's death, the speaker's sympathy for the young cop takes on a bitter edge (©Cheryl Casey / Shutterstock.com)

that define him only by the color of his skin in line 3, line 7, line 13, line 15, and line 22. The failure to identify the dead man as an individual dehumanizes him. This dehumanization is what allowed the officer to fire without even considering the idea that the man is innocent of any crime.

In addition to the unnamed young man, the other people in the area at the time of the shooting are completely devoid of individuality. In line 21, the speaker describes the officer's listening to the unnamed man die and the unnamed women mourning his passing. The women are referred to in the final two words of line 21. Again, the reference does not consider them to be individuals or equals. It is clear in these lines that the officer as well as the white community of the Jim Crow South attempt to negate the lives and feelings of African Americans, and the only feeling that they seem to inspire is fear.

Even though the police officer who pulled the trigger lives in a world where he has more power and authority than the African Americans around him, he still fears to be alone in an African American suburb. By going into a community that is kept separate from his own, he faces the unknown. Jim Crow laws kept people apart, which also prevented African Americans from being viewed as human beings with equal standing. The officer is not scared because he faces any threat; he is scared because he does not see the people around him as human beings capable of the same thoughts and feelings that he has.

Burns notes that by reinforcing the officer's guilt and the injustice of society throughout "Southern Cop," Brown succeeds in evoking an emotional response in his readers. "By ironically focusing on the officer's guilty plight, the narrator makes us participate all the more acutely in the great, ineffable pang of loss felt by the women." In this way, he paints the unknown dead man and the women who mourn him as people with individual thoughts and feelings. By humanizing the victims of this violent act, the poet emphasizes the current injustice and the need for change.

Source: April Paris, Critical Essay on "Southern Cop," in *Poetry for Students*, Gale, Cengage Learning, 2017.

"BROWN LOCATES HIS REPRESENTATION OF BLACK SPEECH WITHIN THE SPECIFIC HISTORICITY OF RURAL AFRO-LINGUISTIC PRACTICES."

Tony Bolden

In the following excerpt, Bolden looks at how Brown's style is influenced by blues music.

Bessie Smith's recording of "Gimme a Pigfoot" can serve as a metaphor for Sterling Brown's approach to blues culture in *Southern Road*. Where previous renditions were mere showbiz pop tunes, Smith infused it with a blues quality. She complemented her concern for style—both in terms of her sound and in her attire—with an equally impressive dedication to her audience and a sense of courage that prompted her once to confront the Klan. Like Smith, Brown revised popular forms, demonstrated a dedication to his audience, and displayed courage in championing the cause of black peasants in America.

It is fitting that Sterling Brown identified himself as a New Negro and distanced himself from the concept of the Harlem Renaissance. The focus on Harlem denied the richness of the rural black culture in the South where Brown had discovered the sources for his art. More importantly, the New Negro movement was one of resistance. Black soldiers had fought valiantly for democracy abroad in World War I only to be denied first-class citizenship upon returning home. The number of lynchings approached that of the 1890s, and the Ku Klux Klan had gained in popularity. But there were also requitals. Riots occurred in Longview, Texas, Washington, D.C., and Chicago. Hence, Rollin Harte quipped, "'The New Negro: you hit him, and he strikes back.'" Of course, African Americans had fought against unfair treatment since European ships arrived on the coasts of Africa. What was different in the late 1910s and 1920s was a new sense of collective consciousness and maturity. W. E. B. Du Bois illustrates this new fighting spirit in an essay entitled "Returning Home": "'we are cowards and jackasses if now that the war is over we do not

marshal every ounce of our brain and brawn to fight a sterner, longer, more unbending battle against the forces of hell in our own land. *We return. We return from fighting. We return fighting.*'"

At the same time, however, this consciousness was framed largely in Eurocentric terms. The conservative essayist George Schuyler's comment that African Americans were no more than "'lampblacked Anglo-Saxon[s]'" (qtd. in Lewis 192) was a bit extreme, but the truth is that many African Americans despised Afrovernacular culture, particularly blues music. The black elite's antipathy toward black music was nothing new (173). But this was a new age, a time for blacks to claim their rightful status as American citizens, and such a claim required sophistication—which meant the symphony, certainly not Bessie Smith or even Louis Armstrong. As Paul Oliver points out, "To the 'New Negro' and most of all to the Black recently arrived from the South who was earnestly seeking to acquire the worldly Northerner's veneer of sophistication, there were overtones of the 'Uncle Tom' element in the blues. Southern blues, folk music and talk, jive speech, and other creative forms that reinforce the morale of the under-privileged signified an acceptance of segregation and may even have appeared as devices that gave it support." Even James Weldon Johnson, whose *God's Trombones* had demonstrated the poetic possibilities of black folk culture, declared in 1931 that dialect could only produce pathos and humor.

Brown, however, was shrewd enough to reconceptualize sophistication in terms of the elegance of blues music, and he understood that the real "Uncle Toms" were those who embraced the forms of the dominant society simply because they were ashamed of the people who created the blues culture. Writing less than twenty years after *The Birth of a Nation* appeared, Brown, as Joanne Gabbin points out, understood the politics of representation: the degree to which a marginalized group is misrepresented is directly related to its subjugation in real life. Thus Brown's question was, how could he help build a literature to describe cultural history from the viewpoint of a largely illiterate people?

His challenge was to create a new poetic language that captured the feelings and insights of his people. Hughes's *Weary Blues* (1926) and *Fine Clothes to the Jew* (1927) proved that vernacular expression and minstrelsy are not synonymous. However, while Hughes's poetry represented urban black culture, Brown sought to depict black folk life in the rural South. More specifically, he sought to penetrate the psyche of black southern peasantry. For Brown, this entailed experimenting with a wider selection of forms than Hughes. "'Dialect, or the speech of the people,'" Brown said, "'is capable of expressing whatever the people are. And the folk Negro is a great deal more than a buffoon or a plaintive minstrel. Poets more intent upon learning the ways of the folk, their speech, and their character, that is to say better poets, could have smashed the mold. But first they would have had to believe in what they were doing.'"

Brown's search for what Lorenzo Thomas calls an "authentic poetic voice" of southern black peasants led to a blend of radical politics and mimetic revisions, that is, riffing on black oral and aural forms. In "Odyssey of Big Boy," Brown riffs on the black vernacular speaking voice and the ballad form to counter the misrepresentation of itinerant black workers. In his essay "Negro Characters as Seen by White Authors," Brown quotes Thomas Nelson Page, who says of black freedmen: "'for the most part, [they] are lazy, thriftless, intemperate, insolent, dishonest, and without the most rudimentary element of morality.'"

As a title, "Odyssey of Big Boy" blends the name of the Greek hero with that of the bluesman Big Boy, who helped initiate Brown in his first-hand study of the black lore in and around Virginia Seminary. In referring to Greek and African American art simultaneously, Brown provides an important clue to his own creative process. Just as bluesmen like Big Boy spoke English according to African grammatical rules, so Brown interprets the Western concept of literature in a uniquely African American style.

"Oddysey of Big Boy" should be read as a praise-poem for the heroic exploits of black workers: hence, the reference to Odysseus. Given their limited social mobility in the 1930s, the very idea of finding heroism among black workers is an act of resistance. At the outset of the poem, the persona evokes the folk heroes Casey Jones and Stagolee and expresses his desire to be with men like these when he dies . . .

The "skinning" image reflects Big Boy's rural locale. "Skinning," in black vernacular, often refers to swimming nude in water holes— away from man-made beaches and swimming

pools. But here the term probably refers to mule skinning.

Brown locates his representation of black speech within the specific historicity of rural Afro-linguistic practices. Mark Sanders has cautioned against misreading Brown as a sort of romantic folk poet. But while I accept the thrust of his point, I contend that it is possible to read the Harvard man's self-conscious positioning within Afro-vernacular as an indication of his political identification with black peasants and his struggle against the bourgeois superstructure in America. Given the poetic form with which Brown is experimenting, his employment of "Done skinned," for instance, rather than the Standard English phrase "I have skinned," reveals the material conditions under which Big Boy toils and therefore exposes the contradictions that confine him to such an existence.

In its stanzaic construction, "Odyssey of Big Boy" does not follow the typical four-line stanza pattern. While Brown uses the abcb rhyme scheme that is typical of ballads, he riffs on the John Henry ballad, which consists of five-line stanzas that conclude with two repeating lines . . .

In addition to enacting resistance by his reshaping of the ballad form, Brown adopts John Henry as a model for resisting misrepresentation. Part of John Henry's appeal is that he is a cultural rebel. Though he does not resist white authority, his conceptualization of his own identity compels him to engage in symbolic battle against the white world . . .

His bulging biceps notwithstanding, John Henry is not unlike other folk heroes, such as Brer Rabbit and The Signifying Monkey, who triumph against insurmountable odds. What is unique about John Henry is that the folk, as toilers of the soil, could interpret his victory over the steam drill as a triumph over technology and thereby reaffirm their own integrity.

Equally importantly, Brown fuses the tone of the blues song with the ballad form, creating a blues-ballad. As Gabbin says, "the blues-ballad combines the narrative framework of the ballad and the ethos of the blues" (159). Both "John Henry" and "The Odyssey of Big Boy" celebrate the labor of black workers, and both begin by recounting boyhood experiences. Unlike "John Henry," though, Brown personalizes his poetic narrative. The result is a comic-heroic narrative whose central character is not a nebulous, mythic hero but rather Big Boy himself, who describes his own exploits in the context of heroic myth.

The next stanza accentuates the realism that distinguishes Brown's work from the dialect poetry of Dunbar. Although there is a strand of humor here, there is no image of the minstrel. Rather, Brown describes Big Boy's experiences without idealizing him: . . .

The reader or listener is caught unsuspecting by the third line, which vividly describes the physical danger of working in a mine. Not surprisingly, Big Boy expresses his refusal to work in mines and demonstrates some control over his life.

More importantly, Brown debunks the myth of laziness and thriftlessness. Note, for instance, that Big Boy initially *enjoys* working in mines. Brown's point is that the economics of slavery have prevented black workers from attaining economic stability. Consequently, workers like Big Boy wandered from job to job. Having worked as a dishwasher, Big Boy expresses his distaste for the job: "Done busted suds in li'l New York,/ Which ain't no work o' mine—/ Lawd, ain't no work o' mine." Big Boy emphasizes his choice for outdoor physical labor. While he could simply be expressing his preference for a kind of work, one might note a bit of male chauvinism in his repulsion toward dishwashing. It is not difficult to find the implication here that dishwashing is a type of labor that befits women better than men.

Big Boy's inability to find steady work makes it difficult for him to establish stable relationships with women. Roaming the countryside and traversing the cities, he has played the role of both two-timer and two-timee . . .

The foregoing passage, including the sly, sexual innuendo involved with "Four'n half and M," points up the problem of gender in Afro-vernacular culture generally and Brown's work in particular. James Smethurst has argued that Brown envisioned the vernacular in masculinist terms. However, without contesting Smethurst's point, it is important to remember that realism itself is a restrictive mode of representation. Brown's objective in *Southern Road*, however problematic, was to show "whatever the people are," which includes their own contradictions. Naturally, one might pose the question: To what extent does Brown share Big Boy's

views? Admittedly, Brown's representation of gender in such poems as "Long Gone" reflects a masculinist viewpoint. But "Ma Rainey," as we shall see, was sufficiently stirring to prompt Angela Davis to quote it as part of an introduction to her discussion of Rainey "because it so successfully conveys the southern flavor of her appeal." More fundamentally, the multiple relationships in "Odyssey of Big Boy" are symptoms of underlying social problems that contribute to tensions in sexual relationships. Note that John Henry's status as an itinerant worker also limits his ability to maintain a stable relationship. And while some readers might point to the preslavery origins of male privilege in traditional African societies, it seems abundantly clear that, in addition to problems related to ideology, capitalism's treatment of black workers as slaves and, later, a reserve labor force has only exacerbated conflicts between black men and women . . . .

Source: Tony Bolden, "Early Blues Poetics: Riffing in Sterling Brown's *Southern Road*," in *Afro-Blue: Improvisations in African American Poetry and Culture*, University of Illinois Press, 2004, pp. 74–80.

James E. Smethurst

In the following excerpt, Smethurst explains Brown's distinction between the Harlem Renaissance and the New Negro Renaissance.

Sterling Brown's own critical distinction between the term "Harlem Renaissance," which he dismisses as strictly box office, and the term "New Negro Renaissance," which describes a literary moment with which Brown identifies, is not just a question of semantics or geographical accuracy. It is in fact a distinction between the values derived from a nationalism embodied in his 1932 collection of poetry *Southern Road* and similar to that which produced the Irish language Gaelic League and those of the allegedly transnational values of modernism. In making this distinction, Brown accepts the premise of Eliot and Pound— and of the Comintern for that matter, at least so far as life under modern capitalism was concerned— that modern urban life is afflicted by a sickness of the spirit caused to a large extent by rampant individualism and the breakup of social and moral consensus; in fact, this spiritual malaise is in Brown's view perhaps more intense for African Americans in the northern urban centers than for other Americans.

"

FOR BROWN, COMMERCIALIZED BLUES
AND JAZZ ARE BOTH ALIENATING AND A MARK OF
THE ALIENATION OF THE BLACK INDIVIDUAL FROM
COMMUNITY AND FROM HISTORY, WHILE FOLK
FORMS ARE SIGNS OF COMMUNAL RESISTANCE AND IN
FACT PERHAPS THE MOST IMPORTANT
COMMUNITY-BUILDING ACTIVITY."

Brown rejects the notion, however, that such a sickness was universal in "the West" and instead posits an essential African American culture in the South that is able to resist the sickness of modern society if only black Americans are willing to hold on to their history and the cultural forms of expression and resistance that developed in the intense racial oppression of the South. Though African American writers and intellectuals in the North do not directly figure in *Southern Road*, the book, then, is a direct challenge to a "Harlem Renaissance." *Southern Road* is consciously antimodernist in its explicitly thematized opposition to Jazz Age primitivist fantasies, which Brown connected to a feminized mass consumer culture. Yet *Southern Road* could be termed modernist in its use of that gendered construct of mass culture and in its implicit attempt to solve the crisis of identity posed by "high" modernism. Of course, Brown's particular engagement with history, race, nationality, and place was quite at odds, and quite consciously at odds, with "high" modernism insofar as his solution of the particular crisis of the African American intellectual, and of the folk, involved not the embracing of a vision of the Holy Roman Empire or modernity itself as embodied, say, by the Brooklyn Bridge, but the embracing of the African American folk, whose consciousness of itself and its needs is in turn raised by the "returning" intellectual. The terms of engagement of *Southern Road* with society and with aesthetics, however, is very closely bound up with those of the "high" modernists.

The very title *Southern Road* is a declaration of independence from the "Harlem Renaissance," specifically set in opposition to the

poem "Bound No'th Blues" by Langston Hughes, a writer who is often connected to Brown because of Hughes's exploration of African American vernacular English and expressive culture as the basis of literature that went beyond the humor and sentimentality of nineteenth century "dialect" and "regional" poetry. In "Bound No'th Blues," from the 1927 collection *Fine Clothes to the Jew*, Hughes creates a black narrator who rejects his former life in the South and surrenders himself to the uncertainty and cultural dislocation of the immigrant on the "northern road": . . .

Here is a rendering of the most common type of "folk blues," wherein the first line of a stanza is repeated in the second line (sometimes with a slight variation or "worrying"), setting a scene and/or identifying a conflict, followed by a third rhyming line that is generally a resolution of, and conclusion to, the first two lines. Hughes splits each of the usual three lines in this type of blues stanza to create six-line stanzas, with the break between Hughes's lines corresponding to the caesura characteristic of lines as they are actually performed in the "folk blues." Thus, in what Hughes himself saw as a traditional southern rural blues form, the narrator clearly articulates a rejection of the South and the narrator's past life there. It is clear that the narrator is not simply rejecting southern racism and poverty, but also the black communities of the rural and small-town South, in which not a single sympathetic or supportive person can be found.

This alienation contrasts with *Southern Road*, where, even in Brown's road poems and poems of individual portraiture set in the South, the protagonists' generally positive connections to other members of the southern African American community are emphasized. If the narrators and characters of *Southern Road* move around, it is not the linear and unidirectional movement of the emigrant, but rather a circular movement that generally terminates back home in the South—sometimes after trial and disillusionment in the North, as in the poem "Tin Roof Blues." Ironically, Hughes's use of a folk blues form and rhetoric as the vehicle for this declaration of alienation from the South and of a search for a new community—"to find somebody / To help me carry this load"—by a southern emigrant suggests a certain continuity of culture between North and South—a continuity that Brown would basically deny in *Southern Road*.

Thus the emigrant narrator of "Bound No'th Blues," who has detached himself practically and psychologically from his former community in the South, seeks another, more nurturing community in the North while remaining emphatically and even traditionally "Negro" in culture.

Brown's choice of *Southern Road*, as opposed to Hughes's "Northern Road," as a title indicates that he is following a different path in writing. Brown focuses on the endurance of African Americans in the rural South, which occasionally flashes into anger and heroic, and fatal, self-defense, but more often finds expression in more oblique forms of cultural resistance. The opposition to Hughes's poem suggested by the collection's title is further emphasized in the form of the title poem. "Southern Road" is unusual in that it, as Joanne Gabbin and Henry Louis Gates Jr. point out, is a work song with its stanzas cast in the form of a blues—the first published instance of Brown's use of the blues form. As in the Hughes poem, the lines of the basic three-line blues stanza are split to create six-line stanzas: . . .

Though the form of Brown's stanzas here resembles that of Hughes's, the implications of the work song—blues hybrid are far different. The "hunh" that punctuates the first and third lines of each stanza is a reminder that the narrator is a member of a community engaged in a common effort, albeit against its will. (The focus on the coercive power of the state operating on a group of people, as opposed to individual acts of racism or "unofficial" social attitudes, also distinguishes this poem from most of the poetry of the Harlem Renaissance concerning racism and racist violence (e.g., Cullen's "The Black Christ" or Hughes's "Song for a Black Gal"), though it does link the poem to much poetry of the 1930s, such as Hughes's verse play *Scottsboro Limited*. The "hunh," of course, marks the moment when all the men on the chain gang swing their hammers together. The injunction "Steady bo'" of the first stanza is directed by the narrator not to himself but to the rest of the crew he is presumably leading, as is "Ain't no rush, bebby, / Long ways to go." This injunction is a call to communal self-preservation, endurance, and a type of resistance that attempts to negotiate the terms of the community's exploitation by setting a limit to the work pace. Thus the voice of the narrator is speaking a communal story in which

the narrator's individual story (or what might be considered the blues aspect of the poem) is inextricably bound up with the group's common experience and activity, signified by elements drawn from the work song. While the dominant sentiment of the poem seems to be that of personal despair, the hybrid of blues and work song, and of individual and community, emphasizes communal resistance and survival in the face of crushing oppression from which there is no immediate escape.

However, that there is no immediate escape does not imply, as Jean Wagner and Alain Locke have suggested, that there is no hope or that resistance is futile. The narrator does not accept his situation stoically, as Wagner puts it; his condition weighs "on his min'." Rather, when read with the other poems of the "Road So Rocky" section of *Southern Road* grouped under the epigraph from this old spiritual ("Road may be rocky / Won't be rocky long"), "Southern Road" implies that the survival of community and a communal expression that authorizes and frames the individual narrative, even on the chain gang, is a form of resistance. Unlike Hughes's poem, wherein the narrator denies the possibility of community in the South and leaves for the North seeking a new type of community, Brown's speaker in "Southern Road" recounts in much more detail than Hughes's the disruption of community through the loss of family and freedom while at the same time affirming his relationship to other black men in the South. He could not sunder this relationship even if he wished to do so, since it is not merely a matter of a common culture or shared past but is actually enforced by the power of the state, as embodied in the shackles and guards of the chain gang. What obtains is a masculinist reconstruction of the African American family in which the folk becomes totally male. Such a recasting of the folk as male appears again and again in Brown's work, from "Strong Men" to "Side by Side."

. . . Thus Brown is authorized to create new "folk" forms such as the blues work song in "Southern Road" and feels free to ridicule black folk religion and even black sacred rhetoric and music while recognizing a secular value in the religion and its rhetoric and music. In this sense Alain Locke is certainly correct that Brown does establish "a sort of common denominator between the old and new Negro," however critical Brown may have been of those aspects of the New Negro movement associated with Harlem by such black intellectuals as Locke and Johnson. If it can be said that Brown's work is in a sense curatorial, in that it seem[s] to valorize older rural "folk" cultural forms while rejecting newer more urban and commercial forms, Brown does not have the feel of the "moldy fig" about him. He is not claiming that there has not been a good song since 1898. Rather, he is attempting to promote what he sees as a vital oppositional culture rather than a residual one— one that is largely, though not entirely outside the orbit of the supply-and-demand commercial culture. For Brown, commercialized blues and jazz are both alienating and a mark of the alienation of the black individual from community and from history, while folk forms are signs of communal resistance and in fact perhaps the most important community-building activity.

Southern Road is also a rejection of what Brown perceives as the cosmopolitan values of the Harlem Renaissance. His collection contains criticism and commentary on specific African American writers as well as what he perceived as the general values of the scene associated with Harlem. Brown examines Harlem and the writers around it in view of his newly defined canon and finds it, and them, wanting. However, unlike Wallace Thurman and the critical descendants of his views on the period expressed in *Infants of the Spring*—Nathan Huggins, for example, in his seminal work on the Harlem Renaissance— who found the New Negro writers too parochial in their material and their standards, Brown found them insufficiently grounded in the struggles, traditions, and aesthetics of the masses of their own people in the rural South, as well as far too pretentious. From this perspective, Brown in *Southern Road* could be said to have much in common with eighteenth-century English neoclassical satire in that his bitter attacks on various sorts of economic and intellectual "strivers" are measured against an idealized past, though in Brown's case it is not a neoclassical idealization of Greece and Rome, but that of the rural folk, that is the measuring stick. Thus, again, Brown's enterprise can be said to be both deeply radical and deeply conservative. His location of the locus of authentic African American culture in the South, his emphasis on authenticity itself, his opposition to mass culture (and the modernism that is an agent of mass culture) set against a residual folk culture, his radical yet curatorial

approach to folklore and his notion of the vanguard intellectual who rejoins the folk remain a pole of attraction for African American writers, even the neomodernist writers of the late 1940s and early 1950s such as Melvin Tolson, Robert Hayden, and Gwendolyn Brooks, whose works would seem as far from the spirit of *Southern Road* as one could imagine.

Source: James E. Smethurst, "The Strong Men Gittin' Stronger: Sterling Brown's *Southern Road* and the Representation and Re-Creation of the Southern Folk Voice," in *Race and the Modern Artist*, edited by Heather Hathaway, Josef Jarab, and Jeffrey Melnick, Oxford University Press, 2003, pp. 69–72, 86–87.

SOURCES

"Anti-Lynching Efforts," Virginia Center for Digital History website, http://www2.vcdh.virginia.edu/afam/reflector/historicalb.html (accessed May 10, 2016).

Brown, Sterling A., "Southern Cop," in *The Collected Poems of Sterling A. Brown*, edited by Michael S. Harper, Triquarterly Books, 1980, pp. 185–86.

Burns, Allan, *Thematic Guide to American Poetry*, Greenwood Press, 2002, p. 50.

Dumenil, Lynn, ed., "Jim Crow Era," in *The Oxford Encyclopedia of American Social History*, Oxford University Press, 2012, p. 576.

"Freedom Riders: Jim Crow Laws," in *American Experience*, http://www.pbs.org/wgbh/americanexperience/freedomriders/issues/jim-crow-laws (accessed on April 2, 2016).

Gates, Henry Louis, Jr., Review of *The Collected Poems of Sterling A. Brown*, in *New York Times*, January 11, 1981, http://www.nytimes.com/1981/01/11/books/songs-of-a-racial-self.html?pagewanted=all (accessed on May 15, 2016).

"Harlem Race Riot of 1935," in *Encyclopædia Britannica*, http://www.britannica.com/topic/Harlem-race-riot-of-1935 (accessed May 15, 2016).

Harmon, William, "Enjambment," "Hyperbole," and "Irony," in *A Handbook to Literature*, ninth edition, Prentice Hall, 2003, pp. 182, 253, 271.

Harper, Michael S., ed., Introduction to *The Collected Poems of Sterling A. Brown*, Triquarterly Books, 2002, p. 5.

Hirsch, Jerrold, *Portrait of America: A Cultural History of the Federal Writers' Project*, University of North Carolina Press, 2003, p. 120.

Jackson, Walter A., *Gunnar Myrdal and America's Conscience: Social Engineering and Racial Liberalism, 1938–1987*, University of North Carolina Press, 1990, p. 3.

Kapai, Leela, "Sterling A. Brown (1901–1989)," in *African American Authors, 1745–1945: A Bio-Bibliographical Critical Sourcebook*, edited by Emmanuel S. Nelson, Greenwood Press, 2000, pp. 57–63.

Powell, Michael, "Wealth, Race, and the Great Recession," in *New York Times*, http://economix.blogs.nytimes.com/2010/05/17/wealth-race-and-the-great-recession/?_r=0 (accessed May 15, 2016).

Richards, Phillip M., "Sterling Brown, Past and Present," in *Massachusetts Review*, Vol. 53, No. 1, Spring 2012, University of Massachusetts, pp. 68–89.

Sanders, Mark A., *Afro-Modernist Aesthetics and the Poetry of Sterling Brown*, University of Georgia Press, 1999, p. 111.

Stepto, Robert, "Sterling A. Brown's Life and Career," in *Modern American Poetry*, http://www.english.illinois.edu/maps/poets/a_f/brown/life.htm (accessed on May 3, 2016); originally published in *American National Biography Online*, 2000, http://www.anb.org/articles/16/16-00200.html.

Tidwell, John Edgar, "Sterling A. Brown's Life and Career," in *Modern American Poetry*, http://www.english.illinois.edu/maps/poets/a_f/brown/life.htm (accessed on May 3, 2016); originally published in *The Oxford Companion to African American Literature*, Oxford University Press, 1997.

FURTHER READING

Brown, Sterling, and Mark Sanders, eds., *A Son's Return: Selected Essays of Sterling A. Brown*, Northeastern Library of Black Literature, 1996.
> Brown was known as a great critic and essayist as well as poet. This collection of essays provides a glimpse of the author's academic writing.

Callan, Jim, *America in the 1930s*, Facts on File, 2005.
> This nonfiction text is created for young adults. The volume provides an overview of the decade in which "Southern Cop" was written.

Gabbin, Joanne V., *Sterling A. Brown: Building the Black Aesthetic Tradition*, Greenwood Publishing Group, 1985.
> Gabbin examines Brown's poetry, criticism, life, and work. Based on interviews and primary documents, the book provides great insight into Brown's work and accomplishments.

Jarret, Gene Andrew, ed., *The Wiley Blackwell Anthology of African American Literature*, Vol. 2, *1920 to the Present*, Wiley Blackwell, 2014.
> This collection of short stories, poems, plays, essays, novellas, and autobiographies dates back to the early twentieth century, featuring Harlem Renaissance authors and showing their artistic development. The text includes the work of Brown and many of his contemporaries.

Sklaroff, Lauren Rebecca, *Black Culture and the New Deal: The Quest for Civil Rights in the Roosevelt Era*, University of North Carolina Press, 2009.
> Sklaroff examines the political and social changes that occurred during the New Deal. The text offers a glimpse into the institutional racism at the time and the steps made toward creating more diverse art.

SUGGESTED SEARCH TERMS

Sterling Brown

Sterling Brown AND biography

Sterling Brown AND "Southern Cop"

Sterling Brown AND Harlem Renaissance

Jim Crow laws

Sterling Brown AND criticism

America AND 1930s

1930s AND civil rights

1930s AND Great Depression

Sterling Brown AND poetry

Sure You Can Ask Me a Personal Question

DIANE BURNS

1983

"Sure You Can Ask Me a Personal Question" is a free-verse poem by Diane Burns. First published in 1983, the poem is a one-sided conversation that exposes the ignorance and assumptions that many people have regarding Native Americans. As in much of Burns's other work, the poet includes elements of humor and sarcasm as she addresses topics related to Native American life and culture in the twentieth century in her poem.

In "Sure You Can Ask Me a Personal Question," the speaker explores the themes of stereotypes and identity as she demonstrates the absurd expectations that accompany the generalizations of entire people groups. The poem is available in *Native American Literature: An Anthology*, published by NTC/Contemporary Publishing Group in 1998.

AUTHOR BIOGRAPHY

Diane Burns was born in Lawrence, Kansas, in 1956, according to Sarah Ferguson's obituary of Burns in the *Villager*. Other sources list her birth date as 1957. The family soon moved to California. Burns's mother was Chippewa, and her father was Chemehuevi. According to Liz Sonneborn in *A to Z of American Indian Women*, "During her childhood, she grew familiar with both Indian traditions as she divided her time between her Chippewa relatives in Wisconsin and her

Someone asks about Navajo rugs, perhaps ignorant of the cultural differences between tribes
(©tobkatrina | Shutterstock.com)

Chemehuevi relations in California." Her parents were teachers, and she was educated at the different boarding schools where they taught.

Burns studied at the Institute of American Indian Arts and earned a Congressional Medal of Merit for her work there. Afterwards, she moved to New York City to study political science at Columbia University's Barnard College. After earning her degree in 1978, she remained in New York, making the Lower East Side her home.

She began writing reviews and poems in college and published in *Greenfield Review*, *Blue Cloud Quarterly*, *White Pine Journal*, *Sunbury*, and others. Burns was also an accomplished illustrator who illustrated her only collected volume of poetry, *Riding the One-Eyed Ford*. The volume was published by a small press in 1981 and nominated for the William Carlos Williams Award. She also contributed to different anthologies, including the 1983 volume *Songs from This Earth on Turtle's Back: Contemporary American Indian Poetry*, which included "Sure You Can Ask Me a Personal Question."

Throughout her career, Burns performed her work at the Bowery Poetry Club, the Poetry Project at St. Mark's Church, and the Nuyorican Poets Cafe. She developed a reputation for her skill, and, according to her obituary, in 1988 "she was among a rather illustrious group of writers—including Allen Ginsberg, Joy Harjo and Pedro Pietri—invited to Nicaragua to take part in the Ruben Dario Poetry Festival, sponsored by the Sandinista government." After struggling with alcoholism, Burns died unexpectedly of kidney and liver failure on December 22, 2006, in New York City, leaving behind her teenage daughter.

POEM SUMMARY

The text used for this summary is from *Native American Literature: An Anthology*, edited by Lawana Trout, NTC/Contemporary Publishing Group, 1998, pp. 49–50. Versions of the poem can be found on the following web page: http://amerinda.org/newsletter/10-2/burns.htm.

"Sure You Can Ask Me a Personal Question" is a thirty-eight-line free-verse poem. In some publications it is divided into stanzas, but the version used for analysis is not clearly divided into stanzas. The poem does not follow a traditional rhyme or metrical pattern. It does, however, repeat words and sounds.

In line 1, the speaker greets someone for the first time, and the rest of the poem shows her side of the conversation. The line ends with a question mark, and the three final words create internal rhyme. Line 2 begins with a negative word that is repeated through line 9. This repetition is an example of anaphora. Additionally, the repeated *n* sound in lines 3 and 5–9 is an example of alliteration. In lines 2 and 3, the speaker informs the other person that she is not the ethnicities guessed. The periods at the end of each line create end stops and also serve to signal the end of the speaker's answers. In line 4, the speaker reveals her heritage, but she begins with one term and shifts to another, indicating confusion over the politically correct term. She goes on to explain in which country her family originated to the person who failed to pay attention to the answer from line 4.

In lines 6–8, the speaker lists people groups that she does not belong to. She battles stereotypes in line 9 by saying Native Americans still exist. The speaker repeats a less than politically correct term for Native American, ending this portion of the conversation in line 10.

A single questioning interjection makes up line 11. The speaker is clearly listening to the other person talk. The tone grows more annoyed and sarcastic. In line 11, the other person has claimed Native American ancestry by virtue of her facial features. Line 11 has an end stop with a period. Lines 13 and 14 are further examples of repetition. In line 13, the speaker responds to the revelation of the family member the other individual claims as Native American. The question mark at the end of the line creates an incredulous tone, and the final word expresses doubt. The speaker repeats the claim that the individual's family was royalty and again expresses disbelief with the final word and punctuation.

The stereotypes continue in line 15, where the speaker again repeats a physical stereotype, specifically long hair. The speaker guesses the ancestry of the relative, a commonly claimed connection in people outside of the Native

American community. Again, the questioning tone is created by the punctuation.

The speaker continues to question the veracity of the claims of ties to the Native American community that the other person makes between lines 17 and 22 by using question marks that continue the suspicious tone. The first six words of lines 17, 19, and 21 repeat. The first word in each of the two-word lines 18, 20, and 22 also repeats. This repetition creates a connection with readers, who can anticipate the coming lines.

In line 17, the speaker restates a claim of friendship, and in line 18, the speaker repeats the claim that it was a close relationship. Lines 19 and 20 introduce the claim of a romantic relationship that is extremely intimate. Line 21 switches to a relationship between employer and a Native American employee. The claim of high pay is echoed in line 22. The sentence from line 23 refers back to the atrocities Native Americans suffered at the hands of European colonists. Line 24 references an apology for the events referenced in line 23.

In lines 25–27, the first two words create anaphora, and first four words repeat in lines 25 and 26. These lines are said in response to the stereotyping questions. Line 25 refers to peyote, a drug that is legal for certain Native American ceremonies. Line 26 equates Native Americans with handcrafts. The idea that all Native Americans are artistic carries over to line 27, where the speaker has to inform the person she is conversing with that she does not make all of her own clothes and instead bought them at a department store.

Line 27 comprises two sentences. The period creates a long pause or caesura. Line 28 is also made up of two sentences. Here, the speaker is obviously answering remarks made by the person she is talking to. The long sentence that makes up line 29 is referencing a celebrity who sang about a Native American and wore a headdress and costume, claiming that she had Cherokee in her family background.

Line 30 begins by repeating the same negative word found throughout the poem. It also references rain dances, which are associated with Native Americans. The three single-word sentences in line 31 are repeated through the end of line 33. The caesura in these lines creates pauses. There is no punctuation at the end of line 32, which creates enjambment between lines 32 and 33. The speaker's impatience with answering questions based on stereotypes is apparent in this change of rhythm. Here the stereotype of Native Americans and spirituality is presented.

Line 34 has eye rhyme with line 33 because they both end in *y*, though the words do not truly rhyme. Line 34 repeats the same negative first word used that began previous lines and rebuffs the idea that Native Americans know how to use bows and arrows. Line 35 references alcoholism, which has become a negative stereotype. The speaker sarcastically responds in line 36, implying that this level of racial profiling inspires drinking.

The first words of lines 37 and 38 match, creating another instance of anaphora. Line 37 answers another stereotype that Native Americans are unemotional. The final line of the poem continues to address this stereotype of stoicism when the annoyed speaker asserts her personal identity.

THEMES

Stereotypes

Stereotyping is one of the main themes in "Sure You Can Ask Me a Personal Question." According to *Merriam-Webster*, to stereotype is "to believe unfairly that all people or things with a particular characteristic are the same." The one-sided conversation that the speaker of the poem has is clearly responding to questions and statements based on assumptions and stereotypes. Many of the assumptions are beyond inaccurate; they are insulting.

One of the stereotypes that the poet addresses is the trope of the wise, spiritual Native American, who is intimately connected to the natural world. The short, repetitive replies in lines 31–33 indicate that the speaker has addressed the topic before and is bored by the assumptions made about her personal spiritual journey. The connection between nature and the spiritual world is also dealt with in line 30 when the speaker is forced to explain that she did not perform a rain dance and change the weather. Ignorance about the different Native American cultures and ceremonies is also apparent in the question answered in line 25. Just because peyote, a plant that is classified as a drug, is legal for certain traditional rituals does not mean that all Native Americans use it or know where to find it.

By the end of the poem, the speaker is clearly annoyed by answering the ignorant and intrusive

TOPICS FOR FURTHER STUDY

- Read *American Born Chinese*, by Gene Luen Yang. This graphic novel for young adults blends mythology with modern narrative as Jin Wang finds his identity in American contemporary society. Write a short story or comic in which Diane Burns meets one or more characters from *American Born Chinese*. What would the characters say to each other? Post your story on a blog.

- Research the history of indigenous people in the United States from colonization to today. Create a web page that provides a brief overview of important dates and people. Be sure to include the events of the 1980s.

- Research the common stereotypes of Native Americans found in popular culture, such as movies, books, and television. How have they changed over the years, and what is the effect of stereotyping people? Write a report and present it to the class using easel.ly to create the graphics.

- Read the young-adult volume *Poetry Speaks Who I Am: Poems of Discovery, Inspiration, Independence, and Everything Else* (2010), edited by Elise Paschen and Dominique Raccah. Choose a poem to compare and contrast with "Sure You Can Ask Me a Personal Question." Pay attention to the themes and style of each poem. Write an essay that examines the differences and similarities between the poems.

- Work with a partner to fill in the missing lines from "Sure You Can Ask Me a Personal Question." Create your side of the conversation in any poetic style you choose. Record yourselves reading the two poems as a conversation using EDPuzzle.

questions that the other person continues to ask. When she answers the question about Native Americans being alcoholics, she sarcastically replies that some people need to drink. She insinuates that this need to drink is necessary because of outside influences, such as people asking annoying and insulting questions. At this point, her tone is growing more and more caustic.

The final stereotype that the speaker addresses is the stoicism people associate with Native American people groups. According to *Cambridge English Dictionaries Online*, stoicism is "the quality of experiencing pain or trouble without complaining or showing your emotions." The speaker, however, is not attempting to hide any deep emotional pain in order to appear strong throughout the conversation. Her face, however, is viewed through the lens of stereotype by the other party in the conversation.

Identity

Throughout Burns's poem, the speaker is attempting to separate herself from the numerous stereotypes placed on her from people who are not Native American. In this way, she is trying to demonstrate that her identity has no basis in contemporary generalizations. The complexity of her cultural and individual identity first appears in line 4 when she begins using one term to define her ethnicity but quickly shifts to another. This change of terminology implies that the term she uses to describe herself may not be recognized by someone outside of her community. In fact, there is no universally accepted term. Additionally, the speaker fails to identify her personal heritage. Instead, she responds in the negative when asked if she is part of commonly known groups in lines 6–8. She clearly has no desire to share her ancestry with the impertinent stranger making assumptions based on stereotypes.

The speaker successfully displays her humor within the poem, identifying this part of herself for her audience. The sarcasm of the final four lines are particularly revealing. For example, her comment about drinking in line 36 implies that the attempt to maintain a real identity apart from cultural myths can drive people to alcoholism. In lines 37 and 38, however, the speaker finally demands that she be seen as an individual rather than a caricature. She claims her facial expression as her own rather than the reflection of an entire group of people. In this way, she emphasizes the fact that she has her personal thoughts, feelings, and life. Although she claims her Native American ancestry, placing the expectation on her to conform to ethnic stereotypes reduces her to a two-dimensional trope and diminishes her identity.

Some people who ask personal question want to share their own stories, such as one who insists she has an "Indian Princess" among her ancestors (©Sergey Novikov / Shutterstock.com)

STYLE

Repetition

Burns repeats many words and phrases throughout "Sure You Can Ask Me a Personal Question." For example, the words in line 31 are repeated in different order till the end of line 33. As readers see this repetition, they come to anticipate the words and phrases, which connects them with the author's work. Additionally, the purpose and meaning of the poem are reinforced in the repetitive words and phrases.

One method of repetition that the poet uses is anaphora. According to William Harmon and Hugh Holman's *A Handbook to Literature*, anaphora is "one of the devices of repetition in which the same expression (word or words) is repeated at the beginning of two or more lines." An obvious example of

COMPARE & CONTRAST

- **1980s:** After the work of the American Indian Movement and other organizations, Native Americans gain greater autonomy. The federal government also provides payments for seized land, including 81.5 million dollars to the Passamaquoddy.

  Today: Native Americans are a growing people group with many accomplishments. While there are still legal conflicts regarding land rights and use, tribal self-determination is improving.

- **1980s:** Federal funding for Native Americans is severely cut back because of budget constraints. Many programs are negatively affected by the loss, and people work towards improving sources of income.

  Today: There is still conflict concerning federal government funding of Native Americans.

President Barack Obama requests an increase in funding for Indian Affairs in 2016.

- **1980s:** Native American tribes take contracts with the government and other companies. They also increase the number of casinos, but unemployment rates remain high among Native Americans.

  Today: Unemployment rates for Native Americans are still high. Jens Manuel Krogstad of the Pew Research Center reported that one of four Native Americans lives in poverty. Native American businesses can take advantage of a variety of federal contracts, such as for construction. The needs of the government determine the contracts awarded. Casinos continue to draw money, but some tribes are more successful than others.

---

anaphora is in lines 2–9, in which the same first word occurs in every line.

Caesura

According to Harmon and Holman, a caesura is a "pause or break in a line of verse." This pause is often created through the use of punctuation. For example, the periods in lines 31–33 are instances of caesura. These one-word breaks in the rhythm of the line display the monotony that the speaker feels during her discussion. It also serves to create a bored and annoyed tone.

Tone

The speaker's tone is essential to understanding "Sure You Can Ask Me a Personal Question." The poem is an informal conversation that quickly becomes an interrogation about racial and cultural stereotypes. The speaker's tone shifts as the conversation continues. For example, the speaker is clearly annoyed in line 9 when the other conversationalist mentions extinction, and her annoyance builds until the final two lines, where she defends her facial

expressions. She is sarcastic as she listens to the other person claim connections with Native American culture in lines 11–22. In lines 31–33, she is obviously bored with the assumptions shared and repeats the same answers. The tone of the poem shifts between bored and sarcastic to demonstrate the discomfort and annoyance that the speaker feels.

HISTORICAL CONTEXT

American Indian Movement

"Sure You Can Ask me a Personal Question" was first published in 1983, following the events of the American Indian Movement (AIM) and during the financial cuts of the Reagan era. The American Indian Movement was a national organization that led numerous political protests. As *Encyclopædia Britannica* points out, "Its original purpose was to help Indians in urban ghettos who had been displaced by government programs that had the effect of forcing them from the reservations."

The organization stood in support of the Indians of All Tribes and other Indian groups in their occupation of Alcatraz (1969–1971), sending a delegation to assess progress and study the protestors' methods. The next year, AIM led a cross-country caravan to focus attention on Indian issues. The Trail of Broken Treaties ended at the Bureau of Indian Affairs in Washington, DC, where, during a weeklong occupation of the building, Indian leaders sought to lay out to federal officials a twenty-point plan to redress grievances. The protest ended when government representatives made some concessions to the Indians and promised further treaty negotiations. On February 27, 1973, the group occupied Wounded Knee, the site of a massacre of the Lakota people. This occupation resulted in a two-month standoff. According to *Encyclopedia of Native American History*, "Shoot-outs between the activists and law enforcement continued during the standoff, resulting in the deaths of two Indians and the wounding of two federal agents." The conflict ended on May 8, 1973, but created a number of legal battles. Legal worries combined with internal struggles eventually led to the national group's end in 1978. However, local chapters remained active.

According to the University of Houston's *Digital History*, "Militant protests paid off. The 1972 Indian Education Act gave Indian parents greater control over their children's schools. The 1976 Indian Health Care Act sought to address deficiencies in Indian health care." Additionally, the federal government began to pay for seized tribal land. For example, 81.5 million dollars was paid to the Passamaquoddy and Penobscot of Maine in 1980.

Native Americans in the 1980s

The budget cuts of the 1980s had a profound impact on Native American communities, which often relied on federal funding. The logic was based on the Indian Self-Determination Act, which was enacted in 1975 and allowed Native American tribes to apply for grants and enter into contracts with the federal government. The act was meant to improve self-determination. In the 1980s, however, Native American communities were encouraged to apply for grants and contracts as they lost funds from the federal government. The amount of money allocated

The speaker is polite to those who ask her about her heritage, but she clearly loses patience
(©Aila Images | Shutterstock.com)

to Native Americans fell 22 percent between 1982 and 1983, according to Sandra Faiman-Silva in "The Native Americans' Struggle for Economic Self-Sufficiency." Faiman-Silva goes on to say, "Essential tribal programs including health-related Community Health Representatives, CETA programs, 'mutual help' home construction monies, and BIA-funded education entitlements have all been targets of Reagan/Bush-era budget cutting measures."

In an effort to combat the lost federal support, some tribes considered gambling as a source of income. "During the 1980s, several state governments endowed some reservations with special rights for hunting, fishing, and high-stakes casino gaming," according to the Library of Congress. Native American communities also contracted with the Department of Defense, General Dynamics, and other organizations. John H. Barnhill notes in *Encyclopedia of American Indian Issues Today*, "Early indicators were that economic development on or near reservations was vigorous in the 1980s. At the same time, economic indicators showed little or no improvement in individual well-being."

CRITICAL OVERVIEW

Diane Burns published only one volume of poetry in her lifetime, "Riding the One-Eyed Ford" in 1981. The collection was nominated for a William Carlos Williams Award. Much of her other poetry, however, was published in journals and anthologies. Although she did not have a long career, critics agree that her work had a profound influence on the landscape of Native American literature.

According to Rodney Simard in *Native American Women: A Biographical Dictionary*, Burns's nomination for the William Carlos Williams award made her "one of the most important contemporary Indian poets." Burns was known for addressing issues of conformity, stereotypes, and identity in much of her poetry through humor. John Lowe defines her characteristic style as "a common ground in many aspects of the humor employed. Especially in the contemporary era." Lowe further describes "Sure You Can Ask Me a Personal Question," published in 1983 in *Songs from This Earth on Turtle's Back: Contemporary American Indian Poetry*, as a work that "epitomizes the wry humor used to skewer white attitudes towards Indians."

Besides humor, Burns was known for rooting her work in oral tradition, particularly because she preferred to perform her poetry. As she said in her interview with Joseph Bruchac, "That Beat, That Pulse," "I would rather read poetry in front of an audience than almost anything else. I feel the most real when I am doing that because it is really expressing myself and what I am." The oral tradition in her work was always apparent. Lawana Trout notes that Burns "creates rhythm by combining sounds from contemporary music and images from popular culture."

CRITICISM

April Paris
Paris is a freelance writer with a degree in classical literature and a background in academic

WHAT DO I READ NEXT?

- Published in 2008, *My Own True Name: New and Selected Poems by Young Adults*, by critically acclaimed Latina writer Pat Mora, is a collection of her work created for young adults. The volume presents themes of identity.

- *Native-American Literature: A Brief Introduction and Anthology*, edited by Gerald Vizenor and Ishmael Reed, includes a wide range of literature and genres. Published in 1997, the text allows readers to better understand the way Native Americans have shaped the landscape of American literature.

- Edited by Joseph Bruchac, *Songs from This Earth on Turtle's Back* was originally published in 1983 and rereleased in 2009. The collection includes some of Burns's poems and also offers an opportunity to compare her work with that of other modern Native American writers.

- Published in 1996, *Native American History: A Chronology of a Culture's Vast Achievements and Their Links to World Events*, by Judith Nies, is a young-adult history text. The volume provides an excellent introductory overview.

- *Riding the One-Eyed Ford*, by Diane Burns, is the only collection of her poetry. Originally published in 1981, the collection was reprinted in 1984.

- *Love Medicine*, by Louise Erdrich, is a novel originally published in 1984 and republished in 2005. Erdrich's humor and themes of identity are often compared to Burns's.

writing. In the following essay, she explores how Diane Burns uses humor in "Sure You Can Ask Me a Personal Question" to combat stereotyping.

Diane Burns displays her wit and her humor as she examines the effects that cultural stereotypes have on Native Americans in her poem

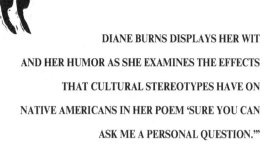

DIANE BURNS DISPLAYS HER WIT
AND HER HUMOR AS SHE EXAMINES THE EFFECTS
THAT CULTURAL STEREOTYPES HAVE ON
NATIVE AMERICANS IN HER POEM 'SURE YOU CAN
ASK ME A PERSONAL QUESTION.'"

"Sure You Can Ask Me a Personal Question." Over the years, popular cultural representations of Native American have changed. As "Overview for Films in First Americans" explains, "The images of Indians in early motion pictures were highly derogatory.... These included the bloodthirsty savage, the noble primitive, the violent and unstable 'half-breed,' and the sexually-alluring Indian maiden." Over time, stereotypes began to change. Much of this has to do with the countercultural movements of the 1960s. "Overview for Films in First Americans" goes on to say, "Movies featured a growing number of wise Indian shamans" and depicted Native Americans "as a noble and dignified people who lived in harmony with nature and cherished spiritual values rather than material possessions." Even though many twentieth-century tropes about Native American people might appear favorable, they trap people into false expectations and drive a wedge between different cultures, keeping them apart.

On the surface, some of the stereotypes addressed in "Sure You Can Ask Me a Personal Question" may appear complimentary because they reflect the later views of Native Americans. For example, in lines 31–33, the speaker listens to someone discuss the spiritual aspects of her culture along with an assumed respect for and connection with the natural world. The topic, however, seems to annoy the speaker more than many of the other subjects in the conversation do. She simply repeats one-word answers over and over as she mentally disengages with the questions that are directed towards her.

The annoyed repetition in these lines insinuates that the speaker is bored by the idea of addressing the same Native American stereotype yet again. This trope of the nature-guided Native American was extraordinarily common when the poem was first published in 1983. As Sarah Fowler explains in "The Commodification of the Native in the 21st Century," "a new utopian fascination with Native American life began in the 1970s and 1980s." Part of the growing interest was centered on a desire to return to nature. Fowler continues: "This trend was pervasive and focused on Native American 'spiritual purity' and relation to the land." As popular culture embraced this view of Native Americans, many people began to accept the stereotype as an undeniable fact.

The person on the other side of this conversation clearly praises what she assumes to be an integral part of the speaker's life. Unfortunately, the idea that the speaker is a spiritually attuned individual who lives on the land and makes her own clothes is far from the truth. As lines 26 and 27 reveal, she purchases her clothes at a nationally known store and does not have any connections with the local Native American artisans. In this way, the speaker shatters some of the assumptions that society and the unheard conversationalist have about her.

Given that the poet lived in New York City at the time when the poem was written, there was little chance for her to separate herself from modern city life and maintain a close connection with the natural world. This concept may seem to be self-explanatory, but it never occurs to the individual conversing with the speaker. As Fowler says, "American Indians struggle to exist as culturally complex individuals in a world that perceives them as homogenously Indian." Still, the stereotype that all Native Americans are one with nature persists even in urban settings.

The expectations that stereotypes create lead to conflicts between people of different cultures. This idea holds true when the caricatures appear to be complimentary as well as when they are obviously insulting. Making assumptions about an entire people group places expectations on them and diminishes their value as distinct individuals with their own personal interests and identities. The person talking with the speaker has no interest in getting to know her; it is a conversation with an idea of a Native American. By failing to treat people as individuals and getting to know them, the ability to connect across cultures and develop respect is lost. This loss of respect is apparent in the way that the speaker responds to a conversation based on assumptions and stereotypes.

The poet's weapon against ignorance and generalizations is comedy. She successfully highlights the absurdity of the expectations placed on Native Americans by those outside their culture. The speaker voices her frustration at being viewed as a trope using her wit and her humor, as the poet addresses important topics such as her own alienation as a Native American in the United States, cultural misunderstandings, and alcoholism. As John Lowe explains in "Coyote's Jokebook: Humor in Native American Literature and Culture," the use of humor in darker themes and ideas is not unique. Counter to the argument that all Native Americans refrain from showing emotion, he notes that they often "create comic treatments for underlying tragic themes such as drunkenness, alienation, aimless lives, poverty, and clashes among cultures." The use of comedy allows the poet to address negativity in a more palatable way.

Negative words permeate "Sure You Can Ask Me a Personal Question," demonstrating the speaker's anger and desire to separate herself from the barrage of demeaning stereotypes the other woman throws at her. It is interesting to note that the speaker uses affirmative words in the poem sparingly: four times, to be precise. The first time occurs in line 10 when the other person in the conversation finally accepts her identity as a Native American. She also agrees, in line 23, that the atrocities indigenous people suffered at the hands of European colonists were terrible.

The speaker repeats a positive word between lines 31 and 33, but, as already addressed, the agreement is half-hearted and disengaged. In her final affirmative statement, the speaker grudgingly agrees that some Native Americans have problems with alcoholism in line 35. While the speaker appears to be supporting a stereotype in this line, she quickly follows her statement with a joke in line 36. As Lowe points out, the poem contains a "bitter humor," and this is one example of it. After fielding intrusive and ignorant questions and comments, the speaker jokes that Native Americans need to drink. By using the first-person plural pronoun in line 36, the speaker includes herself in this group. Her personal inclusion implies that the current conversation is driving her to drink.

Humor is an effective teaching tool, but in this case, it also serves to counter another stereotype that the author faces. The woman talking with the speaker certainly embraces the idea that Native Americans practice a cultural stoicism. Rather than play a caricature, the speaker chooses to display her playful and clever sense of humor. Throughout the poem, she uses a sarcastic and incredulous tone, but this mood appears to be lost on the person talking with her. After over thirty lines, the conversation turns to the speaker's apparent stoicism. In the final two lines of the poem, the speaker counters the stereotype directly to highlight her emotion and lack of stoicism. Here, she demands that the other conversationalist looks at her as a person and not a stereotype of another culture.

By asserting her individuality at the end of the poem, the speaker displays what is wrong with accepting stereotypes as facts, even seemingly positive stereotypes. Although the speaker had a lengthy encounter with a stranger, they failed to communicate. The stranger saw an opportunity to meet a Native American and display understanding of the speaker's culture. Unfortunately, the stranger's knowledge is based on fiction and popular culture, not fact. She does not take the opportunity to make a new friend or learn about a traditionally marginalized people group. This individual does not see the speaker as a three-dimensional person but as a physical representation of an idea.

What is a novelty for the unheard conversationalist is obviously boring repetition for the speaker. Culturally accepted stereotypes keep her from genuinely connecting with new people. Her normal introduction in line 1 quickly deteriorates into an awkward encounter. As the discussion begins, it is clear that the speaker wants the topic of conversation to shift away from her cultural heritage. For example, in the first few lines, she refuses to name her ethnicity, and the subsequent conversation clearly reveals why. Once her Native American identity is revealed, there is no hope of having a normal conversation in which she is not subjected to a barrage of stereotypes and intrusive questions.

Fowler points out that stereotyping "is forcing American Indians to exist within culturally contrived territories, prohibiting the self-determination of modern Indians," which Burns explores in "Sure You Can Ask Me a Personal Question." While the speaker does embrace her Native American heritage, she is not a stereotype and refuses to be reduced to one. Although the other individual in the conversation might believe she is supportive and complimentary, she is belittling

Near the end of the poem, the text makes it clear that the speaker is hardly paying attention when asked about Native American spirituality, which has been co-opted by so many European Americans
(©chevu / Shutterstock.com)

the speaker's heritage and preventing her from expressing herself as an individual.

Source: April Paris, Critical Essay on "Sure You Can Ask Me a Personal Question," in *Poetry for Students*, Gale, Cengage Learning, 2017.

Sarah Ferguson

In the following obituary, Ferguson describes Burns's struggles with addiction, which stifled her talent.

Slowly people drifted into the parish room at St. Mark's Church on Jan. 27 to celebrate the life of Native American poet and longtime Lower East Side resident Diane Burns. They were reluctant, it seemed, to remember the light that burned inside Burns was gone, and that she drank herself to death at age 50, leaving behind a beautiful 15-year-old daughter with shy almond eyes and a scattering of poems so fierce they continue to churn up in literary anthologies two decades later.

Maybe the light inside Burns burned too brightly?

Consider the opening lines of her first and only book of poetry, "Riding the One-Eyed Ford," published in 1981: ...

Illustrated with her own fine pen-and-ink drawings, that slim collection established Burns as a formidable presence in the New York poetry scene and beyond. Though she didn't publish much more than that, her witty, sardonic takes on Native stereotypes are still cutting enough to be taught alongside more famous contemporaries like Sherman Alexie:

> I am Tequila Mockingbird. Yes, I am related to Isaiah Mockingbird, and yes, I am that face in the moon on the cover of the Carson's record album. And the Marshmallow beer girl, and that's me on every stick of Land O'Lakes butter. . . I can trace my lineage back to the beginning of time when the world was nothing but a scrap of mud on the tip of a loon's nose. (from her 1993 essay "Tequila Mockingbird")

Born in 1956 in Lawrence, Kan., to a Chemehuevi father and an Anishinabe mother, Burns was raised with her two brothers in

IN 1988, SHE WAS AMONG A RATHER
ILLUSTRIOUS GROUP OF WRITERS—INCLUDING ALLEN
GINSBERG, JOY HARJO AND PEDRO PIETRI—INVITED
TO NICARAGUA TO TAKE PART IN THE RUBEN DARIO
POETRY FESTIVAL, SPONSORED BY THE SANDINISTA
GOVERNMENT."

Riverside, Cal., where her parents got work teaching at a Native American boarding school. When she was about 10 years old, the family moved to the Lac Corte Oreilles reservation in Hayward, Wis., then on to Wahpeton, N.D., when her parents began teaching at another boarding school there.

"Even in grade school, she was always writing and drawing," recalls Diane's mother, Rose Burns. "In third grade she won the first-place prize for her poem, 'A Pencil Can Travel.'"

Evidently, Diane discovered early on that writing could be a ticket to elsewhere. She spent her senior year of high school at the American Indian Art Institute in Santa Fe, N.M., then got a scholarship from Barnard College, with the aim of becoming a lawyer.

She dropped out of Barnard her senior year—no one remembers why. Perhaps the life of a poet seemed more enthralling. In a video-taped interview with Emilio Murillo for his Manhattan cable show, "Earth Bird," Burns described how she came into her profession somewhat by accident, when the American Indian Community House called up looking to book a Native American poet for an event they were hosting.

"I didn't have anything, so I stayed up all night scribbling and ended up onstage with Audre Lorde," Burns recalled. "I actually got paid $50. I'm the only poet I know who got into the field for money," she joked.

Burns moved to the East Village in the late '70s and quickly became enmeshed in the Downtown arts scene.

"I used to run into Diane all the time on Avenue B back in the day when I could see, and she was a very attractive lady," recalls Steve Cannon, the now-blind publisher of *A Gathering of the Tribes* magazine.

Beyond her striking features, which got Burns work as a model, people were immediately impressed by the force of her words.

"She was like a fresh wind, the clarity of her work was so beautiful," says Josh Gosciak, founder of the multicultural poetry journal *Contact*, who was one of the first to publish Burns's work. "A lot of young Native Americans were coming on the scene in New York and also breaking into film and publishing. It was an exciting period. We haven't seen anything like it since."

"It was a total explosion," says Bowery Poetry Club founder Bob Holman, remembering the first time he heard Burns read in 1980. "All of us down here thought our scene had everything in the world we needed. But Diane literally blew the lid off our little place and set it up as a whole new encampment."

In those days, many poets in the 'hood were earning salaries with benefits under the federal CETA (Comprehensive Employment and Training Act) program, which President Reagan immediately canned when he came into office. Former *Cover* magazine publisher Jeff Wright remembers traveling around with Burns as part of a state-funded CETA spinoff called POET (Poets' Overland Expeditionary Troupe), staging readings at schools and community centers across New York. . . .

"She was like an Indian princess living on the Lower East Side," says Wright. "She was like the best bad girl that ever lived, and when she walked around she made everyone else wild. I fell in love with her immediately, like everyone else. But I was always afraid to get too close, because of the dark side."

Besides a thirst for liquor, Burns landed a dope habit early on, and never really shook it. She didn't seem to wrestle with her demons so much as accommodate them, though her 1981 poem "Booze 'N' Loozing Blues" hints at the pain she felt inside: . . .

Of course back then it seemed like everyone was high on one thing or another, and for many years, Burns was the life of the party.

In 1988, she was among a rather illustrious group of writers—including Allen Ginsberg, Joy Harjo and Pedro Pietri—invited to Nicaragua to take part in the Ruben Dario Poetry Festival, sponsored by the Sandinista government. (Poet Tom Savage remembers Burns pulling out an "enormous gun" on the plane. "It was just amazing to me; it was so bizarre.")

The Sandinistas revered poetry and welcomed the group like foreign dignitaries, especially Burns, who Holman recalls was "sort of the star of our little troupe down there."

"Little did they know what trouble they were getting into," Holman laughs. Apparently Burns and Pietri got so soused at the presidential palace that Pietri interrupted a meeting between the Sandinista government and the Soviet ambassador to look for his shoes.

They then convinced Minister of Culture Ernesto Cardenal to marry them and took off honeymooning, much to the dismay of Pietri's wife back in New York and members of the American Indian Movement, who called up Holman worried Burns had been kidnapped. . .

For many years, Burns carried on giving readings at the Nuyorican Poets Café and hanging out at local bars.

"She was one of the smartest people I ever knew. We met at the Village Idiot," says Steve Ruona, who lived with Burns from 1991 to 2002 and fathered their daughter, Britta.

Steve Cannon credits her with helping him launch *Tribes* magazine and gallery from his ramshackle brownstone on E. Third St.

"When my house burned down in 1990, I was half-blind and didn't have the money to fix the damn thing up, so Diane got her husband Steve to put this house back in order," says Cannon. "She would come over here through thick and thin, scrambling for money, calling people, helping me set things up. That's what kept this place going all those years. The only reason *A Gathering of the Tribes* exists 15 years later is because of Diane Burns."

Cannon also kept Burns going, paying her to keep the books even when others considered her a lost cause. In her latter years as her drinking worsened and she lost custody of Britta, Diane drifted from couch to couch, even berthing for a while with the Hare Krishnas on First Ave.

"They've taken me on as a project," she joked to friends.

Burns kept her sense of humor and her pride through it all, and unlike most folks with bad habits, she never stole.

"Kind," "loving," "modest," "warm but not effusive," "private," "funny," "not one to be captured"—these were some of the words people offered up at the memorial as folks struggled to reconcile Diane's startling talent and her steadfast presence on the scene with the sorry place she ended up.

Though she'd complained of excess fluids in recent weeks, friends say her collapse on Nov. 29 was unexpected. She was taken to Beth Israel Hospital, where she fell into a coma and died of kidney and liver failure on Dec. 22.

If her daughter Britta is any measure, her life was far from hopeless. Britta is now studying acting and has a job performing skits as a teen advocate for Planned Parenthood three days a week.

Cannon says he's hoping to collect Burns's unpublished writings into a book—she was supposedly working on a satirical novel about a Native American beauty queen. Some of her film and poetry reviews can be found on the *Tribes* Web site, www.tribes.org.

After she died, her family held a three-day funeral on the reservation in Wisconsin, with a feast and prayers sung in her tribal tongue.

"You have to stay with the body for the whole time, so on the last night I played poker with her brothers till 5 a.m.," laughs Ruona. "I lost $100, but I know Diane would have been happy to know we were playing poker.

She always wanted people to have a good time." . . .

Source: Sarah Ferguson, "Diane Burns, Native American Lower East Side Poet," in *Villager*, Vol. 76, No. 38, February 14–20, 2007, p. online.

SOURCES

"American Indian Movement," in *Encyclopædia Britannica*, http://www.britannica.com/topic/American-Indian-Movement (accessed May 7, 2016).

Barnhill, John H., "Unemployment," in *Encyclopedia of American Indian Issues Today*, edited by Russell M. Lawson, Greenwood, 2013, pp. 117–18.

Bruchac, Joseph, "That Beat, That Pulse," in *A to Z of American Indian Women*, by Liz Sonneborn, Facts on File, 2007, pp. 33–34; originally published in *Survival This Way: Interviews with American Indian Poets*, University of Arizona Press, 1994, pp. 43–56.

Burns, Diane, "Sure You Can Ask Me a Personal Question," in *Native American Literature: An Anthology*, edited by Lawana Trout, NTC/Contemporary Publishing Group, 1998, pp. 49–50.

Cope, Jenel. "American Indian Movement," in *Encyclopedia of Native American History*, Vol. 1, Facts on File, 2011.

"Diane Burns," Poetry Foundation website, http://www.poetryfoundation.org/poems-and-poets/poets/detail/diane-burns (accessed May 3, 2016).

Faiman-Silva, Sandra, "The Native Americans' Struggle for Economic Self-Sufficiency," in *Bridgewater Review*, Vol. 9, No. 1, April 1992, pp. 6A–8A.

Ferguson, Sarah, "Diane Burns, Native American Lower East Side Poet," in *Villager*, Vol. 76, No. 38, February 14–20, 2007, http://thevillager.com/villager_198/dianeburnsnative.html (accessed on May 3, 2016).

Fowler, Sarah, "The Commodification of the Native in the 21st Century," in *Global Societies Journal*, No. 1, 2013, pp. 44–53.

"The Future for Native Americans?," Library of Congress website, http://www.loc.gov/teachers/classroommaterials/presentationsandactivities/presentations/immigration/native_american9.html (accessed on May 7, 2016).

Harmon, William, and Hugh Holman, "Anaphora," in *A Handbook to Literature*, 9th ed., Prentice Hall, 2003, p. 24.

———, "Caesura," in *Handbook to Literature*, 9th ed., Prentice Hall, 2003, p. 74.

Krogstad, Jens Manuel, "One-in-four Native Americans and Alaska Natives Are Living in Poverty," Pew Research Center, http://www.pewresearch.org/fact-tank/2014/06/13/1-in-4-native-americans-and-alaska-natives-are-living-in-poverty/ (accessed on August 4, 2016).

Lowe, John, "Coyote's Jokebook: Humor in Native American Literature and Culture," in *Dictionary of Native American Literature*, edited by Andrew Wiget, Garland Publishing, 1994, pp. 192, 195.

"The Native American Power Movement," Digital History website, http://www.digitalhistory.uh.edu/disp_textbook_print.cfm?smtid=2&psid=3348 (accessed May 7, 2016).

"Overview for Films in First Americans," Digital History website, http://www.digitalhistory.uh.edu/disp_film.cfm?mediatypeid=1&eraid=1&psid=2948 (accessed May 7, 2016).

Simard, Rodney, "Burns, Diane M.," in *Native American Women: A Biographical Dictionary*, edited by Gretchen M. Bataille and Laurie Lisa, Routledge, 2001, pp. 60–61.

Sonneborn, Liz, *A to Z of American Indian Women*, Facts on File, 2007, pp. 33–34.

"Stereotype," in *Merriam-Webster*, http://www.merriam-webster.com/dictionary/stereotype (accessed on May 11, 2016).

"Stoicism," in *Cambridge Dictionaries Online*, http://dictionary.cambridge.org/us/dictionary/english/stoicism (accessed on May 6, 2016).

Trout, Lawana, Introduction to "Sure You Can Ask Me a Personal Question," in *Native American Literature: An Anthology*, edited by Lawana Trout, NTC Publishing Group, 1999, pp. 49–50.

FURTHER READING

Kumar, J. G. Ravi, *Native American Fiction of the 1970s and 1980s: A Study of History, Culture and Society*, LAP Lambert Academic Publishing, 2013.
> This collection of fictional stories originally published in the 1970s and 1980s focuses on the history of culture of the time in which they were written.

Lincoln, Kenneth, *Native American Renaissance*, University of California Press, 1992.
> This collection assesses the works of prominent twentieth-century Native Americans in the light of their culture, background, and influence on literature.

Targ Brill, Marlene, *America in the 1980s*, Twenty-First Century Books, 2009.
> The nonfiction text provides an overview of the 1980s, using images and quotes to display the history and culture. The book is written for young-adult readers but provides useful information to any student.

Wilson, James, *The Earth Shall Weep: A History of Native America*, Grove Press, 1999.
> This expansive history book examines events from the sixteenth century to the end of the twentieth. Wilson incorporates oral traditions with archaeology and historical sources.

SUGGESTED SEARCH TERMS

Diane Burns

Diane Burns AND "Sure You Can Ask Me a Personal Question"

1980s AND Native Americans

American Indian Movement

poetry AND dialogue form

Native Americans AND stereotypes

ethnicity AND identity

Bureau of Indian Affairs AND history

Unbidden

RAE ARMANTROUT

2009

"Unbidden" is a free-verse poem by the influential East Coast poet and professor Rae Armantrout. It first appeared in the award-winning collection *Versed*, published in 2009. Composed in the latter half of a literary career spanning more than three decades, the poem is a finely tooled representation of Armantrout's unique and innovative style, dressing otherworldly and unfathomable themes in the language of everyday discourse. In keeping with the views of the language school of poetry, the literary movement with which Armantrout is most often associated, the structure of the poem is controlled and elegant. With its evocative and enigmatic imagery, direct second-person appeal, and embedded questions, "Unbidden" demands rather than invites the interpretation of its intended audience. The poem's emotional gravity, undeniable and yet indistinct, is given definition almost entirely through the experience of the individual reader.

"Unbidden" and the other poems in *Versed* were composed largely while Armantrout was undergoing cancer treatment. The poems of this period are considered among Armantrout's most serious and self-aware. They are marked by piercing insight, instances of grim realization punctuated by dark humor, and a preoccupation with the frailty of human life. Far from being static, the poetry of the collection grapples head-on with contemporary realities and adapts itself to the frenetic realities of the modern age.

Rae Armantrout (©*Denis Poroy / AP Images*)

"Unbidden" is a poem at peace with uncertainty. It dwells in the margins of the known and the unknown, the corporeal and the ethereal, the immutable and the ever-changing.

AUTHOR BIOGRAPHY

Armantrout was born on April 13, 1947, in Vallejo, California. She was an only child and endured a stern, insular upbringing at the hand of a career military father with unyielding fundamentalist ideals. Armantrout spent a disjointed childhood in the San Diego area moving from base to base with her family, a lifestyle that made it difficult for her to form lasting friendships with children her age. To cope with the pervasive loneliness of her early years, the future poet gained an early appreciation of the comfort afforded by reading and writing. When her seventh grade teacher gave her an anthology of modern poetry, Armantrout soon came to value poetry above prose and to apply her budding talents to the composition of verse. She modeled her initial forays into poetry on the work of

modernist masters such as T. S. Eliot and William Carlos Williams, both of whom were enduring influences on her mature style.

Armantrout began her college career at San Diego State University studying anthropology but transferred to the University of California at Berkeley to pursue her creative ambitions and major in literature. While at Berkeley, Armantrout studied under the renowned poet Denise Levertov and met future members of the language poetry movement she would later help to pioneer. After a long relationship with him, Armantrout married Chuck Korkegian a year after her graduation in 1970.

Armantrout's success as a poet began with the acceptance of her work by well-known publications and her decision to pursue a master's degree in creative writing at San Francisco State University. In 1978, the aspiring poet published her first independent collection, *Extremities*, which signaled the start of three decades of immense productivity and growing critical acclaim. Armantrout's eleventh collection, *Versed*, which contains "Unbidden," was published in 2009 and recognized as a landmark achievement in the poet's already impressive career. The collection won the 2010 Pulitzer Prize for Poetry, received the 2009 National Book Critics Circle Award, and was a finalist for the National Book Award.

Although she was found to have a rare and particularly deadly form of cancer in 2006, Armantrout underwent successful treatment and continued to write as of 2016. In addition to releasing new volumes of poetry, Armantrout was participating in collaborative writing projects with her fellow language poets, writing essays on the poetic craft, and helping to translate her work into German. Armantrout released her autobiography, *True*, in 1998. As of 2016, she held a professorship in creative writing at the University of California, San Diego.

POEM TEXT

> The ghosts swarm
> They speak as one
> person. Each
> loves you. Each
> has left something   5
> undone.
>
> Did the palo verde
> blush yellow
> all at once?
>
> Today's edges   10
> are so sharp
>
> they might cut
> anything that moved.
>
> The way a lost
> word   15
>
> will come back
> unbidden
>
> You're not interested
> in it now,
>
> only   20
> in knowing
> where it's been.

POEM SUMMARY

The text used for this summary is from *Versed*, Wesleyan University Press, 2010, p. 70. A version of the poem can be found on the following web page: https://www.poets.org/poetsorg/poem/unbidden.

Lines 1–3
The speaker describes the spectacle of swarming ghosts. Despite their great number and varied intents, the spectral multitude speaks with a single voice.

Lines 3–6
Each spirit feels great love for the subject of the poem, and each regrets having left some deed undone in life.

Lines 7–9
The speaker asks whether the palo verde, a rugged species of tree that predominates in the American Southwest, bursts into vivid bloom all at once.

Lines 10–13
The edges of today are described as so sharp as to be a danger to all that moves.

Lines 14–17
The speaker evokes a lost word that once forgotten will resurface unexpectedly and unasked for.

Lines 18–22
The second-person addressee no longer cares for the importance of the word and is only concerned with where it has been in its absence.

THEMES

Ghosts
The elegiac tone of "Unbidden" is established in lines 1–6 with an evocative description of swarming ghosts. The restless nature of these lost souls speaking as one and their disembodied yearning for affections of the flesh strike an emotional chord of loss and unrequited desire. Armantrout describes these ghosts in language both hungry and ethereal, granting them the power of speech but not of action. Powerless to fulfill the deeds left unfinished in life, the spirits can only mourn and appeal to the world of flesh and possibility they will never again experience for themselves.

By the same token, the living, second-person subject of the poem is afflicted by loss of a different sort. In a striking inversion of the plight experienced by the swarming spirits, the urgency of the flesh precludes the luxury of contemplation and of remembrance. Thoughts and words

TOPICS FOR FURTHER STUDY

- The language poetry movement, which Armantrout helped to pioneer, sought to supply poetic meaning through the experiential and emotional framework of the reader. Bring to mind a time when words failed you or were lost and describe the circumstances surrounding the memory in a personal journal entry. Discuss in an essay whether the mere act of recalling the incident adds significance to the meaning of the poem. Explain why or why not.

- Armantrout deals heavily in personification, a device by which human action or adjectives are assigned to an object or abstraction. Reread "Unbidden" and attempt to visualize a today with sharp edges, capable of cutting anything that moves. Create an artistic representation of lines 10–13 using either drawing implements or a computer-based art program. Present and explain your choice to your classmates.

- The image of the blooming palo verde dominates "Unbidden" and evokes connotations of beauty, longevity, and spontaneous creation. Do research online and select your favorite tree, formulating a lesson or aspect of personal significance from its appearance and characteristics. Compose a brief single-stanza poem that articulates the beauty and significance in simple but powerful language.

- The unrequited shades of lines 1–6 are at once troubling and compelling. Armantrout compels the reader to hear the combined voice of these ghosts but not their words, lending an air of mystery to the composition. With a partner, attempt to dispel this mystery at the heart of the poem and brainstorm a list of possible utterances to share with your classmates. Explain your reasoning behind each.

- Read the surreal and irresistible classic of young-adult poetry Shel Silverstein's *Where*

the Sidewalk Ends (1974), and select a single poem for comparison with "Unbidden." Create a Venn diagram of the similarities and differences between the two. As a class, discuss possible defining characteristics of the language poets school to which Armantrout belonged.

- "Unbidden" is a poem of things left unsaid and undone. What are some of your own burning life ambitions? Use the website challengecreator.com to compose your own list of challenges and triumphs you envision for yourself in years to come. If you feel comfortable doing so, share your list with your peers.

- Among her other poetic gifts, Armantrout is famed for her ability to inspire meaning through juxtaposition and to unite, through sentiment, seemingly jarring and discordant images. Using your personal journal, brainstorm a series of vivid, unrelated images, selecting three of your favorites for the activity. Next, choose a partner and exchange your three selections. Use your partner's list to compose a brief story linking the three images in a way that seems natural and implies, but does not directly express, underlying emotional significance. Take turns sharing your compositions with the class and gauge your success at the activity from their reactions.

- Armantrout has been hailed as a great poet of the theme of death and her collection *Versed* as the ultimate expression of that theme. Read Emily Dickinson's famous and unsettling composition "I Heard a Fly Buzz—When I Died" for comparison and craft a brief but insightful review analyzing the relative strengths and weaknesses of the two works. If time allows, engage in a classroom debate to give voice to your individual findings and opinions.

are lost forever and rendered inconsequential by the world's relentless assault on the consciousness. The sharp immediacy of the present moment and the dizzying cycle of action and reaction conspire to make the short-lived flesh oblivious to the more lasting secrets of the soul.

Silence

Representations of the said and the unsaid figure largely in "Unbidden," contributing to the poem's examination of both the immense power and the inadequacy of articulation. The ability of speech afforded the ghosts of lines 1–6 is so great as to bridge the gap between the living and the dead and unite many voices through the strength of a single will. In a similar display of otherworldly power, the stanzas are positioned in such a way that they imply a connection between the words of lines 1–6 and the startling, instantaneous blooming of the majestic palo verde in lines 7–9. In this way, the poem suggests that words have power beyond mortal understanding—they bend the rules of reality and conjure marvels into existence.

At the same time that she acknowledges the boundless possibilities of speech, Armantrout establishes its limitations. The unremembered word of the latter half of the poem and the almost arbitrary manner in which it resurfaces locate the source of vocal expression beyond human consciousness. The unbidden nature of the word and its implied defiance of the will of the speaker establish speech not only as unfathomable to the mortal mind but also as ungovernable.

Time

The poem is fashioned as a rumination on time and the complex interplay between past, present, and future. The thronging ghosts and the forgotten utterance represent that which has passed away while the present, almost cutting in its vivid intensity, looms as a persistent reminder of the immediacy of today. The return of the lost word, its journey through time and consciousness only to resurface as inconsequential in the present, suggests a cyclical, unknowable, and even mischievous quality of time. The poet questions the validity of human perceptions regarding the passage of time by evoking an enduring symbol of longevity and regeneration in the form of a blooming palo verde tree.

This symbol of spontaneity seems to span the rushing river of time represented by the chronological flow of the poem and to provide fleeting refuge between its two halves. The insistent tug of unfulfilled ghosts battles with a sharpened and deadly present for control of the reader's imagination, simulating the immediate and indistinct blending of the past, the present, and the future from which there is no escape.

Uncertainty

In "Unbidden," the poet denies the reader the satisfaction of certainty or even full comprehension. Armantrout's intent is confused by the unexpected juxtaposition of concrete image with abstraction, beauty with desolation, and the speech that saturates the poem is deprived of its basic units of meaning, words themselves. The unified voice of the ghosts remains unheard and yields no revelations, whereas the prodigal word of the second half of the poem, coming and going according to some secret and rebellious will, remains unuttered.

In keeping with the spirit of mystery, Armantrout's composition is structurally divided by an evocative but unanswerable question of ambiguous import. Seemingly rhetorical in its nature, the question nevertheless stirs the shadow of doubt in the mind of the reader and simultaneously asks for and defies logical connection between the two halves of the poem. Caught between the shades of the past, the unrequited urgency of the present, and an indistinct future, the reader is forced to choose between terror or acceptance of an unknowable outcome.

Free Will

The theme of personal volition, and more often its limits, figures largely in "Unbidden" and imbues the poem with a sense of inevitability and helplessness. The ethereal nature of the ghosts relegates them to the plane of emotion and intent but denies them the ability to act and fulfill unrequited desires. Eternally hungry and yet eternally impotent, the spectral multitude throngs around the flesh-and-blood narrator of the poem and pleads its case with a single voice devoid of individuality or the fire of personal conviction. Armantrout's choice of indecisive language and verbs tainted with passivity further amplifies this impression. The sharp

The first stanza invokes ghosts, but rather than being frightening, they are loving (©Lario Tus /
Shutterstock.com)

edges of the present have the potential only to
cut and inflict damage, whereas the palo verde
tree, resplendent with yellow blossoms, colors
unconsciously as if under the influence of flat-
tery or embarrassment introduced by some off-
stage source.

Most striking of all, even the will to
speak is denied the narrator of the poem. In
a bizarre reversal of the expected, Armantrout allows the words to express themselves
through the narrator rather than vice versa,
crediting escaped utterances with the quality
of unruly defiance. Rather than interrogate
the word and make sense of its actions, the
narrator is left to helplessly guess at its former whereabouts.

Even the unusual second-person address of
"Unbidden" contributes to its pervasive air of
helplessness. Any distinction between the narrator and the reader is eroded by the oddly inclusive and yet commanding tone of the narrator.
As a consequence, the reader is told what to
think and how to react and feels constantly

acted upon and absolved of any personal responsibility or volition.

STYLE

Abstract

Contributing to the rampant uncertainty of
"Unbidden" is its reliance upon abstractions,
intangible concepts without an easily defined
form, to catch readers off guard and further
immerse them in the ambiguity of the verse. To
this end, Armantrout's composition maintains a
delicate balance between these bizarre, abstract
images and powerful visualizations rooted in
concrete, everyday experience. The physical
bulk of the immense multicolored palo verde
tree, for instance, is almost immediately under-
mined by the difficult-to-grasp concept of the
present moment. Further complicating this
abstraction, the poet applies physical form, in
this case a sharpened edge, to a concept otherwise without form.

In much the same way, Armantrout appropriates voice, the vehicle through which humans give definition to their surroundings and attach meaning to both physical objects and abstractions, and empties it of all possible significance. The collective drone of the ghosts and the rebellious word of the poem's end are both without discernible form or substance. The source of meaning itself is transformed into an abstraction through the force of Armantrout's artistry.

Cadence

The cadence of "Unbidden," or the pattern of its intonation and flow of its verse, is notable in several respects. Armantrout's lines are intentionally terse and powerful, resisting musicality in favor of gravity. The poet makes frequent use of enjambment, the continuation of a sentence across two or more lines of verse, to string the reader along and heighten the poem's disquieting effect with unusual emphasis. The resultantly disjointed cadence of "Unbidden" contributes to its blurring of the lines between the immediate and the eternal, the past and the present, the living and the dead.

Image

Although painted in simple, spare language, the image of the budding palo verde tree that bifurcates the poem is singularly striking. Aglow with vibrant yellow blossoms, the tree stands alone as a splash of color in an otherwise dismal landscape populated by ghosts and words left unsaid. Paired with connotations of natural beauty and renewal, the longevity of the palo verde serves as a counterbalance to the pettiness and brevity of human concerns.

Mood

The mood of "Unbidden" is as complex and ambiguous as its subject matter. Despite the grim sentiments of lines 1–6 and the narrator's hesitant and uncertain engagement with the sharp-edged present, an air of acceptance and even peace makes itself felt through the progression of the poem. The semirhetorical and ultimately unanswerable question addressed to the palo verde tree, for instance, hints at a degree of disengagement and indifference on the part of the poem's speaker. Although it is outwardly preoccupied with the urgency of the moment, the poem dwells on unalterable realities, the unfulfilled desires of the departed and the unchanging truths of the natural world. The air of casual detachment with which the narrator regards the wayward utterance, gone one moment and returned the next, also contributes to the interpretation of the composition as placid reflection over urgent anxiety.

Personification

Personification, the joining of traditionally human descriptors with nonhuman objects or abstractions, is used to great and often unsettling effect in this poem. The central image of the palo verde tree that dominates the poem is rendered in language both modest and sensual, linking the emergence of buds with the flushing of skin. The here and now of today, a chronological abstraction, is transformed by the poet's skill into an object sharp and unyielding, capable of slicing any who approach.

Subject

The unclear second-person subject of "Unbidden" lends an inclusive, accusatory tone to the poem. The reader is drawn in by the direct appeal and made to question the intent of the swarming ghosts and the reason for their love in a personal context. The inclusive nature of the poem's address imbues its central plight—namely, the sharp immediacy of the present—with a degree of universality and inescapability. By writing in the second rather than the first person, Armantrout makes a pointed break with the lyric tradition, downplaying the narrator in preference to the implied subject.

HISTORICAL CONTEXT

Although the language poetry movement took flight in subsequent decades, most of the poets were of the baby boom generation, so called because of the marked increase in birth rate in the two decades after World War II. They came of age in an America shaped by the Cold War and the Vietnam War and the counterculture revolution of the 1960s and 1970s and took their influences from those events.

The baby boomers continue to represent a powerful ideological and financial force in contemporary America. Fueled in large part by increased emphasis on education and a sense of national ascendency after the victory of America on the world stage, children of Armantrout's generation were born into a legacy of optimism and opportunity, but they exhibited a certain skepticism toward and perhaps disregard of the more rigid societal expectations of the past.

Among other things, Armantrout cited her fractured belief in high ideals and governmental policy during the two major conflicts of her youth in shaping the tenor of her poetry. Beginning the year of her birth, 1947, and extending into her mature adulthood in 1991, the Cold War between the United States and the Soviet Union was a war of paranoia and unchecked imperial ambitions, a conflict without bloodshed, easily assigned blame, or a conceivable end. The standoff originated in disagreements between the two powers during World War II and the loss of millions of Russian lives due to the delayed military participation of the United States. It blossomed into a feud and arms race in the decades after the war. As a child, Armantrout was bombarded with exaggerated and often false rhetoric concerning the evils of communism, the technological and ideological inferiority of the Russian people, and even the imminent end of the world.

In a similarly controversial effort to combat the spread of communism and Soviet ideals, the United States entered the Vietnam War in 1954 and remained a foreign presence in Southeast Asia for almost two decades. The mounting casualties, high incidence of mutilation and psychological trauma, and ambiguous political motivations underlying the conflict all contributed to a widespread loss of faith in the U.S. government.

Partly in response to the wanton bloodshed of the Vietnam War and the perceived need for a new social order, the counterculture movement of the 1960s and 1970s provided American youth with a new source of meaning and conviction. Accompanying the movement was a newfound belief in the suitability of widespread promiscuity, the acceptable use of drugs in mind-expanding capacities, the promotion of peace through adherence to nonviolent religions and communal living, and, most important to aspiring poets like Armantrout and Ron Silliman, a disproportionate emphasis on pushing the established boundaries in literature, art, and music.

Reaching its zenith of popularity and expression in the 1970s and early 1980s still steeped in the convictions of the counterculture movement, the language school of poetry posed a challenge to formerly established modes of writing and sought to engage audiences through

The palo verde tree grows in the American Southwest (©chloe7992 | Shutterstock.com)

the power of language and the poignancy of their own experiences alone. The movement gained momentum in literary communities on both coasts of the United States, in New York and especially in San Francisco. Deriving its name not only from its avowed mission but also from the short-lived but influential $L=A=N=G=U=A=G=E$ magazine edited by Charles Bernstein and Bruce Andrews, the school of poetry included such notable writers as Armantrout, her college associate and lifelong friend Silliman, and other notable figures in contemporary American poetry.

Credited with bringing about a renaissance in the readership of modern poetry, the movement was instrumental in redefining the role of language in writing and pioneering a poetic aesthetic to fit the present age. Many of the school's original participants, including Armantrout, were still composing verse and pushing the boundaries of poetic expression in 2016.

CRITICAL OVERVIEW

As befitting a Pulitzer Prize–winning collection from a renowned poet, initial reviews of *Versed* were overwhelmingly positive. Dan Chiasson of the *New Yorker* praised Armantrout's work for its true spirit of experimentation and the poet's ability to reflect constant movement and fluidity through her verse. He admired this particular collection for its fearless and frenetic portrayal of the modern age that was equally susceptible to sadness and to the humor inherent in a short, brutal existence. Chiasson writes:

> *Versed* is a book about illness, and about the jargon-replete culture of being kept alive. There are wigs, drugs, and cells, all jumbled up with philosophy, string theory, the Iraq War, the tabloids, the TV.

The *New York Times* Art Beat, in an article written by Jennifer B. McDonald, reported the praise of many contemporary reviewers, including Tim Griffin of *Book Forum*, who remarked on the newfound gravity of Armantrout's most recent collection, and Stephen Burt, also of the *New York Times*, who likened the poet to Emily Dickinson in her refusal to mince words or compromise a broad range of possible meanings.

A *Publisher's Weekly* reviewer remarked on the unique stylistic elements of *Versed* and the harmonious juxtaposition of the poet's more familiar engagement with society at large and the darkness within. The review also pays homage to Armantrout's ability to dispense with poetic frills and strike with visceral precision to the heart of feeling, referring to "Armantrout's concentrated, crystalline voice, with a predilection for skipping some steps along the way to sense."

Rob Stanton in *Jacket* explored Armantrout's ambivalent stance about lyric and antilyric poetry through her work. He lauds the poet for her absolute control of the verse and subsequent ability to affect lightning-fast "reversals and fluctuations." In a style he describes as a unique blend of the bleak, pragmatic, and hilarious, Stanton heralds Armantrout as "a (if not *the*) great contemporary poet of death."

Framing the stylistic and thematic observations of many of Armantrout's critics is an intriguing, unknowable quality that Paul Holler, in a 2010 interview with the poet, described as both enervating and obscuring. This effect, Holler posited, was achieved by Armantrout's measured balance of the familiar and the unsettling in her work that grounded readers in relatable experience while enticing them with the allure of the unknown. Holler writes of the perfection of this technique in *Versed*:

> There are numerous examples of these juxtapositions in Ms. Armantrout's most recent work, *Versed*. One of the poems in that collection, "In Place," pairs such themes as life and death, the spiritual and the temporal, and the abstract and the concrete. These contrasting images create energy as well as a sense of mystery. A reader can see that mystery as an end in itself or he or she can try to reconcile those juxtapositions.

CRITICISM

Jeffrey Eugene Palmer

Palmer is a scholar, freelance writer, and high school English teacher. In the following essay, he examines Armantrout's unique spin on lyric poetry as demonstrated through "Unbidden."

Armantrout traces her poetic aesthetic to the groundbreaking developments of the modernist movement of the early twentieth century, crediting literary giants such as William Carlos Williams and T. S. Eliot for influencing her work. In sentiment if not in structure, however, Armantrout's work contains compelling echoes of the far earlier romantic period of the early to mid-1800s.

In an 1817 letter to his brothers, Tom and George, the ill-fated romantic poet John Keats coined the enigmatic term *negative capability* to describe a particular aspect of his artistic ideals. Although the full implications of negative capability for poetry have fascinated modern academics and been the subject of endless scholarly debates, Keats originally used the term to describe his unique take on the role of the lyrical I as an implicit narrator of a poem. Rather than conform to a fixed identity, Keats believed it the poet's duty to act as a conduit for artistic inspiration, embracing a permeability of being that allowed other entities, even objects, to be given voice through the narrator. Keats also wrote of the necessity of embracing the unknown and the indistinct, of trading fleeting convictions and human considerations for the immutable truth underlying all things. Keats explains,

> I mean *Negative Capability*, that is when man is capable of being in uncertainties, Mysteries, doubts, without any irritable reaching after fact & reason...with a great poet the sense

> **ALL PERSONAL CONSIDERATIONS OF UNBEING, OF WORDLESSNESS, OF REGRET HINTED AT BY THE REST OF THE POEM ARE, FOR AN INSTANT, SUBLIMATED INTO NATURE'S ETERNAL WISDOM AND BEAUTY."**

of Beauty overcomes every other consideration, or rather obliterates all consideration.

The unconventional and gripping poetry of Armantrout, as evidenced by pieces like "Unbidden" shares many of the defining characteristics of the philosophy of Keats. Although she is often grouped with the radical language school by association, Armantrout cultivated her unique signature unfettered by, and often in opposition to, the artistic principles of her contemporary peers. While rejecting the florid, structured nature of the earlier poet's style, Armantrout expressed something of the Keatsian longing and deep sadness in "Unbidden"—a willing surrender to forces and mysteries far larger than herself.

In particular, Armantrout admitted to an uneasy relationship with the attempt of the language poetry school to obliterate the narrator altogether and wage war on the lyric. In "Unbidden" the poet's persona can be better described as porous, even amorphous, than as nonexistent. The second-person voice of the poem straddles the line between the exclusive and the inclusive, blurring the distinction between narrator and reader and universalizing the anxieties and concerns expressed. Although the words and images of the verse originate in the mind of their creator, the audience is called to interpret and make relevant their importance by the poem's utter lack of explanation and the entreating, even accusing, second-person address. As with the shades that throng her opening verse, the writer and the reader consolidate their voices into a single poetic identity. This striking move on the part of the poet is consistent with what, in the article *"'See Rae Armantrout for an Alternate View': Narrative and Counternarrative in the Poetry of Rae Armantrout,"* the critic Michael Leddy describes as Armantrout's essential deviance from her fellow language poets:

> Rae Armantrout has emerged as one of the most artful and inventive poets identified with the terms "Language writing" and "language-centered poetry." Armantrout herself has qualms about the usefulness of such labels, and indeed her own work often seems to bear a tenuous relation to familiar language-writing practices. Her poems are typically grounded in the lyric, albeit lyrics of an elliptical and disjunctive sort.

The unique relationship with the lyric to which Leddy referred is strikingly consistent with the ideal of negative capability that Keats championed two centuries earlier. The uncertainty of being and of speaker is further augmented by the direct and unanswerable question that bifurcates the poem. Armantrout also delights in the recurring imagery of the lost and the ungovernable, the ethereal and the invisible. She begins her composition with the image of ghosts pressing in against an ill-defined narrator, intent and yet without the ability to act. The ghosts, like the poet herself, are mere conduits for a single voice that seems to speak through them. Later, in lines 20–22, the lost word is afforded volition denied elsewhere and confounds the narrator with its unfathomable intent. Reversals of action and voice, animate and inanimate all heighten the comparison between Armantrout's evident susceptibility to distortion and Keats's negative capability. In keeping with their mutual understanding of the role of the poet both not only tolerate but also revel in the unknown and the unknowable.

Armantrout articulates a form of negative capability pervasive in her poetry on a stylistic as well as a thematic level. Readers of *Versed*, in particular compositions like "Unbidden," are cast adrift in the unpredictable and often unsettling progression of Armantrout's verse. In "Unbidden," each new stanza bears little resemblance to the previous one, and yet through this seemingly random collection of images and emotions, the poet achieves a perfect harmony of sentiment. The thronging spirits of lines 1–6, the wayward utterance of lines 20–22, and the palo verde tree that roots itself firmly and inexplicably in the center defy the obvious logic of connection and require a leap of faith, rather than careful dissection, to be understood.

WHAT DO I READ NEXT?

- Published and assembled in 2013 for a new generation of readers of verse, *The Collected Poems of Denise Levertov* encompasses the literary contributions of Armantrout's most influential mentor.

- *The Waste Land*, by T. S. Eliot, has been a classic of modern poetry since its initial publication in 1922. Haunting, obscure, and at times unfathomable, *The Waste Land* helped to redefine the poetic craft for a whole new generation of brilliant literary pioneers.

- An exchange of ten correspondences between the famous Austrian poet Rainer Maria Rilke and a young aspirant, *Letters to a Young Poet* was first published in English in 1934 and details the poetic exchange between a master and his pupil.

- Written by Nikki Grimes and published in 2002, *Bronx Masquerade* is a celebration of spoken-word poetry in a diverse, sometimes troubled inner-city environment.

- *A Poet's Glossary* (2014) is Edward Hirsch's up-to-date, comprehensive guide to the poetic craft.

- In his ambitious 1998 masterwork, *Lives of the Poets*, the writer and professor Michael Schmidt weaves together seven centuries of poetic history and exchange from medieval times to the modern age.

- A celebration in verse of the 1980s San Francisco experienced by Armantrout, *The Golden Gate* (1986) is a well-received experiment by Vikram Seth.

- A haunting young-adult classic published in 1999, Janet Fitch's *White Oleander* paints a portrait of a troubled and lonely girlhood in California.

- Famed for her skill not only as a poet but also as a literary critic, lecturer, and essayist, Armantrout has published extensive prose works across the many decades of her career. Compiled and published in 2007, *Rae Armantrout: Collected Prose* is available in a single, exhaustive edition for a modern age of aspiring writers.

Although Armantrout attributes this quality to her loose affiliation with the language poets and by extension their modernist precursors, her comfort in writing poetry divorced from easy comprehension or explanation hints at an origin of an altogether different sort. In a 2010 interview with the reviewer Christopher Lydon, Armantrout shed light on the sporadic spontaneity of her composition style. Her explanation of this process, resonant with the language of uncertainty, owes as much to the negative capability introduced to the world of poetry by Keats as it does to the stream-of-consciousness writing championed by the modernist masters of the following century:

> I do think that I do have elements in common still with the Language Poets, and I think that it's something about the way my poems jump

from thought to thought or image to image without explicitly narrating the connection between. That kind of juxtaposition. Which actually you can see all the way back into modernism, but it's something that also became very much a hallmark of Language Poetry.

The final point of comparison between the language and the romantic poets is evidenced by their willing surrender to forces beyond their ken. As Keats transcended and even obliterated all considerations but for the lofty abstraction of beauty, Armantrout deferred her poem's central question to a majestic, moving symbol in the form of a blooming palo verde tree. All personal considerations of unbeing, of wordlessness, of regret hinted at by the rest of the poem are, for an instant, sublimated into nature's eternal wisdom and beauty. In keeping with the Keatsian

The knowledge that the speaker seeks is no longer wanted when it finally comes, "unbidden"
(©ESB Professional | Shutterstock.com)

conception of negative capability, the uncertainty of the answer embodied by the tree's wisdom is, in itself, a form of poetic solace and fulfillment.

In much the same way, Armantrout and Keats bow to another immutable yet far more terrifying force than nature. Appearing in a collection so steeped in mortality as *Versed*, "Unbidden" is an appropriately complex and ambiguous celebration of death itself. Populated by unrequited shades, words left unsaid, and the sharp edges of a soon-discarded present, Armantrout's poem is as capable of dwelling in the uncertainty of life as it is the certainty of death. The poet's surrender to the theme of mortality is an acceptance of the creed of negative capability, a poetic offering to the greatest mystery of all. The disembodied, ethereal quality of the narrator and her easy communion with the hereafter contribute to what the critic Rob Stanton refers to as "an obvious truth about Armantrout's work: that she has made herself a (if not *the*) great contemporary poet of death."

Further heightening the comparison between Keats and Armantrout is the manner in which they deal with this prospect of death and engage with it on a poetic, philosophical level. In a letter to his brother and sister-in-law in 1819, Keats succumbed to the awful weight of his imminent mortality and advanced a vision of poetry intended to combat these fears. He imagined his craft as a means not only of spiritual salvation but also of personal generation that transformed what he perceived as the crude material of a human soul into a complex and self-aware identity. Keats referred to the world as the vale of soul-making. He premised this spiritual alchemy on the three base ingredients of the heart, the intelligence, and the world itself, as expressed through the work of the poet. He concludes his argument with a poignant plea for approval, imbuing the poetry of weakness, suffering, and death with an otherworldly significance: "Do you not see how necessary a World of Pains and troubles is to school an Intelligence and make it a Soul?"

Although Armantrout seems less assured of the prospect of self-discovery and salvation in poems like "Unbidden," her Keatsian perception of an amorphous and evolving identity remains distinct. In her relentless probing of reality, of questioning the elemental aspect of nature, and in her openness and outright obliteration of personal identity, the modern poet mimics this view of the world as a vale of soul-making. In his review of Armantrout's mature aesthetic and poetic sensibility in *Versed*, Chiasson articulates this quality:

> Poetry shouldn't reveal the soul of a unique individual: there's no such thing as a unique individual. Poetry was there to countermand, rather than to express, identity, to reveal the hand-me-down nature of what we take to be deeply personal memories.

In all these things—her complex relationship with the lyric, comfort within uncertainty, and submission to vast and elemental forces—Armantrout established herself as an heir to another great poet of death, sharing his uncanny ability to slip the bonds of the corporeal and inhabit many identities at once. Her own brand of negative capability, the source of her popularity and singularity even among a school of poets renowned for being singular, seems inspired, effortless, and spontaneous. The poetry that speaks through Armantrout is as timeless and yet immediate as the blossoms of the palo verde or, as Keats writes two centuries earlier in a letter to his friend John Taylor, "as naturally as the leaves to a tree."

Source: Jeffrey Eugene Palmer, Critical Essay on "Unbidden," in *Poetry for Students*, Gale, Cengage Learning, 2017.

Manuel Brito and Rae Armantrout

In the following interview, Armantrout talks about her poems, characterizing them as focusing on perception.

Rae Armantrout's case is particularly fascinating for me since her poetry seems to be apparently dislocated, characterized by a deindividualized substance. In spite of this I think she plays intuitively with her own ontologization and the ultimate projection on the reader. Though the text appears as the leit motif of her poetry, I suspect that her final narrative intention is to picture her life and society through dispersed images. That's why the tension between the individual and the crowd deserves immediate recognitions for we assume that the event/text will be continually reinterpreted.

I FIND THAT, HOWEVER IT'S FRAMED, I RESIST THE SYSTEMATIZATION OF MASCULINITY AND FEMININITY. PARADOXICALLY, I FEEL MOST FEMALE WHEN I AM RESISTING OR SUBVERTING SYSTEMS."

Even in this questionnaire she does not answer categorically but prefers to show herself as a bricoleur with the confidence that she has to take risks in order to gain visibility and honesty in her approach to the text itself. Born in Vallejo (CA) in 1947 she graduated from San Francisco State University. Among her books of poetry we have *Extremities* (1978), *The Invention of Hunger* (1979), *Precedence* (1985), and *Necromance* (1991).

Q: How would you describe your method of writing which is determined by that multiple edgeness that sends us to different centers of perception?

A: You seem to be asking about the role of disjunction (and coherence) in my poems. It's true that they seldom manifest a single image, scenario or procedure. What I am most interested in are complex, oblique relations between stanzas or sections. Typically one of my poems would deal with an abstract *subject* in a series of discrete and concrete ways. An example might be the second section of the poem "Character Development" from my new book *Necromance.* . . .

These two stanzas are very different in tone and in the type of discourse they suggest. One can't imagine the same voice speaking them. The first is intimate and experiential while the second is a quote from a comic book. On the other hand, both stanzas deal with some sort of parental care and both refer (in different ways) to the title concept—character development. Their juxtaposition *appears logical*—if the child can still cry then he must not be dead—but since these are different types of characters, the second actually undercuts the first. The parts are working against as well as with one another. Perhaps this is the *multiple edgeness* to which you refer.

Q: I've observed that in your poetry there are encounters and miscounters, an entrance into the private that is dissolved into the materiality of words and incomplete units, is there an intent of writing self-mirroring poems?

A: Well, my poems are composed, to a great extent, of what I happen to see and hear—and then, immediately, what those sights and sounds cause me to think about. So my personal (home and neighborhood) experience is very much part of the poems. Does that mean they are *self-mirroring* or autobiographical? That depends on how we define the self—which is a question which usually interests me. I'm interested in the conjunction of self and culture. Are our thoughts our own? We are discrete genetic entities and yet each of us had her first words put in her mouth by her parents and grew up to join the pre-existing discourse of her time.

Many Americans would know that Fruity Pebbles is a breakfast cereal advertised on television. Here even the seemingly private element of sleep is inscribed by social text. I heard this commercial as I was drowsing. It's impossible to say whether the poem mirrors my life or the life of our age.

Q: Usually the addressee in your poems is a you *who is verbalized ghostly since there's little context for his/her formalization, in this sense you seem to follow Sapir when he says 'ideation reigns in supreme language...'*

A: The pronouns are fairly arbitrary in my poetry. I would imagine this is so for many other writers as well. Like the characters in dreams, pronouns are aspects of oneself. I may choose a pronoun for the tone it creates. For instance, using *you* can make a poem sound either seductive or confrontational. I provide *little* context for these pronouns partly because I am not necessarily trying to establish them as solid identities, separate from myself. I'm interested in the multiplicity, and also the duplicity, of inner voices. I am not quite sure how your quote from Sapir follow[s] from your observation on my work, however, the ideation is the process of forming ideas—that is more than one. Thinking may be mainly sensing relations. I can connect ideation in this way with my interest in internal voices.

Q: You seem very conscious on non interpreting but of suggesting reflections through questions, open sentences, etc. But also it seems to be an instinctive discourse looking for the pleasure of now and some emotional impasses...

A: I want poetry to have the speed and urgency of thought. I could say that I am neither *interpreting* nor *suggesting reflections*—rather I am, in fact, reflecting. But that ignores the problem of audience. Poetry involves displaying one's mental processes first to oneself and then to others. In the context of display, sincerity is problematic, yet I would agree with Oppen that, however elusive, sincerity is the measure and goal of the poem. That may sound strange coming from someone who has written "*Ventriloquy/ is the mother tongue.*" That line shows the extent of my pessimism. I don't believe we'll ever arrive at truth or sincerity, but I think we'd better keep trying. There *is* a pleasure in encountering an impasse (emotional or otherwise). It is paradoxically, an indication that we are on the way. This is beginning to sound like *Pilgrim's Progress.* Speaking of ventriloquy, this must be the voice of my protestant upbringing. I think people often impose unity on a poem (or a nation for that matter) in order to look good before some imagined audience. I try to avoid that.

Q: I think you try to transcend the polemics about writing like a woman or concerning exclusively to archetypal functions, is there recognitions of a more communal experience?

A: I think a close reading of my work reveals that it is the product of a woman's life. Still, when I was in my twenties, I was actually told by two separate men that I "*wrote like a man.*" All they meant, I suspect, is that I didn't write as exclusively about romantic difficulties as they imagined a woman would or should. Such prescriptions seem arbitrary. These days there is a more sophisticated attempt to define the feminine. Feminist theories have said that a female writing, for instance, might have a kind of limitless sensuousity. It would eschew logic and have no real beginning or end. That's an attractive idea, but I still distrust definitions. At any rate, the writing they describe is not exactly like my own. I am compelled by starts and stops, silences, and (the trappings of) logic. I often use logic comedically, but I am perversely fascinated by it. I don't think it will be easily jettisoned. I find that, however it's framed, I resist the systematization of masculinity and femininity.

Paradoxically, I feel most female when I am resisting or subverting systems.

Q: One of the most consistent commentaries about your poetry comes from Ron Silliman who emphasizes your sensibility in exploring unnoticed facets of the verbal art, is there a special grammar for inventing those mysteries without boundaries?

A: I always thought Silliman was talking about exploring unnoticed facets of social reality in general, not only the *verbal art.* Certainly his own writing renders the sights, sounds and smells of a neighborhood as well as the vicissitudes of the writing process. That's something I very much admire in Ron's work. Likewise, when I want to write poetry (as opposed to some other kind of writing) the first thing I do is "*stop, look, and listen*" as the kindergartners are instructed to do before they cross a street.

I would like a grammar to produce "*mysteries without boundaries.*" I'm attracted by things I don't understand and often write about them. I like ending a poem with a statement which is satisfactory at first, but troubling on second thought. At that point, one has to go back—but how far?

Source: Manuel Brito and Rae Armantrout, "Rae Armantrout," in *A Suite of Poetic Voices: Interviews with Contemporary American Poets,* Kadle Books, 1992, pp. 15–22.

SOURCES

Armantrout, Rae, *Versed,* Wesleyan University Press, 2010, p. 5

"A Brief Guide to Language Poetry," Poets.org, May 18, 2004, http://www.poets.org/poetsorg/text/brief-guide-language-poetry (accessed May 15, 2016).

Burt, Stephen, "The New Thing," in *Boston Review,* http://bostonreview.net/poetry/new-thing (accessed May 15, 2016).

Chiasson, Dan, "Entangled: The Poetry of Rae Armantrout," in *New Yorker,* May 17, 2010, http://www.newyorker.com/magazine/2010/05/17/entangled (accessed May 15, 2016).

Griffin, Tim, "Liberal Mediation," *Book Forum,* http://www.bookforum.com/inprint/016_01/3536 (Accessed May 15, 2016).

Holler, Paul, "An Interview with Rae Armantrout," in *Bookslut,* July 2010, http://www.bookslut.com/features/2010_07_016299.php (accessed July 6, 2016).

Keats, John, "Selections from Keats's Letters (1817)," Poetry Foundation website, http://www.poetryfoundation.org/resources/learning/essays/detail/69384 (accessed May 15, 2016)

———, "To George and Georgina Keats," in *The Complete Works of John Keats,* Vol. 5, edited by H. Buxton Forman, Thomas Y. Crowell, 1901, p. 54.

Kiderra, Inga, "A Life-Changing Year," in *UCSD News,* April 25, 2011, http://ucsdnews.ucsd.edu/archive/thisweek/2011/04/25_Armantrout.asp (accessed May 15, 2016).

Leddy, Michael, "'See Armantrout for an Alternate View': Narrative and Counternarrative in the Poetry of Rae Armantrout," in *Contemporary Literature,* Vol. 35, No. 4, Winter 1994, pp. 739–60.

Lydon, Christopher, "Pulitzer Poet Rae Armantrout," in *Huffington Post,* May 19, 2010, http://www.huffingtonpost.com/christopher-lydon/pulitzer-poet-rae-armantr_b_582301.html (accessed July 8, 2016).

McDonald, Jennifer B, "*Versed* by Rae Armantrout: California Poet, National Recognition," in *New York Times,* April 12, 2010, http://artsbeat.blogs.nytimes.com/201”0/04/12/versed-by-rae-armantrout-california-poet-national-recognition/?comments (accessed May 15, 2016).

Messerli, Douglas, "'Language' Poetries," PIP (Project for Innovative Poetry) Blog, February 24, 2013, http://pippoetry.blogspot.com/2013/02/language-poetries.html (accessed May 15, 2016).

"Rae Armantrout," Poetry Foundation website, http://www.poetryfoundation.org/poems-and-poets/poets/detail/rae-armantrout (accessed May 15, 2016).

Review of *Versed,* in *Publisher's Weekly,* http://www.publishersweekly.com/978-0-8195-6879-3 (accessed May 15, 2016).

Stanton, Rob, "This," in *Jacket,* No. 39, Early 2010, http://jacketmagazine.com/39/r-armantrout-rb-stanton.shtml (accessed May 15, 2016).

FURTHER READING

Andrews, Bruce, and Charles Bernstein, *The L=A=N=G=U=A=G=E Book,* Southern Illinois University Press, 1984.
    This collection includes noteworthy essays, articles, and poems influential to the rise and success of the language school pioneered by Armantrout, Silliman, and others.

Armantrout, Rae, *Extremities,* Figures, 1978.
    Extremities is Armantrout's first full-length collection of verse and presents a compelling counterpoint to her more mature work.

Armantrout, Rae, *True*, Atelos, 1998.

    This memoir remains the foremost example of Armantrout's experimentation with prose and the narrative genre.

Kalaidjian, Walter B, *The Cambridge Companion to Modern American Poetry*, Cambridge University Press, 2014.

    This volume is a comprehensive overview of the numerous literary currents that contributed to the school of language poetry in the 1970s and 1980s.

Silliman, Ronald, *The Alphabet*, University of Alabama Press, 2008.

    Silliman, Armantrout's fellow language poet and close college companion, labored on this collection for over two decades. It is widely considered his groundbreaking and most intriguing poetic contribution.

SUGGESTED SEARCH TERMS

Rae Armantrout

"Unbidden" AND Armantrout

Versed AND Armantrout

Ron Silliman AND Rae Armantrout

language poets

antilyric poetry

L=A=N=G=U=A=G=E magazine AND Charles Bernstein

West Coast poets

language poets AND romantic poets

Valentine

CAROL ANN DUFFY

1993

Carol Ann Duffy's "Valentine" appeared originally in her 1993 collection *Mean Time*. Written during a period of cultural upheavals in post-Thatcher Britain, it is a poem that invites, and perhaps even compels, a reader to rethink the language of romance that shapes contemporary views of love and relationships. On one hand, a poem that engages traditional metaphors and symbols with hope of finding comfort and stability, it is, on the other hand, a poem that recognizes, ultimately, the power of such language to make sense of a relationship defined by an absence of trust and the perpetual threat of violence and disintegration.

AUTHOR BIOGRAPHY

Duffy was born on December 23, 1955, in Glasgow, Scotland. She was the first child (and only daughter) of Frank Duffy, an electrician, and Mary Black. The couple would add four sons to the family, which lived for the first six years of Duffy's life in an economically challenged neighborhood known as the Gorbals. Relocating 260 miles south to Stafford, England, the family settled nicely into their new home, and Duffy began her schooling at Saint Austin's Roman Catholic Primary School. She continued her education at St. Joseph's Convent School

Carol Ann Duffy *(©David Collingwood | Alamy Stock Photo)*

before graduating from Stafford's Girls' High School in 1974.

It was during these formative years that Duffy's love of writing was encouraged by teachers and other poets, including the Liverpool poet Adrian Henri (1932–2000), with whom Duffy began a personal relationship. She applied to the University of Liverpool in 1974, living with Henri and receiving an honors degree in philosophy in 1977.

To say that Duffy is a productive writer is an understatement. Her first volume of poems, *Fleshweathercock and Other Poems*, was published in 1974. Her major poetry collections include *Mean Time* (1993, which includes the

poem "Valentine"), *Standing Female Nude* (1985), *Selling Manhattan* (1987), and *Rapture* (2005). Duffy is also a well-respected writer of illustrated children's books, including *Meeting Midnight* (1999), *The Oldest Girl in the World* (2000), *Queen Munch and Queen Nibble* (2002), *Another Night before Christmas* (2005), and *The Princess' Blankets* (2009).

Duffy's career has been varied and diverse, including a stint as poetry critic for the *Guardian* (1988–1989), editor of the poetry magazine *Ambit*, and lecturer in poetry at Manchester Metropolitan University, where she later became creative director of its writing school. Duffy was appointed England's Poet Laureate in May 2009, which allowed her the opportunity to write a poem celebrating the 2011 wedding of Prince William and Catherine Middleton. Significantly, she is the first woman and openly lesbian poet to ever hold the post. She has also been an active playwright, and her work has been produced at the Liverpool Playhouse and the Almeida Theater in London. Among her dramatic titles are *Take My Husband* (1982), *Cavern of Dreams* (1984), *Little Women Big Boys* (1986), *Loss* (1986), and *Casanova* (2007). Duffy's collaboration with composer Sasha Johnson Manning has produced the very popular *The Manchester Carols*, a series of Christmas songs that premiered in Manchester Cathedral in 2007.

Much celebrated throughout her career, Duffy holds honorary doctorates from the University of Dundee, the University of Hull, the University of St. Andrews, and the University of Warwick. The list of awards she has received is long, including the Scottish Arts Council Book Award (1986, 1990, 1993), Dylan Thomas Prize (1989), Cholmondeley Award (2992), Whitebread Awards (1993), and a National Endowment for Science, Technology and the Arts Award (2001). She was appointed an Officer of the Order of the British Empire (OBE) in 1995, Commander of the Order of the British Empire (CBE) in 2002, and Dame Commander of the Order of the British Empire (DBE) in 2015.

POEM SUMMARY

The text used for this summary is from *Mean Time*, Anvil Press, 1993, p. 34. Versions of the poem can be found on the following web pages: http://www.scottishpoetrylibrary.org.uk/poetry/poems/valentine, http://genius.com/Carol-ann-duffy-valentine-annotated, and http://famouspoetsand poems.com/poets/carol_ann_duffy/poems/8116.

Line 1

The opening stanza of "Valentine" is a single incomplete sentence shaped by the word *not*, which is employed to negate two classic symbols of love: the rose and the heart.

Lines 2–5

The second stanza is an unrhymed quatrain in which the speaker of the poem gives his or her love interest an unusual but powerful symbol:

MEDIA ADAPTATIONS

- Duffy collaborated with Aaron Jay Kernis on a musical adaptation of "Valentine," which was published as part of *Valentines: For Voice and Orchestra*, Associated Music Publishers, 2000.

- Duffy read "Valentine" herself as part of her audiobook edition *Selected Poems 1985–1993*, Hachette Audio, 2006.

the onion. The speaker moves directly into a metaphor that compares an onion to a moon that is wrapped in very commonplace brown paper. The speaker then shifts to a simile that states that the onion as a symbol of love brings with it a promise of light, which illuminates the thoughtful, almost philosophic uncovering of the contours and subtleties of love.

Lines 6–10

The third stanza begins with a confident, and very intimate, offering of the onion to the intended recipient. This stanza also begins to unravel the traditional conception of love by highlighting the obviously negative experiences associated with the unpeeling of an onion, most notably the accumulation of tears and the blurred perception of the world that love (and heartbreak) brings. Love is suggested in this stanza to produce an uncertain and somewhat unstable picture of grief.

Lines 11–12

The next two stanzas both comprise single lines that emphasize how the speaker is determined to approach love with a truthfulness that is neither common nor particularly welcome in contemporary society. In the first of the two lines, the speaker states this assertion simply and directly. In the second, which echoes the opening line/stanza of the poem, the speaker positions the gift of the onion in terms of being an antithesis to such clichés as a traditional card and the more contemporary (though nonetheless clichéd) novelty gesture of a kissogram.

Lines 13–17

The sixth stanza iterates the assertion that the onion is the perfect symbol for the romance that has developed between the speaker and the *you* in the poem. It is a romance that is open to the potentially damaging energies of possessiveness as well as concerns about faithfulness and the resilience of the romance to survive the various pressures that will inevitably appear.

Lines 18–20

The seventh stanza introduces one pressure that the speaker is most concerned about: the pressure on romance that comes with marriage. This stanza envisions the onion in a different way, as a series of loops—as when one slices an onion crosswise—that tighten into a traditional wedding ring.

Lines 21–23

The eighth stanza transforms the image of the wedding ring into something deadly. The ring is further likened to that of a newly sliced onion, which leaves its strong, pungent scent on everything it touches. The scent proves to be a kind of branding, marking the recipient as owned by— or at least committed to—the speaker of the poem. The final line of the poem introduces the image of the knife, which may be commonplace when slicing onions but introduces to the poem a direct reference to the violence and sense of threat that has started to corrupt the romance (and the idea of romance) upon which this relationship has been built.

THEMES

Language

Duffy is a poet for whom the power of language is always of interest, whether in its relationship to the traditional sexual politics that defined Britain through her early life or as a tool for puncturing class assumptions around writing. In "Valentine," Duffy takes direct aim at the language of love and romance that has become clichéd over time. The poem is controlled, in fact, by a negation (*not*), which carries enough impact across the poem to undercut even the most traditional of romantic symbols: flowers

or the image of the heart. These words are de-emphasized in this poem, with emphasis placed on such counteractive (that is, antiromantic) words as *fierce* and *lethal*. Figuratively the valentine offered by the speaker of the poem is not soft or gentle or loving; it is sharp-edged, dangerous, and constrictive.

Marriage

Given that Duffy is a lesbian who published "Valentine" during the final months of Margaret Thatcher's deeply conservative reign over British politics, it is not surprising that she challenges the most powerful and traditional marker of heterosexual relationships: marriage. Again, her weapon of choice is the shrewd juxtaposition of the classic symbol of marriage (the wedding band) with constrictive verbs ("shrink" and "cling") as well as with adjectives and nouns that resonate with danger and the threat of death ("lethal" and "knife").

Looking earlier in the poem, readers can find clues about the origin of the concerns that the speaker has around this relationship. The words "possessive" and "faithful" resonate in the poem as both fearsome and a threat. The implication is relatively clear: marriage is, in part, a strategy by which the speaker hopes to ensure that the person being celebrated understands his or her role of possession, and understands, too, that faithfulness is an assumed characteristic of this relationship.

Romantic Love

The concept of romantic love, which drives the tradition of exchanging valentines with one's love interest, was popularized in Western culture via the understanding of courtly love in the Middle Ages. In this period, cavaliers (knights) engaged in nonsexual relationships with women of nobility, often whom they served. The relations were elaborately scripted by social convention and a deeply held code of moral conduct.

The exploits of these men and their women were captured in stories and songs that circulated freely as reminders of the ideals by which gentlemen and women were expected to live within this society. Courtly love permitted expressions of emotional closeness, which may have been lacking from the union between husband and wife, which enhanced the ideal of courtly love as an act of caring and emotional intimacy rather than a sexual relationship.

Traditional Valentine images are pushed aside (©Valentina_G / Shutterstock.com)

STYLE

Metaphor

Drawn loosely from the Greek term *metaphora* ("to transfer" or "to carry across"), metaphor is a type of figurative language that effectively carries a meaning associated with one subject across a point of comparison to connect with another, typically unrelated object. More specifically (and simply), a metaphor compares two very unlike objects with each other without using the words *like* or *as* (as in "love is an open rose"). Most theories of metaphor suggest that all language contains within it a kind of metaphoric energy, most of which is overlooked or ignored in everyday use, during which the connection between ideas and thoughts is much more direct than in poetry. Nonetheless, metaphor, even when left dormant, is central to how individuals think about and perceive the world.

In poetry, the use of metaphor opens language and perception outwards, effectively cracking the edges of language so that possibilities of meaning cascade to previously unimagined opportunities. Comparing the onion to a moon wrapped in very prosaic brown wrapping paper, Duffy refers both directly and indirectly to the romantic symbolism that the moon has carried for centuries. In ancient mythology, for instance, the moon, which governs the tides, was ruled by the goddess Diana, whose influence also extended to the realm of human emotions, given that the human body is composed mostly of water.

Symbol

Broadly defined, a symbol is a literary device that functions very much like an onion, with various layers of meaning wrapping over each other, often concealed at first sight, but unfolding to reveal themselves (and their interrelationships) through the readings or viewings of a work of art. More simply, a symbol is an object that stands for much more than its literal meaning.

In "Valentine" Duffy challenges the conventional symbols associated with love, specifically the red rose and the heart, both of which are introduced by the word *not* in the opening stanza. With the traditional symbols negated,

TOPICS FOR FURTHER STUDY

- "Poetry is the music of being human," Duffy posited in a *New Statesman* interview in 2011, which makes perfect sense given her own interest in adapting "Valentine" for various arrangements, ranging from voice and piano to full orchestral. Create a musical representation of Duffy's poem (use of the words proper is optional), with a clear articulation of its form as well as its primary theme or message.

- Performance is an essential part of poetry, and Duffy is well known for delivering exceptionally entertaining readings of her poems. The performative qualities of "Valentine" are obvious given the number of readings that can be found on a site like YouTube. Add to this catalogue by creating your own video performance of Duffy's poem. Feel free to use multiple voices, sound effects, and whatever else you feel will help your video convey the complexities and subtleties of "Valentine" while at the same time respecting its key message.

- Read Anne Waldman's "Matriot Acts, Act 1," and in a well-structured and thoughtful essay compare and contrast Waldman's and Duffy's poems with respect to their approaches to love, romance, marriage, and language.

- Duffy is recognized as a skilled and respected visual artist as well as writer and performer. She is also adept at finding very powerful visual artists to work with for her books, especially those written for children. On a poster-size sheet of paper or using a digital drawing program (ArtRage, for example), represent visually (in paint, colored pencil, or any other media) your interpretation of the powerfully visual poem "Valentine." Feel free to incorporate words or symbols into your final product, and be prepared to show your work as part of a class exhibition.

- Create your own version of a food-as-symbol poem, using "Valentine" as your model. Think about a specific emotion (sadness, for instance) or concept (such as a fulfilled life), and then think about what food could be best paired with that choice and why.

- Read Rosemary Norman's "Lullaby," written from the perspective of a devoted daughter or son, which also takes on a familiar tradition and gives it a new twist. In a well-written and considered essay, compare or contrast one or more of the following in both "Lullaby" and "Valentine": tone, language, imagery, the use of traditional symbols.

Duffy introduces her own unusual symbol of love: an onion. Through this symbol, Duffy is able to represent the various layers of love, from the idyllic first moments through the pungent depths that bring with them the hint of danger.

HISTORICAL CONTEXT

Given Duffy's family and personal history of political activism, it is important to note that the early nineties in Britain were very much an era of a country divided. Struggling to rebuild in the aftermath of a decade of Margaret Thatcher's leadership, the 1990s began under a long shadow of dramatically high unemployment and deep social unrest.

Driven by an unrelenting policy of privatization (the selling of previously nationalized industries to private interests) and a commitment to reducing the power of the country's trade unions, Thatcher set in motion a cultural upheaval that saw several of the largest unions launching strikes in response to proposed changes to legislation.

COMPARE
&
CONTRAST

- **1993:** John Major is prime minister of Britain, having replaced the deeply disliked Conservative Margaret Thatcher. Despite his success in overseeing the revival of the British economy, as well as his initiation of the beginnings of the Northern Ireland peace process, Major faces intense criticism of his leadership: by the mid-1990s the conservatives are embroiled in ongoing sleaze scandals involving various MPs, including cabinet ministers. Criticism of Major's leadership reaches such a pitch that he chooses to resign as leader in June 1995, challenging his critics to either back him or oppose him in a new election; he is duly challenged by John Redwood but is easily reelected.

  Today: The office of the British prime minister remains in the shadow (albeit weakening) of the Thatcher era, with every person and party elected to the office forced to distance themselves from the history of economic policy and, to a lesser extent, political brokering of power and influence, that defined the era of the woman known colloquially as "the Iron Lady."

- **1993:** Same-sex relationships, however common, are not recognized formally within British law, forcing a writer like Duffy, a lesbian, to acknowledge the restrictive sexual politics that continue to shape her personal life and career. Indeed, Duffy's sexual orientation is a lingering, albeit never openly acknowledged, issue in the years leading up to her selection as the poet laureate.

  Today: Since 2005, same-sex couples have been allowed to enter into civil partnerships in Britain, which is a clearly defined but separate union providing the legal consequences of marriage. Still, the path to full recognition has remained fraught with debates. In 2006, for instance, the British High Court of Justice rejected a legal bid by a British lesbian couple who had married in Canada to have their union recognized as a marriage rather than a civil partnership.

- **1993:** Kissograms and other variants of the traditional singing telegram enjoy a brief renaissance across Europe. Only two years earlier, in 1991, the movie *The Fisher King* included a scene in which the character of Parry (played by the late Robin Williams) sends a singing telegram to the character of Lydia (Amanda Plummer).

  Today: Kissograms and all the related derivatives have become outdated owing, in part, to shifting cultural concerns around unwanted or unexpected physical contact with strangers and, in larger part, to the increased use of technology as the platform of choice for sending surprises to people.

The miners' strike was the broadest and deepest confrontation between the unions and the Thatcher government. In March 1984 the National Coal Board (NCB) had proposed to close twenty of the 174 state-owned mines and cut 20,000 of the 187,000 jobs in the sector.

Two-thirds of the country's miners, led by the National Union of Mineworkers, put down their tools in protest, despite the action's being declared illegal, as union leaders refused to hold a vote on the strike. Thatcher, in turn, refused steadfastly to meet the unions' demands, forcing the unions to concede and return to work without a deal. The cost to the already struggling British economy was estimated to be at least £1.5 billion. In the poststrike world, the governments of Thatcher and John Major closed a total of ninety-seven coal mines that were deemed unprofitable. By 1994, all remaining mines had been privatized. But the bad news did not end there. Dozens of mines, some of which were clearly profitable, were subsequently closed in

Instead of hearts and flowers, the speaker offers an onion (©pullia | Shutterstock.com)

the 1990s, resulting in the loss of tens of thousands of jobs and the erasure of traditional rural cultures and communities.

The year leading into 1990 was a period rife with challenges to Thatcher's leadership and politics. A direct challenge occurred during the 1989 leadership campaign, but Thatcher easily overcame any threats to her control of the country and party. Regardless, Thatcher's premiership was defined by the second-lowest average approval rating (40 percent) of any postwar prime minister.

By November 1990 the stage was set for the final collapse of Thatcherite Britain. Geoffrey Howe, the literal last man standing from Thatcher's original cabinet of 1979, resigned from his position as deputy prime minister, effectively triggering a full leadership review. Howe's disavowal of his longstanding support proved decisive, with Thatcher coming up a mere four votes short of sustaining support. She was replaced as prime minister and party leader by her chancellor, John Major, who oversaw an upturn in Conservative support in the seventeen months

leading up to the 1992 general election and led the Conservatives to their fourth successive victory on April 9, 1992.

CRITICAL OVERVIEW

Duffy is generally recognized as having achieved what few contemporary poets can: finding a balance between critical and commercial success. As Jody Allen-Randolph celebrated in 1995, Duffy is generally seen as "a sparkling exception" to the mundanity of contemporary British verse, "one of the most courageous and original talents to emerge in British poetry for years." More than a decade later, David Whitley iterated Duffy's continued success, positioning her as "one of the most popular poets working in Britain today." Although some critics have accused her of being a populist poet, most critics celebrate the fact that her works are both literary and accessible. As Peter Forbes of the *Guardian* summarizes so elegantly,

> Duffy is a Scot brought up in the Midlands, politically left-wing, in a gay relationship, and

with a wonderful feel for idiom and contemporary culture, especially low-life, she has been able in her work to unite timeless themes to a sense of life as it is lived now.

Writing in *Children's Literature in Education* (2007), Whitley points out that "Duffy is a poet whose work has always been acutely attuned to the social dimensions of human experience." Her poetry is rich with "many voices" that are "not just explorations of individuals, caught, at times, at a point of crisis." And although these poems are aptly drawn with "social nuances," they can also be read "as symptomatic of attitudes and shifts in sensibility that are responses to changing social structures."

Focusing on Duffy's poems about love specifically, he notes that "love touches the centre of Duffy's speakers' lives in varied ways that encompass male as well as female, joy as well as pain." "Duffy is too good a writer," Whitley concludes, "to be easily pigeon-holed and, if the predominant effect of her poems tends towards questioning or critiquing romantic love, the forms and perspectives offered are diverse."

Writing of the collection *Mean Time* specifically, Forbes celebrates its "nostalgic vein" and Duffy's move to include "poems about broken and budding relationships." It is a volume, Forbes concludes, that showcases "what are perhaps her finest short lyric poems" to date.

CRITICISM

Klay Dyer

Dyer is a freelance writer specializing in topics relating to literature, popular culture, and the relationship between creativity and technology. In the following essay, he explores Duffy's short poem "Valentine" as a site of struggle between traditional language of romantic love and a real relationship that is anything but traditional or, ultimately, romantic.

Romantic love, as both ideal and social construction, is a persistent and determined driver of popular culture. Whether in the novels of such a writer as Nicholas Sparks (*The Notebook*, 1996) or in such generational films as *Casablanca* (1942), *When Harry Met Sally* (1989), and *Love Actually* (2003), romantic themes and symbols continue to drive book and box-office sales while at the same time skirting the edge of a pool that would see them sink into becoming clichés.

TAKING ON THE DUAL ROLE OF ROMANTIC PARTNER AND INTERROGATOR OF ROMANTIC TRADITIONS, DUFFY'S SPEAKER STRUGGLES WITH A CONUNDRUM THAT POETS HAVE FACED FOR CENTURIES: HOW TO NEGOTIATE THE CLICHÉS OF ROMANTIC LOVE WHILE WRITING HONESTLY ABOUT RELATIONSHIPS PLAYED OUT IN A WORLD FAR REMOVED FROM COURTLY TRADITIONS AND MOVIE SCREENPLAYS."

A *cliché* is an expression, idea, or element of a creative work that becomes overused to the point of losing its original impact, especially to the point of being trite or even irritating. It is the threat of this slippage towards triteness that Carol Ann Duffy interrogates in her "Valentine," a poem that moves readers away from the traditional and reassuring comfort zone of romance towards something more dramatic, more risky, and ultimately more honest in its representation than cliché would allow.

Most traditional societies privilege an understanding of romantic love that is, for lack of a better term, comfortable. The role of explicit sexual attraction, while present, is contained by focusing on the uniqueness of the ideal match (the term *soulmate* comes to mind) and by privileging the ideal of a single, eternal love captured in a ceremony that celebrates, as Duffy's poem highlights, faithfulness, and by implication, monogamy.

In "Valentine," however, romantic love is never allowed to become a comforting or even comfortable state. Rather, the poem takes readers to an imagined relationship defined by a sense of lethalness that dances along a knife's edge of possessiveness and potential violence. In short, this poem moves from iterating the comforting cultural ideal of romantic love to exposing that same ideal to what might be considered a postmodern lens. Through this lens, the very act of writing a poem about romantic love interrogates the long tradition of poems about that subject and reconsiders how individuals define

WHAT DO I READ NEXT?

- Duffy is also a prolific children's writer, and her recent fairy tale *The Princess' Blankets* (2009) is a wonderful representative of this side of her work. In this case, the story is illustrated by haunting and mysterious paintings created by Catherine Hyde.

- Pablo Neruda's *Love Poems* (2008) work, like Duffy's "Valentine," to challenge traditional notions of love, romance, passion, and sexual attraction. The poems were translated for this edition by Donald D. Walsh.

- Michael Ondaatje's poem "The Cinnamon Peeler," from his book *Running in the Family* (1982), combines sensuality, food, the power of scent, and a hint of violence in ways very similar to Duffy's "Valentine."

- Philosopher Simon May's *Love: A History* (2011) is a nonfiction study of the longstanding cultural understanding of love as unconditional, selfless, unchanging, sincere, and totally accepting. Tracing over 2,500 years of human thought and history, May shows how our ideal of love developed from its Hebraic and Greek origins alongside Christianity until, during the last two centuries, it evolved to encompass an influential set of expectations and untruths that tend to constrain rather than reinforce human relationships.

- Nicole Krauss's *The History of Love: A Novel* (2005) was a finalist for the Orange Prize for Fiction in 2006. It explores love as a powerful force that connects people across time, tragedy, and a world of distance.

- The late Gabriel García Márquez's novel *Love in the Time of Cholera* (1985) remains one of the definitive works that sets out to explore a love so powerful and unusual as to defy time and the threat of death itself.

themselves as romantic partners. More specifically, it demands a deep rethinking about how the language of romantic love (some of which has been long forgotten) continues to impact contemporary understandings of love, romance, and marriage. It is this deep rethinking that is at the center of Duffy's poem, as the speaker (readers are never clear on the sex) moves seamlessly across the linguistic terrain of his/her feelings for the recipient of the gifts, the ring, and the words of the poem itself. In the end, the speaker is unable to connect in meaningful ways to the traditional language of romantic love poems, and slides not towards cliché but towards the pungency of an onion and the sharp edge of a chef's knife. At poem's end, Duffy's speaker is trapped in a spiral of language, moving in ever-widening circles away from the ideal of the red rose and satin heart and towards an emptiness of language (and relationship) that is more than mere cliché. It is an emptiness that leaves a reader at best uncomfortable and, worse still, pondering a world in which the speaker's spiral is the new norm, the new reality of romance.

Taking on the dual role of romantic partner and interrogator of romantic traditions, Duffy's speaker struggles with a conundrum that poets have faced for centuries: how to negotiate the clichés of romantic love while writing honestly about relationships played out in a world far removed from courtly traditions and movie screenplays. More specifically, the speaker struggles with how to bring some sense of comfort and stability (the twin goals of traditional romance) to a relationship that seems determined to resist providing comfort owing to underlying concern over the faithfulness of the recipient of the gifts and the threatened pressures that come with the ultimate expression of true love: marriage, the ceremony that gives a relationship the sheen of unwavering meaning and a sense of ordered clarity.

One possible answer to the speaker's dilemma is to move beyond thinking of the relationship in traditional terms and to reimagine it as perhaps the least romantic symbol available: an onion, with its pungent, painful scent and its many layers of complexity, all of which can, in skilled hands, be rendered delicious. Romantic love is reimagined in this poem as a series of layers, each capturing a short burst of emotion that might (or might not) be aligned with the one that came before and that might (or might not) gather together into a smooth, understandable progression towards a romantic ideal. Perhaps, the speaker is suggesting, this is a relationship that demands radical rethinking of the language through which it defines itself, moving away from the traditional goal of comfort in order to better understand this relationship in this time and this place. Perhaps romantic love is not a single, coherent set of words and images but is a confused, unstructured flow of potentially random emotions, some good, others not so good.

Untethered from the imperative to resolve romantic love into a comfort-making, comprehensible picture, the speaker is left to deal with the reality of a complex relationship that has become unhooked from the expectations of such foundational concepts as trust, truthfulness, and respect. Unable to connect to past concepts of romance, the speaker ends up in a kind of free fall through the relationship, unpeeling each layer of the onion quickly and fully aware of the stinging eyes and tears that follow.

At the same time, the speaker cannot seem to imagine, let alone look to live, a life totally outside the traditional guidelines for romantic love. The poem opens with two classic images, but only to negate them. It later evokes the equally traditional symbol of the wedding ring, only to undermine its comforting stability with verbs of constriction and discomfort. Finally, the ultimate gesture of romantic love, the marriage proposal, is undercut by the questionable sincerity of the offer and the connection of it to a word that implies that it is something fatal or deadly.

Unlike the speaker in a traditional love poem, Duffy's speaker never finds a sense of certainty or comfort in the articulations of the poem. Instead, he/she seems left in search of answers to some of the more important questions about the relationship, his or her own sense of its legitimacy and the pathway that it might provide in the future. In the journey of the traditional romance, the goal is maturity, insight, and understanding. In Duffy's speaker's journey, the endpoint is a knife's edge tainted by an onion, fear, and threat; it revolves around power, control, and destruction.

The speaker's wandering from the traditions of romantic idealism haunts this poem. As the layers of symbolic onion are peeled away, the poem is increasingly troubled and troubling. The relationship is doomed, it seems, to remain discomforting and fueled by angst, anger, and even paranoia. Never stable or certain, the speaker is forced to a position of perpetual doubt and worry. Divided between wanting to believe and remaining unable to do so, the speaker is forced to live in a state of flux, lacking security and a sense of belonging in the relationship he/she seems determined to celebrate, if ambivalently.

Trapped in this unsettling relationship, as well as in the equally unsettling language, the speaker is forced, too, to reflect upon his/her own role in its trajectory to this place. Unable to embrace the traditional words and symbols of romantic love, the speaker is left with two choices: admit the irrelevance of such language and create a new one or continue to the seemingly logical conclusion that this is not a relationship worthy of such language. The choice, it seems, is to acknowledge that this relationship is more a proliferation of meaningless moments than a movement towards emotional depth and comfort.

Exhausted and without hope, the speaker collapses in the final lines of the poem onto an image of threat and potential violence. Overwhelmed by the struggle to find the right language to capture the full emotions shaping this relationship, the speaker is left vulnerable to a resignation that something is deeply wrong. There is a hopelessness to this poem that stems from a time long ago and from an unwillingness in each generation to carve out a language of romance that has strong roots in the sexual politics and cultural expectations of the here and now. In this sense, the poem pushes readers to reflect and to reconsider their own use of the language and symbolic traditions that populate "Valentine." Like all powerful literature, this is writing that demands that readers reconnect with language, and in doing so resist the impulse to cliché and stagnation that comes from allowing the past to shape, without challenge, the present and the future. This is writing that recognizes that nothing about the human condition is sufficiently strong to construct a full and comprehensive view of love and that the real power of the romance lies in its ability to keep us in touch with the questions that we struggle with and to work towards a serenity that includes, rather than banishes, the bitter tastes that linger from our own experiences.

Source: Klay Dyer, Critical Essay on "Valentine," in *Poetry for Students*, Gale, Cengage Learning, 2017.

The onion is an extended metaphor: its clinging odor as strong as true love and the rings of a slice echo a wedding band (©Ruslan Ivantsov / Shutterstock.com)

London Evening Standard

In the following review, the anonymous author faults Duffy's overuse of alliteration.

The Bees is Carol Ann Duffy's first new collection of poetry to be published since she was appointed our Poet Laureate in 2009, in succession to Andrew Motion. It's also her first since *Rapture*, the ecstatic sequence about the rise and fall of a lesbian love affair which won her the T S Eliot Prize in 2005.

The Bees is not so ruthlessly focused but it has nonetheless been artfully organised around the bee as a symbol, boasting a cover honeycombed in gilt around a glittery bee. The book begins and ends with specific poems about bees and there are others scattered here and there, such as, for example, a lovely riff on Book IV of the Georgics, "Virgil's Bees," which she wrote in response to the 2009 climate change conference in Copenhagen. Throughout, bees stand for endangered nature—and they appear glancingly in the book in other poems, as do allusions to flowers, pollen and honey.

However, there are many other themes. The volume includes, for example, such commissioned poems as "Last Post," marking the deaths of the last First World War veterans, and "Big Ask," a sarcastic question and answer piece about Saddam and Iraq. There are poems about the Cockermouth floods of 2009, about the vanished elms, Dorothy Wordsworth, the joys of Scotch, the river Nile, the Arvon foundation near Loch Ness, and Luke Howard, the Londoner who named cloud formations.

There are poems once more briskly revising classical myth—"Echo," "Leda," "Atlas," "Achilles"—and others glossing anthology pieces by Shakespeare. "Where the bee sucks..." was never going to be missed out and has been turned into a rough assault on modern farming: "Where the bee sucks/ neonicotinoid insecticides/ in a cowslip's bell lie..."

The best, because most personally felt, poems are those mourning the death of her mother from cancer and rejoicing in the life of her teenage daughter, Ella. "Water," for example, beautifully recalls this being her mother's last word to her, calling for a drink—just as the poet herself had called out to her mother when a child, and as her own child does to her now: "Water./ What a mother brings/through darkness still/ to her parched daughter." An inevitable and touching rhyme.

Duffy's predecessor as the Poet Laureate, Sir Andrew, was in important ways not suited to the job, for, although he could act the poet dashingly and represent poetry in general admirably in public, he never managed to write a single memorable line himself. He couldn't make words do anything, simply.

Duffy has almost the opposite problem. Her poems are not just well worked, they are nonstop workouts. Each and every one of them is like a creative exercise taken to the limit. They nearly all take up the kind of challenge that could be set to a whole class, and then go for it absolutely. It all feels very GCSE, in the end. Thus Parliament is an updating of "The Parlement of Fowles," in which each bird describes how its particular environment has been devastated by pollution. "The Woman in the Moon"—"How could you think it ever a man up here?"—also sorrowfully contemplates the mess we've made of the earth: "deserts / where forests were, sick seas."

Sometimes Duffy's careful charms, or as she says, "spells," are appealingly modest. There's a nice series of three-line epigraphs on the joys of whisky, called "Drams": "Barley, water, peat,/ weather, landscape, history:/ malted, swallowed neat."

But the ways she has to show how deliberately she has woven her words soon become tiresome. She uses far too much alliteration, never a tasteful activity at the best of times. "Cockermouth and Workington" begins: "No folk fled the flood,/ no flags furled or spirits failed—/ one brave soul felled" and carries on in that vein.

She has far too many word combinations designed to prove her attentiveness to the way their sounds interknit with each other. Those elms have been "overwhelmed." "So glide,/ gilded, glad, golden," she commands the bees, in the first poem. In the last, she hears of "honey so pure,/ when pressed to the pout of a poet/ it made her profound." Please!

She overdoes lists and names. "Oxfam" poignantly lists items that have been donated for sale; "John Barleycorn" cheerily runs through evocative pub names; "The Counties" trips through, well, the counties...

"Luke Howard, Namer of Clouds," ends in the doting recitation: "Cirrus. Cumulus. Stratus. Nimbus." It's a pretty effect but it's exactly the same cadence she used in her anthology piece, the shipping forecast poem, "Prayer" (voted the nation's second favourite in a poll, trailing only "The Whitsun Weddings"): "Rockall. Malin. Dogger. Finisterre."

Both Duffy and Motion show clear influence from the man who refused the Laureateship, Philip Larkin (better digested in her case than his) but neither has anything like his authority and memorability. With Carol Ann Duffy, there's too much verbal prancing, too little that's original being said, particularly when the poems are not personal. You end the book thinking that if this is poetry, it's a trivial art. But it is not.

Source: Review of *The Bees*, in *London Evening Standard*, September 22, 2011.

Adam O'Riordan

In the following review, O'Riordan praises Duffy's use of imagery and language.

A cursory look at the contents list tells us the term "love poem" is to be taken broadly here, with "Adultery" and "Disgrace" gathered alongside "Valentine" and "New Vows." The selection, drawn from Carol Ann Duffy's first collection through to her forthcoming one, reminds us of her uncommon gift for accessibility coupled with profound artistry; characteristics she shares with Philip Larkin and perhaps, as Poet Laureate, a gift she does not want to be forgotten. This book might be seen as an assertion of the private poet now that Duffy is cast in the public role (or it might be viewed cynically as a stop-gap from her publisher before her next collection).

The book showcases Duffy's breathtaking control of language and imagery. "If I was dead/and my bones adrift/like dropped oars/in the deep, turning earth," she imagines in one poem. Duffy examines love in its modern forms: "I tend the mobile now/like an injured bird," she tells us in "Text." This transforming imagination and eye for the unexpected is seen again in "Valentine" where she offers an onion as a gift for her lover as "it promises light/like the careful undressing of love."

From her earliest poems Duffy writes with a compelling mixture of bravura and tenderness. In "Girlfriends" she describes the excitement and wonder of two lovers discovering their sexuality—"on our frail bodies the sweat cooled"—while in "Warming Her Pearls," an electrifying and much anthologised piece of erotic verse, the narrator tells us: "I lie here awake/knowing the pearls are cooling even now/in the room where my mistress sleeps. All night/I feel their absence and I burn."

Larkin once dismissed the confessional poets—such as Robert Lowell and Sylvia Plath, who emphasised and dramatised the often messy details of their personal lives—telling an interviewer that it was "the big sane boys" who won the medals. Duffy seems to have taken up the challenge of bridging the two; combining the charge and intensity of confessional poetry with the directness and lyricism embodied in Larkin's tradition.

Duffy is fearless when engaging with her literary forebears; Keats's "This Living Hand," with its voice from beyond the grave, can be seen as the model for Duffy's "If I Was Dead," in which the "living hand" becomes "your living kiss." "Leda" carries on a theme begun in her collection "The World's Wife" as Duffy re-imagines the myth of Leda and the Swan. Duffy's Leda is "obsessed by faithfulness" and the act "a chaos of passion," she is empowered—"pierced by love"—and no longer the passive victim of W.B Yeats's poem.

"Leda" is one of four poems included from Duffy's forthcoming collection, *The Bees*. Equally striking is "At Ballynahinch," a sonnet in which the repetition of the name of a town in County Down takes on an incantatory, almost shamanic, power with its "star-thrashed river," where the voice in the poem goes on to confront the "wounded sprawl—of the one who did not love me at all."

Mysterious yet accessible; both truthful and beautiful; this selection is a paean to the power of love and of language's ability to capture it.

Source: Adam O'Riordan, Review of *Love Poems*, in *Telegraph*, February 14, 2010.

Dennis Lee

In the following review, Lee points out that Duffy's children's poetry is appropriate for almost any age group.

Three loud cheers for Carol Ann Duffy. And two and a half quieter cheers for her new collection of children's poetry, *The Good Child's Guide to Rock 'n' Roll*.

Duffy is already celebrated in Britain as an adult poet. As a *Guardian* reviewer observed, "In the world of British poetry, Carol Ann Duffy is a superstar." A Scot raised in London, she writes with a racy, in-your-face candour that gives the finger to hidebound decorum. But she's not just a literary bad girl. She's won all the major British prizes, and there were many who objected when she wasn't named Poet Laureate after Ted Hughes's death.

With the recent birth of a daughter, Duffy has come boogieing into children's poetry as well. *The Good Child's Guide* is her third collection for young people in the past five years. Of the hundred or so poems they contain, a good handful could slide into the unofficial canon of children's verse.

What's her kids' stuff like? Duffy seems never to have met a boundary she didn't want to transgress, so she eludes conventional categories. She breaks the rule about writing for one age level at a time, for instance. I would hand her books to a lively eight-year-old, or a 15-year-old, or anyone in between. Not knowing who would like what, but confident that something would click for everyone.

One of Duffy's trademarks is the way she swings from mood to mood: from bratty to tender, goofy to pensive, formal to free verse. Here's a sampler from the new book, starting with a little courtship lyric. (In Duffy's world, girls get equal-opportunity crushes on boys and girls alike.) . . .

So far, so good: Stevie Smith meets Pippi Longstocking, But the book is more uneven than I'm suggesting. Too often, Duffy seems unable to distinguish an out-take from a real poem. Here's how she ends her tribute to the Everly Brothers in the 10-part title sequence: . . .

Ouch! Unfortunately, there's more where that came from. Duffy is so good that it demeans her talent to include every jingle and misfire she tosses off. But this gifted, wayward poet does things her own way. Since the results are often wonderful, it's pointless to grumble too long.

And as I've discovered recently, there's very little good poetry being written for children in the age range Duffy speaks to. Thanks to Mother Goose, English has something unique: a treasury of verse for the very young. Every culture has songs and tales for its small fry, but no other language I know has produced anything like our nursery rhymes. At the other end of the spectrum, young people from their mid-teens on—providing they're still reading for pleasure—are ready to tuck into Tennyson and Ginsberg and Plath.

But in the middle years, the pickings are pretty slim. In fiction, there's lots; in poetry, with notable exceptions, there's lots of nothing. It's all earnest, heavy-handed tracts on social issues; amateurish nature rhapsodies; formulaic comic verse; and misbegotten attempts to replicate rock or rap on the page.

Which makes Carol Ann Duffy's work close to indispensable. And in fact, I have a suggestion. If you want to explore her children's poetry, don't stop with *The Good Child's Guide*. The first two collections are even better. You may have to order them through your bookstore, since Duffy is a well-kept secret here. But it's worth the effort.

Meeting Midnight (Faber & Faber, 1999) is her first collection, and my own favourite....

In the world of children's poetry, Carol Ann Duffy is decidedly a superstar.

Source: Dennis Lee, "Literary Chick Shakes, Rattles and Rolls," in *Globe & Mail*, December 6, 2003.

SOURCES

Allen-Randolph, Jody, "Remembering Life before Thatcher," in *Women's Review of Books*, Vol. 12, No. 8, May 1995, p. 12.

Duffy, Carol Ann, "Valentine," in *Mean Time*, Anvil Poetry Press, 1993, p. 34.

Elmhirst, Sophie, "Carol Ann Duffy, Poet: 'I Used to Be Called a Poetess—It Was Stuffy and Sexist,'" in *New Statesman*, December 19, 2011, pp. 38–39.

Forbes, Peter, "Winning Lines," in *Guardian* (London, England), August 31, 2002, http://www.theguardian.com/books/2002/aug/31/featuresreviews.guardianreview8 (accessed May 7, 2016).

Martin, Ben, "Carol Ann Duffy: Profile of the new Poet Laureate," in *Telegraph* (London, England), May 1, 2009, http://www.telegraph.co.uk/culture/culturenews/5245613/Carol-Ann-Duffy-Profile-of-the-new-Poet-Laureate.html (accessed May 7, 2016).

Whitley, David, "Childhood and Modernity: Dark Themes in Carol Ann Duffy's Poetry for Children," in *Children's Literature in Education*, Vol. 38, No. 2, June 2007, pp. 103–14.

FURTHER READING

Dowson, Jane, *Carol Ann Duffy: Poet for Our Times*, Palgrave Macmillan, 2016.

> Considering Duffy's entire thirty-year career, this book outlines her impact on trends in contemporary poetry and establishes a clear focus on her primary concerns and techniques.

McRae, Susan, *Changing Britain: Families and Households in the 1990s*, Oxford University Press, 1999.

> The nineties saw major changes in the ways that households functioned and people's lives were lived across Britain. Marriage rates were falling, divorce was on the rise, women were having fewer children and doing so later in life, and one in four families with children was headed by a single parent. These changes carried a cultural significance that went well beyond individual families. *Changing Britain* provides a comprehensive portrait of the implications of these deep social changes, with particular focus on such issues as the impact on Britain's elderly, the dynamics of nonheterosexual families, and the trends of young mothers, single parents, and divorce.

Rees-Jones, Deryn, *Carol Ann Duffy*, 3rd ed., Northcote House, 2010.

> *Carol Ann Duffy* is a brief but useful study of Duffy presented as part of the publisher's Writers and Their Works series. Rees-Jones emphasizes many diverse influences that can be seen in Duffy's work as well as her use of everyday language (which he traces back to William Wordsworth) and her interest in dramatic monologue (linked to Robert Browning and T. S. Eliot). Her writing is also considered in light of the works of such writers as Philip Larkin, Dylan Thomas, the Beat poets, and the Liverpool poets.

Turner, Alwyn W., *A Classless Society: Britain in the 1990s*, Aurum Press, 2013.

> With the defeat of Margaret Thatcher in November 1990, eleven years of bitter social and economic conflict seemed poised to come to an end. But the reality proved that the forces that had warred over the country during the 1980s were going to make moving forward far

more difficult than many predicted. The "New Britain" to emerge under John Major and Tony Blair would be the contradiction of a population that was economically unequal but culturally classless. Opening with the 1991 war in the Persian Gulf and ending with the attack on New York City's World Trade Center on September 11, 2001, *A Classless Society* goes in search of the decade when modern Britain came of age. What it finds is a nation anxiously grappling with new technologies, tentatively embracing new lifestyles, and, above all, forging a new sense of what it means to be British.

SUGGESTED SEARCH TERMS

Carol Ann Duffy

"Valentine" AND Duffy

Mean Time AND Duffy

Scottish poetry

romance AND poetry

food AND metaphor

satire AND poetry

love AND poetry

The Walk

THOMAS HARDY

1914

"The Walk" is an elegiac poem written by British author Thomas Hardy. The poem, written in late 1912 or early 1913, is part of an elegiac sequence titled "Poems of 1912–13." This sequence, which initially included eighteen poems, was first published in 1914 with other groups of poems in a collection titled *Satires of Circumstance*. In his 1919 *Collected Poems*, Hardy made a number of minor revisions and added three poems to the sequence. Sometimes the sequence is referred to by its Latin epigraph, a brief quotation from Virgil's *Aeneid*, "Veteris Vestigia Flammae," meaning "Vestiges of an Old Flame."

In "Poems of 1912–13," Hardy mourns the passing of his wife Emma Gifford Hardy, who died on November 27, 1912. In the months and years following Emma's death, Hardy wrote a number of poems in response to visits he made to places he and Emma had frequented in the earlier years of their marriage. That marriage began as an exhilarating love affair, but by the 1890s the two had drifted apart. Emma's devout Anglicanism, along with her eccentricities and personal frustrations, put her at odds with her husband, whose later novels were regarded by many as scandalous because of their (for the time) frank avowal of sexual passion. In the new century the couple drifted farther apart, to the point where Emma kept largely to herself on the second story of their Dorchester home, Max Gate, while Hardy secluded himself in his study below. Hardy, however, remained devoted to

Thomas Hardy *(©Bettmann / Getty Images)*

Emma, deeply mourned her death, and harkened back to earlier days when he regarded Emma as his muse. For many readers, "The Walk," along with other poems in the sequence, is not only a lament for the passing of Emma but also a meditation on the nature of loss and on the contingency of life, a cry lamenting the human subject's diminishing significance in the new century.

AUTHOR BIOGRAPHY

Thomas Hardy was born on June 2, 1840, in Upper (or Higher) Bockhampton, a village in the county of Dorset, England. His father, Thomas, was a mason and building contractor; his mother, Jemima, had been a maid and cook, and although she came from a poor background, she loved to read Latin poets and French romances (in translation), and she passed this love of literature on to her son. As a child, Hardy attended a local school conducted by the National Society for Promoting the Education of the Poor in the Principles of the Established Church. After

completing his formal schooling in 1856, he was apprenticed to John Hicks, an architect and church restorer in the town of Dorchester. In 1862 he relocated to London, where he took a position as an architectural assistant, and it was during this period that he began writing poetry in earnest.

In 1867 Hardy returned to his home village and again worked with Hicks, but after Hicks died in 1869, Hardy moved to Weymouth, a seaside town in Dorset. In 1870 he was in Cornwall looking into plans for a church restoration project when he met Emma Lavinia Gifford, the sister-in-law of the local rector. He was immediately captivated by her vivacity and good looks, and the two were married in 1874. During the early years of their marriage, the Hardys were happy. In 1885 they took up residence at Max Gate, the home in Dorchester that Hardy himself had designed and where he would live for the rest of his life. As time went on, however, Emma increasingly disapproved of her husband's fiction—and of his infatuations with younger women—and the two became estranged, although they continued to live together until her death in 1912.

Hardy believed that his true vocation was that of a poet and that poetry was a nobler art form than fiction, yet in the twenty-first century he is more likely to be known for his novels. His first published novel, *Desperate Remedies*, appeared in 1871. He began to create his fictional county of Wessex (which reflected the counties of Dorset, Wiltshire, and Somerset) with *Under the Greenwood Tree* in 1872, and in 1873 *A Pair of Blue Eyes* was the first of his novels to be published under his name rather than anonymously. His first popular success was *Far from the Madding Crowd* (1874). In the years that followed, Hardy wrote five major novels on which his reputation as a novelist largely rests: *The Return of the Native* (1878), *The Mayor of Casterbridge* (1886), *The Woodlanders* (1887), *Tess of the D'Urbervilles* (1891), and *Jude the Obscure* (1895).

In these novels, Hardy flouted Victorian conventions of sexual morality, but he became disgusted by the heated reaction to *Jude the Obscure*. The novel, in some quarters called "Jude the Obscene," appalled an English bishop so much that he announced publicly that he had thrown it into the fire. In response to the broader reaction, Hardy abandoned fiction for poetry. Over the remaining years of his life he published a number of collections, among them *Wessex Poems and Other Verses* (1898), *Poems of the Past and the Present* (1901), and *Satires of Circumstance* (1914), which includes "Poems of 1912–13," which in turn includes "The Walk." In 1914, two years after Emma's death, he married the much younger Florence Dugdale, whom he had known before the death of his first wife and who was infatuated with the famous writer. Meanwhile, by 1908, Hardy had published a major, three-part poetic work, *The Dynasts*, an epic verse drama (not intended for stage production) about the Napoleonic Wars. In all, Hardy published fourteen novels, almost 950 poems, and nearly fifty short stories. Although he never won, he was a Nobel Prize nominee in twelve different years beginning in 1910, the same year he was awarded the Order of Merit.

During World War I, Hardy supported the war effort, visiting military hospitals and POW camps. In his later years, he entertained numerous writers of note at Max Gate. During the 1920s he wrote his autobiography, which was published posthumously in two volumes (under Florence Hardy's name). In late 1927 Hardy fell ill with pleurisy and took to his bed. He died at his home in Dorchester on January 11, 1928, from what his death certificate called "cardiac syncope." Still mourning Emma, he had wanted to be buried next to her in the churchyard of St. Michael's Church in Stinsford, a village just outside of Dorchester. Florence opposed this wish, but Hardy's executor hit on a compromise. Hardy's ashes were interred in the south transept of Westminster Abbey, known as Poets' Corner; his heart had been removed, however, and in a simultaneous ceremony, it was buried next to Emma.

POEM TEXT

> You did not walk with me
> Of late to the hill-top tree
> By the gated ways,
> As in earlier days;
> You were weak and lame,   5
> So you never came,
> And I went alone, and I did not mind,
> Not thinking of you as left behind.
>
> I walked up there to-day
> Just in the former way;   10
> Surveyed around
> The familiar ground

MEDIA ADAPTATIONS

- Alan Bates reads "The Walk" on an audio CD titled *Thomas Hardy: Readings by Alan Bates* (Droffig, 2003). The readings are accompanied by music performed by the Melstock Band on instruments that would have been used in rural England in the nineteenth century.

- "The Walk" can be heard read by an unidentified actress in a clip at the Poetry Foundation website (http://www.poetryfoundation .org/features/audio/detail/77044), with a running time of forty-three seconds.

- Several of the other poems in "Poems of 1912–13" are read by British actor Martin Jarvis on *Thomas Hardy: Selected Poems*, released by TextbookStuff.com in 2012. Each of the poems can be heard as an MP3 download.

> By myself again:
> What difference, then?
> Only that underlying sense   15
> Of the look of a room on returning thence.

POEM SUMMARY

The text used for this summary is from *Thomas Hardy: The Complete Poems*, edited by James Gibson, Palgrave, 2001, p. 340. Versions of the poem can be found on the following web pages: http://www.poemtree.com/poems/Walk.htm and http://www.poemhunter.com/poem/the-walk-30/.

"The Walk" consists of two stanzas, each made up of eight lines. In the first stanza, the poet speaks to *you*, taken to refer to his deceased wife, Emma. He begins by noting that in recent days she has not walked with him up to a tree on a local hilltop, following a path through gates, as the two of them had in earlier days. He notes that recently she was weak and lame, so she did not accompany him on his walk. He went alone, but he says that he did not mind because he did not really think that he had left her behind; he thought this perhaps in knowing that she would be there when he returned home.

In the second stanza, the poet says that he walked up to the hilltop today, just as he had in former times, again taking the walk alone. He looked about on the well-known ground by himself. He then asks what the difference was between former walks and this walk. In the final two lines he answers his question by saying that today, unlike before, he had a vague feeling about what the room to which he would return would look like—that is, he knew that she would not be there in the room when he returned.

THEMES

Loss

"The Walk" is an elegiac poem. An *elegy* is a poem that expresses sorrow about the death of a loved one, although it should be acknowledged, first, that elegies can be written in prose and, second, that the loss being lamented can be of anything of value: the loss of innocence, the loss of a way of life, the loss of a cultural value. Further, some elegies are written to mourn the passing of a particular person, while others lament death in general, often with philosophical reflections. Typically, the tone of elegies reflects melancholy and lament, with a pervading atmosphere of loss and regret.

The elegy as a poetic type dates back to ancient Greece and Rome, where elegies were not necessarily laments but were in some cases love poems written in a particular metrical form. Elegies written in response to loss, however, have been written throughout literary history and into the modern era. In the eighteenth century, for example, the so-called graveyard school of poets wrote oftentimes gloomy poetry with reflections on mortality and impermanence; a noteworthy example is Thomas Gray's "Elegy Written in a Country Churchyard" (1751). In the modern period, A. E. Housman's "To an Athlete Dying Young" (1896), W. H. Auden's "In Memory of W. B. Yeats" (1940), and Robert Lowell's "The Quaker Graveyard in Nantucket" (1946) are noteworthy examples of elegiac poems.

One form that elegies have taken is that of the pastoral elegy, which features an idealized

rural setting. Perhaps one of the most famous examples in literary history is John Milton's "Lycidas" (1638). While "The Walk" is not strictly speaking a pastoral elegy, it has something of the tone of one. Clearly, the setting of the poem is rural. The author recollects the walks that he and his loved one took through the Dorset countryside. He references a tree on a hilltop, and the paths that took them through gates. (The English countryside was and still is laced with walking paths open to the public, and various forms of gates and stiles prevent grazing livestock from wandering away.) For Hardy, the path that he and Emma might have taken was part of an idealized landscape, one that reminds the poet of the love that he shared with Emma. In later years, Hardy and his wife were estranged and spent little time together. From this point of view, the loss that Hardy mourns can be seen as not only Emma's death but also the loss of the closeness and exhilaration the two felt earlier in their marriage. Thus, when the author walks the familiar fields and hills and notes the absence of Emma, the feeling he has is no different from what he feels when he walks into a room from which she is absent; there remains a melancholy feeling of bereavement and emptiness.

Memory

Closely related to the theme of loss is that of memory. "The Walk" is suffused with the poet's memories of former times with his wife. In the first stanza, he describes, in swift short strokes, the rural walk that he used to take with his wife and that he has taken in recent days. Although he does not describe the walk in any detail, the reader has the sense that this walk was a source of particular enjoyment for the poet and his wife, one that they often took together. The reader's sense of the poet's melancholy is palpable as, in very spare and restrained diction, he conjures up memories of the walk, the hilltop, and the familiar ground that he surveys. The poet notes that in recent days he took the walk alone, but he did not mind, for his wife would be there when he returned home; he did not feel as though he had left her behind. Today he has followed the same path again, remembering walks of former days. He tries to understand the difference between his recent walks and the walk that he has taken today, relying on memory to re-create the walk in his imagination.

The surroundings sound ideal, with quiet gated lanes to wander down, but the speaker finds little pleasure in his walk (©Raymond Llewellyn / Shutterstock.com)

STYLE

Meter

Hardy remains known and admired for his metrical experimentation. Throughout the body of his poetry—some 950 poems—he employed an expansive array of metrical schemes, placing a unique stamp on each of his poems. "The Walk" exemplifies this metrical experimentation. Each of the two stanzas of "The Walk" consists of eight lines. The first two lines of each stanza consist of three metrical feet each—in particular, three iambic feet, made up (with variations) of an unstressed syllable followed by a stressed syllable (da-DUM, da-DUM, da-DUM). The middle four lines of each stanza are made up of two metrical feet; in most cases, these are anapests, or feet consisting of two unaccented syllables followed by one accented syllable (da-da-DUM, da-da-DUM). The final two lines of each stanza are irregular, with a mix of iambic and anapestic feet. It could be maintained that the meter of the poem is imitative. That is, anapests have a sort of

marching, dogtrot feel to them, suggesting the process of walking. The short lines give the poem a simplicity and directness that can be found in the sequence as a whole and that reinforce the sharp immediacy of the poet's grief.

Rhyme

"The Walk" makes use of a simple rhyme pattern. Using conventional notation, the rhyme scheme of each stanza is *aabbccdd*. Thus, each pair of lines rhymes, and all of the rhymes are true rhymes. (Examples of "true rhyme" are the single-syllable words *trees* and *breeze* or the two-syllable words *array* and *display*; so-called feminine rhymes, or double rhymes, shift the accented syllable back from the end of the line, as in a pair such as *bubble* and *trouble*, but Hardy in this poem avoids this type of rhyme.) This rhyme scheme, in conjunction with the meter, gives "The Walk" a narrative simplicity and directness that perhaps reflects the poet's frame of mind as he ponders the absence of his companion on the walk that they took in the past.

TOPICS FOR FURTHER STUDY

- If you have artistic talent, sketch or paint a picture of the setting of "The Walk" as you imagine Hardy might have envisioned it. Share your picture with your classmates on hard copy or using a technological tool such as Snapfish.

- Conduct Internet research on Dorset County, England, the setting for "The Walk" and most of the other "Emma" poems. Take your classmates on a visual tour of the countryside as Hardy might have experienced it, using a tool such as Jing or Flickr.

- Write your own elegiac poem or prose piece. The poem does not have to be written in response to the death of a loved one, although you might consider writing your elegy about the passing of a beloved public figure: John Lennon, Robin Williams, Prince, or any other celebrated individual. The poem could otherwise reflect a sense of loss over anything—a pet, a romance, a best friend, a goal, a favorite keepsake. Consider posting your poem on the Protagonize website at http://www.protagonize.com/category/poetry/teen_or_young_adult.

- Locate a recording of "Elegy (Song of Mourning)," by French composer Jules Massenet. (In French, the title is "Elégie.") Numerous versions can be found on the Internet. Play a recording of the piece for your classmates and invite them to comment on characteristics of the music that have an elegiac feel; be prepared to share your own thoughts on the topic.

- In 1912, the year in which Hardy wrote "The Walk," Austrian poet Rainer Maria Rilke began work on an elegiac sequence titled *Duineser Elegien* (1923), or *Duino Elegies* ("Duino" being the name of a castle in Trieste, Italy, that inspired the poems). The sequence consists of ten elegies with philosophical themes. Read one of the elegies, perhaps the first one, in English translation and then write an essay in which you compare and contrast its themes with those suggested in Hardy's "The Walk."

- Rita Dove is a Pulitzer Prize–winning poet and the author of "Elegy for Miss O." The poem is an elegy commemorating a beloved English teacher, and it references Thomas Hardy's novel *The Return of the Native*. Dove introduces her poem and then reads it on a YouTube video at https://www.youtube.com/watch?v=HYFhZb8L1cs. Watch/listen to the video, then write a brief essay in which you discuss the role of memory in Dove's poem and in "The Walk."

- Naomi Shihab Nye is the editor of *What Have You Lost?* (2001), a collection of poetry for young adults by 140 poets, all bearing on the theme of loss. Browse the collection, then give an oral presentation for your classmates of one or more poems that you believe share themes or techniques with "The Walk." After reciting the poem(s), invite your listeners to comment on similarities with the Hardy poem and be prepared to share your own thoughts.

HISTORICAL CONTEXT

"The Walk" makes no reference to particular historical events. Two cultural matters, however, had an impact on Hardy's life in ways affecting this poem. The first pertains to the setting. In 1885 Hardy, an architect and builder early in his adult life, moved with his wife into Max Gate, the home in Dorchester, England, that he had designed and that his brother had built (and around which Hardy planted an immense number of trees to give him privacy). Dorchester is

COMPARE
&
CONTRAST

- **1912:** The population of Dorset, a rural and agricultural county in southwestern England, is about 223,000.

  Today: Dorset remains a largely rural county, with a population of about 418,000.

- **1912:** Divorce in Great Britain is rare, requiring proof of adultery or violence; only about one in 450 marriages ends in divorce.

  Today: Each year in the United Kingdom, there is one divorce for every two marriages.

- **1912:** Marital infidelity among the upper classes is common and tolerated but kept out of the public eye. In the first decade of

the century, Alice Keppel is a favored mistress of King Edward VII.

  Today: Camilla Parker-Bowles, the great-granddaughter of Alice Keppel—for years a fixture in the sensationalized tabloid press as the mistress of Charles, the Prince of Wales and heir to the British throne—marries Charles in 2005 and is given the title Duchess of Cornwall.

- **1912:** Hardy continues to live in Max Gate, his home in Dorchester, England, after the death of his wife Emma.

  Today: The Hardy home, Max Gate, is preserved as a National Trust property.

---

a town in the county of Dorset, located in southwestern England. At the time, Dorset was largely a rural and agricultural county, with a sparse population, and Dorchester, itself a small country town, was the model for Casterbridge in Hardy's novel *The Mayor of Casterbridge.* Throughout his novels, stories, and poetry, Hardy captured the rhythms, settings, livelihoods, and ways of life of rural England in the nineteenth century, particularly in "Wessex," the fictional county he created (and, incidentally, the name that he gave to his dog late in life). He depicted the fields and fens, the paths and byways, the heaths and hedgerows of a rural, agricultural region, and many of his characters were the farmers, woodlanders, small merchants, and laborers who inhabited it and spoke its distinctive dialect. The rural Dorset of Hardy's imagination was something of a primitive place, far removed from the modern contrivances of London and other larger cities. It was this corner of the world—isolated, steeped in tradition and history, suffused with superstition and folklore—that Hardy and his wife, an accomplished horsewoman, scoured and explored. "The Walk" captures a moment of that immersion in Dorset.

Also of relevance are the circumstances surrounding the marriage of Hardy and Emma. The two met in 1870 in Cornwall, after Hardy's employer sent him to the St. Joliot Church to make plans for a church restoration project. Hardy was immediately captivated by Emma's dash and impulsiveness, as well as her rosy complexion and blue eyes. The two were married in 1874 and enjoyed contentment in the early years of their marriage, but by the mid-1880s the marriage was beginning to fray. In 1886 Hardy published *The Woodlanders*, a novel that explores marital estrangement and the problems that arise when one of the parties to the marriage begins to feel that someone else is better suited for him or her. This estrangement continued until Emma's death in 1912. The couple, however, continued to live together, without seeking a divorce. In the early years of the twentieth century, divorce in Great Britain was still rare, for it was widely believed that the sanctity of marriage had to be preserved at all costs. Divorce was an expensive proposition, and the grounds for divorce were restricted to adultery and violence. Accordingly, many people like the Hardys continued to cohabit without having any meaningful marital relationship. Further, in this

The speaker walks on his own, not eager to return home (©Sander van der Werf / Shutterstock.com)

social climate, marital infidelity among the aristocracy and royalty was tolerated but never openly discussed. Thus, as the Hardy marriage was deteriorating, King Edward VII, who gave his name to the Edwardian era, consorted with numerous mistresses (among them Winston Churchill's mother and the actresses Lily Langtry and Sarah Bernhardt) with the full knowledge of his wife, Queen Alexandra. Again, divorce would have been unthinkable, a view that filtered throughout British society and likely had its effect on Hardy and his wife in their resolve to remain married.

CRITICAL OVERVIEW

"The Walk" was first published as part of a sequence titled "Poems of 1912–13," which in turn was part of a larger collection titled *Satires of Circumstance*. An appreciative early review of the collection was written for the *New Statesman* by Lytton Strachey, who commented on the mood of the volume:

The prevailing mood in this volume . . . is not a cheerful one. And, in the more reflective and personal pieces, the melancholy is if anything yet more intense. It is the melancholy of regretful recollection, of bitter speculation, of immortal longings unsatisfied; it is the melancholy of one who has suffered. . . . Mortality, and the cruelties of time, and the ironic irrevocability of things—these are the themes upon which Mr. Hardy has chosen to weave his grave and moving variations.

Another appreciative early review, written by Laurence Binyon, appeared in *Bookman*:

Mr. Hardy is an artist, and has the artist's vivid sensitiveness to the inexhaustible beauties of earth and sky, in stable form and changeful colour; but he has also the artist's deeper power, the shaping instinct.

Reflecting on Hardy's technique, in comments that easily apply to "The Walk," Binyon wrote:

He is never seduced by sound; firm delineation, even in the shades and subtleties of feeling, is for him essential. The result is sometimes disconcerting; the mechanism of a stanza creaks and groans with the pressure of its working. There is something incongruous between the prosaic plainness of the speech and the tight structure of rather elaborate lyric form to which it is trimmed.

R. P. Blackmur, in a later essay titled "The Shorter Poems of Thomas Hardy," declares that "Poems of 1912–13."

give, as a unit, Hardy's most sustained invocation that rhythm, so strong that all that was personal—the private drive, the private grief—is cut away and the impersonal is left bare, an old monument, mutilated or weathered as you like to call it, of that face which the personal only hides.

Referring specifically to "The Walk," Blackmur states: "Like the others in the series, it is a poem almost without style; it is style reduced to anonymity, reduced to riches: in the context of the twenty [poems in the sequence], precisely the riches of rhythm."

Patricia Ingram, in an essay titled "Hardy and the 'Cell of Time,'" observes that Hardy's treatment of the theme of time in his poetry is invariably "retrospective, denaturing, static, claustrophobic and largely inescapable." Ingram then notes:

It [the imprisoning "cell of time"] accounts perhaps for the added sense of release found in some of Hardy's best poems in the 1912–1913 sequence, written after Emma's death and recalling the past in a way which in almost every respect differs from that outlined above; it is more vivid than the present and more alive, full of a sense of movement and freedom and usually in an outdoor setting. . . . For once the way out of the present was the past which here expanded instead of dwindling. So, the 1912–13 poems seem to constitute stepping out of the cell.

In the *Oxford Reader's Companion to Hardy*, James Gibson comments on *Satires of Circumstance* generally and "Poems of 1912–13" in particular:

In what, then, lies the greatness of this particular book of verse? Most important of all, it has at its centre the finest group of elegies written in our language. When Emma died in 1912, Hardy was at the peak of his poetic powers, and his grief, his remorse for the wasted years of their marriage, his nostalgia for the past, and his need to relive that past and eternalize the memories of Emma, all inspired his poetical creativity and resulted in these poems of 1912–13 with their passion and deeply felt emotion. But these feelings are powerfully controlled by poetic techniques which Hardy had brought to perfection.

Tim Armstrong, in an essay titled "Thomas Hardy: *Poems of 1912–13*," examines the sequence in the context of the elegiac tradition. He concludes:

But it is the intensity and immediacy of the "Poems of 1912–13" which give them their power, as well as the honesty with which Hardy faces up to his own evasions. He may dissemble in saying that he had no hint that Emma was unwell, he may efface his own duplicities in his marriage, but that dissembling is presented to us for judgement; like the "look of a room on returning thence" described in "The Walk," the empty spaces and negations of the poems speak to us.

CRITICISM

Michael J. O'Neal

O'Neal holds a PhD in English. In the following essay, he examines "The Walk" as a lament for the passing of an era.

That "The Walk," along with the other poems in "Poems of 1912–13," is an elegiac poem written in response to the death of Hardy's wife Emma is readily apparent to those who have even a passing familiarity with the author's life. In the first stanza, the poet addresses *you*, clearly referring to his deceased wife. He indicates that in recent days he has taken a particular walk near their Dorset home by himself, for his wife seems to have been too weak to accompany him. In the second stanza, *you* is never mentioned, reinforcing the sense of bereavement and mourning that suffuses the poem: Emma is gone, and all that is left is a kind of emptiness. The poem takes up, in quick brushstrokes, themes of loss and memory as the author reflects back on the earlier days of his marriage, to a time when he and Emma enjoyed a close relationship, sharing the natural wonders of England's Dorset County. Now, when the author takes the walk, he has the same feeling of emptiness that he has when he returns home to an empty room, a room no longer filled with the presence of his wife.

This much is obvious, but one of the marks of a great poet is the ability to transcend purely personal circumstances and create verse that captures a larger reality. Put simply, the typical reader may no longer be able to share the grief of a husband over the loss of his wife more than a century ago. Emma is in a way a kind of footnote to literary history, significant in the twenty-first

> JUST AS HARDY GRIEVED THE LOSS OF HIS
> WIFE, THE CULTURAL ATMOSPHERE OF THE
> EDWARDIAN ERA LED HIM TO REFLECT MORE
> GENERALLY ON LOSS, ON THE PASSING OF A WAY OF
> LIFE, ON EMPTINESS, ON FEELINGS OF INSIGNIFICANCE
> AND POWERLESSNESS IN THE FACE OF CHANGE AND
> THE TIDES OF HISTORY."

century only in relation to Hardy. But the poems of the elegiac sequence Hardy wrote in response to her passing continue to move readers precisely because they capture something bigger, something that readers a century later can share with the author. That "something" is the passing of an age, a sense that the world is in flux, that permanence is elusive, and that the human subject is ephemeral during a time when public events overshadow and subsume private griefs. Sometimes the German term *Zeitgeist* is used to refer to "the spirit of the age." It is a term that refers to a dominant set of values and ideals permeating a culture and reflected in its art. "The Walk" emerges from a particular spirit of the age prevailing at the time it was written.

It is worth considering why Hardy gave the bland, unassuming title "Poems of 1912–13" to the sequence of which "The Walk" is a part. The title is dull. It strikes one as nothing more than a heading, a designation, a jotting at the top of a homework assignment, not a true title from the pen of a top-tier poet. One would expect the sequence to be given a title that captures in some way the essence of Hardy's grief (although the epigraph accomplishes this, with its reference to "vestiges of an old flame"). What it does, however, is immediately call attention to history, to time, to a moment grasped and held in an onrushing tide of events—or better, to a point in history when the fires of the past are burning low and, in the author's imagination, are about to be extinguished. The poem makes no reference to these events, but the events are there, part of the atmosphere surrounding Hardy and his readers, and those readers would have felt the same somber sense of loss and of passing that

Hardy would have felt as the twentieth century was beginning to unfold.

The Edwardian era has often been described as a "twilight" period in British history, or perhaps as a sunlit afternoon, a period of elegant tea parties on expansive lawns attended by carefree, corseted women and urbane men in jaunty suits and Panama hats. The comparison is apt. During the nineteenth century, and through much of Hardy's childhood and adult life, England was a major imperial power. With colonies worldwide, it was said that "the sun never set on the British Empire." Although problems remained, England had liberalized its institutions—trade, voting rights, education, sanitation, health, marriage laws—to such an extent that the nation was the envy of much of the world. At the same time, however, England remained steeped in her traditions and folkways, which Hardy re-created and celebrated in his novels set in the fictional county of Wessex. It was a world of grizzled furze cutters and rosy-cheeked milkmaids dancing around the maypole, of farmers and herders who passed their evenings smoking their pipes and drinking strong ale in pubs and taverns, chewing over the events of the day. It was the world of the reddleman, who traveled the back roads and cart paths of rural England to be hired by sheep farmers to mark their sheep with reddle, a red dye. The faces and hands of these hardy itinerants were stained by this dye, and when they appeared in a community, their diabolical aspect was so fearsome that mothers would scare misbehaving children into compliance with threats of summoning the reddleman.

This was a world that was rapidly passing into history by developments in the new century. Humans had recently taken flight, and soon the hum of automobiles would begin to replace the clip-clop of horse-drawn vehicles. In 1901, electricity came to Dorchester. During the first decade of the new century, homes were being outfitted with indoor plumbing, wiring, and a newfangled device called the telephone. The country's productivity was high, and it was a world leader in manufacturing, mining, shipping, and trade. London was the financial capital of the world.

But all was not rosy hued. The brutalities, waste, and humiliations of the Second Boer War of 1899–1902 were still fresh in the British imagination. In 1908 the first crisis in the Balkans exacerbated tensions between Serbia and the

WHAT DO I READ NEXT?

- "Beeny Cliff" (1914) is one of the poems in "Poems of 1912–13," available in, for example, *Thomas Hardy: The Complete Poems* (2001). In vivid imagery, it captures Hardy's remembrances of his deceased wife.

- *A Pair of Blue Eyes* (1873) is generally classed as one of Hardy's minor novels. It is also the one that contains the most autobiographical elements, and it was the first of his novels that he did not publish anonymously. The novel's heroine, Elfride Swancourt, is an attractive but naïve character based closely on Emma. The novel mentions a "cliff without a name," which is likely Beeny Cliff, the setting of Hardy's poem of that title.

- *That This* (2010) is an elegiac sequence written by American poet Susan Howe on the death of her husband. The title refers to "that" world of those who have passed and "this" world of the living.

- In June 1985 a terrorist bomb destroyed Air India Flight 182 over the Atlantic Ocean on a flight from Montreal, Canada, to London on its way to Delhi, India. Most of the 329 people who lost their lives were of Indian origin. In 2013 Renée Sarojini Saklikar, an Indian poet living in Canada, published *Children of Air India: Un/authorized Exhibits and Interjections*, a series of elegiac sequences that explore the nature of loss in the context of a public tragedy.

- One of the most famous long elegiac poems of the Victorian period is *In Memoriam A.H.H.* (1850), by Alfred, Lord Tennyson, written over a period of seventeen years after the premature death of Tennyson's close Cambridge friend Arthur Henry Hallam. The poem, made up of 133 sections of varying lengths, examines loss against the backdrop of many of the social, scientific, and religious concerns of the Victorians.

- *The Convert's Passion: An Anthology of Islamic Poetry from Late Victorian and Edwardian Britain* (2009), edited by Brent D. Singleton, collects the poetry of 140 Muslims living in Britain during Hardy's lifetime. Some of the poems are single pieces written by amateurs, while others were written by published authors. Most initially appeared in periodicals.

- The Edwardian era is the period in British history coinciding with the reign of Britain's King Edward VII, who ruled from 1901 to 1910; the era, however, is generally held to extend through the years leading up to the start of World War I in 1914. In *The Edwardians* (2005), Roy Hattersley offers a social and cultural history of the era.

- *Elegies for the Brokenhearted* (2010), by Christie Hodgen, is a young-adult novel structured as five elegies that the narrator, a young woman named Mary Murphy, addresses to the five people who had major influences on her life.

- "The Funeral Service of the Late Thomas Hardy, O.M.," from 1928 at Westminster Abbey, can be found in portable document format (PDF) at http://westminster-abbey.org/__data/assets/pdf_file/0006/86073/Hardy,-Thomas-funeral.pdf.

- *Max Gate* (2013), by Damien Wilkins, is a novel narrated from the point of view of a character named Nellie Titterington, a maidservant in Hardy's household during his final days, as arguments rage over where the famous author is to be buried.

Austro-Hungarian Empire, and in 1912–1913 much of the world was girding its loins for war as a second Balkan crisis led to open warfare in the region, warfare that would soon engulf Europe—and change it forever. A resurgent, unified, industrializing, and hostile Germany

The speaker mentions a particular tree on a hill as a frequent destination of past walks
(©Gwoeii | Shutterstock.com)

was rattling sabers, posing a threat to its European neighbors, including Britain, which grew increasingly suspicious of Germany's expanding naval power in the North Sea and the English Channel. Earlier in the year of Emma's death, the RMS *Titanic* had sunk on its maiden voyage, an event Hardy examined in one of his better-known poems, "The Convergence of the Twain," where he saw the ship as a symbol of England's wealth, power, and industrialization but also of its vanity and technological overreach.

The world in which Hardy grew up was changing in other respects as well. Labor unions, particularly those representing miners, railway workers, and gas workers, were newly resurgent, and the nation was brought nearly to a standstill in 1911 by striking dock workers, miners, and railway workers. Women were clamoring for the vote, staging protests and marches that attracted considerable public attention. The power of the House of Lords in Parliament was reduced by the Parliament Act of 1911, and leftist labor

unionists and Irish nationalists were gaining power in the House of Commons. Ongoing advances in science, in particular the work of physicists such as Albert Einstein and Max Planck, were continuing to undermine traditional religious faith. In the arts, art nouveau and postimpressionism challenged more traditional artistic forms and ushered in the period now referred to loosely as modernism.

Hardy's world was changing rapidly indeed.

Again, none of these developments is mentioned in "The Walk." But "The Walk" is a poem about memory and loss. It is a poem about something that is not what it used to be: The walk that Hardy took became different in the face of time and loss. The melancholy of the poem arises from memory and nostalgia, for an earlier time when things were as they should be. So just as Hardy grieved the loss of his wife, the cultural atmosphere of the Edwardian era led him to reflect more generally on loss, on the passing of a way of life, on emptiness, on feelings of insignificance and powerlessness in the face of change and the tides of history. It is this very human feeling of lamentation for the loss of what was that makes "The Walk" and indeed all of the "Poems of 1912–13" continue to resonate with readers.

Source: Michael J. O'Neal, Critical Essay on "The Walk," in *Poetry for Students*, Gale, Cengage Learning, 2017.

Patricia Clements

In the following excerpt, Clements examines Hardy's exploration of perception in his poetry.

Hardy's later work is dominated by its inquiry into the relation of the mind to the world it inhabits. *Jude the Obscure* carries his inquiry to its most successful expression in fiction. Jude's vision of Christminster, his purely personal mental act, is the steady surface against which the novel's events are imaged, the unchanging measure of the shifting realities of his life. Jude renews his vision again and again, in spite of evidence returned to him by his experience, and the novel derives its resonance from its steadily maintained discrepancy between Jude's dream and his life. The book takes Hardy's dominant theme to its best balance in imaginative prose: it shows the mind locked in permanent contest with the world, focusing each in relation to the other, and it does that without tempting us to see the objects of the real world as merely the objects of consciousness and without throwing into doubt the conventions of its own realism. In other work of about the same time, Hardy dismantled the equipoise, in what appears as experiment or witty play, placing his perfected powers now at the disposal of a fictional treatment of the mind wielding its triumphs over the "real," now of a treatment of the "real" as sufficient. Though he said that he hoped that Jocelyn Pierston would not appear to readers of *The Well-Beloved* as merely a "fantast," he did describe him as "one that gave objective continuity and a name to a delicate dream," and he said that the story itself was "of an ideal or subjective nature, and frankly imaginative, verisimilitude . . . [having] been subordinated to [that] aim." In other late prose works, Hardy tipped the balance of *Jude* in the other direction, boldly clinging to the conventions of realistic fiction by the unusual means of simply converting the "dream" to the "real," of simply asserting the impossible as fact. The fine story, "An Imaginative Woman," for instance (which mentions in passing the French Symbolist

IN THESE MOMENTS OF RE-VISION, HARDY ISOLATES THE MIND IN AN EXPERIENCE OF SHOCK, OF THRILLING PERCEPTION, AND HE FORCES IT TO REORGANIZE OR RETREAT."

school), offers Hardy's symbolism *as* science, and he claims in the preface to *Life's Little Ironies* that the tale's central event (which a reader must recognize as symbolically eloquent but physically preposterous) was "well known to medical practitioners." In the preface to *Wessex Tales*, too, Hardy treats his reader to a witty demonstration of his concern for facts, confessing what he calls an error in his memory of the story which he turned into "The Withered Arm." It was in the afternoon, he says, and not in the evening, that Rhoda Brook was "oppressed" by an incubus. He offers his error in remembering as an example of the inevitable divergence of the mind from the world, as

> an instance of how our imperfect memories insensibly formalize the fresh originality of living fact—from whose shape they slowly depart, as machine-made castings depart by degrees from the sharp hand-work of the mould.

The unceasing play between the mind's "formalizations" and the world's "originality" occupies every side of Hardy's art. His description here of that play reverses expectation: it may be a surprise to hear, from this "novelist of the imagination," this poet of vision, that it is the world, and not the mind, which is shifting, original, alive; that it is the mind, and not the world, which tends mechanically, by degrees, to stiffen experience with pattern.

When Hardy moved entirely to poetry, he did not abandon his dominant theme. The mastered antitheses of *Jude*, which he had split into singleness in some of his other late fiction, provide the counterpoint and the balance of the poems—and if the poems do aim at a multiplied counterpoint, as Hardy's prefaces frequently suggest, they also aim at balance, at a presentation of the mind *in* the world. Their concern with balance makes them consistent not only with Hardy's fiction, but also with other aspects of his thought. It is the relation of the mind to the world which fascinates his notebooks, occupies as its central aesthetic question his late essay on "The Science of Fiction," constitutes the focus of his reading in psychology. At about the same time as Yeats was drawing up his powerful design for a poetry which would exclude "mere reality," Hardy was striving to write poems which would be, as he said more than once, an "exploration of reality"; and while Yeats was making room for Eliot to appear as his natural opposite by rejecting utterly a poetry of "observations," Hardy was taking care to present his "series of feelings and fancies" together with "diverse readings of [life's] phenomena." His poems, Hardy said in the year in which *The Waste Land* was published, were mediations between kinds of experience, attempts to embody the unifying dream of "an alliance between religion, which must be retained unless the world is to perish, and complete rationality, which must come, unless the world also is to perish, by the interfusing effect of poetry." In spite of his several comments about its "lack of concords," Hardy's poetry does aim at a precarious wholeness, at "interfusion" of kinds of experience, and at observation of the complex inter-lacings of the mind and the world.

Hardy's poems create their central drama, their drama of many characters and impersonations, out of the conflict between an actively searching intelligence and the evidence which is returned to it by experience. They are fascinated by observation of the "interaction between seeing and knowing and expecting." They include of course moments of vision, in which experience delivers directly an intense or sufficient feeling. But what the mind sees, with whatever degree of intensity, is, as a dramatic or personative poetry is calculated to show, only part of what exists to be seen, and many of Hardy's poems record the consequences of a second glance, of information uncovered after conclusions have already been drawn. They present moments in which experience expands, so that the mind must in response either open or close, re-draw its design of the world or confirm its isolation in its formalization of what it has seen before. Hardy's poems detail a process of the un-making and re-making of meaning—or of a "frail-witted" and "illuded" refusal to do that—and they show the poet, as himself or as a character in whom he masks his quest, obliged, over and over, to abandon conclusion and start again. The characters of Hardy's poems, like One-Eyed Riley's patients, very often learn that they are "strangers," very often discover from their confrontations with the fresh originality of living fact that they are "nothing but a set / Of obsolete responses." In this essay, I want to examine some of the ways in which Hardy measures and corrects the mind's formalizations by submitting its experience to reconsideration.

Hardy treats the experience of the reconstruction of meaning dramatically in his almost obsessive pattern of repetition or return. Like Jude, whose heavenly vision draws him back in a painful rhythm to his earthly city, or like Jocelyn, whose fantasy drives him restlessly back to Portland, the characters in his poems come back. Sometimes they come back to voice a simple *ubi sunt* theme, to learn that "Time's transforming chisel" has been at work on the scene; sometimes they come back to find that the scene itself has been held static, but that it measures change in them. In both cases, they return to discover, and sometimes to correct, the shocking separateness of the life of the mind from the life of things, to learn how the mind has, insensibly, stylized its own experience. In these moments of re-vision, Hardy isolates the mind in an experience of shock, of thrilling perception, and he forces it to reorganize or retreat.

Hardy's poems of return make their effect by exploiting a natural "tension" or "conflict" between "the perception of order and the perception of things." Repetition creates pattern, of course: the kaleidoscope, as E. H. Gombrich points out, transforms our "messy environment" into "a thing of lawful beauty." But repetition also creates a precise expectation of order and it deprives individual things of their identities. When Hardy sends his questing figure back, he pits a clearly defined expectation against his character's capacity to see what is before him, and he submits that "order" to the possibility of complete revision. In repetition, the mind's stiff patterning can be shattered as it cannot be in experience which involves no very rigid expectation. Ordinary experience in time can merely confirm or extend or amplify or qualify a hypothetical order, but repetition can submit an achieved pattern to total judgement. (It can also permit a poet to treat time as though it were space and experience as though it were design.) Since it can result in a complete destruction of pattern and order, can leave a returning figure naked of artifice, there is a sense in which repetition can offer the only really *new* experience.

Hardy pares his poems of return to the barest possible shape. They consist of the pattern and the perceiver, and they make their shattering point simply by failing to repeat one element in the pattern. Hardy underlines the repeated elements carefully. In "The Revisitation," for instance, he details the similarities between the present night and the night of twenty years before: the pee-wits, the bridge, the lane, the "upper roadway," the "open drouthy downland," the "spry white scuts of conies," the Sarsen stone—all of those things are "the same." They are, the speaking soldier tells us, things "I knew so well"; they are "familiar"; they exist "as before." The speaking wanderer in "The Voices of Things" returns three times to the same spot to create in *us* the clear expectation that the waves of the sea will continue to voice his feelings. The speaker of "My Cicely" rides twice along the same path, forth and back through a landscape whose important details are repeated. In "Where the Picnic Was," the poet climbs to the empty circle by the straight line by which he gained the hill a year before. It is, he says, "the same." The emphasized repetitions are important. "The perception of regularity, of repetition and redundancy," E. H. Gombrich writes, "presents a great economy":

> Faced with an array of identical objects, whether they are the beads of a necklace, the paving stones of a street, or the columns of a building, we rapidly form the preliminary hypothesis that we are confronted with a lawful assembly. . . .

It is for the purpose of establishing that preliminary hypothesis that Hardy's poems are so carefully repetitive. Their patterning is precise, insistent, emphasized: his characters have a right to expect that it will also be complete. . . .

Source: Patricia Clements, "'Unlawful Beauty': Order and Things in Hardy's Poems," in *The Poetry of Thomas Hardy*, edited by Patricia Clements and Juliet Grindle, Barnes & Noble, 1980, pp. 137–41.

SOURCES

Armstrong, Tim, "Thomas Hardy: *Poems of 1912–13*," in *A Companion to Twentieth-Century Poetry*, edited by Neil Roberts, Blackwell, 2001, pp. 359–68, http://personal. rhul.ac.uk/uhle/012/Poems%20of%201912-13.pdf (accessed April 16, 2016).

Binyon, Laurence, Review of *Satires of Circumstance*, in *Thomas Hardy: The Critical Heritage*, edited by R. G. Cox, Routledge & Kegan Paul, 1970, pp. 440–43; originally published in *Bookman*, No. 47, February 1915, pp. 143–44.

Blackmur, R. P., "The Shorter Poems of Thomas Hardy," in *Thomas Hardy: Critical Assessments*, Vol. 2, *The Writer and the Poet*, edited by Graham Clarke, Helm Information, 1993, p. 251; originally published in *Southern Review*, Vol. 6, 1940–1941, pp. 20–48.

"Census of 1911," A Vision of Britain through Time, June 10, 1911, http://www.visionofbritain.org.uk/census/ SRC_P/2/EW1911PRE (accessed April 21, 2016).

Davies, Serena, "The Heart of Thomas Hardy," in *Telegraph* (London, England), September 3, 2008, http:// www.telegraph.co.uk/culture/tvandradio/3559654/The-Heart-of-Thomas-Hardy.html (accessed April 16, 2016).

Dilley, Ryan, "Camilla's Inherited Role as Royal Mistress," BBC News website, July 11, 2003, http://news. bbc.co.uk/2/hi/uk_news/magazine/3055376.stm (accessed April 21, 2016).

Diniejko, Andrzej, "Thomas Hardy: A Biographical Sketch," Victorian Web, 2010, http://www.victorianweb. org/authors/hardy/bio.html (accessed April 16, 2016).

"Divorce since 1900," UK Parliament website, http://www. parliament.uk/business/publications/research/olympic-britain/housing-and-home-life/split-pairs/ (accessed April 22, 2016).

"Dorset (County)," City Population, http://www.city population.de/php/uk-england-southwestengland.php? adm2id = E10000009 (accessed April 22, 2016).

Gibson, James, "*Satires of Circumstance*," in *Oxford Reader's Companion to Hardy*, edited by Norman Page, Oxford University Press, 2000, p. 387.

Hardy, Thomas, "The Walk," in *Thomas Hardy: The Complete Poems*, edited by James Gibson, Palgrave, 2001, p. 340.

Ingram, Patricia, "Hardy and the 'Cell of Time,'" in *Thomas Hardy: Critical Assessments*, Vol. 4, *A Twentieth Century Overview*, edited by Graham Clarke, Helm Information, 1993, pp. 547–48; originally published in *The Poetry of Thomas Hardy*, edited by Patricia Clements and Juliet Grindle, Vision Press, 1980, pp. 119–36.

"Max Gate," Discover Dorchester, http://www.dorches terdorset.com/max-gate.php (accessed April 22, 2016).

"Nomination Database," NobelPrize.org, http://www. nobelprize.org/nomination/archive/show_people.php?id = 3892 (accessed April 18, 2016).

Simkin, John, "Emma Gifford Hardy," Spartacus Educational, September 1997, http://spartacus-educational. com/JgiffordEH.htm (accessed April 16, 2016).

Strachey, Lytton, Review of *Satires of Circumstance*, in *Thomas Hardy: The Critical Heritage*, edited by R. G. Cox, Routledge & Kegan Paul, 1970, pp. 435–39; originally published in *New Statesman*, December 19, 1914.

"Thomas Hardy," in *Merriam-Webster's Encyclopedia of Literature*, Merriam-Webster, 1995, pp. 514–15.

Warren, Jane, "The Love That Haunted Thomas Hardy," in *Express* (London, England), December 30, 2010, http://www.express.co.uk/expressyourself/220065/The-love-that-haunted-Thomas-Hardy (accessed April 16, 2016).

FURTHER READING

Dalziel, Pamela, and Michael Millgate, eds., *Thomas Hardy's "Poetical Matter" Notebook*, Oxford University Press, 2009.

    Readers interested in Hardy's creative processes will find this volume of interest. To the dismay of Hardy scholars, Hardy or his executors destroyed most of his papers, but a few notebooks survived. This volume is one of them. It has a large number of ideas for new poems or poetic sequences, showing that even in his eighties, Hardy was still a productive artist who believed he could go on writing poetry indefinitely.

Grafe, Adrian, and Laurence Estanove, eds., *Thomas Hardy, Poet: New Perspectives*, McFarland, 2015.

    This collection of critical essays examines Hardy's poetry. Taken together, the essays make clear that critical recognition of Hardy's skill as a poet is catching up to recognition of his skill as a novelist.

Hardy, Florence Emily, *The Life of Thomas Hardy, 1840–1928*, Wordsworth Editions, 2007.

    This "biography" of Hardy, originally published in two volumes in 1928 and 1930, was nominally written by his second wife, Florence. Scholars generally hold, however, that the book is an *auto*biography, written largely by Hardy himself in the 1920s, although Florence, herself a published author, made significant contributions to it and oversaw its publication.

Taylor, Dennis, *Hardy's Metres and Victorian Prosody: With a Metrical Appendix of Hardy's Stanza Forms*, Oxford University Press, 1988.

    Hardy's poems represent many experiments in poetic meter. This volume examines the range of Hardy's metrics while offering a history of metrical theory and its apogee in the Victorian period. The volume includes a metrical glossary of Hardy's stanzaic forms.

Tomalin, Claire, *Thomas Hardy*, Penguin Books, 2008.

    This volume is a biography of Hardy by an acclaimed literary biographer. Tomalin examines Hardy's rise from his rural origins to become one of the best-selling authors of the day. She provides a detailed account of Hardy's marriage to Emma Gifford, showing how the exhilarating courtship devolved into a troubled marriage. She examines Hardy's outpouring of poetry after Emma's death, when he continued to see her as his beloved muse.

SUGGESTED SEARCH TERMS

Dorset, England AND Wessex

Edwardian era AND morality

elegy

Emma Lavinia Gifford

Florence Dugdale

Max Gate

Poets' Corner AND Westminster Abbey

Thomas Hardy

Thomas Hardy AND "The Walk"

Thomas Hardy AND Max Gate

When I Was Growing Up

NELLIE WONG

1981

Nellie Wong's "When I Was Growing Up" is a foundational work of third-wave feminism. In the poem, Wong relates her experiences growing up in the Chinatown of Oakland, California, during the 1930s and 1940s, not solely as a member of the oppressed Chinese minority nor solely as a woman but, significantly, as an Asian woman. She shifts the focus in the direction taken by modern feminism: onto the intersection of sexism and racism. In the poem, she describes how mass culture had essentially brainwashed her into wanting to be white, into wanting to reject her Asian identity. However, the speaker of the poem eventually sees that the only way out of her situation is to quit trying to live according to the racial and gender stereotypes imposed by the dominant culture.

AUTHOR BIOGRAPHY

Nellie Wong was born on September 12, 1934, in Oakland, California. Her parents were Chinese immigrants; her father had come to America in 1912. Her family lived in the Oakland Chinatown (separate from the larger Chinatown in San Francisco across the bay). They worked in a grocery store and eventually opened a Chinese restaurant called Great China. During her high school years, Wong worked as a waitress at the family business. Wong has mentioned how her

The speaker plans to run away from Chinatown, which she learns is a ghetto (©Ken Wolter | Shutterstock.com)

political awakening began during World War II when she saw Japanese Americans deported from the San Francisco area to internment camps for the duration of the war. Wong did well in high school and after graduation began to work as a secretary at U.S. Steel. During the 1970s, she took advantage of the company's offer to pay tuition for its workers to take creative writing courses at San Francisco State University. At school, she was further radicalized, in part by hostility against professors who rejected her anger-filled poetry but also by exposure to socialist student groups. She joined the Women Writer's Union and eventually the Freedom Socialist Party. This is a splinter group that broke off from the United States Socialist Workers Party to move further to the left, supporting the violent overthrow of capitalist institutions, including the government. She also cofounded with Merle Woo a group called Unbound Feet (in reference to the traditional Chinese practice of binding women's feet to make them unnaturally small), which was dedicated to public readings of their revolutionary poetry.

Wong began to write poetry that was devoted to feminist themes but was equally meant to address the injustice suffered in America by racial minorities and by workers. She found outlets for publication in radical periodicals, and in 1977 she published her first book of poetry, *Dreams in Harrison Railroad Park*, though the Kelsey Street Press, a feminist publishing house. She soon gained acclaim in feminist circles and was invited to contribute to the important feminist anthology, *This Bridge Called My Back* (1981), where she published "When I Was Growing Up." She found new employment in the administration of San Francisco State University as an analyst for affirmative action, a position she would hold until her retirement in 1998. In 1983, Wong went on a reading tour in China as part of a group of American women writers (which included Alice Walker) sponsored by the US-China People's Friendship Association. She has also given readings in Cuba as well as throughout the United States. She also taught women's studies and creative writing as a visiting professor at several American universities, including the University of Minnesota. Wong has published three other books of poetry: *The Death of Long Steam Lady* (1986), the privately published chapbook *Stolen*

Moments (1997), and another chapbook, *Break-fast Lunch Dinner* (2012). Her early poems are frequently anthologized and appear in more than two hundred collections and college text-books. Since retiring from San Francisco State, Wong has served as the Bay Area organizer for the Freedom Socialist Party and was a leader in protesting against the Gulf War as a member of Bay Area United against War, an activism that led her to take up the theme in her more recent poetry of the oppression of women by Islam. She lives in San Francisco.

POEM SUMMARY

The text used for this summary is from *The Oxford Book of Women's Writing in the United States*, edited by Linda Wagner-Martin and Cathy N. Davidson, Oxford University Press, 1995, pp. 294–96. A version of the poem can be found on the following web page: http://www.heydays.ws/?where = authors&author = Nellie%20Wong.

Wong's "When I Was Growing Up" is div-ided into thirteen units. Each one is between three and eight lines. They are separated by a skipped line and are nested one under another by three levels of indentation. The first and last sections begin with the same phrase, and the remaining sections each begin with a repetition of the title of the poem.

Lines 1–3
The narrator of the poem states that sometime in the past she wanted to be white. She then addresses the reader directly, suggesting the reader will want to know not why she wanted this but *how*. She then offers to count the ways, referencing Elizabeth Barrett Browning's Sonnet 43, which begins, "How do I love thee? Let me count the ways."

Lines 4–6
The speaker specifies that she is describing her youth, in a phrase that begins each section until the end of the poem. At that time, people—she does not say who—told her that she was dark. She believed what she was told and observed her own dark skin in the mirror, but she also imagined that her soul was dark, taking the word in both its literal and metaphorical senses. She blames this on the limitation of her vision, which must also be taken both literally and metaphorically.

Lines 7–10
The speaker says that her sisters, whose skin was evidently lighter than her own, were praised for their beauty. The reader must infer that she was not praised. Now she says that she was in the dark and falling, invoking metaphors drawn from Christian theology. She felt trapped in a confining, restricting space, perhaps in a canyon of skyscrapers, and utterly lost.

Lines 11–15
When she was growing up, the speaker of the poem saw magazines and popular films that fea-tured white actresses and models, particularly blonde women. In order to be raised up out of the pit of depression into which she had fallen, in order to become a woman with the type of beauty that she saw represented, she began to imagine she had lighter skin.

Lines 16–20
The speaker contrasts her depression and apparent hatred of her own racial identity with some slightly more positive memories from her childhood. Wong's parents must have learned English as a second language, and presumably many Chinese immigrants would never have mastered English or would have spoken with an accent. The speaker of the poem, however, excelled in her command of English and spelling. Likewise, in school, she is grouped with gifted students and praised for her ability to conform. This passage suggests the crushing of individuality that in the 1960s was often attributed to the American education system.

Lines 21–25
In high school, the speaker shifted to a school that was mostly white, though with some other Asian students. The white girls seemed rich to her and were also different in their appearance: they had curly hair and sophisticated clothes. She wished she had the same things as the white girls. The line has a double meaning: she did not want merely nicer clothes like them but their fortunate lives also.

Lines 26–31
The speaker says that when she was growing up, she was hungry for American culture. This, she realizes, is a code word: by *American* she means *white*. Even as a child she realized that being Chinese meant not being American, that she was foreign and limited in American culture compared with whites.

Lines 32–35

The speaker recalls the first time she dated a white man. He approached her as something exotic but, at the time, she was happy and flattered to play the part of that stereotype.

Lines 36–41

The speaker says that when she was younger she was ashamed of some Chinese men. She describes them as *yellow*. She perceives them as smaller than white men, and they have the disgusting habit of spitting on the sidewalk. These are characteristics of stereotypes, which the reader is to assume the speaker of the poem embraced in her youth. The next fault of Chinese men is their coughing. This is probably due to tuberculosis, a once more common and fatal disease in America, but the antibiotics to cure the disease came after the time of the speaker's childhood memories. It was just as common among whites and other groups as Chinese, however. The last class of Chinese men she is ashamed of is heroin addicts.

Lines 42–45

People would ask the speaker what race she was, whether she was from the Philippines or Polynesia or even Portugal. They asked her about every possibility except whether she was white, because although she felt her soul had a white covering, her skin was too dark for the question to occur.

Lines 46–51

The speaker expresses her concern over her perception that her skin is dark. She conceived of herself as dirty. She thought God had cleaned the skins of white people, but there was nothing she could do to clean herself. Even the water in which she bathed was dull and dirty.

Lines 52–59

The speaker wanted to run away to the countryside or to the coast of the ocean where she could live in wide open spaces and never see a yellow person, never see a place called Chinatown in Oakland. Only later did she learn to think of her neighborhood as a ghetto, one replicated wherever Chinese people lived in America.

Lines 60–63

The final section begins with the repetition of the first line, expressing that the speaker now understands that she once wanted to be white.

Continuing the parallel with the first section, she repeats the question that inspired her litany: in how many ways did she want to be white? In some frustration, she suggests that she has told the reader enough.

THEMES

Feminism

Wong is principally regarded as a feminist and, indeed, a foundational figure in third-wave feminism. This view is based on the strength of her poetic identity, not merely as an oppressed woman but as an oppressed Asian woman. She lacks privilege even in comparison with the white women she idolizes. Wong is pressured into thinking that her identity as a woman means she has to become a white woman, with blonde hair like the fashion models and movie stars, so it is racist stereotypes as well as sexist stereotypes that prevent the actualization of her authentic identity. She is led to envy the white girls in her high school precisely because they have more privilege than she (symbolized by their attractive clothing): even if they are girls, they are at least white. For Wong, as a contemporary feminist, her experiential world is arranged on a scale of privilege with white men at the top and women of color at the bottom, so feminism and racism are inextricably entangled, the oppression working itself out from the top down. As a young woman, the speaker of Wong's poem desperately wished she could escape from that process, but so long as it existed inside her own consciousness, she could not.

Racism

"When I Was a Growing Up" expresses Wong's wish as a young woman to be white. This wish has many connotations, but her essential complaint is that she feels like an outsider in her own country. The end of the poem expresses a fantasy of an ideal America where race does not exist and there is no such thing as a Chinatown. The only way the speaker, as a young person, knew how to envision race not mattering was for everyone to be white. The young Wong hated being Chinese because she had learned from the mass culture around her—from the movies and magazines of white American culture—that a Chinese person is something to be despised. She was filled with self-loathing and wanted to wash away her Chinese identity. The speaker's

As a girl, the speaker grows to hate the way she looks (©*Old box studio / Shutterstock.com*)

imagining of white skin and a white shell around her soul could almost be schizophrenic fantasies in another context, but here they are shown as the result of uncritically accepting the messages about race that pervade American culture. An interesting episode in the poem (lines 32–35) concerns the time when the speaker dated a white man. It is clear that he was interested in her as an exotic *other*. He had not disregarded or even forgiven her alien racial character but rather had fetishized it, as if she were a character from a comic book or other pop-culture representation. She was, at the time, happy to play along because she could pretend to herself that she was moving nearer the white identity.

The real story of the poem is Wong's resentment over being forced to internalize American culture's racism. The fact that the poem is presented in the past tense—her thoughts and feelings when she was growing up—suggests that she now feels differently and has grown beyond that damaged worldview.

STYLE

Figurative Language

Many readers will recognize that modern poetry is different from the poetry of John Keats's or William Shakespeare's day in that it often lacks the elements of meter and rhyme that, at a superficial level, seem to be the defining characteristics of poetry. Poets in the twentieth century realized that although those characteristics have a history going back three thousand years and are present in the poetry of all Indo-European languages (as well as many other languages, such as Arabic), they are not the essence of poetry. They saw the heart of poetry instead in the poet's skillful use of figurative language. *Figurative language* means both the standard figures of similes and metaphors (which are used in prose as well as poetry) and the use of language in a way different from ordinary speech, to evoke meaning that the ordinary use of words cannot produce. In "When I Was Growing Up," Wong evokes the physical appearance of older poetic texts, dividing her text into lines of arbitrary length and using a complicated system of nested indents in the printed text; however, it is only in her use of figurative language that the poem can be considered a poem. For example, if one were to restate lines 9 and 10 of the poem in simple language, it would be something like "I became depressed." Neither those words nor anything like them appear in the poem; instead, she uses images of falling and being crushed, frightening ideas that convey the emotional reality of her state better than a more literal description could. In another example, Wong is able to convey the rigidity of the American school system by showing the students reduced to merely being a line rather than individuals (line 20).

Intertexuality

Everyone is familiar with the practice of quotation, where a writer reproduces the exact words of another writer, with those words set off in quotation marks with some indication of the source. Very well-known fragments of poetry, such as "To be or not to be" or "A thing of beauty is a joy forever," might even be quoted without these formal signs, relying on the reader to recognize them based on the general knowledge that it is assumed the writer and the audience share. This is hardly the full range of reference to other authors that exists in the work of sophisticated writers. Often an author

TOPICS FOR FURTHER STUDY

- Wong's older sister, Li Keng Wong, a former grade school teacher, wrote a memoir aimed at young adults: *Good Fortune: My Journey to Gold Mountain* (2008). She had been left in China when her father emigrated to the United States and was brought over in 1933. The memoir covers her voyage and the first decade of her life in America, overlapping with the period described in "When I Was Growing Up." Write a paper comparing the two sisters' descriptions of their childhood experiences.

- In the nineteenth and early twentieth centuries, many American families lived in China so that the parents could work as Christian missionaries. Find accounts written by whites who spent their childhood in the China missions and compare their attitudes about race with Wong's in an essay. Scholarly accounts of the American missions, such as Jane Hunter's *The Gospel of Gentility* (1989) or Dana L. Robert's *American Women in Mission* (1997), will guide you to primary sources.

- Many readings of Wong's "When I Was Growing Up" have been filmed as class assignments and posted to social media websites. Some feature an independent reader, while in others the poem is read by an entire class as a chorus. Some simply show the reading, while others illustrate the poem with a montage of images. Create a video recording of your own presentation of the poem, individually or with others.

- Janet S. Gold's *Good Luck Gold and Other Poems* (1994) is a collection of poems for young adults about the racism encountered by a Chinese American girl growing up in San Francisco's Chinatown. Make a presentation to your class using images gathered from the Internet showing scenes from San Francisco's and Oakland's Chinatowns and comparing the poetry in this collection with Wong's.

will refer to another text in a way that is not a direct quotation but will nevertheless call that text to the reader's mind. The way that the author comments on or reshapes the other text, with the reader following along based on his or her own knowledge, becomes a kind of conversation between the author and reader about the other text. The success of this technique depends on the reader's being familiar with the other text. Without that familiarity, the full depth of meaning will be lost, although this does not necessarily make the intertextual passage meaningless or incomprehensible. It will simply evoke a different response in the reader. The intertextual reference itself might be a description or summary of the original text or the reuse of a few of the original's unmistakable words in a new configuration of language that sparks the recognition.

There are two notable examples of intertextuality in Wong's "When I Was Growing Up." In the third line of the poem, she asks the reader to let her (the author) tell her listener (the reader) the ways she wanted to be white when she was growing up. This recalls the opening of Elizabeth Barrett Browning's Sonnet 43, which begins, "How do I love thee? Let me count the ways." Browning then proceeds to tell her lover all the many different ways in which she loves him (a list that itself makes an intertextual reference to Paul's Epistle to the Romans, 8:39, incidentally). Wong's reference here is a parody, however, because what she is going to recount has nothing to do with love; rather, the list chronicles her rejection and abuse by white society. Wong reprises the reference in the final section of the poem, suggesting that while there may be no limit to love (the implication of Browning's poem), she has finally brought an end to the self-loathing imposed on her by seeking acceptance in white-dominated culture.

Another intertextual reference occurs in the next-to-last section of the poem. In this section, the speaker of the poem wishes that she could escape to an America where she is accepted as white and be released from the burden of the oppression directed against her Chinese American identity. This ideal land is characterized as being in "purple mountains," recalling the "purple mountain majesties" from the well-known patriotic hymn "America the Beautiful." This poem, written in its popular form in 1911 by Katherine Lee Bates and set to music by Samuel A. Ward, indeed envisages an ideal America,

COMPARE
&
CONTRAST

- **1980s:** Students are generally grouped by ability in their elementary school classrooms, particularly with respect to reading, as Wong recalls in connecting with her own youth.

  Today: Grouping by ability fell out favor in the late 1980s, since it was viewed as dooming lower-achieving students (especially those from poor and minority families) to never catching up with their better-prepared peers. Recently, however, the practice has been returning, according to national surveys of teachers, in an attempt to tailor instruction to students' abilities.

- **1980s:** Feminism is focused on second-wave issues such as gaining access to the

  workplace for women and electing female politicians.

  Today: Third-wave feminism concentrates on the intersection of lines of oppression in American cultures, such as the convergence of racism and sexism in the oppression of women of color.

- **1980s:** Asian Americans are beginning a demographic upturn in areas such as education and income.

  Today: In average statistics of education and income, Asians surpass all other groups in America, including whites, although Asian cultural identity is still often pushed to the margin by mass culture.

symbolized by the beautiful scenery of Pike's Peak, which inspired the poem. Wong's reference is again parodic, pointing out that no such ideal America exists and she could not escape the racist world described in "When I Was Growing Up."

HISTORICAL CONTEXT

Chinese Immigration to the United States

Prior to the California gold rush in 1848, only a few hundred Chinese people had come to America. When prospecting for gold seemed to promise the hope of making a fortune, though, tens of thousands of Chinese (mostly men, but some families) immigrated from China to California. America is called the *golden mountain* in Chinese as a holdover from that era. While they were attracted by the lure of gold, most Chinese in America took more ordinary jobs in factories and agriculture and provided the labor to build the western section of the transcontinental railroad. By 1882, Chinese immigrants constituted about 10 percent of the population of California.

Most of the immigrants had not learned English and formed their own communities, cities in microcosm where the new language was not necessary, though they would hardly have been allowed to live in white neighborhoods in any case. Racism built up into a kind of panic in the white community, resulting in the Chinese Exclusion Act of 1882, which almost ended Chinese immigration until 1943. Some exceptions were still allowed, and these included Wong's family, which came to the United States between 1912 and 1933.

Throughout the United States and especially in California, there was widespread racism against the Chinese; they were called the "yellow peril." Jack London's 1910 science-fiction short story "The Unparalleled Invasion" describes a world war between China and the West in the 1970s that results in the genocide of the entire nation of China through biological warfare—presented in the story as a happy ending. The Chinese had burdensome restrictions placed on their business activity and employment and were generally prevented from becoming citizens. Chinese men were legally barred from marrying white women.

Pictures of movie stars and models in magazines taught and reinforced a narrow standard of beauty
(©Bohbeh / Shutterstock.com)

A stereotype developed that made out China-towns to be centers of prostitution and opium use as well as organized crime, although this was far from the truth. Public perception and the legal status of Chinese began to change during World War II when China became an ally of the United States in the war against Japan. In "When I Was Growing Up," Wong describes the poverty of the Chinese American community that was a result of the legal restrictions imposed upon them and the drug use that is perceived as one result of that poverty. However, since World War II, Chinese Americans have been perceived as a "model minority," surpassing whites in nearly every demographic category, including college and graduate school education, median income, and home ownership. In negative traits, such as drug use and smoking, rates are much lower in the Chinese community. In recent years, however, this model minority concept has been seen as another form of racism, allowing the discrimination faced by the Chinese to be denied.

CRITICAL OVERVIEW

Wong's "When I Was Growing Up" was originally published in *This Bridge Called My Back* (1981), a collection of essays and other works meant to highlight the particular needs of black, Asian, and Latina women within the feminist movement. The anthology became an important founding document of third-wave feminism, giving Wong's poem a very high profile and resulting in its being republished in more than two hundred places, including many standard college and high school textbooks. Also in 1981, Wong and Japanese American poet Mitsuye Yamada became the subject of the short documentary film *Mitsuye and Nellie: Asian American Poets* by Allie Light and Irving Saraf. The two poets recall in interviews for the film the various ways they were radicalized by the internment of Japanese Americans during World War II from their Japanese and Chinese perspectives.

Since then, however, Wong's significance in the scholarly community has sharply declined, although "When I Was Growing Up" continues to be anthologized. After her 1986 anthology *The Death of Long Steam Lady*, Wong has been unable to find even a small press or academic press to publish her poetry and has published in chapbooks instead. Scholarly literature devoted to Wong consists of biographical sketches of one or two paragraphs meant to contextualize "When I Was Growing Up," either in introductions to the poem in anthologies and textbooks or in feminist or Asian American studies reference works. A particularly insightful specimen of this kind of work is provided by the editors Linda Wagner-Martin and Cathy N. Davidson in *The Oxford Book of Women's Writing in the United States*. They helpfully add an apparently original comment about the poem itself: "Nellie Wong's parodic use of Elizabeth Barrett Browning's famous poem [Sonnet 43] gave a new dimension to her lament for her Asian-American adolescence." Otherwise, many of these mini-biographies that introduce the poem in anthologies tend to be copied one from the other, creating an accepted view of Wong's work, heavily informed by the Light and Saraf film but leaving many questions about her family history unanswered.

The only sustained scholarly discussion of Wong is in Young Sook Jeong's 2006 unpublished dissertation, "Daughtering Asian American Women's Literature in Maxine Hong Kingston, Nellie Wong, and Ronyoung Kim." In a general assessment of Wong, Jeong notes that she has published

> numerous poems that present her political consciousness as a socialist feminist Chinese American and her poetic sensibility exploring various issues of Asian Americans, labor, family, and socio-political matters, and some of them are autobiographical poems revealing her and her family's experiences.

With regard to "When I Was Growing Up," Jeong merely specifies that it is one of "her many autobiographical poems of her adolescent experience and family history."

CRITICISM

Rita M. Brown

Brown is an English professor. In the following essay, she analyzes Wong's "When I Was Growing Up" as a foundational work of third-wave feminism.

> SHE NO LONGER WANTS TO BE THE WHITE ANGEL AND THEREFORE NO LONGER HAS TO FEAR BEING THE DARK-SKINNED MONSTER."

Wong's "When I Was Growing Up" was originally published in 1981. It is important in coming at the very beginning of third-wave feminism, both in its time and in its subject matter. First-wave feminism, beginning in the nineteenth century and, in America, extending until the passage of the Nineteenth Amendment to the Constitution (women's suffrage) in 1920, sought to obtain basic legal equality for women and eventually secured for them the right to own their own property and to vote. With these rights in place, feminism more or less entered into a dormant state in the years of the Great Depression and World War II. During the 1950s, women like Betty Freidan formed the core of second-wave feminism, rebelling against the ideal image of the housewife that was strongly imposed on American women's identities. The goal of this movement was to achieve actual social equality, with middle-class women going to college to train for their own careers, not merely to find a husband (a stereotype of the 1950s). These gains would have been codified by the Equal Rights Amendment, but it was never passed. Nevertheless, women quickly made vast strides in entering the workforce and politics and in freeing themselves from restrictive stereotypes that controlled their social roles and behaviors. It was recognized that full equality might take a generation or more to achieve.

After the relative success of second-wave feminism, the movement that would emerge as the third wave made a probing critique of the feminist movement itself. It found that the feminist movement to a large degree was a movement of middle-class white women. There was, for example, very little contact with the civil rights movement in the African American community that had been occurring at the same time as second-wave feminism and that aimed for many of the same goals of equality. Third-wave feminists conceived that the movement ought to be one of resistance to every form of oppression

WHAT DO I READ NEXT?

- Merle Woo's *Yellow Woman Speaks* (2003) is a collection of poems by Wong's associate. These poems take as their themes the creation of a new feminism directed as much against racism and capitalism as the patriarchy.

- *This Bridge Called My Back: Writings by Radical Women of Color* (1981), edited by Cherrie Moraga and Gloria E. Anzaldúa, is an anthology of feminist essays and poetry that is considered one of the foundational documents of third-wave feminism because it shifts its focus from the oppression of women to the double portion of oppression by women who belong to minority groups. Many of the contributions are by Latinas and Asians, including Wong's "When I Was Growing Up."

- *Dreams in Harrison Railroad Park* (1977) was Wong's first collection of poetry. The poems are often ornamented with references to Chinese culture, and some poems imitate Asian verse forms.

- Chun Yu's *Little Green: A Memoir of Growing Up during the Chinese Cultural Revolution* (2015) is a memoir in verse form intended for a young-adult audience. It explores the experience of growing up in a society undergoing dislocations upon implementing the Leninist-Trotskyist social policies that Wong promotes.

- Shelley Burdgeon's *Third-Wave Feminism and the Politics of Gender in Late Modernity* (2011) outlines a program for transforming feminism into (or *back* into) a practical program for meaningful social change to be brought about by political means.

- *Three Asian Women Writers Speak Out on Feminism* is a collection of essays by Nellie Wong, her close associate Merle Woo, and Mitsuye Yamada. It was published in 2003 by Red Letter Press, which handles the publications of the Freedom Socialist Party. The authors suggest that feminism needs to be reconfigured as a more radical form of political resistance.

---

and those with the power to perpetuate what is known within the movement as *privilege*. Accordingly, the position of minority women takes on a special interest in third-wave feminism, since they are doubly oppressed as women and as minorities.

A foundational critical text of third-wave feminism was *The Madwoman in the Attic*, by Sandra Gilbert and Susan Gubar, first published in 1979. This text analyzed the figure of the feminine in Victorian literature by women; it takes its title from Charlotte Brontë's 1847 novel *Jane Eyre*, in which a character imprisons his mentally ill wife in the attic so that he can enjoy the use of her property and marry a younger woman who is of a lower class (and hence, arguably, more easily controlled). Gilbert and Gubar categorized the female characters they studied into two groups. The first was the *angel*, epitomized by the

character of Jayne Eyre herself, a virtuous, self-denying woman, devoted to helping, even mothering, men and representing everything an aristocratic young man would want in a wife. The other type they called the *monster*, represented by the madwoman in the attic. This kind of woman was destructive and uncontrollable, possessed of a devouring sexual aggression. The kind of feminine dichotomy is hardly localized in the Victorian writers Gilbert and Gubar studied. Klaus Theweleit, in his groundbreaking anthropological study *Male Fantasies* (originally published in German in 1977), analyzed the proto-fascist literature produced by the generation of young German men who had fought in World War I and later in militia organizations (*Freikorps*) in Germany, Poland, and the Baltic states, against movements that aimed at a communist revolution. For these writers, the two archetypes were the *white nurse* and the *red nurse*. The *white nurse*, providing medical aid for the anti-communist fighters, was generally someone from a background similar to the fighters themselves; they were seen as essentially pure and idealistic healers. The *red nurse*, in contrast, was typically a former prostitute whose main duty was not healing but mutilating the bodies of captured fascist militia men. The same dichotomy can be found elsewhere, such as in Samuel Taylor Coleridge's long poem "Christabel" (1816) in the characters of the angelic Christabel and the literally reptilian Geraldine or in the speaker of the ancient Gnostic poem "Thunder: Perfect Mind," who identifies herself simultaneously as a virgin and a prostitute. Countless other examples can be found in literature.

It is obvious that the *monster* archetype is meant to degrade and control women, and some third-wave feminist poets, like Sandra Cisneros in her poem "Loose Woman," attempt to strike back against the patriarchal image and reclaim the monster as a positive model for themselves, reveling in its dangerous sexual power. But Gilbert and Gubar suggest another approach: women must free themselves from both stereotypes. The angel archetype, no less than the monster, is a patriarchal device that controls and limits women's lives. However, as third-wave feminism progressed and became a more clearly defined movement, Gilbert and Gubar's ideas also evolved. In the 2000 introduction to the second edition of their book, they acknowledge, "*The Attic* of our title should be identified as the site of the disenfranchised Third World female character on the borders of, or outside, Western Civilization, not as that of the relatively privileged First World heroine." In other words, no matter how much European and American women believed they were oppressed, the ones who are truly oppressed are not merely women but women of color and those in other marginalized groups.

Wong's "When I Was Growing Up" follows Gilbert's and Gubar's original typology of patriarchal feminine archetypes so closely that she may well have been influenced by their book, published two years before she wrote the poem. Wong was taking creative writing classes at the time, and *The Madwoman in the Attic* was a widely used sensation among English faculty across the country. In her poem, Wong describes the angel and the monster archetypes quite clearly. The angel is pretty, beloved by men, and wears nice clothes. The monster, on the

other hand, is a dark, seething, ugly mass of emotions; her soul feels so dirty that it can never be cleaned. Wong, or at least the narrative voice of the poem, asserts that she spent her childhood and adolescence wanting desperately to be the angel but fearing that she was in fact the monster. Wong goes further, pointing the way toward third-wave feminism. It is very clear that the angel is white, like white movie stars and white high school girls, while the monster has dark skin. It is the darkness of the skin that infects the soul with depression and hopelessness, a darkness that cannot be washed off. She claims that even her own sisters had lighter skin than she and therefore were considered pretty (perhaps by their parents), leaving the monster to be merely grotesque. It is her status of being a racial minority that sets Wong's speaker apart, makes her part of Chinatown rather than America, makes her fellow Chinatown residents into weak and despicable drug addicts. In wishing to become the angel, she wishes to leave Chinatown for America, to become clean instead of dirty, to leave her Chinese identity and skin color to become white.

The final section of the poem points to the way out of her dilemma of being Chinese but wanting to be white, and it is the one suggested by Gilbert and Gubar. Wong emphasizes that the conflict she describes is in the past, something she has moved beyond. She no longer wants to be the white angel and therefore no longer has to fear being the dark-skinned monster. She has moved beyond the two male-created and imposed archetypes. Just as the angel and monster archetypes are by no means original with Gilbert and Gubar (as one would hardly expect since they derive them from literary history), their solution was already suggested long ago. The angel and the monster are judgments imposed on women by the patriarchy and which women must escape by refusing to internalize them as their own judgments about themselves. Precisely this advice was offered not merely to women but to everyone by the second-century Stoic philosopher Epictetus, at the very beginning of his *Handbook* (*Enchiridion*). He says:

> Some things are up to us and some things are not up to us. Our opinions are up to us, and our impulses, desires, aversions—in short, whatever is our own doing. Our bodies are not up to us, nor are our possessions, our reputations, or...whatever is not our own doing....So remember, if you think that things naturally not your own are you own, you will be thwarted, miserable, and upset.

At school, the speaker finds some comfort in being a good, obedient student (©*Blend Images | Shutterstock.com*)

Epictetus's recognition that our bodies and our reputations are not up to us and that we must be indifferent to them if we are not to be doomed to misery, sums up the message of Wong's poem.

Source: Rita M. Brown, Critical Essay on "When I Was Growing Up," in *Poetry for Students*, Gale, Cengage Learning, 2017.

Jolie Sheffer

In the following review, Sheffer describes the collection as an "often-refreshing" recollection of feminist writing.

First published in 1986, this reprint from Radical Women Publications offers an often-refreshing, occasionally dated look back to an earlier moment in feminist and ethnic writing and politics. *3 Asian American Writers Speak Out on Feminism* combines poetry, essays, drama, and book reviews by three major figures in the development of the field of Asian American literature and cultural studies. Its slim size (under 50 pages) makes it appealing as a primer for students and others interested in the history of feminist and Asian American literature and activism.

Clearly responding to the explosion of work by feminists and African American, Chicana, and other women of color in the 1970s and 1980s, this booklet also marks an important moment in the development of Asian American identity politics. For example, Nellie Wong offers an alternative appraisal of Maxine Hong Kingston's *The Woman Warrior*. Refuting Frank Chin's and others' criticisms of the novel's complicated form and the liberties Kingston takes with Chinese myths, Wong embraces the feminist sensibility driving much of Kingston's work. Wong especially lauds Kingston's commitment to addressing both racism and sexism, and the complicated relationship between the two, both in China and in America.

Nellie Wong's poem "Under Our Own Wings" asks the fundamental question of late second-wave feminism: how do we express the complicated matrix of race and ethnicity, gender and sexuality? Wong voices the frustration of women of color who feel the contradictory tug of two distinct struggles against oppression.

The answer for all three authors is that this is not an either/or proposition. Rather, the two struggles are mutually constitutive and equally important. The experiences of Asian American women cannot be understood without attention to both issues.

Just as Kingston seeks to give voice to her silenced female ancestors, Merle Woo seeks to give voice to the women of previous generations, imagining the voices of her female relatives who could not speak of their experiences or did not believe their stories worth telling. Woo explains, "The gallery of voices I hear are old women's voices of my family and my people, all 'auntie' and 'see-nai'—women I rarely see anymore, or never saw, but hear, clamoring for me to give them affirmation." The voices of elderly and first-generation Asian immigrants speak of madness, silence, and interethnic rivalries. For Woo, writing is akin to "the chiming of [her] own unconscious, just waiting to be acknowledged and used, waiting to ring out, waiting for [her] to untie the rope so these bells can swing and clang with fearsome awfulness."

The authors' purpose for writing and their call to action for readers is right there in the title—they write to encourage Asian American women to "speak out." Mitsuye Yamada calls on Asian American women to break the cultural codes that demand women be silent and well behaved. These gendered values create the conditions for the elision of Asian American women's experience, both within feminism and in American culture at large. "We need to raise our voices a little more, even as they say to us, 'This is so uncharacteristic of you.' To finally recognize our own invisibility is to finally be on the path toward visibility. Invisibility is not a natural state for anyone."

If the text feels dated by the language of "oppression" and "rage," that outmoded diction can be understood as a testament to the development of the debate in the past two decades. The widespread creation of Asian American studies programs in universities and a boom in recent fiction by Asian American authors at mainstream publishing houses are signs of the increasing visibility of and vocalization by Asian Americans. Contemporary writers such as Chang-rae Lee, Karen Tei Yamashita, Jhumpa Lahiri, and Bharati Mukherjee have achieved both critical acclaim and best-seller status.

In such a marketplace, Woo, Wong, and Yamada's preoccupation with having to choose between struggles or between identities seems a bit irrelevant. Today, women's studies classes

MY MOM AND DAD CAME FROM A SMALL VILLAGE IN SOUTH CHINA. I HOPE I'M NOT DEALING IN STEREOTYPES HERE, BUT I THINK A LOT OF MY STRENGTH COMES FROM WHO MY ANCESTORS WERE."

routinely address a multiplicity of identity categories; race, class, gender, sexuality, and ethnicity are practically a mantra for attentive cultural analysis. Furthermore, globalization and postcolonial studies have changed the language of current cultural debates, emphasizing "hybridity," "liminality," "situational identity," and the multiplicity of relations and experiences that shape our world. Power is always relative, and our attentiveness to the many kinds, degrees, and means by which power is manifested has increased exponentially. My greatest criticism is that this reprint does not recontextualize the work in light of these changes. A new introduction that addresses these present debates seems far more important and necessary than current photographs of the authors.

In a way, Woo, Wong, and Yamada's call to action has been answered—by the ongoing, continually expanding commitment to raising voices and speaking out. *3 Asian American Writers Speak Out on Feminism* stands as in important document in the development of feminism and Asian American writing. As an introduction to its moment of production and the key issues of political/cultural debates of the mid-1980s, *3 Asian American Writers Speak Out on Feminism* is an important contribution to feminism and ethnic studies.

Source: Jolie Sheffer, Review of *3 Asian American Writers Speak Out on Feminism*, in *Iris*, Vol. 47, Fall–Winter 2003, p. 91.

Serena Turley
In the following interview, Wong talks about writing and politics.

...GS: Since you spent the majority of your life working in an administrative capacity, do you feel that your work helped prepare you for your activism? Additionally, do you feel that your

employment helped contribute to your sense of socialist consciousness?

NW: I do feel that my work in an administrative capacity helped prepare me for my activism. A political organizer needs administrative skills although at the time I was a secretary, I had no notion of how valuable my skills would become. As a secretary and administrative assistant, I learned to coordinate meetings and conferences, make travel arrangements, organized reports, the whole gamut.

Yes, my employment contributed to my sense of socialist consciousness. I learned about racism and sexism on the job. I was excluded from learning more about the company and was expected to type and just keep quiet. A former boss asked me to translate Korean for him. I told him I spoke Cantonese, but he insisted that somehow I understood the Korean visitor! While the women I worked with at the corporation in the 1970s (before I worked at UC San Francisco) were dedicated workers, we were not politically conscious when sexist behavior and practices came down. The workforce also was not unionized.

GS: In the poem "It's in the Blood," you say that "those who remain silent own their own tongues." What exactly do you mean by this? Can silence be used by an oppressed group as a weapon against their oppressors? For instance, in Maxine Hong Kingston's The Woman Warrior, *the girl who remains silent by choice while the narrator is abusing her seems to use her silence as a weapon or an act of defiance. On the other hand, authors like Noam Chomsky have argued that silence in the face of atrocity (specifically in the face of the US government's policy towards Iraq) is the same thing as complicity. In your opinion, is silence always negative or does it also have some positive aspects?*

NW: In my poem, "It's in the Blood," when I say that, "those who remain silent own their own tongues," I meant that I was only speaking for myself and not necessarily for all Asian American women or men. Taking classes in Asian American Studies and Feminist Studies, in addition to Creative Writing, at SF State in the 1970s opened up a whole world for me. When I learned about the collective history of Asian Pacific Americans, I could not remain silent. I felt that I had to tell the story of my family, how and why my parents immigrated to the U.S., and that being Chinese or Chinese American meant that we were part of an oppressed group.

Yes, I believe that in Maxine Hong Kingston's *The Woman Warrior*, the girl who remained silent by choice used her silence as a weapon against her oppressor or as act of defiance. In my opinion, silence is not always negative. As a socialist feminist activist, I would never fink on my comrades. But my breaking my own silences is related to my growing up with a lot of silence. First of all, I never knew how to argue or debate. Everyone else seemed knowledgeable or knew how to communicate. If I had an opinion about anything, it was safer not to state it. Even though I graduated from high school, there was a long, long gap between high school and when I attended San Francisco State University in the 1970s. Sometimes I think I learned to speak at SF State. The poetry writing helped. Taking Feminist Studies helped. Learning about the history of people of color and women and the working class all helped.

GS: You mentioned in both of your speeches that you enjoy martial arts films, such as Crouching Tiger, Hidden Dragon. *What exactly was it about* CTHD *that appealed to you?*

NW: I liked *Crouching Tiger, Hidden Dragon*, because of the martial arts prowess of the women. Even Jen, the young princess who was betrothed, secretly wanted to become a fighter. Michelle Yeoh is tops in her roles as she fights for justice and no man is going to get a compliant or passive response from her. Some of the Hong Kong films like *The East is Red* feature women as heroes. Blind swordswomen fly up roofs and take matters into their own hands. What a difference from old, racist Hollywood films that show Asian women as submissive. But then there's *Charlie's Angels* that gives Lucy Liu, an Asian American woman, a chance to show off her kung fu along with her white compatriots.

GS: What about Zhang Yimou's work? Do you feel that films such as Raise the Red Lantern, To Live, *and* Red Firecracker, Green Firecracker *help to deconstruct the stereotype of the passive Asian womyn?*

NW: I'm a fan of Zhang Yimou's work. Yes, films such as *Raise the Red Lantern*, *To Live*, and *Red Firecracker, Green Firecracker*, help to deconstruct the stereotype of passive Asian women. Michelle Yeoh in *Wing Chun*, a Hong Kong film, also breaks stereotypes of helplessness and passivity. In fact, this was based on a real woman who created a specific type of martial arts fighting. Wing Chun not only defends her village, but fights and defeats the meanest man with superior martial arts skills who wants to dominate her and make her his woman.

Not One Less, is a fairly recent film by Zhang. A 13-year-old girl who teaches kids a few years younger than she is the hero in this one. It's powerful, especially when she goes searching for an unruly boy who runs away from school. The girl's job was to keep the class the same size; otherwise, she wouldn't be paid.

Now, in talking about American films, however, we don't see any images of ourselves. Lucy Liu will recreate her role in another *Charlie's Angels*, but that's about it. Margaret Cho, an outstanding comedienne of Korean American ancestry, has a couple of films. But unless a conscious Asian American filmmaker pays attention, we're not going to see images of many women of color in commercial films. Fortunately, the annual International Asian American Film Festival held in San Francisco showcases films about the Asian Pacific American experience in all it diversity.

GS: How did you become involved with the Freedom Socialist Party? Were you versed in socialist theory before you joined or did your consciousness come as a result of your membership?

NW: I joined both Radical Women and the Freedom Socialist Party in 1981. I wasn't versed in socialist theory until I became a member, if I had waited until I learned everything about socialism, I wouldn't have become a socialist. I was already a feminist, but didn't identify with mainstream feminism. I met Karen Brodine, my late comrade and poet friend, at SF State. We worked together on campus where the feminist movement was exciting and strong. She introduced me to both RW and FSP. Part of the joy in my becoming politically conscious is being in the movements as a woman, as a Chinese American, as a feminist, as a worker, and as a socialist. I have learned much from being involved in these political organizations and they have learned from me. Women's leadership is taken seriously and the men in the FSP are feminists. As a woman of color, I'm not expected to leave my ethnicity or race outside the door. Every aspect of me counts and the party's program is inclusive, not exclusive. Other political organizations—and they were on campus—did not approach me. I'm just glad that I was at SF

State in my mid-30s and with my interests in Creative Writing, Feminism, and Asian American Studies, I found opportunities to expand my horizon and the movement was there, waiting.

GS: You say that your are a Trotskyist rather than a Maoist or a Lenninist. For those who are unfamiliar with socialist theory, how would you explain the difference? What are the political ramifications of such a distinction?

NW: Yes, I'm a Trotskyist, but I'm also a Leninist. Clara Fraser, known as the architect of socialist feminism, was a founder of the FSP. She also helped found RW. Trotskyist theory calls for world revolution and socialism. It also calls for a revolution here in the U.S., the heart of capitalism and imperialism. The Stalinists and Maoists don't talk about the American Question and by that I mean that the Stalinist theory of "socialism in one country" pretty much allows one workers' state to be surrounded by capitalist nations. So we're not going to turn capitalism upside down if capitalism co-exists with socialism. There's no such thing as peaceful co-existence. Look at the world right now. Chaos everywhere and our government and its allies are waging a "War on Terrorism." We bomb Afghanistan and still the enemy is nowhere to be found. We can build for a society that's feminist and socialist, but capitalism has to go. And we need a working class party to do this work. We need to end systems everywhere that allow death and destruction, violence against women and lesbians and gays, against the poor, against youth, elders, immigrants and people with disabilities. It's possible for all of us to live here on earth. We could use the military budget to build schools and training centers, to cure AIDS and cancer. But our profit system is inhumane. We can have a better world. That's why I'm involved.

GS: Where do you see the feminist and socialist movements 20 years from now? What do you think will have to happen in order for the movement(s) to reach that point?

NW: It's difficult to say where the movements will be 20 years from now. But things are changing. From the Battle of Seattle in 1999, we've seen a surge of the anti-globalization forces. Environmentalists, feminists, anti-racist groups, youth, the movement of disability activists, workers, the homeless, seniors—people know what war mongering has done. Everyone knows how CEOs lie and cheat and get away with murder, whether they're cooking the books or scrambling for more markets that just aren't there. A friend of mine says, "Let's take everything we have in the Costco warehouses and ship them to Cuba and other countries that need things." People are looking for answers. Remember, Bush did not get elected! But we can't put faith in the Democratic Party either because they're a part of the problem—they're pro-war just like the Republicans. Since I'm in my late 60s, I have revolutionary optimism because I'm involved. I know I can make a difference along with my comrades and all those who wish for a healthier life.

GS: I am impressed that a womyn of your age/experience is so full of energy! A lot of times, we often grow weary from burning our candles on so many different ends. How do you stay so energetic and remain so active, even after all of these years?

NW: Yes, I'm energetic. Maybe it's because I eat a lot of fruit and vegetables? I don't know what being burned out is. What keeps me going is my revolutionary optimism—that things will get better if we organize, not mourn. Guess what? I used to mourn, not organize! I was a late bloomer, so to speak. I started university when I was in my mid-30s. I got married in my mid-30s and got divorced in my 40s. I began writing poems at SF State and I worked for 46 years! Wages were very low for clericals. Retirement agrees with me because I now am a full-time revolutionary and I still find time to write. I make time to write even though the writing often comes late at night or in the early morning hours. Politics and art, for me, go hand in hand. I read a lot (theory, poetry, novels, newspapers). I love reading political cartoons like Aaron McGruder who writes *Boondocks*. I'm crazy about jazz, food and films and not necessarily in that order. I used to be so sad because I didn't have a husband. Then I married and found that marriage didn't work. I'm not saying that people don't have some good relationships, I know some. Sometimes I think I'm energetic because I come from peasant stock, you know? My mom and dad came from a small village in south China. I hope I'm not dealing in stereotypes here, but I think a lot of my strength comes from who my ancestors were. My parents worked their whole lives and never got rich. The rich, rich history of my people—who fought exclusion laws, who built the railroads, who fought being excluded from going to school with white people—I keep uppermost in my mind. The victories, the triumphs of working people all over the world—that also sustains me. I also think I'm ornery, tough, because I was so passive when I was young.

GS: What advice would you give to young writers? How can they use their talents for the broader social good?

NW: Young writers should write and be active. If you can't find a group to join, start one. Working together in concert with others towards a common goal—that's power in the making. Well, maybe a few writers live on their income as writers, but I don't know them. I'm a worker-writer- revolutionary. They're all linked. Writing is a solitary act, but you don't need to live a solitary life. American culture teaches us to be "rugged individualists." That's okay, but not at the expense of going up the corporate ladder and stomping on everybody but yourself and your rich cohorts. Children can teach us a lot so respect them, love them and they'll thrive. Have faith in humankind. Keep writing and rewriting. You'll know when a poem or a story is done. When I began to write poems, I didn't think about winning prizes. I don't think about that now. The very act of writing is powerful. Writing has everything to with love for language, with learning about life and joy in the struggle, in the joy of creating. Writing is a part of making revolution.

Source: Serena Turley, "The Pen Is Mightier: An Interview with Poet/Activist Nellie Wong," in *G-Spot*, August 6, 2002.

SOURCES

Browning, Elizabeth Barrett, *Sonnets from the Portuguese*, Riccardi, 1914, p. 26.

Cisneros, Sandra, "Loose Woman," in *Loose Woman*, Alfred A. Knopf, 1994, pp. 112–15.

Epictetus, *The Handbook*, translated by Nicholas P. White, Hackett, 1983, pp. 11–12.

Fong, Timothy W., and John Tsuang, "Asian-Americans, Addictions, and Barriers to Treatment," in *Psychiatry*, Vol. 4, No. 11, 2007, pp. 51–59.

Gilbert, Sandra, and Susan Gubar, *The Madwoman in the Attic: The Woman Writer and the Nineteenth-Century Literary Imagination*, 2nd edition, Yale University Press, 2000, pp. xv–xlv.

Jeong, Young Sook, "Daughtering Asian American Women's Literature in Maxine Hong Kingston, Nellie Wong, and Ronyoung Kim," PhD diss., Indiana University of Pennsylvania, 2006, pp. 34, 98, https://books.google.com/books?id = hUAAHFRnKhoC&source = gbs_nav links_s (accessed May 18, 2016).

Theweleit, Klaus, *Male Fantasies, Volume 1: Women, Floods, Bodies, History*, translated by Stephen Conway in collaboration with Erica Carter and Chris Turner, University of Minnesota Press, 1987, pp. 79–99.

Wagner-Martin, Linda, and Cathy N. Davidson, eds., "Contemporary Poetry," in *The Oxford Book of Women's Writing in the United States*, Oxford University Press, 1995, p. 291.

Wong, Nellie, "When I Was Growing Up," in *The Oxford Book of Women's Writing in the United States*, edited by Linda Wagner-Martin and Cathy N. Davidson, Oxford University Press, 1995, pp. 294–96.

Yee, Vivian, "Grouping Students by Ability Regains Favor in Classroom," in *New York Times*, June 9, 2013, http://www.nytimes.com/2013/06/10/education/grouping-students-by-ability-regains-favor-with-educators.html (accessed May 16, 2016).

FURTHER READING

Chang, Iris, *The Chinese in America: A Narrative History*, Penguin, 2004.
> Chang presents an introductory historical account of the American Chinese community from its beginnings more than 150 years ago until the turn of the millennium.

Crisman, Robert, Stephen Durham, Monica Hill, and Merle Woo, *Permanent Revolution in the U. S. Today*, Red Letter, 2003.
> This pamphlet is the manifesto of the Freedom Socialist party and envisions an imminent worldwide Trotskyist revolution that must begin in the United States as the most advanced industrial nation.

Gillis, Stacy, Gillian Howie, and Rebecca Munford, eds., *Third Wave Feminism: A Critical Exploration*, Palgrave Macmillan, 2007.
> This volume is an annotated collection of sources illustrating the history of third-wave feminism and interviews with leading feminists.

Wong, Nellie, *The Death of Long Steam Lady*, West End Press, 1986.
> This is Wong's second collection of poetry. In it, she deals with subjects related to feminism and socialism.

SUGGESTED SEARCH TERMS

Nellie Wong

"When I Was Growing Up"

third-wave feminism

racism AND Chinese Americans

Trotskyist-Leninist

coming of age AND Asian American AND literature

Chinatown

Asian American poets

Yellow Light

GARRETT HONGO
1982

In an interview published in *Because You Asked: A Book of Answers on the Art & Craft of the Writing Life*, poet Garrett Hongo explains that he is "constantly inspired by the great works of literature not to give in, to find inspiration in the humble regions of my own memory" and in the "commonplaces of mild existence." He continues, "I write from lost places, neighborhoods I have been taken away from I feel a need to return to." Hongo's poem "Yellow Light," which first appeared in his 1982 collection of the same name, is a perfect example of this drive to revisit "lost places" in his memory. The poem shows a simple scene: a woman—some critics assume she is the poet's mother—returns home on the city bus with her arms full of groceries and climbs up the steps to her home under the yellow light of the moon. What makes the poem remarkable is the vivid, revealing details Hongo includes, which bring to life a moment in an evening in the Japantown of his youth.

AUTHOR BIOGRAPHY

Hongo was born in Volcano, Hawaii, on May 30, 1951. In the Japanese American community, he is called *yonsei*, a fourth generation Japanese American, and he grew up speaking Japanese as well as English. Being a fourth-generation Japanese American, he grew up speaking Japanese as

The hiss of bus brakes adds atmosphere to the urban setting *(©Juanan Barros Moreno | Shutterstock.com)*

well as English. His family lived on the island of Oahu in Hawaii until he was six, when they moved to California, near Los Angeles. He struggled to adjust to the urban environment after the relaxed pace of life in Hawaii.

Hongo wrote his first poetry at age eighteen: love poems to his girlfriend. She was European American, and they felt they had to hide their feelings for each other. The poems were a way to privately honor their relationship. When he enrolled in Pomona College in Claremont, California, he began to study poetry more seriously, reading voraciously, attending poetry readings, and working with generous mentors to create his own work. Hongo graduated with honors in 1973.

After college, Hongo spent a year in Japan. While he traveled, exploring his heritage, he continued to write poetry. When he returned to the United States, he started graduate school, taking classes in Japanese language and literature at the University of Michigan. He then taught in Seattle for a few years before continuing his graduate studies at the University of California at Irvine, earning a master of fine arts degree in 1980. His

first poetry collection, *Yellow Light*, which includes the poem of the same title, was published in 1982.

Though he began taking courses toward his doctorate in critical theory, he left school in 1984 before earning his degree. He took a teaching position and got married. He and his wife started a family, and he continued writing poetry. He published two more collections: *The River of Heaven* (1988) and *Coral Road: Poems* (2011). Hongo held several teaching positions at universities around the country before settling at the University of Oregon in Eugene, where he is a Distinguished Professor of the College of Arts and Sciences and a professor of creative writing. From 1989 to 1993, he also was the director of the university's creative writing program. As of 2016, Hongo still lives in Eugene.

In addition to being nominated for a Pulitzer Prize, Hongo has received many awards, including fellowships from the National Endowment for the Arts, the Guggenheim Foundation, and the Rockefeller Foundation. He has also edited several acclaimed literary anthologies and wrote a memoir: *Volcano: A Memoir of Hawai'i* (1995).

POEM TEXT

One arm hooked around the frayed strap
of a tar-black patent-leather purse,
the other cradling something for dinner:
fresh bunches of spinach from a J-Town *yaoya*,
sides of split Spanish mackerel from Alviso's,   5
maybe a loaf of Langendorf; she steps
off the hissing bus at Olympic and Fig,
begins the three-block climb up the hill,
passing gangs of schoolboys playing war,
Japs against Japs, Chicanas chalking sidewalks   10
with the holy double-yoked crosses of hopscotch,
and the Korean grocer's wife out for a stroll
around this neighborhood of Hawaiian
          apartments
just starting to steam with cooking
and the anger of young couples coming home   15
from work, yelling at kids, flicking on
TV sets for the Wednesday Night Fights.

If it were May, hydrangeas and jacaranda
flowers in the streetside trees would be
blooming through the smog of late spring.   20
Wisteria in Masuda's front yard would be
shaking out the long tresses of its purple hair.
Maybe mosquitoes, moths, a few orange
          butterflies
settling on the lattice of monkey flowers
tangled in chain-link fences by the trash.   25

But this is October, and Los Angeles
seethes like a billboard under twilight.
From used-car lots and the movie houses
          uptown,
long silver sticks of tight probe the sky.
From the Miracle Mile, whole freeways away,   30
a brilliant fluorescence breaks out
and makes war with the dim squares
of yellow kitchen light winking on
in all the side streets of the Barrio.

She climbs up the two flights of flagstone   35
stairs to 201-B, the spikes of her high heels
clicking like kitchen knives on a cutting board,
props the groceries against the door,
fishes through memo pads, a compact,
empty packs of chewing gum, and finds her keys.   40

The moon then, cruising from behind
a screen of eucalyptus across the street,
covers everything, everything in sight,
in a heavy light like yellow onions.

POEM SUMMARY

The text used for this summary is from *Yellow Light*, Wesleyan University Press, 1982, pp. 11–12. A version of the poem can be found on the following web page: http://workingclasspoems.blogspot.com/2009/03/yellow-light.html.

Stanza 1

The poem opens with a description of a woman carrying an old black purse with an unraveling strap. She is also carrying ingredients for her family's supper: spinach, a loaf of bread, and a fresh fish. The produce comes from a *yaoya*, which is the Japanese word for "greengrocer." This, along with the term *J-Town*, for "Japantown," makes it clear that the woman lives in that specific neighborhood of her city and is likely Japanese American herself. She returns from her errands, riding the municipal bus, and walks up the hill from the bus stop. As she walks, she passes children playing: young Japanese American boys pretending to fight a war and young Mexican American girls drawing hopscotch patterns on the pavement. It is early evening when people are arriving home after a day at work, preparing their dinners, and settling in front of their televisions.

Stanza 2

The second stanza imagines what the neighborhood would look like if it were spring. Flowers would be thriving in the trees along the street and in the neighbors' yards. Insects would be drawn to the blooms. Lines 24 and 25 contrast the images of the beautiful, lush flowering plants with a utilitarian fence and the area where residents leave their trash.

Stanza 3

Stanza 3 makes it clear that it is not spring. Instead, it is October—early autumn. Instead of a riot of color from flowers, the city of Los Angeles is decorated only with artificial lights of all kinds. Searchlights at car dealerships and theaters are compared to metal rods prodding the air. The fluorescent lights of the Miracle Mile, a busy part of the city with stores, offices, museums, and lots of traffic, compete with the warm lights in the homes in the barrio (a Hispanic neighborhood).

Stanza 4

The woman nears home. As she mounts the stairs to her apartment, her high-heeled shoes strike the stone steps, making a sound like a knife hitting a cutting board. She rests her purchases on the ground while she searches among the odds and ends in her purse for her keys.

TOPICS FOR FURTHER STUDY

- Read a few of the stories in the young-adult collection *First Crossing: Stories about Teen Immigrants* (2004). Think about which protagonist interests you most, whether because you identify with that character's experiences or because his or her life is completely different from your own. Then imagine the scenes that this character sees every day. Write a poem from your chosen character's point of view, imitating the style Hongo uses in "Yellow Light," in which detailed images are more important than action and the vivid details create the mood.

- "Yellow Light" is set in Japantown in Los Angeles. Using print and online resources, research that neighborhood and others like it in cities across the United States. Think about why immigrants settle in certain neighborhoods. Do you think it is a good idea for immigrants to remain in such areas, where they can be among comforting, familiar food, language, and culture? Or do you believe immigrants should assimilate into mainstream culture as much as possible?

Work with a small group of classmates to stage a debate on this topic.

- Light is a common theme and image in poetry. It often represents truth or purity, but not always. Working with a partner or a small group, develop a website that gathers poems in which light is a central element. With each poem, include a brief biography of the poet and an explanation of how that particular poem uses light to enhance its message.

- Read several other poems by Hongo, perhaps "I Got Heaven . . ." (https://www.poets.org/poetsorg/poem/i-got-heaven), "The Legend" (http://www.poetryoutloud.org/poem/178868), or "What For" (http://www.poemhunter.com/poem/what-for-11/). Think about Hongo's style as you read. How does he use structural elements, such as line breaks, punctuation, and stanzas, to enhance the meaning of his poems? Select one poem to compare to "Yellow Light" and write an essay that analyzes the structure and other formal elements of the poems.

Stanza 5

The moon emerges from behind a nearby group of eucalyptus trees, bright enough to overtake the other, artificial lights in the neighborhood. The moon's light is also yellow, leading the poet to compare it to the color of onions.

THEMES

Immigrant Life

Much of Hongo's work draws on his own experiences and those of his friends and family as Asian Americans. Although Hongo himself is a fourth-generation American, his family maintained close ties with their heritage and lived in a predominantly Japanese

American neighborhood in Los Angeles for much of his youth. In "Yellow Light," Hongo offers many images of life in an immigrant community. For example, the woman buys her produce at a *yaoya*, a Japanese greengrocer. Though people may settle in neighborhoods with people from their home country, they also mix with people of differing backgrounds. This is reflected in "Yellow Light" when the Japanese American boys play war next to Mexican American girls playing hopscotch. Also, as the woman walks home from the bus stop, she passes the wife of the local Korean grocer. Though the evening seems peaceful, the poem hints at the cultural conflicts that can arise between groups. The "gangs" of boys pretending to fight in a war have the potential to erupt into real violence, and bright fluorescent light of the "Miracle

Artificial light from signs and kitchen windows brighten the night (©Take Photo | Shutterstock.com)

Mile," a prosperous Los Angeles neighborhood, "makes war" with the warm, homey light from the kitchens in the Hispanic neighborhood, suggesting possible class conflict.

Urban Life

The poem is filled with details of life in an urban neighborhood. Rather than buying her food at a huge supermarket, as is common in the suburbs, the woman makes her purchases at smaller stores—produce at one shop and fish at another. She rides a bus while running her errands because in the city owning a car is less practical and more expensive than using public transportation. In the spring, the neighbors have blooming flowers to enjoy, showing that they have tried to beautify their new homes. However, the poem reveals the parts that are not beautiful. All around are hard surfaces: the pavement, the freeways, the flagstone steps leading to her apartment, and the chain-link fence. Artificial light illuminates the sky. Also, the flowering plants climb the fencing near the garbage; in a large suburban yard, people likely find it easier to

hide their trash cans away from their gardens. The tight quarters of urban life are also highlighted by the phrasing in lines 14–17, in which the area begins to "steam" not only with the heat of cooking but also with the "anger" of the people who live there. It is easier for tempers to flare when people live in crowded conditions, which is reinforced in the poem by parents scolding their children and people watching fights on television for entertainment.

Light and Darkness

The poem's title is a clue to the reader that light is an important element. There are also images of darkness, such as the night sky and the exterior of the woman's "tar-black" pocketbook, as well as the interior of the purse, where the woman has to search for her keys. However, the images of light are more prominent, threading throughout the stanzas. As evening falls, the darkness is banished by multiple light sources: the flickering televisions, searchlights from uptown businesses, warm light from family kitchens, and finally the rising moon. In poetry, light often represents truth. Here, Hongo seems to use the light to illuminate the meticulous details in his description of the woman and her neighborhood—it is true in being true to life rather than tackling truth as an abstract concept.

Nature

Although the poem is set in an urban neighborhood, elements of nature shine through, in spite of the "smog." In stanza 2, the natural images are particularly evident. The flowers come out on the trees, and the butterflies gather in spite of the nearby trash. The structure of the phrasing in this stanza also highlights the uncontrollable temperament of nature: it is suggested to be "blooming" and "shaking" out its flowers like long hair. As Hongo portrays nature bursting out in the urban environment, it reflects the vibrancy of life in the neighborhood. Even the sight of children playing in stanza 1 seems a natural image, because all children engage in play, all over the world—it is their natural state. In the final stanza comes another strong symbol of nature: the moon. Just as the moon rises and sets, waxes and wanes, so does life in the neighborhood—even in a city—run in cycles.

STYLE

Imagery

Critics often praise the images Hongo creates in his poems. He uses concrete images, portrayed in vivid and specific detail. This style of poetry aligns Hongo with the imagist movement in poetry, which favored precise visual images and precise, everyday language. This school of poetry was a direct reaction against the abstract, verbose style popular in the nineteenth century. Poet William Carlos Williams famously summed up the philosophy of the imagists in his 1927 poem *Paterson*: "No ideas but in things." It is not that these poets did not think about emotions and abstract concepts; they simply used their images to evoke emotion and thought in the reader rather than directly discussing them. As Samuel Maio writes in his essay "On Garret Hongo's Poetry" in analyzing "Yellow Light," "The combination of lyrical description with the narrative is representative of Hongo's technique. The plain language and unsheathed images contain, within the control of the voice, the emotions this scene evokes for the speaker."

Proselike Language

Many modern poems use short phrases or have lines that contain only a single word. Hongo's poems, however, often use complete sentences with standard punctuation, as can be seen in "Yellow Light." The long descriptive sentences allow the poet to create his meticulously detailed images. Upon reading or hearing a poem like this for the first time, it might seem to be prose. The stanzas even divide the whole into separate ideas, much like paragraphs in prose. Therefore a reader might wonder why Hongo chose to publish this work as a poem rather than a prose description of the scene. Even though Hongo sometimes includes complete sentences in his poems, he also uses some of the elements of poetry. For example, he strategically plans line breaks to stress certain words, such as in stanza 2 of "Yellow Light." Lines 20, 22, and 24 all begin with words ending in *-ing*, which makes the natural growth in May seem to come to life, with each line bursting out as yet another example of the energy of flowers and insects in the spring. Although "Yellow Light" is a narrative poem of a sort, in that it describes the woman as she comes home from her errands and climbs the steps to her apartment, it is not truly a story. Indeed, nothing much happens. Rather than a prose narrative, "Yellow Light" is a series of images better suited to a poem than a prose piece.

HISTORICAL CONTEXT

Little Tokyo: Los Angeles' Japantown

Japantown in Los Angeles, where "Yellow Light" is set, is often called Little Tokyo. The neighborhood traces its origins back to 1886, when former seaman Charles Kame opened a Japanese restaurant on East First Street. A small community of Japanese immigrants had gathered in the area by the turn of the century, and the population grew more when approximately two thousand workers for the Pacific Electric Railway settled there. The 1906 San Francisco earthquake led to racial tensions in the city that chased many Japanese Americans to Los Angeles, further swelling the population, and many of the young male immigrants began to arrange marriages, bringing their brides from Japan and starting families. Agriculture was a common means of earning a living among the immigrants, and several produce markets were

COMPARE
&
CONTRAST

- **1980s:** Over the last two decades, Los Angeles County has become more diverse. Though the county's population in 1960 was 80 percent white, by the close of the 1980s, whites make up only about 40 percent of Los Angeles County residents, while the numbers of Asian and Hispanic/Latino residents have increased greatly (approximately 10 and 38 percent, respectively).

  Today: The population of Los Angeles County continues to diversify. According to the 2010 census, less than 28 percent of county residents are white, and almost half are Hispanic/Latino. Immigration from Asia has increased the Asian population (now almost 14 percent), with the Filipino, Chinese, Korean, and Japanese communities growing rapidly.

- **1980s:** Although there are a few prominent Asian American authors in the first two-thirds of the twentieth century, they are not the subject of serious study by the literary community. After the publication of *The Big Aiiieeeee! An Anthology of Asian-American Writers* in 1974, more attention is paid to Asian American writers by both critics and readers. The 1980s see a blossoming in the works of Asian American women, such as Maxine Hong Kingston and Amy Tan. However, Frank Chin, one of the editors of *The Big Aiiieeeee!*, openly criticizes some of these authors, particularly Kingston, for portraying a Westernized view of Asian culture and reinforcing stereotypes about

  Asian Americans by not standing up to racist assumptions.

  Today: The field of Asian American literature continues to expand. Long-time favorite authors like Kingston and Tan still publish and are joined by new writers, including Chang-rae Lee, Viet Thanh Nguyen, Jhumpa Lahiri, Bharati Mukherjee, Celeste Ng, and many others. Many Asian American authors do not like to be categorized as such, preferring to be thought of simply as "American authors" rather than being defined and judged by their heritage rather than on literary merit.

- **1980s:** New low-wattage metal halide light bulbs are developed for household use, but most people continue to use incandescent bulbs because, though they are less energy efficient, they are cheaper to buy. High-pressure sodium bulbs are most commonly used for streetlights because of their energy efficiency, though many dislike the artificial appearance of the orange light they provide.

  Today: High-pressure sodium lights are still commonly used in urban areas across the United States. Technological developments in solar power allow for compact, efficient panels and rechargeable batteries, making solar-powered streetlights economically feasible. Solar streetlights are likely to use energy-efficient bulbs like low-pressure sodium bulbs, LEDs, or induction lights.

---

established near Little Tokyo where the local farmers could sell their wares. The residents of Little Tokyo also founded other businesses, as well as churches, hospitals, and community organizations.

The start of World War II was devastating for the Little Tokyo community. The attack on Pearl Harbor led many to question the loyalty of

Americans of Japanese descent. On February 19, 1942, President Franklin Roosevelt signed Executive Order 9066, which ordered over a hundred thousand Japanese Americans to be detained in internment camps. Despite the fact that many Japanese Americans enlisted in the military and used their knowledge of the Japanese language in the service of national intelligence, the

The sound of the woman's shoes on the pavement is compared to a knife striking a cutting board
(© Africa Studio / Shutterstock.com)

majority of Japanese Americans spent the war years in concentration camps in remote areas, forced to abandon their homes and jobs. Little Tokyo became a ghost town. Some houses and businesses were taken over by African Americans, and the neighborhood briefly became known as Bronzeville. After the war, many Japanese Americans returned to their homes in Little Tokyo, and most of the African American residents sought other neighborhoods.

In the 1950s and 1960s, Americans nationwide moved out of cities and bought houses in the suburbs. Japanese Americans were no exception, and the population of Little Tokyo decreased again. As older residential buildings were torn down to make way for the new Los Angeles Police Department headquarters and new businesses, local leaders were dismayed at the disappearing character of the neighborhood. In 1969, the Little Tokyo Community Development Advisory Committee was founded, and the following year saw the establishment of the Little Tokyo

Redevelopment Project. The Little Tokyo Historic District was placed on the National Register of Historic Places in 1986. The registered area includes about a dozen commercial buildings, the Union Church on San Pedro Street, and the Nishi Hongwangi Buddhist Temple at First and Central Streets, which now is home to the Japanese American National Museum. Today, Little Tokyo is more a commercial center and tourist attraction than a residential community, but new businesses, guided by the numerous community associations, make efforts to fit into the community not only with architectural embellishment but also by displaying a respect for the community and its values.

CRITICAL OVERVIEW

Critical reception of Hongo's work is overwhelmingly positive. A *World Literature Today* review of *Coral Road* describes the included poems as "powerful compositions." In a *Library Journal* review of the same collection, Sadiq Alkoriji compares Hongo to legendary American poet Walt Whitman, as have other critics. Alkoriji notes that "Hongo's lyricism echoes Whitman's, and his shaping of life experiences through poetic stories generates a tremendous feeling of intimacy." In a 1997 monograph on Hongo, Laurie Filipelli (quoted by Roy Osamu Kamada in *Asian-American Poets: A Bio-Bibliographical Critical Sourcebook*) also sees similarities between Hongo and his predecessors, highlighting "Hongo's increasing homage to the Romantics" in his attention to landscape and how it reflects the thoughts and emotions of the inner self. Filipelli makes clear that though he is influenced by great poets of the past, Hongo is not restricted by the poetic tradition. She concludes that he is "eclectic in his openness to other influences, both literary and nonliterary ... at once conservative and modern."

In a review of the collection *Yellow Light*, Diane Wakoski (quoted by Roy Osamu Kamada in *Asian-American Poets: A Bio-Bibliographical Critical Sourcebook*) compares him with some of her own favorite poets: Galway Kinnell, Denise Leverton, and Federico García Lorca. She raves about his talent, writing that "Hongo is astonishing" and describing the poem "Off from Swing Shift" as "the best poem I have seen on the American treatment of native Japanese during the Second World War because it is not really written about that subject." Here, Wakoski refers to Hongo's knack for using historical events to explain and expose prejudice and trauma in the present. Throughout his work, he draws from his own life as an Asian American, as well as the experiences of his family and community, to illuminate the immigrant experience as a whole.

Alkoriji explains how Hongo uses personal history and experience to great effect in his poems. Hongo "relies on narrative, with meaning emanating from the constant stream of places, colors, names, and anecdotes," Alkoriji writes. However, he is quick to add that "Hongo's lively images and fluid tone prevent the reportorial style from slipping into passive documentation, and his language embodies the local as a way of connecting with the vast outside world." Phoebe Pettingell, in a *New Leader* review of *The River of Heaven*, agrees that Hongo uses elements of the Asian American experience masterfully. "The exotic places he describes—seedy Chinatowns, Pacific ports with their international jumble of peoples and customs—might sound, in paraphrase, like backdrops for Mr. Moto or Charlie Chan," Pettingell notes. However, she asserts that "they are really nothing like that," explaining that his work portrays in vivid detail "what it feels like to grow up as the child of unassimilated immigrants, to be soaked with values incompatible with those of one's ancestors, yet not fully accepted by the new culture."

Hongo's memoir was received just as enthusiastically by critics as his poetry. In a review of *Volcano: A Memoir of Hawai'i*, Mark Jarman describes the book as "remarkable, profound, and haunting." In considering what it is that "makes this book more than a search for roots, more than another immigrant memoir," Jarman concludes that it is "the passion of the writing." *Los Angeles Times* writer Sigrid Nunez compares Hongo's memoir to *The Autobiography of William Butler Yeats* because she feels

> Hongo takes to heart Yeats's assertion ... that the poet who wishes to create a work that will last must first find metaphors in the natural landscape he was born to. This will give the reader some idea of the scope of Hongo's ambition.

CRITICISM

Kristen Sarlin Greenberg

Greenberg is a freelance writer and editor with a background in literature and philosophy. In the following essay, she examines the juxtaposition of natural and unnatural images in Hongo's "Yellow Light."

Poet Hongo is often praised by critics for the detailed images in his work. His attention to detail when he describes natural landscapes has earned comparisons with great poets like William Butler Yeats and Walt Whitman. The vivid details in his poem "Yellow Light" create an interesting juxtaposition between natural and unnatural images, and a careful analysis of these images illuminates the meaning of the poem.

The poem's first image is of the woman getting off the bus. She is clearly in a city, with the list of shops she has visited, the "hissing" brakes of the bus, and the street names. Even the pocketbook she carries is a manufactured thing. It is black like tar, and the fact that it is patent leather

"

WITH HONGO'S PRECISE, STRAIGHTFORWARD
LANGUAGE AND HIS VIVID DESCRIPTIONS, HE SHOWS
THAT BEAUTY AND SATISFACTION DO NOT HAVE TO BE
SOUGHT ONLY IN DRAMATIC NATURAL IMAGES LIKE
BEAMING MOONLIGHT OR GLORIOUS SPRING
FLOWERS. THEY CAN ALSO BE FOUND IN SIMPLE,
EVERYDAY ITEMS LIKE SPINACH LEAVES AND
YELLOW ONIONS."

means that it has an unnatural shine to it from being processed, taking it further away from its natural state. In contrast to this are the foods she carries. The greens she has bought are specifically described as "fresh," and the loaf of bread and the fish are also simple, wholesome sustenance. These basic food staples bring a hint of nature into the urban environment.

As the woman walks home, she passes groups of children playing, as children do everywhere, in every culture. Though perhaps hopscotch is a game played more often where there are sidewalks to draw on with chalk, the patterns might be traced in the dirt in the countryside, and certainly children fight pretend battles no matter where they live. The playfulness of the children also brings some of the energy of nature into the city, making it clear that even surrounded by pavement and buildings, life can be vibrant and lively.

Similarly, the evening activities of the neighborhood reflect the natural course of family life everywhere: preparing supper, tired parents bickering and scolding their children—an inevitable state of affairs when people live in close quarters. However, these natural human interactions are interrupted by the unnatural glow of the television. Rather than interact with each other, even if that interaction involves squabbling, they are watching televised fights.

One of the most striking juxtapositions of natural and unnatural elements in the poem appears in lines 23–25, especially coming after the profusion of spring growth described in the first part of stanza 2. The reader is likely

imagining the neighborhood bursting with colorful flowers, and in addition to this flood of new plant life, insects appear, including bright butterflies drawn by the blossoms. However, the butterflies alight on flowers growing in a fence, and the fence is not even an attractive, natural wood fence. Instead, the fencing is made of utilitarian—many would say ugly—chain link, and the fence is a barrier to an area where garbage is kept. The structure of the poem adds to the starkness of the image because the stanza begins with the jubilant description of spring flowers and ends with the word *trash*.

The following stanza distances the reader even more from the beautiful, natural image of the flowers, making it clear that the poem is set not in May, as imagined in stanza 2, but October. It is not spring, when the natural world reawakens, but fall, when many plants die or slow their growth before winter. Whereas stanza 2 mostly contained natural images, stanza 3 mostly describes unnatural things. Perhaps the one word that suggests nature is *twilight*. It is a poetic sort of word to describe the time between day and night, having an almost magical connotation. However, the descriptions surrounding the word are unnatural and jarring. The surrounding city is compared to a "billboard," a commercial advertisement that is designed to catch the eyes of potential customers. The city is also filled with light.

Indeed, light is an essential element of the poem, as the title suggests. At first, all of the light mentioned is artificial: the searchlights from car dealerships and movie theaters, the fluorescent lights from busy shopping and business areas, and the headlights of the cars on the freeways. In the last few lines of the third stanza, however, Hongo introduces a different kind of light—a homey, warm light from kitchens in the barrio. In contrast with the garish light of the businesses, the kitchen light evokes a feeling of familiarity and comfort in the reader. Though this light is electric and therefore artificial, it is clearly set apart from the other light in the city from business and traffic, which "makes war" with the kitchen light. This choice of words echoes the gangs of children playing in the first stanza, but, more important, it highlights the juxtaposition between the two kinds of light: one anonymous and commercial and the other warm and inviting.

WHAT DO I READ NEXT?

- Hongo's work often highlights various aspects, both good and bad, of the immigrant experience. The poems collected in *Island: Poetry and History of Chinese Immigrants on Angel Island, 1910–1940* (1991) show how new arrivals to America's shores were not always greeted with open arms. Angel Island sits in San Francisco Bay and is sometimes called the "Ellis Island of the West." Between 1910 and 1940, when the Chinese Exclusion Act prevented many immigrants from finding a new home in the United States, thousands of hopeful immigrants were detained on Angel Island. Some were held there for weeks or even months, and many were deported back to China. This volume documents the poems that were written or carved in the walls of the barracks, reflecting the humiliation, frustration, and desperation felt by the island's inmates.

- In addition to his poetry, Hongo wrote a memoir focusing on his childhood titled *Volcano: A Memoir of Hawai'i* (1995). Critics praise the book's intense focus on the landscape around him and the vivid descriptions.

- Hongo's relationship with the landscape, as described in his memoir, led some critics to compare his sensibility to that of William Butler Yeats, who is widely considered to be one of the greatest poets of the twentieth century. Editor Robert Mighall gathers many of Yeats's best-known works in the Collector's Library volume *Collected Poems* (2013).

- In her 1999 young-adult novel *Name Me Nobody*, Lois-Ann Yamanaka explores the themes of family, friendship, and identity. Yamanaka's style is unique, heavily influenced by the rhythms of Hawaiian dialect. The novel's protagonist is thirteen-year-old Emi-Lou, who is being raised by her grandmother after her mother ran away from their Hawaii home to California. Overweight Emi-Lou is teased mercilessly by her classmates— even other Japanese American girls— because of how she looks. She also struggles to accept her friend Von's lesbian relationship with a girl on their softball team.

- Editor Victoria Change provides a broad sampling of works in *Asian American Poetry: The Next Generation* (2004). Both well-known poets and new voices are featured.

- Hongo's third collection, *Coral Road: Poems* (2011), is centered on his Japanese American family and their experiences making a new home in Hawaii.

- Critic Diane Wakoski compares Hongo's work with that of Spanish poet and playwright Federico García Lorca. In the volume *Collected Poems* (1991), published by Farrar, Straus and Giroux, editor Christopher Maurer gathers several of García Lorca's most important works, including both the original Spanish and the English translations.

The reader may at first assume that this warm kitchen light is the "Yellow Light" of the poem's title, and certainly Hongo, a poet who is always precise with his language and references, would not allow such an association to stand unintentionally. Yet the end of the poem introduces another light source that becomes even more important than the homey light mentioned in line 33: the moon.

Before Hongo introduces the moon in the final stanza, he again lists a series of unnatural things in the fourth stanza to continue the alternating natural and unnatural images. The woman walks on flagstone, a natural material that has been placed in an unnatural position: the man-made staircases of an apartment complex. Then she must sift though the detritus in her purse, all of which are modern, somewhat unnatural items: notepads, face powder, and gum packages. Finally, in sharp contrast to this urban, unnatural description, the final stanza describes the moon rising from behind a group of eucalyptus trees.

The moon is a completely natural image. Therefore its light is the most pure, and the penultimate line of the poem stresses its power. The repetition of the word *everything* makes clear that all aspects of the landscape are under the blanket of the moon's light; nothing can compete with it. All other light becomes insignificant, swallowed up by the brightness of the moonlight. Surely the bright moonlight gave the poem its title.

However, the poem's final line introduces a puzzling bit of figurative language. The moon is a powerful natural symbol and the subject of countless poems for its beauty and mystery. Yet here Hongo compares its light to common yellow onions. It is hardly an elegant image. Onions are infamous for their strong smell, and yellow onions are a particular unexciting and inexpensive variety. They are undeniably natural, but why does Hongo choose to link the moon with an everyday onion?

Hongo's choice for the final image of the poem fits with his practice of portraying the details of life in his poems. There is much in life that is common, but an item does not have to be rare to be important. The inexpensive yellow onion, for instance, is used to flavor many basic recipes in many cultures all around the globe. The comparison of the moon to a common food staple also brings the poem full circle, back to the simple ingredients brought home by the woman to her apartment. This circling back to the first lines of the poem also echoes the cycle of life, like the phases of the moon.

With Hongo's precise, straightforward language and his vivid descriptions, he shows that beauty and satisfaction do not have to be sought only in dramatic natural images like beaming moonlight or glorious spring flowers. They can also be found in simple, everyday items like spinach leaves and yellow onions. Hongo blends images of the natural and the unnatural—the positive and the negative—to display the richness of life. We can live our lives, enjoy our families—even while bickering with them—and have some beauty in spite of inescapable negative things in life. Humans are natural creatures under our modern trappings, and like the light of

When the moon rises, it makes all other light seem insignificant (©Joseph Sohm / Shutterstock.com)

the moon overtaking the dimmer, unnatural lights in a city, nature is stronger than manmade things. The moon has no light of its own. It only reflects the light of the sun. In "Yellow Light," Hongo suggests that perhaps we must live in the unnatural environments of cities and perhaps we must accept that there will be ugliness because of the necessities of life, but we can be like the moon, reflecting something greater and brighter.

Source: Kristen Sarlin Greenberg, Critical Essay on "Yellow Light," in *Poetry for Students*, Gale, Cengage Learning, 2017.

Garrett Hongo

In the following interview, Hongo talks about what inspires him.

What is it that you write from? What are your inspirations?

I constantly find myself having to counteract what pop and postmodern culture provides me as scenic and narrative identities, backdrops for the play of consciousness, yet these manufactured things have the appeal of mass (mis)recognition, visual referents others can attach to a story I'm telling, in prose or poetry, about the past and its places. And I am likewise constantly inspired by the great works of literature not to give in, to find inspiration in the humble regions of my own memory, in a homebound ethicality, in the sere commonplaces of mild existence. I have *Walden* as our American version of the great Japanese *eremitic zuihitsu* (poetic essay) tradition practiced by Kamo-no-Chomei, Yoshida Kenko, and Matsuo Basho. And I know that, like them, I write from lost places, neighborhoods I have been taken away from I feel a need to return to.

I write from Kahuku, the plantation village on Oàhu in Hawaiì where I grew up as a child, remembering its Buddhist temple, tofu makers, rows of shotguns, and sandy village square, remembering the fields of sugar cane, the tractors and trailers hauling burned and cut cane down the Kamehameha Highway to the smoking mill at the center of everything. I write from the rocky beaches and sandy promontories where the separate graveyards were for Filipino, Chinese, and Japanese workers. I write from the blossoming plumeria trees, from the ironwoods by the beaches, and my memory of street vendor calls and my grandfather singing in Hawaiian and Japanese as he washed dishes for his roadside café. I write from this world I left at the age of six, returned to when I was ten, that was lost to everyone as a re-capitalized Hawaiì turned itself away from sugar to embrace tourism.

I write from the small tract home my parents bought for us in Gardena, near Los Angeles, its symmetrical grid of suburban streets, its corner gas stations and liquor stores, the barbed wire around my high school, the razor wire around wrecking yards and auto shops, the tiny

Japanese *okazuyas* and gaudy poker parlors, the rat-nests of palm trees, and the long, cooling, fog-banked and wind-tunneled seaward-bound road at the center of town. I write from my memories of all us in high school—black kids bused in from Compton, Chicanos from "The Tracks" near Gardena Boulevard, and we Buddhaheads from all over town, worried about dress and the latest dances, worried about cool and avoiding addiction to glue and Robitussin even as we hoped we were college bound. I write about the summer evening Festival for the Dead at Gardena Hongwanji and the intimate spaces for dinnertime cooking my mother and grandmother made, my father watching football and boxing on the TV, exhausted after work and stymied by his social isolation. I write from people who work and want better for themselves and their children.

And I write from what was an intellectual native ground—my years away at Pomona College, where I studied literature, languages, and philosophy and was allowed to develop my deep love for learning and reflection. I found "the better nature" of literary practice there, sponsored in my soul a feel for the finish of language, the finer tone of contemplative emotions. What was better than reading Keats and Kawabata in the mornings, hearing a lecture on jazz operas and *Moby Dick* by the fiery and signifying Stanley Crouch, browsing through the home library of the poet Bert Meyers, and listening to him hold forth on the Spanish civil war and the last poems of Miguel Hernandez? What was better than reading *A Primer of Tu Fu* late at night, having a cup of Burgundy, and practicing ideograms until I fell asleep over the smearing ink on the soft, absorbent pages of my copybook? A rhyme from Yeats runs through my head as I walk across the yellowing grass of the college soccer field. In the distance, I see the moon ascend over a snow-streaked Mt. Baldy, and I feel a studious complacency rousing into passion in the late Spring twilight.

Volcano, the little village where I was born on the island of Hawaiì, is, finally, the first lost neighborhood of my soul. I did not grow up there in that preternatural rainforest and sublime volcanic landscape, but I moved back many times these last years, writing from the ache of my love for that place. It exceeds all the praise and lyric description I can muster

Poet, take nothing from this world but awe and a longing to return to the magnificent beginnings of first things.

How did you come to write your last book, Coral Road?

I wrote *Coral Road* as an homage to my mother's side of my family, the Shigemitsu and Kubota who worked as contract laborers on the North Shore of Oàhu in Hawaiì during the early part of the 20th century, after arriving there as immigrants from southern Japan. They were a tough, stoical lot, marrying themselves to tough lives on land they occupied for three generations, rootlessly, as the land was never theirs and could never be. They were there for reasons of history and diaspora—the land belonging to capitalism or the lost Kingdom of Hawaiì. What I have of our time there are fragments of stories, songs my grandparents sang washing dishes, a meager handful of documents and a few phrases in Hawaiian and Japanese, and the sparkle of the sea or on the tassels of sugar cane as I drive by whenever I take a survey of those old seaside lands along what is now Kamehameha Highway. I am not a native son nor prodigal one, consequently, but a kind of swallow who has lost his mud home on an island thought by so many to be a paradise.

The people in this book are the legends from my childhood—my grandmother who walked, as a twelve-year old and by night, twenty-five miles along coral roads and railroad tracks from Waialua Plantation to Kahuku so she could escape a bad labor contract, her path lit by the moon as she made her way in secret as a runaway; my uncles who fought for America in Europe during World War II, while a family elder was taken from Hawaiì and spent the war years in a DOJ detention center in Arizona; my father, who brought back from Italy and his time in military service an affection for Renaissance painting and American big band music. And I am there too—a fourth-generation American hankering for these lives to be known and celebrated, for the music of my language to sing of them.

The quick thing to say is that the book is about "heritage" where there is no legacy except love and memory.

With poems structured by long lines and narrative arcs, Coral Road *reads like an epic poem written in the classic tradition. The "ink-dark ocean" described at the end of "Pupukea Shell"* recalls the wine-dark sea of Homer's *Odyssey. The narrator of the title poem nods to Dante's* Inferno *when he asks, "Where is the Virgil who might lead me through the shallow underworld of this history?" How do you see these poems—and their culturally diverse, dislocated characters longing to define their histories and traditions—in relation to their European predecessors?*

First of all, it is not only in relation to European predecessors that the characters define themselves. There are homegrown traditions too—Blind-Boy Lilikoi harkens back to the *chang-a-lang* bar music Puerto Ricans brought to Hawaii, the *shamisen* that Japanese brought, the slack-key and slide guitar styles that emerged from the islands perhaps out of these and other legacies in music. Fresco in "The Art of Fresco" learns Native Hawaiian traditions from Moana and invokes Hawaiian mythology in "Soul's-Leap" as well as passages from Robert Frost's "Directive." In my own voice, I invoke Wang Wei in "Kawela Studies" as well as Emerson. Finally, I've myself learned as much from Japanese poetry and drama as anything in Western literature, having studied the New Zealand theater and classical Japanese poetry in Japan, and as a graduate student at Michigan.

But, I also locate tradition in European literature and music—that's very correct. Kubota writes to Miguel Hernández, Nazim Hikmet, and Tadeusz Rózewicz—a Spaniard, a Turk, and a Pole—as well as Pablo Neruda and Charles Olson, both "Americans," one South and the other North. The plot of "Pupukea Shell" derives from a scene in Giacamo Puccini's opera *La bohème* and the poetry of Virgil (his *Eclogues*), Theocritus (*Idylls*), and Dante (*Divina Commedia*) were much on my mind as I wrote *Coral Road*. As was Derek Walcott's poetry, as a matter of fact. What this poetry does for me is give me inspiration and a kind of roadmap for working on a subject that has *not* been written about—the immigrant history of Japanese Americans in Hawaiì as a topic for a kind of foundational literature as are the works of Virgil, Neruda, Whitman, Walcott, and a few others. Neruda once said, in an interview with Robert Bly, I think, that South Americans have the project of having to write about landscape and flora never having been described before, that they are engaged in a kind of epic task, whereas Europeans and North Americans have had their lands, plants, animals, and even their societies well documented and described in an "advanced" literature. I feel my position a bit akin to Neruda's and his South Americans, as just about all of Japanese American history has not been written about in poetry, that much of the landscape of Hawaiì has not been described except in bullshit tourist brochures and ad copy terms. Furthermore, what faced Theocritus at the beginning of the *Idylls* is something I see too—an archive from a regional, largely oral tradition; a sense his native dialect and identity (he was from Syracusa) were marginalized and undervalued in metropolitan Alexandria; and a wish to celebrate a world perhaps already gone as he wrote about it. My bucolics are derived from him and from Virgil, who described the rural Umbrian landscape and its workers upon it. Wordsworth wrote so too in *The Prelude*, that, in his youth, he chanced to see the beauty in lives battered mainly by necessity and subsistence. With Walcott, I see a forerunner who brought together a love for the traditions of English poetry with his own powers to describe, document, and sing of his own island lands and people.

What I mean to say in these allusions, derivations, claims, and displays of poetic legacy is that all of it is ours to inherit, that nothing isn't our literary legacy, that even a Japanese American poet from Hawaiì can claim his voice part of a large matrix of traditional poetic culture—Western, local, and Eastern all at once. No one "locality" of identity or literature defines, but they all hybridize together as do the shards of pottery, grout, and stray shells from the sea make up the broken and then repaired Caribbean urn Walcott celebrates in his Nobel speech...

What are you thinking about nowadays?

I'm beginning to think about narration in terms of obliquity—that which slips through the major matrices of representation into the margins, that only seem to enter into story in odd symbolic compressions or awkwardly phrased angular meta-narratives seemingly off the point. I'm thinking of micro-histories and repressed narrations and how they are debased and condensed into an arcana of symbols by the master narratives of culture.

N. Scott Momaday's *The Way to Rainy Mountain* is my example of how micro-narrative breaks out of these confinements. Told partly in

memoir, partly in poetry, partly in myth and fragments of history and lore gathered in a personal quest for a foundational story, this book has fascinated me for over thirty years now.

It is a kind of story that is anti-typologically told, yet partakes of typological method in that it is sequenced, proposes narrative linkages in the silent spaces between its episodic "panels" of narration and exposition.

I'm looking also at *Sepharad* by Antonio Munoz Molina and, perhaps oddly, at *The English Patient* by Michael Ondaatje. Ron Slate's review of the new novel *Director's Cut* by Arthur Japin has caught my attention as well.

I'm uncertain where this thinking will lead—which is why I'm intrigued. There isn't a formula or an answer I'm searching for. There isn't a storyline.

Source: Garrett Hongo, "Garrett Hongo," in *Because You Asked: A Book of Answers on the Art & Craft of the Writing Life*, edited by Katrina Roberts, Lost Horse Press, 2015, pp. 359–65.

Samuel Maio

In the following excerpt, Maio characterizes Hongo as a confessional poet.

Other younger poets who continue to employ the confessional mode of voice, however, do not necessarily write such proselike lines as Weigl does. These poets are, as suggested earlier, more concerned with sound and rhythms. Garrett Hongo, for example, has used in his two books—*Yellow Light* (1982) and *The River of Heaven* (1987)—the confessional voice in many poems that are less narrative and more reliant on images than are Weigl's poems. Perhaps, too, they are more given to sound. The principal concerns of *Yellow Light*, a book of carefully ordered poems, are: the discovery of the history of the Issei (the first generation of Japanese immigrants to America), the forging of myths regarding the Issei and succeeding families, and the ethnicity peculiar to the poet's ancestral beginning. Structured in five movements, the poems' central speaker travels through his home neighborhoods, Japan, and America's western region. Engaged in searches that lead to the creation of myths and the recreation of ancient ones, these poems ultimately record the process by which the speaker learns to understand the importance of the immediate.

ENGAGED IN SEARCHES THAT LEAD TO THE
CREATION OF MYTHS AND THE RECREATION OF
ANCIENT ONES, THESE POEMS ULTIMATELY RECORD
THE PROCESS BY WHICH THE SPEAKER LEARNS TO
UNDERSTAND THE IMPORTANCE OF THE IMMEDIATE."

"Yellow Light," the opening poem, takes us to inner-city Los Angeles, the setting for the book's first movement, where a woman with groceries passes "gangs of schoolboys playing war" on her way home to cook dinner. This is what she sees:

> From the Miracle Mile, whole freeways away,
> a brilliant fluorescence breaks out
> and makes war with the dim squares
> of yellow kitchen light winking on
> in all the side streets of the Barrio....
> The moon then, cruising from behind
> a screen of eucalyptus across the street,
> covers everything, everything in sight,
> in a heavy light like yellow onions.

The combination of lyrical description with the narrative is representative of Hongo's technique. The plain language and unsheathed images contain, within the control of the voice, the emotions this scene evokes for the speaker remembering his mother's daily routine. Given the book's purpose of scheme, it is appropriate that the poems of this first movement address the speaker's early life and condition of home.

The subject of the nine-section poem "Cruising 99," marking the second movement of the book, is a pilgrimage toward the uncovering of the possibility for mythmaking. The voice, now detached from the personal memories of home and family, is relaxed, sometimes playful (as in "A Samba for Inada"), and is, finally, a voice seemingly of wonder, one caught in discovery. The poem begins with a "porphyry of elements," an "aggregate of experiences" of the speaker and two friends joy riding down the two-lane Highway 99. This porphyry (literally, a rock containing the minerals of two generations) comes to signify the primary theme of a collection of

poems that, in subject and craft, embodies differing elements of the old and present-day Orient.

In the section "On the Road to Paradise," the fourth part of "Cruising 99," the speaker suggests that he will be wishing continually for "paradise" because his conception of it must somehow include "landscapes / in brocades, mist, wine, and moonlight," like a poem by Tu Fu, all conjuring mystery and all missing from Highway 99 *en route* through the desert: ...

His desire to transcend the restrictions of place and past can be read metaphorically as the speaker's yearning to create poetic landscapes, mystery, and myth from the barrenness of the desert.

Although the actual journey leads nowhere, a commitment to the creation of myth is born. The book's third movement, then, takes the speaker to Japan, the origin of his personal history, to begin his search to recover, expiate, create, mythify, and learn why the past acts as a "skin of cement." As the conclusion of "Postcards for Bert Meyers," a prayer is proposed for the restoration of a heritage, as it was at an earlier time, uncorrupted by history and migration: ...

Yet in the next poem, another part of the speaker's culture is treated less seriously. A Japanese dinner is described with savor and it holds a peculiar importance for him that cannot be shared: ...

Coming in a sequence of poems about the significance of the speaker's experience in Japan, these lines suddenly change the tone of the book's middle movement. At a point where Hongo easily can begin to sentimentalize (as Lowell's confessional verse is often accused of doing) the older world's culture, or to state a bitterness towards an America for failing to embrace this culture in order to enrich its own, or to lament the loss of the past, he evaluates the beauty of a sensual pleasure with grace and with an aggressive, yet tonally light, voice.

Japan has given the speaker, now back in America, a base from which he can confront the meaning of his life in relation to his cultural origin, one of the subjects of the fourth movement of the book. In the poem "Roots," the resolution of self and past is equated to a spiritual enlightenment: ...

Far from the discolored moon "stained with nicotine" that repulses the speaker of "Cruising 99," the desert moon, rising "over the salt flats near Manzanar," is now seen with a beauty befitting a Chinese landscape in a Tu Fu poem. The porphyry, the blending of the old man with the speaker, emerges, and the poem ends in a comforting peace, somewhat closer to "paradise."

Myths for the present, arising from the past, must be written, as called for in the long poem "Stepchild." Interspersed with passages by Carlos Bulosan and others regarding the history of Japanese immigrants, . . .

The task defined, the speaker meets his responsibility in the last movement by creating stories about his childhood, the memories being summoned by looking at a photograph ("The Hongo Store 29 Miles Volcano Hilo, Hawaii"), about a failed labor strike attempt, written in haiku ("C&H Sugar Strike Kahuku, 1923"), about old men and friends ("Kubota" and "And Your Soul Shall Dance"), and, finally, about coming to peace with the history of personal experience and circumstance ("Something Whispered in the *Shakuhachi*"), . . .

Hongo utilizes the confessional voice as a means of personal discovery, much as Lowell did in *Life Studies*. The blending of the old man and the younger speaker (this "porphyry") is part of such a discovery.

Source: Samuel Maio, "Personal Poetry in the 1990s: Garrett Hongo," in *Creating Another Self: Voice in Modern American Personal Poetry*, Thomas Jefferson University Press, 1995, pp. 231–36.

SOURCES

Alkoriji, Sadiq, Review of *Coral Road: Poems*, in *Library Journal*, Vol. 136, No. 16, October 1, 2011, p. 82.

Allen, James P., and Eugene Turner, "Ethnic Change and Enclaves in Los Angeles," American Association of Geographers website, March 8, 2013, http://www.aag.org/cs/news_detail?pressrelease.id = 2058 (accessed May 15, 2016).

"Garrett Hongo," in *American Diversity, American Identity*, edited by John K. Roth, Henry Holt, 1995, pp. 595–98.

"Garrett Hongo," Poetry Foundation website, http://www.poetryfoundation.org/poems-and-poets/poets/detail/garrett-hongo (accessed May 9, 2016).

"History," Little Tokyo Community Council website, http://www.littletokyola.org/index.php?option = com_content&view = article&id = 34%3Ahistory&catid = 13%3Abasic-info&Itemid = 67&lang = en (accessed May 15, 2016).

"History of the Light Bulb," *Bulbs.com*, http://www.bulbs.com/learning/history.aspx (accessed May 15, 2016).

"History of Street Lights in the United States of America," *ISGLighting.com*, http://www.isglighting.com/files/History%20of%20Street%20Lights%20in%20the%20United%20States%20Of%20America.pdf (accessed May 15, 2016).

Hongo, Garrett Kaoru, "Yellow Light," in *Yellow Light*, Wesleyan University Press, 1982, pp. 11–12.

Jarman, Mark, Review of *Volcano: A Memoir of Hawai'i*, in *Southern Review*, Vol. 32, No. 2, Spring 1996, p. 337.

Kamada, Roy Osamu, "Garrett Hongo," in *Asian-American Poets: A Bio-Bibliographical Critical Sourcebook*, edited by Guiyou Huang and Emmanuel Sampath Nelson, Greenwood Press, 2002, pp. 139–40.

Maio, Samuel, "On Garret Hongo's Poetry," in *Modern American Poetry*, http://www.english.illinois.edu/maps/poets/g_l/hongo/about.htm (accessed May 15, 2016).

Nunez, Sigrid, "The Consolations of a Garlanded Isle: The Life of Poet Garrett Hongo," in *Los Angeles Times*, July 23, 1995, http://articles.latimes.com/1995-07-23/books/bk-26763_1_garrett-hongo (accessed May 9, 2016).

Pettingell, Phoebe, Review of *The River of Heaven*, in *New Leader*, Vol. 71, No. 10, June 13, 1988, p. 16.

"Racial/Ethnic Composition: Los Angeles County, 1990–2010 Census," Los Angeles Almanac website, http://www.laalmanac.com/population/po13.htm (accessed May 15, 2016).

Review of *Coral Road: Poems*, in *World Literature Today*, Vol. 86, No. 1, January–February 2012, p. 67.

Roberts, Katrina, "Garrett Hongo," in *Because You Asked: A Book of Answers on the Art & Craft of the Writing Life*, Lost Horse Press, 2015, p. 359.

Row, Jess, "*The Woman Warrior* at 30: Maxine Hong Kingston's Secrets and Lies," in *Slate*, March 27, 2007, http://www.slate.com/articles/news_and_politics/memoir_week/2007/03/the_woman_warrior_at_30.html (accessed May 15, 2016).

Several, Michael, *Little Tokyo: Historical Background*, January 1998, http://www.publicartinla.com/Downtown/Little_Tokyo/little_tokyo.html (accessed May 15, 2016).

"Solar Street Lights," Solar Power Beginner website, http://www.solarpowerbeginner.com/solar-street-lights.html (accessed May 15, 2016).

FURTHER READING

Bruchac, Joseph, ed., *Breaking Silence: An Anthology of Contemporary Asian-American Poets*, Greenfield Review Press, 1983.

In this groundbreaking anthology, Bruchac gathers the work of dozens of Asian American poets, including Hongo, Richard Oyama, Traise Yamamoto, Marilyn Mei Ling Chin, Cyn Zarco, Jeff Tagami, Nellie Wong, Arthur Sze, Gail N. Harada, Yuri Kageyama, Alan Chong Lau, and Dianne Hai-jew.

Fujimoto, Jack, *Sawtelle: West Los Angeles's Japantown*, Arcadia Publishing, 2007.
This volume offers a history of Japantown in Los Angeles—like the "J-Town" of Hongo's poem—complete with pictures and personal stories from residents.

Hongo, Garrett, *The River of Heaven*, Knopf, 1988.
This collection, Hongo's second, won the 1987 Lamont Poetry Prize of the Academy of American Poets. Hongo's elegant poems evoke the beauty of Hawaii and the grit of urban Los Angeles.

Kinnell, Galway, *When One Has Lived a Long Time Alone*, Knopf, 1990.
Critic Diane Wakoski compares Hongo's poems with those of Galway Kinnell, an American poet who has won both the Pulitzer Prize and the National Book Award and was also the Vermont state poet laureate from 1989 to 1993. When asked about literary influences, Kinnell cited Walt Whitman, to whom Hongo has also been compared. In this collection, Kinnell's work touches on themes of reconnecting with nature.

Whitman, Walt, *Leaves of Grass*, Wisehouse Classics, 2016.
Hongo's work is sometimes likened to that of nineteenth-century American poet Walt Whitman. This edition of Whitman's definitive work *Leaves of Grass* is a reproduction of the original 1855 version, for which the poet himself did much of the typesetting.

SUGGESTED SEARCH TERMS

Garrett Hongo

Garrett Hongo AND "Yellow Light"

Garrett Hongo AND literary criticism

Garrett Hongo AND awards

Issei AND Nisei AND Sansei AND Yonsei

poems about immigrant life

narrative poems

Asian American poets

Japantown

Glossary of Literary Terms

A

Abstract: Used as a noun, the term refers to a short summary or outline of a longer work. As an adjective applied to writing or literary works, abstract refers to words or phrases that name things not knowable through the five senses.

Accent: The emphasis or stress placed on a syllable in poetry. Traditional poetry commonly uses patterns of accented and unaccented syllables (known as feet) that create distinct rhythms. Much modern poetry uses less formal arrangements that create a sense of freedom and spontaneity.

Aestheticism: A literary and artistic movement of the nineteenth century. Followers of the movement believed that art should not be mixed with social, political, or moral teaching. The statement "art for art's sake" is a good summary of aestheticism. The movement had its roots in France, but it gained widespread importance in England in the last half of the nineteenth century, where it helped change the Victorian practice of including moral lessons in literature.

Affective Fallacy: An error in judging the merits or faults of a work of literature. The "error" results from stressing the importance of the work's effect upon the reader—that is, how it makes a reader "feel" emotionally, what it does

as a literary work—instead of stressing its inner qualities as a created object, or what it "is."

Age of Johnson: The period in English literature between 1750 and 1798, named after the most prominent literary figure of the age, Samuel Johnson. Works written during this time are noted for their emphasis on "sensibility," or emotional quality. These works formed a transition between the rational works of the Age of Reason, or Neoclassical period, and the emphasis on individual feelings and responses of the Romantic period.

Age of Reason: See *Neoclassicism*

Age of Sensibility: See *Age of Johnson*

Agrarians: A group of Southern American writers of the 1930s and 1940s who fostered an economic and cultural program for the South based on agriculture, in opposition to the industrial society of the North. The term can refer to any group that promotes the value of farm life and agricultural society.

Alexandrine Meter: See *Meter*

Allegory: A narrative technique in which characters representing things or abstract ideas are used to convey a message or teach a lesson. Allegory is typically used to teach moral, ethical, or religious lessons but is sometimes used for satiric or political purposes.

Alliteration: A poetic device where the first consonant sounds or any vowel sounds in words or syllables are repeated.

Allusion: A reference to a familiar literary or historical person or event, used to make an idea more easily understood.

Amerind Literature: The writing and oral traditions of Native Americans. Native American literature was originally passed on by word of mouth, so it consisted largely of stories and events that were easily memorized. Amerind prose is often rhythmic like poetry because it was recited to the beat of a ceremonial drum.

Analogy: A comparison of two things made to explain something unfamiliar through its similarities to something familiar, or to prove one point based on the acceptedness of another. Similes and metaphors are types of analogies.

Anapest: See *Foot*

Angry Young Men: A group of British writers of the 1950s whose work expressed bitterness and disillusionment with society. Common to their work is an anti-hero who rebels against a corrupt social order and strives for personal integrity.

Anthropomorphism: The presentation of animals or objects in human shape or with human characteristics. The term is derived from the Greek word for "human form."

Antimasque: See *Masque*

Antithesis: The antithesis of something is its direct opposite. In literature, the use of antithesis as a figure of speech results in two statements that show a contrast through the balancing of two opposite ideas. Technically, it is the second portion of the statement that is defined as the "antithesis"; the first portion is the "thesis."

Apocrypha: Writings tentatively attributed to an author but not proven or universally accepted to be their works. The term was originally applied to certain books of the Bible that were not considered inspired and so were not included in the "sacred canon."

Apollonian and Dionysian: The two impulses believed to guide authors of dramatic tragedy. The Apollonian impulse is named after Apollo, the Greek god of light and beauty and the symbol of intellectual order.

The Dionysian impulse is named after Dionysus, the Greek god of wine and the symbol of the unrestrained forces of nature. The Apollonian impulse is to create a rational, harmonious world, while the Dionysian is to express the irrational forces of personality.

Apostrophe: A statement, question, or request addressed to an inanimate object or concept or to a nonexistent or absent person.

Archetype: The word archetype is commonly used to describe an original pattern or model from which all other things of the same kind are made. This term was introduced to literary criticism from the psychology of Carl Jung. It expresses Jung's theory that behind every person's "unconscious," or repressed memories of the past, lies the "collective unconscious" of the human race: memories of the countless typical experiences of our ancestors. These memories are said to prompt illogical associations that trigger powerful emotions in the reader. Often, the emotional process is primitive, even primordial. Archetypes are the literary images that grow out of the "collective unconscious." They appear in literature as incidents and plots that repeat basic patterns of life. They may also appear as stereotyped characters.

Argument: The argument of a work is the author's subject matter or principal idea.

Art for Art's Sake: See *Aestheticism*

Assonance: The repetition of similar vowel sounds in poetry.

Audience: The people for whom a piece of literature is written. Authors usually write with a certain audience in mind, for example, children, members of a religious or ethnic group, or colleagues in a professional field. The term "audience" also applies to the people who gather to see or hear any performance, including plays, poetry readings, speeches, and concerts.

Automatic Writing: Writing carried out without a preconceived plan in an effort to capture every random thought. Authors who engage in automatic writing typically do not revise their work, preferring instead to preserve the revealed truth and beauty of spontaneous expression.

Avant-garde: A French term meaning "vanguard." It is used in literary criticism to describe new writing that rejects traditional approaches to literature in favor of innovations in style or content.

B

Ballad: A short poem that tells a simple story and has a repeated refrain. Ballads were originally intended to be sung. Early ballads, known as folk ballads, were passed down through generations, so their authors are often unknown. Later ballads composed by known authors are called literary ballads.

Baroque: A term used in literary criticism to describe literature that is complex or ornate in style or diction. Baroque works typically express tension, anxiety, and violent emotion. The term "Baroque Age" designates a period in Western European literature beginning in the late sixteenth century and ending about one hundred years later. Works of this period often mirror the qualities of works more generally associated with the label "baroque" and sometimes feature elaborate conceits.

Baroque Age: See *Baroque*

Baroque Period: See *Baroque*

Beat Generation: See *Beat Movement*

Beat Movement: A period featuring a group of American poets and novelists of the 1950s and 1960s—including Jack Kerouac, Allen Ginsberg, Gregory Corso, William S. Burroughs, and Lawrence Ferlinghetti—who rejected established social and literary values. Using such techniques as stream of consciousness writing and jazz-influenced free verse and focusing on unusual or abnormal states of mind—generated by religious ecstasy or the use of drugs—the Beat writers aimed to create works that were unconventional in both form and subject matter.

Beat Poets: See *Beat Movement*

Beats, The: See *Beat Movement*

Belles-lettres: A French term meaning "fine letters" or "beautiful writing." It is often used as a synonym for literature, typically referring to imaginative and artistic rather than scientific or expository writing. Current usage sometimes restricts the meaning to light or humorous writing and appreciative essays about literature.

Black Aesthetic Movement: A period of artistic and literary development among African

Americans in the 1960s and early 1970s. This was the first major African-American artistic movement since the Harlem Renaissance and was closely paralleled by the civil rights and black power movements. The black aesthetic writers attempted to produce works of art that would be meaningful to the black masses. Key figures in black aesthetics included one of its founders, poet and playwright Amiri Baraka, formerly known as LeRoi Jones; poet and essayist Haki R. Madhubuti, formerly Don L. Lee; poet and playwright Sonia Sanchez; and dramatist Ed Bullins.

Black Arts Movement: See *Black Aesthetic Movement*

Black Comedy: See *Black Humor*

Black Humor: Writing that places grotesque elements side by side with humorous ones in an attempt to shock the reader, forcing him or her to laugh at the horrifying reality of a disordered world.

Black Mountain School: Black Mountain College and three of its instructors—Robert Creeley, Robert Duncan, and Charles Olson—were all influential in projective verse, so poets working in projective verse are now referred as members of the Black Mountain school.

Blank Verse: Loosely, any unrhymed poetry, but more generally, unrhymed iambic pentameter verse (composed of lines of five two-syllable feet with the first syllable accented, the second unaccented). Blank verse has been used by poets since the Renaissance for its flexibility and its graceful, dignified tone.

Bloomsbury Group: A group of English writers, artists, and intellectuals who held informal artistic and philosophical discussions in Bloomsbury, a district of London, from around 1907 to the early 1930s. The Bloomsbury Group held no uniform philosophical beliefs but did commonly express an aversion to moral prudery and a desire for greater social tolerance.

Bon Mot: A French term meaning "good word." A *bon mot* is a witty remark or clever observation.

Breath Verse: See *Projective Verse*

Burlesque: Any literary work that uses exaggeration to make its subject appear ridiculous, either by treating a trivial subject with profound seriousness or by treating a dignified subject frivolously. The word "burlesque"

may also be used as an adjective, as in "burlesque show," to mean "striptease act."

C

Cadence: The natural rhythm of language caused by the alternation of accented and unaccented syllables. Much modern poetry—notably free verse—deliberately manipulates cadence to create complex rhythmic effects.

Caesura: A pause in a line of poetry, usually occurring near the middle. It typically corresponds to a break in the natural rhythm or sense of the line but is sometimes shifted to create special meanings or rhythmic effects.

Canzone: A short Italian or Provencal lyric poem, commonly about love and often set to music. The *canzone* has no set form but typically contains five or six stanzas made up of seven to twenty lines of eleven syllables each. A shorter, five- to ten-line "envoy," or concluding stanza, completes the poem.

Carpe Diem: A Latin term meaning "seize the day." This is a traditional theme of poetry, especially lyrics. A *carpe diem* poem advises the reader or the person it addresses to live for today and enjoy the pleasures of the moment.

Catharsis: The release or purging of unwanted emotions—specifically fear and pity—brought about by exposure to art. The term was first used by the Greek philosopher Aristotle in his *Poetics* to refer to the desired effect of tragedy on spectators.

Celtic Renaissance: A period of Irish literary and cultural history at the end of the nineteenth century. Followers of the movement aimed to create a romantic vision of Celtic myth and legend. The most significant works of the Celtic Renaissance typically present a dreamy, unreal world, usually in reaction against the reality of contemporary problems.

Celtic Twilight: See *Celtic Renaissance*

Character: Broadly speaking, a person in a literary work. The actions of characters are what constitute the plot of a story, novel, or poem. There are numerous types of characters, ranging from simple, stereotypical figures to intricate, multifaceted ones. In the techniques of anthropomorphism and personification, animals—and even places or things—can assume aspects of character. "Characterization" is the process by which an author creates vivid, believable characters in a work of art. This may be done in a variety of ways, including (1) direct description of the character by the narrator; (2) the direct presentation of the speech, thoughts, or actions of the character; and (3) the responses of other characters to the character. The term "character" also refers to a form originated by the ancient Greek writer Theophrastus that later became popular in the seventeenth and eighteenth centuries. It is a short essay or sketch of a person who prominently displays a specific attribute or quality, such as miserliness or ambition.

Characterization: See *Character*

Classical: In its strictest definition in literary criticism, classicism refers to works of ancient Greek or Roman literature. The term may also be used to describe a literary work of recognized importance (a "classic") from any time period or literature that exhibits the traits of classicism.

Classicism: A term used in literary criticism to describe critical doctrines that have their roots in ancient Greek and Roman literature, philosophy, and art. Works associated with classicism typically exhibit restraint on the part of the author, unity of design and purpose, clarity, simplicity, logical organization, and respect for tradition.

Colloquialism: A word, phrase, or form of pronunciation that is acceptable in casual conversation but not in formal, written communication. It is considered more acceptable than slang.

Complaint: A lyric poem, popular in the Renaissance, in which the speaker expresses sorrow about his or her condition. Typically, the speaker's sadness is caused by an unresponsive lover, but some complaints cite other sources of unhappiness, such as poverty or fate.

Conceit: A clever and fanciful metaphor, usually expressed through elaborate and extended comparison, that presents a striking parallel between two seemingly dissimilar things—for example, elaborately comparing a beautiful woman to an object like a garden or the sun. The conceit was a popular device throughout the Elizabethan Age and Baroque Age and was the principal technique of the seventeenth-century English metaphysical poets. This usage of the word conceit is unrelated to the best-known definition of conceit as an arrogant attitude or behavior.

Concrete: Concrete is the opposite of abstract, and refers to a thing that actually exists or a description that allows the reader to experience an object or concept with the senses.

Concrete Poetry: Poetry in which visual elements play a large part in the poetic effect. Punctuation marks, letters, or words are arranged on a page to form a visual design: a cross, for example, or a bumblebee.

Confessional Poetry: A form of poetry in which the poet reveals very personal, intimate, sometimes shocking information about himself or herself.

Connotation: The impression that a word gives beyond its defined meaning. Connotations may be universally understood or may be significant only to a certain group.

Consonance: Consonance occurs in poetry when words appearing at the ends of two or more verses have similar final consonant sounds but have final vowel sounds that differ, as with "stuff" and "off."

Convention: Any widely accepted literary device, style, or form.

Corrido: A Mexican ballad.

Couplet: Two lines of poetry with the same rhyme and meter, often expressing a complete and self-contained thought.

Criticism: The systematic study and evaluation of literary works, usually based on a specific method or set of principles. An important part of literary studies since ancient times, the practice of criticism has given rise to numerous theories, methods, and "schools," sometimes producing conflicting, even contradictory, interpretations of literature in general as well as of individual works. Even such basic issues as what constitutes a poem or a novel have been the subject of much criticism over the centuries.

D

Dactyl: See *Foot*

Dadaism: A protest movement in art and literature founded by Tristan Tzara in 1916. Followers of the movement expressed their outrage at the destruction brought about by World War I by revolting against numerous forms of social convention. The Dadaists presented works marked by calculated madness and flamboyant nonsense. They stressed total freedom of expression, commonly through primitive displays of emotion and illogical, often senseless, poetry. The movement ended shortly after the war, when it was replaced by surrealism.

Decadent: See *Decadents*

Decadents: The followers of a nineteenth-century literary movement that had its beginnings in French aestheticism. Decadent literature displays a fascination with perverse and morbid states; a search for novelty and sensation—the "new thrill"; a preoccupation with mysticism; and a belief in the senselessness of human existence. The movement is closely associated with the doctrine Art for Art's Sake. The term "decadence" is sometimes used to denote a decline in the quality of art or literature following a period of greatness.

Deconstruction: A method of literary criticism developed by Jacques Derrida and characterized by multiple conflicting interpretations of a given work. Deconstructionists consider the impact of the language of a work and suggest that the true meaning of the work is not necessarily the meaning that the author intended.

Deduction: The process of reaching a conclusion through reasoning from general premises to a specific premise.

Denotation: The definition of a word, apart from the impressions or feelings it creates in the reader.

Diction: The selection and arrangement of words in a literary work. Either or both may vary depending on the desired effect. There are four general types of diction: "formal," used in scholarly or lofty writing; "informal," used in relaxed but educated conversation; "colloquial," used in everyday speech; and "slang," containing newly coined words and other terms not accepted in formal usage.

Didactic: A term used to describe works of literature that aim to teach some moral, religious, political, or practical lesson. Although didactic elements are often found in artistically pleasing works, the term "didactic" usually refers to literature in which the message is more important than the form. The term may also be used to criticize a work that the critic finds "overly didactic," that is, heavy-handed in its delivery of a lesson.

Dimeter: See *Meter*

Dionysian: See *Apollonian and Dionysian*

Discordia concours: A Latin phrase meaning "discord in harmony." The term was coined by the eighteenth-century English writer Samuel Johnson to describe "a combination of dissimilar images or discovery of occult resemblances in things apparently unlike." Johnson created the expression by reversing a phrase by the Latin poet Horace.

Dissonance: A combination of harsh or jarring sounds, especially in poetry. Although such combinations may be accidental, poets sometimes intentionally make them to achieve particular effects. Dissonance is also sometimes used to refer to close but not identical rhymes. When this is the case, the word functions as a synonym for consonance.

Double Entendre: A corruption of a French phrase meaning "double meaning." The term is used to indicate a word or phrase that is deliberately ambiguous, especially when one of the meanings is risque or improper.

Draft: Any preliminary version of a written work. An author may write dozens of drafts which are revised to form the final work, or he or she may write only one, with few or no revisions.

Dramatic Monologue: See *Monologue*

Dramatic Poetry: Any lyric work that employs elements of drama such as dialogue, conflict, or characterization, but excluding works that are intended for stage presentation.

Dream Allegory: See *Dream Vision*

Dream Vision: A literary convention, chiefly of the Middle Ages. In a dream vision a story is presented as a literal dream of the narrator. This device was commonly used to teach moral and religious lessons.

E

Eclogue: In classical literature, a poem featuring rural themes and structured as a dialogue among shepherds. Eclogues often took specific poetic forms, such as elegies or love poems. Some were written as the soliloquy of a shepherd. In later centuries, "eclogue" came to refer to any poem that was in the pastoral tradition or that had a dialogue or monologue structure.

Edwardian: Describes cultural conventions identified with the period of the reign of Edward VII of England (1901-1910). Writers of the Edwardian Age typically displayed a strong reaction against the propriety and conservatism of the Victorian Age. Their work often exhibits distrust of authority in religion, politics, and art and expresses strong doubts about the soundness of conventional values.

Edwardian Age: See *Edwardian*

Electra Complex: A daughter's amorous obsession with her father.

Elegy: A lyric poem that laments the death of a person or the eventual death of all people. In a conventional elegy, set in a classical world, the poet and subject are spoken of as shepherds. In modern criticism, the word elegy is often used to refer to a poem that is melancholy or mournfully contemplative.

Elizabethan Age: A period of great economic growth, religious controversy, and nationalism closely associated with the reign of Elizabeth I of England (1558-1603). The Elizabethan Age is considered a part of the general renaissance—that is, the flowering of arts and literature—that took place in Europe during the fourteenth through sixteenth centuries. The era is considered the golden age of English literature. The most important dramas in English and a great deal of lyric poetry were produced during this period, and modern English criticism began around this time.

Empathy: A sense of shared experience, including emotional and physical feelings, with someone or something other than oneself. Empathy is often used to describe the response of a reader to a literary character.

English Sonnet: See *Sonnet*

Enjambment: The running over of the sense and structure of a line of verse or a couplet into the following verse or couplet.

Enlightenment, The: An eighteenth-century philosophical movement. It began in France but had a wide impact throughout Europe and America. Thinkers of the Enlightenment valued reason and believed that both the individual and society could achieve a state of perfection. Corresponding to this essentially humanist vision was a resistance to religious authority.

Epic: A long narrative poem about the adventures of a hero of great historic or legendary importance. The setting is vast and the action is often given cosmic significance through the intervention of supernatural forces such as gods, angels, or demons. Epics are typically written in a classical style of grand simplicity with elaborate metaphors and allusions that enhance the symbolic importance of a hero's adventures.

Epic Simile: See *Homeric Simile*

Epigram: A saying that makes the speaker's point quickly and concisely.

Epilogue: A concluding statement or section of a literary work. In dramas, particularly those of the seventeenth and eighteenth centuries, the epilogue is a closing speech, often in verse, delivered by an actor at the end of a play and spoken directly to the audience.

Epiphany: A sudden revelation of truth inspired by a seemingly trivial incident.

Epitaph: An inscription on a tomb or tombstone, or a verse written on the occasion of a person's death. Epitaphs may be serious or humorous.

Epithalamion: A song or poem written to honor and commemorate a marriage ceremony.

Epithalamium: See *Epithalamion*

Epithet: A word or phrase, often disparaging or abusive, that expresses a character trait of someone or something.

Erziehungsroman: See *Bildungsroman*

Essay: A prose composition with a focused subject of discussion. The term was coined by Michel de Montaigne to describe his 1580 collection of brief, informal reflections on himself and on various topics relating to human nature. An essay can also be a long, systematic discourse.

Existentialism: A predominantly twentieth-century philosophy concerned with the nature and perception of human existence. There are two major strains of existentialist thought: atheistic and Christian. Followers of atheistic existentialism believe that the individual is alone in a godless universe and that the basic human condition is one of suffering and loneliness. Nevertheless, because there are no fixed values, individuals can create their own characters—indeed, they can shape themselves—through the exercise of free will. The atheistic strain culminates in and is popularly associated with the works of Jean-Paul Sartre. The Christian existentialists, on the other hand, believe that only in God may people find freedom from life's anguish. The two strains hold certain beliefs in common: that existence cannot be fully understood or described through empirical effort; that anguish is a universal element of life; that individuals must bear responsibility for their actions; and that there is no common standard of behavior or perception for religious and ethical matters.

Expatriates: See *Expatriatism*

Expatriatism: The practice of leaving one's country to live for an extended period in another country.

Exposition: Writing intended to explain the nature of an idea, thing, or theme. Expository writing is often combined with description, narration, or argument. In dramatic writing, the exposition is the introductory material which presents the characters, setting, and tone of the play.

Expressionism: An indistinct literary term, originally used to describe an early twentieth-century school of German painting. The term applies to almost any mode of unconventional, highly subjective writing that distorts reality in some way.

Extended Monologue: See *Monologue*

F

Feet: See *Foot*

Feminine Rhyme: See *Rhyme*

Fiction: Any story that is the product of imagination rather than a documentation of fact. Characters and events in such narratives may be based in real life but their ultimate form and configuration is a creation of the author.

Figurative Language: A technique in writing in which the author temporarily interrupts the order, construction, or meaning of the writing for a particular effect. This interruption takes the form of one or more figures of speech such as hyperbole, irony, or simile. Figurative language is the opposite of literal language, in which every word is truthful, accurate, and free of exaggeration or embellishment.

Figures of Speech: Writing that differs from customary conventions for construction, meaning, order, or significance for the purpose of a special meaning or effect. There are two major types of figures of speech: rhetorical figures, which do not make changes in the meaning of the words, and tropes, which do.

Fin de siecle: A French term meaning "end of the century." The term is used to denote the last decade of the nineteenth century, a transition period when writers and other artists abandoned old conventions and looked for new techniques and objectives.

First Person: See *Point of View*

Folk Ballad: See *Ballad*

Folklore: Traditions and myths preserved in a culture or group of people. Typically, these are passed on by word of mouth in various forms—such as legends, songs, and proverbs—or preserved in customs and ceremonies. This term was first used by W. J. Thoms in 1846.

Folktale: A story originating in oral tradition. Folktales fall into a variety of categories, including legends, ghost stories, fairy tales, fables, and anecdotes based on historical figures and events.

Foot: The smallest unit of rhythm in a line of poetry. In English-language poetry, a foot is typically one accented syllable combined with one or two unaccented syllables.

Form: The pattern or construction of a work which identifies its genre and distinguishes it from other genres.

Formalism: In literary criticism, the belief that literature should follow prescribed rules of construction, such as those that govern the sonnet form.

Fourteener Meter: See *Meter*

Free Verse: Poetry that lacks regular metrical and rhyme patterns but that tries to capture the cadences of everyday speech. The form allows a poet to exploit a variety of rhythmical effects within a single poem.

Futurism: A flamboyant literary and artistic movement that developed in France, Italy, and Russia from 1908 through the 1920s. Futurist theater and poetry abandoned traditional literary forms. In their place, followers of the movement attempted to achieve total freedom of expression through bizarre imagery and deformed or newly invented words. The Futurists were self-consciously modern artists who attempted to incorporate the appearances and sounds of modern life into their work.

G

Genre: A category of literary work. In critical theory, genre may refer to both the content of a given work—tragedy, comedy, pastoral—and to its form, such as poetry, novel, or drama.

Genteel Tradition: A term coined by critic George Santayana to describe the literary practice of certain late nineteenth-century American writers, especially New Englanders. Followers of the Genteel Tradition emphasized conventionality in social, religious, moral, and literary standards.

Georgian Age: See *Georgian Poets*

Georgian Period: See *Georgian Poets*

Georgian Poets: A loose grouping of English poets during the years 1912-1922. The Georgians reacted against certain literary schools and practices, especially Victorian wordiness, turn-of-the-century aestheticism, and contemporary urban realism. In their place, the Georgians embraced the nineteenth-century poetic practices of William Wordsworth and the other Lake Poets.

Georgic: A poem about farming and the farmer's way of life, named from Virgil's *Georgics*.

Gilded Age: A period in American history during the 1870s characterized by political corruption and materialism. A number of important novels of social and political criticism were written during this time.

Gothic: See *Gothicism*

Gothicism: In literary criticism, works characterized by a taste for the medieval or morbidly attractive. A gothic novel prominently features elements of horror, the supernatural, gloom, and violence: clanking chains, terror, charnel houses, ghosts, medieval castles, and mysteriously slamming doors. The term "gothic novel" is also applied to novels that lack elements of the traditional Gothic setting but that create a similar atmosphere of terror or dread.

Graveyard School: A group of eighteenth-century English poets who wrote long, picturesque meditations on death. Their works were designed to cause the reader to ponder immortality.

Great Chain of Being: The belief that all things and creatures in nature are organized in a hierarchy from inanimate objects at the bottom to God at the top. This system of belief was popular in the seventeenth and eighteenth centuries.

Grotesque: In literary criticism, the subject matter of a work or a style of expression characterized by exaggeration, deformity, freakishness, and disorder. The grotesque often includes an element of comic absurdity.

H

Haiku: The shortest form of Japanese poetry, constructed in three lines of five, seven, and five syllables respectively. The message of a *haiku* poem usually centers on some aspect of spirituality and provokes an emotional response in the reader.

Half Rhyme: See *Consonance*

Harlem Renaissance: The Harlem Renaissance of the 1920s is generally considered the first significant movement of black writers and artists in the United States. During this period, new and established black writers published more fiction and poetry than ever before, the first influential black literary journals were established, and black authors and artists received their first widespread recognition and serious critical appraisal. Among the major writers associated with this period are Claude McKay, Jean Toomer, Countee Cullen, Langston Hughes, Arna Bontemps, Nella Larsen, and Zora Neale Hurston.

Hellenism: Imitation of ancient Greek thought or styles. Also, an approach to life that focuses on the growth and development of the intellect. "Hellenism" is sometimes used to refer to the belief that reason can be applied to examine all human experience.

Heptameter: See *Meter*

Hero/Heroine: The principal sympathetic character (male or female) in a literary work. Heroes and heroines typically exhibit admirable traits: idealism, courage, and integrity, for example.

Heroic Couplet: A rhyming couplet written in iambic pentameter (a verse with five iambic feet).

Heroic Line: The meter and length of a line of verse in epic or heroic poetry. This varies by language and time period.

Heroine: See *Hero/Heroine*

Hexameter: See *Meter*

Historical Criticism: The study of a work based on its impact on the world of the time period in which it was written.

Hokku: See *Haiku*

Holocaust: See *Holocaust Literature*

Holocaust Literature: Literature influenced by or written about the Holocaust of World War II. Such literature includes true stories of survival in concentration camps, escape, and life after the war, as well as fictional works and poetry.

Homeric Simile: An elaborate, detailed comparison written as a simile many lines in length.

Horatian Satire: See *Satire*

Humanism: A philosophy that places faith in the dignity of humankind and rejects the medieval perception of the individual as a weak, fallen creature. "Humanists" typically believe in the perfectibility of human nature and view reason and education as the means to that end.

Humors: Mentions of the humors refer to the ancient Greek theory that a person's health and personality were determined by the balance of four basic fluids in the body: blood, phlegm, yellow bile, and black bile. A dominance of any fluid would cause extremes in behavior. An excess of blood created a sanguine person who was joyful, aggressive, and passionate; a phlegmatic person was shy, fearful, and sluggish; too much yellow bile led to a choleric temperament characterized by impatience, anger, bitterness, and stubbornness; and excessive black bile created melancholy, a state of laziness, gluttony, and lack of motivation.

Humours: See *Humors*

Hyperbole: In literary criticism, deliberate exaggeration used to achieve an effect.

I

Iamb: See *Foot*

Idiom: A word construction or verbal expression closely associated with a given language.

Image: A concrete representation of an object or sensory experience. Typically, such a representation helps evoke the feelings associated with the object or experience itself. Images are either "literal" or "figurative." Literal images are especially concrete and involve little or no extension of the obvious meaning of the words used to express them. Figurative images do not follow the literal meaning of the words exactly. Images in literature are usually visual, but the term "image" can also refer to the representation of any sensory experience.

Imagery: The array of images in a literary work. Also, figurative language.

Imagism: An English and American poetry movement that flourished between 1908 and 1917. The Imagists used precise, clearly presented images in their works. They also used common, everyday speech and aimed for conciseness, concrete imagery, and the creation of new rhythms.

In medias res: A Latin term meaning "in the middle of things." It refers to the technique of beginning a story at its midpoint and then using various flashback devices to reveal previous action.

Induction: The process of reaching a conclusion by reasoning from specific premises to form a general premise. Also, an introductory portion of a work of literature, especially a play.

Intentional Fallacy: The belief that judgments of a literary work based solely on an author's stated or implied intentions are false and misleading. Critics who believe in the concept of the intentional fallacy typically argue that the work itself is sufficient matter for interpretation, even though they may concede that an author's statement of purpose can be useful.

Interior Monologue: A narrative technique in which characters' thoughts are revealed in a way that appears to be uncontrolled by the author. The interior monologue typically aims to reveal the inner self of a character. It portrays emotional experiences as they occur at both a conscious and unconscious level. Images are often used to represent sensations or emotions.

Internal Rhyme: Rhyme that occurs within a single line of verse.

Irish Literary Renaissance: A late nineteenth- and early twentieth-century movement in Irish literature. Members of the movement aimed to reduce the influence of British culture in Ireland and create an Irish national literature.

Irony: In literary criticism, the effect of language in which the intended meaning is the opposite of what is stated.

Italian Sonnet: See *Sonnet*

J

Jacobean Age: The period of the reign of James I of England (1603-1625). The early literature of this period reflected the worldview of the Elizabethan Age, but a darker, more cynical attitude steadily grew in the art and literature of the Jacobean Age. This was an important time for English drama and poetry.

Jargon: Language that is used or understood only by a select group of people. Jargon may refer to terminology used in a certain profession, such as computer jargon, or it may refer to any nonsensical language that is not understood by most people.

Journalism: Writing intended for publication in a newspaper or magazine, or for broadcast on a radio or television program featuring news, sports, entertainment, or other timely material.

K

Knickerbocker Group: A somewhat indistinct group of New York writers of the first half of the nineteenth century. Members of the group were linked only by location and a common theme: New York life.

Kunstlerroman: See *Bildungsroman*

L

Lais: See *Lay*

Lake Poets: See *Lake School*

Lake School: These poets all lived in the Lake District of England at the turn of the nineteenth century. As a group, they followed no single "school" of thought or literary practice, although their works were uniformly disparaged by the *Edinburgh Review*.

Lay: A song or simple narrative poem. The form originated in medieval France. Early French *lais* were often based on the Celtic legends and other tales sung by Breton minstrels—thus the name of the "Breton lay." In fourteenth-century England, the term "lay" was used to describe short narratives written in imitation of the Breton lays.

Leitmotiv: See *Motif*

Literal Language: An author uses literal language when he or she writes without exaggerating or embellishing the subject matter and without any tools of figurative language.

Literary Ballad: See *Ballad*

Literature: Literature is broadly defined as any written or spoken material, but the term most often refers to creative works.

Lost Generation: A term first used by Gertrude Stein to describe the post-World War I generation of American writers: men and women haunted by a sense of betrayal and emptiness brought about by the destructiveness of the war.

Lyric Poetry: A poem expressing the subjective feelings and personal emotions of the poet. Such poetry is melodic, since it was originally accompanied by a lyre in recitals. Most Western poetry in the twentieth century may be classified as lyrical.

M

Mannerism: Exaggerated, artificial adherence to a literary manner or style. Also, a popular style of the visual arts of late sixteenth-century Europe that was marked by elongation of the human form and by intentional spatial distortion. Literary works that are self-consciously high-toned and artistic are often said to be "mannered."

Masculine Rhyme: See *Rhyme*

Measure: The foot, verse, or time sequence used in a literary work, especially a poem. Measure is often used somewhat incorrectly as a synonym for meter.

Metaphor: A figure of speech that expresses an idea through the image of another object. Metaphors suggest the essence of the first object by identifying it with certain qualities of the second object.

Metaphysical Conceit: See *Conceit*

Metaphysical Poetry: The body of poetry produced by a group of seventeenth-century English writers called the "Metaphysical Poets." The group includes John Donne and Andrew Marvell. The Metaphysical Poets made use of everyday speech, intellectual analysis, and unique imagery. They aimed to portray the ordinary conflicts and contradictions of life. Their poems often took the form of an argument, and many of them emphasize physical and religious love as well as the fleeting nature of life. Elaborate conceits are typical in metaphysical poetry.

Metaphysical Poets: See *Metaphysical Poetry*

Meter: In literary criticism, the repetition of sound patterns that creates a rhythm in poetry. The patterns are based on the number of syllables and the presence and absence of accents. The unit of rhythm in a line is called a foot. Types of meter are classified according to the number of feet in a line. These are the standard English lines: Monometer, one foot; Dimeter, two feet; Trimeter, three feet; Tetrameter, four feet; Pentameter, five feet; Hexameter, six feet (also called the Alexandrine); Heptameter, seven feet (also called the "Fourteener" when the feet are iambic).

Modernism: Modern literary practices. Also, the principles of a literary school that lasted from roughly the beginning of the twentieth century until the end of World War II. Modernism is defined by its rejection of the literary conventions of the nineteenth century and by its opposition to conventional morality, taste, traditions, and economic values.

Monologue: A composition, written or oral, by a single individual. More specifically, a speech given by a single individual in a drama or other public entertainment. It has no set length, although it is usually several or more lines long.

Monometer: See *Meter*

Mood: The prevailing emotions of a work or of the author in his or her creation of the work. The mood of a work is not always what might be expected based on its subject matter.

Motif: A theme, character type, image, metaphor, or other verbal element that recurs throughout a single work of literature or occurs in a number of different works over a period of time.

Motiv: See *Motif*

Muckrakers: An early twentieth-century group of American writers. Typically, their works exposed the wrongdoings of big business and government in the United States.

Muses: Nine Greek mythological goddesses, the daughters of Zeus and Mnemosyne (Memory). Each muse patronized a specific area of the liberal arts and sciences. Calliope presided over epic poetry, Clio over history, Erato over love poetry, Euterpe over music or lyric poetry, Melpomene over tragedy, Polyhymnia over hymns to the gods, Terpsichore over dance, Thalia over comedy, and Urania over astronomy. Poets and writers traditionally made appeals to the Muses for inspiration in their work.

Myth: An anonymous tale emerging from the traditional beliefs of a culture or social unit. Myths use supernatural explanations for natural phenomena. They may also explain cosmic issues like creation and death. Collections of myths, known as mythologies, are common to all cultures and nations, but the best-known myths belong to the Norse, Roman, and Greek mythologies.

N

Narration: The telling of a series of events, real or invented. A narration may be either a simple narrative, in which the events are recounted chronologically, or a narrative with a plot, in which the account is given in a style reflecting the author's artistic concept of the story. Narration is sometimes used as a synonym for "storyline."

Narrative: A verse or prose accounting of an event or sequence of events, real or invented. The term is also used as an adjective in the sense "method of narration." For example, in literary criticism, the expression "narrative technique" usually refers to the way the author structures and presents his or her story.

Narrative Poetry: A nondramatic poem in which the author tells a story. Such poems may be of any length or level of complexity.

Narrator: The teller of a story. The narrator may be the author or a character in the story through whom the author speaks.

Naturalism: A literary movement of the late nineteenth and early twentieth centuries. The movement's major theorist, French novelist Emile Zola, envisioned a type of fiction that would examine human life with the objectivity of scientific inquiry. The Naturalists typically viewed human beings as either the products of "biological determinism," ruled by hereditary instincts and engaged in an endless struggle for survival, or as the products of "socioeconomic determinism," ruled by social and economic forces beyond their control. In their works, the Naturalists generally ignored the highest levels of society and focused on degradation: poverty, alcoholism, prostitution, insanity, and disease.

Negritude: A literary movement based on the concept of a shared cultural bond on the part of black Africans, wherever they may be in the world. It traces its origins to the former French colonies of Africa and the Caribbean. Negritude poets, novelists, and essayists generally stress four points in their writings: One, black alienation from traditional African culture can lead to feelings of inferiority. Two, European colonialism and Western education should be resisted. Three, black Africans should seek to affirm and define their own identity. Four, African culture can and should be reclaimed. Many Negritude writers also claim that blacks can make unique contributions to the world, based on a heightened appreciation of nature, rhythm, and human emotions—aspects of life they say are not so highly valued in the materialistic and rationalistic West.

Negro Renaissance: See *Harlem Renaissance*

Neoclassical Period: See *Neoclassicism*

Neoclassicism: In literary criticism, this term refers to the revival of the attitudes and styles of expression of classical literature. It is generally used to describe a period in European history beginning in the late seventeenth century and lasting until about 1800. In its purest form, Neoclassicism marked a return to order, proportion, restraint, logic, accuracy, and decorum. In England, where Neoclassicism perhaps was most popular, it reflected the influence of seventeenth-century French writers, especially dramatists. Neoclassical writers typically reacted against the intensity and enthusiasm of the Renaissance period. They wrote works that appealed to the intellect, using elevated language and classical literary forms such as satire and the ode. Neoclassical works were often governed by the classical goal of instruction.

Neoclassicists: See *Neoclassicism*

New Criticism: A movement in literary criticism, dating from the late 1920s, that stressed close textual analysis in the interpretation of works of literature. The New Critics saw little merit in historical and biographical analysis. Rather, they aimed to examine the text alone, free from the question of how external events—biographical or otherwise—may have helped shape it.

New Journalism: A type of writing in which the journalist presents factual information in a form usually used in fiction. New journalism emphasizes description, narration, and character development to bring readers closer to the human element of the story, and is often used in personality profiles and in-depth feature articles. It is not compatible with "straight" or "hard" newswriting, which is generally composed in a brief, fact-based style.

New Journalists: See *New Journalism*

New Negro Movement: See *Harlem Renaissance*

Noble Savage: The idea that primitive man is noble and good but becomes evil and corrupted as he becomes civilized. The concept of the noble savage originated in the Renaissance period but is more closely identified with such later writers as Jean-Jacques Rousseau and Aphra Behn.

O

Objective Correlative: An outward set of objects, a situation, or a chain of events corresponding to an inward experience and evoking this experience in the reader. The term frequently appears in modern criticism in discussions of authors' intended effects on the emotional responses of readers.

Objectivity: A quality in writing characterized by the absence of the author's opinion or feeling about the subject matter. Objectivity is an important factor in criticism.

Occasional Verse: Poetry written on the occasion of a significant historical or personal event. *Vers de societe* is sometimes called occasional verse although it is of a less serious nature.

Octave: A poem or stanza composed of eight lines. The term octave most often represents the first eight lines of a Petrarchan sonnet.

Ode: Name given to an extended lyric poem characterized by exalted emotion and dignified style. An ode usually concerns a single, serious theme. Most odes, but not all, are addressed to an object or individual. Odes are distinguished from other lyric poetic forms by their complex rhythmic and stanzaic patterns.

Oedipus Complex: A son's amorous obsession with his mother. The phrase is derived from the story of the ancient Theban hero Oedipus, who unknowingly killed his father and married his mother.

Omniscience: See *Point of View*

Onomatopoeia: The use of words whose sounds express or suggest their meaning. In its simplest sense, onomatopoeia may be represented by words that mimic the sounds they denote such as "hiss" or "meow." At a more subtle level, the pattern and rhythm of sounds and rhymes of a line or poem may be onomatopoeic.

Oral Tradition: See *Oral Transmission*

Oral Transmission: A process by which songs, ballads, folklore, and other material are transmitted by word of mouth. The tradition of oral transmission predates the written record systems of literate society. Oral transmission preserves material sometimes over generations, although often with variations. Memory plays a large part in the recitation and preservation of orally transmitted material.

Ottava Rima: An eight-line stanza of poetry composed in iambic pentameter (a five-foot line in which each foot consists of an unaccented syllable followed by an accented syllable), following the ababab cc rhyme scheme.

Oxymoron: A phrase combining two contradictory terms. Oxymorons may be intentional or unintentional.

P

Pantheism: The idea that all things are both a manifestation or revelation of God and a part of God at the same time. Pantheism was a common attitude in the early societies of Egypt, India, and Greece—the term derives from the Greek *pan* meaning "all" and *theos* meaning "deity." It later became a significant part of the Christian faith.

Parable: A story intended to teach a moral lesson or answer an ethical question.

Paradox: A statement that appears illogical or contradictory at first, but may actually point to an underlying truth.

Parallelism: A method of comparison of two ideas in which each is developed in the same grammatical structure.

Parnassianism: A mid nineteenth-century movement in French literature. Followers of the movement stressed adherence to well-defined artistic forms as a reaction against the often chaotic expression of the artist's ego that dominated the work of the Romantics. The Parnassians also rejected the moral, ethical, and social themes exhibited in the works of French Romantics such as Victor Hugo. The aesthetic doctrines of the Parnassians strongly influenced the later symbolist and decadent movements.

Parody: In literary criticism, this term refers to an imitation of a serious literary work or the signature style of a particular author in a ridiculous manner. A typical parody adopts the style of the original and applies it to an inappropriate subject for humorous effect. Parody is a form of satire and could be considered the literary equivalent of a caricature or cartoon.

Pastoral: A term derived from the Latin word "pastor," meaning shepherd. A pastoral is a literary composition on a rural theme. The conventions of the pastoral were originated by the third-century Greek poet Theocritus, who wrote about the experiences, love affairs, and pastimes of Sicilian shepherds. In a pastoral, characters and language of a courtly nature are often placed in a simple setting. The term pastoral is also used to classify dramas, elegies, and lyrics that exhibit the use of country settings and shepherd characters.

Pathetic Fallacy: A term coined by English critic John Ruskin to identify writing that falsely endows nonhuman things with human intentions and feelings, such as "angry clouds" and "sad trees."

Pen Name: See *Pseudonym*

Pentameter: See *Meter*

Persona: A Latin term meaning "mask." *Personae* are the characters in a fictional work of literature. The *persona* generally functions as a mask through which the author tells a story in a voice other than his or her own. A *persona* is usually either a character in a story who acts as a narrator or an "implied author," a voice created by the author to act as the narrator for himself or herself.

Personae: See *Persona*

Personal Point of View: See *Point of View*

Personification: A figure of speech that gives human qualities to abstract ideas, animals, and inanimate objects.

Petrarchan Sonnet: See *Sonnet*

Phenomenology: A method of literary criticism based on the belief that things have no existence outside of human consciousness or awareness. Proponents of this theory believe that art is a process that takes place in the mind of the observer as he or she contemplates an object rather than a quality of the object itself.

Plagiarism: Claiming another person's written material as one's own. Plagiarism can take the form of direct, word-for-word copying or the theft of the substance or idea of the work.

Platonic Criticism: A form of criticism that stresses an artistic work's usefulness as an agent of social engineering rather than any quality or value of the work itself.

Platonism: The embracing of the doctrines of the philosopher Plato, popular among the poets of the Renaissance and the Romantic period. Platonism is more flexible than Aristotelian Criticism and places more emphasis on the supernatural and unknown aspects of life.

Plot: In literary criticism, this term refers to the pattern of events in a narrative or drama. In its simplest sense, the plot guides the author in composing the work and helps the reader follow the work. Typically, plots exhibit causality and unity and have a beginning, a middle, and an end. Sometimes, however, a plot may consist of a series of disconnected events, in which case it is known as an "episodic plot."

Poem: In its broadest sense, a composition utilizing rhyme, meter, concrete detail, and expressive language to create a literary experience with emotional and aesthetic appeal.

Poet: An author who writes poetry or verse. The term is also used to refer to an artist or writer who has an exceptional gift for expression, imagination, and energy in the making of art in any form.

Poete maudit: A term derived from Paul Verlaine's *Les poetes maudits* (*The Accursed Poets*), a collection of essays on the French symbolist writers Stephane Mallarme, Arthur Rimbaud, and Tristan Corbiere. In the sense intended by Verlaine, the poet is "accursed" for choosing to explore extremes of human experience outside of middle-class society.

Poetic Fallacy: See *Pathetic Fallacy*

Poetic Justice: An outcome in a literary work, not necessarily a poem, in which the good are rewarded and the evil are punished, especially in ways that particularly fit their virtues or crimes.

Poetic License: Distortions of fact and literary convention made by a writer—not always a poet—for the sake of the effect gained. Poetic license is closely related to the concept of "artistic freedom."

Poetics: This term has two closely related meanings. It denotes (1) an aesthetic theory in literary criticism about the essence of poetry or (2) rules prescribing the proper methods, content, style, or diction of poetry. The term poetics may also refer to theories about literature in general, not just poetry.

Poetry: In its broadest sense, writing that aims to present ideas and evoke an emotional experience in the reader through the use of meter, imagery, connotative and concrete words, and a carefully constructed structure based on rhythmic patterns. Poetry typically relies on words and expressions that have several layers of meaning. It also makes use of the effects of regular rhythm on the ear and may make a strong appeal to the senses through the use of imagery.

Point of View: The narrative perspective from which a literary work is presented to the reader. There are four traditional points of view. The "third person omniscient" gives the reader a "godlike" perspective, unrestricted by time or place, from which to see actions and look into the minds of characters. This allows the author to comment openly on characters and events in the work. The "third person" point of view presents the events of the story from outside of any single character's perception, much like the omniscient point of view, but the reader must understand the action as it takes place and without any special insight into characters' minds or motivations. The "first person" or "personal" point of view relates events as they are perceived by a single character. The main character "tells" the story and may offer opinions about the action and characters which differ from those of the author. Much less common than omniscient, third person, and first person is the "second person" point of view, wherein the author tells the story as if it is happening to the reader.

Polemic: A work in which the author takes a stand on a controversial subject, such as abortion or religion. Such works are often extremely argumentative or provocative.

Pornography: Writing intended to provoke feelings of lust in the reader. Such works are often condemned by critics and teachers, but those which can be shown to have literary value are viewed less harshly.

Post-Aesthetic Movement: An artistic response made by African Americans to the black aesthetic movement of the 1960s and early '70s. Writers since that time have adopted a somewhat different tone in their work, with less emphasis placed on the disparity between black and white in the United States. In the words of post-aesthetic authors such as Toni Morrison, John Edgar Wideman, and Kristin Hunter, African Americans are portrayed as looking inward for answers to their own questions, rather than always looking to the outside world.

Postmodernism: Writing from the 1960s forward characterized by experimentation and continuing to apply some of the fundamentals of modernism, which included existentialism and alienation. Postmodernists have gone a step further in the rejection of tradition begun with the modernists by also rejecting traditional forms, preferring the anti-novel over the novel and the anti-hero over the hero.

Pre-Raphaelites: A circle of writers and artists in mid nineteenth-century England. Valuing the pre-Renaissance artistic qualities of religious symbolism, lavish pictorialism, and natural sensuousness, the Pre-Raphaelites cultivated a sense of mystery and melancholy that influenced later writers associated with the Symbolist and Decadent movements.

Primitivism: The belief that primitive peoples were nobler and less flawed than civilized peoples because they had not been subjected to the tainting influence of society.

Projective Verse: A form of free verse in which the poet's breathing pattern determines the lines of the poem. Poets who advocate projective verse are against all formal structures in writing, including meter and form.

Prologue: An introductory section of a literary work. It often contains information establishing the situation of the characters or presents information about the setting, time period, or action. In drama, the prologue is spoken by a chorus or by one of the principal characters.

Prose: A literary medium that attempts to mirror the language of everyday speech. It is distinguished from poetry by its use of unmetered, unrhymed language consisting of logically related sentences. Prose is usually grouped into paragraphs that form a cohesive whole such as an essay or a novel.

Prosopopoeia: See *Personification*

Protagonist: The central character of a story who serves as a focus for its themes and incidents and as the principal rationale for its development. The protagonist is sometimes referred to in discussions of modern literature as the hero or anti-hero.

Proverb: A brief, sage saying that expresses a truth about life in a striking manner.

Pseudonym: A name assumed by a writer, most often intended to prevent his or her identification as the author of a work. Two or more authors may work together under one pseudonym, or an author may use a different name for each genre he or she publishes in. Some publishing companies maintain "house pseudonyms," under which any number of authors may write installations in a series. Some authors also choose a pseudonym over their real names the way an actor may use a stage name.

Pun: A play on words that have similar sounds but different meanings.

Pure Poetry: Poetry written without instructional intent or moral purpose that aims only to please a reader by its imagery or musical flow. The term pure poetry is used as the antonym of the term "didacticism."

Q

Quatrain: A four-line stanza of a poem or an entire poem consisting of four lines.

R

Realism: A nineteenth-century European literary movement that sought to portray familiar characters, situations, and settings in a realistic manner. This was done primarily by using an objective narrative point of view and through the buildup of accurate detail. The standard for success of any realistic work depends on how faithfully it transfers common experience into fictional forms. The realistic method may be altered or extended, as in stream of consciousness writing, to record highly subjective experience.

Refrain: A phrase repeated at intervals throughout a poem. A refrain may appear at the end of each stanza or at less regular intervals. It may be altered slightly at each appearance.

Renaissance: The period in European history that marked the end of the Middle Ages. It began in Italy in the late fourteenth century. In broad terms, it is usually seen as spanning the fourteenth, fifteenth, and sixteenth centuries, although it did not reach Great Britain, for example, until the 1480s or so. The Renaissance saw an awakening in almost every sphere of human activity, especially science, philosophy, and the arts. The period is best defined by the emergence of a general philosophy that emphasized the importance of the intellect, the individual, and world affairs. It contrasts strongly with the medieval worldview, characterized by the dominant concerns of faith, the social collective, and spiritual salvation.

Repartee: Conversation featuring snappy retorts and witticisms.

Restoration: See *Restoration Age*

Restoration Age: A period in English literature beginning with the crowning of Charles II in 1660 and running to about 1700. The era, which was characterized by a reaction against Puritanism, was the first great age of the comedy of manners. The finest literature of the era is typically witty and urbane, and often lewd.

Rhetoric: In literary criticism, this term denotes the art of ethical persuasion. In its strictest sense, rhetoric adheres to various principles developed since classical times for arranging facts and ideas in a clear, persuasive, appealing manner. The term is also used to refer to effective prose in general and theories of or methods for composing effective prose.

Rhetorical Question: A question intended to provoke thought, but not an expressed answer, in the reader. It is most commonly used in oratory and other persuasive genres.

Rhyme: When used as a noun in literary criticism, this term generally refers to a poem in which words sound identical or very similar and appear in parallel positions in two or more lines. Rhymes are classified into different types according to where they fall in a line or stanza or according to the degree of similarity they exhibit in their spellings and sounds. Some major types of rhyme are "masculine" rhyme, "feminine" rhyme, and "triple" rhyme. In a masculine rhyme, the rhyming sound falls in a single accented syllable, as with "heat" and "eat." Feminine rhyme is a rhyme of two syllables, one stressed and one unstressed, as with "merry" and "tarry." Triple rhyme matches the sound of the accented syllable and the two unaccented syllables that follow: "narrative" and "declarative."

Rhyme Royal: A stanza of seven lines composed in iambic pentameter and rhymed *ababbcc*. The name is said to be a tribute to King James I of Scotland, who made much use of the form in his poetry.

Rhyme Scheme: See *Rhyme*

Rhythm: A regular pattern of sound, time intervals, or events occurring in writing, most often and most discernably in poetry. Regular, reliable rhythm is known to be soothing to humans, while interrupted, unpredictable, or rapidly changing rhythm is disturbing. These effects are known to authors, who use them to produce a desired reaction in the reader.

Rococo: A style of European architecture that flourished in the eighteenth century, especially in France. The most notable features of *rococo* are its extensive use of ornamentation and its themes of lightness, gaiety, and intimacy. In literary criticism, the term is often used disparagingly to refer to a decadent or over-ornamental style.

Romance: A broad term, usually denoting a narrative with exotic, exaggerated, often idealized characters, scenes, and themes.

Romantic Age: See *Romanticism*

Romanticism: This term has two widely accepted meanings. In historical criticism, it refers to a European intellectual and artistic movement of the late eighteenth and early nineteenth centuries that sought greater freedom of personal expression than that allowed by the strict rules of literary form and logic of the eighteenth-century neoclassicists. The Romantics preferred emotional and imaginative expression to rational analysis. They considered the individual to be at the center of all experience and so placed him or her at the center of their art. The Romantics believed that the creative imagination reveals nobler truths—unique feelings and attitudes—than those that could be discovered by logic or by scientific examination. Both the natural world and the state of childhood were important sources for revelations of "eternal truths." "Romanticism" is also used as a general term to refer to a type of sensibility found in all periods of literary history and usually considered to be in opposition to the principles of classicism. In this sense, Romanticism signifies any work or philosophy in which the exotic or dreamlike figure strongly, or that is devoted to individualistic expression, self-analysis, or a pursuit of a higher realm of knowledge than can be discovered by human reason.

Romantics: See *Romanticism*

Russian Symbolism: A Russian poetic movement, derived from French symbolism, that flourished between 1894 and 1910. While some Russian Symbolists continued in the French tradition, stressing aestheticism and the importance of suggestion above didactic intent, others saw their craft as a form of mystical worship, and themselves as mediators between the supernatural and the mundane.

S

Satire: A work that uses ridicule, humor, and wit to criticize and provoke change in human nature and institutions. There are two major types of satire: "formal" or "direct" satire speaks directly to the reader or to a character in the work; "indirect" satire relies upon the ridiculous behavior of its characters to make its point. Formal satire is further divided into two manners: the "Horatian," which ridicules gently, and the "Juvenalian," which derides its subjects harshly and bitterly.

Scansion: The analysis or "scanning" of a poem to determine its meter and often its rhyme scheme. The most common system of scansion uses accents (slanted lines drawn above syllables) to show stressed syllables, breves (curved lines drawn above syllables) to show unstressed syllables, and vertical lines to separate each foot.

Second Person: See *Point of View*

Semiotics: The study of how literary forms and conventions affect the meaning of language.

Sestet: Any six-line poem or stanza.

Setting: The time, place, and culture in which the action of a narrative takes place. The elements of setting may include geographic location, characters' physical and mental environments, prevailing cultural attitudes, or the historical time in which the action takes place.

Shakespearean Sonnet: See *Sonnet*

Signifying Monkey: A popular trickster figure in black folklore, with hundreds of tales about this character documented since the 19th century.

Simile: A comparison, usually using "like" or "as," of two essentially dissimilar things, as in "coffee as cold as ice" or "He sounded like a broken record."

Slang: A type of informal verbal communication that is generally unacceptable for formal writing. Slang words and phrases are often colorful exaggerations used to emphasize the speaker's point; they may also be shortened versions of an often-used word or phrase.

Slant Rhyme: See *Consonance*

Slave Narrative: Autobiographical accounts of American slave life as told by escaped slaves. These works first appeared during the abolition movement of the 1830s through the 1850s.

Social Realism: See *Socialist Realism*

Socialist Realism: The Socialist Realism school of literary theory was proposed by Maxim Gorky and established as a dogma by the first Soviet Congress of Writers. It demanded adherence to a communist worldview in works of literature. Its doctrines required an objective viewpoint comprehensible to the working classes and themes of social struggle featuring strong proletarian heroes.

Soliloquy: A monologue in a drama used to give the audience information and to develop the speaker's character. It is typically a projection of the speaker's innermost thoughts. Usually delivered while the speaker is alone on stage, a soliloquy is intended to present an illusion of unspoken reflection.

Sonnet: A fourteen-line poem, usually composed in iambic pentameter, employing one of several rhyme schemes. There are three major types of sonnets, upon which all other variations of the form are based: the "Petrarchan" or "Italian" sonnet, the "Shakespearean" or "English" sonnet, and the "Spenserian" sonnet. A Petrarchan sonnet consists of an octave rhymed *abbaabba* and a "sestet" rhymed either *cdecde, cdccdc,* or *cdedce.* The octave poses a question or problem, relates a narrative, or puts forth a proposition; the sestet presents a solution to the problem, comments upon the narrative, or applies the proposition put forth in the octave. The Shakespearean sonnet is divided into three quatrains and a couplet rhymed *abab cdcd efef gg.* The couplet provides an epigrammatic comment on the narrative or problem put forth in the quatrains. The Spenserian sonnet uses three quatrains and a couplet like the Shakespearean, but links their three rhyme schemes in this way: *abab bcbc cdcd ee.* The Spenserian sonnet develops its theme in two parts like the Petrarchan, its final six lines resolving a problem, analyzing a narrative, or applying a proposition put forth in its first eight lines.

Spenserian Sonnet: See *Sonnet*

Spenserian Stanza: A nine-line stanza having eight verses in iambic pentameter, its ninth verse in iambic hexameter, and the rhyme scheme ababbcbcc.

Spondee: In poetry meter, a foot consisting of two long or stressed syllables occurring together. This form is quite rare in English verse, and is usually composed of two monosyllabic words.

Sprung Rhythm: Versification using a specific number of accented syllables per line but disregarding the number of unaccented syllables that fall in each line, producing an irregular rhythm in the poem.

Stanza: A subdivision of a poem consisting of lines grouped together, often in recurring patterns of rhyme, line length, and meter. Stanzas may also serve as units of thought in a poem much like paragraphs in prose.

Stereotype: A stereotype was originally the name for a duplication made during the printing process; this led to its modern definition as a person or thing that is (or is assumed to be) the same as all others of its type.

Stream of Consciousness: A narrative technique for rendering the inward experience of a character. This technique is designed to give the impression of an ever-changing series of thoughts, emotions, images, and memories in the spontaneous and seemingly illogical order that they occur in life.

Structuralism: A twentieth-century movement in literary criticism that examines how literary texts arrive at their meanings, rather than the meanings themselves. There are two major types of structuralist analysis: one examines the way patterns of linguistic structures unify a specific text and emphasize certain elements of that text, and the other interprets the way literary forms and conventions affect the meaning of language itself.

Structure: The form taken by a piece of literature. The structure may be made obvious for ease of understanding, as in nonfiction works, or may be obscured for artistic purposes, as in some poetry or seemingly "unstructured" prose.

Sturm und Drang: A German term meaning "storm and stress." It refers to a German literary movement of the 1770s and 1780s that reacted against the order and rationalism of the enlightenment, focusing instead on the intense experience of extraordinary individuals.

Style: A writer's distinctive manner of arranging words to suit his or her ideas and purpose in writing. The unique imprint of the author's personality upon his or her writing, style is the product of an author's way of arranging ideas and his or her use of diction, different sentence structures, rhythm, figures of speech, rhetorical principles, and other elements of composition.

Subject: The person, event, or theme at the center of a work of literature. A work may have one or more subjects of each type, with shorter works tending to have fewer and longer works tending to have more.

Subjectivity: Writing that expresses the author's personal feelings about his subject, and which may or may not include factual information about the subject.

Surrealism: A term introduced to criticism by Guillaume Apollinaire and later adopted by Andre Breton. It refers to a French literary and artistic movement founded in the 1920s. The Surrealists sought to express unconscious thoughts and feelings in their works. The best-known technique used for achieving this aim was automatic writing—transcriptions of spontaneous outpourings from the unconscious. The Surrealists proposed to unify the contrary levels of conscious and unconscious, dream and reality, objectivity and subjectivity into a new level of "super-realism."

Suspense: A literary device in which the author maintains the audience's attention through the buildup of events, the outcome of which will soon be revealed.

Syllogism: A method of presenting a logical argument. In its most basic form, the syllogism consists of a major premise, a minor premise, and a conclusion.

Symbol: Something that suggests or stands for something else without losing its original identity. In literature, symbols combine their literal meaning with the suggestion of an abstract concept. Literary symbols are of two types: those that carry complex associations of meaning no matter what their contexts, and those that derive their suggestive meaning from their functions in specific literary works.

Symbolism: This term has two widely accepted meanings. In historical criticism, it denotes an early modernist literary movement initiated in France during the nineteenth century that reacted against the prevailing standards of realism. Writers in this movement aimed to evoke, indirectly and symbolically, an order of being beyond the material world of the five senses. Poetic expression of personal emotion figured strongly in the movement, typically by means of a private set of symbols uniquely identifiable with the individual poet. The principal aim of the Symbolists was to express in words the highly complex feelings that grew out of everyday contact with the world. In a broader sense, the term "symbolism" refers to the use of one object to represent another.

Symbolist: See *Symbolism*

Symbolist Movement: See *Symbolism*

Sympathetic Fallacy: See *Affective Fallacy*

T

Tanka: A form of Japanese poetry similar to *haiku*. A *tanka* is five lines long, with the lines containing five, seven, five, seven, and seven syllables respectively.

Terza Rima: A three-line stanza form in poetry in which the rhymes are made on the last word of each line in the following manner: the first and third lines of the first stanza, then the second line of the first stanza and the first and third lines of the second stanza, and so on with the middle line of any stanza rhyming with the first and third lines of the following stanza.

Tetrameter: See *Meter*

Textual Criticism: A branch of literary criticism that seeks to establish the authoritative text of a literary work. Textual critics typically compare all known manuscripts or printings of a single work in order to assess the meanings of differences and revisions. This procedure allows them to arrive at a definitive version that (supposedly) corresponds to the author's original intention.

Theme: The main point of a work of literature. The term is used interchangeably with thesis.

Thesis: A thesis is both an essay and the point argued in the essay. Thesis novels and thesis plays share the quality of containing a thesis which is supported through the action of the story.

Third Person: See *Point of View*

Tone: The author's attitude toward his or her audience may be deduced from the tone of the work. A formal tone may create distance or convey politeness, while an informal tone may encourage a friendly, intimate, or intrusive feeling in the reader. The author's attitude toward his or her subject matter may also be deduced from the tone of the words he or she uses in discussing it.

Tragedy: A drama in prose or poetry about a noble, courageous hero of excellent character who, because of some tragic character flaw or *hamartia*, brings ruin upon him- or herself. Tragedy treats its subjects in a dignified and serious manner, using poetic language to help evoke pity and fear and bring about catharsis, a purging of these emotions. The tragic form was practiced extensively by the ancient Greeks. In the Middle Ages, when classical works were virtually unknown, tragedy came to denote any works about the fall of persons from exalted to low conditions due to any reason: fate, vice, weakness, etc. According to the classical definition of tragedy, such works present the "pathetic"—that which evokes pity—rather than the tragic. The classical form of tragedy was revived in the sixteenth century; it flourished especially on the Elizabethan stage. In modern times, dramatists have attempted to adapt the form to the needs of modern society by drawing their heroes from the ranks of ordinary men and women and defining the nobility of these heroes in terms of spirit rather than exalted social standing.

Tragic Flaw: In a tragedy, the quality within the hero or heroine which leads to his or her downfall.

Transcendentalism: An American philosophical and religious movement, based in New England from around 1835 until the Civil War. Transcendentalism was a form of American romanticism that had its roots abroad in the works of Thomas Carlyle, Samuel Coleridge, and Johann Wolfgang von Goethe. The Transcendentalists stressed the importance of intuition and subjective experience in communication with God. They rejected religious dogma and texts in favor of mysticism and scientific naturalism. They pursued truths that lie beyond the "colorless" realms perceived by reason and the senses and were active social reformers in public education, women's rights, and the abolition of slavery.

Trickster: A character or figure common in Native American and African literature who uses his ingenuity to defeat enemies and escape difficult situations. Tricksters are most often animals, such as the spider, hare, or coyote, although they may take the form of humans as well.

Trimeter: See *Meter*

Triple Rhyme: See *Rhyme*

Trochee: See *Foot*

U

Understatement: See *Irony*

Unities: Strict rules of dramatic structure, formulated by Italian and French critics of the Renaissance and based loosely on the principles of drama discussed by Aristotle in his *Poetics*. Foremost among these rules were the three unities of action, time, and place that compelled a dramatist to: (1) construct a single plot with a beginning, middle, and end that details the causal relationships of action and character; (2) restrict the action to the events of a single day; and (3) limit the scene to a single place or city. The unities were observed faithfully by continental European writers until the Romantic Age, but they were never regularly observed in English drama. Modern dramatists are typically more concerned with a unity of impression or emotional effect than with any of the classical unities.

Urban Realism: A branch of realist writing that attempts to accurately reflect the often harsh facts of modern urban existence.

Utopia: A fictional perfect place, such as "paradise" or "heaven."

Utopian: See *Utopia*

Utopianism: See *Utopia*

V

Verisimilitude: Literally, the appearance of truth. In literary criticism, the term refers to aspects of a work of literature that seem true to the reader.

Vers de societe: See *Occasional Verse*

Vers libre: See *Free Verse*

Verse: A line of metered language, a line of a poem, or any work written in verse.

Versification: The writing of verse. Versification may also refer to the meter, rhyme, and other mechanical components of a poem.

Victorian: Refers broadly to the reign of Queen Victoria of England (1837-1901) and to anything with qualities typical of that era. For example, the qualities of smug narrowmindedness, bourgeois materialism, faith in social progress, and priggish morality are often considered Victorian. This stereotype is contradicted by such dramatic intellectual developments as the theories of Charles Darwin, Karl Marx, and Sigmund Freud (which stirred strong debates in England) and the critical attitudes of serious Victorian writers like Charles Dickens and George Eliot. In literature, the Victorian Period was the great age of the English novel, and the latter part of the era saw the rise of movements such as decadence and symbolism.

Victorian Age: See *Victorian*

Victorian Period: See *Victorian*

W

Weltanschauung: A German term referring to a person's worldview or philosophy.

Weltschmerz: A German term meaning "world pain." It describes a sense of anguish about the nature of existence, usually associated with a melancholy, pessimistic attitude.

Z

Zarzuela: A type of Spanish operetta.

Zeitgeist: A German term meaning "spirit of the time." It refers to the moral and intellectual trends of a given era.

Cumulative Author/Title Index

Cumulative Author/Title Index

Cumulative Nationality/Ethnicity Index

Graham, Jorie
The Hiding Place: V10
Mind: V17
Gregg, Linda
A Thirst Against: V20
Gunn, Thom
The Missing: V9
H.D.
Helen: V6
Sea Rose: V28
Song: V48
Hacker, Marilyn
The Boy: V19
Hahn, Kimiko
Pine: V23
Hall, Donald
Names of Horses: V8
Harjo, Joy
Anniversary: V15
Grace: V44
Remember: V32
Harper, Frances Ellen Watkins
Bury Me in a Free Land: V55
The Slave Mother: V44
Hashimoto, Sharon
*What I Would Ask My Husband's
Dead Father:* V22
Hass, Robert
*The World as Will and
Representation:* V37
Hayden, Robert
Runagate Runagate: V31
Those Winter Sundays: V1
The Whipping: V45
Hecht, Anthony
"More Light! More Light!": V6
Hejinian, Lyn
*Yet we insist that life is full of
happy chance:* V27
Hillman, Brenda
Air for Mercury: V20
Hirsch, Edward
Omen: V22
Hirshfield, Jane
Three Times My Life Has Opened:
V16
Hoagland, Tony
Social Life: V19
Holmes, Oliver Wendell
The Chambered Nautilus: V24
Old Ironsides: V9
Hongo, Garrett
And Your Soul Shall Dance: V43
The Legend: V25
What For: V33
Yellow Light: V55
Howe, Marie
The Boy: V46
What Belongs to Us: V15
Hudgins, Andrew
*Elegy for My Father, Who is Not
Dead:* V14

Hughes, Langston
Democracy: V54
Dream Variations: V15
Dreams: V50
Harlem: V1
I, Too: V30
Let America Be America Again:
V45
Mother to Son: V3
The Negro Speaks of Rivers: V10
Theme for English B: V6
The Weary Blues: V38
Hugo, Richard
For Jennifer, 6, on the Teton: V17
Inez, Colette
*Back When All Was Continuous
Chuckles:* V48
Jackson, Major
Urban Renewal: XVIII: V53
Jarman, Mark
Ground Swell: V49
Jarrell, Randall
*The Death of the Ball Turret
Gunner:* V2
Losses: V31
Jeffers, Robinson
Carmel Point: V49
Hurt Hawks: V3
Shine, Perishing Republic: V4
Johnson, James Weldon
The Creation: V1
Lift Every Voice and Sing: V54
Justice, Donald
Counting the Mad: V48
Incident in a Rose Garden: V14
Kelly, Brigit Pegeen
The Satyr's Heart: V22
Kenyon, Jane
Having it Out with Melancholy:
V17
Let Evening Come: V39
Reading Aloud to My Father: V52
*"Trouble with Math in a One-
Room Country School":* V9
Kerouac, Jack
Nebraska: V52
Kim, Sue (Suji) Kwock
Monologue for an Onion: V24
Kinnell, Galway
Another Night in the Ruins: V26
Blackberry Eating: V35
Saint Francis and the Sow: V9
Kizer, Carolyn
To An Unknown Poet: V18
Knight, Etheridge
The Idea of Ancestry: V36
Koch, Kenneth
Paradiso: V20
Komunyakaa, Yusef
Blackberries: V55
Camouflaging the Chimera: V37
Facing It: V5

Ode to a Drum: V20
Slam, Dunk, & Hook: V30
Kooser, Ted
At the Cancer Clinic: V24
The Constellation Orion: V8
Kumin, Maxine
Address to the Angels: V18
400-Meter Freestyle: V38
Nurture: V46
Kunitz, Stanley
The War Against the Trees: V11
Kyger, Joanne
September: V23
Lanier, Sidney
Song of the Chattahoochee: V14
Lauterbach, Ann
Hum: V25
Laux, Dorianne
For the Sake of Strangers: V24
Lazarus, Emma
The New Colossus: V37
Lee, Li-Young
Early in the Morning: V17
*For a New Citizen of These United
States:* V15
The Gift: V37
A Story: V45
The Weight of Sweetness: V11
Levertov, Denise
The Blue Rim of Memory: V17
In the Land of Shinar: V7
A Tree Telling of Orpheus: V31
What Were They Like: V42
Levine, Philip
Starlight: V8
Lim, Shirley Geok-lin
Ah Mah: V46
Pantoun for Chinese Women: V29
Longfellow, Henry Wadsworth
The Arsenal at Springfield: V17
The Children's Hour: V52
Paul Revere's Ride: V2
A Psalm of Life: V7
The Tide Rises, the Tide Falls:
V39
The Wreck of the Hesperus: V31
Lorde, Audre
Coal: V49
Hanging Fire: V32
What My Child Learns of the Sea:
V16
Lowell, Amy
Lilacs: V42
The Taxi: V30
Lowell, Robert
Hawthorne: V36
For the Union Dead: V7
*The Quaker Graveyard in
Nantucket:* V6
Loy, Mina
Luna Baedeker: V54
Moreover, the Moon: V20

Subject/Theme Index

H

Harlem Renaissance
  Southern Cop: 167, 169–172
Healing
  Bury Me in a Free Land: 62
Helplessness
  The Fence: 72
  Incident: 104–105
Home
  Yellow Light: 268
Hopelessness
  Bury Me in a Free Land: 53
Human experience
  Love Song: 153
Human spirit
  Bury Me in a Free Land: 50
Humanism
  Bury Me in a Free Land: 51
Humiliation
  Blackberries: 33
Humor
  In the Bazaars of Hyderabad: 132
  Love Song: 137, 139, 144–150, 153
  *Sure You Can Ask Me a Personal
    Question:* 174, 178, 181–184
  Unbidden: 188
Hyperbole
  Southern Cop: 159, 161
Hypocrisy
  Southern Cop: 156, 159–160, 165

I

Identity
  I Am Not I: 89, 90
  Love Song: 149
  *Sure You Can Ask Me a Personal
    Question:* 177, 178, 181, 183–184
  Unbidden: 199
  When I Was Growing Up: 236, 248
Ignorance
  *Sure You Can Ask Me a Personal
    Question:* 174
Imagery
  Blackberries: 35–36, 41, 43–44,
    47–48
  Bury Me in a Free Land: 55
  The Fence: 75, 78, 80–81, 84
  Love Song: 148
  Unbidden: 188, 193, 197
  Valentine: 207, 214, 216–217
  Yellow Light: 258, 261–264, 268
Immigrant life
  When I Was Growing Up: 238,
    242–243
  Yellow Light: 256–260, 268–269
Impotence
  The Walk: 232
Indian culture
  In the Bazaars of Hyderabad: 116,
    126–129
Indian history
  In the Bazaars of Hyderabad: 123–125

Inequality
  Blackberries: 35
  Love Song: 151
  Southern Cop: 164
Injustice
  Bury Me in a Free Land: 59, 61,
    62
  Southern Cop: 156, 166
Innocence
  Southern Cop: 156, 159, 160, 164,
    165
Insecurity
  Valentine: 214
Insignificance
  The Walk: 232
Insincerity
  Southern Cop: 158
Inspiration
  Yellow Light: 264–266
Integrity
  Bury Me in a Free Land: 68
Intertextuality
  When I Was Growing Up: 240–242
Intimacy
  Valentine: 206, 207
Invasion
  The Fence: 70, 73–74, 78, 80
Iraqi history
  The Fence: 70, 75–78, 80, 81–83
Irony
  Love Song: 140, 147, 153, 154
  Southern Cop: 158–161, 164–166,
    170
Isolation
  Alone: 3
  Love Song: 147–148

J

Jazz
  Blackberries: 39–40
Juxtaposition
  Blackberries: 38, 41
  Unbidden: 200
  Yellow Light: 261

K

Knowledge
  Blackberries: 43
  At the San Francisco Airport: 22

L

Lament
  The Walk: 232
Language
  Blackberries: 43
  The Fence: 83, 84
  I Am Not I: 92, 93, 96–97, 99
  Love Song: 134, 140, 152–154
  Southern Cop: 163, 168, 170
  Valentine: 204, 207, 208, 213–214,
    216–217

Light and darkness
  At the San Francisco Airport: 22
  Yellow Light: 257–258, 262–264
Logic
  Unbidden: 200, 201
Longing
  Unbidden: 197
Loss
  At the San Francisco Airport: 27
  The Walk: 221, 223, 231
Love
  Love Song: 154
  Valentine: 204, 206–209, 212–214
Lyric poetry
  Unbidden: 196–200

M

Manners. *See* Social conventions
Marriage
  Valentine: 207, 213
  The Walk: 226–228
Masculinity
  I Am Not I: 98
  Love Song: 136
Melancholy
  Alone: 16
  The Walk: 227
Memory
  The Fence: 84
  The Walk: 223
  Yellow Light: 253
Metaphors
  Alone: 3
  Blackberries: 38, 41, 43, 44
  The Fence: 72
  Valentine: 204, 208
  When I Was Growing Up: 238, 240
Metaphysics
  Alone: 4
  I Am Not I: 87
Middle Eastern culture
  The Fence: 81–83
Mind and body
  I Am Not I: 90
Modernism
  Southern Cop: 169, 170
  Unbidden: 196, 198
Modernity
  Alone: 12, 13
  Unbidden: 188
Monsters
  When I Was Growing Up: 246
Mood
  The Fence: 75
  Unbidden: 194
  Valentine: 217
  The Walk: 227
Morality
  Bury Me in a Free Land: 56
Mortality
  Unbidden: 199
Mother-child relationships
  Love Song: 148

Subject/Theme Index

Cumulative Index of First Lines

For a long time the butterfly held a prominent place in psychology (Lepidopterology) V23:171–172

For God's sake hold your tongue, and let me love, (The Canonization) V41:26

For Jews, the Cossacks are always coming. (The Cossacks) V25:70

For three years, out of key with his time, (Hugh Selwyn Mauberley) V16:26

Forgive me for thinking I saw (For a New Citizen of These United States) V15:55

Frogs burrow the mud (Winter) V35:297

From childhood's hour I have not been (Alone) V55:3

From my mother's sleep I fell into the State (The Death of the Ball Turret Gunner) V2:41

From the air to the air, like an empty net, (The Heights of Macchu Picchu) V28:137

G

Gardener: Sir, I encountered Death (Incident in a Rose Garden) V14:190

Gather ye Rose-buds while ye may, (To the Virgins, to Make Much of Time) V13:226

Gazelle, I killed you (Ode to a Drum) V20:172–173

Get up, get up for shame, the Blooming Morne (Corinna's Going A-Maying) V39:2

Glory be to God for dappled things— (Pied Beauty) V26:161

Go, and catch a falling star, (Song) V35:237

Go down, Moses (Go Down, Moses) V11:42

God of our fathers, known of old, (Recessional) V42:183

God save America, (America, America) V29:2

Grandmother was smaller (Ah Mah) V46:19

Grandmothers who wring the necks (Classic Ballroom Dances) V33:3

Gray mist wolf (Four Mountain Wolves) V9:131

Green, how I want you green. (Romance sonámbulo) V50:224

Grown too big for his skin, (Fable for When There's No Way Out) V38:42

H

"Had he and I but met (The Man He Killed) V3:167

Had I the heavens' embroidered cloths, (He Wishes for the Cloths of Heaven) V51:125–126

Had we but world enough, and time (To His Coy Mistress) V5:276

Hail to thee, blithe Spirit! (To a Sky-Lark) V32:251

Half a league, half a league (The Charge of the Light Brigade) V1:2

Having a Coke with You (Having a Coke with You) V12:105

He clasps the crag with crooked hands (The Eagle) V11:30

He hears her (Maestro) V47:153

He seems to be a god, that man (He Seems to Be a God) V52:76

He was found by the Bureau of Statistics to be (The Unknown Citizen) V3:302

He was seen, surrounded by rifles, (The Crime Was in Granada) V23:55–56

Hear the sledges with the bells— (The Bells) V3:46

Heard you that shriek? It rose (The Slave Mother) V44:212

Heart, you bully, you punk, I'm wrecked, I'm shocked (One Is One) V24:158

Her body is not so white as (Queen-Ann's-Lace) V6:179

Her eyes the glow-worm lend thee; (The Night Piece: To Julia) V29:206

Her eyes were coins of porter and her West (A Farewell to English) V10:126

Here, above, (The Man-Moth) V27:135

Here, she said, *put this on your head.* (Flounder) V39:58

Here they are. The soft eyes open (The Heaven of Animals) V6:75

His Grace! impossible! what dead! (A Satirical Elegy on the Death of a Late Famous General) V27:216

His house was exposed to dust from the street. (The Fence) V55:72

His speed and strength, which is the strength of ten (His Speed and Strength) V19:96

His vision, from the constantly passing bars, (The Panther) V48:147

Hog Butcher for the World (Chicago) V3:61

Hold fast to dreams (Dream Variations) V15:42

Home's the place we head for in our sleep. (Indian Boarding School: The Runaways) V43:102

Hope is a tattered flag and a dream out of time. (Hope is a Tattered Flag) V12:120

"Hope" is the thing with feathers— ("Hope" Is the Thing with Feathers) V3:123

How do I love thee? Let me count the ways (Sonnet 43) V2:236

How is your life with the other one, (An Attempt at Jealousy) V29:23

How shall we adorn (Angle of Geese) V2:2

How soon hath Time, the subtle thief of youth, (On His Having Arrived at the Age of Twenty-Three) V17:159

How would it be if you took yourself off (Landscape with Tractor) V10:182

Hunger crawls into you (Hunger in New York City) V4:79

I

I am fourteen (Hanging Fire) V32:93

I am not a painter, I am a poet (Why I Am Not a Painter) V8:258

I am not with those who abandoned their land (I Am Not One of Those Who Left the Land) V36:91

I am silver and exact. I have no preconceptions (Mirror) V1:116

I am the Smoke King (The Song of the Smoke) V13:196

I am trying to pry open your casket (Dear Reader) V10:85

I am—yet what I am, none cares or knows; (I Am) V50:126

I ask them to take a poem (Introduction to Poetry) V50:167

I became a creature of light (The Mystery) V15:137

I, being born a woman and distressed (I, being born a woman and distressed (Sonnet XVIII)) V41:203

I Built My Hut beside a Traveled Road (I Built My Hut beside a Traveled Road) V36:119

I cannot love the Brothers Wright (Reactionary Essay on Applied Science) V9:199

I caught a tremendous fish (The Fish) V31:44

Cumulative Index of Last Lines

and fear lit by the breadth of such calmly turns to praise. (The City Limits) V19:78

And Finished knowing—then— (I Felt a Funeral in My Brain) V13:137

And gallop terribly against each other's bodies (Autumn Begins in Martins Ferry, Ohio) V8:17

And gathering swallows twitter in the skies. (To Autumn) V36:295–296

and go back. (For the White poets who would be Indian) V13:112

And handled with a Chain— (Much Madness is Divinest Sense) V16:86

And haply may forget. (Song) V54:221

And has not begun to grow a manly smile. (Deep Woods) V14:139

And his own Word (The Phoenix) V10:226

And I am Nicholas. (The Czar's Last Christmas Letter) V12:45

And I let the fish go. (The Fish) V31:44

And I was unaware. (The Darkling Thrush) V18:74

And in the suburbs Can't sat down and cried. (Kilroy) V14:213

And it's been years. (Anniversary) V15:3

and joy may come, and make its test of us. (One Is One) V24:158

And kept on drinking. (Miniver Cheevy) V35:127

And laid my hand upon thy mane— as I do here. (Childe Harold's Pilgrimage, Canto IV, stanzas 178–184) V35:47

and leaving essence to the inner eye. (Memory) V21:156

and let them pull it free. (Reading Aloud to My Father) V52:182

And life for me ain't been no crystal stair (Mother to Son) V3:179

And like a thunderbolt he falls (The Eagle) V11:30

And makes me end where I begun (A Valediction: Forbidding Mourning) V11:202

And 'midst the stars inscribe Belinda's name. (The Rape of the Lock) V12:209

And miles to go before I sleep (Stopping by Woods on a Snowy Evening) V1:272

And moulder in dust away! (The Children's Hour) V52:17

and my anger! (Identity Card) V52:91–92

and my father saying things. (My Father's Song) V16:102

And no birds sing. (La Belle Dame sans Merci) V17:18

And not waving but drowning (Not Waving but Drowning) V3:216

And now, like a posy, a pretty one plump in his hands. (Catch) V50:61

And oh, 'tis true, 'tis true (When I Was One-and-Twenty) V4:268

And reach for your scalping knife. (For Jean Vincent D'abbadie, Baron St.-Castin) V12:78

and retreating, always retreating, behind it (Brazil, January 1, 1502) V6:16

And School-Boys lag with Satchels in their Hands. (A Description of the Morning) V37:49

And settled upon his eyes in a black soot ("More Light! More Light!") V6:120

And shuts his eyes. (Darwin in 1881) V13: 84

and so cold (This Is Just to Say) V34:241

And so live ever—or else swoon to death (Bright Star! Would I Were Steadfast as Thou Art) V9:44

and strange and loud was the dingoes' cry (Drought Year) V8:78

and stride out. (Courage) V14:126

and sweat and fat and greed. (Anorexic) V12:3

And that has made all the difference (The Road Not Taken) V2:195

And the deep river ran on (As I Walked Out One Evening) V4:16

And the dying Negro moan. (Southern Cop) V55:158

and the first found thought of you. (First Thought) V51:87

And the horse on the mountain. (Romance sonámbulo) V50:224

And the midnight message of Paul Revere (Paul Revere's Ride) V2:180

And the mome raths outgrabe (Jabberwocky) V11:91

And the Salvation Army singing God loves us.... (Hopeis a Tattered Flag) V12:120

And then moves on. (Fog) V50:110

And therewith ends my story. (The Bridegroom) V34:28

and these the last verses that I write for her (Tonight I Can Write) V11:187

And the tide rises, the tide falls, (The Tide Rises, the Tide Falls) V39:280

And the worst friend and enemy is but Death. (Peace) V45:169

and thickly wooded country; the moon. (The Art of the Novel) V23:29

And those roads in South Dakota that feel around in the darkness ... (Come with Me) V6:31

and to know she will stay in the field till you die? (Landscape with Tractor) V10:183

and two blankets embroidered with smallpox (Meeting the British) V7:138

and waving, shouting, *Welcome back.* (Elegy for My Father, Who Is Not Dead) V14:154

And we gave her all our money but our subway fares. (Recuerdo) V49:225

And—which is more—you'll be a Man, my son! (If) V22:54–55

and white, still undeveloped. (Postcard from Kashmir) V54:206

and whose skin is made dusky by stars. (September) V23:258–259

And wild for to hold, though I seem tame.' (Whoso List to Hunt) V25:286

And would suffice (Fire and Ice) V7:57

And yet God has not said a word! (Porphyria's Lover) V15:151

and you spread un the thin halo of night mist. (Ways to Live) V16:229

and your dreams, my Telemachus, are blameless. (Odysseus to Telemachus) V35:147

And Zero at the Bone— (A Narrow Fellow in the Grass) V11:127

(answer with a tower of birds) (Duration) V18:93

Around us already perhaps future moons, suns and stars blaze in a fiery wreath. (But Perhaps God Needs the Longing) V20:41

aspired to become lighter than air (Blood Oranges) V13:34

As any She belied with false compare (Sonnet 130) V1:248

As ever in my great Task-Master's eye. (On His Having Arrived at the Age of Twenty-Three) V17:160

As far as Cho-fu-Sa (The River-Merchant's Wife: A Letter) V8:165

as it has disappeared. (The Wings)
V28:244

As the contagion of those molten
eyes (For An Assyrian Frieze)
V9:120

As they lean over the beans in their
rented back room that is full of
beads and receipts and dolls
and clothes, tobacco crumbs,
vases and fringes (The Bean
Eaters) V2:16

as we crossed the field, I told her.
(The Centaur) V30:20

As what he loves may never like too
much. (On My First Son)
V33:166

at home in the fish's fallen heaven
(Birch Canoe) V5:31

away, pedaling hard, rocket and
pilot. (His Speed and Strength)
V19:96

B

back towards me. (The Cord)
V51:34–35)

Back to the play of constant give and
change (The Missing) V9:158

Beautiful & dangerous. (Slam,
Dunk, & Hook) V30:176–177

Before God's last *Put out the Light*
was spoken. (Once by the
Pacific) V47:195–196

Before it was quite unsheathed from
reality (Hurt Hawks) V3:138

Before they started, he and she, to
play. (The Guitarist Tunes Up)
V48:115

before we're even able to name them.
(Station) V21:226–227

behind us and all our shining
ambivalent love airborne there
before us. (Our Side) V24:177

Bi-laterally. (Legal Alien) V40:125

Black like me. (Dream Variations)
V15:42

Bless me (Hunger in New York City)
V4:79

bombs scandalizing the sanctity of
night. (While I Was Gone a
War Began) V21:253–254

Burning with thorns among berries
too ripe to touch. (Blackberries)
V55:35

But a dream within a dream? (A
Dream within a Dream) V42:80

But, baby, where are you?" (Ballad
of Birmingham) V5:17

But be (Ars Poetica) V5:3

But endure, even this grief of love.
(He Seems to Be a God) V52:76

But for centuries we have longed for
it. (Everything Is Plundered)
V32:34

but it works every time (Siren Song)
V7:196

but the truth is, it is, lost to us now.
(The Forest) V22:36–37

But there is no joy in Mudville—
mighty Casey has "Struck Out."
(Casey at the Bat) V5:58

But we hold our course, and the wind
is with us. (On Freedom's
Ground) V12:187

by a beeswax candle pooling beside
their dinnerware. (Portrait of a
Couple at Century's End)
V24:214–215

by good fortune (The Horizons of
Rooms) V15:80

By the light of the moon. (So We'll
Go No More a Roving)
V52:232–233

C

Calls through the valleys of Hall.
(Song of the Chattahoochee)
V14:284

Can rob no man of his dearest right;
(Bury Me in a Free Land)
V55:52

cherry blossoms (A Beautiful Girl
Combs Her Hair) V48:20

chickens (The Red Wheelbarrow)
V1:219

clear water dashes (Onomatopoeia)
V6:133

clenched in his stranger's fever. (Ah
Mah) V46:19

Columbia. (Kindness) V24:84–85

Come, my *Corinna*, come, let's goe a
Maying. (Corinna's Going
A-Maying) V39:6

come to life and burn? (Bidwell
Ghost) V14:2

comfortless, so let evening come.
(Let Evening Come) V39:116

Comin' for to carry me home (Swing
Low Sweet Chariot) V1:284

coming out. All right? Mama might
worry. (To My Brother Miguel)
V48:225

cool as from underground springs
and pure enough to drink. (The
Man-Moth) V27:135

crossed the water. (All It Takes)
V23:15

D

Dare frame thy fearful symmetry?
(The Tyger) V2:263

"Dead," was all he answered (The
Death of the Hired Man) V4:44

deep in the deepest one, tributaries
burn. (For Jennifer, 6, on the
Teton) V17:86

Delicate, delicate, delicate,
delicate—now! (The Base
Stealer) V12:30

delicate old injuries, the spines of
names and leaves. (Indian
Boarding School: The
Runaways) V43:102

designed to make the enemy nod off.
(The History Teacher) V42:101

Die soon (We Real Cool) V6:242

dispossessed people. We have seen it.
(Grace) V44:68

Do what you are going to do, I will
tell about it. (I go Back to May
1937) V17:113

Does thy life destroy. (The Sick
Rose) V47:211

down from the sky (Russian Letter)
V26:181

Down in the flood of remembrance, I
weep like a child for the past
(Piano) V6:145

Downward to darkness, on extended
wings. (Sunday Morning)
V16:190

drinking all night in the kitchen. (The
Dead) V35:69

Driving around, I will waste more
time. (Driving to Town Late to
Mail a Letter) V17:63

dry wells that fill so easily now (The
Exhibit) V9:107

dust rises in many myriads of grains.
(Not like a Cypress) V24:135

dusty as miners, into the restored
volumes. (Bonnard's Garden)
V25:33

E

endless worlds is the great meeting of
children. (60) V18:3

Enjoy such liberty. (To Althea, From
Prison) V34:255

Eternal, unchanging creator of earth.
Amen (The Seafarer) V8:178

Eternity of your arms around my
neck. (Death Sentences) V22:23

even as it renders us other to each
other. (Enlightenment) V52:35

even as it vanishes—were not our
life. (The Litany) V24:101–102

ever finds anything more of
immortality. (Jade Flower
Palace) V32:145

I, too, am America. (I, Too) V30:99

I turned aside and bowed my head and wept (The Tropics in New York) V4:255

I would like to tell, but lack the words. (I Built My Hut beside a Traveled Road) V36:119

I'd understand it all— (Nebraska) V52:147–148

If Winter comes, can Spring be far behind? (Ode to the West Wind) V2:163

I'll be gone from here. (The Cobweb) V17:51

I'll dig with it (Digging) V5:71

Imagine! (Autobiographia Literaria) V34:2

In a convulsive misery (The Milkfish Gatherers) V11:112

In a heavy light like yellow onions. (Yellow Light) V55:255

In an empty sky (Two Bodies) V38:251

In balance with this life, this death (An Irish Airman Foresees His Death) V1:76

in earth's gasp, ocean's yawn. (Lake) V23:158

In Flanders fields (In Flanders Fields) V5:155

In ghostlier demarcations, keener sounds. (The Idea of Order at Key West) V13:164

In hearts at peace, under an English heaven (The Soldier) V7:218

In her tomb by the side of the sea (Annabel Lee) V9:14

in the family of things. (Wild Geese) V15:208

in the grit gray light of day. (Daylights) V13:102

In the rear-view mirrors of the passing cars (The War Against the Trees) V11:216

In these Chicago avenues. (A Thirst Against) V20:205

in this bastion of culture. (To an Unknown Poet) V18:221

In this old house. (Sadie and Maud) V53:195

in winter. (Ode to My Socks) V47:173–174

in your unsteady, opening hand. (What the Poets Could Have Been) V26:262

Inns are not residences. (Silence) V47:231

iness (l(a) V1:85

Into blossom (A Blessing) V7:24

Is breaking in despair. (The Slave Mother) V44:213

Is Come, my love is come to me. (A Birthday) V10:34

is love—that's all. (Two Poems for T.) V20:218

is safe is what you said. (Practice) V23:240

is going too fast; your hands sweat. (Another Feeling) V40:3

is still warm (Lament for the Dorsets) V5:191

It asked a crumb—of Me ("Hope" Is the Thing with Feathers) V3:123

It had no mirrors. I no longer needed mirrors. (I, I, I) V26:97

It hasn't let up all morning. (The Cucumber) V41:81

It is always brimming May. (A Golden Day) V49:129

It is Margaret you mourn for. (Spring and Fall: To a Young Girl) V40:236

It is our god. (Fiddler Crab) V23:111–112

it is the bell to awaken God that we've heard ringing. (The Garden Shukkei-en) V18:107

it over my face and mouth. (An Anthem) V26:34

It rains as I write this. Mad heart, be brave. (The Country Without a Post Office) V18:64

It takes life to love life. (Lucinda Matlock) V37:172

It was your resting place." (Ah, Are You Digging on My Grave?) V4:2

it's always ourselves we find in the sea (maggie & milly & molly & may) V12:150

its bright, unequivocal eye. (Having it Out with Melancholy) V17:99

It's funny how things blow loose like that. (Snapping Beans) V50:244–245

It's the fall through wind lifting white leaves. (Rapture) V21:181

its youth. The sea grows old in it. (The Fish) V14:172

J

Judge tenderly—of Me (This Is My Letter to the World) V4:233

Just imagine it (Inventors) V7:97

K

kisses you (Grandmother) V34:95

L

Laughing the stormy, husky, brawling laughter of Youth, half-naked, sweating, proud to be Hog Butcher, Tool Maker, Stacker of Wheat, Player with Railroads and Freight Handler to the Nation (Chicago) V3:61

Learn to labor and to wait (A Psalm of Life) V7:165

Leashed in my throat (Midnight) V2:131

Leaving thine outgrown shell by life's un-resting sea (The Chambered Nautilus) V24:52–53

Let my people go (Go Down, Moses) V11:43

Let the water come. (America, America) V29:4

life, our life and its forgetting. (For a New Citizen of These United States) V15:55

Life to Victory (Always) V24:15

like a bird in the sky … (Ego-Tripping) V28:113

like a shadow or a friend. *Colombia.* (Kindness) V24:84–85

like it better than being loved. (For the Young Who Want To) V40:50

Like nothing else in Tennessee. (Anecdote of the Jar) V41:3

Like Stone— (The Soul Selects Her Own Society) V1:259

like the evening prayer. (My Father in the Navy) V46:87

Little Lamb, God bless thee. (The Lamb) V12:135

Look'd up in perfect silence at the stars. (When I Heard the Learn'd Astronomer) V22:244

love (The Toni Morrison Dreams) V22:202–203

Love is best! (Love Among the Ruins) V41:248

Loved I not Honour more. (To Lucasta, Going to the Wars) V32:291

Luck was rid of its clover. (Yet we insist that life is full of happy chance) V27:292

M

'Make a wish, Tom, make a wish.' (Drifters) V10: 98

make it seem to change (The Moon Glows the Same) V7:152

May be refined, and join the angelic train. (On Being Brought from Africa to America) V29:223

may your mercy be near. (Two Eclipses) V33:221

midnight-oiled in the metric laws? (A Farewell to English) V10:126

Monkey business (Business) V16:2

More dear, both for themselves and for thy sake! (Tintern Abbey) V2:250

More simple and more full of pride. (I Am Not One of Those Who Left the Land) V36:91

must always think good thoughts. (Letter to My Wife) V38:115

My foe outstretchd beneath the tree. (A Poison Tree) V24:195–196

My love shall in my verse ever live young (Sonnet 19) V9:211

My skin alive with the pitch. (Annunciation Overheard from the Kitchen) V49:24

My soul has grown deep like the rivers. (The Negro Speaks of Rivers) V10:198

My soul I'll pour into thee. (The Night Piece: To Julia) V29:206

N

never to waken in that world again (Starlight) V8:213

newness comes into the world (Daughter-Mother-Maya-Seeta) V25:83

Nirvana is here, nine times out of ten. (Spring-Watching Pavilion) V18:198

No, she's brushing a boy's hair (Facing It) V5:110

No winter shall abate the abate the spring's increase. (Love's Growth) V53:131

no—tell them *no*— (The Hiding Place) V10:153

Noble six hundred! (The Charge of the Light Brigade) V1:3

nobody,not even the rain,has such small hands (somewhere i have never travelled,gladly beyond) V19:265

Nor swim under the terrible eyes of prison ships. (The Drunken Boat) V28:84

Not a roof but a field of stars. (Rent) V25:164

not be seeing you, for you have no insurance. (The River Mumma Wants Out) V25:191

Not even the blisters. Look. (What Belongs to Us) V15:196

Not of itself, but thee. (Song: To Celia) V23:270–271

Not to mention people. (Pride) V38:177

Nothing, and is nowhere, and is endless (High Windows) V3:108

Nothing gold can stay (Nothing Gold Can Stay) V3:203

Now! (Alabama Centennial) V10:2

nursing the tough skin of figs (This Life) V1:293

O

O Death in Life, the days that are no more! (Tears, Idle Tears) V4:220

O Lord our Lord, how excellent is thy name in all the earth! (Psalm 8) V9:182

O Roger, Mackerel, Riley, Ned, Nellie, Chester, Lady Ghost (Names of Horses) V8:142

o, walk your body down, don't let it go it alone. (Walk Your Body Down) V26:219

Of a demon in my view— (Alone) V55:3

Of all our joys, this must be the deepest. (Drinking Alone Beneath the Moon) V20:59–60

of blackberry-eating in late September. (Blackberry Eating) V35:24

of blood and ignorance. (Art Thou the Thing I Wanted) V25:2–3

of blood on the surface of muscle. (En Route to Bangladesh, Another Crisis of Faith) V53:82

of existence (Constantly Risking Absurdity) V41:60

of gentleness (To a Sad Daughter) V8:231

of love's austere and lonely offices? (Those Winter Sundays) V1:300

Of Oxfordshire and Gloucestershire. (Adlestrop) V49:3

of peaches (The Weight of Sweetness) V11:230

of pimpled mud and your eyes (The Tall Figures of Giacometti) V50:271

Of the camellia (Falling Upon Earth) V2:64

Of the Creator. And he waits for the world to begin (Leviathan) V5:204

Of the look of a room on returning thence. (The Walk) V55:222

of our festivities (Fragment 2) V31:63

Of what is past, or passing, or to come (Sailing to Byzantium) V2:207

Of which the chronicles make no mention. (In Music) V35:105

Oh that was the garden of abundance, seeing you. (Seeing You) V24:244–245

Old Ryan, not yours (The Constellation Orion) V8:53

On rainy Monday nights of an eternal November. (Classic Ballroom Dances) V33:3

On the dark distant flurry (Angle of Geese) V2:2

on the frosty autumn air. (The Cossacks) V25:70

On the look of Death— (There's a Certain Slant of Light) V6:212

On the reef of Norman's Woe! (The Wreck of the Hesperus) V31:317

on their melting shoulders. (Snowmen) V46:175

On your head like a crown (Any Human to Another) V3:2

One could do worse that be a swinger of birches. (Birches) V13:15

"Only the Lonely," trying his best to sound like Elvis. (The Women Who Loved Elvis All Their Lives) V28:274

or a loose seed. (Freeway 280) V30:62

Or does it explode? (Harlem) V1:63

Or every man be blind— (Tell all the Truth but tell it slant) V42:240

Or hear old Triton blow his wreathed horn. (The World Is Too Much with Us) V38:301

Or help to half-a-crown." (The Man He Killed) V3:167

Or if I die. (The Fly) V34:70

Or just some human sleep. (After Apple Picking) V32:3

or last time, we look. (In Particular) V20:125

or last time, we look. (In Particular) V20:125

Or might not have lain dormant forever. (Mastectomy) V26:123

or nothing (Queen-Ann's-Lace) V6:179

Or pleasures, seldom reached, again pursued. (A Nocturnal Reverie) V30:119–120

Or the dazzling crystal. (What I Expected) V36:313–314

or the one red leaf the snow releases in March. (ThreeTimes My Life Has Opened) V16:213

Or whistling, I am not a little boy. (The Ball Poem) V47:24

ORANGE forever. (Ballad of Orange and Grape) V10:18

our every corpuscle become an elf. (Moreover, the Moon) V20:153

Our love shall live, and later life renew." (Sonnet 75) V32:215

outside. (it was New York and beautifully, snowing . . . (i was sitting in mcsorley's) V13:152

owing old (old age sticks) V3:246

P

patient in mind remembers the time. (Fading Light) V21:49

Penelope, who really cried. (An Ancient Gesture) V31:3

Perhaps he will fall. (Wilderness Gothic) V12:242

Petals on a wet, black bough (In a Station of the Metro) V2:116

Plaiting a dark red love-knot into her long black hair (The Highwayman) V4:68

plunges into the heart and is gone. (The Panther) V48:147

Powerless, I drown. (Maternity) V21:142–143

Práise him. (Pied Beauty) V26:161

Pressed to the wall, dying, but fighting back! (If We Must Die) V50:145

Pro patria mori. (Dulce et Decorum Est) V10:110

Q

Quietly shining to the quiet Moon. (Frost at Midnight) V39:75

R

Rage, rage against the dying of the light (Do Not Go Gentle into that Good Night) V1:51

Raise it again, man. We still believe what we hear. (The Singer's House) V17:206

Remember. (Remember) V32:185

Remember the Giver fading off the lip (A Drink of Water) V8:66

Ride me. (Witness) V26:285

rise & walk away like a panther. (Ode to a Drum) V20:172–173

Rises toward her day after day, like a terrible fish (Mirror) V1:116

S

Sans teeth, sans eyes, sans taste, sans everything. (Seven Ages of Man) V35:213

Shall be lifted—nevermore! (The Raven) V1:202

shall be lost. (All Shall Be Restored) V36:2

Shall you be overcome. (Conscientious Objector) V34:46

Shantih shantih shantih (The Waste Land) V20:248–252

share my shivering bed. (Chorale) V25:51

she'd miss me. (In Response to Executive Order 9066: All Americans of Japanese Descent Must Report to Relocation Centers) V32:129

Show an affirming flame. (September 1, 1939) V27:235

Shuddering with rain, coming down around me. (Omen) V22:107

Simply melted into the perfect light. (Perfect Light) V19:187

Singing of him what they could understand (Beowulf) V11:3

Singing with open mouths their strong melodious songs (I Hear America Singing) V3:152

Sister, one of those who never married. (My Grandmother's Plot in the Family Cemetery) V27:155

Sleep, fly, rest: even the sea dies! (Lament for Ignacio Sánchez Mejías) V31:128–30

slides by on grease (For the Union Dead) V7:67

Slouches towards Bethlehem to be born? (The Second Coming) V7:179

so like the smaller stars we rowed among. (The Lotus Flowers) V33:108

So long lives this, and this gives life to thee (Sonnet 18) V2:222

So prick my skin. (Pine) V23:223–224

so that everything can learn the reason for my song. (Sonnet LXXXIX) V35:260

Somebody loves us all. (Filling Station) V12:57

someone (The World Is Not a Pleasant Place to Be) V42:303

Speak through my words and my blood. (The Heights of Macchu Picchu) V28:141

spill darker kissmarks on that dark. (Ten Years after Your Deliberate Drowning) V21:240

Stand still, yet we will make him run (To His Coy Mistress) V5:277

startled into eternity (Four Mountain Wolves) V9:132

still be alive. (Hope) V43:81

Still clinging to your shirt (My Papa's Waltz) V3:192

Stood up, coiled above his head, transforming all. (A Tall Man Executes a Jig) V12:229

strangers ask. *Originally?* And I hesitate. (Originally) V25:146–147

Surely goodness and mercy shall follow me all the days of my life: and I will dwell in the house of the Lord for ever (Psalm 23) V4:103

sweet land. (You and I) V49:274

sweet on the tongue. (Maestro) V47:153

sweet things. (Problems with Hurricanes) V46:157

switch sides with every jump. (Flounder) V39:59

syllables of an old order. (A Grafted Tongue) V12:93

T

Take any streetful of people buying clothes and groceries, cheering a hero or throwing confetti and blowing tin horns . . . tell me if the lovers are losers . . . tell me if any get more than the lovers . . . in the dust . . . in the cool tombs (Cool Tombs) V6:46

Take it, no one will know. (My Heart Is Heavy) V50:204

Than from everything else life promised that you could do? (Paradiso) V20:190–191

Than that you should remember and be sad. (Remember) V14:255

Than the two hearts beating each to each! (Meeting at Night) V45:137

that does not see you. You must change your life. (Archaic Torso of Apollo) V27:3

that dying is what, to live, each has to do. (Curiosity) V47:43–44

that floral apron. (The Floral Apron) V41:141

that might have been sweet in Grudnow. (Grudnow) V32:74

That story. (Cinderella) V41:43

That then I scorn to change my state with Kings (Sonnet 29) V8:198

that there is more to know, that one day you will know it. (Knowledge) V25:113

That watches and receives. (The Tables Turned) V54:237

That when we live no more, we may live ever (To My Dear and Loving Husband) V6:228

That's the word. (Black Zodiac) V10:47

The benediction of the air. (Snow-Bound) V36:248–254

To beat real iron out, to work the bellows. (The Forge) V41:158

To every woman a happy ending (Barbie Doll) V9:33

To find they have flown away? (The Wild Swans at Coole) V42:287

To find out what it really means. (Introduction to Poetry) V50:167

to float in the space between. (The Idea of Ancestry) V36:138

to glow at midnight. (The Blue Rim of Memory) V17:39

to its owner or what horror has befallen the other shoe (A Piéd) V3:16

To live with thee and be thy love. (The Nymph's Reply to the Shepherd) V14:241

To mock the riddled corpses round Bapaume. ("Blighters") V28:3

To perfume the sleep of the dead. (In the Bazaars of Hyderabad) V55:118

To see the cherry hung with snow. (Loveliest of Trees, the Cherry Now) V40:160

To strengthen whilst one stands." (Goblin Market) V27:96

To strive, to seek, to find, and not to yield (Ulysses) V2:279

To the moaning and the groaning of the bells (The Bells) V3:47

To the temple, singing. (In the Suburbs) V14:201

To wound myself upon the sharp edges of the night? (The Taxi) V30:211–212

too. (Birdfoot's Grampa) V36:21

torn from a wedding brocade. (My Mother Combs My Hair) V34:133

Tread softly because you tread on my dreams. (He Wishes for the Cloths of Heaven) V51:125–126

True to our God, true to our Native Land. (Lift Every Voice and Sing) V54:136

Turned to that dirt from whence he sprung. (A Satirical Elegy on the Death of a Late Famous General) V27:216

U

Undeniable selves, into your days, and beyond. (The Continuous Life) V18:51

under each man's eyelid. (Camouflaging the Chimera) V37:21

unexpectedly. (Fragment 16) V38:62

until at last I lift you up and wrap you within me. (It's like This) V23:138–139

Until Eternity. (The Bustle in a House) V10:62

unusual conservation (Chocolates) V11:17

Uttering cries that are almost human (American Poetry) V7:2

W

Walt Whitman shakes. This game belongs to him (Defending Walt Whitman) V45:42

War is kind (War Is Kind) V9:253

watching to see how it's done. (I Stop Writing the Poem) V16:58

water. (Poem in Which My Legs Are Accepted) V29:262

We are satisfied, if you are; but why did I die?" (Losses) V31:167–68

we tread upon, forgetting. Truth be told. (Native Guard) V29:185

We wear the mask! (We Wear the Mask) V40:256

Went home and put a bullet through his head (Richard Cory) V4:117

Were not the one dead, turned to their affairs. (Out, Out—) V10:213

Were toward Eternity— (Because I Could Not Stop for Death) V2:27

What will survive of us is love. (An Arundel Tomb) V12:18

When I died they washed me out of the turret with a hose (The Death of the Ball Turret Gunner) V2:41

When I have crost the bar. (Crossing the Bar) V44:3

When locked up, bear down. (Fable for When There's No Way Out) V38:43

When the plunging hoofs were gone. (The Listeners) V39:136

when they untie them in the evening. (Early in the Morning) V17:75

when you are at a party. (Social Life) V19:251

When you have both (Toads) V4:244

Where deep in the night I hear a voice (Butcher Shop) V7:43

Where ignorant armies clash by night (Dover Beach) V2:52

where it's been. (Unbidden) V55:190

Where things began to happen and I knew it. (Ground Swell) V49:149

Which caused her thus to send thee out of door. (The Author to Her Book) V42:42

Which Claus of Innsbruck cast in bronze for me! (My Last Duchess) V1:166

Which for all you know is the life you've chosen. (The God Who Loves You) V20:88

which is not going to go wasted on me which is why I'm telling you about it (Having a Coke with You) V12:106

which only looks like an *l*, and is silent. (Trompe l'Oeil) V22:216

whirring into her raw skin like stars (Uncoiling) V35:277

white ash amid funereal cypresses (Helen) V6:92

White-tipped but dark underneath, racing out (Saturday at the Canal) V52:197–198

Who may revel with the rest? (In the Orchard) V45:105

Who toss and sigh and cannot rest. (The Moon at the Fortified Pass) V40:180

who understands me when I say this is beautiful? (Who Understands Me But Me) V40:278

Why am I not as they? (Lineage) V31:145–46

Wi' the Scots lords at his feit (Sir Patrick Spens) V4:177

Will always be ready to bless the day (Morning Walk) V21:167

will be easy, my rancor less bitter . . . (On the Threshold) V22:128

Will hear of as a god." (How we Heard the Name) V10:167

Wind, like the dodo's (Bedtime Story) V8:33

windowpanes. (View) V25:246–247

With courage to endure! (Old Stoic) V33:144

With gold unfading, WASHINGTON! be thine. (To His Excellency General Washington) V13:213

with my eyes closed. (We Live by What We See at Night) V13:240